THE DIMENSIONS OF THE PAST

ESSAYS PRESENTED TO THE
AMERICAN HISTORICAL ASSOCIATION'S
COMMITTEE ON QUANTITATIVE DATA

THE DIMENSIONS OF THE PAST

Materials, Problems, and Opportunities
for Quantitative Work in History

Edited by

VAL R. LORWIN AND JACOB M. PRICE

New Haven and London, Yale University Press, 1972

CONTENTS

INTRODUCTION

by Jacob M. Price and Val R. Lorwin

The past decade has seen a heightening of interest in the United States in the use of quantitative materials and quantitative methods in historical research. In part, this interest reflects the general fascination with numbers and their manipulation generated in American culture by the rapid developments in computer technology in the past generation. In part, too, it reflects a growing sophistication among American historians about their own discipline and a growing desire to move closer to the other social sciences in methods and concerns. This new interest in quantification has manifested itself not only in methodological discussions, conferences, symposia, and other such prolegomena to serious work, but also in a significant number of individual and group projects of data collection and analysis. By and large, however, these projects have been confined to the history of the United States, economic, social, and political.

American economic historians have long been collectors and users of quantitative data. It was largely with their interests in mind that the Census Bureau was persuaded to prepare the pioneering *Historical Statistics of the United States* (1945). Most of the pioneers in economic history earlier in this century tended to use quantitative data simply to report facts or trends —much as a good business journalist might. Few attempted levels of analysis above those one might find in the commercial press. Nor was there much effort among the economic historians of the first decades of this century to go beyond quantitative data already readily available (usually in government publications) and to create additional data from quantifiable materials. A great expansion of the categories of material regarded as usable came in the 1920s with the creation of the International Scientific Committee on Price History. This group sponsored the compilation in many countries of new price series, from the Middle Ages to the twentieth century, based upon hitherto neglected data assembled from institutional records, business accounts, and newspapers, as well as from governmental sources. The American contributors to this project, headed by Arthur H. Cole, prepared valuable price series for leading American commercial centers. Broader horizons were opened up to economic historians by the work of economists and statisticians in the National Bureau of Economic Research who were pushing their national income and other time series backward into the nineteenth century. Such work required greater economic and statistical sophistication than anything hitherto attempted by economic historians. By the 1960s, however, the techniques of even more advanced mathematical economics were being applied to economic history by a new generation of controversial economist-historians, the best known of whom include Robert Fogel, Lance Davis, Albert Fishlow, and J. R. T. Hughes. Ever-widening circles of young economic historians are taking up the new methods as innovating graduate programs turn out a new generation of economic historians (and historical economists) sympathetic to and trained in quantitative and mathematical methods.

An even more striking break with the past involves the expanding quantitative interests of political historians in the United States. Elections by their very nature require quantitative reporting, and there was an historiographic tradition in the United States of electoral studies emphasizing the geographical variations so well loved by historians of the Turner school. After the Second World War, a new generation of scholars—including V. O. Key, Jr., Richard P. McCormick, Lee Benson, and others—sought out neglected electoral records in state and local archives and attempted much more sophisticated quantitative analyses of elections, relating electoral behavior to class, religious, and ethnic patterns as well as older geographic ones.

Just as the work of the postwar economic historians found encouragement and methodological inspiration in the retrospective economics of the National Bureau *atelier,* so the work of the new quantitative political historians found aid and comfort in the "behavioral persuasion" which has been such a marked feature of political science since 1945. As the historians pushed forward in time and methodology, the political behaviorists, anxious to put their current survey and electoral data into the richer context of time series of past elections and their attendant ecological data, pushed backward in time and were forced to familiarize themselves with essentially historical approaches. The two armies linked up in the 1960s in the work of the Inter-University Consortium for Political Research at Ann Arbor, Michigan. Under the directorship of a political scientist (Warren Miller, of the University of Michigan Survey Research Center), the consortium was a cooperative effort of ultimately more than one hundred institutions to create a machine data bank to handle and provide wider access to the survey data of the Survey Research Center. Researchers at any of the subscribing institutions have access to the information stored at Ann Arbor and deliverable in card, tape, or printout form. It soon became evident to the political scientists responsible for the consortium data bank that they might attempt broader questions and deeper analysis if they added data on earlier electoral and legislative behavior extending as far back as possible to their survey data. (Such a retrospective data bank would, of course, be of use not just to political scientists but to historians and historical sociologists as well.) Thus the consortium or ICPR came to create a machine historical archive storing almost all American electoral data for presidential, guber-natorial, and congressional elections. Related economic, social, and demo-graphic data would be added later, as would all available congressional roll-call votes. With the consortium data bank, three important develop-ments of the postwar decades were joined in fruitful collective action—the political historians' search for quantitative rigor, the political behaviorists' search for temporal depth, and the postwar developments in computer technology.

As long as quantification had been simply one approach which some individual historians employed, there was no reason for the historical pro-fession to become collectively involved in such work. The consortium, how-ever, with its many member institutions and its necessarily substantial bud-get, required some more formal participation by organized historians. In 1963, the American Historical Association (AHA) set up under Lee Benson of the University of Pennsylvania an ad hoc Committee to Collect the Quan-titative Data of History (later the Committee on the Quantitative Data of History). Originally the almost exclusive purpose of this committee was to assist and counsel the great historical data-collection projects of the Inter-University Consortium. Gradually, however, the committee evolved into a general policy advisory committee on quantitative projects requiring col-lective action and substantial financial support. By 1967, the supervision of the consortium projects was transferred from the parent (now policy) com-mittee to a subcommittee under Professor Allan G. Bogue of the University of Wisconsin.

One of the problems which the AHA Committee on Quantitative Data faced arose from the phenomenon that for a time almost all the quanti-tative work in the United States was being done in American history; this was particularly true of the big machine-data projects, foremost of which was the consortium. This was somewhat paradoxical, since fewer than half the professional historians in this country are specialists in United States history. Intellectually this was disturbing, for, if thinking and proceeding quantitatively had proved rewarding for American students of United States history, obviously such procedures could prove equally rewarding for American students of other fields of history. In the few cases where a sig-nificant number of American historians had done quantitative work in foreign history (most notably, the "Berkeley School" of colonial Latin American demographic historians), the results were heartening.

It was easy enough to say that American historians working on the his-tory of other countries should be encouraged to think and work quanti-tatively; it was almost as easy to suggest that the AHA should encourage, for foreign history, large-scale data collection projects and machine archives comparable to those of the consortium for United States political history. But where, when, how, and in what order? As soon as it left the relatively comfortable confines of United States history, the committee encountered countless thorny problems, particularly when contemplating large group projects. With what countries and periods should one start? Should one look for relatively rich data or relatively neglected data, or for data analogous to those already being collected for the United States and hence useful for comparative purposes? (A machine archive of data immediately comparable with some of the data being assembled by the consortium offered obviously exciting possibilities.)

The American Historical Association is, of course, primarily an organization of historians in the United States, but, when one turns to the history of other countries, one enters areas where American historians are only a small proportion of the community of researchers. The number of Britons working in British history, Frenchmen working in French history, Indians working in Indian history, Japanese working in Japanese history, and so forth far exceeds the number of Americans working in those areas. Were the American Historical Association actively to encourage and commission large-scale data-collection projects in foreign history, it would have to decide immediately whether such encouragement would go only to American historians and to projects involving and reflecting their current interests and not to projects involving and reflecting the interests of the larger international community of researchers. Specifically, if the projects of American scholars were to be the primary concern of the AHA, they could not be planned and executed without the active cooperation of historians and archivists in the countries under study.

These were some of the problems facing the AHA Committee on Quantitative Data after its enlargement and reconstitution in 1967 to include scholars in fields outside of United States history. The committee did not feel itself competent to pass on problems of research strategy for quantitative historical investigations all over the world. First it needed some basic information. In which countries were there already bodies of quantitative and quantifiable data suitable for use in historical research? What were the major qualitative and other technical problems in their use? To what extent and in what ways were such data now being exploited by historians of their own and other lands? Where current historiography was quantitatively oriented, what vital problems, methods, and materials were still in need of attention? Were there projects under way to produce compilations similar to the *Historical Statistics of the United States* or the *Abstract of British Historical Statistics*? In which countries were there machine historical archives, either in operation or in the planning stages, analogous to those of the Inter-University Consortium at Ann Arbor? Although members of the committee could give partial answers to most of these basic questions, fuller and more systematic answers were required. Before the committee could offer suggestions on policy, its first task would have to be fact finding on the current state of quantitative historical work in countries outside the United States.

In November and December of 1967 the AHA Committee on Quantitative Data held two exploratory conferences at Ann Arbor. The first conference was devoted to European (excluding Russian) history; the second, to Latin American, Asian and Russian history. The papers commissioned in preparation for these conferences were intended to be arduous surveys of the current state of quantitative history in different countries or on different problems, not the casual "think pieces" often expected as conference papers. The contributors were provided with resources with which to engage research assistants to help in the preparation of supporting bibliographies, which were integral features of their reports. They were invited to consider the following questions:

1. What kinds of quantitative data (printed or manuscript) are available for the period or country under discussion?
2. What are some of the more important and characteristic problems involved in using such data?
3. What uses have hitherto been made of the various kinds of data mentioned?
4. What seem to be the most fruitful directions for further work (substantive and methodological)?

From the first planning stages, the committee saw the papers to be commissioned not simply as working papers for the committee and its conferees but as significant scholarly essays—with valuable bibliographical apparatus and discussion—of interest to the profession generally and to students of particular fields. As such, their publication was one of the original objectives. Discussion at the 1967 conferences indicated that the scholarly utility of the envisaged volume would be greatly enhanced if the papers prepared to meet the conferences' tight calendar could be revised, expanded, and polished in the light of conference discussions and if additional papers could be commissioned. Additional commissions accepted by other scholars in 1968 greatly increased the scope and interest of the planned collection.

For technical and budgetary reasons, it was not possible to commission papers covering every historical subdiscipline and every major area of the globe or to publish all the papers received. But the table of contents reveals that the papers selected cover a wide variety of emphases (economic, social, and political) and extend in time from the Middle Ages to yesterday and geographically from Latin America to Russia, from Scandinavia to Japan. The omission of the United States was deliberate. The volume, intended first and foremost for an American audience, was designed as a collection of introductory methodological and bibliographic surveys that would examine current quantitative work, explore some of the problems associated with such work, and suggest promising areas outside the United States for future historical investigation. Since much well-publicized quantitative work on United States history is already being done in this country, there was less need for such an introductory and heuristic survey here.

For similar reasons, the commissioning of chapters did not emphasize work in other relatively familiar English-speaking countries. Admirable collections of historical statistics for Great Britain and Canada, containing extremely valuable bibliographical apparatus, have already been published. The British tradition of quantitative work in economic, demographic, and electoral studies is relatively (even if not sufficiently) well known in this country. The one paper commissioned for Britain therefore restricted itself to the feasibility of a new type of investigation and archive—a machine data bank on parliamentary recruitment and behavior. For countries whose quantitative resources and work were less well known to our prospective readers, more comprehensive surveys were intended. The planned irregularity of the volume was meant to maximize the chances that the various chapters would, in their different ways, serve as introductions, guides, suggestions, and stimuli for researchers and serious students of quantitative historical work.

The planning and preliminary editing for this volume were largely the work of Jacob Price (aided by helpful suggestions from several members of the AHA Committee on Quantitative Data); the final editing was almost entirely the responsibility of Val Lorwin.

We wish to express our thanks to the secretarial staffs of the History Department and Survey Research Center of the University of Michigan and of the History Department at the University of Oregon for valued help over many years, often under great pressure of time. We also thank the other members of the American Historical Association's Committee on Quantitative Data for invaluable help on many administrative and editorial points. The project owes much in particular to the efforts of Warren Miller and Lee Benson. We are also extremely grateful for the warm interest in this project shown by the Yale University Press, particularly by its editors, Merle Spiegel and Robert L. Zangrando. Last, but far from least, we gladly acknowledge the substantial financial assistance this project has received from the International Business Machines Company and especially from the National Endowment for the Humanities.

Statistics has a very modern sound to it, associated in the public mind with modern bureaucracies, printed forms, required reports, university-trained experts, electric calculators, and electronic computers. Even distinguished historians have assumed that no statistical or even quantitative historical work can be done for periods antedating the establishment of the first bureaus and statistical societies. It is particularly good, then, that our volume should open with David Herlihy's illuminating study of quantitative work in medieval history. Even the terribly sparse records of Carolingian times have lent themselves to occasional projects of quantification, though it is only in the High Middle Ages that documentation becomes available for any significant number of quantitative projects. By the late Middle Ages (fourteenth and fifteenth centuries), archival resources, though still quite spotty, permit the gathering of "data, and series of data, on numerous topics: prices, wages, rents, yields, commerce and industry, public revenues, population, and 'social indicators.' " By then, according to Herlihy, the quantitative and quantifiable archives are, if anything, unmanageably rich.

It is less of a surprise that, when we come to the early modern period (sixteenth through eighteenth centuries), an *embarras de richesses* turns up in more than one quarter of the globe. The fullest treatment of this period is given in John Te Paske's chapter (10) on colonial Latin America. Here we find abundant materials in both Latin America and Iberia for an historiography rich in work and opportunities for work on many topics, including demography, social structure and social conditions, external trade, public finance, mining, and ecclesiastical activities. Though materials for these centuries are much sparser in Scandinavia and Japan, both Birgitta Odén and Kozo Yamamura (with Susan Hanley) suggest how, under quite different conditions, fragmentary fiscal, estate, and village records have been used for significant quantitative work in early modern Scandinavia (chap. 6) and Japan (chap. 12) respectively. The most highly developed historiographical tradition of quantitative work in the early modern period is that of France, associated in particular with the Sixth Section of the Ecole Pratique des Hautes Etudes. The principal works of this school are indicated by Louise Tilly in her survey of French studies (chap. 4 and bibliography), although she concentrates on the period after 1789. Many important closely related works on Spain are discussed by Juan Linz in the first half of chapter 5.

As we come to the late eighteenth and early nineteenth centuries, we enter into what is for historical quantification an era of transition between the early modern and the modern in conditions of data accumulation and publication. This transitional or "protostatistical" age, discussed by David Landes in chapter 2, may be seen as starting with the foundation of the English office of the Inspector-General of Imports and Exports in 1696 and extending to the establishment of essentially modern statistical bureaus and publications in the mid-nineteenth century. The greatest innovations of this period were the beginnings of regular censuses, starting with Sweden in the 1740s. Governments collected great masses of data somewhat unsystematically, and they published very little. It thus fell to an interesting race of political arithmeticians and protostatisticians, discussed by Landes, to extract what they could from the governments' hoarded papers and, acting on their own, to venture into both calculations and publication. In the Scandinavian countries, and perhaps even in Russia and India, the proto-statistical period saw significant innovations in record keeping that have made possible the rich historiography discussed by Odén and have—for Russia and India—at least opened up the prospects for future work suggested by Arcadius Kahan (chap. 9) and Morris D. Morris (chap. 13). In India, it is the centralized records and accounts of the East India companies which are protostatistical; by contrast, the intriguing indigenous records of this time are still prestatistical, though quantifiable nonetheless.

When, in the mid-nineteenth century, we pass into the modern statistical age, new problems face the historian. Government census and other statistical bureaus (subnational, national, and international) publish hundreds and thousands of pages of quantitative material yearly; tens of thousands of pages of other data lie unpublished in the archives, sometimes already aggregated, sometimes quite raw (e.g., original census returns). For Belgium alone, the published data for one year, 1968, for the single domain of foreign commerce cover over 5,000 pages of dense type. The historian is less concerned with whether he can find what he wants than with how to use what he finds.

Though modern data are as a rule more carefully assembled than almost all types of earlier data, they are released in more highly aggregated or processed forms. There is, obviously, a world of difference between the simple head counting of the early censuses and current national income calculations. Every stage in the processing and manipulation of data creates new opportunities for losing information, introducing distortions, and compounding errors. The quantitative historian must familiarize himself not only with the technical stages through which data pass in processing but also with the cultural, institutional, and political factors which affect both collection and processing and thus govern the reliability of the end product. The data of the Scandinavian countries—with their long traditions of statistical compilation and established civic morale—were seemingly prepared under the most nearly ideal of circumstances, yet Odén describes how modern scholars in those countries, subjecting class after class of data to very close scrutiny, have found many wanting. At quite the other extreme, the new countries of Latin America could draw upon no such long tradition of expert record making or selfless public service. In his chapter (11) on modern Latin America, William McGreevey discusses some of the external checks that must be applied to such data. For Germany, where statistical services and civic traditions were infinitely stronger, James Sheehan takes up (in chap. 7) a different range of problems, those arising from factors as diverse as local and federal traditions and frequent boundary changes. Still other sorts of distortion and even suppression can arise from deliberate public policy. In the section of chapter 9 devoted to Soviet data,

Arcadius Kahan examines at some length the unhappy fate under Stalin of the once-strong Russian statistical services and their gradual restoration in the post-Stalin years. Series by series, they are seen reflecting the turmoil and changes in high policy of the Soviet state in the 1930s and 1940s.

The ostensible richness of modern data poses problems not only of choice and quality but also of proper use. Valuable data may be under- or improperly utilized by careless or methodologically ingenuous investigators. The extremely interesting chapter by Charles Tilly (3), although it focuses on France for its examples of data and methods, has the widest general significance. Tilly discusses the importance of system in data accumulation for both computer and manual processing, as well as the subtle union of method and imagination needed to extract the fullest meaning from data once assembled. The acquisition of such technique can be most rewarding, and Tilly demonstrates effectively the variety of things one can do only by quantitative operations.

In many of the individual countries discussed, quantification is no new frontier in historical work. The reader cannot help but be impressed by the great amount of published work reported by Odén and Yamamura for the areas, relatively unfamiliar to English-language scholars, of Scandinavia and Japan. In Scandinavia, there have been substantial accomplishments in the study of population, migration, elites, agriculture, industry, and trade. Less is reported from Japan on political and social developments, but the economic work is impressive, and the amount of collected historical-statistical data published is surely unsurpassed anywhere. Almost as impressive are the achievements in the more familiar fields of modern France and colonial Latin America, reported by Louise Tilly and John Te Paske.

Other chapters place their emphasis on the work to be done. William Aydelotte (chap. 8) concentrates entirely on the creation (yet to be started) of a machine data bank to facilitate the study of British political behavior —electoral and parliamentary—in the past century and a half. Juan Linz is concerned primarily with work to be done on a range of fresh and old problems of national and comparative history in Spain and comparable countries, notably Portugal and Italy. In chapter 5 he offers us a rich and imaginative catalog of social, institutional, and political projects lending themselves to—indeed, requiring—quantification. Similar interests are expressed in James Sheehan's chapter (7) on political and social historical studies on modern Germany. He can report a larger amount of work already accomplished than Linz can for Spain, but the thrust of his discussion is toward work yet to be done. The chapters by William McGreevey and Morris D. Morris are also oriented toward future work, but their emphases are on economic history. McGreevey reports interesting beginnings in Argentina and Colombia in large-scale quantitative projects, but for most Latin American countries the compilation of the basic series for the century after liberation is yet to be started. Morris reports interesting starts on a wide variety of topics in India, where the raj encouraged relatively strong traditions and institutions of data accumulation from the late nineteenth century, but he reminds us of some of the pitfalls of many series of raj statistics. The time is now ripe, Morris argues, for the cooperative compilation of a collection of Indian economic-historical statistics. Among Asian countries, this would represent a stage which Japan has long since reached but which apparently no other country except India may yet contemplate.

For the working historian, the lessons of these papers are probably clear. From France to Scandinavia to Japan, quantitative ways of thinking, quantitative approaches, and quantitative methods have entered the mainstream of historical investigation. In all areas, major quantitative work is now being done, and even more is likely to be done in the immediate future. The neglect of the possibilities of quantitative research by so many American historians working on topics outside of United States history leads to an unnecessary restriction of their analytical techniques and an unfortunate enfeeblement of their results. Not all problems are equally suitable for quantification; nor will quantification ever become the exclusive or even preponderant form or mood of historical investigation. Yet if historians in the United States and other English-speaking lands working on the history of other countries wish to move to exciting frontiers of research endeavor in their respective areas of interest, a greater proportion of them than at present will have to think and work in part quantitatively.

Not all the quantitative work attempted will, of course, be elegant, rigorous, satisfying, or even necessary. Some, yielding perhaps unwittingly to what looks like a mode, will rush into numbers without a sufficient awareness of the problems inherent in the materials they are using or the methods they are attempting. Others, fascinated with method mastered, may use it to play games that are not worth the candle. Nor may the technically proficient always sense the unnecessarily limited scope of the adequate work they are doing; thus they may fail to perceive the rich pastures waiting outside the walls of their carefully tended but limited quantitative gardens. Demographers and macroeconometricians may do work that is inherently almost entirely quantitative, but most large historical problems—even those which best lend themselves to quantitative approaches—are rarely solved by quantification alone. Nonquantitative materials and judgments are almost always needed to explain the forces behind the trends in a time series, the accidents that account for fluctuations, the logic manifest in a correlation.

Thus, in the years to come, for a wide range of historical problems the crucial questions will not be whether to use quantification but when and how and how far and for what purpose. What Charles Tilly writes now of France will tomorrow surely be true of most countries with developed historiographical traditions:

Today's historians have no doubt engaged in a certain amount of heed-less, and even erroneous, quantification. . . . Quantification couples its benefits with large risks. . . . Yet the French experience of the last few decades points to the capacity of intelligent quantification to renew, clarify, and enrich history. . . . The fundamental division of tactics and opinion among today's students of French history is not between quanti-fiers and qualifiers; it is between those whose inquiries begin with the questions of economics, demography, or some other generalizing discipline outside history and those who draw their quantitative questions from the logic of historical inquiry itself. . . . disagreements among the proponents of both procedures will rage for years to come, reshaping historiography in France and elsewhere. The debaters will rarely debate *whether* to quantify; they will, instead, argue over what, when, how, and to what end. [p. 125 below]

1

QUANTIFICATION AND THE MIDDLE AGES

by David Herlihy

The union of the words *quantification* and *the Middle Ages* in my title may seem to many incongruous if not monstrous.[1] Quantification requires data which are abundant, precise, and homogenous. Medieval statistics are notoriously random, hard to collect, hard to interpret, and often, it seems, more likely to breed contention than contentment among scholars. But in spite of the lean and truculent documentation, studies based on some sort of statistical analysis have proliferated in recent years. I shall in fact have difficulty surveying this substantial bibliography with the limited time, competence, and experience at my disposal. Stringent limits are required to accomplish even this bare and rapid survey.

The span of time I hope to cover includes the centuries between 500 and 1500, the conventional Middle Ages. But the late-ancient world merits a brief backward glance. Even for that apparently unpromising epoch, statistical studies of great ingenuity have been accomplished, which give hope and instruction to historians working in similar periods of documentary dearth. Many medieval civilizations—Islamic, Byzantine, Ottoman, Balkan-Slavic, and Russian, as well as Western—have recently attracted quantitative studies, but I will keep my gaze fixed steadily on the West.[2] Even within the narrow confines of western Europe, I shall have to neglect some statistical methods. I cannot discuss the many interesting uses of quantification by literary historians, analyzing by word counts the vocabulary and style of medieval authors. Nor can I examine recent efforts to reconstruct weather patterns in the Middle Ages, in spite of their evident fascination.[3] Some comments concerning archeology and the data it is yielding will be made, but not enough to do this science justice. Here my attention will be focused principally on documentary materials, specifically the private acts and administrative records which have survived, in greater quantities than is sometimes realized, from the Middle Ages.

In finding our way across these thousand years of history, the traditional name and concept Middle Ages is itself a stumbling block. The changing quantity and character of archival records do not justify the hoary conception, or misconception, of a single medieval period, fixed and changeless. Rather, they demand that we distinguish at least two Middle Ages. The transition between them comes at various times in various places, but most commonly in the late thirteenth or early fourteenth centuries. Before approximately 1250, with only a few major exceptions, statistical documents are sparse, scattered, and meager in the data they contain. They are also overwhelmingly ecclesiastical in their origins. The views, interests, and needs of churchmen offer us, and sift for us, nearly all we know concerning the economy and society of this early period. Then, in the later thirteenth and fourteenth centuries, the documentation changes radically across Europe, both in quantity and character. There is a huge expansion, nearly an explosion, in the volume of surviving materials. If he has the ambition and the taste, the medieval historian can still hope to read in the course of his scholarly life all surviving private acts and administrative records which antedate the thirteenth century. But the historian of the late Middle Ages must frequently face a mountain of documents quite beyond his capacity to dominate, even within limited geographic areas.

This great increment in archival survivals in the late Middle Ages is only partly the result of the diminished attrition suffered by newer documents. It also reflects the changing character of medieval government and social life. Before the thirteenth century, educated laymen formed only a tiny segment of society in most parts of Europe. The unlettered laity, and hence the great mass of society, neither needed nor produced written records in substantial quantities. This situation changed in the late Middle Ages; both government and business became very much the concerns of professional men, who were literate and trained for the tasks they were fulfilling. Historians have long spoken of a "laicization" of medieval society in the course of the thirteenth century and of an emergent "lay spirit" which transformed the goals and practices of government.[4] The terms may be inexact and even misleading, but it is at least certain that the professional administrative and business classes were expanding in numbers and assuming an unprecedented social weight and influence. In government, in business, and often in the management of their own households, these literate men made the redaction and preservation of written records a part of established routine. The new professional competence evident in both government and private affairs bequeathed to us this wealth of documentation from the late Middle Ages.

In these later centuries, too, documentation took on a new face. No longer must we view the medieval world primarily through ecclesiastical lenses, although filters do remain. Statistics were collected and recorded not for their own interest but to serve fiscal or administrative purposes or to suit the needs of private businesses or households. In interpreting this material, we must constantly keep in mind the technical purposes for which it was gathered. But we still can be grateful for the much wider, deeper appreciation of medieval society which the new archival bounty makes possible.

From the late thirteenth century, then, a new Middle Ages began. By measure of surviving archives, the last two centuries of the traditional Middle Ages were not that different, in most western-European countries, from the opening centuries of the modern epoch. The documentation offers the medievalist very nearly the same opportunities—and the same difficulties—which his colleague encounters working in the sixteenth or seventeenth century. The conventional divisions of Western history correspond poorly with the patterns of documentary survival. In this chapter I shall consider separately these two Middle Ages: the early period, lasting approximately to the end of the thirteenth century; and the late Middle Ages, especially the fourteenth and fifteenth centuries, which with much justification could already be called modern.

THE EARLY MIDDLE AGES

For the first several centuries of the Middle Ages, up to about 750, the state of statistical records amply justifies the period's reputation for darkness. Statistical documentation is, in direct terms, nonexistent. A few private acts and estate surveys have survived, but these number hardly more than a hundred. They are scattered over time and place. Even comparisons among them are difficult, and there is no hope of forming from them any statistical series.

Archeological Data

But the early Middle Ages are not totally devoid of statistics. Scholars have succeeded in measuring some aspects of late-ancient and early-medieval society. For these quantitative data they are indebted not to documentary archives but to archeology and its related disciplines of epigraphy and numismatics.

Inscriptions from the ancient world have survived in vast quantities. Those of interest to us, dating from between the second and seventh centuries after Christ, that are published and available to scholars today must be numbered at well over 100,000, and new excavations continuously provide more. Many of these inscriptions are taken from tombs. They frequently record the sex and age of the deceased and sometimes his accomplishments in life, which point to his social status.

These tomb inscriptions, of course, give no aggregate figures concerning late-antique populations, and they probably do not safely support even rough estimates of population size. They can be used, with confidence if still with some risk, in judging statistically the ethnic composition of an ancient population.[5] But the most remarkable contribution of tomb in-

scriptions has been the light which they have cast on mortality rates and
life expectancies within ancient society. Given the great number of inscriptions available, it is possible to estimate and contrast mortality rates among
the various provinces; between men and women, Christians and pagans; and
amid the various social classes.[6] The Hungarian scholar J. Szilágyi has recently undertaken a systematic statistical survey of tombstone inscriptions
from the provinces of the western empire. The results of this analysis are
of interest not only for purposes of historical demography but also for their
invaluable commentary on social conditions within the late empire, on
the treatment accorded women and slaves, and on the contrasting standards
of living—and chances of dying—which marked the lives of the free and
the unfree, the rich and the poor, the urban residents and their rural counterparts. This sort of information—fundamentally demographic but with
strong social implications—further invites comparison with other historic
societies; it is the stuff from which a sound comparative history of human
societies can be built.

Another set of archeological data now throws some faint but welcome
light over the murky centuries which divide the ancient world from the
Carolingian age: coins. For coins too have survived in fairly voluminous
quantities. Those dating from the eighth century number about 5,500, and
ninth-century specimens are still more numerous, at least by several thousand. Many statistical studies have been devoted to this stock of coins,
measuring their weights, their metallic properties, and the composition of
the hoards in which most of them were found. Numismatic statistics have
served to illuminate the nature of the Carolingian mint reforms—a subject
of great import not only for monetary history but for the entire tangled
topic of medieval metrology.[7] Scholars have used numismatic evidence to
locate trade routes, investigate the flow of precious metals, and even determine whether the West was gaining or losing gold in the exchange. Even
more recently, numismatists have tried to estimate the volume of early-
medieval monetary issues—notably the coinage of Anglo-Saxon England
and also, though less rigorously, that of Merovingian France.[8] The ingenious
methods rest on a determination of the number of dies used to strike the
surviving coinage; an estimate of the number of coins each die could strike;
and, finally, a calculation of what the mint, using that number of dies, could
have produced. A lively scholarly debate has settled over, or rather rages
about, all these uses of numismatic evidence. Here I shall only comment
that modern numismatic science is very much open to new methods and
techniques, very much alive, and very promising.

I should add one short postscript to this rapid treatment of the statistical
use of archeological data in the Middle Ages. After about 750, written
records of a statistical character begin to appear in the archives, and as their
numbers grow, the historical use of archeology seems to wane. Archeology
retains its importance chiefly in those countries poorly served by documen-

tary archives—Iceland, the Scandinavian countries, Poland, and Hungary. This is unfortunate, as medieval archeology continues to offer sometimes unique information. Recently, a group of Hungarian scholars have studied the burial grounds of an eleventh-century community and the skeletal remains of its members.[9] They were able to construct from their data a life table. Vital statistics of this sort are unavailable for the age in lands farther west, in spite of a greater abundance of written records. I cannot consider the uses of medieval archeological data further, but I must at least point to its continuing interest and importance.

Documentary Data

From the Carolingian age, from about 750 on, we have, for the first time in usable quantities, documents which allow for statistical research. Between 750 and 900—that is, between the formation and disintegration of the Carolingian empire—there probably have survived 50,000 of these acts, chiefly property conveyances. Many of them are, unfortunately, only a line or two in length and have reached us in the form of highly condensed abstracts of documents preserved in monastic *Libri Traditionum,* or Books of Donations; but full charters have also survived by the thousands. These Carolingian documents are the first of a continuing series of charters and administrative records which in subsequent generations grew alternately thick and thin, now favoring one region and now another, but never entirely breaking over the entire length of the Middle Ages. It is hard to give a firm estimate of their volume, but those acts antedating 1200 A.D. certainly surpass 100,000 and come from well over 500 archival collections.

These charters and administrative records are overwhelmingly ecclesiastical in provenience and are almost as overwhelmingly concerned with agricultural transactions. They fall into two general categories. The smaller part, which is actually comprised of longer documents, is made up of surveys, *censiers,* or, in their usual English title, manorial extents. These are inventories, sometimes redacted with exacting detail, listing and describing the lands or estates belonging to a particular monastery. *Censiers* are especially abundant in the north of Europe. Certainly the most impressive and exhaustive of these Carolingian surveys is the Polyptych of the monastery of St.-Germain-des-Prés near Paris, redacted under the abbot Irminon probably between 803 and 829.[10] It describes with scrupulous detail more than twenty manor houses and 1,646 servile farms dependent upon them, lists by name all the serfs and dependent cultivators (men, women, and children), and minutely records their varied obligations. Irminon's survey offers a brilliant —and unfortunately rare—insight into agricultural settlement, manorial organization, and the composition of servile families in the ninth century.

In the south of Europe, the great estates were never so well established nor so well organized as in the north. The region offers fewer, poorer surveys, but, as if in compensation, it has preserved much richer collections of charters—those of the second category. One Italian monastery alone, for example, that of Farfa near Rome, has more than 4,000 charters antedating 1150. Unlike the manorial surveys, these charters do not provide a comprehensive view of ecclesiastical holdings at any given time. But they usually offer a better means of observing, measuring, and dating changes in ecclesiastical holdings.

This series of private acts and administrative records, dating from about 750 and continuous thereafter, is probably more voluminous than most nonmedievalists and many medievalists realize, but the charters yield quantifiable data only stubbornly. They do not, of course, give aggregate statistics on population or production. Losses have been considerable over the centuries, and changes in notarial practices have also affected the series in its numbers and character. They reflect lay interests only indirectly and ecclesiastical interests only partially. Even the information they give on prices, rents, or agricultural yields is frequently difficult to interpret. The metrology used is often baffling and usually uncertain. Charlemagne, at least in law and aspiration, had standardized weights and measures across his empire, but whatever unity had actually been achieved soon disappeared with the disintegration of the empire. Almost every region of Europe developed its own peculiar ways of measuring. Confusion is compounded by the practice, even on the part of petty lords, of altering by fiat the measures used by their subjects. We cannot always be certain that a *modius* of grain, or an *arpent* of land, even in the same area, contained the same quantities in 1150 as in 950. Sporadic price series, largely concerned with land values, can be constructed, but there is no possibility of compiling a continuous and reliable history of price movements during the early Middle Ages.

With all these deficiencies, can this documentation be used at all in a statistical sense? The answer, in my opinion, is yes, definitely, even though we cannot answer the kinds of questions which might first occur to historians of modern societies. And, further, for all its deficiencies, this series still contains a huge amount of information. The alternative to measured analysis is random selection, in which results are much dependent on the historian's personal impressions. Quantification is an antidote to impressionism; it permits an entire range of documents, not just a few, to lend support to the conclusion. These documents, for example, readily support studies devoted to particular regions or estates. My bibliography (pp. 35–37 below) gives numerous examples of such studies, and many of them, particularly those most recently published, contain considerable statistical material.[11]

It is further possible, in my estimation, to subject to a kind of statistical analysis the surviving private acts from extensive regions of Europe. We can, for example, consider all the documents of Italy, southern France, or Spain as forming a single corpus and proceed to measure certain simple but revealing changes in the character and content of these documents. The following questions can be asked: [12] How important are payments in money substitutes, in comparison with payments in coin? How important are rents in kind or in labor, in contrast to rents in money? How fluid, or how stable, are agricultural holdings? How frequently do women appear as principals in contracts or as property owners, in comparison with men? How frequently does a man use a matronymic, rather than a patronymic, to identify himself? Quantification of this sort essentially evaluates the relative importance of alternate answers to the same question and measures the changing content of the documentation rather than the changing social realities. But even this is something; often the hardest task of the medieval social historian is simply to prove that there are changes occurring in the dim centuries he studies. Measured analysis of the documentary record can give the historian an extended view of his sources not otherwise attainable, a new awareness of change, new problems to answer, and, it is to be hoped, new insights into the character and experience of medieval society.

England

The documentation of the early Middle Ages, overwhelmingly ecclesiastical in origin, can illustrate change, but it supplies almost no aggregate figures on population and production, and it tells very little about agricultural yields, rents, and prices. But one country, England, does not quite fit into this broad characterization. To be sure, ecclesiastical archives are of major importance in England as everywhere in Europe. They are especially inviting to statistical analysis, in that they have preserved, most notably in the thirteenth century, numerous and lengthy manorial extents and other manorial records. The archives of the great Benedictine houses and, to a lesser extent, of the episcopal sees provide the foundations of our knowledge of English manorial history. No other properties anywhere in thirteenth-century Europe can be studied so intensively as these English ecclesiastical manors.

England also possessed, sooner than other Western governments, archives serving the needs of royal administration. Here the great treasure is, of course, the Domesday Book of 1086; in addition, series of fiscal and judicial records, initiated in the early twelfth century, became with time more and more varied and exploded in volume from the late thirteenth century. Domesday is a wonder for its age and remains, even in England, unique for centuries thereafter. The studies exploiting its inexhaustible statistical wealth would fill a small library. Galbraith and Finn have recently written excellent introductions to its character and use.[13] A mine of information for local historians and geographers, Domesday also provides (though not without some ambiguity) a basis for estimating England's total population in 1086.[14] It is by all odds the richest, and deservedly the most famous, of the statistical compilations left to us from the early Middle Ages.

These sources illuminate the English countryside and its rural society with unique clarity, and they have been rigorously analyzed by several generations of scholars—Vinogradoff, Postan, Hilton, Hallam, Finberg, Lennard, Raftis, Titow, Sylvia Thrupp, and others. Soviet historians—E.A. Kosminsky and, more recently, M. A. Barg—have continued the traditional Russian interest in English rural history.[15] The studies of all these scholars, many of them dense with figures, have investigated such subjects as yields, rent levels, size of holdings, density of settlement, population movements, demographic replacement ratios, and peasant mobility. Only in more recent years have continental scholars developed a comparable interest in agricultural history, and only for a later period do they have comparable documentation.

THE LATE MIDDLE AGES

From the later thirteenth century, the explosion in documentation gives the statistical historian new and unprecedented capabilities. He can gather data, and series of data, on numerous topics: prices, wages, rents, yields, commerce and industry, public revenues, population, and "social indicators" which provide some insight into the character of late-medieval society. Of course, the available data faithfully reflect the fund of documentation and its peculiarities. That fund is rich and getting richer, but its accumulation is still subject to wide and frequent interruptions and remains unevenly distributed across the face of Europe. The historian cannot expect to find measurable information for all the places, all the times, and all the subjects that may interest him. But neither must he struggle with a poor and miserable documentation. His real embarrassment has become one familiar to historians of modern societies: the nearly unmanageable size of archives.

Yields, Prices, Wages, Money

In the late Middle Ages, the new documentary abundance—and a greater metrological consistency—allows the construction, really for the first time in medieval history, of fairly full, continuous, and reliable series of wages, prices, and yields. Here too, England has the advantage over the rest of Europe, by virtue of its archives and its energetic researchers. The huge, pioneering study by Thorold Rogers, devoted to both yields and prices, has suffered much criticism over the years, but it remains a landmark in the history of statistical compilation. Numerous recent studies have maintained Rogers's interests while correcting some of his omissions and errors.

Continental countries are more poorly endowed with published data concerning prices; and with great regional contrasts in weights, measures, and money, price series are harder to construct. But N. W. Posthumus's recent study of the history of prices in Holland is a model of what can be done. Slicher van Bath has given us a general survey of yield ratios which spans the late Middle Ages. In France, D'Avenel's old study of wages and prices is even more vulnerable to criticism than that of Thorold Rogers. But regional and local studies are now giving a good view of price movements there too. Guy Fourquin's recent work on agriculture in the neighborhood of Paris between the thirteenth and sixteenth centuries is packed with information concerning prices and much else. German lands, in contrast, seem poorly served by price studies. Italy possesses huge archives which could serve for price history, but there too the work progresses slowly, and information must be sought primarily in local studies. Some years ago, E. J. Hamilton produced a pioneering study on prices and wages in Valencia, Aragon, and Navarre from 1351 to 1500. We thus know something concerning price movements, and we shall learn more once the great archives of Europe are made to yield their still untouched harvests.

The new data also illuminate the history of money. Some figures recording mint output have survived: Miskimin has provided a recent, convenient compilation of those figures for France and England. Exchange ratios among important coins are also available. This makes possible analyses of monetary phenomena more sophisticated—and more certain—than can be accomplished for any prior age.[16]

Commerce and Industry

Statistical documents illustrating commerce and industry are virtually nonexistent in the early Middle Ages, but here too, starting in the thirteenth century—and even a little earlier in Italy—the documents begin to yield quantitative data. The Genoese notarial chartularies, surviving from the mid-twelfth century, provide a vivid portrayal of trade through that great port—the earliest close view we have of medieval commercial exchange. Many scholars—Robert Reynolds, Robert Lopez, Erik Bach, and others—have worked with these materials, and some have supported their arguments with measurements. The notarial chartularies reveal no firm aggregate figures, but they do give some statistical information concerning relative trade volumes and prices. From the middle of the thirteenth century, similar chartularies have come down to us from ports and from the major inland commercial centers of Italy and southern Europe. A little later in the century, the first private account books came into use, and from the fourteenth century these replace the notarial chartularies as our best record of private business enterprises. The mountain of documents left by the merchant of Prato, Francesco di Marco Datini, is world-famous; Federigo Melis's study of Datini's business ventures overflows with informative statistics. Raymond de Roover made use of the business records of the Medici bank to analyze its fluctuating fortunes. Many Italian banks and businesses left large archives in the fourteenth and fifteenth centuries, but most of these have not yet been investigated by historians.

Notarial chartularies or business accounts do not provide aggregate statistics showing total volumes of commercial exchange or production, but tariff and other tax records do. Tariff receipts illustrating trade volumes have survived sporadically for the port of Genoa from the late thirteenth century; a recent, solid study by John Day examines the Genoese tariffs for 1376–77. One of the richest series of tariff accounts has been preserved from England; these have been frequently used, most recently in the fine analysis of E. M. Carus-Wilson and O. Coleman. We have some production figures, unfortunately scattered and sporadic, on mining and woolen manufacture.[17] In keeping with the continuing political and administrative divisions of the late Middle Ages, there are no records showing trade movements across national (or what were to become national) borders, or production within them, with the sole exception of England. But commercial historians have studied many major centers of medieval trade—Genoa, Geneva, Antwerp, Marseilles, Dieppe, Toulouse, and others.

Private and Public Finances

Historians have also been studying the income and expenses of the great noble houses; the churches; the papacy; and the major cities, principalities, and monarchies of Europe. Fiscal records allowing for such investigations appear only sporadically and are at times difficult to interpret. But they do give a wide, if still spotty, picture of the movement of private and governmental revenues and expenses.[18] These in turn can be related to approximate population to gain some impression of per capita tax burdens and the role of ecclesiastical and political authorities in the economic life of the community.

Population

Estimates of total population for large areas in Europe before the thirteenth century are possible only for England, on the basis of its Domesday Book, and population movements must be judged from indirect evidence. But the clouds obscuring European population history lift, if still only partially, in the late Middle Ages. Indirect evidence proliferates. German scholars, for example, have made highly technical, skillful statistical studies of Wüstungen, or abandoned habitations;[19] and a recent cooperative work has examined, using many techniques, the phenomenon of deserted villages in European history.[20] In addition, surviving poll tax records in England and France give some direct evidence of population size in the fourteenth century.

More detailed than the poll taxes, but covering smaller geographic areas, are the property surveys—*estimes, estimi,* or *catasti.* They have survived, again sporadically, from the mid-thirteenth century and are especially numerous in southern Europe. The recently growing interest in historical demography has won for them the warm attention of scholars. In France, Philippe Wolff at Toulouse has been one of the pioneers in the systematic analysis of these *estimes.* Baratier's survey of population movements in

Provence between the thirteenth and sixteenth centuries and Mme Higounet-Nadal's examination of the population of Périgueux in the fourteenth century are examples of recent and excellent studies by French scholars. In Italy, Enrico Fiumi has been producing remarkably significant analyses of demographic history devoted to San Gimignano, Volterra, Prato, and the countryside of Florence.

To illustrate the sometimes extraordinary wealth of these surveys, I would like to comment briefly on one, in the study of which I am personally involved: the Catasti of Florence. The oldest of these surveys was redacted in 1427 and completed by 1430. It included in its purview the population not only of Florence itself but also of the towns and countrysides subject to it— Arezzo, Pisa, Pistoia, Prato, San Gimignano, and other communities, stretching over the entire length of the Arno valley. It thus assumes gigantic proportions. The survey lists approximately 50,000 families, or more than 200,000 persons, all by name. For each family, it states the ages, occupation, and residence of the members; the marital status of females; whether the family head is an immigrant in the area or resides elsewhere; and at times even the health, physical and mental, of adults and children. It further notes recent changes in the family membership through births, deaths, and marriages—becoming, at least for a year, a register of vital statistics unique for the age. It lists with equal thoroughness the property owned, distinguishing assets in land, animals, commercial and business investments, and shares in the public debt. And it tells what the family owed as well as owned. The Catasto thus gives an extraordinary statistical view of a population of nearly a quarter million more than two generations before Columbus's great voyages. Its range, wealth, and comprehensiveness offer final proof that the Middle Ages are rich in figures.

Many historians have made use of this opulent source. Most recently and notably, the Italian scholar Elio Conti has used the Catasto (and many other documents) to compile a book of statistics concerning the Florentine countryside in the late Middle Ages and early modern period. Bruno Casini, archivist of the city of Pisa, has published a compilation of the principal data in the Catasto relating to the city of Pisa in 1428. Further, the Catasto has contributed to Fiumi's several demographic studies and to my own recent book on Pistoia.

No scholar, however, has yet attempted to survey the Catasto, even the single version of 1427–30, in all its breathtaking dimensions. It is simply too overwhelming. But, clearly, much could be learned from a consideration of its entire range of information. To meet this need, an international team of scholars has been formed, under the auspices of the sixth section of the Ecole Pratique des Hautes Etudes in Paris, with additional support from the University of Wisconsin. The plan was to enter onto perforated cards, and then onto magnetic tape, the principal demographic and economic data contained in the entire Catasto of 1427, to make possible its analysis by computer. The work of converting the data into machine-readable form was finished in 1970, and the analysis is now beginning. Duplicates of the cards and tape are deposited at Paris and at Madison, where they are available to scholars.

The Catasto is only one of many huge statistical compilations surviving from the late Middle Ages and early modern times. They offer great quantities of statistical information, but it has remained awkward for individual scholars to use them efficiently. They are too large to be edited and published in a conventional sense, and in manuscript form they present paleographical difficulties to the researcher, and he often must lose much time in extracting from their mass the kinds of data he wants. It seems to me worthwhile to explore the possibilities of preparing partial, machine-readable editions of these large compilations, which could tell the researcher quickly and accurately what he wants to know, or at least give him a better indication of where to search in the manuscript itself to find the desired information. It is hoped that the experience gained in preparing a partial, machine-readable edition of the Florentine Catasto of 1427 will help enlist more of the techniques of data storage and retrieval in the service of historians.

Social Indicators

All these sources offer quantitative measurements of numerous aspects of late-medieval society. It would be possible, in some areas and for some times, to calculate the relative importance of particular professional groups— clergy, notaries, and artisans, for example. We could even occasionally investigate the kinds of diseases prevalent in the medieval population, the number of hospital beds available for the sick, and hospital occupancy rates. Professor Sylvia Thrupp has suggested as a dissertation subject to one Ph.D. candidate a statistical study of the crimes prevalent in medieval English society and the relationship between the number and character of crimes to periods of famine or social stress.

Much of what we can do depends on the surviving documents, and not everything is possible. But we still have a rich choice.

Proposals

Thus the techniques of quantification have already been widely applied in medieval studies, for nearly the entire length of the Middle Ages. To make the quantitative data of medieval history more readily available to historians, whether medievalists or not, I have three proposals to present. First, we need a much more thorough, and more accessible, bibliographical control over statistical sources and the studies based on them. There exists, for example, no single, comprehensive bibliography of monastic chartularies and other private acts, upon which statistical investigations in the early Middle Ages chiefly depend. Probably the most convenient arrangement would be to compile a bibliography based on geographic regions, a kind of "topo-bibliography," which would list published chartularies and other statistical records, note the existence of major unpublished surveys, and record the studies based upon the available data.

Secondly, I would emphasize again the value of preparing, and depositing in an accessible data library, partial, machine-readable editions of the great statistical compilations of medieval and early modern history. That way they could yield the enormous volume of statistical data they contain far more readily than is at present possible.

Finally, it would be useful to consolidate in a "data bank" information gathered from various sources illuminating a single topic. We have, for example, some information regarding life expectancies, sex ratios, and the like for nearly every period of the Middle Ages. But the data remain scattered in a great range of publications and unpublished sources. The difficulty of making comparisons means that this information has not yet contributed, as it might contribute, to social history.

I have touched many bases in this short chapter, and I run the risk of being ruled safe at none. But this conclusion at least is safe. Quantification is already a proven tool of medieval research. Its more intensive and extended use promises still more information, which should interest not only medievalists but all scholars committed to the comparative study of human development and social change.

NOTES

1   I would like to express my gratitude to Professors Sylvia L. Thrupp of the University of Michigan and Harry A. Miskimin of Yale University and to Mme Christiane Klapisch of the Centre de Recherches Historiques of the Ecole Pratique des Hautes Etudes, all of whom graciously responded to my requests for information concerning present uses of quantification in medieval research. I would also like to thank Richard Ring, now of Ripon College, who labored long and hard over the bibliography. It goes without saying, however, that I assume full responsibility for both text and bibliography. They doubtless contain errors and omissions, and the wrath of critics should be directed against me alone.

2   For examples of statistical studies devoted to medieval civilizations other than Western, see A. Andréadès, "De la population de Constantinople sous les empereurs byzantins," *Metron* 1 (1920): 68–119; idem, *A History of Greek Public Finances;* E. Ashtor, "Prix et salaires dans l'Espagne musulmane aux Xe et XIe siècles," *Annales: Economies-Sociétés-Civilisations* 20 (1965): 664–79; idem, "La recherche des prix dans l'Orient médiéval," *Studia Islamica* 21 (1964): 101–44; O. M. Barkan, "Essai sur les données statistiques de registres de recensement dans l'Empire Ottoman aux XVe et XVIe siècles," *Journal of the Economic and Social History of the Orient* 1 (1957): 9–36; P. Charanis, "A Note on the Population and Cities of the Byzantine Empire in the Thirteenth Century," in *The Joshua Starr Memorial Volume;* Walter J. Fischel, "The City in Islam," *Middle Eastern Affairs* 7 (1956): 227-32; S. D. Goitein, "The Exchange Rate of Gold and Silver Money in Fatimid and Ayyubid Times," *Journal of the Economic and Social History of the Orient,* vol. 8, no. 1 (1965), pp. 1–46;

Philip Grierson, "The Monetary Reforms of Abd al-Malik," *Journal of the Economic and Social History of the Orient* 3 (1960): 241–64; D. Jacoby, "La population de Constantinople à l'époque byzantine," *Byzantion* 31 (1961): 81–110; idem, "Phénomènes de démographie rurale à Byzance aux XIIIe, XIVe, et XVe siècles," *Etudes Rurales*, nos. 5–6 (July-Sept. 1962), pp. 161–86; R. Janin, *Constantinople byzantin;* A. Kriesis, "Ueber die Wohnhaustyp des früheren Konstantinopel," *Byzantinische Zeitschrift* 53 (1960): 322–27; Ira Marvin Lapidus, *Muslim Cities in the Later Middle Ages;* F. Lot, *L'art militaire et les armées au Moyen Age en Europe et dans le Proche-Orient;* G. C. Miles, *The Coinage of the Umayyads of Spain;* Daniel Sperber, "Costs of Living in Roman Palestine," *Journal of the Economic and Social History of the Orient* 8 (1965): 248–71; M. Tikhomirov, *The Towns of Ancient Russia.*

3 For an effective review of what is now known concerning the history of climate, see Emmanuel Le Roy Ladurie, *Histoire du climat depuis l'an mil* (Paris: Flammarion, 1967).

4 Cf. Joseph R. Strayer, "The Laicization of French and English Society in the Thirteenth Century," *Speculum* 15 (1940): 76–86, reprinted in *Change in Medieval Society*, ed. Sylvia L. Thrupp (New York: Appleton-Century-Crofts, 1964), pp. 103–15; G. de Lagarde, *La naissance de l'esprit laïque au déclin du Moyen Age*, 3d ed. (Louvain: Nauwelaerts, 1956–63).

5 See L. Barkóczi, "The Population of Pannonia from Marcus Aurelius to Diocletian," *Acta Archaeologica Academiae Scientiarum Hungaricae* 16 (1964): 257–356.

6 For a discussion of the method, see F. G. Maier, "Römische Bevölkerungsgeschichte und Inschriftenstatistik," *Historia* 2 (1953–54): 318–51; R. Etienne, "Démographie et épigraphie," *Atti del III Congresso Internazionale di Epigrafia Greca e Latina* (Rome, 1959), pp. 415–24; A. Degrassi, "L'indicazione dell'età nelle iscrizioni sepolcrali latine," *Akte des IV Internationalen Kongresses für griechische und lateinische Epigraphie* (Vienna, 1964), pp. 72–98. But for a criticism of certain uses of the inscriptions, see K. Hopkins, "On the Probable Age Structure of Roman Population," *Population Studies* 20 (1966–67): 245–64.

7 See, most recently, Harry A. Miskimin, "Two Reforms of Charlemagne?" *Economic History Review*, 2d ser. 20 (1967): 35–52.

8 See D. M. Metcalf, "How Large was the Anglo-Saxon Currency?" *Economic History Review*, 2d ser. 18 (1965): 475–82; idem, "The Prosperity of North-Western Europe in the Eighth and Ninth Centuries," *Economic History Review*, 2d ser. 20 (1967): 344–57; Philip Grierson, "Mint Output in the Tenth Century," *Economic History Review*, 2d ser. 9 (1957): 462–66; idem, "The Volume of Anglo-Saxon Coinage," *Economic History Review*, 2d ser. 20 (1967): 153–60.

9 G. Acsadi, J. Nemeskéri, and L. Harsányi, "Le cimetière du XIe siècle de Kerpuszta," *Acta Archaeologica Academiae Scientiarum Hungaricae* 11 (1959): 418–55. On the method, see J. Nemeskéri, J. Hardanyi, and G. Acsadi, "Methoden zur Diagnose des Lebensalters von Skelettfunde," *Anthropologische Anzeiger* 24 (1960): 70–95.

10 *Polyptyque de l'abbé Irminon ou dénombrement des manses, des serfs, et des revenus de l'abbaye de Saint-Germain-des-Prés sous le règne de Charlemagne*, ed. B. Guérard (Paris: Imprimerie royale, 1844).

11 See section II, B.

12 See my "The Agrarian Revolution in Southern France and Italy, 801–1150," *Speculum* 33 (1958): 23–41; "Church Property on the European Continent, 701–1200," *Speculum* 36 (1961): 81–99; "The History of the Rural Seigneury in Italy, 701–1200," *Agricultural History* 33 (1959): 58–71; "Land, Family, and Women in Continental Europe, 701–1200," *Traditio* 18 (1962): 89–120; "Treasure Hoards in the Italian Economy, 960–1139," *Economic History Review* 10 (1957): 1–14.

13 V. H. Galbraith, *The Making of Domesday Book* (Oxford: Oxford University Press, Clarendon Press, 1961); R. Weldon Finn, *An Introduction to Domesday Book* (New York: Barnes and Noble, 1963); Henry Ellis, *A General Introduction to Domesday Book*, 2 vols. (London: Eyre and Spottiswoode, 1833).

14 See Russell, *British Medieval Population.*

15 See bibliography, especially section II.

16 See, for example, C. M. Cipolla, *Studi di storia della moneta*, vol. 1, *I movimenti dei*

cambi in Italia dal secolo XIII al XV; Harry A. Miskimin, "Monetary Movements and Market Structure Forces for Contraction in Fourteenth and Fifteenth Century Europe," *Journal of Economic History* 24 (1964): 470–90; idem, *Money, Prices, and Foreign Exchange in Fourteenth Century France;* idem, "Two reforms of Charlemagne?"

17 See bibliography, section IV, B.
18 See bibliography, section V.
19 W. Abel, *Die Wüstungen des ausgehenden Mittelalters;* M. W. Beresford, *The Lost Villages of England;* H. Pohléndt, *Die Verbreitung der mittelalterlichen Wüstungen*
20 *Villages désertes et histoire économique, XIe-XVIIIe siècle.*

BIBLIOGRAPHY

This bibliography is not exhaustive. Quantification is so widespread in medieval studies today that many more works might have been included. But if it is not comprehensive, it is at least representative of the many uses to which statistics are now being put.

For the convenience of those using the bibliography, the titles have been grouped in six principal sections: Demography; Medieval Agrarian Society; Money, Credit, Prices, and Wages; Commerce and Industry; Finances; Social Structures and Social Indicators. I do not pretend to have infallibly shepherded all my titles into their appropriate pens. Data on tariffs, for example, appear under the categories of both Commerce and Finances. Those who wish to use this bibliography to best effect should seek their references under several related topics. In their search, they may become further convinced of the plenitude of statistical studies in an age even today widely considered prestatistical.

I. DEMOGRAPHY

A. Studies of Medieval Populations

Ammann, H. "Die Bevölkerung von Stadt und Landschaft Basels am Ausgang des Mittelalters." *Baseler Zeitschrift* . . . 49 (1950): 25–52.
Andréadès, A. "De la population de Constantinople sous les empereurs byzantins." *Metron* 1 (1920): 68–119.
Arnould, M. A. *Les dénombrements de foyers dans le Comté de Hainaut, XIVe-XVIe siècles.* Brussels: Palais des Académies, 1956.
Baratier, E. *La démographie provençale du XIIIe au XVIe siècle (avec chiffres de comparaison pour le XVIIIe siècle).* Paris: SEVPEN (Société d'Editions et Vente des Publications de l'Education nationale), 1961.
Barkan, O. M. "Essai sur les données statistiques de registres de recensement dans l'Empire Ottoman aux XVe et XVIe siècles." *Journal of the Economic and Social History of the Orient* 1 (1957): 9–36.
Barkóczi, L. "The Population of Pannonia from Marcus Aurelius to Diocletian. *Acta Archaeologica Academiae Scientiarum Hungaricae* 16 (1964): 257–356.
Bautier, Robert. "Feux, population, et structure sociale au milieu du XVe siècle.

L'exemple de Carpentras." *Annales: Economies-Sociétés-Civilisations* 14 (1959): 255–68.

Bellettini, A. *La popolazione di Bologna dal XV secolo all' unificazione italiana.* Bologna: Zanichelli, 1961.

Beloch, J. *Bevölkerungsgeschichte Italiens.* 3 vols. Berlin: De Gruyter, 1937, 1939, 1961.

———. "Die Bevölkerung Europas im Mittelalter." *Zeitschrift für Sozialwissenschaft* 3 (1900): 405–23.

———. "Die Bevölkerung Europas zur Zeit der Renaissance." *Zeitschrift für Sozialwissenschaft* 3 (1900): 765–86.

———. "La popolazione di Venezia nei secoli XVI e XVII." *Nuovo Archivio Veneto* 3 (1902): 5–49.

Bergier, J.-F., and Solari, L. "Histoire et élaboration statistique. L'exemple de la population de Genève au XVe siècle." In *Mélanges d'histoire économique et sociale en hommage au Professeur Antony Babel,* edited by Jean-François Bergier and Anne-Marie Piuz. 2 vols. Geneva, 1963.

Biraben, J. N. "La population de Reims et son arrondissement et la vérification statistique des recensements anciens." *Population* 16 (1961): 722–30.

———. "La population de Toulouse au XIVe et XVe siècles." *Journal des Savants* (Paris), Oct.-Dec. 1964, pp. 284–300.

Buckatzsch, E. J. "The Constancy of Local Populations and Migration in England before 1800." *Population Studies* 5 (1951–52): 62–69.

Burn, A. R. *"Hic Breve Vivitur:* The Expectation of Life in the Roman Empire." *Past and Present* 4 (1953): 2–31.

Casini, Bruno. *Aspetti della vita economica e sociale di Pisa dal Catasto del 1428-1429.* Biblioteca del "Bollettino Storico Pisano," Collana Storica, 3. Pisa: Giardini, 1965.

———, ed. *Il Catasto di Pisa del 1428-29.* Pubblicazioni della Società Storica Pisana, Collana Storica, 2. Pisa: Giardini, 1964.

Charanis, P. "A Note on the Population and Cities of the Byzantine Empire in the Thirteenth Century." In *The Joshua Starr Memorial Volume.* Jewish Social Science Publications, 1. New York, 1953.

Cipolla, C. M. "Profilo di storia demografica della città di Pavia." *Bollettino Storico Pavese* 6 (1943): 5–87.

———. "Popolazione e proprietari della campagna secondo un ruolo di contribuenti del sec. XII." *Bollettino della Società Pavese di Storia Patria* 46 (1947): 85–97.

Cooper, T. M. "The Numbers and Distribution of the Population of Medieval Scotland." *Scottish Historical Review* 26 (1947): 2–9.

Cuvelier, J. "Contribution à l'histoire financière et démographique de Louvain au Moyen Age." *Bulletin de la Commission Royale d'Histoire* (Belgium) 108 (1943): 1–61.

Dollinger, P. "Le chiffre de population de Paris au XIVe siècle: 210,000 ou 80,000?" *Revue Historique* 216 (1956): 35–44.

Duncan-Jones, R. P. "Human Numbers in Towns and Town Organizations of the Roman Empire: The Evidence of Gifts." *Historia* 13 (1964): 199–208.

Ekwall, E. *Studies on the Population of Medieval London.* Stockholm: Almqvist and Wiksell, 1956.

Fiumi, E. "Il computo della popolazione di Volterra nel medio evo secondo il 'sal delle bocche.' " *Archivio Storico Italiano* 107 (1949): 3–16.

———. *Demografia, movimento urbanistico, e classi sociali in Prato dall' età comunale ai tempi moderni.* Florence: Olschki, 1968.

———. 'La demografia fiorentina nelle pagine di Giovanni Villani." *Archivio Storico Italiano* 108 (1950): 78–158.

———. 'Fioritura e decadenza dell' economia fiorentina." *Archivio Storico Italiano* 115 (1957): 385–439; 116 (1958): 443–510; 117 (1959): 427–502.

———. 'Note di storia medievale volterrana." *Archivio Storico Italiano* 103 (1945–46): 82–112.

———. "Sui rapporti economici tra città e contado nell' età comunale." *Archivio Storico Italiano* 114 (1956): 18–68.

———. "La popolazione del territorio volterrano-sangimignanese ed il problema demografico dell'età comunale." In *Studi in onore di Amintore Fanfani,* 1:249–90. Milan: Giuffrè, 1962.

———. "Stato della popolazione e distribuzione della ricchezza in Prato secondo il Catasto del 1428–29." *Archivio Storico Italiano* 123 (1965): 277–303.

———. *Storia economica e sociale di San Gimignano.* Florence: Olschki, 1961.

Fort, José Iglésies. *El fogaje de 1365–1370. Contribución al conocimiento de la población de Cataluña en la segunda mitad del siglo XIV.* Memorias de la Real Academia de Ciencias y Artes de Barcelona, 34, no. 11. Barcelona, 1962.

Fourquin, Guy. "La population de la région parisienne aux environs de 1328." *Le Moyen Age* 62 (1956): 63–91.

Frugoni, A. "G. Villani, 'Cronica,' XI, 94." *Bollettino dell' Istituto Storico Italiano per il Medio Evo e Archivio Muratoriano* 77 (1965): 229–55.

Gejvall, N. G. *Westerhus. Medieval Population and Church in the Light of Skeletal Remains.* Lund: Ohlsson, 1960.

Genicot, L. "On the Evidence of Growth of Population in the West." In *Change in Medieval Society,* edited by Sylvia L. Thrupp, pp. 14–29. New York: Appleton-Century-Crofts, 1964.

———. "Sur les témoignages d'accroissement de la population en occident du XIe au XIIIe siècle." *Cahiers d'Histoire Mondiale* 1 (1953): 446–62.

Gyorffy, G. "Einwohnerzahl und Bevölkerungsdichte in Ungarn bis zum Anfang des XIV. Jahrhunderts." *Studia Historica* 42 (1960): 1–31.

Hallam, H. E. "Some Thirteenth Century Censuses." *Economic History Review,* 2d ser. 10 (1957): 341–61.

———. "Population Density in Medieval Fenland." *Economic History Review,* 2d ser. 14 (1961): 71–81.

Harley, J. B. "Population Trends and Agricultural Developments from the Warwickshire Hundred Rolls of 1279." *Economic History Review,* 2d ser. 11 (1958): 8–18.

Herlihy, David. "Population, Plague, and Social Change in Rural Pistoia, 1201–1430." *Economic History Review,* 2d ser. 17 (1965): 225–44.

Higounet-Nadal, Arlette. *Les comptes de la taille et les sources de l'histoire démographique de Périgueux au XIVe siècle.* Ecole Pratique des Hautes Etudes, VIe section, Centre de Recherches Historiques, Démographie et Sociétés, 9. Paris: SEVPEN, 1965.

Hörl, Irmgard. *Die Zusammensetzung und Schichtung der ältesten Münchner Bevölkerung, von 1158, dem Gründungsjahr der Stadt, bis 1403, dem Jahr der Neuordnung der Stadtverfassung.* Munich, 1952.

Hoskins, W. G. "The Population of an English Village, 1086–1801: A Study of Wigston Magna." *Transactions of the Leicestershire Archeological and Historical Society* 33 (1957). Reprinted in *Provincial England. Essays in Social and Economic History.* London: Macmillan, 1963.

Jacoby, D. "La population de Constantinople à l'époque byzantine: Un problème de démographie urbaine." *Byzantion* 31 (1961): 81–110.

———. "Phénomènes de démographie rurale à Byzance aux XIIIe, XIVe, et XVe siècles." *Etudes Rurales*, nos. 5–6 (July-Sept. 1962), pp. 161–86.

Keyser, E. *Bevölkerungsgeschichte Deutschlands.* 2d ed. Leipzig: Hirzel, 1941.

Kirchgässner, Bernhard. *Wirtschaft und Bevölkerung der Reichsstadt Esslingen im Spätmittelalter. Nach den Steuerbüchern, 1360–1460.* Esslinger Studien, 9. Esslingen: Stadtarchiv, 1964.

Krause, J. "The Medieval Household: Large or Small?" *Economic History Review,* 2d ser. 9 (1956): 420–32.

Kriesis, A. "Ueber die Wohnhaustyp des früheren Konstantinopel." *Byzantinische Zeitschrift* 53 (1960): 322–27.

Kronshage, W. *Die Bevölkerung Göttingen: Ein demographischer Beitrag zur Sozial- und Wirtschaftsgeschichte von 14. bis 17. Jahrhundert.* Göttingen: Vandenhoeck and Ruprecht, 1960.

Landgraf, H. *Bevölkerung und Wirtschaft Kiels im 15. Jahrhundert.* Quellen und Forschungen zur Geschichte Schleswigs-Holsteins, 39. Neumünster: Wachholtz, 1959.

Lot, F. "L'état des paroisses et des feux en 1328." *Bibliothèque de l'Ecole des Chartes* 90 (1929): 51–107, 256–315.

———. *Recherches sur la population et la superficie des cités remontant à la période gallo-romaine.* Bibliothèque de l'Ecole des Hautes Etudes, fasc. 287, 296, 301. Paris: Champion, 1945–53.

Luzzatto, G. "L'inurbamento delle popolazioni rurali in Italia nei secoli XII e XIII." In *Studi in onore di Enrico Besta,* 2:183–205. Milan, 1938.

Mols, R. "Die Bevölkerungsgeschichte Belgiens im Lichte der heutigen Forschung." *Vierteljahrsschrift für Sozial- und Wirtschaftsgeschichte* 46 (1959): 491–511.

———. *Introduction à la démographie historique des villes d'Europe du XIVe au XVIIIe siècle.* 3 vols. Louvain: Gembloux-Duculot, 1954–56.

Montanari, Paolo. *Documenti sulla popolazione di Bologna alla fine del trecento.* Fonti per la storia di Bologna, Testi, 1. Bologna: Istituto per la Storia di Bologna, 1966.

Pasero, C. "Dati statistici e notizie intorno al movimento della popolazione bresciana durante il dominio veneto, 1426–1797." *Archivio Storico Lombardo* 88 (1961): 71–97.

Perrin, C. Edmond. "Note sur la population de Villeneuve-Saint-Georges au IXe siècle." *Le Moyen Age* 69 (1963): 75–86

Phelps Brown, E. H., and Hopkins, Sheila V. "Wage-Rates and Prices: Evidence for Population Pressure in the Sixteenth Century." *Economica* 24 (1957): 289–306.

Postan, M. M. "Some Economic Evidence of Declining Population in the Later Middle Ages." *Economic History Review*, 2d ser. 2 (1950): 221–46.

Reinke, H. "Bevölkerungsprobleme der Hansestädte." *Hansische Geschichtsblätter* 70 (1951): 1–33.

Rice, Eugene. "Recent Studies on the Population of Europe, 1348–1620." *Renaissance News*, vol. 18, no. 2 (1965), pp. 180–87.

Robinson, W. C. "Money, Population, and Economic Change in Late Medieval Europe." *Economic History Review*, 2d ser. 12 (1959): 63–76.

Russell, J. C. "Aspects démographiques des débuts de la féodalité." *Annales: Economies-Sociétés-Civilisations* 20 (1965): 1118–27.

———. *British Medieval Population.* Albuquerque: University of New Mexico Press, 1948.

———. "Demographic Limitations of the Spaulding Serf Lists." *Economic History Review*, 2d ser. 15 (1962): 138–44.

———. "L'évolution démographique de Montpellier au Moyen Age." *Annales du Midi* 74 (1962): 345–60.

———. *Late Ancient and Medieval Population.* Transactions of the American Philosophical Society, n. s. 48. Philadelphia: American Philosophical Society, 1958.

———. "Late Medieval Balkan and Asia Minor Population." *Journal of the Economic and Social History of the Orient* 3 (1960): 265–74.

———. "Late Medieval Population Patterns." *Speculum* 20 (1945): 151–71.

———. "Medieval Midland and Northern Migration to London, 1100–1365." *Speculum* 34 (1959): 341–45.

———. "The Medieval Monedatge of Aragon and Valencia." *Proceedings of the American Philosophical Society* 106 (1962): 483–504.

———. "The Metropolitan City Region of the Middle Ages." *Journal of Regional Science* 2 (1960): 55–70.

———. "The Pre-Plague Population of England." *Journal of British Studies* 5 (1966): 1–21.

———. "A Quantitative Approach to Medieval Population Change." *Journal of Economic History* 24 (1964): 1–21.

———. "Recent Advances in Medieval Demography." *Speculum* 40 (1965): 84–101.

Smith, R. S. "Barcelona 'Bills of Mortality' and Population, 1457–1590." *Journal of Political Economy* 44 (1936): 84–93.

———. "Fourteenth Century Population Records of Catalonia." *Speculum* 19 (1944): 494–501.

Spiess, Werner. *Die Ratsherrn der Hansestadt Braunschweig, 1231–1671.* Braunschweig: Waisenhaus, 1940.

Szilágyi, J. "Beiträge zur Statistik der Sterblichkeit in den westeuropäischen Provinzen des römischen Imperiums." *Acta Archaeologica Academiae Scientiarum Hungaricae* 13 (1961) : 125–55.

———. "Beiträge zur Statistik der Sterblichkeit in der illyrischen Provinzgruppe und in Nord-Italien (Gallia Padana)." *Acta Archaeologica Academiae Scientiarum Hungaricae* 14 (1962): 297–396.

———. "Die Sterblichkeit in den nordafrikanischen Provinzen." *Acta Archaeologica Academiae Scientiarum Hungaricae* 17 (1965): 310–34; 18 (1966): 235–77; 19 (1967): 24–59.

———. "Die Sterblichkeit in den Städten Mittel- und Süditaliens sowie in Hispanien (in der römischen Kaiserzeit)." *Acta Archaeologica Academiae Scientiarum Hungaricae* 15 (1963): 127–224; 16 (1964): 129–224.

Thrupp, Sylvia L. "The Problem of Replacement Rates in Late Medieval English Population." *Economic History Review,* 2d ser. 18 (1965): 101–19.

———. "A Survey of the Alien Population in England in 1440." *Speculum* 32 (1957): 262–73.

Titow, J. Z. "Some Evidence of Thirteenth Century Population Increase." *Economic History Review,* 2d ser. 14 (1961): 218–224.

Torres-Balbás, Leopoldo. "Extension y demografia de las ciudades hispano-musulmannas," *Studia Islamica* 3 (1955): 35–59.

Vannerus, J. "Dénombrements luxembourgeoises du XVe siècle." *Bulletin de la Commission Royale d'Histoire* 106 (1941): 237–314.

Vielrose, E. *Die Bevölkerung Polens vom X. bis XVIII. Jahrhundert.* Marburg: Lahn, 1958.

B. Studies Containing Demographic Materials

Emery, R. W. *The Jews of Perpignan in the Thirteenth Century.* New York: Columbia University Press, 1959.

Février, Paul-Albert. *Le développement urbain en Provence de l'époque romaine à la fin du XIVe siècle. Archéologie et histoire urbaine.* Bibliothèque des Ecoles Françaises d'Athènes et de Rome, 202. Paris: de Boccard, 1964.

Fischel, Walter J. "The City in Islam." *Middle Eastern Affairs* 7 (1956): 227–32.

Ganshof, F. L. *Etude sur le développement des villes entre Loire et Rhin au Moyen Age.* Paris: Presses Universitaires de France, 1943.

Heers, Jacques. *Gênes au XVe siècle. Activité économique et problèmes sociaux.* Ecole Pratique des Hautes Etudes, VIe section, Centre de Recherches Historiques, Affaires et Gens d'Affaires, 24. Paris: SEVPEN, 1961.

Herlihy, David. *Medieval and Renaissance Pistoia: The Social History of an Italian Town, 1200–1480.* New Haven: Yale University Press, 1967.

Herzog, Erich. *Die Ottonische Stadt: Die Anfänge der mittelalterlichen Stadtbaukunst in Deutschland.* Frankfurter Forschungen zur Architekturgeschichte, 2. Berlin: Mann, 1964.

Hill, J. W. F. *Medieval Lincoln.* Cambridge: Cambridge University Press, 1948.

Janin, R. *Constantinople byzantin.* Paris: Institut français d'études byzantines, 1950.

Joris, A. *La ville du Huy au Moyen Age, des origines à la fin du XIVe siècle.* Bibliothèque de la Faculté de Philosophie et Lettres de I'Université de Liège, 152. Paris, 1959.

Keyser, E., ed. *Deutsches Städtebuch.* 4 vols. Stuttgart: Kohlhammer, 1939–62.

Lapidus, Ira Marvin. *Muslim Cities in the Later Middle Ages.* Joint Center for Urban Studies, Harvard Middle Eastern Studies, 11. Cambridge, Mass.: Harvard University Press, 1966.

Lesage, G. *Marseille angevine, 1264–1348.* Paris: de Boccard, 1950.

Nudi, Giacinto. *Storia urbanistica di Livorno.* Venice: Pozza, 1959.

Rothert, Hermann, ed. *Das älteste Bürgerbuch der Stadt Soest, 1302–1449.* Veröffentlichungen der Historischen Kommission für Westfalen, 27. Münster, 1958.

Salvini, J. *Le diocèse de Poitiers à la fin du Moyen Age.* Publications de l'Université de Poitiers. Etudes régionales, 1. Poitiers, 1946.

Schmidt, Bertold. *Die späte Völkerwanderungszeit in Mitteldeutschland.* Veröffentlichungen des Landesmuseums für Vorgeschichte in Halle, 18. Halle, 1961.

Schneider, J. *La ville de Metz aux XIIIe et XIVe siècles.* Nancy: Thomas, 1950.

Slicher van Bath, B. H. "The Economic and Social Conditions in the Frisian Districts, 900–1500." [Wageningen Landbouwhoogeschool], *Afdeling Agrarische Geschiedenis Bijdragen* 13 (1965): 97–133.

Tikhomirov, M. *The Towns of Ancient Russia.* Moscow: Foreign Languages Publishing House, 1959.

Williams, Gwyn A. *Medieval London from Commune to Capital.* London: Athlone, 1963.

Wittwer, D. *Le Livre de Bourgeoisie de la ville de Strasbourg, 1440–1530.* 3 vols. Strasbourg, 1961.

Wolff, Philippe. *Les "estimes" toulousaines des XIVe et XVe siècles.* Bibliothèque de l'Association Marc Bloch de Toulouse, Documents d'Histoire Méridionale. Toulouse: Laboureur, 1956.

C. Agricultural Settlement

Abel, W. *Die Wüstungen des ausgehenden Mittelalters. Ein Beitrag zur Siedlungs- und Agrargeschichte Deutschlands.* Quellen und Forschungen zur Agrargeschichte, 1. 2d ed. Stuttgart: Fischer, 1955.

Beresford, M. W. *The Lost Villages of England.* New York: Philosophical Library, 1954.

Boutrouche, R. "Les courants de peuplement dans l'Entre-Deux-Mer." *Annales d'Histoire Economique et Sociale* 7 (1935): 13–37, 124–54.

Donkin, R. A. "Settlement and Depopulation on Cistercian Estates during the Twelfth and Thirteenth Centuries, Especially in Yorkshire." *Bulletin of the Institute of Historical Research* 33 (1960).

Fournier, Gabriel. *Le peuplement rural en Basse-Auvergne durant le Haut Moyen Age.* Publications de la Faculté des Lettres et Sciences Humaines de Clermont-Ferrand, 2d ser., fasc. 12. Paris: Presses Universitaires de France, 1962.

Higounet, Charles. "Mouvements de population dans le Midi de la France du XIe au XVe siècle d'après les noms de personne et de lieu." *Annales: Economies-Sociétés-Civilisations* 8 (1953): 1–24.

Hoskins, W. G., and Stamp, L. D. *The Commons Land of England and Wales.* London: Collins, 1963.

Ourliac, P. *Les sauvetés du Comminges: Etudes et documents sur les villages fondés par les hospitaliers dans la région des côteaux commingeois.* Toulouse: Boisseau, 1947.

Pohlendt, H. *Die Verbreitung der mittelalterlichen Wüstungen in Deutschland.* Göttingen: Geographisches Institut der Universität Göttingen, 1950.

Sawyer, P. H. "The Density of Danish Settlement in England." *University of Birmingham Historical Journal* 6 (1957).

Villages désertes et histoire économique, XIe-XVIIIe siècle. Ecole Pratique des Hautes Etudes, VIe section, Centre de Recherches Historiques, Les Hommes et la Terre, 11. Paris: SEVPEN, 1965.

D. Medieval Plagues, Diseases, and Famines

Amulree, Lord. "Monastic Infirmaries." In *The Evolution of Hospitals in Britain,* edited by F. N. L. Poynter. London: Medical Books, 1964.

Bean, J. M. W. "Plague, Population, and Economic Decline." *Economic History Review,* 2d ser. 15 (1963): 423–36.

Bowsky, William M. "The Impact of the Black Death upon Sienese Government and Society." *Speculum* 39 (1964): 1–34.

Campbell, Anna M. *The Black Death and Men of Learning.* New York: Columbia University Press, 1931.

Capra, P. J. "Au sujet de famines en Aquitaine au XIVe siècle." *Revue Historique de Bordeaux et du Département de la Gironde* 4 (1955): 1–36.

Carpentier, E. *Une ville devant la peste: Orvieto et la peste noire de 1348.* Paris: SEVPEN, 1963.

Celli, Angelo. *The History of Malaria in the Roman Campagna.* London: Bale and Danielsson, 1933.

Deaux, George. *The Black Death, 1347.* London: Hamilton, 1969.

Dubled, Henri. "Consequences économiques et sociales de mortalités du XIVe siècle, essentiellement en Alsace." *Revue d'Histoire Economique et Sociale* 37 (1959): 273–294.

Fisher, J. L. "The Black Death in Essex." *Essex Review* (1943), pp. 13-21.

Fourquin, G. "La population de la région parisienne aux environs de 1348." *Le Moyen Age* 62 (1956): 63–91.

Graus, F. "Autour de la peste noire au XIVe siècle en Bohême." *Annales: Economies-Sociétés-Civilisations* 18 (1963): 720–24.

Kelter, E. "Das deutsche Wirtschaftsleben des 14. und 15. Jahrhunderts im Schatten der Pestepidemien." *Jahrbuch für Nationalökonomie und Statistik* 165 (1953): 160–208.

Larenaudie, Marie-Joseph. "Les famines en Languedoc aux XIVe et XVe siècles." *Annales du Midi* 64 (1952): 27–39.

Levett, Ada E. *The Black Death on the Estates of the See of Winchester.* Oxford Studies in Social and Legal History, 5. Oxford: Oxford University Press, Clarendon Press, 1916.

MacArthur, W. P. "The Identification of Some Pestilences Recorded in Irish Annals." *Irish Historical Studies* 6 (1949): 169–88.

Mollat, M. "Notes sur la mortalité à Paris au temps de la Peste Noire, d'après les comptes de l'oeuvre de Saint-Germain l'Auxerrois." *Le Moyen Age* 69 (1963): 505–27.

Møller-Christensen, Vilhelm. *Ten Lepers from Naestved in Denmark: A Study of Skeletons from a Medieval Danish Leper Hospital.* Copenhagen: Danish Science Press, 1953.

Prat, G. "Albi et la peste noire." *Annales du Midi* 64 (1952): 15–25.

Renouard, Y. "Conséquences et intérêt démographiques de la peste noire de 1348." *Population* 3 (1948): 459–66.

———. "La peste noire de 1348–1350." *Revue de Paris* 57 (1950): 107–19.

Robbins, H. "A Comparison of the Effects of the Black Death on the Economic Organization of France and England." *Journal of Political Economy* 36 (1928): 447–79.

Russell, J. C. "Effects of Pestilence and Plague, 1315–1385." *Comparative Studies in Society and History* 8 (1966): 464–73.

Saltmarsh, J. "Plague and Economic Decline in the Later Middle Ages." *Cambridge Historical Journal* 7 (1941): 23–41.

Schreiner, Johan. *Pest og Prisfall i Senmiddelalderen.* Oslo: Dybwad, 1948.

Thompson, A. Hamilton. "The Registers of John Glynwell, Bishop of Lincoln, for the Years 1347–50." *Archaeological Journal* 68 (1911): 301–60.

———. "The Pestilences of the Fourteenth Century in the Diocese of York." *Archaeological Journal* 71 (1914): 97–154.

Thrupp, Sylvia L. "Plague Effects in Medieval Europe." *Comparative Studies in Society and History* 8 (1966): 474–83.

Ziegler, Philip. *The Black Death.* London: Collins, 1969.

II. MEDIEVAL AGRARIAN SOCIETY

A. Yield Ratios

Bennett, M. K. "British Wheat Yield per Acre for Seven Centuries." *Economic History* 3 (1937): 12–29.

Beveridge, W. H. "The Yield and Price of Corn in the Middle Ages." *Economic History* (a supplement to the *Economic Journal*) 1 (May 1927): 155–67.

Hoskins, W. G. "Harvest Fluctuations and English Economic History, 1480–1619." *The Agricultural History Review* 12 (1964): 28–42.

Lennard, R. "Statistics of Corn Yields in Medieval England." *Economic History* 3 (1937): 173–92.

Mertens, J. A., and Verhulst, A. E. "Yield-Ratios in Flanders in the Fourteenth Century." *Economic History Review*, 2d ser. 19 (1966): 175–82.

Slicher van Bath, B. H. "Yield Ratios, 810–1820." [Wageningen Landbouwhooge-school], *Afdeling Agrarische Geschiedenis Bijdragen,* no. 10 (1963).

B. Studies of Particular Estates and Areas

Baker, A. R. H. "Open Fields and Partible Inheritance on a Kent Manor." *Economic History Review*, 2d ser. 17 (1964): 1–23.

Bishop, T. A. M. "The Rotation of Crops at Westerham, 1297–1350." *Economic History Review*, vol. 9, no. 1 (1938–39), pp. 38–44.

Boutruche, R. *La crise d'une société: Seigneurs et paysans du Bordelais pendant la Guerre de Cent Ans.* Publications de la Faculté des Lettres de l'Université de Strasbourg, fasc. 110. Paris: Belles Lettres, 1947.

———. "La dévastation des campagnes pendant la guerre de Cent Ans et la reconstruction agricole de la France." In *Mélanges 1945,* 3: 127–63. Publications de l'Université de Strasbourg, Faculté des Lettres, 106. Paris: Belles Lettres, 1947.

Chibnall, A. C. *Sherington: Fiefs and Fields on a Buckinghamshire Village.* Cambridge: Cambridge University Press, 1965.

Conti, Elio. *La formazione della struttura agraria moderna nel contado fiorentino.* Vol. 1, *L'età precomunale.* Vol. 3, pt. 2, *Monografie e tavole statistiche, secoli XV–XIX.* Istituto Storico Italiano per il Medio Evo, Studi Storici, fasc. 51–55, 64–68. Rome: Sede dell'Istituto, 1965.

Coopland, G. W. *The Abbey of St. Bertin and Its Neighborhood, 900–1350.*

Oxford Studies in Social and Legal History, 4. Oxford: Oxford University Press, Clarendon Press, 1914.

Darby, H. C., ed. *The Domesday Geography of Eastern England.* Cambridge: Cambridge University Press, 1952.

———, and Campbell, Eila M. J., eds. *The Domesday Geography of South-East England.* Cambridge: Cambridge University Press, 1962.

———, and Maxwell, I. S., eds. *The Domesday Geography of Northern England.* Cambridge: Cambridge University Press, 1962.

———, and Terrett, I. B., eds. *The Domesday Geography of Midland England.* Cambridge: Cambridge University Press, 1954.

Davenport, F. G. *The Economic Development of a Norfolk Manor, 1086–1565.* Cambridge: Cambridge University Press, 1906.

Déléage, A. *La vie rurale en Bourgogne jusqu'au début du onzième siècle.* 3 vols. Mâcon: Protat, 1941.

Dollinger, P. *L'évolution des classes rurales en Bavière depuis la fin de l'époque carolingienne jusqu'au milieu du XIIIe siècle.* Paris: Belles Lettres, 1949.

———. "Les transformations du régime domanial en Bavière au XIIIe siècle d'après deux censiers de l'abbaye de Baumburg." *Le Moyen Age* 56 (1950): 279–306.

Donnelly, J. S. "Changes in the Grange Economy of English and Welsh Cistercian Abbeys, 1300–1540." *Traditio* 10 (1954): 399–458.

Duby, G. "Un inventaire des profits de la seigneurie clunisienne à la mort de Pierre le Vénérable." *Studia Anselmiana* 40 (1956): 128–40.

———. *La société aux XIe et XIIe siècles dans la région mâconnaise.* Paris: Colín, 1963.

Finberg, H. P. R. *Tavistock Abbey. A Study in the Social and Economic History of Devon.* Cambridge Studies in Medieval Life and Thought, n.s. 2. Cambridge: Cambridge University Press, 1951.

Fourquin, Guy, *Les campagnes de la région parisienne à la fin du Moyen Age, du milieu du XIIIe siècle au début du XVIe siècle.* Publications de la Faculté des Lettres et Sciences Humaines de Paris, Série "Recherches," 10. Paris: Presses Universitaires de France, 1964.

Genicot, L. *L'économie rurale namuroise au Bas Moyen Age, 1199–1429.* Louvain: Bibliothèque de l'Université, 1943.

———. "L'étendue des exploitations agricoles dans le comté de Namur à la fin du XIIIe siècle." *Etudes rurales,* nos. 5–6 (1962), pp. 5–31.

Guérin, I. *La vie rurale en Sologne aux XIVe et XVe siècles.* Les hommes et la terre, 5. Paris: SEVPEN, 1960.

Hallam, H. E. *Settlement and Society: A Study of the Early Agrarian History of South Lincolnshire.* Cambridge Studies in Economic History. Cambridge: Cambridge University Press, 1965.

Harvey, P. D. A. *A Medieval Oxfordshire Village, Cuxham, 1240 to 1400.* London: Oxford University Press, 1965.

Higounet, Charles. *La grange de Vaulerent: Structure et exploitation d'un terroir cistercien dans la plaine de France, XIIe–XVe siècles.* Paris: SEVPEN, 1965.

Hilton, R. H. *The Economic Development of Some Leicestershire Estates in the Fourteenth and Fifteenth Centuries.* Oxford: Oxford University Press, 1947.

Hunt, T. J., ed. *The Medieval Customs of the Manors of Taunton and Bradford on Tone.* Somerset Record Society, 66. Frome: Butler and Tanner, 1962.

Jones, P. J. "An Italian Estate, 900–1200." *Economic History Review,* 2d ser. 7 (1954): 18–34.

Kleiminger, Rudolf. *Das Heiligengeisthospital von Wismar in sieben Jahrhunderten. Ein Beitrag zur Wirtschaftsgeschichte der Stadt, ihrer Höfe, und Dörfer.* Abhandlungen zur Handels- und Sozialgeschichte, Ed. im Auftrag des Hansischen Geschichtsverein, 4. Weimar: H. Böhlaus Nachfolger, 1962.

Kosminsky, E. A. *Studies in the Agrarian History of England in the Thirteenth Century.* Edited by R. H. Hilton; translated by Ruth Kisch. Oxford: Blackwell, 1956.

Lennard, R. "The Economic Position of the Bordars and Cottars of Domesday Book." *Economic Journal* 61 (1951): 342–71.

———. "The Demesnes of Glastonbury Abbey in the Eleventh and Twelfth Centuries." *Economic History Review,* 2d ser. 8 (1956): 355–63.

Levett, A. E. "The Financial Organization of the Manor." *Economic History Review,* vol. 1, no. 1 (1927–28), pp. 65–86.

Lodge, Eleanor C. *The Estates of the Archbishop and Chapter of Saint André of Bordeaux under English Rule.* Oxford Studies in Social and Legal History. Oxford: Oxford University Press, Clarendon Press, 1912.

Morgan, M. *The English Lands of the Abbey of Bec.* Oxford Historical Series. London: Oxford University Press, 1946.

Page, F. M. *The Estates of Croyland Abbey: A Study in Manorial Organization.* Cambridge Studies in Economic History. Cambridge: Cambridge University Press, 1934.

———, ed. *Wellingborough Manorial Accounts, A.D. 1258–1323. From the Account Rolls of Croyland Abbey.* Northamptonshire Record Society, 8. Kettering, 1936.

Postan, M. M. "Glastonbury Estates in the Twelfth Century." *Economic History Review,* 2d ser. 5 (1953): 358–67.

———. "Glastonbury Estates in the Twelfth Century: A Reply." *Economic History Review,* 2d ser. 9 (1956): 106–18.

Raftis, J. A. *The Estates of Ramsey Abbey. A Study in Economic Growth and Organization.* Pontifical Institute of Medieval Studies, Studies and Texts, 3. Toronto, 1957.

Sclafert, T. *Cultures en Haute-Provence. Déboisements et pâturages au Moyen Age.* Les hommes et la terre, 4. Paris: SEVPEN, 1959.

Slicher van Bath, B. H. "The Economic and Social Conditions in the Frisian Districts from 900 to 1500." [Wageningen Landbouwhogeschool], *Afdeling Agrarische Geschiedenis Bijdragen,* no. 13 (1965).

Strayer, J. R. "Economic Conditions in the County of Beaumont-le-Roger, 1261–1313." *Speculum* 26 (1951): 277–87.

Thiele, Augustinus. *Echternach und Himmerod. Beispiele benediktinischer und zisterziensischer Wirtschaftsführung im 12. und 13. Jahrhundert.* Forschungen zur Sozial- und Wirtschaftsgeschichte, 7. Stuttgart: Fischer, 1964.

C. *Studies of Large Areas*

Abel, W. *Agrarkrisen und Agrarkonjunktur: Eine Geschichte der Land- und Ernäh-rungswirtschaft Mitteleuropas seit dem hohen Mittelalter.* 2d ed. Hamburg: Parey, 1966.

———. *Geschichte der deutschen Landwirtschaft vom frühen Mittelalters bis zum 19. Jahrhundert.* Deutsche Agrargeschichte, 2. Stuttgart: Ulmer, 1962.

Baker, A. R. H. "Evidence in the 'Nonarum Inquisitiones' of Contracting Arable Lands in England during the Early Fourteenth Century." *Economic History Review,* 2d ser. 19 (1966): 518–32.

Barg, M. A. *Issledovaniia po istorii angliiskogo feodalizma v XI–XIII vv.* Studies in the History of English Feudalism in the Eleventh to Thirteenth Centuries. Moscow: Academy of Science, 1962.

Duby, Georges. *L'économie rurale et la vie des campagnes dans l'Occident médiéval.* 2 vols. Paris: Aubier, 1962.

———. *Rural Economy and Country Life in the Medieval West.* Translated by Cynthia Postan. Columbia: University of South Carolina Press, 1968.

Hannestad, K. *L'évolution des ressources agricoles de l'Italie du 4ème au 6ème siècle de notre ère.* Historisk-filosofiske Meddelelser, Danske Videnskabernes Selskab, Bind 40, nr. 1. Copenhagen: I kommision hos Munksgaard, 1962.

Herlihy, David. "The Agrarian Revolution in Southern France and Italy, 801–1150." *Speculum* 33 (1958): 23–41.

———. "Church Property on the European Continent, 701–1200." *Speculum* 36 (1961): 81–99.

———. "The History of the Rural Seigneury in Italy, 701–1200." *Agricultural History* 33 (1959): 58–71.

———. "Land, Family, and Women in Continental Europe, 701–1200." *Traditio* 18 (1962): 89–120.

Lennard, R. "The Long and Short Hundred in Agrarian Statistics." *Agricultural History Review* 8 (1960): 75–81.

———. *Rural England, 1086–1135. A Study of Social and Agrarian Conditions.* Oxford: Oxford University Press, Clarendon Press, 1959.

Postan, M. M., ed. *The Cambridge Economic History of Europe.* Vol. 1, *The Agrarian Life of the Middle Ages.* 2d ed. Cambridge: Cambridge University Press, 1966.

Ruggini, Lellia. *Economia e società nell' 'Italia Annonaria'. Rapporti fra agricoltura e commercio dal IV al VI secolo dopo Cristo.* Milan: Giuffrè, 1961.

Slicher van Bath, B. H. "Accounts and Diaries of Farmers before 1800 as Sources for Agricultural History." [Wageningen Landbouwhoogeschool], *Afdeling Agrarische Geschiedenis Bijdragen* 8 (1962): 5–33.

———. *The Agrarian History of Western Europe, A.D. 500–1850.* London: Arnold, 1963.

Titow, J. Z. "Some Differences between Manors and the Effects on the Condition of the Peasant in the Thirteenth Century." *Agricultural History Review* 10 (1962): 1–13.

Verhulst, A. "L'économie rurale de la Flandre et la dépression économique du bas Moyen Age." *Etudes rurales* 10 (1963): 68–80.

D. Studies of Livestock and Particular Crops

Dion, Roger. *Histoire de la vigne et du vin en France des origines au XIXe siècle.* Paris, 1959.

Donkin, R. A. "Cattle on the Estates of Medieval Cistercian Monasteries in England and Wales." *Economic History Review,* 2d ser. 15 (1963): 31–63.

————. "Cistercian Sheep-Farming and Wool Sales in the Thirteenth Century." *Agricultural History Review* 6 (1958): 2–8.

Lennard, R. "Statistics of Sheep in Medieval England." *Agricultural History Review* 7 (1959): 75–81.

Postan, M. M. "Village Livestock in the Thirteenth Century." *Economic History Review,* 2d ser. 15 (1962): 219–49.

Ryder, M. "Livestock Remains from Four Medieval Sites in Yorkshire." *Agricultural History Review* 9 (1961): 105–10.

Skeel, C. "The Cattle Trade between Wales and England from the 15th to the 19th Centuries." *Transactions of the Royal Historical Society,* 4th ser. 9 (1926): 135–58.

Trow-Smith, R. *A History of British Livestock Husbandry to 1700.* London: Routledge and Kegan Paul, 1957.

III. MONEY, CREDIT, PRICES, AND WAGES

A. Money and Credit

Ames, E. "The Sterling Crisis of 1337–1339." *Journal of Economic History* 25 (1965): 496–522.

Bigwood, G. *Le régime juridique et économique du commerce de l'argent dans la Belgique du Moyen Age.* Académie Royale de Belgique, Classe des Lettres et des Sciences Morales et Politiques, Mémoires, 2ème sér. 14. 2 vols. Brussels, 1921–22.

Bisson, T. N. "Coinage and Royal Monetary Policy in Languedoc during the Reign of Saint Louis." *Speculum* 32 (1957): 443–69.

Bolin, Sture, "Muhammed, Charlemagne, and Ruric." *The Scandinavian Economic History Review* 1 (1953): 5–39.

————. *State and Currency in the Roman Empire to 300 A.D.* Stockholm: Almqvist and Wiksell, 1958.

Cipolla, C. M. *Studi di storia della moneta.* Vol. 1, *I movimenti dei cambi in Italia dal secolo XIII al XV.* Pavia, 1948.

Craig, John. *The Mint. A History of the London Mint from A.D. 287 to 1948.* Cambridge: Cambridge University Press, 1953.

De Roover, R. "*Cambium ad Venetias:* Contribution to the History of Foreign Exchange." In *Studi in Onore di Armando Sapori,* 1:629–48. Milan: Istituto editoriale cisalpino, 1956.

————. *L'évolution de la lettre de change, XIVe–XVIIIe siècles.* Paris: Colin, 1953.

————. *The Rise and Decline of the Medici Bank, 1397–1494.* Cambridge, Mass.: Harvard University Press, 1963.

Gaettens, Richard. *Die Wirtschaftsgebiete und der Wirtschaftsgebietspfennig der Hohenstaufenzeit.* Lübeck: Riechmann, 1963.

Girard, Albert. "La guerre des monnaies." *Revue de synthèse historique* 19 (1940–46): 83–101.

———. "La guerre monétaire, XIVe et XVe siècles." *Annales d'histoire sociale* 2 (1940): 207–18.

Goitein, S. D. "The Exchange Rate of Gold and Silver Money in Fatimid and Ayyubid Times: A Preliminary Study of the Relevant Geniza Material." *Journal of the Economic and Social History of the Orient,* vol. 8, no. 1 (1965), pp. 1–46.

Grierson, Philip. "Mint Output in the Tenth Century." *Economic History Review,* 2d ser. 9 (1957): 462–66.

———. "The Monetary Reforms of Abd al-Malik." *Journal of the Economic and Social History of the Orient* 3 (1960): 241–64.

———. "The Volume of Anglo-Saxon Coinage." *Economic History Review,* 2d ser. 20 (1967): 153–60.

Haenens, Albert d'. "Les mutations monétaires du XIVe siècle et leur incidence sur les finances des abbayes bénédictines: Le budget de Saint-Martin de Tournai de 1331 à 1348." *Revue Belge de Philologie et d'Histoire* 37 (1959): 317–42.

Herlihy, David. "Treasure Hoards in the Italian Economy, 960–1139." *Economic History Review* 10 (1957): 1–14.

Jankuhn, Herbert. *Haithabu. Ein Handelsplatz der Wickingerzeit.* 4 ergänzte Auflage. Neumünster: Wachholtz, 1963.

Laurent, Henri. *La Loi de Gresham au Moyen Age. Essai sur la circulation monétaire entre la Flandre et le Brabant à la fin du XIVe siècle.* Brussels: Editions de la Revue de l'Université de Bruxelles, 1933.

Lesage, G. "La circulation monétaire en France dans la 2éme moitié du XVe siècle." *Annales: Economies-Sociétés-Civilisations* 3 (1948): 304–17.

Metcalf, D. M. "How Large was the Anglo-Saxon Currency?" *Economic History Review,* 2d ser. 18 (1965): 475–82.

———. "The Prosperity of North-Western Europe in the Eighth and Ninth Centuries." *Economic History Review,* 2d ser. 20 (1967): 344–57.

Miles, G. C. *The Coinage of the Umayyads of Spain.* New York: American Numismatic Society, 1950.

Miskimin, Harry A. "Monetary Movements and Market Structure-Forces for Contraction in Fourteenth and Fifteenth Century Europe." *Journal of Economic History* 24 (1964): 470–90.

———. *Money, Prices, and Foreign Exchange in Fourteenth Century France.* Yale Studies in Economics, 15. New Haven and London: Yale University Press, 1963.

———. "Two Reforms of Charlemagne? Weights and Measures in the Middle Ages." *Economic History Review,* 2d ser. 20 (1967): 35–52.

Morrison, K. F. "Numismatics and Carolingian Trade: A Critique of the Evidence." *Speculum* 38 (1963): 403–32.

Reddaway, T. F. "The King's Mint and Exchange in London, 1343–1543." *English Historical Review* 82 (1967): 1–23.

Sawyer, P. H. *The Age of the Vikings.* London: Arnold, 1962.

Sisto, A. *Banchieri feudatari subalpini nei secoli XII–XIV.* Pubblicazioni della Facoltà di Lettere e Filosofia dell' Università di Torino, 14, fasc. 1. Turin: Giappichelli, 1963.

Suhle, A. *Deutsche Münz- und Geldgeschichte von den Anfängen bis zum 15. Jahrhundert.* Berlin: Deutsche Verlag der Wissenschaften, 1955.

Watson, A. M. "Back to Gold—and Silver." *Economic History Review*, 2d ser. 20 (1967): 1–34.

Zerbi, T. *Studi e problemi di storia economica: Credito ed interesse in Lombardia nei secoli XIV e XV.* Milan: Marzorati, 1955.

B. Prices

Ashtor, E. "Prix et salaires dans l'Espagne musulmane aux Xe et XIe siècles." *Annales: Economies-Sociétés-Civilisations* 20 (1965): 664–79.

———. "La recherche des prix dans l'Orient médiéval." *Studia Islamica* 21 (1964): 101–44.

Avenel, Georges d'. *Histoire économique de la propriété, des salaires, des denrées et de tous les prix . . . depuis l'an 1200 jusqu'en l'an 1800.* 7 vols. Paris: Imprimerie Nationale, 1894–1926.

Beveridge, William, with the collaboration of L. Liepmann, F. J. Nicholas, M. E. Reyner, M. Wretts-Smith, and others. *Prices and Wages in England from the Twelfth to the Nineteenth Century.* Vol. 1, *Price Tables: Mercantile Era.* London: Longmans, Green, 1939.

Brenner, Y. S. "Prices and Wages in England, 1450–1550." *Bulletin of the Institute of Historical Research* 34 (1961): 101–05. (Summary of thesis.)

Chittolini, G. "I beni terrieri del capitolo della cattedrale di Cremona fra il XIII e il XIV secolo." *Nuova Rivista Storica* 49 (1965): 213–74.

Coppejans-Desmedt, H., et al., under the direction of C. Verlinden. *Dokumenten voor de geschiedenis van prijzen en lonen in Vlaanderen en Brabant, XVe–XVIIIe eeuw.* Rijksuniversiteit te Gent, Werken uitgegeven door de faculteit van de letteren en de wijsbegeerte, 125. Bruges: De Tempel, 1959–65. (With French summaries.)

Elsas, M. J. *Umriss einer Geschichte der Preise und Löhne in Deutschland, vom ausgehenden Mittelalter bis zum Beginn des neunzehnten Jahrunderts.* 3 vols. Leiden: Sijthoff, 1936–49.

Farmer, D. L. "Some Grain Price Movements in Thirteenth Century England." *Economic History Review*, 2d ser. 10 (1957): 207–20.

———. "Some Price Fluctuations in Angevin England." *Economic History Review*, 2d ser. 9 (1956): 34–43.

Godding, P. *Le droit foncier à Bruxelles au Moyen Age.* Etudes d'Histoire et d'Ethnologie Juridiques, 1. Brussels: Université libre, Institut de Sociologie Solvay, 1960.

Gould, J. D. "Y. S. Brenner on Prices: A Comment." *Economic History Review*, 2d ser. 16 (1963): 351–60.

Grass, N. S. B. *The Evolution of the English Corn Market from the Twelfth to the Eighteenth Century.* Harvard Economic Studies, 13. Cambridge, Mass.: Harvard University Press, 1915.

Hamilton, E. J. *Money, Prices, and Wages in Valencia, Aragon, and Navarre, 1351–1500.* Cambridge, Mass.: Harvard University Press, 1936.

Heers, Jacques. "Le prix de l'assurance maritime à la fin du Moyen Age." *Revue d'Histoire Economique et Sociale* 37 (1959): 7–19.

Kneisel, E. "The Evolution of the English Corn Market." *Journal of Economic History* 14 (1954): 46–52.

Koenigsberger, H. G. "Property and the Price Revolution: Hainault, 1474–1573." *Economic History Review*, 2d ser. 9 (1956): 1–15.

Longden, J. "Statistical Notes on Winchester Heriots." *Economic History Review*, 2d ser. 11 (1959): 392–411.

Phelps Brown, E. H., and Hopkins, Sheila V. "Seven Centuries of the Prices of Consumables, Compared with Builders' Wage-Rates." *Economica*, n.s. 33 (1956): 296–314.

Postan, M. M., and Titow, J. "Heriots and Prices on Winchester Manors." *Economic History Review*, 2d ser. 11 (1959): 392–411.

Posthumus, N. W. *Inquiry into the History of Prices in Holland.* 2 vols. Leiden: Brill, 1946–64.

Richardson, Harold. *The Medieval Fairs and Markets of York.* St. Anthony's Hall Publications, 20. York: St. Anthony's Press, 1961.

Rogers, J. E. Thorold. *A History of Agriculture and Prices in England from the Year after the Oxford Parliament (1259) to the Commencement of the Continental War (1793).* 7 vols. in 8. Oxford: Oxford University Press, Clarendon Press, 1866–1902.

Ross, Alan S. C. "The Assize of Bread." *Economic History Review*, 2d ser. 9 (1956): 332–42.

Sapori, Armando. *Una compagnia di Calimala ai primi del trecento.* Florence: Olschki, 1932.

Scholliers, E. *Loonarbeid en honger. De levensstandaard in de XVe en XVIe eeuw te Antwerpen.* Antwerp: De Sikkel, 1960. (With French summary.)

Schreiner, J. "Wages and Prices in England in the Later Middle Ages." *Scandinavian Economic History Review* 2 (1954): 61–73.

Usher, A. P. "The General Course of Wheat Prices in France, 1350–1788." *Review of Economic Statistics* 12 (1930): 159–69.

———. "Prices of Wheat and Commodity Price Indexes for England, 1259–1930." *Review of Economic Statistics* 13 (1931): 103–13.

Uytven, R. Van. *Stadsfinanciën en stadsekonomie te Leuven van de XIIe tot het einde der XVIe eeuw.* Verhandelingen van de Koninklijke Vlaamse Academie voor Wetenschappen Letteren en Schone Kunsten van België, Klasse der Letteren, 44. Brussels, 1961.

Van der Wee, Hermann. "Prix et salaires. Introduction méthodologique." In *Cahiers d'Histoire des Prix—Bijdragen voor de Prijzengeschiedenis*, 1:5–42. Louvain, 1956.

Zanetti, Dante. *Problemi alimentari di una economia preindustriale-cereale a Pavia dal 1398 al 1700.* Collezione di studi dell'Istituto di Storia Economica dell' Università di Torino, Facoltà di Economia e Commercio. Turin: Boringhieri, 1964.

C. Wages

Beveridge, William. "Wages in the Winchester Manors." *Economic History Review*, vol. 7, no. 1 (1936–37), pp. 22–43.

———. "Westminster Wages in the Manorial Era." *Economic History Review*, 2d ser. 8 (1955): 18–35.

Kenyon, N. "Labour Conditions in Essex in the Reign of Richard II." *Economic History Review*, vol. 4, no. 4 (1932–34), pp. 429–51.

Knoop, D., and Jones, G. P. "Masons and Apprenticeship in Medieval England." *Economic History Review,* vol. 3, no. 3 (1931–32), pp. 346–66.

Lewis, N. B. "The Recruitment and Organization of a Contract Army, May to November, 1337." *Bulletin of the Institute of Historical Research* 37 (1964): 1–79.

Mellows, W. T.; King, P. I.; and Brooke, C. N. L., eds. *The Book of William Morton, Almoner of Peterborough Monastery, 1448–1467.* Northamptonshire Record Society. Hereford, 1954.

Perroy, E. "Wage Labor in France in the Later Middle Ages." In *Change in Medieval Society,* edited by Sylvia L. Thrupp, pp. 237–46. New York: Appleton-Century-Crofts, 1964. Reprinted from *Economic History Review* 8 (1955).

Phelps Brown, E. H., and Hopkins, Sheila V. "Seven Centuries of Building Wages." *Economica,* n.s. 22 (1955): 195–206.

Postan, M. M. "The Chronology of Labour Services." *Transactions of the Royal Historical Society,* 4th ser. 20 (1937): 169–93.

―――. *The Famulus: The Estate Labourer in the Twelfth and Thirteenth Centuries. Economic History Review,* Supplements, 2. London: Cambridge University Press, 1954.

Prince, A. E. "The Payment of Army Wages in Edward III's Reign." *Speculum* 19 (1944): 137–60.

IV. COMMERCE AND INDUSTRY

A. Commerce

Ahvenainen, Jorma. *Der Getreidehandel Livlands im Mittelalter.* Societas Scientiarum Fennica, Commentationes Humanarum Litterarum, 34, 2. Helsinki, 1963.

Babel, Antony, *Histoire économique de Genève. Des origines au début du XVIe siècle.* 2 vols. Geneva: Jullien, 1963.

Bach, Erik. "Etudes génoises: Le minutier de Lanfranco." In *Studi in onore di Armando Sapori,* 1:373–90. Milan: Istituto editoriale cisalpino, 1956.

Beardwood, A. *Alien Merchants in England, 1350 to 1377: Their Legal and Economic Position.* Publications of the Mediaeval Academy, 8. Cambridge, Mass.: Mediaeval Academy of America, 1931.

Bergier, Jean-François. *Genève et l'économie européenne de la Renaissance.* Paris: SEVPEN, 1963.

Böhnke, Werner. "Der Binnenhandel des deutschen Ordens in Preussen und seine Beziehung zum Aussenhandel im 1400." *Hansische Geschichtsblätter* 80 (1962): 26–95.

Bridbury, A. R. *Economic Growth: England in the Later Middle Ages.* London: Allen and Unwin, 1962.

―――. *England and the Salt Trade in the Later Middle Ages.* Oxford: Oxford University Press, Clarendon Press, 1955.

Burwash, D. *English Merchant Shipping, 1460–1540.* Toronto: University of Toronto Press, 1947.

Cahen, Claude. "Notes sur l'histoire des Croisades et de l'Orient latin. III: L'Orient latin et commerce du Levant." *Bulletin de la Faculté des Lettres de Strasbourg,* 29me année, no. 8 (1951).

Carus-Wilson, E. M. *The Expansion of Exeter at the Close of the Middle Ages.* Exeter: University of Exeter, 1963.

————. *Medieval Merchant Venturers. Collected Studies.* London: Methuen, 1954.

————. *The Overseas Trade of Bristol in the Later Middle Ages.* Bristol Record Society Publications, 7. Bristol, 1937.

————, and Coleman, Olive. *England's Export Trade, 1275–1547.* Oxford: Oxford University Press, Clarendon Press, 1963.

Coornaert, Emile. *Les français et le commerce internationale à Anvers, fin du XVe–XVIe siècles.* 2 vols. Paris: M. Rivière, 1961.

Craeybeckx, J. *Un grand commerce d'importation: Les vins de France aux anciens Pays-Bas, XIIIe–XVIe siècles.* Paris: SEVPEN, 1958.

De Roover, Florence Edler. "Andrea Banchi, Florentine Silk Manufacturer and Merchant in the Fifteenth Century." *Studies in Medieval and Renaissance History* 3 (1966): 221–86.

Dollinger, Philippe. *The German Hansa.* Translated by D. S. Ault and S. H. Steinberg. Stanford: Stanford University Press, 1970.

Engel, Eva Maria. "Bürgerlichen Lehnsbesitz, bauerliche Produktenrente, und altmarkisch-hamburgische Handelsbeziehungen im 14. Jahrhunderts." *Hansische Geschichtsblätter* 82 (1964): 21–41.

Espinas, G. *Les origines du capitalisme.* Vol. 3, *Deux fondations de villes dans l'Artois et la Flandre française, Xe–XVe siècles: Saint Omer, Lannoy du Nord.* Lille: E. Raoust, 1946.

Gray, H. L. "The Production and Export of English Woolens in the Fourteenth Century." *English Historical Review* 39 (1924): 13–35.

Heers, Jacques. *Gênes au 15e siècle. Activité économique et problèmes sociaux.* Ecole Pratique des Hautes Etudes, VIe section, Affaires et gens d'affaires, 24. Paris: SEVPEN, 1961.

————. *Le Livre de comptes de Giovanni Piccamiglio, homme d'affaires génois, 1456–1459.* Paris: SEVPEN, 1959.

————. *L'occident aux XIVe et XVe siècles: Aspects économiques et sociaux.* Nouvelle Clio, 23. 3d ed. Paris: Presses Universitaires de France, 1970.

Histoire du commerce de Marseille. Edited by Gaston Rambert. Vol. 1, *L'Antiquité,* by R. Busquet; *Le Moyen Age jusqu'en 1291,* by R. Pernoud. Vol. 2, *De 1291 à 1423,* by E. Baratier; *De 1423 à 1480,* by F. Reynaud. Vol. 3, *De 1480 à 1515,* by R. Collier; *De 1515 à 1599,* by J. Billioud. Paris: Plon 1949–51.

James, Margery K. "The Fluctuations of the Anglo-Gascon Wine Trade during the Fourteenth Century." *Economic History Review,* 2d ser. 4 (1951): 170–96.

————. "A London Merchant of the Fourteenth Century." *Economic History Review,* 2d ser. 8 (1956): 363–76.

Kerling, N. J. *Commercial Relations of Holland and Zeeland with England from the Late 13th Century to the Close of the Middle Ages.* Leiden: Brill, 1954.

Krekic, B. *Dubrovnik (Raguse) au Moyen Age.* Paris: Mouton, 1961.

Krueger, Hilmar C. "Genoese Merchants, Their Partnerships and Investments, 1155 to 1164." In *Studi in onore di Armando Sapori,* 1:255–72. Milan: Istituto editoriale cisalpino, 1956.

Lavergne, G. "La pêche et le commerce du corail à Marseille aux XIVe et XVe siècles." *Annales du Midi* 64 (1952): 199–212.

Lopez, R. S. "Market Expansion: The Case of Genoa." *Journal of Economic History* 24 (1964): 445–64.

———, and Miskimin, H. A. "The Economic Depression of the Renaissance." *Economic History Review,* 2d ser. 14 (1962): 408–26.

Lütge, F. *Strukturwandlungen im ostdeutschen und osteuropäischen Fernhandel des 14. bis 16. Jahrhunderts.* (Bayerische Akademie der Wissenschaften, Philosophische-Historische Klasse, Sitzungsberichte, 1. Munich: Beck, 1964.

Mallett, M. E. "Anglo-Florentine Commercial Relations, 1465–1491." *Economic History Review,* 2d ser. 15 (1962): 250–65.

Marciani, C. "Le relazioni tra l'Adriatico orientale e l'Abruzzo nei secoli XV, XVI, e XVII." *Archivio Storico Italiano* 123 (1965): 14–47.

Melis, F. *Aspetti della vita economica medioevale: Studi nell'Archivio Datini di Prato.* Siena: Monte de Paschi di Siena, 1962.

Mollat, M. "Anglo-Norman Trade in the Fifteenth Century." *Economic History Review,* 2d ser. 17 (1947): 143–50.

———. *Le commerce maritime normand à la fin du Moyen Age.* Paris: Plon, 1952.

Pelham, R. A. "The Foreign Trade of Sussex, 1300–1350." *Sussex Archeological Collections* 70 (1929): 93–118.

———. "Exportation of Wool from Sussex in the Late Thirteenth Century." *Sussex Archaeological Collections* 74 (1933): 131–39.

———. "Some Further Aspects of Sussex Trade during the Fourteenth Century." *Sussex Archaeological Collections* 71 (1930): 171–204.

Penners, Theodor. "Fragen der Zuwanderung in den Hansestädten des späten Mittelalters." *Hansische Geschichtsblätter* 83 (1965): 12–45.

Renken, F. *Der Handel der Königsberger Grosschäfferei des deutschen Ordens mit Flandern um 1400.* Abhandlungen zur Handels- und Seegeschichte, 5. Weimar: Böhlaus, 1937.

Reynolds, R. L. "Genoese Trade in the Late Twelfth Century, Particularly in Cloth from the Fairs of Champagne." *Journal of Economic and Business History* 3 (1931): 362–81.

———. "The Market for Northern Textiles in Genoa, 1179–1200." *Revue Belge de Philologie et d'Histoire* 9 (1930): 495–533.

———. "Merchants of Arras and the Overland Trade with Genoa in the Twelfth Century." *Revue Belge de Philologie et d'Histoire* 9 (1930): 495–533.

Ruddock, A. A. *Italian Merchants and Shipping in Southampton, 1270–1600.* Southampton: University College, 1951.

Scammell, G. V. "English Merchant Shipping at the End of the Middle Ages: Some East Coast Evidence." *Economic History Review,* 2d ser. 13 (1961): 327–41.

Schneider, Jean. *Recherches sur la vie économique de Metz au XVe siècle: Le Livre de Comptes des merciers messins Jean Le Clerc et Jacquemin de Moyeuvre, 1460–61.* Metz: Mutelet, 1951.

Van der Wee, Hermann. *The Growth of the Antwerp Market and the European Economy, Fourteenth to Sixteenth Centuries.* Vol. 1, *Statistics.* Vol. 2, *Interpretation.* Vol. 3, *Graphs.* The Hague: Martinus Nijhoff, 1963.

Veale, Elspeth M. *The English Fur Trade in the Later Middle Ages.* Oxford: Oxford University Press, Clarendon Press, 1966.

Watson, W. B. "The Florentine Galley Trade with England and Flanders in the

Fifteenth Century." *Revue Belge de Philologie et d'Histoire* 39 (1961): 1079–91; 40 (1962): 317–47.

Williams, Gwyn A. *Medieval London: From Commune to Capital.* University of London, Historical Studies, 11. London: Althone Press, 1963.

Wolff, Philippe. *Commerces et marchands de Toulouse, vers 1350 vers 1450.* Paris: Plon, 1954.

B. Industry

Braunstein, P. "Les entreprises minières en Vénétie au XVe siècle." *Mélanges d'archéologie et d'histoire* 77 (1965): 529–608.

Britnell, R. H. "Production for the Market on a Small Fourteenth Century Estate." *Economic History Review,* 2d ser. 19 (1966): 380–87.

Carus-Wilson, E. M. "The English Cloth Industry in the Late Twelfth and Early Thirteenth Centuries." *Economic History Review* 14 (1944): 32–50.

———. "An Industrial Revolution of the Thirteenth Century." *Economic History Review* 11 (1941): 39–60.

Delumeau, Jean. *L'alun de Rome, XVe–XIXe siècle.* Paris: SEVPEN, 1962.

Espinas, G. *La draperie dans la Flandre française au Moyen Age.* 2 vols. Paris: Picard, 1923.

Heitz, Gerhard. *Ländliche Leinenproduktion in Sachsen, 1470–1555.* Deutsche Akademie der Wissenschaften zu Berlin, Schriften des Instituts für Geschichte, serie 2, Landegeschichte, 4. Berlin: Akademie-Verlag, 1961.

Lejeune, Jean. *La formation du capitalism moderne dans la principauté de Liège au XVIe siècle.* Liège: Faculté de philosophie et lettres, 1939.

Levitsky, Ya. A. *Goroda i gorodskoe remeslo v Anglii v X–XII vv.* [Towns and Urban Industry in England from the Tenth to the Twelfth Centuries]. Moscow: Academy of Sciences, 1960.

Nef, J. U. "Silver Production in Central Europe, 1450–1618." *Journal of Political Economy* 49 (1941): 575–91.

Perry, R. "The Gloucestershire Woolen Industry, 1100–1690." *Transactions of the Bristol and Gloucestershire Archeological Society* 66 (1947): 49–138.

Schubert, John R. T. *History of the British Iron and Steel Industry from c. 459 B.C. to A.D. 1775.* London: Routledge and Kegan Paul, 1957.

Sicard, Germain. *Aux origines des sociétés anonymes: Les moulins de Toulouse au Moyen Age.* Ecole Pratique des Hautes Etudes, VIe section, Affaires et gens d'affaires, 5. Paris: SEVPEN, 1953.

V. FINANCES

A. Ecclesiastical Institutions

Bauer, Clement. "Studi per la storia delle finanze papali durante il pontificato di Sisto IV." *Archivio della Reale Società Romana di Storia Patria* 50 (1927): 319–400.

Beresford, M. W. "Six New Towns of the Bishops of Winchester, 1200–1255." *Medieval Archaeology* 2 (1959): 187–215.

Burne, R. V. H. *The Monks of Chester: The History of St. Werburgh's Abbey.* London: SPCK, 1962.

Du Boulay, F. R. H. "A Rentier Economy in the Later Middle Ages: The Archbishopric of Canterbury." *Economic History Review,* 2d ser. 16 (1964): 427–38.

Favier, Jean. *Les finances pontificales à l'époque du grand schisme d'Occident, 1378–1409.* Bibliothèque des Ecoles françaises d'Athènes et de Rome, fasc. 211. Paris: de Boccard, 1966.

Gottlob, A. *Aus der Camera apostolica des XV. Jahrhunderts: Ein Beitrag zur Geschichte des päpstlichen Finanzwesens des Enden Mittelalters.* Innsbruck: Wagner, 1889.

Guillemain, Bernard. *La cour pontificale d'Avignon, 1309–1376. Etude d'une société.* Bibliothèque des Ecoles françaises d'Athènes et de Rome, 201. Paris: de Boccard, 1962.

————. *La politique bénéficiale du pape Benoît XII, 1334–1342.* Bibliothèque de l'Ecole des Hautes Etudes, Sciences Historiques et Philologiques, 229. Paris: Champion, 1952.

Holt, N. R., ed. *The Pipe Roll of the Bishopric of Winchester, 1210–1211.* Manchester: Manchester University Press, 1964.

Jones, Douglas. *The Church in Chester, 1300–1540.* Chetham Society, 3d ser. 7. Manchester, 1957.

Knowles, D., and Hadcock, R. N. *Medieval Religious Houses: England and Wales.* London: Longmans, Green, 1953.

Lunt, William E. *Financial Relations of England with the Papacy, 1327–1534.* Publications of the Mediaeval Academy, 74. Cambridge, Mass.: Mediaeval Academy of America, 1962.

————. *Financial Relations of the Papacy with England to 1327.* Publications of the Mediaeval Academy, 33. Cambridge, Mass.: Mediaeval Academy of America, 1939.

————. *Papal Revenues in the Middle Ages.* 2 vols. New York: Columbia University Press, 1934.

Mollat, G., and Samaran, C. *La fiscalité pontificale en France au XIVe siècle: Période d'Avignon et Grand Schisme d'Occident.* Bibliothèque des Ecoles françaises d'Athènes et de Rome, 96. Paris: Fontemoing, 1905.

Moorman, John R. H. *Church Life in England in the Thirteenth Century.* Cambridge: Cambridge University Press, 1945.

O'Sullivan, M. D. *Italian Merchant Bankers in Ireland in the Thirteenth Century.* Dublin: Figgis, 1962.

Partner, P. "*Camera papae.* Problems of Papal Finance in the later Middle Ages." *Journal of Ecclesiastical History* 4 (1953): 55–68.

Poliakov, Léon. *Les banchieri juifs et le Saint-Siège du XIIIe au XVIIe siècle.* Ecole Pratique des Hautes Etudes, VIe section, Affaires et gens d'affaires, 30. Paris: SEVPEN, 1965.

Renouard, Yves. *Les relations des papes d'Avignon et des compagnies commerciales et bancaires de 1316 à 1378.* Bibliothèque des Ecoles françaises d'Athènes et de Rome, fasc. 151. Paris: de Boccard, 1941.

Schafer, K. H. *Die Ausgaben der Apostolischen Kammer unter den Papsten Urban V. und Gregor XI, 1362–78.* Vatikanische Quellen zur Geschichte der papstlichen Hof—und Finanzverwaltung, 6. Paderborn: Schöningh, 1937.

Snape, R. H. *English Monastic Finances in the Later Middle Ages.* Cambridge: Cambridge University Press, 1926.

Woodruff, C. E. "The Financial Aspect of the Cult of St. Thomas of Canterbury." *Archaeologica Cantiana* 44 (1932): 3–32.

B. Lay Lords and Governments

Altschul, Michael. *A Baronial Family in Medieval England: The Clares, 1217–1314.* Johns Hopkins Studies in History and Political Science, 83, 2. Baltimore: Johns Hopkins University Press, 1965.

Andréadès, A. M. *A History of Greek Public Finances.* Translated by Carroll N. Brown. Cambridge, Mass.: Harvard University Press, 1933.

Bamberger, Elisabeth. "Die Finanzverwaltung in den deutschen Territorien des Mittelalters, 1200–1500." *Zeitschrift für die gesamte Staatswissenschaft* 77 (1922–23): 168–255.

Bean, J. M. W. *The Estates of the Percy Family, 1416–1537.* London: Oxford University Press, 1958.

Beresford, M. W. *Lay Subsidies and Poll Taxes.* Canterbury: Phillimores, 1963. Reprinted from *Amateur Historian* 3 (1958); 4 (1959).

Blair, C. H. H. "Baronies and Knights of Northumberland, A.D. 1166–1266." *Archaeologia Aeliana,* 4th ser. 30 (1952): 1–57.

Borrelli de Serres, Léon Luis. *Recherches sur divers services publics du XIIIe au XVIIe siècle.* 3 vols. Paris, 1895–1909.

Cazel, F. A. "The Fifteenth of 1225." *Bulletin of the Institute of Historical Research* 34 (1961): 67–81.

Cohn, Henry J. *The Government of the Rhine Palatinate in the Fifteenth Century.* London: Oxford University Press, 1965.

Daviso de Charvensod, M. C. *I pedaggi delle Alpi occidentali nel Medio Evo.* Deputazione Subalpina di Storia Patria, Miscellanea di Storia Italiana, 4th ser. 5. Turin, 1961.

Day, John. *Les douanes de Gênes, 1376–77.* Ecole Pratique des Hautes Etudes, VIe section, Collection "Ports-Routes-Trafics," 17. 2 vols. Paris: SEVPEN, 1963.

Dupont-Ferrier, Gustave. *Etudes sur les institutions financières de la France à la fin du Moyen Age.* 2 vols. Paris: Firmin-Didot, 1930–32.

Fanchamps, M. L. "Etude sur les tonlieux de la Meuse moyenne du VIIIe au milieu du XIIIe siècle." *Le Moyen Age* 70 (1964): 205–63.

Finances et comptabilité urbaines de XIIIe au XVIe siècle. Colloque International. Blankenberge, 6–9–IX–1962. Actes. Brussels: Pro Civitate, 1964.

Fourquin, Guy. *Le domaine royal en Gâtinais d'après la prisée de 1332.* Ecole Pratique des Hautes Etudes, VIe section, Collection "Les hommes et la terre," 7. Paris: SEVPEN, 1963.

Fryde, E. B. "The English Farmers of the Customs, 1343–1351." *Transactions of the Royal Historical Society,* 5th ser. (1959).

————. "Materials for the Study of Edward III's Credit Operations, 1327–1348." *Bulletin of the Institute of Historical Research* 22 (1949): 103–38; 23 (1950): 1–30.

Gras, N. S. B. *The Early English Customs System: A Documentary Study of the Institutional and Economic History of the Customs from the Thirteenth to the Sixteenth Century.* Harvard Economic Studies, 18. Cambridge, Mass.: Harvard University Press, 1918.

Harriss, G. L. " 'Fictitious Loans.' " *Economic History Review,* 2d ser. 8 (1955): 187–99.

Holmes, D. A. *The Estates of the Higher Nobility in Fourteenth Century England*. Cambridge: Cambridge University Press, 1957.

Howell, Margaret. *Regalian Right in Medieval England*. London: Athlone Press, 1962.

Kirby, J. L. "The Financing of Calais under Henry V." *Bulletin of the Institute of Historical Research* 23 (1950): 165–77.

Larner, John. *The Lords of Romagna: Romagnal Society and the Origins of the Signorie*. Ithaca: Cornell University Press, 1965.

Léonard, Emile G. *Les Angevins de Naples*. Paris: Presses Universitaires de France, 1954.

Luzzatto, Gino. *Il debito pubblico della Repubblica di Venezia dagli ultimi decenni del XII secolo alla fine del XV*. Milan: Istituto Editoriale Cisalpino, 1963.

Lydon, J. F. "Edward II and the Revenues of Ireland in 1311–12." *Irish Historical Studies* 14 (1964): 39–57.

Marsh, Frank Burr. *English Rule in Gascony, 1199–1259, with Special Reference to the Towns*. University of Michigan Historical Studies. Ann Arbor: Wahr, 1912.

Mitchell, Sydney Knox. *Taxation in Medieval England*. Edited by Sidney Painter. New Haven and London: Yale University Press, 1951.

Mollat, M. *La comptabilité du port de Dieppe au XVe siècle*. Paris: Colin, 1951.

———. "Recherches sur les finances des ducs Valois de Bourgogne." *Revue Historique* 219 (1958): 285–321.

Morris, W. A., and Willard, J. F., eds. *The English Government at Work, 1327–1336*. Pt. 1, *Central and Prerogative Administration*. Publications of the Mediaeval Academy, 37. Cambridge, Mass.: Mediaeval Academy of America, 1940.

———, and Strayer, J. R., eds. *The English Government at Work, 1327–1336*. Pt. 2, *Fiscal Administration*. Publications of the Mediaeval Academy, 48. Cambridge, Mass.: Mediaeval Academy of America, 1947.

———, and Dunham, W. H., Jr., eds. *The English Government at Work, 1327–1336*. Pt. 3, *Local Administration and Justice*. Publications of the Mediaeval Academy, 56. Cambridge, Mass.: Mediaeval Academy of America, 1950.

Perroy, E. "La fiscalité royale en Beaujolais." *Le Moyen Age* 29 (1928): 5–47.

Pocquet du Haut-Jussé, B. A. "Les chefs des finances ducales en Bourgogne." *Mémoires de la société pour l'histoire du droit et des institutions des anciens pays bourguignons, comtois, et romands* 4 (1937): 5–77.

Pugh, T. B., ed. *The Marcher Lordships of South Wales, 1415–1536. Select Documents*. Cardiff: University of Wales Press, 1963.

Ramsay, Sir James H. *A History of the Revenues of the Kings of England, 1066–1399*. 2 vols. Oxford: Oxford University Press, Clarendon Press, 1925.

Rey, Maurice. *Les finances royales sous Charles VI. Les causes du déficit, 1388–1413*. Bibliothèque générale de l'Ecole Pratique des Hautes Etudes, VIe section. Paris: SEVPEN, 1965.

———. *Le domaine du roi et les finances extraordinaires sous Charles VI, 1388–1413*. Bibliothèque générale de l'Ecole Pratique des Hautes Etudes, VIe section. Paris: SEVPEN, 1965.

Richard, J. *Les ducs de Bourgogne et la formation du duché du XIe au XIVe siècle*. Publication de la Université de Dijon, n. s. 12. Paris: Belles Lettres, 1954.

Richardson, H. G., and Sayles, G. O. "Irish Revenue, 1278–1384." *Proceedings of the Royal Irish Academy* 62 (1962): 87–100.

Rosenthal, Joel T. "The Estates and Finances of Richard, Duke of York, 1411–1460." *Studies in Medieval and Renaissance History* 2 (1965): 115–203.

Ross, C. D., and Pugh, T. B. "Materials for the Study of Baronial Incomes in Fifteenth Century England." *Economic History Review*, 2d ser. 6 (1953): 185–94.

Salzman, L. F. "Early Taxation in Sussex." *Sussex Archaeological Collections* 98 (1960): 29–43; 99 (1961): 1–19.

Somerville, Robert. *History of the Duchy of Lancaster*. Vol. 1, *1265–1603*. London: Chancellor and Council of the Duchy of Lancaster, 1953.

Steel, Anthony. *The Receipt of the Exchequer, 1377–1485*. Cambridge: Cambridge University Press, 1954.

Verhulst, A., and Gysseling, M., eds. *Le Compte général de 1187, connu sous le nom de 'Gros brief,' et les institutions financières du comté de Flandre au XIIe siècle*. Brussels: Palais des Académies, 1962.

Willard, J. F. *Parliamentary Taxes on Personal Property, 1290–1334. A Study in Mediaeval English Financial Administration*. Publications of the Mediaeval Academy, 19. Cambridge, Mass.: Mediaeval Academy of America, 1934.

Wolff, P. "Registres d'impôts et vie économique à Toulouse sous Charles VI." *Annales du Midi* 56 (1944–46): 5–66.

Wolffe, B. P. "Henry VII's Land Revenues and Chamber Finance." *English Historical Review* 79 (1964): 225–54.

VI. SOCIAL STRUCTURES AND SOCIAL INDICATORS

Aleati, G. "Biblioteche e prezzi di codici in Pavia nel tardo Medio Evo." *Bollettino della società pavese di storia patria* 49–50 (1951): 99–107.

Beeler, John. *Warfare in England, 1066–1189*. Ithaca: Cornell University Press, 1966.

Bligny, Bernard. *L'église et les ordres religieux dans le royaume de Bourgogne aux XIe et XIIe siècles*. Paris: Presses Universitaires de France, 1960.

Bonenfant, P., and Despy, G. "La noblesse en Brabant aux XIIe et XIIIe siècles." *Le Moyen Age* 64 (1958): 27–66.

Brown, R. A. "Royal Castle Building in England, 1154–1216." *English Historical Review* 70 (1955): 353–98.

Edwards, Kathleen. "The Social Origins and Provenance of the English Bishops during the reign of Edward II." *Transactions of the Royal Historical Society* 9 (1959).

Gaier, Claude. "Analysis of Military Forces in the Principality of Liège and the County of Looz from the Twelfth to the Fifteenth Centuries." *Studies in Medieval and Renaissance History* 2 (1965): 205–61.

Hewitt, H. J. *The Organization of War under Edward III, 1338–62*. Manchester: Manchester University Press, 1965.

Hillebrand, Werner. *Besitz und Standesverhältnisse des Osnabrücker Adels 800 bis*

1300. Studien und Vorarbeiten zum historischen, Atlas Niedersachsens, fasc. 23. Göttingen: Vandenhoeck and Ruprecht, 1962.

Hilton, R. H. *The Social Structure of Rural Warwickshire in the Middle Ages.* Dugdale Society Occasional Papers, 9. Oxford: Batey, 1950.

Hollister, C. Warren. *The Military Organization of Norman England.* Oxford: Oxford University Press, Clarendon Press, 1965.

Honeybourne, Marjorie B. "The Leper Hospitals of the London Area: With an Appendix on Some Other Medieval Hospitals of Middlesex." *Transactions of the London and Middlesex Archaeological Society* 21 (1963): 1–61.

Lewis, Archibald R. *The Development of South French and Catalan Society, 718–1050.* Austin: University of Texas Press, 1965.

Lot, F. *L'art militaire et les armées au Moyen Age en Europe et dans le Proche-Orient.* 2 vols. Paris: Payot, 1946.

Luzzatto, Gino. "Il costo della vita a Venezia nel trecento." In *Studi di storia economica veneziana,* pp. 285–97. Padua, 1954.

Martines, Lauro. *The Social World of the Florentine Humanists.* Princeton: Princeton University Press, 1963.

Powell, W. R. "The Administration of the Navy and the Stannaries, 1189–1216." *English Historical Review* 71 (1956): 177–88.

Raftis, J. Ambrose. *Tenure and Mobility: Studies in the Social History of the Medieval English Village.* Pontifical Institute of Medieval Studies, Studies and Texts, 8. Toronto, 1964.

———. "Social Structures in Five East Midland Villages." *Economic History Review,* 2d ser. 18 (1965): 83–100.

Sawyer, P. H. "The Wealth of England in the Eleventh Century." *Transactions of the Royal Historical Society* 15 (1965): 145–64.

Schofield, R. S. "The Geographical Distribution of Wealth in England, 1334–1649." *Economic History Review,* 2d ser. 18 (1965): 483–510.

Siedschlag, B. N. *English Participation in the Crusades, 1150–1220.* Menasha, Wis.: Collegiate Press, 1939.

Sperber, Daniel. "Costs of Living in Roman Palestine." *Journal of the Economic and Social History of the Orient* 8 (1965): 248–71.

Thompson, Michael W. *Novgorod the Great.* London: Evelyn, Adams 2nd Mackay, 1967.

Thrupp, Sylvia L. *The Merchant Class of Medieval London, 1300–1500.* Chicago: University of Chicago Press, 1948.

2

STATISTICS AS A SOURCE FOR THE

HISTORY OF ECONOMIC DEVELOPMENT

IN WESTERN EUROPE

THE PROTOSTATISTICAL ERA

by David S. Landes

The scope of a report on quantitative sources for the history of European economic development will necessarily vary with the definition of development and with the range of concerns of the student of development. If one defines "economic development" as primarily the growth of wealth and income over time and confines analysis to the conventional economic variables, one can make do with the traditional indicators—statistics of output, trade, income, scale and structure of enterprise, and the like—plus data on population, of course, to convert aggregates into ratios. If, however, one defines economic development as a larger socioeconomic process, involving human as well as material capital, then the relevant indicators would include figures on health, education, pathological social behavior (crime, suicide, illegitimacy, and the like), and, where available, on social values and attitudes.

For obvious practical reasons, this report will concentrate on the first category of data, without implying in principle any such conceptual limitation of the proper matter of economic analysis.

The quantitative data on European economic development may be classified for quality and coverage in three classes corresponding to historical periods:

1. Those gathered or produced in what we may call the protostatistical era, when governments were as yet desultory and incomplete in their collection and publication of information and much of our knowledge must be derived from the more or less informed speculations of individual

"political arithmeticians" or statisticians. Data of this kind go back to the Domesday survey and the hearth counts of the Middle Ages, but they become a substantial corpus of source material in the late seventeenth and eighteenth centuries, when the mercantilist and cameralist states of Europe sought to promote economic growth for political ends and thereby were led to seek more precise and complete information than before on the condition and economic activities of their subjects.

2. The data collected during what we may call the first statistical era, when the state came to realize that numbers were too important a matter to be left to chance. What were needed were, first, a systematic program of regular and fuller coverage of what were felt to be significant indicators; and second, official bureaus to collect, prepare, preserve, and publish these data for the use of other agencies of the state and, eventually, of the public.

3. The data collected and prepared during what we may call the modern or second statistical era, when new conceptions of the role of the state and the character of economic change have made it desirable to go beyond the collation and arithmetical transformation of simple raw numbers and to create aggregative and analytical indicators of a much more highly processed character. The first products of this new approach were probably composite indexes of prices and wages, which date back to the late nineteenth century. But the great innovation was the introduction in the period after World War I of systematic national income accounting, followed after the Second World War by such techniques as input-output tables. Significantly enough, both these new techniques were developed by private citizens rather than officials, and they remain in considerable part the special province of such private organizations as the National Bureau of Economic Research in the United States, the Department of Applied Economics of Cambridge University in England, the Institut de Sciences Economiques Appliquées in France, and the Institut für Konjunkturfroschung in Germany.[1] These agencies, to be sure, need the raw data collected and collectable only by the state; so that they have come to play the role of informed buyers, constantly ordering new and improved products from the producer, in this instance the various official administrative and statistical bureaus.[2]

This chapter will deal primarily with the first of these three eras and the beginning of the second—roughly the period up to about 1830.

The quantitative sources for the protostatistical period are a function of both the relationship of the state to the economy and the philosophy and technique of the statisticians. Thus the widest range of raw information comes from Prussia, where the monarchy was engaged in a vigorous effort to promote economic growth and was directly involved via subsidies, loans, or direct investment in many if not most of the enterprises in what would today be called the modern sector. Our scantiest information comes from the more backward countries, where the state was not ambitious or capable enough to undertake a deliberate program of economic control and development. Great Britain, which was advancing beyond mercantilism to laissez-faire and where our raw data consist primarily of trade returns and similar by-products of tax collection, falls somewhere in between.

On the other hand, the British compensated for their ignorance with ingenuity and boldness. The political arithmeticians of the seventeenth century, who were the fathers of economic statistics, had recourse from the start to estimated means, population estimates, and multipliers in order to arrive at aggregate figures. Thus William Petty (1623–87) was prepared to offer national totals for income, rents, wages, and consumption, not only for Britain but even for such less familiar lands as Ireland and France.[3] Needless to say, such manipulations, when based on inaccurate information or faulty reasoning, could produce egregious errors: Petty was prepared, for example, to infer from the larger volume of Irish food exports in 1664 as compared with 1641 a comparable increase in Irish population.[4] The trouble with Petty's work was that he wanted to make a point—a characteristic affliction of all social scientists—and that his method gave him too much free rein. He wanted to build up England's strength and wealth relative to those of other countries—"a proposition," as Charles Davenant put it, "not quite right in itself but very grateful to those who governed." [5] Petty was not the last to succumb to this temptation, but some of the men who followed him were more careful workers, and their figures have stood up well to the scrutiny and manipulation of modern statisticians.[6]

The most important of Petty's successors was Gregory King (1648–1712), who, like many other political arithmeticians, acquired his interest in numbers as a government functionary. King was secretary to the comissioners of public accounts and later to the controllers of army accounts, and his effort to construct a quantitative schema of British social structure grew out of the need to assess a new tax on births, burials, and marriages on a graduated scale. And though the returns for this tax have not survived, King probably saw some of them, as well as hearth books and other fiscal records. The result was two essays—*Natural and Political Observations upon the State and Condition of England* and *Of the Naval Trade of England*—neither of which was published integrally until more than a century later, when George Chalmers printed the former as an appendix to his own *Estimate of the Comparative Strength of Great Britain* (1804). But King's estimates were known to Charles Davenant (1656–1714), who made extensive use of them in his own work; [7] and they have stood up well alongside such other evidence as has come to light since, so that the population figures of King and the social accounts explicit and implicit in his breakdown of the population and its income remain the basis of all efforts to quantify British economic growth in the modern period.

King's utilization of tax records as a source of economic intelligence was itself an innovation, even for a government official. At the time, a number of these taxes were still farmed out to private enterpreneurs, who paid a fixed sum for the opportunities and risks of collection and traditionally kept their accounts to themselves. Not until 1674 were the collectors of the excise required to communicate their records to the government; not until 1679, the collectors of hearth money.[8] Even the regular collection of general trade statistics was a novelty. There are long series of customs accounts of exports of raw wool for the period 1275–1547 and of wool cloth for the years 1347–1547; [9] and we have short local runs of trade and shipping figures, more or less marred by exemptions and discontinuities.[10] It was only in 1681 that the customs commissioners were told to furnish the Committee of Trade with quarterly statements of imports and exports; these records have not survived, and there is some doubt whether they were ever complete. Not until 1696, with the appointment of an inspector-general of exports and imports, do we begin to have a complete time series of British trade statistics.[11]

King and Davenant remained the giants of British political arithmetic for the next century. The first half of the eighteenth century was particularly barren of careful, systematic work, most writers either building freely on the estimates of King and Davenant or imagining numbers to suit their arguments. The first serious effort to offer a new analysis of social structure and national income was that of Joseph Massie, a long forgotten political polemicist of the period of the Seven Year's War. The subject matter and technical competence of his work would seem to indicate that Massie had some connection with the sugar trade—much of his polemical effort was directed at attacking the West Indian sugar interest; and it was to support these attacks and a more general opposition to excise duties that he was led to draw up a list of social categories, estimate their respective incomes and their consumption of dutiable products, and then calculate the incidence of the duties. His general schema is patterned after that of King, but there are some crucial differences that make comparison difficult. King's data reflect an economy in which the boundaries between agriculture and industry were still blurred. He lumped his workers into two catch-all categories: "labouring people and out-servants" and "cottagers and paupers." Seventy years later, industry had grown considerably, and with it occupational specialization: Massie, like Colquhoun after him, broke down his working population by sectoral employment.[12]

In the field of trade statistics, the first major advance since Davenant did not come until 1776, when Charles Whitworth extracted from the *Journals* of the House of Commons his tables of imports and exports by source and destination (but not by commodity) for the period 1697–1773.[13] Abstracts for subsequent years (again by source or destination) were printed in David Macpherson's *Annals of Commerce* (1805).[14] For more detailed information the historian has to go to the manuscript ledgers of the inspector-general's

office, available at the Public Record Office in London. In this respect the
student of British economic history enjoys an advantage over his colleague
on the Continent; most of the detailed French records, for example, have
disappeared.

The student of today also has an advantage over the writers of the eighteenth century, who did not have access to these detailed trade figures. The
same holds true for most fiscal accounts; indeed, much of this information
did not become available in print until the retrospective curiosity of the
mid-nineteenth century led officials to resurrect data moldering in the
manuscript records.[15] The manuscript records in turn leave much to be
desired. Whatever contemporaries may have thought, the historian must find
the eighteenth-century state insufficiently curious or rapacious: information
on the aggregate production of those commodities not subject to excise or
duty, either in a finished or unfinished state, was and is nonexistent.[16]
Most serious, the critical foundation for the hypothetical constructions of
political arithmetic was wanting: there were no aggregate data on population. Small wonder, then, that with the exception of Massie's work and an
estimate of 1779 by the famed agronomist Arthur Young, little was done to
quantify national income until the turn of the century.[17]

The first British census, as is well known, was taken in 1801. The statisticians of the eighteenth century were compelled to rely on the data of the
parish registers and such local sources as the London bills of mortality. Some,
like King before, were able to do surprisingly well with small samples; others
allowed their convictions to shape their statistics, so that there was a strong
current of opinion that insisted that population was actually falling.[18] Not
until the 1830s, when Rickman produced global estimates based on a
systematic compilation of recorded births, deaths, and marriages in 1600–
1701 and 1749–51, was a reasonably accurate picture of the course of
population change in the eighteenth century available.[19] Later research had
modified Rickman's results somewhat, particularly for the middle of the
century, but on the whole they have stood up well, in spite of some heroic
assumptions about the fixed relation of parish registrations to actual population and an almost unavoidable neglect of migration.

The subsequent history and use of British population statistics are a good
example of the possibilities and limitations of informed estimates as a tool
in historical research. The calculations of Rickman have been refined and
re-refined by a succession of demographers, beginning a generation later
with William Farr and continuing with J. Brownlee, G. T. Griffith, J. T.
Krause, and W. A. Cole in this century.[20] These results make it possible to
offer useful calculations of the trend in income per head over the course of
the eighteenth century (defining useful calculations as those that would
not be altered significantly by anything but radical changes in the assumptions on which the calculations are based) and of a variety of other indicators of and factors in economic development (consumption per head, tax

burden, urbanization). In regard to urbanization, the recent article by A. E. Wrigley on "London's Importance, 1650–1750" is a good example of "useful" calculations in the sense defined above: Wrigley constructs what he calls a demographic model of London, presenting the city as a kind of heart pumping in a large fraction of the total population (the city's natural increase was not sufficient to sustain its growth) and pumping many out again as carriers of social and economic change.[21] Similarly, calculations of local population trends have dispelled the long-cherished myth that the enclosures emptied the land of its inhabitants and drove them into the cities to serve as factory fodder—dispelled it, that is, for all but those who clung to it as an article of faith.[22] On the other hand, our population figures have not sufficed to settle the argument about the determinants of the increase in population, and the old dispute of the birth-rate and death-rate schools goes on unabated.[23]

The point is that the usefulness of numbers, even imprecise numbers, is a function of their use. Just as the population figures of the precensus period leave much to be desired but lend themselves to all manner of reasonable manipulations and calculations, so the estimates of national income and wealth that proliferate around the end of the eighteenth century (in combination with King's figures for the 1690s) make possible the elaboration of a sequence of discrete statements of Britain's overall economic growth, covering the period from the close of the seventeenth century to the end of the Napoleonic wars. Among the sources for the last part of this period are the works of Arthur Young (particularly informative on agriculture, but on the other sectors of the economy as well), Sir John Sinclair (on Scotland), Sir Frederick Morton Eden (estimates of the insurable wealth of the country), Henry Beeke and Benjamin Bell (based on William Pitt's estimates of the potential return of an income tax), George Chalmers (offering not an explicit calculation of national income or wealth, but an array of data useful in assessing the estimates of others), and above all, Patrick Colquhoun, who occupies the place at the end of the protostatistical era that King does at the start.[24]

The principal contributor to the current effort at a quantitative reconstruction of Britain's economic growth before and during the Industrial Revolution has been Phyllis Deane, and it is instructive to examine her own changing picture of the course of growth for the light it throws on the evidential possibilities and limitations of contemporary estimates. In an early article (1955), which relied primarily, though not exclusively, on this sequence of estimates by political arithmeticians, she offered the following summary of one aspect of the story: [25]

The main conclusion suggested by the estimates which have been examined in this paper is that the average rate of growth in average real incomes apparently did not reach 1 per cent [per year] over any measurable period of the century and a quarter between the Revolution and the second decade of the nineteenth century. They also suggest that the rate of growth was markedly higher in the period before 1770, when it approached 1 per cent, that it was either between 1770 and 1798 or between 1798 and 1812, in both of which periods it appears to have been negligible (possibly negative) when the rise in prices is taken into account. If this is a true reflection of the course of average national output, it implies that real incomes advanced slowly but definitively up to about 1770 and failed to keep pace with the growth of population during the half-century from 1770 onwards.

"If this is a true reflection"—there's the rub. Miss Deane's figures flew in the face of everything we knew of the course of British economic development in those years. In particular, the period from 1770 to 1798 was one of extraordinarily rapid technological change; of fast growth in a number of key industries, among them cotton and iron; of extensive investment in transportation facilities and in enclosure; and of a remarkable increase in trade, especially export trade, after the end of the American War (1783). Under the circumstances, any effort to picture this as a period of stagnant or declining real income per head, on the basis of even the best-informed contemporary guesses, was simply unpersuasive.

This conflict between the aggregated constructs of the historian of national income and the evidence of other indicators, both quantitative and qualitative, is to be found in other places and times and poses a serious problem to scholarship. The difficulty is not one of principle: there is no intrinsic reason why the techniques of modern national income analysis should not yield valid results when applied historically. There are, to be sure, the errors generated by partial and inexact evidence; but these will not account for all the trouble, since these same data support other interpretations more compatible with qualitative evidence. The explanation seems to lie in the execution, that is, in the application of the modern techniques to the old material. Sometimes, as in the Deane article of 1955, there is a failure to use enough of the old evidence and collate the income series with other available indicators. Sometimes, willy-nilly or by choice, the periodization distorts the picture. Thus 1812 was a year of extremely high prices, and the effort to deflate income estimates by price indexes seems to depreciate the gain in real income.

This is not intended as a criticism of Miss Deane. It was not she who chose the terminal date 1812; the availability of Colquhoun imposed it on her. Her aim in the article was to do what she could with contemporary income estimates, and she did a remarkable job of collating, adjusting, and standardizing some very disparate and inconvenient material, while regrouping the data along lines compatible with modern income accounting practice. Yet figures of this kind possess great power, partly because they are numbers in an age that worships even the appearance of precision, partly because they are the kind of numbers that summarize a wide and complex array of information and thus join to seeming precision the seduction of neatness and convenience. What is more, the capacity of the scholar to explain "facts" is almost unlimited. In the years following Miss Deane's work, there were people prepared to argue that the Industrial Revolution was a figment of the historian's imagination: witness the statistics on the growth of national income!

Miss Deane herself, however, warned from the start of the danger of resting too much on so tenuous a base: "In view of the highly tentative nature of the national income estimates on which this conclusion is based, it must be treated as a highly tentative hypothesis. Whether it will be possible to assemble a sufficiently weighty series of quantity indicators from other sources effectively to check this hypothesis remains to be seen." [26] Subsequently, of course, she did assemble such a series of indicators, with very different results. Her revised calculations of real output per head show a slow rise during the first half of the eighteenth century, perhaps ½ percent per year, then a leveling off in the third quarter, and finally a faster rise of about 1 percent over the last quarter.

Even if we admit, however, that the new calculations come closer to the truth, in that they fit our general knowledge of the period better, their significance is not unambiguous. And since we here confront another major hazard of the statistical interpretation of economic history, it is useful to examine the difficulty in some detail.

In 1960 the International Economic Association held a conference in Constance on the economics of the Rostow model of growth, and particularly the concept of take-off. A number of scholars came determined to demolish once and for all a thesis that they found wanting but that had attained in a short time remarkable currency. Miss Deane, in collaboration with H. J. Habakkuk, offered a paper, based largely on her revised calculations of British national income and output, which argued that the rate of growth during the so-called take-off was not significantly higher than that of certain preceding periods and that the modern sector, which admittedly grew much faster than the rest of the economy, did not account for more than a small portion of total output. While conceding that there was some kind of break around 1780 ("by the 1830's, when the railway age gathered momentum, the British economy had been growing rapidly [by preindustrial standards] for nearly half a century"), the authors noted that Nef had "traced the process of industrialization back to the sixteenth century"; that a sustained rise in the rate of growth of total output went back to the 1740s; and that, even after 1780, "it took about a century for the long-term rate of growth in average real incomes (measured over thirty-year periods) to rise from about 1 per cent per annum to just over 2 per cent per annum." In short, "the most striking characteristic of the first take-off was its gradualness." [27]

This interpretation may well be correct; it is certainly defensible. But it raises two interesting methodological problems. The first concerns all aggregative calculations: to what extent do manipulations of this kind, which entail, especially for the protostatistical period, a great deal of interpolation, extrapolation, weighing, and adjustment, inevitably smooth out the breaks in the line of growth and thereby conceal or diminish the significance of certain turning points or critical periods? Aggregative statistics may of their nature tell a tale of gradualness, whatever the real story may have been. Second, statistics do not in themselves give the meaning of a given change. How important was a doubling of the rate of growth of real national output per head? Or an increase in the share of the modern industrial sector from 3 percent to 10 percent of national income in the space of twenty years? [28] The answer in this case is, I think, that these changes were very important. But that is not the point; the point is that the aggregate numbers alone cannot tell the significance of such changes. For that we need a larger understanding of the patterns and ramifications of change within the economy as a whole.[29]

Figures, in short, are data. They are, among other things, an aid in testing hypotheses and in giving exact content to an analysis. But they are not a substitute for analysis; they cannot tell us what we do not ask of them; and they do not constitute an autonomous, unambiguous statement of some kind of objective reality.

FRANCE

Although the French state was far more involved than the British in the control and promotion of economic activity, it was surprisingly slow to collect the data required for an effective policy. The explanation for this negligence lies in the impecuniousness and the self-reinforcing inefficiency of French government. Because the monarchy was always short of funds, it had to mortgage its revenues by selling offices and farming out taxes. Venality of office in turn imposed serious constraints on recruitment and afflicted the country with a swarm of more or less competent (or incompetent) officials, while the farming of taxes and customs duties took collection out of government hands and placed it in the charge of entrepreneurs who had every interest in keeping the results secret. Meanwhile the endemic poverty of the state made it embarrassing for its rulers to know the hard facts about income and expenditure, while the effort to press more revenue out of a population aggrieved by a notoriously inequitable tax burden imbued the subjects of the king with a mistrust of anything connected with the state and an unwillingness to provide any information that might serve the ends of the fisc. In sum, the French state found it hard to collect statistical data; was ill-prepared to collate and process such data as it did have; and since it really did not want to know the unpleasant truth, was prepared to tolerate the falsification of these data.

Not all French officials felt this way. The best of them—Colbert, d'Aguesseau, Trudaine, Necker—were well aware of the need for better information. Marshal Vauban, in his *Projet d'une dix^{me} royale* of 1707 (see p. 70 below), made an eloquent plea for regular censuses of the population, its occupational distribution, and its economic condition. "Would it not be," he wrote, "an extreme pleasure for [the ruler] to be able, from his desk, to review for himself in an hour the present and past state of a great kingdom of which he is the sovereign master, and to be able to know by himself, with certainty, wherein consists its greatness, its wealth, and its force, the welfare and misfortune of his subjects, and what he can do to increase the one and remedy the other?" [30]

Unfortunately, even where the Crown was willing, the wishes of the higher functionaries in Paris had to be translated into action by the clumsy bureaucratic machine, hampered as it was by the renitency of the *parlements* (which constituted a kind of parallel government) and the self-interest of regional and local establishments. Colbert, from 1661 to his death in 1683 Louis XIV's chief minister, was the first to ask for complete trade statistics, but we have no overall data for that period and can only assume that he was not able to realize his wish.[31] In 1693 the young Daguesseau (later d'Aguesseau), who was charged with commercial matters in the office of the controller-general of Finance, Pontchartrain, ordered the head of the general tax farm to instruct the customs agents to keep records and forward them to Paris, where they might be assembled in annual tables of imports and exports. To no avail. In 1700 the customs officials were directed to prepare trimestrial reports to the controller-general; that same year saw the creation of the Conseil de Commerce, which was directly interested in these returns. Still to no effect. When in 1712 the French sat down to negotiate with the British at Utrecht, they found themselves at a serious disadvantage. The British, who, as we have seen, had begun collecting full and regular trade statistics in 1696, were able to use them to good purpose in the transactions; the French had little to offer in rebuttal. This finally moved the French to take action, and in 1716 the administration was able to produce the first general return of imports and exports. What happened after that is not clear. Our next reasonably full return does not come until 1725, but from that point on we have annual statistics.[32]

The quality of these statistics is something else again. The custom agents apparently registered the quantities declared by the merchants (subject, of course, to inspection), and these were converted to values on the basis of prices furnished after the end of the year by the local chambers of commerce. (Often these prices were used in the following year or even two.) That these figures were often far from accurate we know from the reiterated complaints of the higher authorities. In addition, the returns were submitted at first without systematic recapitulation of subtotals and totals; thus numbers got lost in the confusion, and different efforts to sum the data yielded different results. Not until 1756 did Trudaine remedy some of the difficulty by insisting on summaries for each area and commodity. Even so the data left much to be desired, and in 1781, moved by complaints of P. S. Dupont, Necker reorganized the service. This was followed in 1785 by the creation of the Bureau de la Balance du Commerce, which took over the statistical function from the office of the controller-general.

Under the circumstances, it is easy to understand why we do not possess a single reliable time series of French trade figures for the eighteenth century. The one most commonly employed is that prepared by (or for) Ambroise-Marie Arnould, assistant director of the Bureau de la Balance du Commerce, covering the period 1716–88. These figures differ sharply from the incomplete statistics of Bruyard, head of the Bureau de Commerce from 1756. They also differ, for particular years, from the figures presented by such officials as Necker and Chaptal; and for the final years of the Old Regime, from the recapitulative tables published in the nineteenth century.[33]

In addition to these errors and disagreements, the trade figures present other difficulties to the historian who seeks to use them in analyzing French economic development. For one thing, the heterogeneous customs regime made it impossible to obtain full data on the movement of goods in and out of France. The country was divided into four classes of territory:

1. The *cinq grosses fermes,* consisting of Paris and the surrounding provinces, constituted the French customs area proper.
2. The *provinces réputées étrangères,* including the southern half of France, Brittany, Flanders (except Dunkirk), Artois, and the Franche-Comté, which was only partially subject to the national tariff, paid duty on goods imported and exported to the *cinq grosses fermes* and in principle kept records of their own exports to other lands.
3. The *provinces d'étranger effectif,* including the provinces and districts of Marseilles (except the city itself), Bayonne and Labourd (Bayonne itself became a free port in 1784), Gex, Lorraine, Alsace, the Trois-Evêchés, and Dunkirk, were treated as foreign, did not come under the administration of the General Farm, and kept their own records of trade with France and other countries.
4. The free ports—Marseilles, St.-Jean-de-Luz, Lorient, Dunkirk, and Bayonne—as the designation indicates, paid no duties on imports or exports.

The reader will see at once the statistical difficulties posed by such a complex regime. Two examples will suffice. First, it is not clear how the authorities separated shipments between the different customs areas from real exports and imports; there was presumably a serious problem of double counting. The documents seem to make no mention of this, which only increases the historian's disquietude. Second, no records were kept of much of the trade, particularly of movement of goods in and out of the free ports and the *provinces d'étranger effectif.* Arnould made an effort to guess at the totals in question, but he admits that his figures are suppositions. What Bruyard did is not clear. To these lacunae, moreover, should be added the uncertainty of the data on some branches of trade, in particular that with India and the Far East. From 1723 to 1770 this was monopolized by the Compagnie des Indes, whose activity was not included in the official statistics of the balance of trade. Arnould filled the gap by taking over the figures in Raynal's eighteenth-century history of the subject; and although these undoubtedly furnish a reliable picture of the year-to-year fluctuations and trends, it is not clear that the values given were calculated on the same basis as those in the official trade statistics.[34]

A second major problem is the difficulty of distinguishing real from current values. The official figures have not been deflated for changes in the price level, and the process of deflation is complicated by the need first to correct reported values for changes in the content of the coinage. In principle, to be sure, Arnould has already done this for us, converting current values to the livres that were legal tender at the end of the Old Regime, with a silver content equal to $\frac{1}{54}$ of a mark of metal. But when one takes into account the number of alterations in the currency—especially at the start of this period, when five years saw 21 different livres, so that the mark of silver varied in value from 35 to 131 livres—one cannot accept Arnould's results at face value, the less so since we have no idea of his procedure.

It is a brave man, then, who would use the French trade figures as quantitative evidence of the rate and character of French economic development. The only example that comes to mind is to be found in a recent article by François Crouzet, comparing the economic growth of France and Britain in the eighteenth century.[35] Crouzet uses for his base period (1716–20) the Bruyard figures, which are substantially lower than those or Arnould and imply that much more rapid a rate of growth over the course of the century. But Bruyard's figures are clearly incomplete, and as noted earlier, there is reason to believe that the procedures of reporting and collection improved over the course of the century, biasing the nominal returns upwards. In any event, here, as in the case of the British national income estimates, the evaluation of the data is a function not only of their accuracy but of the analytical conceptions of the scholar. The significance of trade figures as a clue to economic growth, for example, may well lie less in their totals than in their composition; and a comparison of Britain and France should lay more stress on the fact that the fastest growing section of the British export trade was manufactures, especially toward the end of the period, whereas in the French case it was reexports of colonial goods (sugar, coffee, tobacco, etc.) and sales of primary products (food, alcoholic beverages, raw materials). Industrial products accounted for two-thirds of British exports in the 1780s, against two-fifths of the French. Crouzet, of course, is well aware of these complications; but he is inclined on balance to dismiss the view that French commerce, however flourishing in some of these years, was a kind of gloss on the national economy and hence essentially irrelevant to the course of economic development. He may well be right. The point I want to make here, however, is simply that once again the statistics by themselves, even if good, are not enough.

When we move from trade to the other typical areas of protostatistical reporting, we are no better off. In regard to public revenues and expenditures, our information for the France of the Old Regime is hopelessly incomplete, for reasons suggested above: in particular, the facts were so painful that even the government could not bear to know. Thus we know that from time to time, what passed for accurate *états au vrai* of the state finances were prepared for the eyes of the king (insofar as the dispersion of authority in matters of revenue collection and expenditure made it possible to prepare such statements). But these balance sheets were never published, and since none of them has come down to us, we may assume that they were destroyed. Not until Necker (who even as director-general of finance took months to find his way through the confusion of the French treasury) published his famous *Compte rendu au Roi* (1781) was the public given any indication of the income and expenditure of the monarchy. Necker was dismissed shortly thereafter, in part (though only in part) because his *Compte rendu* was a vexation and embarrassment to the Court. A few years later he brought out his study, *De l'administration des finances de la France,* which presented a kind of idealized balance sheet of a normal year's income and outgo. These data are a valuable source of information on the social and political structure of the ancien régime, but they do not constitute a time series, and they throw little if any light on the course of economic development. For something comparable in France to the British excise figures, which we have reason to believe are a reliable indicator of the output of certain industries, we would have to look to the accounts of the farmers-general and the records of those local authorities charged with the verification and stamping of manufactures. Some evidence of this kind is available, but it is spotty, incomplete, and of varying reliability. I shall return to this point later.

In general, we are forced to fall back on ingenious guesses and fantasies in all matters concerning the production of specific commodities. The most important branch of activity was agriculture, and one would have thought that the influence of the food supply on public order was such as to incite the authorities to the most zealous curiosity in this domain. In fact, the administration relied primarily on price reports (the so-called *mercuriales*), which go back to the sixteenth century and have been more or less well preserved in the national and departmental archives; and on rough estimates (usually in the form of prognoses) of the state of the crops, prepared in each *élection* and forwarded through the *intendants* to the Contrôle Général in Paris. These have not been preserved and are known to us by the circular instructions concerning their preparation. An effort to collect real output figures in the early 1770s was a failure; as Turgot put it in a circular of 27 December 1774 ordering the abandonment of the attempt, "One had no doubt foreseen only some of the obstacles that might impede an operation so wide in its scope and so complex in its details." We can infer what some of these obstacles were from Turgot's fear that undue inquisitiveness might alarm the population; the French peasant was hardly going to cooperate in a proceeding that might well be the preliminary to new fiscal levies. After this, the authorities fell back on the old *apparences de récolte*. These too have disappeared, except for some of the regional elements that went into the national averages and a summary document, a *"relevé du produit des récoltes"* for the country as a whole from 1774 to 1788, prepared at a later date by the Ministry of the Interior. It is this last series that was utilized by Labrousse in his studies of the French economy on the eve of the revolution to demonstrate the decisive influence of the harvest in an economy dominated by grain and textiles.[36]

For other goods we are usually worse off. The numbers of livestock were no easier to ascertain than the size of the harvest. As for manufactures, the closest thing we have to time series are the *états de l'inspection*, going back as far as 1715 and confined almost exclusively to textiles. These returns were spotty to begin with, and only fragments have survived in the manuscript archives, mixed in with other documents and as yet unindexed. Since these returns were derived from the record of goods produced in the so-called regulated industries (textiles, leather, paper) and submitted to the official inspectors for the stamp of approval, their coverage was necessarily incomplete. Aside from such evasion as inevitably occurred, there was a large and growing sector of unregulated production in these same branches, more dynamic than the other and more important for the course of French economic development.[37]

Alongside these series there are also the results of a number of occasional *enquêtes* into the state and activity of selected industries at particular times. One of the best-documented industries is iron manufacture, for which we have a general *enquête sur les forges* of 1772, and an *enquête sur les bouches à feu* of 1788 that was intended in principle to cover all fuel-using industries.[38] We are considerably less fortunate with other branches, partly because the execution of these inquiries always left much to be desired—the returns to Paris were typically vague and innocent of numbers—and partly because little of this material has survived.[39] As a result, efforts to establish global outputs of the different branches tend to rely heavily on factitious surrogates: estimates of consumption per head multiplied by population; or conversions of the output or consumption of raw materials, often derived in turn by multiplying estimates of averages (like yield per area of cultivation) by estimates of area.[40]

Finally there is the question of population data. In France, as in Britain, there were no regular official censuses before the nineteenth century, and the mistrust of the fisc made not only the common people but even certain levels of official authority hostile to any moves in this direction. When, around 1760, the bishop of Avranches sent a letter to his priests inquiring about the number of people and communicants in their parishes, the *parlement* of Rouen forbade them to reply. When the Abbé Expilly made a similar effort to circularize the province for information about population, trade, industrial output, and the like, the same *parlement* threatened a fine of 500 livres for anyone who replied.[41]

The attitude of the central government toward demographic intelligence was ambivalent. Certainly the authorities, or at least some of them, were hostile to private inquiries. The Abbé Expilly, for example, found it impossible to publish the whole of his population data, which he had collected, as he put it, "with care, trouble, and unbelievable expense." Why? The abbé thought he was the victim of a cabal, presumably a Physiocratic cabal, of those who refused to believe that the population of France was growing (more on this below). In a "Mémoire au Roi" of August 1778, he wrote:

> More than ten years ago I had recognized the fact that France had about 24 million inhabitants, but I neither could nor might publish in entire this important discovery, which I had made on the basis of the enormous research and work I had been carrying out. It is because there *existed a powerful and influential party that had everyone intimidated [en imposait absolument]* and considered as blasphemous, information of a sort that would throw light on the real resources of France, which this same party was doing its best to render unrecognizable or even incomprehensible.[42]

Insofar as Expilly was able to publish some of the results of his circular inquiries, they appeared as appendixes to the separate volumes of his great *Dictionnaire géographique, historique, et politique des Gaules et de la France,* which remains a major source on all aspects of French society and institutions toward the end of the Old Regime.[43] In 1767, when he got to his fifth volume and published the article on "Population," he lamented the neglect and possible reticence of the regime:

> Why, on a subject as important as that of the count of the population, must we confine ourselves to conjectures, to suppositious calculations whose accuracy depends on so many circumstances, most of them little known, when it is easy to obtain each year a report of the persons living in each parish of England, or even of the three kingdoms of England, Scotland, and Ireland? Up to now, reduced to reports of births, deaths, and marriages that are kept for only a few cities, what have we been able to learn of the general state of the kingdom?[44]

Expilly's allusion to reports on a few cities was a reference to, among other things, the *Bulletins du mouvement de la population de Paris,* which

had been published annually since 1664.[45] These, it should be noted, were
not censuses, but summary statements of the items recorded in the parish
records: births, deaths, marriages. The authorities did, however, conduct a
number of local censuses over the course of the late seventeenth and eighteenth centuries, and these, in conjunction with the parish data, then
served as a basis for calculations of the overall population.[46] Necker tells
the story well in his *De l'administration des finances:*

> We are now more surely and exactly informed about the population of
> the Kingdom than we were formerly; and this is the result of the efforts of
> the government. No doubt it was not possible to do a general enumer-
> ation of so large a country; it was even less feasible to renew such an
> enumeration every year. But after ordering partial counts in different
> places, one compared the results with the number of births, deaths, and
> marriages; and these ratios, confirmed to a certain degree by tests made
> in other countries, established a measure of comparison in which it is
> reasonable to have confidence. [1:252]

The problem of calculating such ratios is not so simple as Necker suggests. He himself points out the sharp fluctuations in deaths and marriages,
which make any ratios between these and total population too unstable for
use in this kind of calculation. He also remarks on the incompleteness of
birth statistics, due partly to the unwillingness of certain groups to record
their children in the registers of the Catholic churches and partly to the
negligence of the poor, who were more careless in these matters than the
rich, especially in the event of stillbirth or early death. Even so, once the
problem of a representative ratio has been solved (and it is instructive to
consider the reasoning of Necker in this regard), the time series of recorded
births does make possible a reasonably accurate notion of the change in
population over time. The trouble is that aggregate data on births were
assembled only in the final years of the Old Regime, from 1770 on. For the
earlier period, the bases of estimation are local birth figures, hearth counts,
and local censuses (e.g., Paris in 1694, Alsace in 1697).[47] Given the spottiness
of such information, it is not surprising that many contemporaries were
convinced that the population of the kingdom was falling and had already
fallen sharply from the mid-seventeenth to the mid-eighteenth century.
Among those who advanced this opinion were the Physiocrats, followed in
this respect by most of the Encyclopedists. Even the calculations of Messance
and Moheau in the 1760s and 1770s, which showed a population of at least
22.5 million, were not enough to dissuade Quesnay from his belief that the
number had declined over the period 1650–1750 from about 24 to 16
million.[48]

Necker and other statesmen of the period were more impressed by the
calculations of men like Messance and Moheau than by the unsupported
assertions of men like Quesnay; among other things, the behavior of other

economic indicators, however incomplete, seemed to contradict the depopulationist view. Since then, the work of more sophisticated demographic historians has succeeded in producing a reasonably persuasive time series of French population from the seventeenth century on—full of gaps, to be sure, but comparable in accuracy and usefulness to the one established for Great Britain. If this consensus is correct, population was perhaps 19.5 to 20 million in 1688, a half million lower at the end of the century (the 1690s were years of war, famine, and disease), lower still a decade later (more war, famine, and disease), followed by a turn upward sometime around 1720 and a steady, substantial rise from that point on. By 1776 the number had risen, according to Bourgeois-Pichat, to about 25.6 million, and the first official census, that of 1801, counted 27,350,000.[49]

French historical demography has not confined its attention to macro-demographic problems, that is, to the estimation of aggregate population movements for large regions or for France as a whole. Some of the most interesting and valuable work has taken the form of local studies, based on the reconstitution technique of Louis Henry, which tries to reproduce the course of population change in a small area family by family, person by person. These microdemographic researches are as yet of limited relevance to the analysis of national patterns, because they are too few to form a representative sample; though Henry and his colleagues are currently engaged in remedying that defect.[50] In the meantime, local data tell a great deal more than one would expect a priori—about the influence of economic conditions on demographic behavior; about patterns of mobility; about links between occupation and age of marriage, fertility, and other demographic variables; and, inferentially, about the social and psychological attitudes that help shape population response to environmental change. As such, they are an important element in the burgeoning corpus of regional and local economic and social histories, which constitute the most flourishing and valuable branch of current work on French economic development.[51] (See pp. 74–75.)

The work of the Henry school has found an important echo in England, where Peter Laslett and E. A. Wrigley have established a Cambridge Group for the History of Population and Social Structure. Beginning with detailed studies of a few localities, this center is now engaged in the collection, by correspondence, of sufficient data from all over the country to permit the induction of general population patterns in the early modern period. As its name indicates, the scope of its work is explicitly larger than the pure demographic analysis favored by Henry; the aim is to move from population to social structure, and some of the findings about geographical mobility (surprisingly high) and household size (smaller than would be compatible with the widespread existence of extended families), if confirmed by further research, are among the most important and exciting put forward in British historiography in recent years.[52]

The weaknesses of the data on these three major dimensions of the French economy in this preindustrial era make it very difficult to appreciate and utilize such contemporary estimates of overall growth as have come down to us. As in Britain, the composition and size of the national product or national wealth were of interest and concern to both officers of the Crown and curious private persons engaged in speculation about the ends and means of public policy. As a result, we have an irregular array of assertions and informed guesses about the output of different branches of the economy, or of the economy as a whole, from the late seventeenth century on. The most reliable of these are presumably the reports of the *intendants* to the central government, which were based in principle on direct inquiries in the field; the least reliable are the global estimates proffered by a series of political arithmeticians, some of which are not so much independent appraisals as rehashes of the work of the most plausible predecessor.

The first important general estimate of this kind, interestingly enough, was the work of a military man, Sébastien le Prestre de Vauban, marshal of France and better known for his contributions to military tactics and the engineering of fortifications than for his work in political economy. But money is the sinews of war, and Vauban's military responsibilities had led him to concern himself with the financial resources of the country: when, in his declining years, he lost influence as a man of war, he sought to place his experience at the disposal of the king by offering some advice on questions of tax policy and social justice. In 1698 he wrote an essay pleading for a new and more equitable system of taxation, the *Projet d'une dix^{me} royale*, which was not published until 1707 and then instantly suppressed by order of the king.[53] This is not the place to examine Vauban's plan; the point is that he found it necessary, in presenting his proposal, to offer estimates of population and income as a basis for calculations of the return from such a general tithe. These estimates, which offer some regional breakdowns, would probably play the role in reconstructions of French growth that Gregory King's figures play today in analogous English studies. They are, however, sketchier and seem far more suppositious than King's tables.

Contemporary with Vauban was his cousin, Pierre Le Pesant, seigneur de Boisguilbert (or Boisguillebert), author of *Le détail de la France sous le règne présent* (1695), which appeared a year later in shortened form with the ferociously explicit title, *La France ruinée sous le règne de Louis XIV, par qui et comment* (Cologne, 1696); and of the *Factum de la France, ou moyens très faciles de rétablir les finances de l'Etat* (1707).[54] As the titles of his works indicate, Boisguilbert was a severe critic of the policies of Louis XIV, and his essay postulated a catastrophic decline in French wealth and population over the last third of the seventeenth century and first decade of the eighteenth. Although Boisguilbert was convinced that it was feasible to establish a system of national accounts—if one could do it for a household, an estate, or a village, why not for a nation?—he confined himself to the assertion of a substantial loss in income since 1660: some 500 to 600 million livres by 1695, 1,500 million by 1707. (By way of comparison, Vauban reckoned the entire French national product at 600 million livres in 1701.) By the same token Boisguilbert estimated population in 1707 at 14 to 15 million, well below the 20 million or more of a generation earlier.

Now these were certainly years of war and depression, and both income and numbers fell significantly, though to an extent that is yet to be determined. Yet Boisguilbert's figures are too extreme to be believed. If true, they would imply a collapse comparable to the wasting of certain parts of Germany in the Thirty Years' War, and this seems improbable in a country that saw little fighting within its own boundaries. The difficulty would seem to lie in the polemical and impressionistic character of Boisguilbert's work: he relied heavily on small samples and tended to extrapolate from the circle of his personal experience.[55]

Vauban and Boisguilbert were followed at intervals by a series of amateur economists, moralists, and polemicists, some of whom simply cribbed from their predecessors, others of whom made an effort to build on such official data as were accessible and to add to these by their own inquiries. The most important were the Comte Henri de Boulainvilliers, who published (significantly enough in London) an *Etat de la France . . . extrait des mémoires dressés par les intendants du royaume*,[56] which offers the most convenient collection of the results of the general administrative survey of the late seventeenth century; and, of course, the Abbé Expilly, the greatest of a series of authors of regional or national geographies or "dictionaries." [57] None of these writers, it should be emphasized, made an effort to put the statistical data together in a systematic fashion; and rarely were any of them attentive to the distinction between fact on the one hand and supposition and assumption on the other. It is difficult, therefore, to appraise their assertions or to balance one man's picture against another's. Not until we come to Tolosan and Lavoisier at the end of the century do we have estimates based on real familiarity with such official data as were available, and even then we have nothing comparable to King's or Massie's efforts to reconstruct the nation's economic and social accounts.[58]

The revolutionary and Napoleonic years saw something of an efflorescence of French statistical publication. Much of this was a natural accompaniment of the drastic reforms effected in all aspects of administration. Just as Lavoisier was asked by the National Assembly to draw up a statement of French resources and the distribution of wealth with an eye to revision of the system of taxation, so he and others were called upon to calculate the population of the realm, to make local population counts, and to report on industrial and agricultural output. These projects were initially unsuccessful: political conditions were too unsettled to encourage serious statistical inquiry. Thus, although the law of 22 July 1791 enjoined the local authorities to make periodic censuses of the inhabitants in their charge, it was not until the end of the century that François de Neufchâteau (minister of the interior July–September 1797 and July 1798–June 1799) was able to get the prefects to work on this and not until 1801 that France had her first modern general census.[59] Similarly, an effort in the year V (1796–97) to effect an industrial census by department was premature: it brought in only five returns—from the Corrèze, Creuse, Moselle, Nord, and Pas-de-Calais.[60] Two years later, however, more returns started coming in, and over a period of some years dozens of departmental monographs were published, comparable to the reports furnished by the *intendants* a century before. These monographs have their limitations: in particular, the department is not a significant economic or social unit; but the best of them constitute to this day an invaluable source on the economic and social condition, not only of France, but also of the areas she occupied in the Low Countries, Germany, Switzerland, and Italy, on the eve of the Industrial Revolution.[61]

At the same time, a Bureau de Statistique was established in the Ministry of the Interior, possibly on the initiative of Lucien Bonaparte, who was minister from December 1799 to November 1800. (The circumstances of its creation are not entirely clear.) This was once again a manifestation of the rationality that was among other things a revulsion from the sloppiness and *laisser-aller* of the Old Regime, and it marked one more area (along with technical and scientific education and the introduction of metric weights and measures) in which revolutionary France showed the way to the other countries of Europe.

Lucien Bonaparte's successor as minister of the interior, the chemical manufacturer Chaptal, did much to encourage the work of the Bureau. He had Peuchet prepare an *Essai d'une statistique générale de la France* (Paris, year IX [1800–01]), which was addressed to all prefects and designed to provide a model for returns to a general inquiry into the condition of France in the year IX (1800–01) as compared with 1789.[62] In principle, the Bureau de Statistique was to collate and digest these returns, with a view to preparing a general balance sheet. It never did so, possibly because even with the best of will, the data were incomplete and of uneven quality. But it did make the information available to a number of political arithmeticians, most of them employed by the government in statistical posts, who then brought out a series of special and general studies on the state of the country, its resources and income, the condition of its inhabitants, its demographic characteristics, and so on.

These publications were all entitled *statistiques*. Among them were Alexandre de Ferrière's *Analise de la statistique générale de la France*, 7 fasc. (Paris, 1803–04), Herbin de Halle's *Statistique générale et particulière de la France et de ses colonies*, 7 vols. (1803), Peuchet's *Statistique élémentaire de la France* (1805), the *Description topographique et statistique de la France* of Peuchet and P. G. Chanlaire (3 vols. [Paris, 1810]), and

Charles Ganilh's *La théorie de l'économie politique, fondée sur des faits résultant des statistiques de la France et de l'Angleterre* (Paris, 1815). The repetition of this theme in title after title and the spate of publication on this subject are evidence of a wave of fashion; the French had discovered, as it were, a new form of enlightenment. The government of Napoleon was enamored of numbers, and its encouragement of statistical inquiry produced a generation of political statisticians. The harvest continued to be reaped even after the government dissolved the Bureau de Statistique in 1812 and assigned its duties to a number of different offices, and after the Empire fell and gave way to a regime that tended to look on statistics as a revolutionary abortion and an instrument of despotism. Even the government of the Restoration was concerned to collect the kind of data, principally on grain harvests and prices, which had obvious implications for public order and the stability of the regime. In the same way, a number of ministries found it desirable, with a view to parliamentary legislation, to gather and publish information for the use of legislators and voters. The Ministry of Commerce, which was engaged throughout this period in interminable tariff negotiations with the Chamber of Deputies, brought out, beginning in 1821, annual tables of foreign trade going back to 1819 and, from 1827 on, decennial tables. The Ministry of Justice gathered criminal statistics from 1825; the Ministry of Finance assembled data on revenues and expenditures. At the same time, the Comte de Chabrol, prefect of the Seine, issued a series of volumes of statistics of the city of Paris that constitutes perhaps the earliest and richest source of its kind for urban history in the prerailroad era.[63] All this inevitably suggested the desirability of a new central statistical bureau, to collate, standardize, and preserve the information. The suggestion was already advanced in the closing years of the Restoration; it was not acted upon until 1833, however, at the instigation of Adophe Thiers, then minister of commerce. It was this Service Central that brought out in 1835 and 1836 the first of a long, irregular series of volumes that constitute the *Statistique générale de la France,* a still largely unexploited mine of information on all aspects of the national history over the course of the nineteenth century.[64]

In view of the shortcomings of the French national estimates for the eighteenth century, it is not surprising that we do not as yet have a serious quantitative reconstruction of the course of economic growth in that period. Toutain's study of agriculture, to be sure, takes the story back to 1700 and covers what was far and away the most important branch of the economy.[65] And we are promised a volume by T. J. Markovitch on French industry from 1664 to 1789 in the same series. But this work, impressive though it is in its wide-ranging research (the team at the Institut de Science Economique Appliquée has resurrected sources long forgotten or neglected by the conventional historians) and in the ingenuity of its calculations, is built on so flimsy an evidential base that the historian uses it at his peril.

The Toutain volume in particular has been subjected to searching criticisms by Emmanuel Le Roy Ladurie, who points out that the "marriage" of Gregory King's unreliable and unsupported estimates of French income and consumption with Vauban's "utopian" guesses in other areas seriously deflates the totals for the base year of 1700 and, consequently, exaggerates the French rate of growth over the course of the century.[66] Among the work that has to be reassessed in the light of this bias is Crouzet's comparison of economic growth in France and Britain (see above, p. 64 n. 35) and a fairly substantial body of literature on agricultural progress in France (sometimes characterized as an agricultural revolution) in the eighteenth and early nineteenth centuries.[67]

This primary flaw, moreover, is aggravated by many smaller and no doubt inevitable weaknesses of Toutain's procedure. His method is essentially to assemble such contemporary estimates as can be found (of area under cultivation, for example, and "normal" yield per area), to reject those that seem manifestly improbable, and to build high and low estimates of low chronological specificity out of those that are left. All this seems eminently reasonable; but if the criterion for the historical economist is to be the concordance of the figures with expectation, what should the historian do with those numbers that do not fit such other evidence, qualitative or quantitative, as may be available? What is one to make, for example, of estimates of physical product per head that show France and Britain as more or less equal at the beginning of the nineteenth century, when Britain had already experienced some thirty years of industrial revolution and France, far behind in technology, was trying to make up the income lost during a decade of war and revolution? [68] It is hard to be sure what the answer is. Perhaps all our conceptions of the course of economic development need revision. Or perhaps the figures are wrong. The problem is particularly acute in studying the protostatistical era. But it remains serious for the later period as well and tends to disappear only with the introduction of modern techniques of national accounting and the adaptation of data collection to these techniques.

In view of these difficulties, there is much to be said for relying more on the microdata—the local returns, the short runs, the private records. The France of the Old Regime is rich in this kind of material—richer by far than Britain—because of the pervasive intervention of the government in economic activity and the tendency to see the population (*"les peuples"*) as a resource of the state. Because of this abundance of administrative paper, French scholars have been able to produce a corpus of regional and local histories without compare. (There are very few of these for eighteenth-century Britain.) It would be impossible here to give anything approaching a full list of even the outstanding studies, but an examination of any of these will convey something of the richness of the statistical base. Take the recent volumes by Emmanuel Le Roy Ladurie on *Les paysans de Languedoc* (Paris, 1966): the author is able to put together data on population variables, earnings and income, taxes, landholdings, occupational distribution, prices, and indirectly on output by way of yields. Much of this information rests on the extraordinary richness of the land records of the region: the *compoix* of Languedoc, precise cadastral descriptions of real property and the distribution of ownership, go back to the fourteenth century and make possible a continuous quantitative history from the Middle Ages to the present.[69]

Or consider a local study in urban and industrial history: Jeffry Kaplow's *Elbeuf during the Revolutionary Period: History and Social Structure* (Baltimore, 1964). Kaplow has been able to obtain or put together data on population, occupational distribution, wages, income, marriage patterns, industrial output, and costs of manufacture. The data on output illustrate the strength and weaknesses of these microstatistics. They are of two types: statistics on the amount of raw wool used by the local wool manufacture for the period 1740–63; and semestrial data on the number of pieces inspected, plus a valuation of this output at uniform prices, for the years 1750–71. These are useful series, but they pose as many questions as they answer. For one thing, the valuations of output, presumably based on what was considered the "normal" prevailing price, are at best a distorted reflection of real market values. Kaplow notes that we do not know when these cloths were sold or at what price. A more serious problem, however, relates to the size of output. If we are to believe the Elbeuf series—or that for the entire *généralité,* for that matter—output of woolen cloth diminished over these two decades. Perhaps it did. The data on consumption of raw wool show a very slight decline over the interval. On the other hand, these are years when rural output on the basis of putting-out was presumably increasing, and much of this must have escaped inspection; so that what we may have is a decline of the urban manufacture only, not a decline of the Norman woolen industry. If so, the figures taken *by themselves* obscure rather than illuminate the course of French economic development.

To be sure, data of this kind, drastically limited in their domain (they cover only a small area and only part of the population in that area), are no substitute for accurate aggregates or representative national averages. But there are questions in economic development that can be studied as well on the local level as on the national: the effect of certain changes in technique and organization, the link between social variables and economic activity, the reaction to market changes.[70] And for those problems that should be viewed in a larger framework, there is always the promise that the multiplication of these local studies will permit us one day to piece together a far more detailed and accurate picture than is now possible by way of highly processed estimates of aggregates.

GERMANY, THE LOW COUNTRIES, AND ITALY

When one moves from consolidated, well-defined nation-states like Great Britain and France (even with its customs divisions) to the mosaic of sovereignties that characterized the Low Countries, Italy, and the Germanies of the Old Regime, one enters a different order of statistical complexity and ignorance. As we shall see, the numbers are there—more abundant for some countries than for either Britain or France. The difficulty lies in re-grouping and assembling these protostatistical data so that they cover roughly the same political entities that we have statistics for from the nine-teenth century on. Even if one grants that the nation-state is not always the relevant unit of analysis in the study of economic development, that it would be desirable, for example, to look at industrialization as a common European achievement rather than as the work of separate political units, we would still want to follow the process on the local and regional level, and there shifting sovereignties and boundaries continue to pose a problem.

Fortunately, the accidents of political history have mitigated the diffi-culty. In general, Prussia is not a bad surrogate for Germany. To be sure, the kingdom did not comprise in the eighteenth century some of the most advanced industrial areas which later came within the Prussian or German boundaries. The most serious of these exclusions are the Rhineland and Saxony—the former then, as now, a region of great industrial versatility ranging from mining through metallurgy, hardware, and textiles; the latter probably Germany's greatest center of textile putting-out. Even so, Prussia's share of the larger area's industrial output was substantial, especially in coal mining and ferrous metallurgy, and this share became overwhelming after 1815, when Prussia annexed the Rhineland. The final step was the creation of the Zollverein (1828–34), which brought all but an insignificant portion of Germany's industrial output into the domain of German eco-nomic statistics.

The Prussia of the eighteenth century is a veritable mine of statistics for the economic historian, and it is one of the puzzles of historiography that no effort has been made to put together a quantitative picture of her overall development in these years. Not only are the figures there, but thanks to the diligence of German scholars, we have excellent guides to the raw sources and the literature of the period. For the official statistics, there is Otto Behre's classic *Geschichte der Statistik in Brandenburg-Preussen bis zur Gründung des Königlichen Statistischen Bureaus* (Berlin, 1905), which is far more than a catalog of the material, offering as it does numerous tables from both printed and manuscript sources.[71] For the contemporary economic literature, there is no comparable survey, but we do have Mag-dalene Humpert's invaluable *Bibliographie der Kameralwissenschaften* (Cologne, 1937), which testifies to the unparalleled preoccupation of German writers with questions of political economy in all its aspects in a period when Germany was well behind western Europe in technology and standard of living.[72]

Paradoxically, the abundance of this literature, along with the richness of the statistical record, was a product of this backwardness, for it was the effort of ambitious states like Prussia to promote population growth and economic development as a means to political power that produced this insatiable appetite for figures. The scope and detail of this cameralist curiosity may be judged from one of the great classics of Prussian statistical geography, Friedrich Wilhelm August Bratring's *Statistisch-topographische Beschreibung der gesammten Mark Brandenburg* (3 vols [1804–09]), which, though concerned primarily with the contemporary condition of the province, contains substantial information on earlier periods.[73] If one turns to the section on any given *Kreis* (a small administrative division), one finds first a statement of its boundaries, size, topography and geology, and the distribution of land by quality and use. Then follows population: number at mid-century and end of century, distribution by civil status and occupation, division into urban and rural categories.[74] Next come data on output and capital stock. Figures on grain production are given for a specific year (not a so-called "normal"), broken down into seed, harvest, consumption, and stock—so that it is possible to derive accurate ratios of yields per seed and per area. Livestock data are given for both rural and "urban" areas and include statistics of total stock; numbers used for "productive" purposes; numbers slaughtered, sold, and imported. Separate information is provided where applicable on the output, use, and value of industrial raw materials like wool and linen. Then industrial output is given, enterprise by enterprise—number of workers, size of output, value of output, cost and origin of raw materials (whether home-produced or imported)—so that it is feasible to produce value-added figures for most branches. For the cities, we also have figures of the number and structure of public and private buildings, of tax and excise returns (which are a guide to consumption), of religious composition, of school facilities, and so on; while for most villages, we have a breakdown of residents by tenurial status.[75]

This statistical abundance at the turn of the century does not imply, however, a comparable density of information for earlier periods. Thanks to the avid curiosity of the Prussian crown, which badgered its functionaries ceaselessly for numbers on the largest and smallest aspects of the economy, we do have data on trade, occupations, taxes, population, and the rest going back to the first half of the century.[76] But we also know that there was a gap between intent and performance; that the functionaries found it hard to effect a new census every year; that the general tables of trade and industry were not systematically prepared and submitted (the king often found it necessary to ask for special reports on matters already covered in principle in the overall statistics); and that the fragmentation and dis-

persion of the territories of the state made the collection of certain data,
particularly those on trade, a necessarily imperfect operation. In general,
one has the sense with a ruler like Frederick II ("the Great") that one has
with Napoleon—that even with the best of will, his servants could not keep
up with his demands and may on occasion have manufactured numbers
rather than plead ignorance. Finally, it must be noted that not all the
statistical material that once undoubtedly existed has come down to us.

Even so, there is an extraordinary corpus of raw material for the scholar.
Nothing like it exists for any other European state. A glance at the standard
industrial histories of Saxony in this period, for example, make it obvious
how much less her historians have to go on.[77] Austria, the sundry states of
the Rhineland and what is now Belgium, and Switzerland all present a
spotty array of figures, the adventitious legacy of adventitious policies of
data collection. To be sure, these can be of great value in the study of local
questions, which may in turn be of wider significance—the kind of thing
we have already encountered in French regional and local studies. There
are, for example, substantial local population statistics—of cities such as
Chemnitz, or Basel, or Bruges; or of villages such as those near Zurich
studied by Rudolf Braun in his pioneer work on the impact of industry on
rural society in the prefactory era.[78] In addition, we have the records of
enterprises—state-run, mixed, and private—and these have on occasion
been put to excellent use.[79] There are also data on certain branches of
trade and, in particular, on turnover at the great fairs. Some of these series
go back centuries.[80] Even so, they do not permit—or at least, have not permitted as yet—anything like the kind of aggregation that has been attempted
for Britain and France. It is no accident that the standard economic histories of these areas, including those most quantitative in character, prefer
to begin their discussion at the very end of the eighteenth century, or more
often in the early nineteenth century.[81]

Why this timing? The major factors were political and intellectual. On
the one hand, the extension of French dominion in the 1790s directly and
indirectly promoted the collection of statistical data. French administration
brought with it the incessant demands of the authorities in Paris for accurate intelligence;[82] even in countries that did not come under occupation, the techniques of French administration served as an example. Thus
the history of Dutch official statistics (national, as against local) begins
in effect with the Batavian Republic (1795–1806).[83] Still more important
was the urgent sense that the technological advance of Britain had altered
the balance of economic power and that industrial development was not
only a vehicle of power (in the eighteenth-century cameralist sense) but a
condition of independence. And although there was a retreat from the
extreme cameralist position of development from above (here the same
British example that dismayed the Continent tended to encourage a re-
laxation of the traditional controls), the task of the state had been redefined

to include the collection and sometimes even the dissemination of exact information on the life and activities of the population—the better to guide all concerned.[84]

This redefinition, in turn, while conditioned by political considerations, was essentially an intellectual phenomenon. The methods and concepts of political statistics constituted a new technology, which diffused like any other, only more easily. The studies of the leading political arithmeticians, officials and amateurs, were the common baggage of up-to-date functionaries of the day. Statistical societies proliferated, bringing together both groups, and these not only showed what could be done with home data but brought to the attention of their members the statistics of other countries. The same societies collected libraries of the rapidly growing body of statistical publication, and the catalogs of some of these collections, along with those of the official statistical bureaus, represent to this day our best guide to the literature.[85] But here we are getting ahead of the story. The point is that as a result of intellectual emulation, the statistical function became an essential element of government.

This statistical revolution found expression in central Europe, as in Britain and France, in a few precocious attempts at aggregation. Because of the political fragmentation of the area, such efforts were confined to the larger units and in particular to Prussia, where the data were, as we have seen, far more complete than elsewhere. Even there, this kind of work does not go back far. The population studies of Süssmilch date from the 1740s, and these were followed by a number of international statistical handbooks or geographies comparing the central European states with those of western Europe.[86] But none of these is comparable to the work of the British political arithmeticians, who tried to put the figures together to make a schema or model of the whole.

The first to attempt this kind of thing for one of the German states, to my knowledge, was Johann Leopold Krug (1770–1843), Prussian official and the author of a number of statistical handbooks. In 1805 he brought out two volumes of *Betrachtungen über den National-Reichthum des preussischen Staats and über den Wohlstand seiner Bewohner.*[87] This was an attempt to aggregate the Prussian national product on a value-added basis, which arrived at a total income of 261 million Reichstaler, or 27.5 taler per head.[88] Krug's work was momentarily to exercise a decisive influence on the history and character of Prussian statistics; along with the earlier recommendation of Stein, it induced the king to create a new royal statistical bureau to gather the official data and aggregate them, and it provided a model for the definition and classification of the objects of official inquiry. This was in 1805. At this point the war with France intervened, and after a short start the bureau was suspended, not to be reestablished until 1810. By that time, Krug had been displaced by J. G. Hoffmann, who had other views of the aims and character of government statistics; and though Krug stayed on in a subordinate position, he had lost his appetite for conceptualizing and writing. He also was not happy working under Hoffmann, whom he found unctuous and tyrannical.[89]

Krug's publications are a mine of information and would seem to be the logical starting point for any effort to reconstruct a time series of Prussian national income running backward into the eighteenth century and forward into the first half of the nineteenth century. (The more elaborate calculations of Walther Hoffmann and his collaborators take the middle of the nineteenth century as their point of departure.[90]) But Krug's methods and conceptions pose interesting, though not insurmountable, difficulties. He had his own notion of real and unreal (*unächtes*) income, excluding from his totals what he calls circulating capital (the profits of trade, interest from loans, income from investments) and deducting from the value of Prussian goods sold abroad the cost of imports. As a result of these and other peculiarities of calculation, industry (including craft work) and mining account for only 3.5 percent of total income, which is clearly wrong. The lode, in other words, may be rich, but there is a lot of work to be done before we have for Prussia what Phyllis Deane has given us for Great Britain.

By way of conclusion it is useful to consider the implications of the above discussion for future work. Two tasks confront us. The first is to pull together, standardize as much as possible, and publish the statistics that are now dispersed in hundreds of scarce volumes and pamphlets, to say nothing of manuscript archives. In this connection, it would be desirable to reedit and reprint the most important of these preindustrial studies, especially those, like Krug's, which present data that cannot be understood out of context.[91] The second is to build on this statistical base a quantitative history of preindustrial economic development.

Neither of these is an easy task. At the present time (1967) a team headed by Professor Wolfgang Köllmann of the Ruhr University in Bochum is planning to bring out a handbook of historical statistics for Germany in the period 1815–75, but it will be several years before the task of collection is completed and any publication can be envisaged. As for the protostatistical data, my own guess is that they, though sparser, might take longer to gather and process. The reconstruction of the story will depend, as always, not only on the accuracy and completeness of the information at our disposal, but on the concepts and analytical tools we apply to it. We could conceivably be worse off for having more statistical evidence—if, for example, we allowed ourselves to be governed by this evidence at the expense of other kinds of material. But I think economic history has gone past that point; and I envisage a drastic renewal of our knowledge and understanding of the sources and patterns of industrialization if this program is successfully carried out.

NOTES

1 This is not to imply that these private organizations are completely free of government connections; on the contrary, their work is in greater or less part financed by official or quasi-official agencies. But for various reasons, in particular their ability to hire university scholars on a part-time basis, they are better able than the civil service to attract the top intellectual talent in their fields.

2 In fairness, it should be pointed out that the statistical societies formed in the nineteenth century—in London, Manchester, Paris, and other major centers of administrative and economic activity—also played the role of informed consumers and innovators in technique for the agencies of the state. Their members, for example, made the important advances in the use of index numbers for the study of prices and wages; and their journals contain the pioneer articles on the subject. But this was still the age of the individual craftsman, and the various statistical societies rarely served as corporate centers for the collection, preparation, and publication of quantitative data. On the other hand, these societies did frequently help some of their members to gather data, usually local data, of a kind not available in official documents; and some of our most valuable evidence of economic and social conditions in urban centers in the process of industrialization comes from these surveys.

3 See his *Political Arithmetick, or A Discourse concerning the Extent and Value of Lands, People, Buildings; Husbandry, Manufacture, Commerce, Fishery, Artizans, Seaman, Soldiers; . . .* (London, 1690, 1691). Petty arrived at English national income by multiplying an estimated population of 6 million by an estimated average consumption of £7 per year; this equaled £42 million. He assumed that the British Crown had about 10 million subjects in all, including the inhabitants of overseas plantations (pp. 111, 102). His technique is still being employed in the reconstruction of national income for societies on which we have little statistical information. Cf. Andrzej Wyczański, "Le revenu national en Pologne au XVIᵉ siècle: premiers résultats," *Annales: économies, sociétés, civilisations* 26 (1971): 105–13.

4 On this and other aspects of the work of the British political arithmeticians, see the important articles by Phyllis Deane, "The Implications of Early National Income Estimates for the Measurement of Long-term Economic Growth in the United Kingdom," *Economic Development and Cultural Change* 4 (1955–56): 3–38; and "The Industrial Revolution and Economic Growth: The Evidence of Early British National Income Estimates," ibid., vol. 5 (1956–57), pp. 159–74.

5 Cited in Deane, "Implications of Early National Income Estimates," p. 5. On Davenant, see n. 7 below.

6 More than a century later, one of the most important of the early French statisticians, Jacques Peuchet, was to cite the abuses of speculation and manipulation to draw an invidious distinction between statistics (good) and political arithmetic (bad):

> Statistics also differs from political arithmetic. The latter does not proceed by way of analysis; it in no way seeks to obtain results by the enumeration of things. It substitutes calculation for these other methods, and it derives from a more or less probable or certain datum inferences that it sets up as facts.
>
> Thus, by knowing the annual consumption of grain in a country, the political arithmetician manages to learn the population, because obviously, if, on the basis of particular information, one can establish consumption per head, one can calculate the number of consumers by dividing aggregate consumption by consumption per head. Reciprocally, one can obtain the total amount harvested by the reverse operation, that is, by multiplying individual consumption by the number of consumers.
>
> In the same situation statistics proceeds by enumeration, and that is what distinguishes it from political arithmetic. [*Statistique élémentaire de la France* (Paris, 1805), pp. 24–25]

Yet Peuchet himself did not eschew the speculative techniques he imputed to political arithmetic. His own calculations of total French food consumption were based on hazardous inferences from the French army ration adjusted for the lower average consumption per head of the general population (ibid., pp. 371 ff.).

7 Davenant was commissioner of the excise (1678–89), which had formerly been farmed out but was now collected by the government, and inspector-general of the exports and imports (1705–14). He was the author of a number of tracts in political economy, of which the most important from our point of view is *A Report to the Honourable the Commissioners for Putting in Execution the Act, intituled an Act for the Taking, Examining, and Stating the Publick Accounts of the Kingdom*, 2 vols. (London, 1710, 1712). Davenant did not himself offer estimates of national income, but his data on trade are valuable aids to the correction and completion of King's figures.

8 Deane, "Implications of Early National Income Estimates," p. 5.

9 See the excellent introduction to E. M. Carus-Wilson and Olive Coleman, *England's Export Trade, 1275–1547* (Oxford: Oxford University Press, Clarendon Press, 1963). We are indebted for these figures to the decision of Edward I to nourish his feeble exchequer with a new custom on wool, England's major export, and on hides, which were far less important. Cf. N. S. B. Gras, *The Early English Customs System* (Cambridge, Mass.: Harvard University Press, 1918).

10 Cf. Henry S. Cobb, "Local Port Customs Accounts prior to 1550," *Journal of the Society of Archivists*, vol. 1, no. 8 (October 1958), pp. 213–24, for the earlier records. Also the series of volumes of port books and brokage books of Southampton in the fifteenth century, in the *Southampton Record Series*. These are reprints *in extenso* and have yet to be reduced to statistical tables.

For later material of a similar kind, see especially a valuable article by W. B. Stephens, "The Cloth Exports of the Provincial Ports, 1600–1640," *Economic History Review*, 2d ser. 22 (1969): 228–48; also Raymond W. K. Hinton, ed., *The Port Books of Boston, 1601–1640* (Hereford: Lincoln Record Society, 1956), and his short reconstruction of one aspect of the trade: "Dutch Entrepot Trade at Boston, Lincs., 1600–40," *Economic History Review*, 2d ser. 9 (1956–57): 467–71.

11 The standard work is G. N. Clark, *Guide to English Commercial Statistics, 1696–1782* (London: Royal Historical Society, 1938). The most complete and reliable collection of the eighteenth-century figures is to be found in Elizabeth Schumpeter, *English Overseas Trade Statistics, 1697–1808* (Oxford: Oxford University Press, Clarendon Press, 1960). The raw data, however, pose serious problems for the historian because of the predominance of fixed official values as against fluctuating market values (though this facilitates the calculation of a volume index), the presence of a scattering of items recorded at declared values, and the incompleteness of the returns (the eighteenth century was a period of extensive and fluctuating smuggling, amounting perhaps to one fourth of imports in a peak period such as the years of war with the American colonies). On this whole question, see B. R. Mitchell and Phyllis Deane, *Abstract of British Historical Statistics* (Cambridge: Cambridge University Press, 1962), pp. 274–76; and Phyllis Deane and W. A. Cole, *British Economic Growth, 1688–1959*, 2d ed. (Cambridge: Cambridge University Press, 1967), pp. 41–50. On smuggling, see W. A. Cole, "Trends in Eighteenth-Century Smuggling," *Economic History Review*, 2d ser. 10 (1957–58): 395–409.

12 On Massie, see Peter Mathias, "The Social Structure in the Eighteenth Century: A Calculation by Joseph Massie," *Economic History Review*, 2d ser. 10 (1957–58): 30–45. On Colquhoun, see n. 24 below.

13 Sir Charles Whitworth, *State of the Trade of Great Britain in Its Imports and Exports . . . 1697 [to 1773]* (London, 1776). The book was immediately translated into French and published by the Imprimerie Royale as *Commerce de la Grande-Bretagne, et tableaux de ses importations et exportations progressives, depuis l'année 1697 jusqu'à la fin de l'année 1773* (Paris, 1777). Whitworth was a member of Parliament from 1747 and in 1768 became chairman of Ways and Means of the Commons.

14 David Macpherson, *Annals of Commerce, Manufacture, Fisheries, and Navigation, with Brief Notices of the Arts and Sciences Connected with Them*, 4 vols. (London, 1805). An invaluable compendium, recently reprinted, it includes a wide variety of

statistical material, with fascinating price data going back to the Middle Ages. Macpherson (1746–1816), son of a tailor and clothier and trained as a surveyor, was for a time deputy-keeper of the Public Records.

15 Thus balanced accounts of government income and expenditure for the eighteenth century were not published until 1869, when net accounts appeared for 1688–1802 and gross accounts for 1802–69. These were the result of twelve years' work by H. W. Chisholm, chief clerk of the exchequer, with the advice and help of "the most experienced financial officers of the Government" (Deane, "Implications of Early National Income Estimates," p. 16). The lack of gross figures (that is, figures inclusive of the costs of collection and disbursement) for the earlier period reflects the remarkable *laisser-aller* of eighteenth-century administration, when office was not simply office but a form of enterprise: revenue officers were paid only partly by salaries, partly "by fees and gratuities and other entitlements received by them, of which no account was ever rendered."

16 Among the commodities whose output we can follow by trade or tax returns are tallow candles, soap, hides and skins, glass (from the 1740s), and, above all, cotton (since all the raw material was imported and paid duty). There were also local controls that provide useful information: official stamping of woolen (not worsted) cloths in the West Riding and of Scottish linen produced for market (not for home use); collection of coinage dues on Cornish tin as far back as the twelfth century; sale of most copper in Cornwall and Devon at "public ticketings" (1726 on); taxation of shipments of "sea coal" from the Northeast (a reasonably complete series from 1655 on).

17 Arthur Young's estimates, for the year 1770, are to be found in his *Political Arithmetick,* part 2, *Containing Considerations on the Means of Raising the Supplies within the Year . . .* (London, 1779). This part 2 is really a separate book from the earlier volume of 1774, which spells the title differently: *Political Arithmetic, Containing Observations on the Present State of Great Britain. . . .* It was produced as a refutation of an impressionistic estimate by Sir William Pulteney, *Considerations on the Present State of Affairs, and the Means of Raising the Necessary Supplies,* 1st and 2d eds. (London, 1779). Pulteney estimated the wealth of Great Britain at slightly over a billion pounds: 7 million people consuming an average of £7.10.0 per year gives a total income of 52.5 million, which he then capitalized at 5 percent (ibid. [2d ed.], p. 30).

18 The best of these precensus estimates was probably that of Sir Frederick Morton Eden (best known for his careful and detailed study of *The State of the Poor): An Estimate of the Number of Inhabitants in Great Britain and Ireland* (London, 1800).

19 John Rickman (1771–1840) was secretary to Charles Abbot, M.P. and later Speaker of the House of Commons. In 1814 Rickman became second clerk assistant at the table of the House, and in 1820 clerk assistant. In these capacities he helped prepare the first census act of 1800; prepared the census reports of 1801, 1811, 1821, 1831; and made calculations of population growth in earlier years. The most complete and latest of Rickman's estimates, covering the period 1570–1750, were published in the introduction to the 1841 census. *Parliamentary Papers,* 1843, [496], vol. 22, no. 1, pp. 34–37.

20 For references to these sources, see J. T. Krause, "Changes in English Fertility and Mortality, 1781–1785," *Economic History Review,* 2d ser. 11 (1958–59): 52–53; and Deane and Cole, *British Economic Growth,* chap. 3.

21 *Past and Present,* no. 37 (July 1967), pp. 44–70.

22 An extreme example was William Cobbett, who, in the Goldsmith tradition ("Ill fares the land, to hastening ills a prey . . ."), was convinced that the countryside was being emptied and insisted that the census figures of 1801–21 had been concocted by the government to conceal the facts. On the general issue, the seminal article is J. D. Chambers, "Enclosure and the Labour Supply in the Industrial Revolution," *Economic History Review,* 2d ser. 5 (1953): 318–43.

23 For some of the elements in this debate, see the selections in D. V. Glass and D. C. Eversley, eds., *Population in History* (London: Edward Arnold, 1965); also a new article by David J. Loschky and Donald F. Krier, "Income and Family Size in Three Eighteenth-Century Lancashire Parishes: A Reconstitution Study," *Journal of Eco-*

nomic History 29 (1969): 429–48, which applies probability analysis to a small sample in an effort to test hypotheses about the influence of occupation and wealth on age of marriage and fertility. (The results are discouraging.)

In addition to this work in what we may call macrodemography, there has appeared in recent years a small corpus of research into local population history, using data derived from family-by-family reconstruction. See p. 69 below.

24 Colquhoun (1745–1820), the son of a county registrar in Scotland, was an active businessman, a lobbyist for Scottish commercial interests, and founder of the Chamber of Commerce in Glasgow before becoming police magistrate in London in 1792. His work as magistrate brought him into contact with the poor and drew his attention to a wide range of social problems. His major contribution to political economy was his *Treatise on the Population, Wealth, Power, and Resources of the British Empire in every Quarter of the World* (London, 1814; 2d ed. 1815).

25 Deane, "Implications of Early National Income Estimates," p. 35.

26 Ibid., p. 37.

27 H. J. Habakkuk and Phyllis Deane, "The Take-off in Britain," in *The Economics of Take-off into Sustained Growth*, ed. W. W. Rostow (London: Macmillan, 1963), pp. 81–82.

28 The same problem has arisen in regard to the controversial calculations of Robert Fogel on the contribution of the railway to American economic growth. Assuming that social saving is the relevant measure of this contribution and that his calculation of social saving is correct, how important is the addition of 5 percent to national income? It looks small, but how does one know? Cf. Mark Nerlove, "Railroads and American Economic Growth," *Journal of Economic History* 26 (1966): 107–15; also the discussion of an ingenious article by Peter D. McClelland, "The Cost to America of British Imperial Policy," *American Economic Review* 59 (May 1969): 370–85.

29 In principle, a series of input-output tables would bring us closer to a statistical measure of the significance of growth in the modern sector.

30 As reprinted in Eugène Daire, ed., *Economistes-financiers du XVIIIᵉ siècle* (Paris, 1843), p. 145.

31 Colbert also initiated in 1664 the first general inquiry into the state of the kingdom. The circular sent from Paris to the provinces instructed the officials to prepare what Bertrand Gille has called "descriptive statistics," that is, statistics without numbers. The central government asked for good maps; lists of local officials and clergy, with appraisals of their character and influence; information on Crown estates (one needed an inquiry for this?!) and waterways; a review of fiscal arrangements, with details on the conditions and returns of tax collections; reports of counterfeit money; a survey of natural resources; and news of the development of trade and industry. The categories could have lent themselves to quantification in some instances; but, given the conceptions of the time, the choice of language and the omission of explicit reference to numbers was not an accident. The intelligence that came in from the field took the form of data for an administrative almanac. On all this, see Bertrand Gille, *Les sources statistiques de l'histoire de France: des enquêtes du XVIIᵉ siècle à 1870* (Geneva and Paris: Droz, 1964), pp. 24–25. On publications of these early *mémoires*, see Emile Bourgeois and Louis André, *Les sources de l'histoire de France: XVIIᵉ siècle, 1610–1715*, 8 vols. (Paris, 1913–35), vol. 7, *Histoire économique; histoire administrative*, ed. L. André (Paris: Auguste Picard, 1934), pp. 189–207.

32 Cf. Emile Levasseur, *Histoire du commerce de la France*, 2 vols. (Paris: Arthur Rousseau, 1911), 1:509.

33 The Arnould figures were published in the atlas (third) volume of his *De la balance du commerce et des relations extérieures de la France dans toutes les parties du globe*, 3 vols. (Paris, 1971). This volume is often missing, but the tables were reprinted in France, Ministère des Finances, *Bulletin de statistique et de législation comparée* 13 (1883): 46–80. (The article, which is anonymous, was prepared by A. de Foville.) According to this source, the tables for 1716–76 were also published by César Moreau in the *Bulletin de la Société Française de Statistique Universelle* of August 1830, as derived from a manuscript table prepared for the king "par les soins de Trudaine de Montigny, Conseiller d'Etat, intendant des finances, et l'un des magistrats du Conseil les plus distingués par les lumières, les talents, et l'exactitude." The Bruyard figures

are to be found in manuscript in the Archives Nationales, in F 12, 643, and F 12, 1834 A. (There are some minor differences between the two versions.) They have been published by F. Lohmann in "Die amtliche Handelsstatistik Englands und Frankreichs im XVIII. Jahrhundert," *Sitzungsberichte der Königlichen Preussischen Akademie der Wissenschaften zu Berlin* 2 (1898) 891–92 (only the general totals, as given in the original, that is, incomplete and marred by arithmetic errors, compounded in this case by typographical mistakes); and by Ruggiero Romano in "Documenti e prime considerazioni intorno alla 'balance du commerce' della Francia dal 1716 al 1780," in *Studi in onore di Armando Sapori*, 2 vols. (Milan, [1957]), 2:1267–1300 (the full set of tables, plus documents offering valuable information on the manner of collection).

34   Abbé Guillaume Thomas Raynal, *Histoire philosophique et politique des établissements et du commerce des Européens dans les deux Indes* (numerous editions), *Atlas*, bk. 4, table 2. The volume I used was entitled *Atlas de toutes des parties connues du globe terrestre dressé pour l'Histoire philosophique* . . . and is ascribed to Rigobert Bonne (ed.) and the Geneva edition of 1780.

35   François Crouzet, "Angleterre et France au XVIIIᵉ siècle: essai d'analyse comparée de deux croissances économiques," *Annales: économies, sociétés, civilisations* 21 (1966): 254–91.

36   C. E. Labrousse, *Esquisse du mouvement des prix et des revenus en France au XVIIIᵉ siècle* (Paris: Dalloz, 1932); idem., *La crise de l'économie française à la fin de l'Ancien Régime et au début de la Révolution* (Paris: Presses Universitaires Françaises, 1944). The latter furnishes a long analysis and criticism of these sources. On the hazards and opportunities of processing these data for purposes of microeconomic analysis, cf. David S. Landes, "The Statistical Study of French Crises," *Journal of Economic History* 10 (1950): 195–211; and André Danière, "Feudal Incomes and Demand Elasticity for Bread in Late Eighteenth-Century France" (with accompanying exchange with Landes), ibid., pp. 317–44.

37   On some of the problems occasioned by these figures, see the discussion of the Kaplow monograph on Elbeuf, p. 75 below.

38   The first of these provided the basis for Bertrand Gille's *Les forges françaises en 1772* (Paris, 1960); the second, for Hubert and Georges Bourgin's *L'industrie sidérurgique en France au début de la Révolution* (Paris: Imprimerie Nationale, 1920).

39   Two industries that were the subject of repeated inquiries were paper and leather, both regulated. On the first, we have a typescript *thèse* of the Ecole des Chartes by Mlle A. Gambier, "L'industrie papetière en France au XVIIIᵉ siècle" (1961); on the second, H. Depors, *Recherches sur l'état de l'industrie des cuirs en France pendant le XVIIIᵉ et le début du XIXᵉ siècle* (Paris, 1932).

40   On all the above, the best source is Gille, *Les sources statistiques de l'histoire de France*, an invaluable compendium that ought to be in the library of every student of modern French history.

41   "Statistique," in Marcel Marion, *Dictionnaire des institutions de la France aux XVIIᵉ et XVIIIᵉ siècles* (Paris, 1923; reprinted Paris: A. and J. Picard, 1968). On the Abbé Jean-Joseph Expilly and his career as writer and demographer, see especially E. Esmonin, "L'Abbé Expilly et ses travaux de statistique," *Revue d'histoire moderne et contemporaine* 4 (Oct.–Dec. 1957): 241–80; also R. Le Mée, "Du nouveau sur Expilly," *Annales de démographie historique*, 1968, pp. 172–74.

42   The "Mémoire" of 1778 has not survived; but part of it was published by [Simon N. L.] Linguet, *Annales politiques* (London) 6 (1785): 244–57. The above extract is from p. 255. The article begins with a table of the annual average of marriages, births, and deaths by provinces and *généralités* for the period from 1769 to 1777, and an estimate of total population as of January 1788.

43   Abbé Jean-Joseph Expilly, *Dictionnaire géographique, historique, et politique des Gaules et de la France*, 6 vols. (Paris, 1762–70). The value of the work lies above all in the extensive personal inquiries on which it was based. Expilly sent circular questionnaires to officials throughout the kingdom, at a time when postal charges were very onerous. Some of his correspondents, indeed, begged off on this ground.

44   Esmonin, "L'Abbé Expilly," p. 278.

45   This is Esmonin's starting date (p. 278 n. 1). It does not accord with other statements

on the subject, all of which date these bulletins from 1670. Cf. Jacques Bertillon (then chef des travaux statistiques of the city of Paris), *Des recensements de la population; de la nuptialité, de la natalité, et de la mortalité à Paris pendant le XIXe siècle et les époques antérieures* (Paris, 1907), p. 14; also Emile Levasseur, *La statistique officielle en France* (Nancy, 1885), p. 3 n. 3, who points out that, aside from published summary tables, the library of the Institut de France has two manuscript volumes giving the annual reports for each parish month by month for the years 1713–88, plus a separate fascicle for 1789. The annual summary totals for the city as a whole were published in the second volume (*Année 1823*) of the *Recherches statistiques sur la ville de Paris* (see n. 64 below) as "Recherches sur le mouvement de la population de la ville de Paris dans les XVIIe, XVIIIe et XIXe siècles," tables 53–55. The footnotes to these tables indicate that the reports for some years are missing, as are some of the Protestant data; also, the boundaries of the area covered change.

46   In addition to local returns, there were at least two attempts to obtain information on total population. Both at the end of the seventeenth century and in the middle of the eighteenth, Paris asked the intendants to return reports on the number of people in their *généralités* and on the condition of the population. The second of these was unknown to historians until recently, when a summary was discovered in the archives of the Ministry of Foreign Affairs. It is of interest less for the data on population, which are almost surely incomplete, than for the information it furnishes on the geography of income distribution—what the inquiry calls "*les facultés des peuples.*" Fr. de Dainville, "Un dénombrement inédit au XVIIIe siècle: l'enquête du Contrôleur-Général Orry—1745," *Population* 7 (1952): 49–68. There is also, in the Bibliothèque Nationale in the fonds Delamare, a document entitled "Dénombrement de 1709," which gives for the whole of France a population of 20,339,980 persons. Unfortunately, this is not a true census: some of its data are taken over from earlier counts; some are arrived at by conversion of hearth counts. Jacques Dupaquier, "Sur la population française au XVIIe et au XVIIIe siècle," *Revue historique* 239 (1968): 47.

47   On the problems and opportunities posed by the utilization of hearth counts as a surrogate for censuses, cf. various articles by J. Dupaquier: "Des rôles de tailles à la démographie historique: l'exemple du Vexin français," *Annales de démographie historique*, 1965, pp. 31–41; "Des rôles de tailles à la démographie historique: l'exemple de Crulai," *Population* 24 (1969): 89–104; "Essai de cartographie historique: le peuplement du bassin parisien en 1711," *Annales: économies, sociétés, civilisations* 24 (1969): 976–98 and map.

48   For Quesnay, see his article on "Fermiers" in the *Encyclopédie méthodique* (Section "Economie politique et diplomatique"). This article is reprinted in *François Quesnay et la physiocratie*, 2 vols. (Paris: Institut National d'Etudes Démographiques [INED], 1958), vol. 2. The passage in question is on p. 438. On early French population theories and estimates, see Joseph J. Spengler, *French Predecessors of Malthus* (Durham, N.C.: Duke University Press, 1942). There is an enlarged French edition entitled *Economie et population: Les doctrines françaises avant 1800: de Budé à Condorcet*, INED, "Trauvaux et documents," cahier no. 33 (Paris, 1954).

The relevant works of Messance are *Recherches sur la population des généralités d'Auvergne, de Lyon, de Rouen, et de quelques provinces et villes du royaume, avec des réflexions sur la valeur du bled, tant en France qu'en Angleterre depuis 1674 jusqu'en 1764* (Paris, 1766) and *Nouvelles recherches sur la population de la France* (Lyons, 1788). Messance was *receveur des tailles* (tax collector) in the *élection* of Saint-Etienne.

[Jean-Baptiste] Moheau was the author of *Recherches et considérations sur la population de la France* (Paris, 1778; reprinted 1912). For a long time, Moheau was thought to be a straw man, and the book was attributed to Montyon. It now seems probable that Moheau, who was appointed to a post in the Ministry of War on the morrow of the book's publication, was indeed the author, or at least had the capacity to write such a book. See M. Reinhard, "Notes brèves sur la démographie française au XVIIIe siècle," *Annales de démographie historique, 1966* (Paris, 1967), pp. 211–12.

49   Jean Bourgeois-Pichat suggests the figure of 28,288,000 in 1801. Among the most useful sources on French population history of this period are Emile Levasseur, *La*

population française: histoire de la population avant 1789 et démographie de la France, comparée à celle des autres nations au XIXᵉ siècle, 3 vols. (Paris, 1889–92); Jean Bourgeois-Pichat, "Evolution générale de la population française depuis le XVIIIᵉ siècle," *Population* 6 (1951): 635–62; 7 (1952): 319–29; and J. C. Toutain, *La population de la France de 1700 à 1959* (Paris: 1963), vol. 3 of J. Marczewski, ed., *Histoire quantitative de l'économie française,* in F. Perroux, ed., *Cahiers de l'Institut de Sciences Economiques Appliquées,* suppl. no. 133, Jan. 1963, series AF, no. 3; E. Esmonin, "Statistiques du mouvement de la population en France de 1770 à 1789," *Etudes et chronique de démographie historique, 1964* (Paris: Société de Démographie Historique, [1964]), pp. 27–130; Jacques Dupaquier, "Sur la population française au XVIIᵉ et au XVIIIᵉ siècle," *Revue historique* 239 (Jan.–March 1968): 43–79.

The Institut National d'Etudes Démographiques in Paris is currently engaged in a project to estimate changes in French population since the reign of Louis XIV by reconstituting birth and death rates from a sample of parish registers and civil registers. See Michel Fleury and Louis Henry, "Pour connaître la population de la France depuis Louis XIV; plan de travaux par sondage," *Population* 13 (1958): 663–86; and Yves Blayo, "L'enquête de l'I.N.E.D. sur la population de la France avant 1830," *Annales de démographie historique, 1966,* pp. 193–97.

50 The first results have now appeared; see Y. Blayo and L. Henry, "Données démographiques sur la Bretagne et l'Anjou de 1740 à 1829," in *Annales de démographie historique, 1967* (Paris, 1968); also most of the contents of the 1969 volume of the same yearbook, which takes as its theme "Villes et villages de l'ancienne France."

51 For the work of Henry and his school, see especially Michel Fleury and Louis Henry, *Des registres paroissiaux à l'histoire de la population: manuel de dépouillement et d'exploitation de létat civil ancien* (Paris: INED, 1956); and Etienne Gautier and Louis Henry, *La population de Crulai, paroisse normande: Étude historique* (Paris: INED, "Travaux et documents," cahier no. 33, 1958). There is also a valuable introduction to the general subject of population studies, with copious bibliographical references to the historical literature: C. Legeard, *Guide de recherches documentaires en démographie* (Paris: Gauthier-Villars, 1966).

52 See especially P. Laslett, *The World We Have Lost* (London: Methuen, 1965); idem., "Le brassage de la population en France et en Angleterre au XVIIᵉ et au XVIIIᵉ siècles," *Annales de démographie historique,* 1968, pp. 99–109; E. A. Wrigley, ed., *An Introduction to English Historical Demography* (London: Weidenfeld and Nicolson, 1966); E. A. Wrigley, *Population and History* (New York: McGraw-Hill, 1969); also the still unpublished proceedings of a Conference on the Comparative History of the Family, held in Cambridge on 12–15 September 1969, to be edited by Peter Laslett for the Cambridge Group for the History of Population and Social Structure, Silver Street, Cambridge.

53 A second printing was released that same year, after the death of Vauban on March 30, and by 1708 there were at least eight printings. The essay was reprinted with valuable editorial notes in Daire, *Economistes-financiers du XVIIIᵉ siècle,* and reedited separately by E. Coornaert (Paris: Alcan, 1933).

54 For a complete list of the works of Boisguilbert in their various editions, see Walter Braeuer, *Frankreichs wirtschaftliche und soziale Lage um 1700; dargestellt unter besonderer Berücksichtigung der Werke von Vauban und Boisguillebert* (Marburg: N. G. Elwert, 1968), pp. 178–80.

55 There is a sharp critique of Boisguilbert in Earl J. Hamilton, "The Political Economy of France at the Time of John Law," *The History of Political Economy* 1 (1969): 126–37. Hamilton, it seems to me, goes to the other extreme and argues (p. 136) for a state of prosperity that other students of the period do not recognize. For a more favorable appreciation of the Boisguilbert estimates, see Braeuer's *Frankreichs wirtschaftliche und soziale Lage.*

56 Henri de Boulainvilliers, *Etat de la France . . . extrait des mémoires dressés par les intendants du royaume,* 2 vols. (London, 1727); later published in 6 vols. (London, 1737) and in 8 vols. (London, 1752). Boulainvilliers, who was a man of many parts, was also the author of a history of the Arabs and co-author of a tract on the errors of Spinoza.

57   On some of these other authors and their works, see Esmonin, "L'Abbé Expilly,"
     p. 246.
58   Tolosan, *Mémoire sur le commerce de la France et de ses colonies* (Paris, 1789);
     Antoine Laurent Lavoisier, *De la richesse territoriale du royaume de France* (Paris,
     1791). Cf., on Tolosan's estimates and others, Arnould, *De la balance du commerce,*
     2:216–72. Tolosan was *intendant-général du commerce* and wrote his study in con-
     sultation with a businessman named Béchet. Lavoisier, of course, is far better known
     as a chemist than as a political economist. For years, however, he was a member of
     the General Farm, and it was his income as an entrepreneur of tax collection that
     paid for his laboratory and his scientific experiments. He was also secretary to the
     Committee on Agriculture from 1785 on; from 1787, delegate to the provincial as-
     sembly of Orléans, in which capacity he busied himself with plans for the social and
     economic development of the area; also from 1787, an officer of the Caisse d'Escompte,
     a forerunner of the Bank of France, reporting on its operations to the National
     Assembly in 1789; and, from 1790 to 1791, commissary of the treasury and a member
     of a number of important legislative committees.
59   Neufchâteau ordered the prefects not only to report on the population of their
     departments but also "on the products of agriculture, of trade, on the state of industry,
     of roads, and of canals" (France, Ministère du Travail et de la Prévoyance Sociale,
     *Statistique générale de la France: historique et travaux de la fin du XVIIIe siècle au
     début du XXe siècle* [Paris, 1913], p. 6).
60   Charles Schmidt, "Un essai de statistique industrielle en l'an V," in France, Ministère
     de l'Instruction Publique et des Beaux-Arts, Commission de Recherche et de Publi-
     cation des Documents relatifs à la Vie Economique de la Révolution, *Bulletin tri-
     mestriel,* 1908, pp. 11–205.
61   There is a bibliography of these departmental reports, including those not published,
     in A. de Saint-Léger, "Les mémoires statistiques des départements pendant le Direc-
     toire, le Consulat et l'Empire," *Le bibliographe moderne* 19 (1918–19): 5–43.
62   Peuchet was archivist of the Administration des Droit-Réunis (that is, a keeper of tax
     records) and at that time member of the Conseil du Commerce.
63   *Recherches statistiques sur la ville de Paris et le département de la Seine; recueil de
     tableaux dressés et réunis d'après les ordres de M. le comte de Chabrol, préfet du
     département,* 5 vols. (Paris, 1825–29).
64   This brief history rests largely on Gille, *Les sources statistiques,* pp. 149–51. The
     details are to be found in "La statistique officielle en France," in *25e anniversaire de la
     Société de Statistique de Paris 1860–1885* (Paris, 1886), pp. 145–204. The same volume
     includes chapters on the history of official statistics in Belgium, Holland, Sweden,
     Finland, Denmark, Germany, Austria, Switzerland, and Italy.
65   J. C. Toutain, "Le produit de l'agriculture française de 1700 à 1958, I: Estimation du
     produit au XVIIIe siècle," in J. Marczewski, ed., *Histoire quantitative de l'économie
     française,* no. 1 (Cahiers de l'ISEA, no. 115 [July 1961], AF, 1) (Paris, 1961).
66   Le Roy Ladurie, "Les comptes fantastiques de Gregory King," *Annales: économies,
     sociétés, civilisations* 23 (1968): 1086–102.
67   On this question, the work of Michel Morineau promises to be decisive. See his article,
     "Y a-t-il eu une révolution agricole en France au XVIIIe siècle?" *Revue Historique* 239
     (1968): 299–326; and his new book, *Les faux-semblants d'un démarrage économique:
     agriculture et démographie en France au XVIIIe siècle* (Paris: Colin, 1971).
68   Cf. J. Marczewski, "Le produit physique de l'économie française de 1789 à 1913
     (comparaison avec la Grande-Bretagne)," in *Histoire quantitative de l'économie
     française* (Cahiers de l'ISEA, AF, 4, no. 163 [July 1965]), p. lxxi.
69   The *compoix* are found only in regions of *taille réelle,* that is, where the tax was
     levied on the land rather than on the person. Once again, the fiscal preoccupations
     of the ruler bring the historian his first statistics.
70   One of the weaknesses of the traditional collection of historical statistics is that in its
     concern for national and regional totals or averages it ignores valuable microdata,
     useful not only as illustrations of more general phenomena but also as evidence of
     the more private aspects of economic activity. Business accounts and private budgets
     are good examples of the latter.

71 See also R. Boeckh, *Die geschichtliche Entwicklung der amtlichen Statistik des Preussischen Staates* (Berlin, 1863); Hugo Klinckmüller, *Die amtliche Statistik Preussens im vorigen Jahrhundert* (Jena, 1880); E. Blenck, *Das Königliche Statistische Bureau in Berlin, beim Eintritte in sein neuntes Jahrzehnt* (Berlin, 1885).

72 For all its size, however, the Humpert bibliography is far from exhaustive. It pays little attention, for example, to works dealing with provincial or local units, so that a major study like Bratring's (see p. 77 below) is not mentioned. Nor are the classifications always complete in their coverage; the reader must be prepared to look around.

73 This has now been reprinted, with a valuable biographical and bibliographical introduction, by the Historische Kommission zu Berlin, Otto Büsch and Gerd Heinrich eds. (Berlin: Walter de Gruyter, 1968).

74 This division is deceptive, because urban status was defined legally rather than by an objective criterion like population density or economic and social function. All the so-called *Städte* were small or middling by our standards, and even the largest devoted a portion, sometimes a substantial portion, of land and labor to agriculture. On the other hand, the share of "urban" producers in total agricultural output was small.

75 One example will convey the kind of information offered. For the Havelländische Kreis in the Mittelmark, we are told that for the village and Erbpachts-Vorwerk of Solm there were 1 *Lehnschulze*, 1 *Halbbauer*, 10 *Ganzkossäten*, 4 *Büdner*, 6 *Einlieger*, 1 *Schiffer*, a public house, 26 hearths, and 238 people (Friedrich Wilhelm August Bratring, *Statistisch-topographische Beschreibung*, 2:112).

76 On population, see the summary data in "Statistische Uebersicht der Bevölkerung sämtlicher Städte der Kurmark Brandenburg in ihrer Umgrenzung bis zum Tilsiter Frieden i. J. 1807, in verschiedenen Zeiträumen von 1736 bis 1846," *Mitteilungen des Statistischen Bureaus in Berlin* 2 (1849): 265–77; also "Ueber die frühere (i.d.J. 1617, 1688, 1740, 1774) und gegenwärtige (i.J. 1849) Bevölkerung der jetzigen Provinz Brandenburg," *ibid.*, 3 (1850): 199–231.

77 Cf. especially Rudolf Forberger, *Die Manufaktur in Sachsen vom Ende des 16. bis zum Anfang des 19. Jahrhunderts* (Berlin: Akademie-Verlag, 1958); also Albin König, *Die sächsische Baumwollindustrie am Ende des vorigen Jahrhunderts und während der Kontinentalsperre* (Leipzig, 1899).

78 See Max Flinzer, "Die Bewegung der Bevölkerung in Chemnitz von 1730–1870," *Mittheilungen des Statistischen Bureaus der Stadt Chemnitz* (1872); W. Bickel, *Bevölkerungsgeschichte und Bevölkerungspolitik der Schweiz* (Zürich: Büchergilde Gutenberg, 1947); P. Deprez, "The Demographic Development of Flanders in the Eighteenth Century," Glass and Eversley, eds., *Population in History*, pp. 608–30; Braun, *Industrialisierung und Volksleben: Die Veränderungen der Lebensformen in einem ländlichen Industriegebiet vor 1800* (Erlenbach-Zürich and Stuttgart: Eugen Rentsch, 1960).

79 Thus Pierre Lebrun, *L'industrie de la laine à Verviers pendant le XVIIIᵉ et le début du XIXᵉ siècle* (Liège: Faculté de Philosophie et Lettres, 1948).

80 Cf. the charts in Walter Bodmer, *Schweizerische Industriegeschichte: die Entwicklung der schweizerischen Textilwirtschaft im Rahmen der übrigen Industrien und Wirtschaftszweige* (Zürich: Berichthaus, 1960), between pp. 544 and 545. It should be noted in passing that these charts are given without indication of sources and without accompanying tables.

81 Cf. Johann Slokar, *Geschichte der österreichischen Industrie und ihrer Förderung unter Kaiser Franz I* (Vienna, 1914); Jaroslav Purs, "The Industrial Revolution in the Czech Lands," *Historica II* (Prague, 1960); Wolfgang Köllmann, *Sozialgeschichte der Stadt Barmen im 19. Jahrhundert* (Tübingen: J. C. B. Mohr, 1960). To be sure, as these and other titles indicate, the authors have chosen subjects that do not require them to go back before the nineteenth century. The point is that this choice is not coincidence. What is more, most of these books do look back, if only to provide background for their story, and their treatment of the earlier period is testimony to the absence of statistical evidence.

82 For examples of secondary studies based in greater or lesser part on this statistical revolution in areas under French rule, see Hermann Ringel, *Bergische Wirtschaft*

zwischen 1790 und 1860 (n.p.: Bergische Industrie- und Handelskammer zu Remscheid, 1966); Athos Bellettini, *La popolazione del dipartimento del Reno* (Bologna: Zanichelli, 1965); J. R. Suratteau, *Le département du Mont-Terrible sous le régime du Directoire* (Paris: Les Belles-Lettres, 1965); Roger Darquenne, "Histoire économique du département de Jemappes," *Annales du Cercle Achéologique de Mons* 65 (1962–64): 1–430.

83 Netherlands, Centraal Bureau voor de Statistiek, *Bijdragen tot de Statistiek van Nederland*, Nieuwe Volgreeks, 14, *Geschiedenis van de Statistiek in het Koninkrijk der Nederlanden* (1902).

84 Thus even after the French departed, they left their legacy of statistical curiosity. By way of example, cf. the efforts of the Netherlands in this domain: I. J. Brugmans, ed., *Statistieken van de Nederlandse Nijverheid uit de eerste Helft der 19ᵉ Eeuw*, 2 vols. (The Hague: Nijhoff, 1956); N. Caulier-Mathy, *Statistique de la province de Liège sous le régime hollandais*, Cahiers du Centre Interuniversitaire d'Histoire Contemporaine, no. 25 (Louvain and Paris: Nauwelaerts, 1962).

85 Cf. *Katalog der Bibliothek des Königl. Sächs. Statistischen Bureaus* (Dresden, 1890).

86 Johann Peter Süssmilch, *Die göttliche Ordnung in den Veränderungen des menschlichen Geschlechts*, 2 parts (Berlin, 1740, and subsequent editions); idem., *Der königlichen Residentz Berlin schnelles Wachsthum und Erbauung* (Berlin, 1752). Among the more important of these general statistical compendia are Gottfried Achenwall, *Abriss der neuesten Staatswissenschaft der vornehmsten europäischen Reiche und Republiken* (Göttingen, 1749), 2d and subsequent eds. under the title *Staatsverfassung der heutigen vornehmsten europäischen Reiche und Völker im Grundriss;* A. F. Büsching, *Kurzgefasste Vorbereitung zur europäischen Länder- und Staatskunde* (Hamburg, 1758); G. R. von S[midtburg], *Statistische Tabellen zur bequemen Uebersicht der Grösse, Bevölkerung, des Reichsthums und der Macht der vornehmsten europäischen Staaten* (Prague, 1781); A. F. W. Crome, *Ueber die Grösse und Bevölkerung der europäischen Staaten* (Leipzig, 1785); idem, *Ueber die Culturverhältnisse der europäischen Staaten* (Leipzig, 1792); E. F. von Hertzberg, *Sur la population des états en général et sur celle des états prussiens en particulier* (Berlin, 1785); [A. F. Randel], *Statistische Uebersicht der vornehmsten teutschen und europäischen Staaten, in Ansehung ihrer Grösse, Bevölkerung, ihres Finanz- und Kriegs-Zustandes* (Berlin, 1786); J. A. Remer, *Lehrbuch der Staatskunde der vornehmsten europäischen Staaten* (Braunschweig, 1786); idem, *Tabellen zur Aufbewahrung der wichtigsten statistischen Veränderungen in den vornehmsten europäischen Staaten* (Braunschweig, 1787–94); J. D. A. Hoeck, *Statistische Uebersicht der deutschen Staaten in Ansehung ihrer Grösse, Bevölkerung, Producte, Industrie, und Finanzverfassung*, 4 vols. (Basel, 1800; enl. ed. 1804); idem. *Statistische Darstellung der europäischen Staaten nach ihrem neuesten Zustande* (Amberg, 1805).

87 Johann Leopold Krug was originally a student in theology, and he began his career as a catechist in a small Lutheran community. But he was interested in statistics, attended the lectures of the historian and statistician Krause at Halle, and used his abundant spare time as catechist to attempt a reconstruction of Prussian national accounts. This proved impossible; but he did bring out the more descriptive *Topographisch-statistisch-geographisches Wörterbuch sämmtlicher königlich preussischer Staaten*, 13 vols. (Halle, 1796–1803), and he tried to publish a journal, *Der preussiche Staatsanzeiger,* which got him into trouble with the official censor with the very first issue. All this brought him to the attention of the king, who offered Krug a post in the government service as Geheimer Registrator (registrar). In his new post he had access to the kinds of data he had previously lacked and was able in 1803 to publish the *Abriss der neuesten Statistik des Königlichen Preussischen Staats,* the first general statement of its kind based on official statistics. In that same year, he joined Professor Jakob of Halle in editing a new statistical serial, the *Annalen der preussischen Staatswirtschaft und Statistik,* in which he was to publish his first essays in national income accounts. These in turn provided the raw material for his *Betrachtungen,* discussed above. On the life and work of Krug, see the essay by Inama in the *Allgemeine deutsche Biographie.*

88 One taler equals three marks. If one revalues to take account of inflation since the

early nineteenth century, one might multiply these taler by a factor of six to eight, arriving at a figure of 165–220 taler per head, or $124 to $165 of 1970 money. Even the lower amount seems high.

89 Gerd Heinrich, in his introduction to the reprint of Bratring (see n. 73 above), p. xxiv n. 36. On the creation of the Statistical Bureau, see, in addition to Boeckh and Blenck (n. 71 above), the article of E. Engel, "Zur Geschichte des Kgl. Preuss. Statistischen Bureaus," *Zeitschrift des Königlichen Statistischen Bureaus* 1 (1861): 3–9.

90 See Walther G. Hoffmann, *Das Wachstum der deutschen Wirtschaft seit Mitte des 19. Jahrhunderts* (Berlin, Heidelberg, New York, 1965).

91 A reprint of Krug's *Betrachtungen über den Nationalreichtum* was issued in 1970 by Scientia Verlag in Aalen, Germany.

3

QUANTIFICATION IN HISTORY,
AS SEEN FROM FRANCE

by Charles Tilly

Why should historians worry about numbers? Suppose we take our text from Lawrence Stone:

> If these fleeting appearances are to be given historical significance, it is necessary to be sure that they are typical, a thing which only statistics will reveal. Political history is different, and easier. At any one time there is only one Prime Minister—if that—and at most no more than three foreign or economic policies. But a social group consists of a great mass of men, each an individual human being, and as such a partial variant from the norm. Statistical measurement is the only means of extracting a coherent pattern from the chaos of personal behaviour and of discovering which is a typical specimen and which a sport. Failure to apply such controls had led to much wild and implausible generalization about social phenomena, based upon a handful of striking or well-documented examples.[1]

The original draft of this essay comprised part of a paper my wife Louise and I wrote together, entitled "Quantitative Sources for French History and French Sources for Quantitative History, 1789–1960." Faced with the gargantuan bulk and the claims to generality of that paper, the editors of this volume urged us to cut it in two or three parts. We did the latter, placing the sections which I had substantially written in this essay, those written primarily by my wife in a separate paper, and the bibliography—an inextricably collaborative effort—under a third title. As in all separations of Siamese siblings, each part bears unmistakable marks of its former dependency. Both essays still cite our jointly-constructed bibliography. If they care to make the effort, textual critics will detect my heavy hand at a few points in my wife's paper, and her light touch here and there in this one. Nevertheless, the division of authorship represents the division of labor and responsibility fairly accurately.

The Canada Council supported the work on urbanization and political upheaval in France which lies behind this essay. The Center for Advanced Study in the Behavioral Sciences gave me the leisure to write it. I am grateful to Abdul Qaiyum Lodhi for assistance in locating sources, and to Edward Shorter for well-informed criticism.

All this has long been true. But before the last decade or so, extraordinarily few historians recognized it. When they wrote of a great mass of men they either brushed them into place with the grand gesture of a Macaulay or plucked a few telling cases from the record in the loving manner of an Eileen Power.

Then collective biography, in its many forms, began to take hold of historians. Often the "masses" under study were simply large elites; the analyses of the House of Commons by Namier, of Roman dignitaries by Syme, and of Chinese bureaucrats by Ping-Ti Ho fall into that class. The study of historical demography through the person-by-person analysis of genealogies or parish registers, however, follows the same general logic. So does reconstitution of patterns of social mobility from city directories, manuscript censuses, and notarial records. In fact, many of the most important innovations in historical work since World War II consist of variants of the same procedure: documenting important historical conditions, changes, or relations which are hard to detect in the experience of any particular individual by accumulating the experiences of many individuals in comparable fashion. The "individuals" may actually be firms, villages, or families, but the overall procedure of cumulating and comparing is pretty much the same.

This sort of research does not absolutely require statistical analysis. Namier's books, for example, contain only the crudest quantification. Nevertheless, once started on this path, a historian almost inevitably adopts quantification as a means of clarifying his thought, representing his argument, and summarizing his findings. The increasing availability of data-processing procedures and machines—including computers—eases and encourages the adoption of quantitative procedures.

Innovations outside of collective biography have drawn historians in the same direction. Social scientists examining political, economic, or demographic change in the contemporary world have asked what the historical record of development reveals about similar processes—some in proud confidence that mysteries of the past will yield to laws discovered in the present, others in the humbler hope that the long and often well-documented experiences of old nations will provide some means of anticipating the experiences of new ones. National income analysis, as shaped by Wesley Mitchell and Simon Kuznets, whetted the appetites of economists for series of data extending back into history. When seeking to generalize about "nation building," sociologist Reinhard Bendix undertook thoughtful qualitative comparisons of the historical experiences of Japan, India, Russia, England, France, Germany, and other western European countries. Such efforts have built up a class of adepts in the analysis of historical materials in such fields as sociology, economics, and political science. They have also stimulated historians to consider some of the same questions. Both the questions and the questioners have helped introduce the quantitative styles of these various social sciences into historical analysis.

There is, to be sure, more to the recent rise of quantification in history than the adoption of collective biography and the quest of students of developing nations for historical analogies. For other reasons, economists have taken up some old historical problems—whether, for example, slavery was profitable in the United States before the Civil War. Sociologists have scooped up historical evidence for generalizations held to operate regardless of time or place. Aided by new technologies for the collection, storage, and processing of data, some branches of history have been able to pursue their traditional inquiries into statistics of steel production, election results, or literacy on a greatly expanded scale. Nevertheless the greatest impulses to historical quantification since World War II have come (1) from the widespread adoption of collective biography, in the broad sense, as a means of investigating historical conditions affecting large numbers of people, and (2) from the arrival among historians of outsiders trained in the analytic styles and quantitative techniques of the other social sciences and inspired by pressing questions about the long-run changes of whole societies.

In North America, important branches of historical inquiry—notably intellectual history and the history of science—have virtually escaped these influences.[2] What is more, scholars in these areas frequently hold the social sciences in fear and contempt. Within political, diplomatic, and what passes for social history, there are also plenty of historians who treat quantification as a blight. The greatest enthusiasm for, and comfort with, quantitative procedures shows up among political and social historians of Latin America, Asia, and Africa, among economic historians of most sections of the world and among that newest generation which has had the greatest exposure to the recent work of the other social sciences. North American historians are divided on the issue; the frequency with which they issue pronouncements on quantification, pro and con, attests to this. But let us suppose that the exhortation of Lawrence Stone (whose superb combination of qualitative and quantitative investigation is more widely admired than imitated) carries the day. Consider us all converts. There the work only begins.

Once persuaded that, all things considered, it is better to quantify than to remain in doubt, the historian must return to considering all things. If not why, then how and when? When and how is it worth the effort to use materials which are already in numerical form as historical evidence, or the even larger effort to draw numbers from the memoirs, letters, or bureaucratic files which are the ordinary historian's raw materials? My first general answer is: much more often and in far more ways than today's historians think. My second general answer hedges: still, it depends.

On *what* it depends is the subject of this essay. The essay will present some reflections on the kinds of problems which lend themselves to quantitative treatment, on the sources which are worth quantifying, and on the range of procedures available for doing the job. I will not, however, pretend to catalog all the many varieties of quantitative material and quantitative techniques.

Worse still, I shall draw all my observations concerning these exceedingly general problems from the experiences of the modern historians of a single country, France. Let me offer a quadruple defense of that narrowness. First, I have some firsthand knowledge of French archival materials and essentially secondhand knowledge of the rest. Second, modern France has produced and preserved exceptionally rich series of some of the most eminently quantifiable kinds of sources. Third, her historians have been among the world's leaders in several crucial varieties of quantification. Fourth, some of the problems and promises of historical quantification come out most clearly when one can see the interaction of different kinds of sources from the same period and area. There is enough to analyze in France to keep us busy for quite some time.

WHAT ARE QUANTITATIVE PROBLEMS?

Quantitative analysis strikes in unexpected places. Where it strikes depends more on the investigator's genius than on the intrinsic nature of the problem. Before André Siegfried (1. 118),* for example, writers on French politics were well aware that durable differences in voting behavior existed among France's regions and were somehow related to differences in property, religious practice, and so on. Among others, Charles Seignobos, a leading "conventional" historian, had gone on about these matters at considerable length. Siegfried's contribution was both to develop a coherent argument about the connections between social structure and political behavior and to put together three procedures:

1. Identifying and tabulating series of "typical votes" as a means of judging the political tendency of an area
2. Assembling uniform information about the politics and social structure of whole sets of areas, ranging from very small (communes) to very large (departments)
3. Undertaking systematic comparisons of those areas, mainly through the mapping of their characteristics, with the hope of identifying correspondences between political behavior and social structure

Together, the three procedures amounted to a crude but persuasive quantitative analysis.

Half a century later Paul Bois's reexamination of the same problems (1.011) challenged a number of Siegfried's comparisons and conclusions

---

* Citations in this form refer to "A Selected Bibliography of Quantitative Sources for French History and French Sources for Quantitative History since 1789," by Louise and Charles Tilly (pp. 157–75 below). In this case, for example, Siegfried's *Tableau politique de la France de l'Ouest* is item 118 under heading 1, "Representative Scholarly Works Using Quantitative Sources," hence it is identified as 1.118.

by employing an essentially Siegfriedian analysis. The argument falls; the logic remains. In its time, Siegfried's *Tableau politique de la France de l'Ouest* inspired a generation or more of French scholars (the names Goguel, Dupeux, Le Bras come to mind) to take up similar crude quantitative procedures. Siegfried had recast a well-recognized problem in quantitative form and invented some workable procedures for dealing with it quantitatively. Before his intervention, there was nothing obviously quantitative about the problem; after his intervention, there was.

That is the usual course of events with quantitative analysis in history. The case of Siegfried should warn us that there is no distinct class of "quantitative problems" only more or less quantitative ways of dealing with problems. Nonetheless, some kinds of inquiry lend themselves to quantification more easily than others. In the present state of our knowledge, an historian is more likely to profit from a quantitative statement of his problem if he is concerned with a considerable number of people than if he is concerned with only one or two, if his basic question or explanation has to do with a change or a difference among groups, if that which he is seeking to explain is already in numerical form (as is the case with strike activity, birth rates, or voting in national elections), or if his argument deals with a complicated but well-identified set of interdependencies. To put it more abstractly, the gain from quantification generally rises with—

1. the number of units involved;
2. the importance of variation to the central argument;
3. the quantifiability of the phenomenon to be explained;
4. the complexity of the principal model.

The ideal case for quantification, therefore, would be the attempt to explain how some obviously quantifiable phenomenon observable for many people, households, or communes (like number of children or wealth) changed or varied during a given historical period, the explanation itself involving a half dozen specifiable features of the people, households, or communes. The worst possible case would be the attempt to account for a single act, trait, or event for a particular individual (or, for that matter, a particular nation) by means of some general characteristic of that individual.

CHARACTERISTIC QUANTITATIVE PROBLEMS

Some typical problems already faced by historians of France have quantitative edges to them. We might group them roughly under these headings:

1. Composition of particular populations
2. Group differences
3. Trends and shifts in trends
4. Paths
5. Correlations

Quantification in the French historiography of the last few decades has followed approximately this order, with population composition most often studied quantitatively, correlations least often, and the others as listed in between.

Composition

Questions about the composition of particular populations keep coming up in French history because historians necessarily single out certain groups as crucial actors at a given time and account for their acts, at least in part, in terms of the groups' enduring characteristics. The still-unresolved debate over the politics of the men within the Convention who came to be called the Girondins bears less on what they did than on who they were, whence they came, whom they represented. Sydenham's *The Girondins* (1.125) took some gingerly steps toward quantification of the problem by using several proscription lists as the means of identifying the population in question. But these steps did not take Sydenham very far. Perhaps they led him backward: he finally concluded that the population was neither well enough defined nor sufficiently homogeneous in character to justify calling the Girondins anything more definite than the presumed enemies of Robespierre.

I have begun with a dubious example in order to warn against numerical hubris. The quantitative study of populations like the Girondins, which have blurred boundaries—no clear rules of membership, no corporate identity, no obvious distinguishing marks—will always be risky. Identifying the parliamentary "monarchists" of 1791, the "republicans" of 1848, or even the "Gaullists" of 1946 presents political historians with a challenge which numbers alone cannot meet. Nonetheless, Donald Greer's useful statistical work with the official lists of émigrés and persons sentenced under the Terror (1.063; 1.064) shows that with caution and application one can make sense of such elusive populations as political refugees and victims of repression. Duncan MacRae's recent quantitative analyses of the National Assembly under the Fourth Republic (1.091), furthermore, make even the identification and dissection of parliamentary factions seem feasible.

Where the political population is well defined, the task is much easier. By now we have a number of valuable studies of the composition of different groups of French officeholders. Tudesq's analysis of the 3,500 *conseillers généraux* (members of the elected departmental assemblies) from 1840 to 1848, for example, provides information on their ages, occupations, wealth, and so on (1.131). The information comes from the standard non-quantitative sources of the collective biographer: the individual dossiers of the officeholders stored in the archives, notes of the prefects and their staffs on the elections and the elected, minutes of the *conseils*, biographical dictionaries.

The quantification consists very simply of collecting comparable information about each councillor, classifying all the data in a standard way, and then preparing maps or frequency distributions to represent the characteristics of councils and councillors. Occasionally Tudesq undertakes a simple cross-tabulation—comparing, for instance, the characteristics of opponents and supporters of the regime in 1840. Most of the time he uses his data as but one more form of description. The data show how little the advent of manhood suffrage shook the hold of small-town notables on these honorific offices. A number of the studies of this variety, in fact, point to a greater stability of French political personnel than the *va-et-vient* of regimes has ordinarily led us to imagine. That is one of the important advantages of collective biography and related quantitative procedures: they provide alternative ways of judging the abruptness and extensiveness of changes which may appear catastrophic (or, for that matter, unimportant) when viewed from the top of the system.

It would be illuminating to extend Tudesq's procedures to communal councils, since a number of standard ideas about French political life attach importance to purely local influences. Of course, there are nearly 40,000 communes in France, as compared with only 90-odd departments, and their officials are frequently obscure enough to leave very little written about themselves. One would have to sample, perhaps using the sample of communes which the Institut National d'Etudes Démographiques has set up for the study of demographic history. Communal and departmental archives are richer in data on local administration than on anything else, so there is a reasonable chance of assembling comparable descriptions of most communal councillors over long periods of time. Again the question of how much the local officeholders changed from 1847 to 1851 (when, in a number of communes in the southeast, republican mayors who had been forced out of office by Louis Napoleon appeared at the heads of troops of rebels) would be worth examining; similar questions concerning 1830, 1870, 1940, and 1944 are still pending.

More important in the long run, studies of this kind will eventually make firmer international comparisons of political life possible. Is the problem set for us by Alexis de Tocqueville and Elie Halévy (why the French political system was less stable than many others) a false one? If it turns out that the notorious instability of the French system occurred mainly at its very top, might that not have something to do with the kinds of people who filled positions below the top? A systematic comparison of the political personnel of France, Germany, Italy, and Great Britain since 1800 would help enormously in examining the even bigger enigmas which lie behind the puzzle of French instability.

Of course, the populations studied through collective biography and related procedures need not be sets of officeholders. Tudesq himself made a far more extensive analysis of the rich men he calls the *grands notables* of France than of the *conseillers généraux*. His thesis concerning these

grands notables (whom he defines for most purposes as men paying at least
1,000 francs a year in property taxes) concentrates on their social lives and
political orientations (1.132). But it places them in a framework of comparable, quantified categories. Tudesq's statistical work makes it easy to
compare his two inquiries and to discover how much greater the change
of political personnel in 1848 was at the national than at the departmental
level—and therefore how much greater the shift away from the republicans
at the national level was between 1848 and 1851.

A similar sort of quantification has been overturning established ideas
about French revolutionary crowds and activists. Georges Lefebvre inspired
many of the last few decades' studies of crowds and activists. Albert Soboul's
Sans-culottes parisiens en l'an II (1.123) has been the single most influential
work in this line, but by now George Rudé (1.111; 1.112), Kåre Tønnesson
(1.127), Richard Cobb (1.032), David Pinkney (1.100), and Jacques Rougerie
(1.109), among others, have made significant contributions to the statistical
description of the formerly faceless ordinary participants in the multiple
French revolution. Their work has included far more than statistics.
(Richard Cobb, in particular, has frequently complained about the substi-
tution of enumeration for understanding.) Their tallies of the occupations,
residences, ages, and birthplaces of the revolutionaries have nevertheless
been crucial in identifying the men with their milieus and in clearing away
old notions about their marginality, criminality, and desperation.

The statistical study of ordinary activists is bound to remain controversial
for some time to come, since the sources it requires come into being on two
main occasions: (1) when ordinary people form or take over associations
which maintain records of their proceedings, as happened in the Parisian
sections during the early years of the revolution; and (2) when the government defines and lists them as participants in some notable collective action,
most often by arresting, prosecuting, wounding, or killing them. Soboul's
and Rudé's investigations have shown that the existing records are very
rich and that a bright historian can do wonders with them; they have not
erased the suspicion that the people who get into the record differ from those
who do not. That suspicion can only be confirmed or spiked through much
closer comparison of sources generated in different ways (for example,
dossiers of arrestees vs. records of persons killed and wounded vs. eyewitness
accounts for the June Days or the Commune).

Biases concerning those included in the records are serious when the investigator is attempting to use a statistical summary of the record descrip-
tively—for example, as a characterization of all participants in the Stavisky
riots of 1934. That is the way most of the quantifiers have worked. The
biases are often less important when the point is to detect whether two
groups differed significantly, as in Remi Gossez's comparison of the June
Days' rebels and the troops who put them down (1.060). For example, his
conclusion that the *garde mobile* came more regularly from the so-called

dangerous classes than did the rebels themselves is likely to hold up even if the sources describing both groups underrepresent the dregs of Paris. Likewise, regardless of whether the native Parisians arrested during the June Days accurately represent all Parisians who somehow took part in the rebellion, it is worth knowing that native Parisians, if arrested, were much more likely than outsiders to be convicted and sentenced.

Table 3.1 offers an interesting comparison between arrests in Paris at the time of the insurrection of December 1851 and at the time of the Commune of 1871. It confirms the more definite working-class character of the Commune and indicates that within the working class, the industries and occupations absorbing unskilled workers were exceptionally well represented among the supporters of the Commune.

Table 3.1

Arrests in Paris during Insurrection of December 1851
and Commune of 1871

Industrial category	Percentage of 2,390 persons arrested in 1851	Percentage of 31,717 persons arrested in 1871
Agricultural workers	1.3	1.3
Wood	10.5	8.8
Textiles, clothing	9.4	4.2
Shoemaking	6.9	4.7
Leathers and hides	1.1	1.2
Luxury crafts	8.3	7.6
Printing and publication	3.0	2.9
Metals	8.2	13.0
Construction	7.5	17.2
Day labor	6.2	16.4
Office workers	7.9	8.8
Domestic help, janitors, etc.	3.9	5.4
Retail trade	9.9	4.8
Professions, finance	15.9	3.7

SOURCE: Extract from table published by Jacques Rougerie (1.109, p. 127), adapted for easier reading and corrected for a few computational errors.

That way of putting it, however, raises a question which has rarely been adequately answered in French studies of revolutionary crowds: how do the rebels differ from the general population? Since there were censuses in 1851 and 1866, one can attempt a comparison of the arrestees with the Parisian labor force of the time. Table 3.2 gives numbers of workers arrested per 10,000 workers in each field. The table's weaknesses illustrate the problems of this type of quantification. To make the comparison properly, we would want to arrive at a closer fit between Rougerie's categories and those of the census. The brackets show cases in which we had to combine census categories in order to match arrestees with the labor force; the dashes indicate cases in which even combining categories produced too risky a match. Some of the people Rougerie calls *journaliers* (day laborers) in 1871 almost certainly appeared in another category in the 1866 census, since his figures imply that almost half the city's day laborers were arrested. During the years from 1866 to 1871, the character of the Parisian labor force undoubtedly changed to some extent, and during the revolutionary years of 1870 and 1871 an unknown number of workers left the city.

Table 3.2

Arrests in Paris during Insurrection of
December 1851 and Commune of 1871
(Per 10,000 workers)

Industrial category	1851	1871
Agricultural workers	11	256
Textiles, clothing	85 }	74
Shoemaking	7 }	
Luxury crafts	48	368
Printing and publication	24	171
Metals	109	527
Leather and hides	312	191 }
Wood		1143 }
Construction	20	248
Day labor	100	—
Office workers	—	167
Domestic help, janitors, etc.	6	134
Retail trade	437	293
Professions, finance	18	61

SOURCE: Reworking of Rougerie's data (1.109) plus labor-force data from censuses (5.003; 5.006).

Even these crude figures, however, indicate some features of the two insurrections left unidentified by the percentage distributions: the generally higher involvement of the whole range of industries in the Commune; the waning but still substantial contribution of the shopkeepers to the insurrections; the heavy participation of wood and metal workers, considering their numbers, in both 1851 and 1871; the exceptional rise in arrests within those industries employing the least skilled labor. The calculations provide a first link, if no more than that, between the insurgents and their milieus.

The trick is to compare the participants in an action with the population "at risk," as the epidemiologists would say. Calculating participation in rebellion as a rate (just as labor statisticians have long calculated participation in strikes as a series of rates by industry or locality) opens a simple path from an essentially descriptive to a somewhat more analytical use of the same quantitative data.

The quantitative analysis of population composition reappears in a far wider range of studies than we have discussed. I have just mentioned one application: the study of industrial disputes. Louis Chevalier used compositional analysis widely in his studies of migration to Paris, which are models of ingenuity and thoroughness in the matching of sources with problems (1.029). Studies of the French labor force, too, have ordinarily gone on against the backdrop of compositional analysis. It is true that most writers referring to labor force characteristics have dipped into compendia like the *Annuaire statistique;* they have not faced the problems of quantification directly. But the more detailed historical studies of workers have ordinarily required data not available in published census tables and the like. Quantitative analyses of population composition, used mainly for descriptive purposes, are a standard fixture of French historical works.

Group Differences

The systematic quantitative study of group differences is not quite so widespread as that of population composition. In French historical works it most frequently takes the form of spot maps displaying the variation of some characteristic—religious practice, literacy, cholera, leftist voting, industrial production—among the departments of France or within Paris. Since the time of Siegfried, such maps have recurred persistently in French political, social, and economic histories. The delightful little *Atlas historique de la France contemporaine 1800–1965,* constructed by MM. Bouju, Dupeux, Gérard, Lancelot, Lesourd, and Rémond, is stuffed with them. Rarely have the makers of such maps gone beyond the crudest nonquantitative attempts to get at the covariation of such characteristics. (For methods of doing so, see 2.033.) Although most French scholars are aware, for instance, of the general correspondence among the distributions of modern industry, transportation lines, and literacy, I have not found a single statistical study of the extent and form of their interdependence.

The comparison of major segments of the population defined in terms of occupation or wealth has also concerned a number of quantifiers in French history. Relying especially on records of notarized transactions and of death-duty declarations, Adeline Daumard, François Furet, and their associates in the Sixième Section of the Ecole Pratique des Hautes Etudes have been attempting to piece together the social structure of Paris during the eighteenth and nineteenth centuries. Much of their analysis has been geographic: an investigation of variations from arrondissement to arrondissement, from *quartier* to *quartier.* When they have not been mapping wealth as revealed by marriage contracts or the sale prices of dwellings as reported in the *Petites Affiches,* they have typically been examining the differences in those characteristics among the major occupational groups within the city. This procedure has brought them difficulties and criticism; no one can undertake such comparisons without some a priori decisions as to which occupations fit together, yet nothing is more likely to excite debate than the grouping of the population into presumably homogeneous classes.

Not that French social historians abhor the idea of class; each one simply has his own idea of where and when to draw the dividing lines. It would be possible to use conventional statistical procedures like analysis of variance to examine whether variation within the categories in one classification or another was so great as to cast doubt on the assumption of homogeneity. Or it would be possible to use some single criterion like endogamy to establish the solidarity of one presumed class or another, and then open to investigation how heterogeneous the class was in other respects. So far neither of these procedures has received much serious attention.

Other forms of systematic group comparison are exceedingly rare in French historical writing. Few researchers have attempted to compare special groups like officeholders, rebels, entrepreneurs, artists, and vagabonds with the general population. No one has dealt seriously with the apparent retreat of women from French public life after the revolution, a problem which male-female comparisons would help clarify. Even such much-mooted questions as the differences between large and small industrial firms, the contrasts among the various socialist factions (Guesdistes, Allemanistes, etc.), and the variable impoverishment and mobility of agricultural workers in different sorts of communities have received almost no quantitative treatment. In the present state of technique and documentation, these questions elude pursuit at the national level. They are, nevertheless, quite promising for study at the level of the commune, department, or region.

Trends

The statistical study of trends and shifts in trends is often the first thing that comes to mind when French quantitative history is mentioned. Analysis of "la conjoncture" à la Simiand, Labrousse, and Braudel permeates French historical work. In sheer volume, reconstructions of trends in prices, fertility, crime, or living standards have been much rarer than examinations of population composition and group differences. However, a few such trend studies have had an exceptional impact.

The substantial theses of André Armengaud (on Tarn-et-Garonne, Tarn, Haute-Garonne, and Ariège) (1.005) and Georges Dupeux (on Loir-et-Cher) (1.044) illustrate that influence very well. Each man is seeking to account for the political evolution of his region from about the middle of the nineteenth century. Both books contain three main sections: an area-by-area examination of the region under study at the beginning of the period, a substantial analysis of the *conjoncture* over the entire period, and a discussion of changes in political life over the same period. Obviously the first two are supposed to provide the basic explanations for the third. While in

Armengaud's thesis demographic changes get more attention than in Dupeux's, and while Dupeux works harder to assemble the continuous series of prices, incomes, and production dear to the economic historian, the midsections of both works consist largely of attempts to fashion time series, or, at least, comparable quantitative observations spread over considerable stretches of time) from sources ranging from the census and the *Travaux statistiques de l'Administration des Mines* to mercurials, conscription registers, and tax rolls.

The reader who approaches either of these books from the viewpoint of the social sciences notices two things about the uses of the time series. First, there is no attempt to apply statistical analysis to the covariation of the different series, even in so simple a form as the correlation coefficient. Second, their point is to establish a nonquantitative proposition (most classes of the peasantry of Loir-et-Cher prospered between 1850 and 1870; property was fractionating in the Southwest after mid-century) which will later serve as an explanation of social and political life. Both writers stop short of quantitative analysis as it is ordinarily carried on in the social sciences. This may, of course, reflect no more than the prudence of historians well aware of the flaws in their data or the roughness of their arguments. But I suspect that the example set by such masters as Labrousse has stayed the hands of those who might be capable of more extensive quantitative analyses of trends.

Over the last few decades, the most striking innovations in the quantitative analysis of trends in French history have, in fact, come from outside the school of *conjoncture* and *longue durée*. The controversial national income analyses of François Perroux, Jean Marczewski, and their collaborators are one major example. The family reconstitution approach to demographic history developed by Louis Henry and his co-workers is the other.

Although less frequently debated, the second example is more of a break with past procedures than the first. It involves deliberately employing sampling procedures, squeezing numbers from apparently unquantitative sources like genealogies and parish registers, and aggregating from very small units like households and parishes to large ones like regions and the nation as a whole. The procedure has some obvious difficulties: the use of the families which stay in place to represent all families, the underenumeration of the destitute, drifters, and derelicts, and so on. Nevertheless, once the method has proved itself as a way of establishing national trends in fertility and mortality, it is likely to serve as a model for studies of social mobility, wealth, or even political participation.

Paths

As we turn to the analysis of paths, we enter historical terrain little explored by quantifiers. This includes all those phenomena which can be represented usefully by directed graphs such as that shown in figure 3.1, showing links from A to B, B to C, B to D, D to E, and E to A, not from C to D, and so on. The spread of epidemics, crazes, rebellions, or innovations are obvious cases. Less obviously, patterns of occupational mobility, trade, intermarriage, political influence, or migration also form paths. Not long before his death, André Siegfried wrote a provocative little book called *Itinéraires de contagions, épidémies, et idéologies* (1.117). In it he elaborated the notion that population movements, epidemics, and new ideas follow the same paths around the world and are propagated in similar ways. A related, if somewhat less ambitious, idea had appeared in Georges Lefebvre's famous *Grande Peur* some thirty years before (1.081). It recurs, at least by implication, in George Rudé's *Crowd in History* (1.112). All these books include detailed maps, but none of them goes beyond maps to quantitative analysis of the correspondences among them.

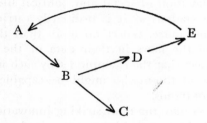

Figure 3.1

The quantitative analysis of paths has three possible applications to French history: (1) the identification of the most common, powerful, and/or persistent links in a complicated set of relations; (2) the investigation of similarities and dissimilarities among different sets of relations; (3) the study of the interdependence between the form of linkage and the behavior of the units linked. One could usefully do the first in attempting to discern the principal channels and most important nodes in a complex set of trading relations like France's grain trade or domestic textile industry. Fernand Braudel's *La Méditerranée* (1.017, e.g. 1:557–75) provides a model for the first stages of such an analysis, as it does for many other forms of quantification. The second type of application would be appropriate as a means of asking whether something like the same pattern of movement among regional cities, trading towns, smaller villages, and open countryside appeared in normal marketing arrangements and in such widespread conflicts as the grain riots of 1789, the 45-Centime Revolt of 1848, or the soi-disant rural uprisings of 1961. The third application would help in assessing the impact of the railroads on local political organization after 1840. Although writers like Georges Duveau, André Siegfried, and Maurice Agulhon have given a number of hints along these lines, no one has converted those hints into quantitative inquiry.

Correlations

The quantitative study of correlation is in about the same condition as that of paths. That comes as a bit of a surprise, since Braudel himself has declared that "to explain, then, is to locate, to imagine correlations between the metabolism of material life and the other multiple fluctuations in the life of men" (1.017, 2:213). Innumerable writers, to be sure, have detected connections between pairs of variables in French society, but almost no one has ever attempted to measure the connections themselves. For example, it is a commonplace of French political history that the electoral strength of the Radicals under the Third Republic rested especially with the small property holders. Yet we have no serious quantitative investigation of the correlation between Radical vote and fragmentation of property from time to time or from area to area. The necessary materials exist and could be analyzed for small units like cantons selected through a sampling procedure.

Most efforts to deal with such problems have been through the crude and deceptive procedure of comparing maps representing the distributions of the two phenomena in question—comparing them by eye, at that. Gordon Marker's little-known work on interregional migration in France is an exception (1.093), as is Robert Goetz-Girey's preliminary attempt to correlate fluctuations in strike activity with variations in wages and business activity (1.058). Few more exceptions are likely until (and unless) French historians develop greater statistical expertise and a stronger interest in explicit verification of statements of relationship. In this case, the main innovations are likely to come from outside history; economists, sociologists, and political scientists have the appropriate questions and technical preparation for the study of correlations—especially when it becomes a matter of relating three or more variables, instead of just a pair.

This is a pity. Much historical argument is relational: A goes with B, A causes B, A and B jointly produce C. A good many relational arguments would benefit from being brought out into the open and subjected to quantitative verification. Albert Soboul's vigorous discussion of 1848 is a case in point:

> While the peasant proprietors, the rural bourgeoisie, the great noble and bourgeois landlords, after a moment of fright, increased their political control and economic domination from 1848 to 1851, the poor peasants responded violently with a true class reflex which led them in 1851 to a genuine *prise de conscience* in favor of that republic which they had formerly misunderstood or maligned. [1.122, p. 55]

The ideas about class consciousness resist quantification, and any division of the rural population into major categories will start an agitated debate. Yet the general assertion of a relationship among wealth, property holding, political alignment, and protest from 1848 to 1851 invites quantitative comparison. Enough records of taxation, voting, and repression exist for the period (as the theses of André Armengaud, Louis Chevalier, and Philippe Vigier have shown) to make such a comparison feasible and profitable.

This survey has focused on the quantification of questions historians are already asking themselves; the typical problems are population composition, group differences, trends, paths, and correlations. If we strayed outside our fence, we would soon stumble across the sorts of problems the "new economic historians" have claimed and have sought to treat with quantitative procedures rather more sophisticated than those mentioned: the French equivalents of the economics of slavery or the contributions of railroads to economic development. The recurring thought that declining fertility slowed economic growth in nineteenth- and twentieth-century France, for instance, might yield to cliometric examination. Still farther away we would come upon the application of complicated models of population growth, industrialization, or political development to the French experience. Does Kaldor's model produce a satisfactory approximation of French economic development? At the very end of the stroll, we might find ourselves quite outside history, in that timeless realm in which situations, persons, or events plucked from the past or the present serve as tests of general statements about social life.

Abundant materials for quantitative analyses of each of these varieties exist in and out of French archives. Whether they are actually undertaken does not depend very heavily on the availability of data or of statistical techniques; it depends on whether French historians become concerned about a different range of questions than those on which they have traditionally fixed their attention.

WHAT ARE QUANTITATIVE SOURCES?

Quantitative problems do not form a distinct class of inquiries in history. Nor do quantitative sources stand out from all others. Historians have quantified the oddest things: funerary inscriptions, baptismal certificates, parliamentary careers, blast furnaces. These phenomena have no intrinsic quantitative character. Indeed, their uses have only five important things in common:

1. They were relevant to questions concerning population composition, group differences, trends, paths, or correlations already being raised by historians.
2. There were several, or many, instances to deal with.
3. It was possible to document those instances in a somewhat comparable fashion.
4. The record appeared sufficiently complete and reliable to make the quantifying effort worthwhile.

5. The historians were able to summon up the will and the abstractions to treat the instances as similar in some important respects.

Only two of these conditions have to do with the sources themselves. Even then the kind of document matters less than the character of the collection of documents.

All these conditions vary over time and space. I have already said that the gain from quantification of any particular historical question rises with the number of units involved, the importance of variation to the central argument, the quantifiability of the phenomena to be explained, and the complexity of the principal model. Now I should add that the questions themselves change. At present the analysis of collective biographies of participants in the great annual bicycle race, the Tour de France, might be diverting, but it would not resolve any currently pressing historical question. Fifty years ago, before Richard Cobb's writing (1.032), who cared about the individual recruits to the militias which marched out from Paris and Lyon in 1793? Now historians do care, and they are well informed by Cobb's work. Questions change.

Likewise, the availability of multiple instances changes. The opening up of the Archives Historiques de la Guerre, in the Fort de Vincennes, has placed within historical reach the dossiers of thousands of nineteenth-century victims of military repression. Thus Jacques Rougerie, Rémi Gossez, and dozens of Parisian candidates for diplomas in modern history have been enabled to carry out statistical studies of rebels and rebellions (cf. 2.050). Yet such studies are at present much harder to conduct for the rebels and rebellions of small-town France, for lack of accessible documentation. The availability of multiple instances not only changes but varies from region to region.

The ability to document the instances in a comparable fashion also varies. Computer technology makes it simpler to keep control of vast files including standard sets of notations for each individual or unit (this is the main use to which students of history have put them). But computer or no computer, it is much easier to assemble uniform documentation when the people who did the original recording also did some standardizing. The efforts of the Office du Travail to organize the reporting of strikes—which are by no means identical events—imposed a relatively constant form on the materials available for the analysis of industrial conflict after 1889. No such standardization occurred in the reporting of electoral campaigns. Every standardization, to be sure, twists events somehow. Real strikes are subtler and more diverse than the *Statistique des Grèves*. And practically no standardizing procedure picks up all instances of the phenomenon it purports to deal with, or even an unbiased sample of the phenomenon.

Historians face a difficulty encountered by almost all consumers of quantitative information generated by other people. The measurement arises from the working of an institution whose activity overlaps but does not coincide completely with the phenomenon measured. In fact, what appears to be an index of the phenomenon is more directly an index of the institution's activity. Crime statistics offer the best-known example of this difficulty. Reporting procedures have an enormous effect on the quantity of crimes recorded. If a serious theft is defined in terms of the value of the object stolen, a statistical increase in crimes of that category will occur as a consequence of an increase in wealth.

The setting of definitions is the weakest form of organizational impact on statistics. The organization can have a stronger influence on the numbers by changing the definitions so as to produce an apparent change in the phenomenon measured. But its own activity shows up most clearly in figures which actually represent the frequency with which its members carried out certain formal procedures: filing of complaints, arrests, bookings, convictions, and so on. Students of crime statistics have often noted the pressure on a patrolman to produce the "right" number of arrests for his particular assignment; they have also observed the production of "crime waves" through the temporary or permanent stepping up of the incentives for reporting infractions previously ignored or handled informally.[3] Jack Douglas (2.030; 2.031) has identified similar difficulties in the reporting of suicide; we might more confidently read suicide statistics as indexes of the willingness of the authorities to label acts of self-destruction publicly than as evidence of the frequency of self-destruction.

In a similar but less obvious fashion, production figures based on the volume of materials inspected and/or taxed by representatives of the central government (as in the case of eighteenth-century cloth manufacturing in France) respond as directly to changes in the punctiliousness of local officials as to changes in the vigor of local industry. Perhaps the hardest cases of all in which to sift out this effect of the specialists in control of an activity on the volume of activity reported are those in which measurement depends on the entry of goods or services into a market. Even if good data were available on the amount of prostitution in a country, for example, no one would presume to estimate the total level of sexual activity, because a high but variable proportion of such activity goes on outside the market. Nevertheless, we do attempt to measure variations in personal services, energy production, or field crops via the part which passes through the market. In this case, the standardizers influence the measurement at least twice: when merchants initiate and record the transactions, and when tax collectors set up procedures for dipping into the record. The standardizers, in short, enslave historians with their largesse. What we need to combat that servitude is a kind of historiography as yet ill developed: the investigation of how organizational conditions themselves affect the character of the documentation produced and available to the historian.

As a result of these processes, the completeness and reliability of the sources vary. Oskar Morgenstern's little book on errors in economic data

(2.073) will quickly sober up any historian who has drunk too deeply of numerical Nepenthe. Even in contemporary, deliberately assembled estimates of production, consumption, or income, Morgenstern points out, errors of 10 percent or more often occur. A fortiori for the estimates of Necker or of nineteenth-century prefects. The numerophilic historian often has one advantage over the economist who also works with numbers: he knows a great deal about the original sources. The classic cautions apply. For the years 1790 and 1791, we can attach greater confidence to the records of church property sales than to estimates of the revenues of the clergy, and greater confidence to those estimates than to the reports of poverty sent to the Constituent Assembly's Committee on Mendicity (see, e.g., 1.050). The first came out of a public occasion involving crucial government funds and a number of parties with an interest in a reliable public record. The second involved a sort of adversary proceeding and considerable public review. In the third case, there were few checks and a potential advantage to the liars. The historian can, of course, use the poverty reports for purposes of comparison if he is willing to assume fairly constant mendacity about mendicity, or if he is able to use the voluminous supporting notes they contained for verification. He will nevertheless want to use them with even greater delicacy than the data on the property sales.

Should we therefore forget numbers? Listen to Oskar Morgenstern:

> The weakness of econometric, mathematical models, when subjected to numerical application is *not* due to the fact that they are mathematical or that a numerical application is made. Rather we are confronted with a property of our reasoning and of our ability to observe and to measure the phenomena which we want to explain. The properly handled mathematical formulation has the virtue of showing us clearly where the limitations of our knowledge are. [2.073, p. 14]

Let that be our text. The sources vary greatly in reliability and completeness; the quantitative historian takes on a special obligation to examine and report that reliability and completeness.

Finally, the acceptable abstractions change. Gradually, if not without growling and baring of fangs, French economic historians are moving toward some sort of agreement on the possibility of, and the means of establishing, cost-of-living estimates for widely spaced points in the nineteenth and twentieth centuries as a step toward the identification of fluctuations in real wages over the entire period. The real wage is a controversial abstraction.

Again, the very first question Annie Kriegel (1.071) and Antoine Prost (1.074) take up in their separate studies of the Confédération Général du Travail after World War I and in the 1930s is: "Qu'est-ce qu'un syndiqué?" What, indeed, *was* a union member during those turbulent years? What sense can the labor historian make of times when union affiliations changed sharply from month to month; when a system of stamps, half-stamps, and quarter-stamps made it easy for workers to "join" part-way or part-time; and when union leaders often disguised the information they did have for tactical purposes? The definition—the abstraction—turns out to affect the numbers seriously. Prost chooses to deal with persons formally enrolled and paying dues; he uses records of dues payments themselves to establish estimates of membership. (That was, in fact, close to what the officials of the CGT did when they were not manufacturing numbers for the sake of propaganda.) Very likely Prost's way of dealing with the problem, and the numbers that go with it, will serve as a standard for other examinations of union strength in France.

All this amounts to an important qualification of my initial statement. "Quantitative sources" still do not form a separate realm. A series of important conditions, however, affects whether quantitative documentation of any particular phenomenon is available or even feasible at a given time. The nature of the phenomenon probably matters less than the way its initial recording occurred and the way its historian goes about his inquiry. If there is a large set of events which the participants or the observers considered to have something in common, and especially if some organization established a routine which defined, treated, and recorded those events uniformly (as parish priests recorded marriages, registry offices recorded deeds, and city officials recorded the price of grain), the quantifier usually has an easier time of it. Indeed, under these conditions some of the material in the archives is quite likely to be in statistical form already, quantified by bureaucrats. For France since 1789, the extreme examples are census data, reports on industrial activity, vital statistics, information on crime and repression, strike materials, conscription records, and tax rolls.

QUANTITATIVE ANALYSIS AS SUCH

Suppose an historian finds some of these sources and their quantification of probable value to his work. What should he do? He cannot stick his hand into the toolbox and come up with a universal statistical wrench. An historian always faces the problem of fitting the sources to his questions, and vice versa.

Fitting them together means finding a quantitative operation which corresponds to the logic of his inquiry. That much is obvious. I feel no compulsion to lay out the full set of quantitative tools likely to help an historian—a useful task, but one which would run on to dictionary length. I wish instead to mention some of the large alternatives the quantifier has open to him, in order to emphasize how wide the range of choice is. It would be a pity if any reader who has borne with me this far came to the conclusion that he could quantify profitably only if his sources resembled those of Louis Henry, André Tudesq, or Duncan MacRae—or that in the event that his sources did resemble those of Henry, Tudesq, or MacRae, his only choice was to use their techniques.

LEVELS OF MEASUREMENT

The first large choice has to do with levels of measurement. Teachers of elementary statistics commonly distinguish among nominal, ordinal, and interval measurement. Nominal measurement consists of placing units in mutually exclusive categories which do not form any particular order (from high to low, large to small, and so on): years, departments, industrial/commercial/administrative, invaded/not invaded. Ordinal measurement consists of placing units of ordered categories whose distance from each other is unspecified: high/medium/low, heavily industrial/moderately industrial/nonindustrial, destroyed/heavily damaged/lightly damaged/undamaged. At the extreme, there may be one category per unit, which means that they are ranked individually. Interval measurement actually states the distances between units along a continuum: prices of 2 sous, 2.5 sous, 4 sous, 8 sous; populations of 350, 650, 1,200, 850,000. Only with the third variety of measurement does it begin to make sense to calculate means, to speak of one unit as being three times as large as another, and so on.

There is nothing esoteric about these three levels of measurement. Historians have been using all of them, without the labels, for generations. But they have usually turned away from ordinal measurement, and they have almost never realized they could perform statistical analyses of data unsuitable for interval treatment but quite amenable to nominal or ordinal measurement. Even in the admirable, highly statistical work of Antoine Prost, there is a reluctance to exploit these lower levels of measurement. His data, for example, make possible a rough test of his speculation that the Communists gained strength mostly in the industrial unions into which workers rushed in response to the Popular Front excitement of the mid-1930s—that they were riding on a "syndicalisme de crise et non de longue

Table 3.3

Tendency of Union Départementale in France, 1939

Ratio of union membership in November 1938 to membership in March 1936	Communist	Balanced/ Undecided	Non-communist	Total
Less than 4	9	6	21	36
4 to 6.5	11	5	8	24
Over 6.5	7	3	12	22
Unknown	2	1	6	9
Total	29	15	47	91 [a]

SOURCE: Data taken from Antoine Prost (1.103, p. 138, maps 5, 13).
[a] Includes Territory of Belfort.

organisation" (1.103, p. 138). Table 3.3 shows the political orientation of these unions. There is some tendency for departments experiencing rapid increases in union membership to opt for Communist leadership, as Prost's argument would lead us to expect. But how strong is the relationship?

Prost's usual statistic, the product-moment correlation coefficient, will not work in this case; it requires interval measurement. The variable "tendency of Union Départementale" is measured only ordinally. There are, however, several statistics appropriate to this problem. One of them is Gamma, a measure of the similarity or dissimilarity in the orderings of two variables, which goes from −1 to 0 to +1. In this case, Gamma =+.14, indicating a weak relationship between the two factors but leaving a great deal of room for the operation of other variables. (In fact, a chi-squared test indicates that a relationship at least this strong could occur about one time in four by chance alone.) Clearly Prost's argument needs further scrutiny. It would be easy and useful to apply the same treatment to a number of the other nominal or ordinal variables which slip into his discussion.

DESCRIPTION AND ANALYSIS

The second large choice is between descriptive and analytic uses of quantification. Here the distinction is a bit looser than in the case of nominal, ordinal, and interval measurement, but it is no less important. Users of statistical methods commonly make a three-way division among procedures for directly describing a body of data (for example, mean, standard deviation, proportion), procedures for measuring the relationship of separate variables to each other (for example, the correlation coefficient), and procedures for inferring from a given body of data to the phenomena the data represent (t-tests, chi-squared). The latter suggests what I mean by analytic uses of quantification. The scanner of French quantitative history sees no more than wisps of inferential statistics and statistics of relationship amid the mounds of descriptive statistics. By and large, he finds the numbers used to buttress statements like "There were many Ps in Poitiers," "Q went up in Quercy from 1910 to 1920," "R was lower in Reims than in Rouen." He will have to search strenuously for quantification of statements like "S varied as a function of T" or "There is a high likelihood that U and V were negatively related to each other in France as a whole," although he will frequently encounter the qualitative versions of these statements. Normally the French quantifier lines up numerical descriptions on the way to conducting an essentially nonquantitative analysis.

An excellent case in point comes from a book I have already hailed for its thoroughness and ingenuity in quantification: Paul Bois's _Paysans de l'Ouest_ (1.011, p. 349). In a section which is crucial to his argument, Bois carefully assembles data on eighteenth-century property holding in a sample of ten communes of the Sarthe. The calculations took a large effort and a

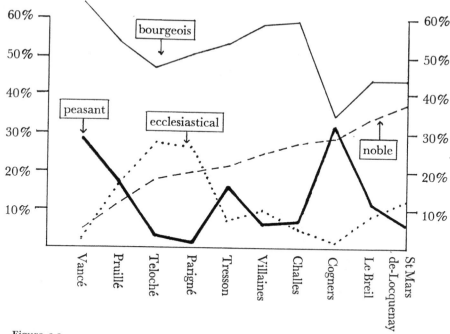

Figure 3.2

great deal of knowledge of the locales. Bois sums them up in the graph in figure 3.2. Then he turns from quantification back to a qualitative inspection of the graph:

> One can see by examining the graph that peasant property is in opposition above all to that of the bourgeoisie. As it happens, the highest point for the bourgeois (Villaines, Challes) corresponds to one of the lowest points for the peasants. Moreover, the bourgeoisie's lowest point (Cogners) corresponds to the peasantry's high point, the two swings in the curve having the same amplitude, as if the peasantry had retained that which the bourgeoisie could not grab. None of the other swings is so striking.
>
> One can see, next, that there is also a fairly strong opposition between peasant and ecclesiastical property, although not so strong as between peasant and bourgeois. [1.011, p. 349]

These interpretations of the graph are, to say the least, misleading. If we calculate a rank-order correlation coefficient comparing peasant property with each of the other three, we get the following result:

peasant: bourgeois	.04
peasant: noble	−.11
peasant: clergy	−.62

In fact, there is no association between peasant and bourgeois property, positive or negative. There is a trivial negative association between noble and peasant property. And there is quite a strong tendency for ecclesiastical property to rise as peasant property falls. By the logic of the argument, we should conclude that the real rivalry for the land was between peasants and priests. A more deliberate analytic use of statistics would have helped Bois correct and clarify this tangled section of his argument.

UNITS OF ANALYSIS

The third large choice comes with the designation of the units to be analyzed. Quantitative analysis almost always requires identifying multiple, comparable, mutually exclusive units which can be documented in a similar fashion. In our survey of French quantitative work, the units we have most frequently encountered are individuals, departments, and France as a whole (the "comparable units" in this case being different years of France's history). Such units as communes, cantons, and arrondissements come into play in detailed regional studies. And on occasion a political analyst will collect data for different departmental councils, different sessions of the Chamber of Deputies, and the like. Quantitative analysis rarely takes firms, families, associations, unions, parties, and the like as the basic units. When the units are not individuals, they tend to be geographic.

The selection of the unit emerges from a transaction between the analyst's argument and the way the relevant data are stored. The preeminence of the geographic principle in French administration, and consequently in French archives, has encouraged historians to assemble their data in terms of departments and arrondissements. This concentration on a relatively small repertoire of units has some advantages: it assures the transfer of expertise, procedures, and data from one study to the next. Its disadvantage, clearly enough, is sometimes to misalign the logic of the statistical analysis and the logic of the argument which contains it.

Agricultural historians seeking to trace the evolution of a particular natural region have perennially contended with this misalignment of administrative and agricultural areas. In his examination of the modernization of farming in the vicinity of Semur in Burgundy, Gérard Martin warns repeatedly of the approximations he has been forced to adopt:

> The study of the specialization of agriculture in the Auxois is made difficult by the lack of continuity of the documents. Often the statistics are prepared for the department or the arrondissement. But our region does not correspond to an arrondissement. It has often happened that we had a usable statistic for the whole region at a given date and could not find a comparable statistic for a later date. . . . Since the Revolution, the name Auxois stands only for an economic and geographic area, and does not correspond to any administrative unit. In his talk given in 1949, titled

"L'Auxois, entité historique, ethnique, géographique et géologique," Louis Bourrhier defined it as a quadrilateral whose sides are made up by the valleys of the Serein on the southwest, of the Oze, continued by those of the Brenne and the Armançon on the northeast, by a hypothetical line connecting Sainte-Magnance with Buffon. But it is practically impossible to carry out an economic study of a region laid out this way; we must find the appropriate administrative divisions and, in our case, the cantonal division is crucial. The rural economy is tied directly to the earth. The Auxois is the geographical system of the Lias. We shall therefore include in our region the cantons in which Liassic terrains occupy a significant part of the territory. [1.095, pp. 87–88]

He then proceeds to list the cantons. Here we witness the transaction between argument and data right out in the open.

The problem is by no means peculiar to agricultural historians. Louis Chevalier has to stretch rather far to connect his data on suicide with the presumed disorganization of Paris under the impact of rapid population increase during the July Monarchy: his data on differentials in suicide among occupational groups deal with France as a whole, and his data on overall suicide rates deal with the department of the Seine as a whole (1.028, pp. 345–46). During the period under study, Paris's share of the Seine's population was decreasing rapidly as the suburbs grew faster than the central city. As a result, the rise in the Seine's reported rate of attempted and completed suicides from 43 per 100,000 in around 1820 to 56 per 100,000 in around 1845 would be consistent with any of the hypothetical situations given in table 3.4. These are very different circumstances. Common sense

Table 3.4

Hypothetical Breakdown of Suicide Rate in
the Seine in 1820 and 1845
(Per 100,000)

| | Hypothesis A | | Hypothesis B | | Hypothesis C | |
	Paris	Rest of Seine	Paris	Rest of Seine	Paris	Rest of Seine
1820	40	63	45	30	45	30
1845	40	110	45	93	60	42

and Louis Chevalier tell us to pick hypothesis C over the other two. Yet the risk is there. And here the fit is fairly good: Paris had about 87 percent of the Seine's population in 1820, about 77 percent in 1845. The worse the fit between units in data and argument, the greater the risk.

Sometimes there is no choice: no matter how the historian pushes and hauls, the gap between data and argument remains. I have no new solution for that difficulty. I wish only to insist that the selection of units of analysis is a major problem, which becomes more obvious and more acute with extensive quantification. For a large-scale quantitative analysis often means long accumulation and preparation of the data, unit by unit. Initial selection of the wrong unit can cost a great deal. Nonhistorical social scientists faced with the same problem tend to assemble their data in terms of the smallest unit possible (the person, the block, the firm), tag each unit according to the larger groupings into which it falls, and thus retain the ability to aggregate and disaggregate as the analysis demands. Historians have something to learn from that procedure.

They also have something to learn from the sociologists' discussions of the problem of "ecological correlation." Sociologists have learned through hard experience that correlations which obtain at the level of a given unit do not necessarily hold for smaller units contained within it or for larger units of which it is a part. The fact that average education and income vary together closely among the neighborhoods of a metropolitan area gives us no warrant to conclude that they are just as closely related for individuals or for municipalities within the metropolis.

Although in general the quantitative historian should match argument, units analyzed, and statistical procedure as closely as possible, there are some occasions for inferring characteristics of units not observed from units observed. One is the estimate of values for the units missing from a set, as in the interpolation of labor-force figures for intercensal years or in the use of a regression equation of income on education to estimate income where the investigator has education data for an entire set of arrondissements but lacks income data for a few of them. The other is the deliberate employment of sampling to expand the range and reduce the cost of an analysis involving many units. Historians tend to be properly wary about interpolation and improperly fearful about sampling. Indeed, the only notable use of sampling procedures I have encountered in my survey of sources is INED's establishment of a national sample of communes for the exploration of demographic history. French historians could gain a great deal by tying other long-range inquiries requiring both local data and national findings to the same sample.

HANDLING THE DATA

The quantitative historian has a final large choice among ways of recording, storing, and processing his data. The choice sequence is shown in figure 3.3. Actually it is quite likely, even desirable, that the choice of quantitative procedure come first. The point of the diagram is to show that the choice of machine data-processing sets important limits on how the data can be reduced, the choice of early data reduction sets limits on the quantitative procedure, and so on.

Some of these terms may be mystifying. For most purposes, at the present time, the historian's choice between machine data processing and work by hand amounts to a decision whether to punch his information onto machine-readable cards via a standard coding procedure. If his pool of information is very small or very irregular, he may well choose to do his work by hand instead. In that case, he still faces a data-reduction problem. Often a student working in the archives takes a dossier of acts like the sales of church properties in 1791 or 1792, prepares a list of major occupational titles likely to appear in the documents, and tallies the titles as they appear. If the occupational classification turns out to be unsatisfactory, or if it turns out to make a big difference whether the buyer bid singly or with a group, the student must return to the original source for another tally. That

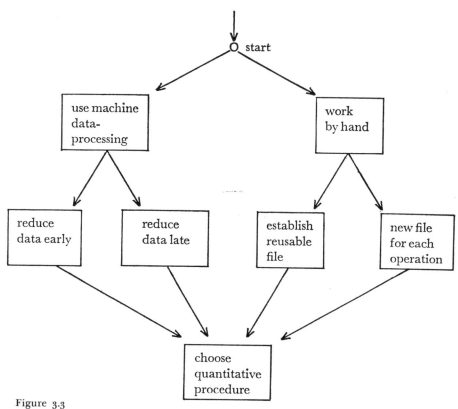

Figure 3.3

is what I mean by establishing a new file for each operation. Preparing a single sheet for each person encountered in the source and then recording each transaction involving that person on the same sheet—a fairly common procedure—has some of the same inflexibility. Even if the description of each transaction is quite detailed, the student who decides to analyze, say, the change in the average value of purchases from one period to the next will have to do much of the work over again.

A reusable file, on the other hand, commonly consists of a separate, detailed sheet or card for each of the smallest units consistently represented in the file. In the case of sales of church properties, parcels or transactions are the likely units. The decision as to how much to record the first time is essentially an economic one, balancing the cost of transcription, the cost of returning to the source, and the probability that one will change his mind about what to ask from the data. In our own painful work, my group has found the marginal costs of recording additional items once one is already working with a source, and of maintaining the larger files required by the selection of small units, modest compared with the costs of changing one's mind later on.

If his pool of data is large, or if he plans an analysis using a number of separate items of information at once, the historian will most likely find it profitable to turn from hand to machine data processing. That presents him with a decision about the timing and character of data reduction. In the present state of technology, it is rarely practical to put an entire source into machine-readable form. The historian must sort out the parts he needs. Sometimes that means transcribing texts or part of texts onto cards or tape. In his enormous project of coding the *cahiers de doléances* of 1789, for example, Gilbert Shapiro actually places key words and abbreviated phrases on punched cards for machine interpretation.

Much more often this reduction of data means another kind of coding: placing the particular unit within a numerically tagged set of categories. Here, for example, are two excerpts from a codebook used for the recording of political disturbances in France:

CARD 82: Formation
A Note on Classifying the Industrial Group of the Formation
A large minority of our formations consist of persons from a single fairly well defined industry—masons, railroad workers, winegrowers or something else. When that is the case, find the appropriate category and code it in columns 18 and 19. If it is a combination of distinct industrial groups, code 02 ("Mixture of industrial categories") and COMMENT if possible. If there is nothing distinctive about its industrial composition (for example, if the formation is a casual crowd or a group of women and children), code 01 ("No distinct industrial category"). Only code 00 ("Insufficient information") when there is too little information in the account to make a choice among the other alternatives reasonable.

The code for columns 18 and 19 is an expanded version of the industrial classification used in the *Statistique des Grèves*. The summary which follows gives all the headings used in 1935, and places all the occupations for which strikes were reported in that year. That means a number of occupations are not on the list; but they are rare, and in any case not usually too hard to match with occupations already shown. This classification emphasizes the industry rather than the job. The code in column 20 ("Detailed occupation") will offer another chance to place the occupation, whether you know the industry or not.

cols. 18–19   *INDUSTRIAL GROUP OF FORMATION*
NOTE: Code   00 Insufficient information
detailed occu-   01 No distinct industrial category
pations in col.   02 Mixture of industrial categories: COMMENT ENCOUR-
20. If there are   AGED

two or more
distinct indus-
trial groups,
consider
whether they
should be
treated as
separate
formations.

11 Farm workers
12 Winegrowers
13 Forest workers
14 Fishermen
20 Extractive industries
   21 Mines
   22 Quarries
30 Textiles and clothing
40 Wood-working industries
   41 Wood-working
   42 Construction in wood
50 Metal-producing and metal-working
60 Commerce
   61 Traders, wholesale merchants
   62 Tradesmen
   63 Retail Merchants
   64 Shopkeepers
   65 Peddlers, etc.
70 Liberal professions
   71 Sciences, letters, arts
   72 Students
   73 Teachers, professors
   74 Priests, monks, nuns
80 Public Services
   81 Government service
   82 Tax collectors, customs officers, etc.
   83 Police
   84 Military
90 Other industries
   91 Food
   92 Chemistry, rubber
   93 Paper and cardboard
   94 Printing and publication
   95 Leathers and hides
   96 Working of stones and earths
   97 Transport and maintenance

   99 Other: MANDATORY COMMENT

CODING IMMEDIATE BACKGROUND

Remember that this formation's participation in the disturbance begins at the moment when it starts to interact either with another formation taking part or with the object of its attack. Determine whether the formation was engaging in any collective activity back to the point of a break of six hours or more. The time from the beginning of that continuous activity to the moment of first participation in the disturbance is the "immediate background."

Out of that immediate background, code the collective activity you judge to be most relevant to the disturbance itself in columns 24–25, the next most relevant in columns 26–27. Remember that you can generalize two or more activities with the same first digit by placing a zero in the second column: picketing (32) plus petitioning (31) plus sending a deputation (33) can be coded 30. If there are three or more important activities, and devising combination codes will not solve the problem, place 90 in columns 26–27, and COMMENT.

cols. 24–27   *IMMEDIATE BACKGROUND OF THIS FORMATION'S*
                PARTICIPATION IN THE DISTURBANCE
        00   Insufficient information
        01   This formation did not exist before the disturbance began
        02   This formation existed, but was not acting collectively just
            before the disturbance began
        03   This formation existed, and was acting collectively in a way
            not directly relevant to the disturbance
        10   Peaceful meeting
            11   Harangue by a speaker
        20   Strike
            21   Sit-down, occupation of premises
        30   Presentation of demands
            31   Petitioning
            32   Picketing
            33   Sending a deputation
        40   Preparations for violence
            41   Arming
            42   Occupation of positions
            43   Show of force
            44   Awaiting arrival of forces/preparing ambush
            45   General security measures
            46   Planning insurrection
            49   Other specific preparation: MANDATORY COMMENT
        50   Obstructive measures
            51   Blocking of streets, entrances, passages
            52   Closing off a public area
            59   Other specific obstructive measures: MANDATORY
               COMMENT
        60   Organizational activity of formation
            61   Election of leaders or officers
            62   Strategy meeting
        70   Parade, ceremony, celebration, fete involving this formation
            and appealing to only a segment of the community
            71   May Day demonstration
            72   Belligerent march
            73   Demonstration
            74   Counter-demonstration
        80   Community activity
            81   Community election
            82   Patriotic holiday festivities
        90   Uncodable combinations: MANDATORY COMMENT
        99   Other uncodable collective activity: MANDATORY COM-
            MENT

When the information concerning the disturbance is adequate, the first of
these codes arouses no great controversy. It adapts one version of the
standard industrial classification used in French censuses, strike statistics,
and other official publications. It therefore lends itself to comparison with
the data in those sources. The subheadings are not exhaustive or even
mutually exclusive, as a glance at the headings under "commerce"—which
are, in the French of the actual codebook, *négociants, commerçants,*

marchands, boutiquiers, colporteurs—will show. Instead, they permit the coder to record the most common labels which appear in the sources. The whole coding scheme is a compromise among the mixed industrial-occupational codes employed in various official publications, the vocabularies of the sources with which the code works, and the needs of the analysis. But it seems to be a viable compromise. Aside from the frequent absence of information and appearance of occupationally mixed crowds, its main weakness is its failure to reflect the changes in the major divisions within the French labor force; the classification applies more neatly to 1930 than it does to 1800 or to 1960.

Many of the judgments made in accordance with the code for "immediate background," on the other hand, are bound to be contestable. That is one reason for having a COMMENT option; it permits (and sometimes requires) the coder to place verbal qualifications, explanations, and specifications on punched cards which form part of the machine record and can be recalled along with the numerical codes. Still, we cannot hope to make all these fine distinctions reliably. Nor do we use all these categories in any one analysis. They serve three purposes:

1. To make coding easier (The strain of choosing among large categories like "preparations for violence" and "obstructive measures" is rather great, and the coder who can match the situation at hand with a descriptive phrase finds the task less arduous.)
2. To make possible a wide variety of recombination of these small items, as further inquiry dictates
3. To make it feasible to recapture the detail when the analysis produces confusing or unexpected results

In short, this codebook rests on the assumption of a very late reduction of the data to the final categories to be used in the quantitative analysis. The coding of political disturbances is so novel and so risky that we could not afford to reduce all the data to stark, simple, immutable categories early in the investigation.

If the fortunate analyst knows exactly what output he will eventually demand from the computer, he can feed just the relevant items and distinctions into the machine record and forget the rest. But rare is the man who knows exactly what he will want. That is why the choice between early and late data reduction is crucial and precarious. Early data reduction is cheap, quick, neat; it tends to hide mistakes. Late data reduction is costly, cumbersome, and untidy, but it is also safer. The choice is not trivial.

CONCLUSIONS

However the data are reduced, the quantitative historian finally comes to the application of a statistical or mathematical procedure. On this weighty matter, I have only a pregnant platitude to offer: the logic of the procedure should correspond to the logic of the argument in which it is embedded. Even in elementary descriptive statistics, each procedure has its own logic and limitations. One extreme value can easily produce an apparently important difference between the means of two distributions which are otherwise substantially the same; the median behaves rather differently. And even the simpler statistics of inference and relationship incorporate varying models of the world as well as varying conceptions of agreement, chance, or causality. There is no way the historian can saunter up to the computer, plug in his file, and walk away with an all-purpose statistical analysis in his fist. Statistics do not supplant thought; they sharpen it.

Not everyone believes that. Louis Chevalier, on whose earlier work I have relied so heavily in this survey of quantitative sources and quantification, has recently issued a series of warnings against numerology in history. "The intrusion into history," he says, "of disciplines and especially of quantitative techniques alien to history is generally accompanied by a pseudo-scientific presentation, with references to concepts borrowed from elsewhere, which cannot even render history the service rendered in the fable by the blind man to the paralytic, and by a ponderous, codified text, whose contents no one will ever check and which testifies, in the absence of scholarship, to the author's determination" (1.031, p. 797). In his recent, brilliant book, *Les parisiens,* Chevalier goes on to reject even those forms of quantification which grow from within the discipline itself. The following passage refers to a survey done in Aubervilliers:

> Finally, instead of displaying our cumbersome measurements and proofs, instead of dissecting our patients in the usual way, in horizontal slices— demographic, economic, and other kinds—and weighing the pieces on properly verified scales, we shall be satisfied to tell the tale and to choose the facts, the figures or just the responses which best summarize the conclusions of our survey on which all the researchers were agreed. It sometimes happens (for periods before our own and also at times for our own time) that the novel, especially the Parisian novel, takes the place of history and of sociological description, nothing being less fictional than some works of fiction. Likewise, contemporary social research has no chance to survive or even to exist unless it borrows its procedures from the novel or, at least, goes up to the point at which the novel begins. [1.030, pp. 43–44]

Indeed, Chevalier's *Parisiens* presents a startling contrast to his number-jammed early writings on the city; Balzac and Zola elbow out the census.

For my part, I love Balzac and Zola. *Le père Goriot* and *Germinal* will far outlive the statistical scribblings of the nineteenth century. They are both works of art and stores of acute observation of social life—thank goodness the two are not incompatible! One of the great merits of Chevalier's earlier *Classes laborieuses et classes dangereuses* (1.028), however, was to show how much inspiration Balzac, Zola, and other nineteenth-century chroniclers of the city drew from the statistical inquiries of their contemporaries. The inspiration is still there.

Today's historians have no doubt engaged in a certain amount of heedless, and even erroneous, quantification; my review of French quantitative work has touched on a few such extravagances. Quantification couples its benefits with large risks, and this survey has identified some of them. Yet the French experience of the last few decades points to the capacity of intelligent quantification to renew, clarify, and enrich history. We could have drawn the same lesson from recent exploits in Chinese history, where numerical description and analysis are helping students reconstruct population and social structure over vaster expanses of space and time than French historians ever dream of. Or Latin American history, where questions about racial composition, urbanization, population growth, and economic structure are compelling historians both to quantify and to broaden their conceptions of history itself, could have illustrated the promise of quantification. Although many historians remain dubious, few fields of history are now untouched by quantitative procedures.

The fundamental division of tactics and opinion among today's students of French history is not between quantifiers and qualifiers; it is between those whose inquiries begin with the questions of economics, demography, or some other generalizing discipline outside history and those who draw their quantitative questions from the logic of historical inquiry itself. I imagine that within a generation the same will be true through most of the historical profession. We must hope for a synthesis and fear a schism. In any case, we can be sure that disagreements among the proponents of both procedures will rage for years to come, reshaping historiography in France and elsewhere. The debaters will rarely debate *whether* to quantify; they will, instead, argue over what, when, how, and to what end.

NOTES

1 Lawrence Stone, *The Crisis of the Aristocracy, 1558–1641* (Oxford: Oxford University Press, Clarendon Press, 1965), pp. 3–4.
2 These bald assertions rest on data from a survey of about 600 members of twenty-nine departments of history in distinguished United States colleges and universities. The survey was conducted in 1968 under my direction for the Behavioral and Social Science Survey of the National Academy of Sciences and the Social Science Research Council. See David S. Landes and Charles Tilly, eds., *History as Social Science* (Englewood Cliffs, N.J.: Prentice-Hall, Inc., 1971).
3 These difficulties of reporting, although part of the lore of criminologists, have apparently failed to get much attention from French historians of crime, judging by the work of such authors as Bercé (1.008).

Note: Bibliography for this chapter is included in "A Selected Bibliography of Quantitative Sources for French History and French Sources for Quantitative History since 1789," by Louise and Charles Tilly, pp. 157–75 below.

4

MATERIALS OF THE QUANTITATIVE
HISTORY OF FRANCE SINCE 1789

by Louise A. Tilly

French historians have been counting things for years, with greater zeal and ingenuity than their Anglo-Saxon confreres. First they counted men. Early in the eighteenth century, informed estimates and speculations concerning France's demographic history and resources began to appear, written by such men as Vauban, Saugrain, Moheau, and Messance. Soon they tried to count men's deeds and misdeeds. Necker gave an early dignity to quantitative reporting of the nation's condition. The regional *statistique* was already a fashionable form of publication at the end of the eighteenth century. By the time of the July Monarchy, dozens of so-called moral statisticians were actively enumerating vice, crime, and working conditions in France. Balzac, Sue, Hugo, and other novelists of the time, as Louis Chevalier has pointed out, relied heavily on the moral statisticians for inspiration and material.

The professional historians, it is true, were slower to build quantities and quantification into their work. Levasseur's rich and still-useful historical studies of the French population and labor force (3.010; 3.011),* which began to appear in the 1880s, belong to a rather different genre from the dominant historical writings of his time: Fustel de Coulanges, Aulard, Renan. Only after 1920 did the influence of André Siegfried, Georges Lefebvre, François Simiand, and Ernest Labrousse make numbering a feature of the standard French historical style. Now readers of French doctoral theses in history expect them to be laden with tables, graphs, and spot maps. Since the Second World War, we have become familiar not only with

---

* Citations in this form refer to "A Selected Bibliography of Quantitative Sources for French History and French Sources for Quantitative History since 1789," by Louise and Charles Tilly (pp 157–75 below). In this case the two major works by Levasseur are items 010 and 011 under heading 3, "Compendia of Sources," hence they are identified as 3.010 and 3.011.

the bulky Sixième Section volume, dragging its statistical appendixes behind it, but also with several competing varieties of quantitative history. In short, there is no shortage of numbers in contemporary French historical research and writing.

As a consequence, my review of quantitative sources for French history and of French sources for quantitative history can rely on real examples. There is much more to be done (and some of the failures and gaps in French quantitative history are especially instructive), but at least we have a lengthy, varied experience to draw on. My study falls into two major sections: (1) experience with quantification in French history, and (2) a survey of quantitative sources. Quantitative sources are there; French historians are using them. The exciting work being done lies in the area of bringing together sources and problems.

Although Americans are still issuing manifestos on behalf of—or against —quantitative history, none of these assertions will bother many French historians. As Albert Soboul says, "Today, except for a few minor qualifications, the case has been won. The necessity for statistical data becomes more and more obvious: is there anything that people don't seek to enumerate, or measure? Men, their occupations or their income, the distribution of property and wealth, their social relations and behavior, their political opinions as well as their religious practice. Every human activity provides a grip for a quantitative analysis; it is the only effective way of going beyond the individual to conclusions of general significance" (2.087, p. 15). Then, however, Soboul goes on to warn against ripping the numbers from their context and regarding them as the sole, full reality. There the inquiry gets tricky. In French history, the question is no longer whether to quantify— it is when, and how.

EXPERIENCE WITH QUANTIFICATION IN FRENCH HISTORY

French historians have already accumulated plenty of experience in quantitative history. My review of that experience will emphasize not the collection of quantitative data as such but the major changes in the historical use of quantitative data. The review falls into three parts: a chronological summary, a report of a small survey of recent important historical work, and a discussion of the present state of the question.

The History of Quantitative History

The political arithmeticians of the seventeenth century were no doubt the earliest to conceive of the statistical method, based on mathematical analysis of large numbers of cases, as opposed to the case-study method. Within the time span we are considering, however, the nineteenth-century moral statisticians mark the beginning. They were largely concerned with measuring or analyzing development and change in their own society. Guerry, for example, dealt mainly with official statistics on crime, suicide, marriage, divorce, and education. Quetelet, a Belgian whose work was more theoretical than Guerry's, had a greater influence in France through his contacts with the Ecole Polytechnique. He argued, among other basic notions, that social organizations were the cause of regularity in personality types and that statistical comparison of large numbers of individual actions was the proper method for studying human actions. Taking from astronomy the term *system*, Quetelet postulated a social system as an integrated unit which generates its own rates or probabilities of social facts independently of other factors. And although Le Play was not an exponent of quantitative methods (in fact, he upheld a monographic approach and personal collection of field data), he did emphasize measurement and selection of facts, thus contributing to later concepts of statistical sampling or indexing. Because he was only a wavering believer in empirical procedures, however, and regularly used his data in a polemical fashion, he had little direct impact on later quantitative sociology.

A second generation of statisticians were contemporaries of Durkheim. Jacques Bertillon's work was directly influenced by the work of Quetelet and of Bertillon's own father, who was director of the statistical bureau of the city of Paris. Bertillon himself also served in this post. He was one of several bureaucrats involved in the collection of statistics in this period who worked out techniques for analyzing large-scale data to throw light on a variety of social questions. His *Cours élémentaire de statistique administrative* (1895) sketched organizational guidelines for statistical bureaus and methods for collecting and analyzing data. Gabriel Tarde, in his later years director of the criminal statistics section of the Ministry of Justice in Paris, developed a more sweeping, explanation-seeking brand of sociology; but he also sought out empirical, quantifiable indicators. His works on the "laws" of imitation and conflict were buttressed by time series and comparative statistics. Durkheim's work grew out of that of the moral statisticians, building the concept of measuring social phenomena into sociological theory. He tried to apply the principles of natural scientific method to social facts, insisting on exact definitions, comparisons, and measurements and breaking down phenomena or situations into single elements or indexes.

Durkheim's influence on sociology was vast and profound; he also influenced developments in history in crucial ways. François Simiand put forward the social scientific method as a tool for history in an attack on the currently influential conception of history (epitomized by Charles Seignobos). Seignobos conceived of history as a verifiably objective description of political facts isolated from their economic and social context. In 1903, Simiand threw down a methodological challenge to the Seignobos school in a famous article which attacked the "idols" of history: acceptance of periodization without consideration for its significance; and concentration of interest on politics and persons rather than on nonpolitical or apolitical groups, institutions, or phenomena. The method he proposed was based on rigorous definitions, careful collection and measurement of data, statistical analysis of changes over time and correlations, and a careful approach to causality, as opposed to more general antecedents. Simiand's convictions of the overpowering validity of his method led to the statement, not dissimilar to claims of the advanced cliometricians of today, that "history, not in the sense of an auxiliary discipline and the grouping of materials, but as an autonomous science complete in itself, has no reason for existence and is bound to disappear: it has no explanatory method of its own" (2.086, p. 483). Thus he claimed that the quantitative measurement which Durkheim had prescribed as the appropriate method of social science was equally applicable to historical questions.

Simiand's monumental work on wages *Le salaire, l'évolution sociale, et la monnaie* [1.120]) and his influential description of long and short economic cycles (*Fluctuations économiques à longue période et la crise mondiale* [1.119]), both published in 1932, were almost contemporaneous with the youthful work of Camille-Ernest Labrousse, who is today the dean of French quantifying historians (*Esquisse du mouvement des prix et des revenus en France au XVIIIe siècle* [1.074]. In Labrousse, familiar methodological concerns appear: defining and measuring "seasonal, yearly, year-to-year, cyclical, intercyclical, long term, very long term . . . fluctuations" (1.073, p. iii). Once economic fluctuations and their social effects had been sketched, patterns discerned, and their explanations proposed, Labrousse sent his students to the various regions of France to buttress his arguments with detailed local data. Although they do not deal with our postrevolutionary period, the great theses of Goubert, Baehrel, and LeRoy Ladurie must be mentioned as influenced by Labrousse's inspiration and direction; sometimes, as in the case of Baehrel, they even turn up data which challenge the master's theories.

In 1955, at the Tenth International Congress of Historical Sciences, Labrousse proposed a group effort to define and trace the French bourgeoisie over the years 1700–1850. He recalled Georges Lefebvre's advice in 1939 to abandon the task of defining the bourgeoisie as a whole and instead concentrate on building a workable definition by aggregating the separate elements which careful evaluation indicated should be included. Labrousse suggested

—counting, classifying by occupation,
—ranking within occupations,
—comparing and ranking from occupation to occupation,
—or regrouping hierarchically,
—all or part of the categories labeled "bourgeois." [2.057, p. 369]

He then supported this summation by a survey of sources available for a quantitative treatment of the question. The sources were grouped as follows:

(1) electoral records, especially voters' lists from the period of the franchise limited by tax-paying qualification; (2) fiscal records (*capitation, taille* rolls, notarial registrations for the Old Regime), direct tax records (such as death tax and registration for the postrevolutionary period); (3) demographic records, the *état-civil*, censuses and other counts, army recruitment records.

Since 1955, another group of theses (for example, those of Daumard, Bois, Dupeux, Tudesq) have given evidence of the fruitfulness of this approach. Labrousse is still advising young historians to look beyond the monographic study in depth of a given place at a given time: "make geographical sacrifices to maintain chronological ambitions"; look for comparable long series, "work preferably in a locality for which long, multiple sources, more or less comparable, are available. . . . I seek ways of resolving our difficulties—in the plurality of sources, methods, and conceptions, and in the refined interpretation of positive or negative findings" (2.057, pp. 110–12).

The postwar Labrousse is concerned with the comparative aspect of Durkheimian method. This aspect was largely overlooked by Simiand but taken up by the more influential Marc Bloch and the entire school of the *Annales*. Bloch and Lucien Febvre, who founded the *Annales d'histoire économique et sociale* in 1929, wished to stimulate a more analytic approach to history, despite an invocation of "collective mentalities" which recalled an older *Geisteswissenschaft*. Foregoing Simiand's rigorous quantitative methods, they went back to Durkheim's emphasis on comparison of cases as a substitute for the experimental method of physical science.

The *Annales* also promoted a broad geographical and temporal range of approaches and subjects, as well as interdisciplinary studies to achieve "a broader and more humane history." The eclectic openness of the *Annales* meant that, from volume 1 on, articles with quantitative data would appear regularly. Bloch himself combined criticism of Simiand's lack of comparative perspective with this assessment of the importance of his work: "The day when there are in our universities, for the use of apprentice historians, practical exercises in statistics . . . one can well imagine the two fundamental diagrams of M. Simiand proposed as explanatory texts, texts sometimes difficult for still inexpert eyes, but profoundly instructive" (2.007, 2:897).

One of the great contemporaries and successors of Simiand, Bloch, and Febvre was Georges Lefebvre, whose long, productive years at the historian's craft produced and encompassed many changes in quantitative history. His *Paysans du Nord pendant la Révolution française* (1.082) linked social and economic structures of prerevolutionary rural France in a study of the distribution of landholding. He spent years studying, and directing students in the study of, the sale of the confiscated church and noble property; his hope was to describe for all France the effect of the French Revolution on the structure of property throughout France. Lefebvre also inspired historians to examine the role of ordinary people in history: "a return to Michelet, but enlightened, renewed by recourse to Marx, at least to certain aspects of sociological Marxism" (1.075, p. 3). Finally, in his last work, *Etudes orléanaises* (1.080), published in 1962 but for which some of the original research had been done over forty years before, Lefebvre opened methodological pathways to social historians through his use of tax records to reconstruct the social structure of the Revolutionary period.

Quantitative historical research in France has been and is at present being carried on most vigorously in a group of autonomous institutes. They are all independent of the universities, responsible directly to ministries, and primarily oriented toward research rather than teaching a course of study. The Ecole Pratique des Hautes Etudes, founded in 1867, was promoted (especially after the disaster of 1870) as the French vehicle for the current German conception of scholarship and research. It serves as an administrative link among specializing institutes, provides support for research seminars and research facilities, and offers student fellowships and posts for advanced scholars. Historians are most familiar with its Sixth Section, Sciences Economiques et Sociales, which contains Fernand Braudel's Centre de Recherches Historiques; in addition, there are five other autonomous sections, each topped by its own council of scholars.

The Fondation Nationale des Sciences Politiques (FNSP), inspired by André Siegfried, has been active in sponsoring work in political geography. In the postwar period François Goguel has organized projects comparing regional political complexion, exemplified by electoral behavior, and social and economic characteristics of the various regions. The FNSP has issued a long series of monographs (Cahiers de la Fondation Nationale des Sciences Politiques), many of which deal quantitatively with historical subjects. It also sponsors a very useful periodical bibliography, the *Bulletin analytique de documentation politique, économique, et sociale contemporaine* (2.098).

In work growing out of political geography, Gabriel Le Bras, the former doyen of the law faculty at the University of Paris and the foremost French sociologist of religion, compared religious practice and votes. Le Bras, whose wide-ranging work also embraces canon law and other branches of the law, has also worked within the Ecole Pratique des Hautes Etudes in both the Sixth Section and the Section for Religious Studies.

In the immediate postwar period, French politicians became concerned with population weakness—qualitative as well as quantitative—and therefore created a special institute in 1945 for the study of population "as an indispensable condition for national recovery." Much of the work of the Institut National des Etudes Démographiques (INED) has been contemporary, as in the careful analysis of recent censuses. Men like Charles Pouthas (1.102) and Abel Châtelain (2.018), however, have used older censuses and other population counts or estimates for historical analysis.

Louis Chevalier, working within the INED as well as at the Collège de

France, has produced a very different sort of demographic history in his *Classes laborieuses et classes dangereuses* (1.028). On the one hand, he paid much attention to literary sources; on the other, he challenged traditional history for its shortcomings while proposing his "biological" demography as the appropriate method for study of the past. Braudel wrote that Chevalier was claiming that "profundities [of the past] are accessible to demography, not to history or economics, which reveals the 'organized community' . . . these statistics do not merely supplement history . . . they extend and transform it" (2.011, pp. 513, 515). But, declared Braudel, Chevalier was beating a dead horse; French history had left behind the traditional forms he attacked. Chevalier's conception of demography goes beyond ordinary definitions. In proportion to results to date, however, his claims are extravagant. In any case, he now seems to have abandoned his proposals for biodemographic history in favor of an antiquantitative cultural history (1.030).

Louis Henry, also associated with the INED, has developed a method of reconstructing family units of the past using baptism, burial, and marriage notations in parish registers, many of which are available after the middle of the seventeenth century (2.034; 2.055). This careful, often tedious recording of the vital events of seventeenth-, eighteenth-, and nineteenth-century families has revealed important characteristics of demographic change, many of them departing strikingly from traditional views of early modern demography. An early criticism by René Baehrel, vigorously questioning the technique, was brushed off by Henry, who nevertheless did not explain why some of the key information to be gathered and basic techniques employed are distrusted or considered misleading by other demographers (2.002; 2.003).

Another important research center is the Institut des Sciences Economiques Appliquées (ISEA), headed by François Perroux. At the ISEA, Jean Marczewski, with what seems to some French economic historians an excessively narrow view of quantitative history, is heading a team of scholars whose goal (following national accounts procedures) is to assemble long aggregate time series portraying the French economy since 1700 (2.068). So far, the works on population and agricultural production have appeared (1.129; 1.130)—to the quick dismay of some reviewers. Pierre Chaunu wrote, "The undeniable progress in conceptualization of the problem is paid for by a fantastic regression in the order of statistical material employed. . . . The intelligent compilations of Toutain are wiped out by the gigantic ambitions of the manifesto; the long-term work plan of Jean Marczewski is undermined by the hasty execution of the plan" (2.020, p. 172; cf. 2.064). The debate, obviously, continues.

The Institut National de la Statistique et des Etudes Economiques (INSEE) is the postwar successor to the Statistique Générale, charged with statistical collection, analysis, and presentation for the government. Within it, Edmond Malinvaud's project (part of an international series edited by Moses Abramovitz and Simon Kuznets) is mostly concerned with analysis of French economic growth since World War II, but there will be historical annexes tracing economic growth back to 1896.

Recent Quantitative Work

To see more precisely how and how often quantitative material is used in current French historical writing, I conducted an elementary survey. I classified the major books on postrevolutionary France reviewed in the *Revue d'histoire moderne et contemporaine* and its *Bulletin* in 1966, 1967, and the first half of 1968 according to whether or not they involved substantial quantification. I eschewed the *Annales* in favor of a more traditional journal, in order not to bias the list toward quantitative works.

Most of the quantification was descriptive and simple in conception, but there was a great deal of it, some of which represented an enormous amount of work. The breakdown by field is given in table 4.1. The categories in the table are rough. For example, I have classified Tudesq's works as economic/social, but there is a case to be made for calling them collective biography or political history. I have called Willard's thesis on the Guesdists political because it deals with party history, but it contains a great deal of quantitative information on the economic characteristics of areas of Guesdist strength and on the social composition of the party.

Table 4.1

Orientation of Current French Historical Writing

	Nonquantitative (no. of vols.)	Quantitative (no. of vols.)
Political history	5	1
Military history	3	0
Biography	5	0
Economic/social	1	11
Intellectual	4	0
Religious	1	0
Total	19	12

Table 4.1 has two interesting points to it. The first is the sample observation that almost two-fifths of the major historical works in this period involved substantial quantification (by which I mean that an important part of the argument depended on the quantitative material and that the book contained a considerable amount of quantitative information presented as such rather than inserted incidentally into the argument). The second is that the quantitative works were almost entirely in economic and social history. Those are, of course, the fields in which the influences of the *Annales* and the Sixième Section have been most felt.

The frequency of quantification appears much greater if we consider only the eight theses on the list. This information is given in table 4.2. The numbers are too few on which to base sweeping analysis. Nevertheless, they fit in with my general impression of French historical work since World War II. The contemporary French historian's thesis subject is likely to be in social or economic history, which involves him in extensive, although not necessarily complicated, quantification.

Table 4.2

Orientation of Eight Recent French Historical Theses

	Nonquantitative (no. of vols.)	Quantitative (no. of vols.)
Political history	1	1
Military history	0	0
Biography	1	0
Economic/social	0	5
Intellectual	0	0
Religious	0	0
Total	2	6

The theses reviewed were:

Gerbod, *La condition universitaire en France au XIXe siècle* (1.055).
Ibarrola, *Structure sociale et fortune mobilière et immobilière à Grenoble en 1847* (1.068).
Lévy-Leboyer, *Les banques européennes* (1.085).
Sorlin, *Waldeck-Rousseau* (1.124).
Tudesq, *Les conseillers généraux en France au temps de Guizot, 1840–1848* (1.131).
———, *Les grands notables en France, 1840–1849* (1.132).
Vasseur, *Les débuts du mouvement ouvrier dans la région de Belfort-Montbéliard, 1870–1914* (1.133).
Willard, *Le mouvement socialiste en France, 1893–1905. Les Guesdistes* (1.138).

The nonquantitative works are Sorlin's biography of Waldeck-Rousseau and Gerbod's study of university professors, although the latter includes mapping of geographical origins of the men under discussion and occasional tables for such topics as the numbers of candidates for the various degrees. Of the others, Ibarrola's book (following the lead of Mlle Daumard) is based on death registrations of property, but for a very limited period and a small city. Willard combines a brief biography of Jules Guesde, a narrative history of the Parti Ouvrier Français, extensive regional analysis of the economic status of party members, and comparisons of general economic structure and labor force of regions where the party was strong; his thesis is complete with tables, graphs, and maps. Vasseur does a somewhat similar charting of union membership, economic indicators, and the social situation, but for a small region. Maurice Lévy-Leboyer's thesis is both sweeping and thorough. He examines the origins of French industry before 1848 with the central question in mind, Why did France lag, compared to Britain and Belgium, in the early stages of industrialization? Some familiar themes are covered, such as the economic consequences of the revolution and the Napoleonic wars, but most impressive is the freewheeling way Lévy-Leboyer assembles information about industry and enterprise and links it, by way of banking history, with the financial situation of the economy. The exhaustive footnotes of *Les banques européennes* are a capsule introduction to a great range of quantitative sources for nineteenth-century economic and social history.

The Question of Quantification Today

Today's French historians have accepted Georges Lefebvre's dictum: to describe is not enough; one must count. Adeline Daumard and François Furet wrote confidently in 1959: "Scientifically speaking, there is no social history except quantitative history. On this point, agreement is almost unanimous. But it is necessary to find, and then exploit, documents which while amenable to quantification are nevertheless complex enough to describe a variety of occupational and family structures" (2.028, p. 676). And Mademoiselle Daumard insisted that "statistics, when they rest on a secure base, are preferable to the 'typical case' which may always be exceptional" (1.035, p. xv). Quantitative data, as far as most French historians are concerned, are a vital part of history; the questions that divide the historians grow out of and beyond this agreement. How far should analysis of quantitative information go? What are the proper techniques for analysis? What methods can historians use to approximate the controls and experimentation of the hard sciences on the data they are using? What are the ultimate objectives of history, and, ultimately, what is history?

Starting with the last question first, here is an unequivocal statement from Fernand Braudel, Ernest Labrousse, and Pierre Renouvin: "History is a social science: it may be defined, after a fashion, as the study of the social timespan [*duration*]. By virtue of this, it is linked to the other sciences of man, its neighbors, attentive to their research, but offering them, or capable of offering them, its services" (2.014, p. 36). The dominance of the social-scientific concept of history is clear in most of the articles in Braudel's *Annales*. This statement, however, is from the *Revue historique,* a journal with a more eclectic orientation; and the signature of Renouvin, political and diplomatic historian par excellence, underscores its significance. As one historian of history wrote:

> We seem to have arrived today at the point where some ask if there exists a real difference of nature between history and sociology. . . . The quarrel of the theme "continuous history"—"discontinuous sociology"

has been simmering long . . . and if history claims, following Lucien Febvre and Fernand Braudel, the quality of "science of the present," it will perhaps not distinguish itself any longer from sociology except by that greater exigency towards the temporal of which Pierre Vilar speaks. [2.047, p. lv]

The convergence of the comparative method and quantification in a kind of checks-and-balances method for history as social science seems to be the major direction of French historical thinking today. The comparisons are on all levels and in all dimensions: Daumard and Furet, once again, feel that multiple sources are crucial: "One must multiply the points of view, search out . . . [and] if necessary sample, when abundance of sources imposes it, all the categories of sources left by the past" (2.029, p. 293). They wrote this in reply to Tirat's criticism of their method—a criticism on both nonquantitative (the neglect of qualitative factors) and quantitative grounds (the need for temporal comparisons and simultaneous use of a range of different documents) (2.090, pp. 211–18). In the main, however, Tirat takes the utility of quantification for granted; he calls for more types of data and for their comparative use. Likewise, Dupeux stresses the importance of integrating multiple quantitative sources into a single analysis of social structure. Demographic and electoral archives, he writes, should in principle be used as mutual controls, although (as he learned to his pain) the principle is easier to advocate than to follow (1.044, pp. 17–18).

In addition to insisting on the comparative use of multiple sources, today's French quantifiers often urge extensive comparisons over space and time and the simultaneous application of the procedures of several disciplines. Chaunu has recently summed up the main drift of such advice: "History, an auxiliary science, gives to the sciences of man in the present that depth in time which, when truly integrated, is the most secure alternative to experimentation" (2.020, p. 171).

The multidisciplinary approach can be seen also in terms of the contrast between *structure*—the long-standing, slow-changing setting in which events happen—and *conjoncture*—the more dynamic picture of the modification and change of a situation at a given time and place. In the introduction to his thesis on Catalonia, Pierre Vilar describes his arrival at a broad comparative view of history by means of his intellectual biography. He relates a pilgrim's progress from geography into economic and social history against the disturbed background of Spain and France in the 1930s and 1940s. His view of quantitative history is broader than Simiand's, but his claims are similar: "Quantitative history, having made its case, tends towards a *total* history" (1.135, 1:17). Again, it is Braudel to whom we turn for the exaltation of this approach. To him, "history is the sum of all possible histories, a collection of skills and points of view, of yesterday, today, and tomorrow" (2.012, p. 734).

Given their acceptance of quantification and their definition of history as social science, the reaction of the French economic historians to Marczewski's quantitative history might seem surprising. But Marczewski, it must be remembered, attacked them, dismissed their work as "timid and fragmentary," and set up his own concept as the only quantitative history. Quantitative history, he wrote, is "a method of economic history which integrates all the facts studied in a system of interdependent accounts and which pulls out conclusions in the form of quantitative aggregates determined entirely and uniquely by the givens of the system" (2.068, p. 15). From this will come an aggregative history, not applicable to isolated historical facts or heroes but describing groups of men over long periods of time.

To the attack (against Marczewski) and defense (of history) went Chaunu, who used the term *serial history* for the attempt of historians to construct series, limited in time and place by their subject matter and sources, but nevertheless quantitative in nature (2,020). Marczewski, less aggressive in his rebuttal, accepted a kind of serial history as the first step toward his quantitative history; but he struck out at monographic "histoire ponctuelle," which is precise but limited in time and space (2.068, pp. 48 ff.).

Vilar, also hostile to Marczewski's claims, tried to delimit the adjacent disciplines of quantitative history and retrospective economics. He conceded that history has no technique to offer to the social sciences, but it has a mode of analysis of social materials which can substitute for experimentation. He objects to the exorbitant claims of Marczewski for his quantitative history but accepts the national-accounts model as a legitimate approach to the economy of the past. To Vilar, Marczewski's work is "retrospective econometrics, in the service of economic analysis, which employs the historical technique for self-enlightenment" (2.096, p. 303). The method of criticism and weighing of sources is what the historian's craft can offer, says Vilar, but the new quantitative history of Marczewski fails to use this method. It goes beyond its sources, deducing its model and building it far beyond the legitimate deductions from its documentation. "A series serves the historian when it exhausts the possibilities of a source and does not go beyond it" (2.096, p. 305). The lines are clearly drawn. Vilar questions whether the new concepts of quantitative history add anything to the historian's knowledge based on the old-fashioned kind of quantification.

This very point, however, turned on its head, has been the most recent argument for a tentative acceptance of Marczewski's work. Denis Richet writes, "Although these reservations are serious, they do not carry conviction unless one can distinguish an astonishing discordance between the results already obtained by the 'quantitative' method and the accumulating facts of 'serial' history. To judge by those which have been written for the eighteenth century—agriculture and population—it is of agreement and confirmation that we must speak" (1.107, p. 784). However, disagreement continues over Toutain's eighteenth-century figures (1.129; 1.130), and

LeRoy Ladurie continues the historians' attack, essentially accusing Toutain of lack of historical perspective and dependence on unreliable sources (2.064). For the nineteenth century, however, the newly constructed time series of Lévy-Leboyer (1.086), compared to those of Marczewski, do not lead to any serious reevaluations.

Nothing like this grand debate has enlivened the literature of demographic, social, or political history so far. One might expect the argument to spread to those fields of inquiry, for they too are experiencing a division between those who are mainly interested in borrowing procedures from the social sciences in order to understand French history better and those who are more concerned to test general sociological hypotheses by the case of France. Vilar could well have spoken of Henry as doing "retrospective demography" or of Furet as doing "retrospective sociology."

As students of contemporary political change turn to the comparative study of the European historical experience (something I expect to happen increasingly in years to come and which Juan Linz advocates forcefully in chapter 5 of this volume), the complaints and counter-complaints will most likely become more common. The two sorts of enterprise need not be contradictory, and they may well enhance each other. Yet their coexistence in other parts of history has ordinarily produced a good deal of strain and misunderstanding. The discussion between retrospective econometrics and economic history is only the opening round of a long debate.

A SURVEY OF SOURCES

My own inventory of quantitative sources deals almost entirely with materials which historians have actually used in numerical form and stresses those which are either readily quantifiable in the present state of the art or already available as statistics. For convenience, I have worked from a classification developed by Wilbert Moore for assembling comparable social indicators for twentieth-century nations (2.071). Moore's classification has a contemporary slant, giving such categories as mass media rather more space than a historian of preceding centuries would assign to them. It also stresses the variables which economists, sociologists, and demographers find most fascinating, at the expense of important features of political structure. I have therefore modified Moore's categories to meet the needs of this inventory.

This is the modified outline used in my review of sources:

I. Productive organization and economic structure
  A. Factors of production
    1. Land—structure of property
    2. Capital
      a) Wealth and savings

        b) Industrial plant
        c) Housing
        d) Capital in agriculture
     3. Labor
        a) Labor force composition
        b) Conditions of labor
          (1) Wages
          (2) Work relationships (intensity of work, etc.)
          (3) Unemployment
        c) Strikes and industrial conflict
     4. Resources
        a) Raw materials
        b) Energy
   B. Organization of productive units
     1. Geographical distribution
     2. Size and complexity
   C. Production
     1. Production indexes
     2. Prices
     3. Other cyclical indicators
   D. Distribution and consumption
     1. Commerce
     2. Transportation
     3. Consumption
     4. Standard of living
   E. Motivation and enterprise
 II. Demographic and ecological structure
   A. Population size and growth
   B. Vital statistics
   C. Migration
     1. Internal
     2. External
   D. Urbanization
III. Social structure
   A. Family and kinship
     1. Marriage
     2. Family patterns
     3. Family breakup
   B. Community organization and problems
     1. Poverty
     2. Social welfare
        a) Public assistance
        b) Hospitals
        c) Municipal pawnshops

      3. Insanity
      4. Crime
      5. Suicide
    C. Popular culture
      1. Communications, mass media
      2. Education, libraries
      3. Entertainment
      4. Folklore
    D. Interest groups and associations
    E. Religious organizations and beliefs
    F. Social stratification and mobility
IV. Organization of the state
    A. Institutions and administration
    B. Legislature
    C. Elections
    D. Personnel
      1. Elected
      2. Members of cabinets
      3. Administrative officials
    E. Taxation and government expenditure
      1. National
      2. Local
    F. Military
      1. Recruitment (except officers)
      2. Composition of officer corps, recruitment, and education of officers
    G. Other government activity and structures

I have given this outline in detail as a possible agenda for further surveys of sources. The accompanying "Selected Bibliography of Quantitative Sources for French History and French Sources for Quantitative History since 1789," by Louise and Charles Tilly (pp. 157–75 below), contains sources dealing with each of these items, but it is laid out in terms of the major headings I to IV. Likewise, my discussion will deal with the larger categories. It will move from general sources to economic structure, demographic and ecological structure, social structure, and, finally, the state.

Bibliographies, Manuals, and Compendia

The most useful general inventories of sources are by Gille (2.046), Dupeux (2.037), and Legeard (2.062). Both Gille's *Sources statistiques de l'histoire de France* and Dupeux's "Guide de recherches de sociologie électorale" arrange material topically and chronologically; they include considerable information about archival series and locations (on all levels) as well as printed volumes. Legeard's *Guide de recherches documentaires en démographie* is especially useful because it analyzes in tabular form not only the subheadings of the population censuses but also the population information in the *Annuaires statistiques*. In addition, it gives bibliographical information in all languages and lists the volumes of the *Statistique générale de la France* and the contents of the *Statistique annuelle* from 1871 to 1906. The reference librarian's standard tool (now somewhat out of date) for locating printed government documents in United States libraries, Gregory's *Serial Publications of Foreign Governments, 1815–1931* (2.054), has the most readily accessible complete analytic listing of these publications, including most that are not available in the United States. Finally, for the researcher in archives, the *Guide du lecteur* of the Archives Nationales (2.001), although not exhaustive, is a compact reference for the contents of the series of the archives.

One of the more forbidding features of the great French doctoral dissertations has tremendous value for the student of quantitative history: the bulky theses always include an extended, systematic discussion of sources, and the citations are almost always meticulous and voluminous. The theses of Dupeux, Armengaud, or Bois can be profitably read at least twice: once for the text and once for the discussion of sources, the footnotes, and the appendixes. For some purposes, the second reading will be the more valuable.

In preparing his thesis on the Alpine region during the period 1848–51, Philippe Vigier examined documents in the national archives, the archives of the Ministry of War, the Bibliothèque Nationale, communal archives, municipal libraries, archives of the Chambre de Commerce of Avignon, and private archives; he drew the largest part of his documentation from a series of departmental archives (1.134). His review of sources combines a detailed enumeration of these groups of documents plus an extensive systematic bibliography. As a result, it could serve as an excellent guide to the sources available for local and regional history under the Second Republic. As it happens, Vigier's thesis contains no more than a respectable amount of quantification. He assembled time series for such matters as changes in the silk industry's labor force in Avignon and Lyon and prepared cantonal maps of such information as election results under the Second Republic, but on the whole his quantitative analysis remains subordinate and elementary. Nevertheless, Vigier's sources from the Archives Nationales alone include a large variety of documents already in quantitative form, quantified by him, or obviously amenable to quantification. Here are some of them, with indications of the series in which they fall:

BB[6]   personal dossiers of judicial personnel
BB[18] general correspondence of the *division criminelle,* including records of arrests
BB[22] detailed dossiers of pardons and amnesties for political offenses

BB³⁰   papers of the Ministry of Justice, again including accounts of distur-
        bances and records of arrests
  C   records of the National Assembly, including both detailed minutes
        of sessions of the assembly and its committees and voluminous
        dossiers on elections and candidates
F¹b   dossiers on government personnel, including not only national and
        departmental officials but also individual communal files
 F⁷   police records of a great variety, including specially prepared *statis-
        tiques* for some of the larger rebellions
F¹⁰   regular, detailed reports of the inspectors of agriculture
F¹¹   *mercuriales* and other indications of local prices and food supply
F¹²   frequent reports on the industrial activity of different departments
        from 1846 to 1856
F¹⁴   detailed regional *états* of roads, canals, railroads
F¹⁷   periodic reports of the inspectors of public education for all parts of
        France
F¹⁸   voluminous reports on provincial newspapers and publishers, with
        special reference to their control
F¹⁹   personal files, *statistiques,* and summary reports concerning the ec-
        clesiastical personnel of the departments
F²⁰   the series actually labeled *Statistique,* which contains a great deal of
        the background data for and from censuses and tax surveys

Each of these, to be sure, presents its own problems of technique and
judgment, but discontinuity and uncertain comparability challenge the
researcher continually throughout. For all that, two things about this incomplete and casual listing are impressive: the sheer volume and variety
of the material for quantitative history, and the extent to which a centralized French administration piled up detailed information about distant
localities in its central files. Vigier, a regional historian, found most of his
documentation in departmental archives, but an indispensable portion of
it came nevertheless from the archives of Paris.

Even for local history on a smaller scale, the central archives hold much
of value. Pierre Pierrard, in his thesis on Lille during the Second Empire
(1.098), had to get around the holes left by the devastating destruction of
departmental archives during the First World War. His unpublished materials came not only from the departmental archives of the Nord but from
the municipal archives of Lille, railroad archives, records of a number of
local religious institutions, and the national archives. Pierrard quantifies
somewhat more willingly and abundantly than Vigier; his numbers tend to
fall into time series representing changes in prices or demographic transformations and into simple tabulations giving labor-force or welfare re-
cipients by period, area, or industry. He, too, finds essential parts of his

documentation in the national archives—within the same general series, in fact, as Vigier.

Compendia of statistical information are more abundant for the period after 1870. I include the histories (of the working class and of the French population) by Levasseur (3.010; 3.011) among the compendia because they reprint great extracts of source material; parts of the *enquête industrielle* of 1848, for example, appear in the appendix of his *Histoire des classes ouvrières*. And his material is largely from before 1870. The early volumes of the *Statistique de la France* (3.008) are a rich collection of detailed inquiries and statistics. Most of them appear in our bibliography under topical headings; the major exception is the first, *Documents statistiques* (3.006), which contains assorted statistics in the style of the later *Annuaires statistiques* (3.003). From 1871 to 1898, the *Statistique annuelle* (3.007) functioned as a compendium of information on population change, localities, agriculture, and industry; from 1899 to 1906, under the title *Statistique annuelle du mouvement de la population* (5.022), it contained only the vital statistics.

The *Annuaire statistique,* published annually since 1878 (except during war years), absorbed the more general items of the *Statistique annuelle;* it includes occasional retrospective volumes rich in historical statistics. The *Annuaire* is the logical starting point for quantitative research because it not only summarizes statistical information but also itemizes sources for further inquiry. The early *Annuaires* have more detailed citations of sources; they also tend not to analyze or adjust information. Thus the first *Annuaire* uses records of the octroi (municipal entry duties) in major cities to give average prices and consumption for a variety of goods. By the 1930s, statistical analysis in the *Annuaires* is much more complicated, and weighted index numbers are more typical than simple price lists. National figures and figures for Paris alone appear most commonly, but much of the material is also broken down by department. The early *Annuaires* contain more diverse and miscellaneous bits of information, such as numbers of adherents of various religious sects; the modern editions are devoted to economic information assembled according to national accounts procedures. For a quick first introduction to French quantitative materials, nothing excels an hour's browsing in one of the *Annuaire's* retrospective volumes— the one published in 1966, for example.

Since 1880, the city of Paris has had its own annual statistical report, but from 1821 to 1860 miscellaneous statistical volumes were issued under the direction of the prefect (3.013; 3.014). Departmental *annuaires* likewise contain comparable information over time: names of officials, teachers, religious associations, communal chambers of commerce, professional organizations, local associations, and the like.

So much for compendia. Let us now turn to more specialized sources, beginning with those treating productive organization and economic structure. (In the text, I shall use short titles and summary designations; complete references appear in the "Selected Bibliography," pp. 157–75 below.)

Productive Organization and Economic Structure

The principal bodies of documentation concerning economic activity available to the historian came into being as by-products of the French state's attempts to regulate or profit from that activity. Tax rolls, census schedules, records of private and commercial transactions subject to duty, and reports on strikes generally fit this pattern. As crucial as they are to economic analysis, the archives and reports of private economic organizations (firms, farm organizations, labor unions, trade associations, cooperatives, consumer groups) and the traces of individual transactions (most commonly found in family papers or notarial minutes) are naturally neither as abundant nor as accessible as the documents generated by the state. As a consequence, the available economic record is weighted toward the public activities of the economy's larger, more readily observable units. The researcher wishing to study entrepreneurial history is almost obliged to seek out the papers of firms successful enough to have remained in business in order to supplement the intermittent light cast by bankruptcy proceedings and life histories of tycoons. (The archives of nationalized firms, e.g., railroads, are sometimes available also.) The student of agrarian structure must depend to a large degree on the residues of the state's efforts to tax the land and to supervise inheritance.

The basic sources for change in the structure of property immediately after 1789—records of the sale of the *biens nationaux*—rest mainly in departmental archives, although there are numerous local studies on the subject. Likewise, the essential sources for the study of transfers of those properties after the initial sales—the *actes d'enregistrement* and notarial minutes—are widely scattered, with departmental archives the most important repositories. The same is true of the nineteenth-century cadaster (which took thirty years to prepare and therefore does not represent the property holding of any precise year). The volumes of the Statistique Générale series report on land use (3.006; 5.002). Starting in the 1840s, agricultural inquiries, including figures on land under cultivation, appeared every ten years. There were agricultural censuses in 1848 (papers lost in fire), 1892, 1929, 1942, and 1955. Special inquiries (such as that in 1908 on small property holdings) are another source of information on property and methods of exploitation.

Fiscal records reveal not only land held but also other forms of wealth of tax-paying individuals. Gonnet argues that fiscal sources include a larger sample of population than do electoral records or registration of property transfers at death—the state having extended its tax power long before it extended the franchise—and thus are more accurate for tracing social and economic structures (2.048; 2.049). But the fiscal materials actually available are scanty before 1914. The death registrations found in the departmental archives are Daumard's chief source (2.025; 2.026; 2.029; 1.036), but they refer only to property owners. Lists of voters up to and including 1848, when property restrictions were lifted, are also found in departmental archives and the Bibliothèque Nationale; they are used by both Daumard and Tudesq to trace wealth and property (1.036; 1.132). For small-scale savings and fluctuations of financial position, the savings bank (*caisse d'épargne*) deposit reports and movements of pawned objects in the *monts de piété* are available from 1835 and 1843 respectively (3.005; 4.023; 6.014; 6.023).

The basic information on labor-force composition can be gathered from industrial inquiries starting with that of 1840–45 and from censuses after 1851. The varying occupational categories and methods of recording occupations are surveyed in Dupeux's "Guide de Recherches" (2.037). There are numerous government surveys on prices and wages, starting with that of 1873, which covers retrospectively the years back to 1849 for wages. If we follow Moore and accept the level of mechanization in industry as an index of the intensity of work, the statistics on motive power would be considered under the heading of labor as well as under indexes of industrialization. Reports on industrial conflict (strikes and lockouts) can be found in the *Statistique annuelle* (3.007); later in the *Statistique des grèves* (4.013); then in the *Bulletin* of the Ministère du Travail (4.037); and, since 1946, in the ministry's *Revue française du travail* (4.052).

For productive organization and production, official series of statistics are available. The most recent works which have constructed time series from them are Lévy-Leboyer (1.086), Markovitch (2.069), and Marczewski (2.068). Information for the period before 1870 appears in several of the volumes of the Statistique générale, including agricultural and industrial inquiries, reports on mines and public works, and price information. (Industrial censuses were taken in 1840, 1861, 1864; there followed a hundred-year hiatus before the next industrial census.)

Data on the price of grain in 1835, and a series for 1756–90, for example, are found in the second volume of the Statistique générale, *Archives statistiques du ministère des Travaux publics, de l'Agriculture, et du Commerce* (3.005). Here also are found figures on silk production and domestic herds as well as lists of savings banks and corporations. (Gille's bibliography [2.046] is more extensive than ours on these matters.) There is a rich *Statistique de l'industrie minérale,* put out by the Direction des Mines, covering a good part of the nineteenth century (4.004). At times it extends to the enumeration of every steam engine in France. Summary reports on commerce, roads, and railroads appear in specialized publications; in early Statistique générale volumes; and, after 1877, in *Annuaires.* Since the information was collected locally after 1835, departmental archives also abound in these data. The *Album de statistique graphique,* issued by the

Ministère des Travaux Publics in 1900, offers graphic information on roads, railroads, bridges, and even traffic in Paris, back to 1855 or so (4.030). Renouard (1.106) provides some excellent examples of the uses of these kinds of material.

Demographic and Ecological Structure

While such problems as tracing the spread of contraception or examining the incidence of particular diseases may drive an investigator to a great variety of sources, two major varieties of documentation provide the great bulk of the available demographic evidence for France. The first is, of course, censuses of one kind or another. The second is the registration of individual vital events by the family, the church, or the state. Both these types of documents miss an unknown proportion of the population, especially among its poorest and most mobile segments. Yet the historian can get far closer to the demography of the mass of the French people than to their political participation or their economic activity. First because it was Catholic, then because it was bureaucratic, France produced and retained an impressively full and continuous demographic record. Demographic historians are now integrating that record into their historical works.

After some exceptional enumerations during the early revolutionary period, the first regular French census took place in 1801. Printed summaries from the early censuses, however, did not appear until 1837, when they formed part of the Statistique générale's third volume, *Territoire et population* (5.002). The legal population of communes, cantons, arrondissements, and departments has ordinarily been published by the Ministry of the Interior. The listings appeared in the *Bulletin des lois* through the 1866 census; the *Dénombrement* has appeared in a separate volume since 1872. Nominal lists (the actual name-by-name recording of population in communes) for the nineteenth century are often available in communal archives but not, unfortunately, in departmental or national depositories. The articles by Biraben (2.006) and Pinchemel (2.079) give bibliographical and methodological assistance in the use of the *listes nominatives*. The movement of population over time is recorded in the vital statistics reports, which summarize birth, death, and marriage registers of the *état-civil*. The population movements of the 1850s and 1860s are reported in print in the second series of the Statistique générale volumes. The handbook by Legeard (2.062) provides the best summaries of the contents of census volumes and related publications. From 1871 to 1906, the *Statistique annuelle* reported vital statistics. From 1907 on, vital statistics appeared in a volume usually called the *Statistique générale de la France,* issued at first by the Ministère du Travail.

For international migration, the figures must be gathered by indirect methods. There are no precise official statistics on movements of persons across frontiers, although there are scattered mid-nineteenth century reports on *Mouvement de l'émigration en France*. By examining population change at successive censuses and comparing it with natural increase as shown through birth and death information, some investigators have been able to estimate net migration. For internal migration, the materials are richer but harder to handle. The work of Laurence Wylie and his students on a single community of Anjou shows the possibility of analyzing migration on a local scale through a species of collective biography (1.138), and the work of Abel Châtelain on electoral records (2.018) provides a related procedure for doing this on a large scale. While relying mainly on census data concerning place of birth for later periods, Louis Chevalier has used an abstract of Parisian death records compiled for the senior Bertillon to estimate the geographic origins of immigrants of the 1820s and 1830s (1.029). Others have used changes in housing stock or the difference between intercensal natural increase and total population growth as evidence.

These studies of migration in preindustrial France have revealed surprisingly high rates of mobility, even though most movements were quite localized. The findings raise a warning about the use of individual communes as the basis of estimates of demographic characteristics and their changes in the population as a whole. Family reconstitution ordinarily excludes both mobile families and mobile members of otherwise nonmobile families as well, since the analyst uses the records of one parish or commune at a time. In their pathbreaking study of Crulai, for example, Gautier and Henry lost 311 of the 608 families in their basic sample, most of them apparently to out-migration. (This is an inference from the various numbers reported in the book; Gautier and Henry do not discuss the issue.) Most of what we know about contemporary populations leads us to expect significant differences in fertility, marriage, and other demographic characteristics between the mobile and immobile segments of the population.

Genealogies present another problem: they are drawn up retrospectively to trace the ancestry of a living person or family. Persons not in the direct line of ancestry can be excluded, and children who die in infancy are underrepresented if not totally excluded. Family reconstitution from parish registers and genealogies has a power to reach into demographic processes previously inaccessible to historical analysis. But, like other powerful quantitative techniques, it requires close attention both to its basic assumptions and to the quality of the data under analysis.

Social Structure

My definition of social stucture covers quite a range: family and kinship, community organization and problems, popular culture, interest groups and associations, religious organizations and beliefs, social stratification, and mobility. The census is the all-purpose source. This is especially true of family structure. In 1901, tables dealing with families as such first appeared in the census volumes. In 1906, 1911, 1926, 1931, and 1936, separate volumes called *Statistique des familles* were issued. Since 1946 similar information has been included in the general volumes of the census. The nominal lists of the census for each commune have more value for work on the small scale, and the same may be said for individual marriage records; both are preserved locally in city halls. These can be treated anonymously, to establish statistical trends and patterns, or individually, to reconstitute families and recreate individual family histories.

Social problems such as poverty and crime are recorded in complete statistical series going back to the 1830s and 1840s, arising out of governmental controls and assistance. The volumes of *Administrations publiques* of the Statistique générale (second series) include tables on public assistance, foundlings, public pawn shops, and similar phenomena; the original documents, in some cases, are still in departmental archives. Local administrations were also required to keep records on hospitalizations (admissions and discharges, at least), orphans, and the insane. While some of these are available in published form (see "Selected Bibliography," p. 173 below), Gille gives archival locations for administrative documents which were never published.

Crime and suicide figures are summarized in the *Annuaire statistique* for the later period, but fuller information is carried in the *Comptes rendus* of criminal justice (which go back to 1827) and of civil justice (from 1831) (6.006; 6.007; 6.008). The criminal justice statistics include tables on suicides (after 1837) and accidental deaths (after 1833).

For education, regular statistics on primary instruction were a by-product of the Guizot law of 1833. (Less complete reports had been prepared on education under the Restoration, concerning such topics as the proportion of students to the population; these became fuller in 1829 and 1830. Guizot's move toward regular statistics culminated a tendency already well under way.) Statistical *Rapports au Roi* (6.009) on primary instruction are available for the 1830s and 1840s. There is also one incomplete report on secondary instruction (6.010). Under the Second Republic, the Empire, and the Third Republic, regular statistical reporting on primary education continued. On the occasion of the 1865 Universal Exposition, university and secondary instruction were reviewed. After 1878, there are summaries of all schools series in the *Annuaire statistique*. In *La Condition universitaire* (1.055), Gerbod uses a group of publications from which names and careers of university professors and alumni of the Ecole Normale Supérieure can be traced; he employs them andecdotally, but they seem to be open to quantitative analysis too. The sources include an 1877 memorial of the Ecole Normale Supérieure reviewing careers of alumni who had died since 1848, an annual *Nécrologie* of the same school, and obituaries of university professors in the *Journal général de l'instruction publique*.

The *Annuaire statistique* gives figures for major communications media. In 1878, the telegraphic service alone is included. With time appear the telephone, the press, radio, and, finally, television.

There are few associations in which the government was sufficiently interested to keep statistical records. These do not include political parties, which have to be studied through their own archives or other sources. Some American libraries contain printed *Annuaires* of parties and other political associations, often including lists of members with their addresses and occupations. Police records (in the archives of the Paris Préfecture de Police, for example; see 2.092), of course, often contain detailed reports and enumerations of suspect and clandestine political societies.

As unions grew, the *Annuaire des syndicats* (4.007) recorded figures or supposed figures of their membership (see also the studies by Kriegel [1.071] and Prost [1.103]). The series of volumes of *Associations professionnelles ouvrières* (4.008) was a retrospective inquiry into unions up to the end of the nineteenth century, industry by industry and place by place. For further studies of working-class activism it would help to begin with the uneven, sometimes inaccurate, but still useful bibliography of *Mouvements ouvriers et socialiste* (2.074) and with Jean Maitron's *Dictionnaire biographique du mouvement ouvrier français* (6.003).

For information on religious practices, Le Bras's *Introduction à l'histoire de la pratique religieuse* (2.061) contains a bibliographical review. Statistics in official documents are limited, but religious callings are an occupational category in census reports, and religious affiliation was asked in some censuses (1851, 1861). In 1861, a special census of religious communities was also incorporated into the regular census. In episcopal archives a researcher can find pastoral visits, ordination lists, statistical information on the clergy, and the famous parish-by-parish figures of *pascalisants*. Here many of the works of Gabriel Le Bras on religious sociology and the "Notes de statistique d'histoire religieuse" of the *Revue d'histoire de l'Eglise de France* (conveniently inventoried by Dupeux [2.037]) are relevant.

There are two kinds of sources that yield names and information about individuals, which are the basic units for a collective biography approach to the history of social structure. The first is the *annuaire* or *almanach,* which may list members of a profession, an institution, or a more loosely defined group. Gaston Saffroy's *Bibliographie des almanachs et annuaires administratifs* (2.054) includes hundreds of such volumes covering a rich variety of people. There are, for example, a series of almanacs on the national guard of the revolutionary period and of the Legion of Honor at different periods. There are also numerous listings of the nobility, of which the *Annuaire de la noblesse de France* (6.001) seems to have had the longest life (1843 to 1957); even a *Société et le high-life* (6.021) was issued, complete with Paris and country addresses, from 1883 to 1950. The various annuals of government employees, elected officials, and diplomatic and officers' corps will be discussed in the last section of this chapter on organization of the state.

All archival records containing names and occupations can yield information on social stratification and mobility when used cumulatively over considerable periods of time. Notarial archives (so useful for *ancien régime* studies of this type) are less often used in nineteenth-century studies than are death registrations of property, because they represent a smaller and wealthier sample of the population. Census nominal lists, marriage contracts, and tax and military recruitment records are other possibilities for tracing class structure and mobility. Over the next few years French collective biographers, who are gaining fast in numbers and enthusiasm, are likely to develop a whole new set of procedures for linking these diverse records.

Some very serious technical problems remain to be mastered. One of them appears in Adeline Daumard's use of the *enregistrements des mutations par décès* as a source of information about family structure, levels of living, and social mobility in early nineteenth-century Paris (1.035; 2.026). She is fully aware of the drawbacks; she has weighed them and found them not to be sufficiently serious to challenge her findings. Yet they are worrisome. The first problem is that not all deaths were accompanied by a declaration of the deceased's property. Most of the nonregistrations, Mademoiselle Daumard feels, are those of children and paupers, who are of minimal importance to her inquiry. (She does, however, discuss poverty; the number of paupers' deaths was of some importance to this topic.) Furthermore, she acquires data concerning the population whose property and family structure she is analyzing at the point of death; hence the population studied is much older than the general population. If the spouse or some of the children died before the subject, they are not mentioned in the declaration. Conclusions on celibacy, marital instability, and family size are therefore unattainable. The advanced age of the persons studied probably also affects the quantity of their property and wealth. They might have more possessions than young people, newly independent in the world; or, under other circumstances, their wealth might have been whittled away by the misfortunes of old age or by inflation. Once again, the conclusion is that more powerful techniques and more complicated sources require a new body of expertise and criticism. The assumptions and inferences made in using such sources as *mutations par décès* become more delicate as they become more interesting.

Organization of the State

Although political history and political biography have been the dominant forms of history, they have by no means exhausted the possible approaches to the history of the state. If the ideal case for quantification is an attempt to explain how some quantifiable phenomenon observable for many people or groups of people changed or varied during a given historical period, the most fruitful areas for a quantitative political history are (1) elections, (2) parliamentary voting, (3) the bureaucracy and governing elite, (4) government finances, and (5) political violence and the residues of government repression. Of these, elite studies and financial analysis can be pursued quite far using mainly printed sources; electoral studies and examination of repression are dependent on archival material.

The institutional and administrative framework of the state and the way it varied over time is the essential setting for political quantification. The standard institutional histories of the revolutionary period and the nineteenth century (Godechot [1.057], Ponteil [1.101], Duverger [1.048]) can be completed by a Fifth Republic government publication, *Les institutions politiques de la France* (7.014), which brings the information up to 1958 but traces changes all the way from the *Ancien Régime*. For the administrative context, Brian Chapman's basic works, *An Introduction to French Local Government* (1.025) and *The Prefects and Provincial France* (1.026), may be bolstered by Maurice Block's *Dictionnaire de l'administration française* of 1898 (7.005). To locate towns and villages, the *Dictionnaire des communes* (3.002) has been essential; a recent pair of books, *Index-atlas des départements français* (3.009A) and *Liste alphabétique des communes et lieux-dits de France métropolitaine* (3.012), do the same job.

For legislative action as opposed to legislative personnel (which will be discussed later), the basic source is the *Journal officiel,* titled also in some periods the *Moniteur universel* (7.010). This includes reports of departmental administrations, laws and decrees, and debates of the Chamber of Deputies and the Senate up to 1881. The *Annales* of the Assemblée Nationale (7.011) report these debates after 1881. The privately published *Année politique,* for the years 1874 to 1905 (7.003), although wholly discursive, gives useful chronology of political events; and the post-1944 *Année politique, économique, sociale, et diplomatique* is more disposed to report numbers, as in roll-call votes (7.002). The *Bulletin de statistique et de législation comparée* (put out by the Ministry of Finance) includes statistical background for legislative projects and also tax, tariff, and budget information (7.031).

There is no central depository for all official election returns, and the problem of describing elections is complicated further by the looseness of party designations, continuing to a large degree into the twentieth century. Campbell (1.020) uses newspaper reports for uniform election returns, but dossiers of the individual legislative elections from 1885 to 1932 can be found in the archives of the National Assembly. For elections before that date, the Archives Nationales contain several relevant series (especially B^{II}, popular votes 1793–1851; C, *procès verbaux* of the Assemblées Nationales; and F^{1cII} and F^{1cIII}, departmental reports on "esprit public et élections").

Dupeux discusses these thoroughly in his "Guide de recherches" (2.037); his thesis on the Loir-et-Cher is a model of effective use of electoral archives together with economic and social information (1.044). To gauge each deputy's political position in the absence of, or in addition to, party designations, there are in print the *Programmes, professions de foi, et engagements électoraux* of the deputies, also known as the "Barodets" (7.012); these are available in the New York Public Library for at least some of the years from 1881 to 1919, and there is a complete set in the archives of the National Assembly. A "Table analytique des *Annales de la Chambre des Députés*," also in the Assembly archives, gives information on each deputy's parliamentary activity, speeches, committee memberships, bills introduced, and so on. More information on candidates is in departmental archives.

Personal information about the legislators of France is available in the *Dictionnaire des parlementaires français* (7.007; 7.008). The first series of five volumes covers 1789–1889; the second series covers 1889–1940, but volumes 1–4, which have been published to date, go only through the letter *D*. In addition, there are dossiers in the Archives Nationales on administrative officials, including departmental officers several degrees below the prefects.

Personnel—elected, cabinet, and administrative—can be traced through several printed listings of officeholders: the *Almanach royal*, later *Almanach national*, published continuously from the last years of the reign of Louis XIV (1700) to 1919, is filled with names (7.001). The nineteenth-century volumes I have examined list all members of the legislature and cabinets; high administrators, including departmental officers; and, for Paris, professional men (notaries, lawyers, doctors, and even members of chambers of commerce). From 1919, the *Annuaire général* filled a similar role in listing personnel of government, but after 1926 increased listings on foreign countries led to decreased richness of detail on France (7.004). Colonial administrators and diplomats can be traced through similar annual registers: the *Annuaire colonial* (1887–97) (7.027; 7.028), the *Annuaire du Ministère des Colonies* (1898–) 7.029, and the *Annuaire diplomatique et consulaire* (1858–) (7.026). The *Annuaire agricole, commercial, et industriel des colonies françaises* (7.028) gives information from 1887 on in quite minute detail, including names of colonists and their businesses, especially for the North African colonies.

The names and numbers of state personnel could be used in at least three ways:

1. By the technique of collective biography, the fairly simple listings could be enriched by information from other sources to build portraits of typical ministers, deputies, prefects, and ambassadors.
2. Continuity or discontinuity of governing elites over the nineteenth-

century changes in regime could be traced with little need for additional information, as some occupational data though no personal or family detail appear with many of these listings.

3. Statistical analyses of size and activity of bureaucratic cadres as they varied over time, regimes, and regions within France could be compared to indexes of industrialization, urbanization, and social change to build a quantified bureaucratic dimension of the process of modernization.

Government finances are most easily approachable through the yearly *Bulletin de statistique et de législation comparée* (7.031), although there are also much more detailed documents on receipts and expenditures in our bibliography. Regional data on taxes paid and government expenditures on local projects could be compared. For local finances, there are yearly reports for departments and communes. Paris is most richly documented, as is to be expected: there are not only the *Annuaire statistique de la ville de Paris* (3.013) since 1880 and the earlier *Recherches statistiques* (3.014), but a multivolume work on the *Régime administratif et financier de la ville de Paris et du départment de la Seine* (1.115), which is up-to-date to 1958 and maintains an historical perspective with many retrospective materials.

The citizen's obligation to military service, one of the revolutionary innovations, has generated a good deal of already-quantified material. Printed volumes of *Comptes présentés en exécution de la loi du 10 mars 1818 sur le recrutement de l'armée* (7.017) start in 1819 and continue, with title variations, to the present; a summary of the statistics can be found in the *Annuaire statistique*. Information on literacy (after 1827) and on physical stature (after 1836) is noted. Departmental archives include lists of contingents for the same periods. Adeline Daumard (1.035) has reported very full information for the Seine department in the Restoration period, giving the name and occupation not only of each recruit but of his parents as well. LeRoy Ladurie and his associates have amply catalogued the varied information available in the dossiers established for military service (1.084A). There are also annual statistics of military justice. Individual members of the officer corps of both army and navy are listed in *Annuaires* whose full titles can be found in "A Selected Bibliography" (p. 174 below).

Another category of state activity is that of the residues of repression and police activity. In order to draw up a uniform list of episodes of political violence of varying degrees, Charles Tilly's project on political disturbances in France from 1830 to 1960 found that newspapers provided a reasonable reportorial coverage. More detailed information on the clash of groups with the state monopoly of force had to be sought in archival material, however. Lists of suspects and arrest and interrogation reports are to be found in several locations. Notable among these are (1) the Archives Nationales, series F[7] and BB[18]; (2) Archives de la Préfecture de Police

(Paris), with which Tulard is working and for which he has published a partial *inventaire sommaire* (2.092; see also 2.085); (3) Archives historiques de l'Armée at Vincennes; (4) *archives hospitalières* for reports on wounded admitted, deaths, and discharges during crucial outbursts of violence. In addition, the Ministry of the Interior of the Third Republic published intriguing statistics of "foreign anarchists" and "foreigners" expelled from France from 1894 to the early 1900s (7.022; 7.023). And reports on anarchists and other suspicious characters are also preserved in departmental archives.

In some respects, almost all the sources I have reviewed provide information about the operation of the French state. Most of the documents came into being as by-products of the state's operations. Their retention and publication depended mainly on officialdom. And today the researcher still approaches the unpublished portions of the documentation through agencies and functionaries of the state. The long action of the state as filter dilutes the accessible record in ways with which we are still learning to deal. Yet the French state was and is an exceptionally active, persistent, bureaucratic seeker and recorder of the facts.

Of course, the historian must play his role of professional skeptic. As David Landes wrote in a critique of Labrousse and Chabert, "There have been few eras in world history when officials have not had one or another axe to grind, axes that tend to change with the notoriously fickle fortunes of politics and personal intrigue" (2.058, p. 202). The historian who opens official records must evaluate the reliability of the information in them, and most quantitative historians of France have taken this critical role seriously. Historians are equipped by training to study sources; the dazzling array of potential quantitative sources will be whittled down by critical examination of the worth of the information in them. For the nineteenth and twentieth centuries there will remain, nevertheless, a vast number of sources which can be used quantitatively to bring new insight to what happened in history.

A SELECTED BIBLIOGRAPHY OF

QUANTITATIVE SOURCES FOR FRENCH

HISTORY AND FRENCH SOURCES FOR

QUANTITATIVE HISTORY SINCE 1789

by Louise A. and Charles Tilly

This bibliography is meant to accompany our individual essays, "Quantification in History, As Seen from France (chap. 3 above, by Charles Tilly) and "Materials of the Quantitative History of France since 1789" (chap. 4 above, by Louise Tilly).* It can also stand alone, if people will make allowances for its origins. We have limited it to published material, with the single exception of a valuable unpublished doctoral dissertation. Attempting to inventory quantitative and quantifiable material in the archives would be an enormous undertaking. It might even be self-defeating.

The list favors serials over single volumes, books over articles, material which has already been quantified over material simply amenable to quantification. The historical works (as distinguished from sources or compendia) included consist mainly of those discussed in our two essays. We have had to slight many excellent books and thousands of relevant articles. As a result, the bibliography is somewhat better than representative, but it falls far short of being comprehensive.

We have tried to select our titles and set up the inventory so that the interested student of France can find any quantitative source of which we are aware—published or not—in no more than two steps. The first step would be to identify and examine the scholarly works (section 1), manuals (section 2), and particular sources (remaining sections) most closely related to the particular topic under investigation. The second step would be to use the inventories of sources in these works.

* We are grateful to the Center for Advanced Study in the Behavioral Sciences for free time and secretarial help and to Abdul Qaiyum Lodhi for assistance in the inventorying of sources.

ABBREVIATIONS

Annales ESC   *Annales: Economies, Sociétés, Civilisations*
       CHESR   Commission d'Histoire Economique et Sociale de la Révolution
        CNRS   Centre Nationale de la Recherche Scientifique
        FNSP   Fondation Nationale des Sciences Politiques
        INSEE   Institut National de la Statistique et des Etudes Economiques
        INED   Institut National des Etudes Démographiques
        ISEA   Institut des Sciences Economiques Appliquées
         PUF   Presses Universitaires de France
      SEVPEN   Société d'Editions et Vente des Publications de l'Education
                Nationale

1. REPRESENTATIVE SCHOLARLY WORKS USING QUANTITATIVE SOURCES

1.001   Adam, G. *Atlas des élections sociales en France.* FNSP, Cahier no. 137. Paris: Colin, 1964.

1.002   Agulhon, Maurice. *La sociabilité méridionale.* 2 vols. Aix-en-Provence: La Pensée Universitaire, 1966.

1.003   Ariès, Philippe. *Histoire des populations françaises et de leurs attitudes devant la vie depuis le XVIIIe siècle.* Paris: Editions Self, 1948.

1.004   Armengaud, André. "Histoire rurale et démographie: Les nourrices du Morvan au XIXe siècle." *Etudes et chronique de démographie historique,* 1964.

1.005   ———. *Les populations de l'Est Aquitain au début de l'époque contemporaine.* Paris: Mouton, 1961.

1.006   Baehrel, René. *Une croissance: La Basse-Provence rurale, fin XVe siècle–1789. Essai d'économie historique statistique.* Paris: SEVPEN, 1961.

1.007   Barral, P. *Le département de l'Isère sous la IIIe République. Histoire sociale et politique.* FNSP, Cahier no. 115. Paris: Colin, 1962.

1.008   Bercé, Yves-Marie. "Aspects de la criminalité au XVIIe siècle." *Revue historique* 239 (Jan.–Mar. 1968): 33–42.

1.009   Bernard, P. *Economie et sociologie de la Seine-et-Marne, 1850–1950.* FNSP, Cahier no. 43. Paris: Colin, 1953.

1.010   Blayo, Y., and Henry, L. "Données démographiques sur la Bretagne et l'Anjou de 1740 à 1829." *Annales de démographie historique,* 1967.

1.011   Bois, Paul. *Paysans de l'Ouest.* Le Mans: Vilaire, 1960.

1.012   Bomier Landowski, P. "Les groupes parlementaires de l'Assemblée Nationale et de la Chambre des Députés de 1871 à 1940." In *Sociologie électorale,* edited by F. Goguel and G. Dupeux. FNSP, Cahier no. 26. Paris: Colin, 1961.

1.013   Boulard, F. *Essor ou déclin du clergé français.* Paris: Editions du Cerf, 1950.

1.014   Bourgeois-Pichat, Jean. "La situation démographique." *Population,* vol. 1, no. 4 (1946), pp. 511–32.

1.015   Boutelet, Bernadette. "Etude par sondage de la criminalité dans le bailliage du Pont-de-l'Arche." *Annales de Normandie* 12 (1962): 235–62.

1.016 Bouvier, Jean; Gillet, Marcel; and Furet, François. *Le mouvement du profit en France au XIXe siècle.* The Hague: Mouton, 1965.

1.017 Braudel, F. *La Méditerranée et le monde méditerranéen à l'époque de Philippe II.* 2d ed. 2 vols. Paris: Colin, 1966.

1.018 Brinton, Crane. *The Jacobins: An Essay in the New History.* New York: Macmillan, 1930.

1.019 Cahen, L. "Evolution de la population active française depuis cent ans." *Etudes et conjoncture,* série rouge (Economie française), May–June, 1953, pp. 230–88.

1.020 Campbell, Peter. *French Electoral Systems and Elections since 1789.* Hamden, Conn.: Archon Books, 1965.

1.021 Canal, S. *Un département exsangue. Etudes démographiques sur le Tarn-et-Garonne.* Paris: Librairie des Etudes Sociologiques, 1934.

1.022 Capronnier, J. *Le prix des meubles d'époque, 1860–1956.* Paris: Colin, 1967.

1.023 Chabert, A. *Essai sur les mouvements des prix en France de 1798 à 1820.* Paris: Librairie de Médicis, 1945.

1.024 ———. *Essai sur les mouvements des revenus et de l'activité économique en France de 1798 à 1820.* Paris: Librairie de Médicis, 1949.

1.024A Chalmin, P. "Le remplacement dans l'armée française au XIXe siècle." *Bulletin de la Société d'histoire moderne,* 12 série, no. 10 (1959), pp. 14–16.

1.025 Chapman, Brian. *Introduction to French Local Government.* London: Allen and Unwin, 1953.

1.026 ———. *The Prefects and Provincial France.* London: Allen and Unwin, 1955.

1.027 Charlot, M., and Dupaquier, J. "Mouvement annuel de la population de la ville de Paris de 1670 à 1821." *Annales de démographie historique,* 1967, pp. 511–19.

1.028 Chevalier, Louis. *Classes laborieuses et classes dangereuses à Paris pendant la première moitié du XIXe siècle.* Paris: Plon, 1958.

1.029 ———. *La formation de la population parisienne.* Paris: PUF, 1950.

1.030 ———. *Les Parisiens.* Paris: Hachette, 1967.

1.031 ———. "A Reactionary View of Urban History." *Times Literary Supplement,* 8 September 1966, pp. 796–97.

1.032 Cobb, Richard. *Les armées révolutionnaires: Instrument de la terreur dans les départements, avril 1793–floréal an II.* 2 vols. Paris: Mouton, 1961, 1963.

1.033 Collinet, Michel. "The Structure of the Employed Classes in France during the Last Fifty Years." *International Labour Review* 67 (1953): pp. 211–35.

1.034 Cotteret, J.-M.; Emeri, C.-R.; and Lalumière, P. *Lois électorales et inégalités de représentation en France, 1936–1960.* FNSP, Cahier no. 107. Paris: Colin, 1960.

1.035 Daumard, Adeline. *La bourgeoisie parisienne de 1815 à 1848.* Paris: SEVPEN, 1963.

1.036 ———. *Maisons de Paris et propriétaires parisiens au XIXe siècle.* Paris: Editions Cujas, 1965.

1.037   ———, and Furet, F. *Structures et relations sociales à Paris au XVIIIe siècle.* Paris: Colin, 1961.

1.038   Davidovitch, André. "Criminalité et répression en France depuis un siècle, 1851–1952." *Revue française de sociologie* 2 (1961): 30–49.

1.039   Delefortrie, N., and Morice, J. *Les revenus départementaux en 1864 et en 1954.* Paris: Colin, 1959.

1.040   Deniel, R., and Henry, L. "La population d'un village au nord de la France: Sainghin-en-Mélantois de 1665 à 1851." *Population,* 1965, pp. 563–602.

1.040A   Désert, G. "Le remplacement dans le Calvados sous l'Empire et les Monarchies censitaires." *Revue d'histoire économique et social* 43 (1965): 66–85.

1.041   Dogan, M. "L'origine sociale du personnel parlementaire français." In *Partis politiques et classes sociales,* edited by M. Duverger. FNSP, Cahier no. 74. Paris: Colin, 1955.

1.042   ———. "Political Ascent in a Class Society: French Deputies, 1870–1958." In *Political Decision Makers,* edited by Dwaine Marvick. Glencoe, Ill.: Free Press, 1961.

1.043   ———. "La stabilité du personnel parlementaire sous la IIIe République." *Revue française de science politique* 3 (April–June 1953): 319 ff.

1.044   Dupeux, Georges. *Aspects de l'histoire sociale et politique du Loir-et-Cher, 1848–1914.* Paris: Mouton, 1962.

1.045   ———. *Le Front Populaire et les élections de 1936.* FNSP, Cahier no. 99. Paris: Colin, 1959.

1.046   Duplessis-Le-Guelinel, G. *Les mariages en France.* FNSP, Cahier no. 53. Paris: Colin, 1954.

1.047   Duveau, Georges. *La vie ouvrière en France sous le Second Empire.* Paris: Gallimard, 1946.

1.048   Duverger, Maurice. *Les institutions françaises.* Paris: PUF, 1962.

1.049   Fasel, George W. "The French Election of April 23, 1848: Suggestions for a Revision." *French Historical Studies* 5 (1968): 285–98.

1.050   Faucheux, Marcel. *L'insurrection vendéenne de 1793. Aspects économiques et sociaux.* Paris: Imprimerie nationale, 1964.

1.051   Festy, Octave. *L'agriculture pendant la Révolution française. Les conditions de production et de récolte des céréales.* Paris: Gallimard, 1947.

1.051A   Fleury, M., and Valmary P. "Le progrès de l'instruction élémentaire de Louis XIV à Napoléon III, d'après l'enquête de Louis Maggiolo, 1877–1879." *Population* 12 (1957): 71–92.

1.052   Fohlen, C. *Une affaire de famille au XIXe siècle: Méquillet-Noblot.* FNSP, Cahier no. 75. Paris: Colin, 1955.

1.053   Fourastié, J. *Documents pour l'histoire et la théorie des prix.* 2 vols. Paris: Colin, 1959, 1962.

1.054   Gautier, Etienne, and Henry, Louis. *La population de Crulai, paroisse normande. Etude historique.* Paris: PUF, 1958.

1.055   Gerbod, P. *La condition universitaire en France au XIXe siècle.* Paris: PUF, 1965.

1.056   Girard, Louis; Prost, Antoine; and Gossez, Rémi. *Les conseillers généraux en 1870. Etude statistique d'un personnel politique.* Travaux de Centre de Recherches sur l'Histoire du XIXe Siècle, 1. Paris: PUF, 1967.

1.057 Godechot, Jacques. *Les institutions de la France sous la Révolution et l'Empire.* Paris: PUF, 1951.

1.058 Goetz-Girey, Robert. *Le mouvement des grèves en France, 1919–1962.* Paris: Sirey, 1965.

1.059 Goguel, François. *Géographie des élections françaises de 1870 à 1951.* FNSP, Cahier no. 27. Paris: Colin, 1951.

1.060 Gossez, Rémi. "Diversité des antagonismes sociaux vers le milieu du XIXe siècle." *Revue économique,* May 1956, pp. 439–57.

1.061 Goualt, J. *Comment la France est devenue républicaine. Les élections générales et partielles à l'Assemblée nationale, 1870–1875.* FNSP, Cahier no. 62. Paris: Colin, 1954.

1.062 Goubert, Pierre. *Beauvais et le Beauvaisis de 1600 à 1730. Contribution à l'histoire sociale de la France du XVIIe siècle.* 2 vols. Paris: SEVPEN, 1960.

1.062A Goreux, L.-M. "Les migrations agricoles en France depuis un siècle et leur relations avec certains facteurs économiques." *Etudes et Conjoncture,* no. 4 (April 1956), pp. 327–76.

1.063 Greer, Donald. *The Incidence of the Emigration during the French Revolution.* Cambridge, Mass.: Harvard University Press, 1951.

1.064 ———. *The Incidence of the Terror during the French Revolution: A Statistical Interpretation.* Cambridge, Mass.: Harvard University Press, 1935.

1.064A Higonnet, Patrick. "La composition de la Chambre des Députés de 1827 à 1831." *Revue historique* 239 (1968): 351–75.

1.065 ———, and Higonnet, Trevor B. "Class, Corruption, and Politics in the French Chamber of Deputies, 1846–1848." *French Historical Studies* 5 (Fall 1967): 204–24.

1.066 Huber, M.; Bunlé, H.; and Boverat, F. *La population de la France.* Paris: Hachette, 1965.

1.067 Hufton, Olwen H. *Bayeux in the Late Eighteenth Century.* Oxford: Oxford University Press, 1967.

1.068 Ibarrola, Jésus. *Structure sociale et fortune mobilière et immobilière à Grenoble en 1847.* Paris: Mouton, 1965.

1.069 INSEE. "La concentration des établissements en France de 1896 à 1936." *Etudes et conjoncture,* no. 9 (1954), pp. 840–81.

1.070 Kindleberger, Charles. *Economic Growth in France and Britain, 1851–1950.* Cambridge, Mass.: Harvard University Press, 1964.

1.071 Kriegel, Annie. *La croissance de la CGT, 1918–1921. Essai statistique.* Paris: Mouton, 1966.

1.072 Labrousse, C.-E., ed. *Aspects de la crise et de la dépression de 1846–1851.* Bibliothèque de la Révolution de 1848, vol. 19. La Roche-sur-Yon: Imprimerie Centrale de l'Ouest, 1956.

1.073 ———. *La crise de l'économie française à la fin de l'ancien régime et au début de la Révolution.* Paris, 1944.

1.074 ———. *Esquisse du mouvement des prix et des revenus en France au XVIIIe siècle.* Paris: Dalloz, 1933.

1.075 ———. "Georges Lefebvre, 1874–1959," *Annales ESC,* 15e année (1961), pp. 1–8.

1.076 Lacassagne, A. *La criminalité comparée des villes et des campagnes.* Lyon, 1882.

1.077 Lane, F. C., and Riemersma, J. C., eds. *Enterprise and Secular Change. Readings in Economic History.* Homewood, Ill.: Irwin, 1953.

1.078 LeBras, Gabriel. *Etudes de sociologie religieuse.* 2 vols. Paris: PUF, 1955.

1.079 Lefebvre, G. *Documents relatifs à l'histoire des subsistances dans le district de Bergues pendant la Révolution, 1788-an V.* 2 vols. Lille: C. Robbe, 1914–21.

1.080 ———. *Etudes orléanaises.* CHESR, Memoires et Documents, 15. 2 vols. Paris: CHESR, 1962, 1963.

1.081 ———. *La Grande Peur de 1789.* Paris: Colin, 1932.

1.082 ———. *Les paysans du Nord pendant la Révolution française.* 2 vols. Paris: F. Rieder, 1924. New ed. Bari: Laterza, 1959.

1.083 Le Guen, Gilbert. "La structure de la population active des agglomérations françaises de plus de 20,000 habitants: Méthode d'étude, résultats." *Annales de géographie* 69 (1960): 355–70.

1.084 LeRoy Ladurie, E. *Les paysans de Languedoc.* 2 vols. Paris: SEVPEN, 1966.

1.084A ———; Bernageau, N.; and Pasquet, Y. "Le conscrit et l'ordinateur. Perspectives de recherches sur les archives militaires du XIXe siècle français." *Studi storici,* anno 10 (1969), pp. 260–308.

1.085 Lévy-Leboyer, Maurice. *Les banques européennes et l'industrialisation internationale dans la première moitié du XIXe siècle.* Paris: PUF, 1965.

1.086 ———. "La croissance économique en France au XIXe siècle. Résultats preliminaires." *Annales ESC,* 23e année (1968), pp. 788–807.

1.087 Lhomme, Jean. "Le pouvoir de'achat de l'ouvrier français au cours d'un siècle, 1840–1940." *Le Mouvement social,* no. 63 (April–June 1968), pp. 41–69.

1.088 Lidderdale, D. W. S. *Le Parlement français.* FNSP, Cahier no. 54. Paris: Colin, 1954.

1.089 Long, R. *Les élections législatives en Côte-d'Or depuis 1870. Essai d'interprétation sociologique.* FNSP, Cahier no. 96. Paris: Colin, 1958.

1.090 Loubère, Leo. "The Emergence of the Extreme Left in Lower Languedoc, 1848–1851: Social and Economic Factors in Politics." *American Historical Review* 73 (1968): 1019–51.

1.091 MacRae, Duncan. *Parliament, Parties, and Society in France, 1946–1958.* New York: St. Martin's Press, 1967.

1.092 Marie, C. *L'évolution du comportement politique dans une ville en expansion: Grenoble, 1871–1965.* FNSP, Cahier no. 148. Paris: Colin, 1966.

1.093 Marker, Gordon. "Internal Migration and Economic Opportunities. France and its Regions." Ph.D. dissertation, University of Pennsylvania, 1964.

1.094 Marnata, F. *Les loyers des bourgeois de Paris, 1860–1958.* Paris: Colin, 1961.

1.095 Martin, Gérard. "Evolution de l'Agriculture en Auxois de 1840 à 1939." In *Etudes sur la vie rurale dans la France de l'Est,* Cahier no. 11, pp. 85–197. Dijon: Association Interuniversitaire de l'Est, 1966.

1.096 Meyer, Jean. *La noblesse bretonne au XVIIIe siècle.* 2 vols. Paris: SEVPEN, 1966.

1.097 Perroux, François. *L'économie du XXe siècle.* 2d ed. Paris: PUF, 1964.

1.098   Pierrard, Pierre. *La vie ouvrière à Lille sous le Second Empire.* Paris: Bloud et Gay, 1965.

1.099   Pinchemel, P. *Géographie de la France.* Paris: Colin, 1966.

1.100   Pinkney, David. "The Crowd in the French Revolution of 1830." *American Historical Review* 70 (1964): 1–17.

1.101   Ponteil, Félix. *Les institutions de la France de 1814 à 1870.* Paris: PUF, 1966.

1.102   Pouthas, C. *La population française pendant la première moitié du XIXe siècle.* Paris: PUF, 1956.

1.103   Prost, Antoine. *La CGT à l'époque du Front Populaire, 1934–1939.* FNSP, Cahier no. 129. Paris: Colin, 1964.

1.104   Rambaud, P., and Vincienne, M. *Les transformations d'une société rurale: La Maurienne, 1561–1962.* Paris: Colin, 1964.

1.105   Rémond, André. *Etudes sur la circulation marchande en France aux XVIIIe et XIXe siècles.* Vol. 1, *Les prix des transports marchands de la Révolution au Premier Empire.* Paris: Rivière, 1956.

1.106   Renouard, Dominique. *Les transports de marchandises par fer, route, et eau, depuis 1850.* Paris: Colin, 1960.

1.107   Richet, Denis. "Croissance et blocages en France, XVe au XVIIIe siècle." *Annales ESC* 23e année (1968): 759–87.

1.108   Rist, Charles, and Pirou, Gaetan, eds. *De la France d'avant-guerre à la France d'aujourd'hui.* Paris: Recueil Sirey, 1939.

1.109   Rougerie, Jacques. *Procès des Communards.* Paris: Juilliard, 1964.

1.110   ———. "Remarques sur l'histoire des salaires à Paris au XIXe siècle." *Le Mouvement Social,* no. 63 (1968), pp. 71–108.

1.111   Rudé, George. *The Crowd in the French Revolution.* Oxford: Oxford University Press, 1959.

1.112   ———. *The Crowd in History.* New York: Wiley, 1964.

1.113   Sauvy, Alfred. *Théorie générale de la population.* Vol. 1, *Economie et croissance.* Paris: PUF, 1963.

1.114   ———. *Histoire économique de la France entre les deux guerres.* 2 vols. Paris: Fayard, 1965–67.

1.114A Schnapper, B. *Le remplacement militaire au XIXe siècle.* Paris: SEVPEN, 1968.

1.115   Seine, Préfecture de la. *Le régime administratif et financier de la ville de Paris et du département de la Seine.* 4 vols. N.p., n.d., but after 1958.

1.116   Siegfried, André. *Géographie électorale de l'Ardèche sous la IIIe République.* FNSP, Cahier no. 9. Paris: Colin, 1949.

1.117   ———. *Itinéraires de contagions, épidémies, et idéologies.* Paris: Colin, 1960.

1.118   ———. *Tableau politique de la France de l'Ouest sous la Troisième République.* Paris: Colin, 1913.

1.119   Simiand, François. *Fluctuations économiques à longue periode et la crise mondiale.* Paris: Alcan, 1932.

1.120   ———. *Le salaire, l'évolution sociale, et la monnaie.* 3 vols. Paris: Alcan, 1932.

1.121   Singer-Kerel, Jeanne. *La coût de la vie à Paris de 1840 à 1954.* Paris: Colin, 1961.

1.122   Soboul, Albert. "La Question paysanne en 1848." *La pensée*, n.s., no. 18 (1948), pp. 55–66.

1.123   ———. *Les sans-culottes parisiens en l'an II: Mouvement populaire et gouvernement révolutionnaire, 2 janvier 1793–9 thermidor an II*. Paris: Clavreuil, 1958.

1.124   Sorlin, Pierre. *Waldeck-Rousseau*. Paris: Colin, 1966.

1.125   Sydenham, M. J. *The Girondins*. London: University of London, Athlone Press, 1961.

1.126   Thuillier, Guy. *Aspects de l'économie niversnaise au XIXe siècle*. Paris: Colin, 1966.

1.126A Tilly, Charles. *The Vendée*. Cambridge, Mass.: Harvard University Press, 1964.

1.127   Tønnesson, Kåre. *La defaite des sans-culottes: Mouvement populaire et reaction bourgeoise en l'an III*. Oslo: Presses Universitaires, 1959.

1.128   Touraine, Alain. *L'évolution du travail ouvrier aux usines Renault*. Paris: CNRS, 1955.

1.129   Toutain, Jean-Claude. *La population de la France de 1700 à 1959*. ISEA, Cahier no. 133 suppl. Paris: ISEA, 1963.

1.130   ———. *Le produit de l'agriculture française de 1700 à 1958*. 2 parts. ISEA, Cahier nos. 115, 115 suppl. Paris: ISEA, 1961.

1.131   Tudesq, A. J. *Les conseillers généraux en France au Temps de Guizot, 1840–1848*. FNSP, Cahier no. 157. Paris: Colin, 1967.

1.132   ———. *Les grands notables en France, 1840–1849: Etude historique d'une psychologie sociale*. Paris: PUF, 1964.

1.133   Vasseur, Daniel. *Les débuts du mouvement ouvrier dans la région de Belfort-Montbéliard, 1870–1914*. Paris: Les Belles Lettres, 1967.

1.134   Vigier, Philippe. *Essai sur la répartition de la propiété foncière dans la règion Alpine: Son èvolution des origines du cadastre à la fin du Second Empire*. Paris, SEVPEN, 1963.

1.135   Vilar, Pierre. *La Catalogne dans l'Espagne moderne. Recherches sur les fondements économiques des structures nationales*. 3 vols. Paris: SEVPEN, 1962.

1.136   Ville-Chabrolle, Marcel de. "La concentration des entreprises en France avant et depuis la guerre (d'après les recensements généraux de mars 1906, 1921, et 1926)." *Bulletin de la Statistique Générale* 22 (1933): 391–462.

1.137   Vincent, G. *Les professeurs du second degré. Contribution à l'étude du corps enseignant*. FNSP, Cahier no. 160. Paris: Colin, 1967.

1.138   Willard, Claude. *Le mouvement socialiste en France, 1893–1905. Les Guesdistes*. Paris: Editions Sociales, 1965.

1.138A Wylie, Lawrence, ed. *Chanzeaux, a Village in Anjou*. Cambridge, Mass.: Harvard University Press, 1966.

2. BIBLIOGRAPHIES AND METHODOLOGICAL DISCUSSIONS

2.001   Archives Nationales. *Guide du Lecteur*. N.p.: Les Amis des Archives, 1964.

2.002   Baehrel, René. "La mortalité sous l'ancien régime. Remarques inquiètes." *Annales ESC*, 12e année (1957), pp. 85–98.

2.003 ——, and Henry, Louis. "Histoire et démographie." Part 1, "A propos des 'Remarques inquiètes' de René Baehrel," by Louis Henry. Part. 2, "Réponse de René Baehrel." *Annales ESC,* 12e année (1957), pp. 628–38.

2.004 Bauer, Raymond A., ed. *Social Indicators.* Cambridge, Mass.: M.I.T. Press, 1966.

2.005 Bautier, R. H. "Les archives." In *Encyclopédie de la Pléiade,* edited by C. Samaran. Vol. 11, *L'histoire et ses méthodes.* Paris: Gallimard, 1961.

2.006 Biraben, J. N. "Inventaire des listes nominatives de recensement en France." *Population* 18 (1963): 305–28.

2.007 Bloch, Marc. "Le salaire et les fluctuations économiques à longue période." In *Mélanges historiques,* 2: 890–914. Paris: SEVPEN, 1963.

2.008 Bois, P., and Bouloiseau, M. *Table analytique des actes, bulletins, notices, inventaires, et documents, 1907–1960.* Paris: Imprimerie Nationale, 1963. A bibliography of recent published sources on the revolutionary period.

2.009 Bouloiseau, Marc. *Etude de l'émigration et de la vente des biens des émigrés.* Paris: Imprimerie Nationale, 1963.

2.010 Bourdon, Jean. "La critique historique appliquée aux documents statistiques et numériques." *Journal de la société de statistique de Paris,* 1956, pp. 24–49.

2.011 Braudel, F. "La démographie et les dimensions des science de l'homme." *Annales ESC,* 15e année (1960), pp. 493–523.

2.012 ——. "Histoire et sciences sociales: La longue durée." *Annales ESC,* 13e année (1958), pp. 725–53.

2.013 ——. "Histoire et sociologie." In *Traité de sociologie,* edited by G. Gurvitch. Paris: PUF, 1967.

2.014 ——; Labrousse, E.; and Renouvin, P. "Les recherches d'histoire moderne et contemporaine." *Revue historique* 222 (1959): 34–50.

2.015 Brimo, Albert. *Méthode de la géo-sociologie électorale.* Paris: Pedene, 1968.

2.016 Caumartin, Jean. *Les principales sources de documentation statistique.* Paris: Dunod, 1935.

2.017 Châtelain, Abel. "Les migrations temporaires françaises au XIXe siècle: Problèmes, Méthodes, Documentation." *Annales de démographie historique,* 1967.

2.018 ——. "Une source nouvelle sur les migrations intérieures françaises. Le fichier électoral." *Annales ESC,* 11e année (1956), pp. 205–12.

2.019 ——. "Valeur des recensements de la population française au XIXe siècle." *Revue de géographie de Lyon* 29 (1954): 273–80.

2.020 Chaunu, Pierre. "Histoire quantitative ou histoire sérielle." *Cahiers Vilfredo Pareto,* no. 3 (1964), pp. 165–76.

2.021 Chen, Y. Y. "Etudes statistiques sur la criminalité en France de 1897 à 1930." In *Etude de Sociologie.* Paris, 1937.

2.022 *Contributions à l'histoire démographique de la Révolution française.* CHESR, Mémoires et Documents, 14. Paris: CHESR, 1962.

2.023 Couturier, M. "Démographie historique et mécanographie électronique." *Annales de démographie historique,* 1966.

2.024 Crécy, M. de. "Bibliographie analytique des enquêtes effectuées par ordre du Ministre du Commerce et de l'Agriculture de 1800 à 1918." *Histoire des Enterprises,* no. 10 (1962), pp. 20–76.

2.025 Daumard, Adeline. "Paris et les archives de l'enregistrement." *Annales ESC,* 13e année (1958), pp. 289–303.

2.026 ——. "Une source d'histoire sociale: L'enregistrement des mutations par décès. Le XIIe Arrondissement de Paris en 1820 et 1847." *Revue d'histoire économique et sociale* 35 (1957): 57–75.

2.027 ——. "Structure sociales et classement socio-professionnel. L'apport des archives notariales au XVIIIe et au XIXe siècle." *Revue historique* 227 (1962): 139–54.

2.028 ——, and Furet, François. "Méthodes de l'histoire sociale. Les archives notariales et la mécanographie." *Annales ESC,* 14e année (1959), pp. 676–93.

2.029 ——. "Problèmes de méthode en histoire sociale. Réflexions sur une note critique." *Revue d'histoire moderne et contemporaine* 11 (1964): 291.

2.030 Douglas, Jack D. *The Social Meanings of Suicide.* Princeton, N.J.: Princeton University Press, 1967.

2.031 ——. "The Sociological Analysis of Social Meanings of Suicide," *Archives européennes de sociologie* 7 (1966): 251–58.

2.032 Duncan, Otis Dudley. "Path Analysis: Sociological Examples." *American Journal of Sociology* 72 (July 1966): 1–16.

2.033 ——; Cuzzort, Ray P.; and Duncan, Beverly. *Statistical Geography.* Glencoe, Ill.: Free Press, 1961.

2.034 Dupaquier, Jacques. "De l'application de la méthode des sondages à l'histoire sociale." In *L'histoire sociale. Sources et méthodes,* pp. 183–93. Paris: PUF, 1967.

2.035 ——. "Des rôles de tailles à la démographie historique: L'exemple du Vexin français." *Annales de démographie historique,* 1965.

2.036 ——. "Sur la population française au XVIIe et au XVIIIe siècle." *Revue historique* 239 (1968): 43–79.

2.037 Dupeux, Georges. "Guide de recherches." In *Sociologie électorale,* edited by F. Goguel and G. Dupeux. FNSP, Cahier no. 26. Paris: Colin, 1951.

2.038 Fleury, Michel, and Henry, Louis. *Des registres paroissiaux à l'histoire de la population. Manuel de dèpouillement et d'exploitation de l'état civil ancien.* Paris: INED, 1956.

2.039 ——. *Nouveau manuel de dépouillement et d'exploitation de l'état civil ancien.* Paris: INED, 1965.

2.040 France, INSEE. *Répertoire des sources statistiques françaises.* Paris: Imprimerie Nationale, 1962.

2.041 France, Statistique générale de la France. *Historique et travaux de la fin du XVIIIe siècle au début de XXe.* Paris, 1913.

2.042 Furet, François. "Structures sociales parisiennes au XVIIIe siècle: L'apport d'une série fiscale." *Annales ESC,* 16e année (1961), pp. 939–58.

2.043 ——. "Sur quelques problèmes posés par le développement de l'histoire quantitative." *Social Science Information,* vol. 7, no. 1 (February 1968).

2.044 Gandilhon, René. "Les archives du cadastre. Un exemple." *Annales ESC,* 11e année (1956), pp. 213–15.

2.045 Gille, Bertrand. *Le conseil général des manufactures: Inventaire analytique des procès verbaux, 1810–1829.* Paris: SEVPEN, 1961.

2.046 ——. *Les sources statistiques de l'histoire de France: Des enquêtes du XVIIe siècle à 1870.* Geneva: Droz, 1964.

2.047 Glénison, Jean. "L'historiographie française contemporaine: Tendances et réalisations." In *La Recherche historique en France de 1940 à 1965*. Paris: CNRS, 1965.

2.048 Gonnet, Paul. "Archives fiscales et histoire sociale." *Revue d'histoire économique et sociale* 36 (1958): 432–43.

2.049 ———. "Archives fiscales et histoire urbaine." *Revue d'histoire économique et sociale* 35 (1957): 41–51.

2.050 Gossez, R.; Kriegel, A.; and Rougerie, J. "Sources et méthodes pour une histoire sociale de la classe ouvrière." *Le mouvement social*, no. 37 (1962), pp. 1–18.

2.051 Goubert, P. "Des registres paroissiaux à l'histoire. Indications practiques et orientation de recherches." *Bulletin d'histoire moderne et contemporaine du Comité des travaux historiques et scientifiques*, 1956.

2.052 ———. "Une richesse historique en cours d'exploitation: Les registres paroissiaux." *Annales ESC*, 9e année (1954), pp. 83–93.

2.053 ———. "Les sources modernes: Les XVIIe et XVIIIe siècles." In *L'histoire sociale. Sources et méthodes*. Paris: PUF, 1967.

2.054 Gregory, Winifred, ed. *List of the Serial Publications of Foreign Governments, 1815–1931*. New York. H. W. Wilson, 1932.

2.055 Henry, Louis. *Manuel de démographie historique*. Geneva and Paris: Droz, 1967.

2.056 ———. "Une richesse démographique en friche: Les registres paroissiaux." *Population*, 1952, pp. 281–90.

2.057 Labrousse, C.-E. "Voies nouvelles vers une histoire de la bourgeoisie occidentale aux XVIIIème et XIXème siècles, 1700–1850." In *Relazioni del X Congresso Internazionale di Scienze storiche*, vol. 4. Florence: Sansoni, [1955].

2.058 Landes, David S. "The Statistical Study of French Crises." *Journal of Economic History* 10 (1950): 195–211.

2.059 Laurent, Robert. "Une source: Les archives d'octroi." *Annales ESC*, 11e année (1956), pp. 197–204.

2.060 Le Bras, Gabriel. "Géographie politique et géographie religieuse." In *Etudes de sociologie electorale*. FNSP, Cahier no. 1. Paris: Colin, 1947.

2.061 ———. *Introduction à l'histoire de la pratique religieuse en France*. 2 vols. Paris: PUF, 1942, 1945.

2.062 Legeard, C. *Guide de recherches documentaires en démographie*. Paris: Gauthier-Villars, 1966.

2.063 Lemaire, Robert. "Les sources contemporaines: Les XIXe et XXe siècles en France." In *L'histoire sociale. Sources et méthodes*, pp. 115–43. Paris: PUF, 1967.

2.064 LeRoy Ladurie, E. "Les comptes fantastiques de Gregory King." *Annales ESC*, 23e année (1968): 1086–102.

2.065 Levasseur, E. "La statistique officielle en France." *Journal de la Société de Statistique de Paris*, 1885.

2.066 Lhomme, Jean. "L'attitude de l'économiste devant l'histoire économique." *Revue historique* 231 (1964): 297–306.

2.067 ———. *Economie et histoire*. Geneva: Droz, 1967.

2.068 Marczewski, Jean. *Introduction à l'histoire quantitative*. Geneva: Droz, 1965.

2.069 Markovitch, Tihomir J. "Les cycles industriels en France. (Essai d'élaboration préalable d'indices annuels de la production industrielle pour le XIXe siècle)." *Le Mouvement Social,* no. 63 (April–June 1968), pp. 11–39.

2.070 Meuvret, Jean. "Les données démographiques et statistiques en histoire moderne et contemporaine." In *Encyclopédie de la Pléiade,* edited by C. Samaran. Vol. 11, *L'histoire et ses méthodes,* pp. 893–936. Paris: Gallimard, 1961.

2.071 Moore, Wilbert. "Industrialization and Social Change." In *Industrialization and Society,* edited by Bert F. Hoselitz and Wilbert Moore. Paris: UNESCO-Mouton, 1966.

2.072 Morazé, Charles. "Quelques problèmes de méthode." In *Etudes de sociologie électorale.* FNSP, Cahier no. 1. Paris: Colin, 1947.

2.073 Morgenstern, Oskar. *On the Accuracy of Economic Observations.* Princeton, N.J., Princeton University Press, 1963.

2.074 *Mouvements ouvriers et socialistes. Chronologie et bibliographie . . . 1750–1918.* Edited by E. Dolléans and M. Crozier. Paris: Editions Ouvrières, 1950.

2.075 Peronet, Michel. "Généalogie et histoire: Approches méthodiques." *Revue historique* 239 (1968): 111–22.

2.076 Perrot, J.-C.; Sutter, J.; and Couturier, M. "Nouveau débat sur démographie historique et mécanographie électronique." *Annales de démographic historique,* 1967.

2.077 Perrot, Michelle. "Grèves, grévistes, et conjoncture. Vieux problème, travaux neufs." *Le Mouvement Social,* no. 63 (1968), pp. 109–24.

2.078 ———. "Le problème des sources pour l'étude du militant ouvrier au XIXe siècle." *Le Mouvement social,* nos. 33–34 (1961), pp. 21–34.

2.079 Pinchemel, P. "Les listes nominatives de recensement de la population." *Revue du Nord* 36 (1954): 419–531.

2.080 Reinhard, Marcel. *Etude de la population pendant la Révolution et l'Empire. Instruction, recueil de textes, et notes.* Paris: CHESR, 1961.

2.081 ———. *Etude de la population pendant la Révolution et l'Empire. Recueil de textes, premier supplément.* Paris: CHESR, 1963.

2.082 ———. "La statistique de la population sous le Consulat et l'Empire. Le bureau de statistique." *Population* 5 (1950): 103–20.

2.083 Rostow, W. W. "Histoire et sciences sociales: La longue durée." *Annales ESC* 14e année (1959): 710–19.

2.084 Saffroy, Gaston. *Bibliographie des almanachs et annuaires administratifs et ecclésiastiques de l'ancien régime; et des almanachs et annuaires généalogiques et nobiliaires du XVIe siècle à nos jours.* Paris: Saffroy, 1959.

2.085 Seine, Préfecture de Police. *Inventaire de la série BA des Archives de la Préfecture de Police.* Paris: Imprimerie Municipale, 1962.

2.086 Simiand, François. "Méthode historique et science sociale." *Annales ESC* 15e année (1960): 83–119. Originally appeared in *Revue de synthèse historique,* 1903.

2.087 Soboul, Albert. "Description et mesure en histoire sociale." In *L'histoire sociale. Sources et méthodes.* Paris: PUF, 1967.

2.088 *Les sociétés rurales françaises. Eléments de bibliographie réunis par le groupe de sociologie rurale du Centre d'Etudes Sociologiques sous la direction de Henri Mendras.* Paris: FNSP, 1962.

2.089 Thuillier, Guy. "Note sur les sources de l'histoire régionale de l'alimentation au XIXe siècle." *Annales ESC,* 23e année (1968), pp. 1301–08.

2.090   Tirat, J.-Y. "Problèmes de méthode en histoire sociale." *Revue d'histoire moderne et contemporaine* 10 (1963): 211–18.

2.091   Tudesq, A. J. "Les listes électorales de la monarchie censitaire." *Annales ESC* 13 (1958): 277–88.

2.092   Tulard, Jean. *La Préfecture de Police sous la monarchie de Juillet, suivi d'un inventaire sommaire et d'extraits das rapports de la Préfecture de Police conservés aux Archives Nationales.* Paris: Imprimerie nationale, 1964.

2.093   United States, Library of Congress and Department of Commerce, Bureau of Census. *National Censuses and Vital Statistics in France between Two World Wars, 1921–1942. A Preliminary bibliography.* Washington, D.C., 1945.

2.094   Vilar, Pierre. "Croissance économique et analyse historique." In *Premiere conférence internationale d'histoire économique. Contributions.* Stockholm: August 1960; Paris: Mouton, 1960.

2.095   ———. "Géographie et historique statistique." In *Eventail de l'histoire vivante. Mélanges offertes à Lucien Febvre*, 1:121–35. Paris, 1953.

2.096   ———. "Pour une meilleure compréhension entre économistes et historiens. 'Histoire quantitative' ou économetrie rétrospective?" *Revue historique* 233 (1965): 293–312.

2.097   Wolfe, A. B. "History of Population Censuses in France." *Journal of the American Statistical Association* 27 (1932).

2.098   France, FNSP. *Bulletin analytique de documentation politique économique et sociale contemporaine.* 1946– (bimonthly).

3. COMPENDIA OF SOURCES

3.001   *Atlas historique de la France contemporaine, 1800–1965.* Paris: Colin, 1966.

3.002   *Dictionnaire des communes: France métropolitaine, départements d'outre-mer, rattachements, et statistiques.* Paris: Berger-Levrault, 1963. Earlier editions date back to 1913.

3.003   France, Institut National de la Statistique et des Etudes Economiques. *Annuaires statistiques régionaux.* Put out by regional directions of INSEE. For details, including retrospective volumes, see Legeard (2.062), 131–34.

3.004   France, Statistique générale de la France. *Annuaire statistique de la France.* 1878–.

3.005   France. *Archives statistiques du ministère des Travaux publics, de l'Agriculture, et du Commerce.* 1837. List of contents is in Gille (2.046), pp. 206–08.

3.006   ———. *Documents statistiques sur la France.* 1835.

3.007   ———. *Statistique annuelle.* Vols. 1–36. 1871–1906.

3.008   ———. *Statistique de la France.* Vols. 1–13; 2nd series, vols. 1–21. 1835–72. Volumes are listed by title in part 4 below.

3.009   Giry, R. *L'atlas industriel de la France.* Paris: Documentation française, 1959.

3.009   *A Index-atlas des départements français.* Rennes and Paris: Oberthur, 1968.

3.010   Levasseur, Emile. *Histoire des classes ouvrières et de l'industrie en France de 1789 à 1870.* 2d ed. 2 vols. Paris, 1904.

3.011   ———. *La population française. Histoire de la population avant 1789 et démographie de la France comparée à celle des autres nations au XIXe siècle.* 2 vols. Paris, 1889, 1891.

3.012   *Liste alphabétique des communes et lieux-dits de France métropolitaine.* Rennes and Paris: Oberthur, 1966.

3.013   Paris. *Annuaire statistique de la ville de Paris.* 1880–.

3.014   ———. *Recherches statistiques sur la ville de Paris et le département de la Seine. Recueil de tableaux dressés d'après les ordres de . . . le Préfet.* Vols. 1–6. 1821–60.

4. ECONOMIC SOURCES

Census. For labor force composition, *see* Census in part 5 below.

4.001   *Etudes et conjoncture. L'espace économique français.* Paris: PUF, 1951; also later editions.

4.002   *Exposition universelle de 1851 à Londres. Travaux de la Commission française sur l'industrie des nations.* 8 vols. Paris, 1854–73. Information on mining and industry.

4.003   France, Direction des Mines. *Compte rendu des travaux des ingénieurs des mines.* 1833–46.

4.004   ———. *Résumé des travaux statistiques de l'administration des mines.* 1836–46. Continues as *Statistique de l'industrie minérale et des appareils à vapeur en France et en Algérie,* issued by Bureau de documentation minière. 1847/52–.

4.005   France, Ministère de l'Industrie et du Commerce, Direction des Mines et de la Sidérurgie. *Statistique de l'industrie minérale.* 1913–64.

4.006   France, Direction des routes et de la navigation. *Statistique de la navigation intérieure.* 1881–1948.

4.007   France, Direction du Travail. *Annuaire des syndicats professionels, industriels, commerciaux, et agricoles.* 1889–1914.

4.008   France. *Les associations professionnelles ouvrières.* 4 vols. 1889–1914.

4.009   ———. *La petite industrie.* 2 vols. 1893, 1896.

4.010   ———. *Répartition des forces motrices à vapeur et hydrauliques en 1899.* 1900–01.

4.011   ———. *Résultats statistiques du recensement des industries et professions en 1896.* 4 vols. 1899–1902.

4.012   ———. *Statistique des forces motrices en 1906.* 1907.

4.013   ———. *Statistique des grèves et des recours à la conciliation.* 1893–1936. Figures for 1890–92 are published as nos. 3 and 7 of France, Direction du Travail, *Notices et comptes rendus.* 1891, 1893.

4.014   France, INSEE. *Bulletin mensuel de statistique.* 1949–. Title varies.

4.015   ———. *L'espace économique français: Population, production, revenus, par département.* 1955.

4.016   ———. *Recensement général de l'agriculture de 1955.* 1955.

4.017   ———. *Statistique agricole.* 1937–66.

4.018   ———. *La structure des exploitations agricoles en France.* 1949.

4.019   France, Ministère de l'Agriculture. *Enquête sur l'industrie laitière en France et à l'étranger.* 1903.

4.020   ———. *Notice sur le commerce des produits agricoles.* 2 vols. 1905.

4.021 ———. *Récoltes des céréales et des pommes de terre de 1815 à 1876.* 1878.

4.022 ———. *Statistique agricole annuelle.* 1881–.

4.023 ———. *Rapport sur les opérations des caisses d'épargne ordinaires.* 1836–79. After 1882, when the last volume of this series was published, it was under Direction de la caisse nationale d'épargne.

4.024 ———. *Statistique agricole de la France. Résultats généraux de l'enquête décennale.* 1840, 1862, 1873, 1882, 1892. See 4.049 for the 1852 volume in this series.

4.025 ———. *Tableaux mensuels des prix moyens, mensuels, et annuels de l'hectolitre de froment par département du 22 septembre 1800 jusqu'au 31 décembre 1870.* 1872.

4.026 France, Ministère des Finances. *Compte définitif des recettes.* 1799–.

4.027 ———. *Compte général de l'administration des finances.* 1841–.

4.028 ———. *Mouvement économique en France de 1929 à 1939.* 1941.

4.029 ———. *Mouvement économique en France de 1938 à 1948.* 1951.

4.030 France, Ministère des Travaux Publics. *Album de statistique graphique de 1900.* 1900.

4.031 ———. *Statistique des ports maritimes de commerce.* 1839.

4.032 ———, Direction Générale des Ponts et Chaussées. *Recueil de documents statistiques sur les routes royales et sur les routes départementales.* 1837.

4.033 ———, Administration Générale des Ponts et Chaussées et des Mines. *Compte rendu des travaux des ingénieurs des mines pendant l'année. . . .* 1836–46.

4.034 ———. *Résumé des travaux statistiques de l'administration des mines en . . .* 1836–46, 1870, 1871, 1872. Continues annually to 1913. Title then changed to *Statistique de l'industrie minérale,* continues to 1964.

4.035 France, Ministère des Travaux Publics, de l'Agriculture, et du Commerce. *Prix et salaires à diverses époques.* 1873.

4.036 France, Ministère du Commerce. *Rapports sur l'application des lois réglementant le travail. Rapports des inspecteurs. . . .* 1893–1913.

4.037 France, Ministère du Travail. (Title of ministry varies.) *Bulletin.* 1894–1939. Includes wage information for 1904 in 1906 issue; other wage reports in 1916, 1929, 1931; strike information after 1914.

4.038 ———. *Les indices du coût de la vie en France.* 1941.

4.039 France, Ministère du Travail et de la Prévoyance sociale. *Salaire et durée du travail, coût de la vie pour certaines catégories d'ouvriers en 1906.* 1907.

4.040 ———. *Salaires et coût de l'existence à divers époques, jusqu'en 1910.* 1911.

4.041 ———. *Salaires, durée du travail, et coût de la vie en 1910.* 1910.

4.042 France, Ministère du Travail et de la Sécurité Sociale. *Statistiques du travail et de la sécurité sociale.* 1958–.

4.043 France, Statistique générale de la France. *Agriculture.* 4 vols. 1840–41. Covers Régions du Nord Oriental, Midi Oriental, Nord Occidental, Midi Occidental.

4.044 ———. *Bulletin.* Articles on wages and cost of living: T.6, fasc. 4 (July 1917), pp. 387–404; T.10, fasc. 4 (July 1929), pp. 339–74 (covers 1911–21); T.14, fasc. 2 (January 1925), pp. 168–92 (for 1911–24). 1911–49, then replaced by *Bulletin mensuel de statistique* (4.014).

4.045 ———. *Commerce extérieur, 1787–1837.* 1838.

4.046   ———. *Enquête industrielle de 1861–1865.* 1873.
4.047   ———. *Indices généraux du mouvement économique en France de 1901 à 1931.* 1932.
4.048   ———. *Industrie en 1840–1845.* 4 vols. Covers Régions du Nord Oriental (1847), Midi Oriental (1848), Nord Occidental (1850), Midi Occidental (1852).
4.049   ———. *Statistique agricole décennale de 1852.* 2 vols. 1860.
4.050   ———. *Statistiques industrielles obligatoires en France.* 1941.
4.051   ———. *Statistique sommaire des industries principales en 1873.* 1873.
4.052   *Revue française du travail.* Published by Ministry of Labor since 1946.

5. DEMOGRAPHIC SOURCES

5.001   France. *Bulletin des lois.* 1793–. Nos. 501 (1822), 154 (1827), 163 (1832), 958 (1842), 1367 (1847), 533 (1852), 469 (1857), 1001 (1862), and 1464 (1867) contain population counts.
Census (arranged chronologically, nos. 5.002 to 5.010)
5.002   France, Statistique générale de la France. *Territoire et population.* 1837. Retrospective census figures to 1801.
5.003   ———. *Territoire et population.* 2 vols. 1855.
5.004   ———. *Résultats du dénombrement de la population en 1856.* 1859.
5.005   ———. *Population. Résultats du dénombrement de 1861.* 1864.
5.006   ———. *Population. Résultats du dénombrement de 1866.* 1869.
5.007   ———. *Résultats généraux du dénombrement de 1872.* Nancy, 1873.
5.008   ———. *Résultats statistiques du dénombrement de. . . .* 1881, 1886, 1891, 1896.
5.009   ———. *Résultats statistiques du recensement général de la population effectué le. . . .* 1901, 1906, 1911, 1921, 1926, 1931, 1936, 1946, 1954.
5.010   France, INSEE. *Recensement de 1962.* 1964.
5.011   France, INED. *Migrations professionnelles: Données sur leur évolution en divers pays de 1900 à 1955.* 1957.
5.012   France, Ministère de l'Intérieur. *Dénombrement de la population de 1872.* Also published in 1876, 1881, etc. (census years). Population by department, arrondissement, canton, and commune.
5.013   ———. *Mouvement de l'émigration en France.* 1865/74–1878/81.
5.014   France, Statistique générale de la France. *Mouvement de la population en 1851–52–53.* 1856.
5.015   ———. *Mouvement de la population en 1854.* 1857.
5.016   ———. *Mouvement de la population pendant les années 1855–56–57.* 1861.
5.017   ———. *Mouvement de la population pendant les années 1858–59–60.* 1863.
5.018   ———. *Mouvement de la population en 1861–62–63–64–65.* 1870.
5.019   ———. *Mouvement de la population en 1866–67–68.* 1872.
5.020   ———. *Dénombrement des étrangers en France. Résultats statistiques du dénombrement de 1891.* 1893.
5.021   ———. *Statistique des familles en 1906.* 1912. *Statistique des familles et des habitations, 1911.* 1918. *Statistique des familles, 1926.* 1932. *Statistique des familles, 1931.* 1939. *Statistique des familles, 1936.* 1945.

5.022 ———. *Statistique annuelle du mouvement de la population.* 1907–. From 1898 on, the *Statistique annuelle* contained only the movement of population; its name was changed in 1907 to indicate this.

6. SOURCES FOR SOCIAL STRUCTURE

6.001 *Annuaire de la noblesse de France.* Paris, 1843–1957.

6.002 Bloch, C., and Tuetey, A. *Procès-verbaux du Comité de Mendicité de la Constituante.* Paris: Imprimerie Nationale, 1911.

6.003 *Dictionnaire biographique de mouvement ouvrier français.* Published under the direction of Jean Maitron. Part 1, vols. 1–3, 1789–1864; part 2, vols. 4–7 (A-MOR), 1864–71. Paris: Editions ouvrières, 1964–70.

6.004 France, Direction de l'Assistance et de l'Hygiène Publique. *Statistique sanitaire des villes de France.* 1886–1905. Title changed in 1906, but report continues.

6.005 France, Ministère de la Justice. *Compte général de la justice civile et commerciale pendant l'année. . . .* 1831.

6.006 ———. *Compte général de l'administration de la justice criminelle pendant l'année. . . .* First volume published in 1827, concerning 1825.

6.007 ———. *Compte général de l'administration de la justice civile et commerciale et de la justice criminelle.* (Alternate title of the preceding two series, 6.005 and 6.006).

6.008 France, Ministère de l'Instruction Publique et des Beaux-Arts. *Annuaire de l'instruction publique et des beaux-arts.* 1851–.

6.009 ———. *Rapports . . . relatifs à l'instruction primaire.* 1832–81.

6.010 ———. *Rapport sur l'instruction secondaire.* 1843, 1865, 1876, 1887. Title changed to *Statistique de l'enseignement secondaire* in 1865.

6.011 ———. *Statistique de l'enseignement primaire.* 1880. Covers 1829–77. Regular statistics by the same title, of which this volume is no. 2, ran from 1876–1906.

6.012 ———. *Résumé des états de situation de l'enseignement primaire.* 1878–95.

6.013 France, Statistique générale de la France. *Administrations publiques.* 2 vols. 1843, 1844.

6.014 ———. *Documents sur l'épidémie de choléra de 1854.* 1862.

6.015 ———. *Statistique annuelle des institutions d'assistance.* 1899–.

6.016 ———. *Statistique des établissements d'aliénés de 1842 à 1853.* 1857.

6.017 ———. *Statistique des asiles d'aliénés pour les années 1854 à 1861.* 1866.

6.018 ———. *Statistique de l'assistance publique de 1842 à 1853.* 1858.

6.019 ———. *Statistique de l'assistance publique pour les années 1854 à 1861.* Strasbourg, 1866.

6.020 Gasparin, de. *Rapport au Roi sur les hôpitaux, les hospices, et les services de bienfaisance.* Paris, 1837.

6.021 *Société et le high-life.* Paris, 1883–1950.

6.022 Watteville, de. *Rapports sur les Monts de Piété.* Paris, 1850.

6.022A ———. *Statistique des établissements et services de bienfaisance.* Paris, 1849.

7. POLITICAL SOURCES

7.001 *Almanach national: Annuaire officiel de la République française.* 1700–1919. Entitled *Almanach royal* during monarchical regimes.

7.002 *L'année politique, économique, sociale, et diplomatique en France.* Paris: PUF, 1944/45–.

7.003 *L'année politique.* Edited by André Daniel. Paris, 1874–1905.

7.004 *Annuaire générale de la France et de l'étranger,* Paris, 1919–.

7.005 Block, Maurice. *Dictionnaire de l'administration française.* Paris and Nancy: Berger-Levrault, 1898.

7.006 Cercle Républicain. *Annuaire.* Paris, 1902, 1903.

7.007 *Dictionnaire des parlementaires français, 1789–1889.* Vols. 1–5. Paris, 1891.

7.008 *Dictionnaire des parlementaires français. Notices biographiques sur les ministres, sénateurs, et députés français de 1889 à 1940.* Edited by Jean Jolly. Paris: PUF, 1964. Vols 1 through 4, covering through letter D, have appeared.

7.009 Lachapelle, G., ed. *Elections législatives de 1910. Résultats officiels.* Paris: Roustan, 1910. Volumes in same series cover elections of 1914, 1919, 1924, 1928.

7.010 France. *Journal officiel de la République française, 1789–.* Also called *Le moniteur universel* in some periods.

7.011 France, Assemblée nationale, Chambre des députés. *Annales . . . Débats parlementaires.* 1881–.

7.012 ———. *Programmes, professions de foi, et engagements électoraux.* 1881–.

7.013 France, Commission des Finances (Chambre des Députés). *Rapport fait au nom de la Commission des finances chargée d'examiner le projet de loi portant fixation du budget général de l'exercise . . .* 1846–. Known as Commission Annuelle du Budget to 1919.

7.014 France, Direction de la documentation. *Les institutions politiques de la France.* 2 vols. N.d., but after 1958.

7.015 France, Ministère de la Guerre. *Annuaire officiel des officiers de l'armée active. . . .* Title varies. 1819–.

7.016 ———. *Compte général de l'administration de la justice militaire.* 1833–87.

7.017 ———. *Comptes généraux présentés par le ministre de la guerre.* 1819–.

7.018 ———. *Compte rendu du Ministère de la guerre sur le recrutement de l'armée pendant l'année. . . .* 1819–.

7.019 France, Ministère de la Marine. *Annuaire de la Marine.* 1890–.

7.020 France, Ministère de la Marine et des Colonies. *Annuaire de la Marine et des Colonies.* 1853–89. Published earlier under the title *Etat général de la marine et des colonies.* 1763–1852.

7.021 France, Ministère de l'Intérieur. *Les élections législatives du 17 juin 1951.* 1953. *Les élections législatives du 2 janvier 1956.* 1957. *Les élections législatives des 1958, 1959.* 1960.

7.022 ———. *Etat signalétique des anarchistes étrangers expulsés de France.* 1894–1901.

7.023 ———. *Etat signalétique des étrangers expulsés de France.* 1894–1907.

7.024 ———. *Situation financière des communes de France et d'Algérie.* 1878–. Published annually.

7.025 ———. *Situation financière des départements.* 1887–.

7.026 France, Ministère des Affaires Etrangères. *Annuaire diplomatique et consulaire de la République française.* 1858–77; n.s., 1879–.

7.027 France, Ministère des Colonies. *Annuaire colonial. Administratif.* 1887–97.

7.028 ———. *Annuaire colonial. Agriculture, commerce, et industrie.* 1887–.

7.029 ———. *Annuaire du Ministère des colonies.* 1898–.

7.030 France, Ministère des Finances. *Annuaire général des finances.* 1890–.

7.031 ———. *Bulletin de statistique et de législation comparée.* 1877–1940. Continued as *Bulletin de législation comparée.*

7.032 Monde, Le. *Elections et référendums des 21 octobre 1945, 5 mai, et 2 juin 1946.* Paris, 1946.

7.033 ———. *Elections et référendums des 13 octobre, 10 et 24 novembre, et 8 décembre 1946.* Paris, 1947.

7.034 Temps, Le. *Elections législatives des 1er et 8 mai 1932.* Paris, 1932.

7.035 ———. *Elections législatives des 26 avril et 3 mai 1936.* Paris, 1936.

5

FIVE CENTURIES OF SPANISH HISTORY:
QUANTIFICATION AND COMPARISON

by Juan J. Linz

PREFATORY NOTE

After writing one version of this paper, I had to ask myself again about the boundaries of my efforts in time and space. The discovery of rich sets of data for earlier periods and a number of outstanding monographs led me to expand its scope backward to the time of Charles V, but excluding the Middle Ages and the reign of Ferdinand and Isabella. At the other terminus, I decided to include the Civil War as history, perhaps because almost half of today's Spaniards already have no other knowledge of it, and many wish it to be relegated to the past. I have excluded those parts of the world that were once part of Spain's empire but now comprise other nations, except when they are discussed in works of direct relevance to the development of peninsular Spain. The history of the transoceanic empire, Flanders, Italy, and Portugal under Spanish kings is not my concern. Finally, I faced the problem of how to delimit quantification. There can be little doubt about the quantitative character of a number of monographs, but other works containing quantitative data do so incidentally and without elaborating them in any special way. In some cases I have included them—when

Without the generous advice, criticism, bibliographic suggestions, and access to the libraries of colleagues and friends, this chapter could not have been written. I want to thank particularly Gonzalo Anes Alvarez, Richard Herr, Clara Lida, Edward Malefakis, Miguel Martínez Cuadrado, Stanley Payne, Nicholás Sánchez-Albornoz, Manuel de Terán, and Iris Zavala. They are obviously not responsible for its imperfections, particularly since they have not had a chance to see the final version. Val Lorwin, with his proverbial generosity, has contributed much in improving the text. He and Jacob M. Price have encouraged me with their patience with a late contributor. Mrs. Alice Gibson and Merle Spiegel contributed their editorial skills. I also want to express my recognition to the libraries of Yale and Columbia University. Much gratitude goes to my wife, Rocío de Terán, for her help, forbearance, and encouragement. The Council for European and Comparative Studies of Yale University has supported my research.

the data seemed particularly relevant, when they were leading to important questions and calling attention to useful sources. For the more modern period, where the number of monographs is smaller, I felt it important to mention information that would lend itself to counting in a way that would refine, add to, or challenge other types of analysis. Quantification obviously does not correlate—positively or negatively—with quality. Some outstanding works are not quantitative, or are hardly so, and therefore will not be discussed or will be mentioned only briefly; others which would rank low on quality deserve our attention because they use quantitative data or call our attention to the possibilities of quantification. The required bias here in favor of quantification should not be mistaken for lack of appreciation of nonquantitative works. In an effort to point to many areas in which countable data could be fruitful, I did not limit myself to a number of outstanding monographs but roamed widely through the literature, mentioning some minor works that happened to come to my attention at the risk of neglecting other efforts. This risk was compounded by difficulties of access, brought about by my working mainly in United States libraries and revising the manuscript over two years.

Modern Spanish history poses many problems for which quantitative data are of great relevance. The classic works of E. J. Hamilton, Pierre Vilar, Huguette and Pierre Chaunu, and Ramón Carande have all used statistical data in the solution of problems in economic history. But important subjects still await quantitative treatment: problems of politics, social conflicts, changes in class structure, religious behavior, education, elite recruitment, and public administration. For many of these we do have quantitative data covering several centuries, or biographical or other information susceptible to quantification, that could contribute not only to Spanish history but also to a comparative historical sociology of European societies in their transition to modernity.

Curiously, or perhaps naturally, the towering achievements of Spanish quantitative history deal not with the nineteenth or twentieth centuries but with the sixteenth, seventeenth, and eighteenth centuries—the period between the discovery of America and the Napoleonic invasion. By contrast, the transition to democracy and delayed industrialization—with its internal conflicts and the division along religious, class, and regional lines that culminated in the civil war of 1936–39—has been neglected. This can perhaps be explained by the fact that study of the earlier period could contribute to the understanding of the consequences of the overseas discoveries upon the general European economy, the shift of the center of gravity of European history from the Mediterranean to the Atlantic (so brilliantly described by Braudel), the influx of precious metals and their impact on prices and trade, the effects of wars, and the emergence of mercantilism and capitalism. To these attractions of subject, one might add the availability of detailed records for long periods of internal peace. In these records the new royal bureaucracies systematically collected information on population, wealth, shipping, migration, and public finances; and the archives of the Indies, Simancas, and the Crown of Aragon, as well as those of convents and hospitals, provide continuous series of them.

THE SIXTEENTH AND SEVENTEENTH CENTURIES

The social, demographic, economic, and financial history of the Spanish empire under the Habsburgs has attracted outstanding scholars, some of whom have devoted extensive and brilliant attention to quantitative data. Some of the works, especially those of E. J. Hamilton and Pierre Vilar, treat the Spanish data as a point of departure for an analysis of the rise of capitalism, influencing the work not only of historians of other countries but also (in the case of Hamilton) the economic theory of Keynes. Others like Braudel and his disciple, Chaunu, have contributed to a better understanding of the emergence of a world economy by analyzing the links of the Spanish empire with the non-Western world.

The social and economic history of this period is discussed in general works by Juan Reglá, Vicens Vives, J. van Klaveren, Carrera Pujal, and Domínguez Ortiz.[1] Here I will refer only to quantitative studies in more monographic form. The monumental, influential work of Fernand Braudel makes a unique contribution by placing Spain in the context of the political, social, and economic history of the second half of the sixteenth century and the struggle of Christian Europe against the Turkish empire for control of the Mediterranean.[2] Data on the time needed for news to travel between different cities by sea or by land, on the budgets of different governments, and on loans taken by the Spanish monarchs are just a few examples of quantitative information skillfully used to clarify historical situations, processes, and events. The long bibliographical essay on archives and printed sources is in itself a valuable instrument.

Finance, Banking, and Commerce

Ramón Carande's study of the economy and finance of Castile from 1516 to 1556 is written in the tradition of the German economic historians.[3] It was begun as a complement to Ehrenberg's 1896 work on the age of the Fuggers. The discovery of rich archival sources, especially in the Archivo de Indias and at Simancas, led to a three-volume study published between 1943 and 1967. The paradox of a great empire at the zenith of its power, enriched by the recently discovered treasures of the Indies and yet, because of its international commitments and financial ineptitude, continuously in dire financial straits, is explored through the operations of the bankers from preliminary contacts to final payments, which often entailed the direct transfer of treasure arriving from overseas. The loans and their amounts by periods, the names of creditors together with their nationalities, and the sums paid are listed chronologically by year for the whole reign, and the graphs based on this information comprise one of the most important contributions to quantitative history by any Spanish scholar. The weakness of the Castilian merchants and their diminishing ability to satisfy the needs of the Emperor at the end of the period are reflected in the figures of their shares of loans to the Emperor. These figures and the costs of loans in Germany and Italy, higher than in Spain, help to explain the rapid dissemination outside Castile of the wealth coming from the Indies as well as the lack of economic growth in the heartland of the empire. The work also includes a detailed analysis of the organization of Castilian finances, deficits, expenditures, income from various taxes and royal domains, customs, silk rent inherited from the Arabs in Granada, church contributions, the subsidies (*servicios*) voted by the Cortes, and the territorial distribution of the tax load. The first volume also gives us an excellent statistical view of population, emigration, agricultural prices, manufacturing, markets, banking and shipping. Each volume concludes with detailed bibliographical references to sources and a critical guide to the relevant literature. Carande has made an additionally valuable contribution in his identification of problems meriting monographic research and for which sufficient data exist.

The finances of the crown continue to attract the attention of Spanish historians. The work of Modesto Ulloa and Antonio Domínguez Ortiz follows along the lines of Carande's.[4] On the basis of archival research, particularly in Simancas, Ulloa presents budgets and detailed accounts of income from taxes, *servicios* of the Cortes, and loans for the kingdom of Castile and the Indies. The reign of Philip IV saw the great projects of political centralization and absolutism initiated by the Conde-Duque de Olivares come to nought because of the rebellion of Catalonia and the secession of Portugal. Domínguez Ortiz shows us the tax burden carried by Castile in the period of Philip IV, which, according to J. H. Elliott, is a basic cause behind the efforts to reform the constitution of the Spanish monarchy, and which in turn led to the revolt of the Catalans. An important section of Domínguez Ortiz's work deals with the relations between the king and his Spanish, Portuguese, Italian, and German bankers. Appendixes and many figures in the text provide quantitative information on all these subjects.

Sedentary merchants were great letter writers. From the archives of the Ruiz family of Medina del Campo, now a small Castilian town but formerly an important center of trade and finance, the historians of early Castilian capitalism, trade, and finance have drawn the data for several excellent monographs. The archives include correspondence between 1558 and 1598, and the practice of filing replies with the letters received makes it possible to follow operations in detail. Henri Lapeyre has published two monographs on the Ruiz operations.[5] The first volume, on the *asientos* between the Castilian merchant-banker and Philip II after a decree of 1575 attempted to exclude the Genoese, contributes to our knowledge of international relations in the banking world, of the need for credit for war and politics, and of the weaknesses of Castilian bankers as compared to their foreign competitors. The second work, inspired by Braudel, is centered on the business relations of the Ruiz brothers, André (in Nantes) and Simón (in Medina del Campo), and their heirs in the 1590s. Twenty-eight tables give data on various transactions, prices, and exchange rates in the different financial capitals of the time. F. Ruiz Martín has analyzed and published the correspondence of the Ruiz with Florentine businessmen—907 letters among some 4,850 exchanged with Italy—along the same lines, including some quantitative series. One of his most interesting tables presents the number of letters exchanged in the period 1564–1606—3,496 in all—between the house of Ruiz and Italian cities. José Gentil da Silva has examined the letters of the Portuguese merchants; Valentín Vázquez de Prada, those coming from Antwerp. The studies based on the Ruiz Archives are the most important contributions to sixteenth-century economic history to be based on private rather than public documentation.[6]

Money, Prices, Wages, Wars, and Economic Development: Hamilton and his Critics

The monumental work of Earl J. Hamilton on money, prices, and wages in different parts of Spain between 1351 and 1800 constitutes the richest and most fundamental source for quantitative information in Spanish history and a towering achievement of economic history.[7] It would be presumptuous to attempt to review here Hamilton's archival and printed sources, methods, research, and calculations, or to evaluate his contributions and hypotheses. Nor is it possible to discuss Hamilton's empirical data and the complex relations between data and theory which have been analyzed by Pierre Vilar, David Felix, John U. Nef, Ingrid Hammarström, and Jorge Nadal, among many others.[8]

Hamilton's unpublished data and his 1929 article were at the root of Keynes's inflationist thought in volume 2 of his *Treatise on Money* (1930). Years later, supported by the Keynesian argument, Hamilton emphasized the relationship between what he called "profit inflation" and capitalist industrial progress.[9] Other economic historians—Parenti and Cipolla, for example—followed the same direction, while some of the French historians were almost alone in resisting the trend. The richness of information on money and prices and the relative lack of data on production, land rent, or even population changes, combined with the difficulty of making comparisons of real wages, have led historians to neglect other factors on the basis of present-day theories. Expressing his uneasiness about the impact of economic theory on the work of historians, Jorge Nadal closes his review of the question of the Spanish price revolution in the sixteenth century by saying, "Rarely will theoretical science have caused so much harm to historical science, which is and has to be a science of fact." [10]

Pierre Vilar (who took some of his hypotheses from Marx), Jorge Nadal, and, more recently, Gonzalo Anes have tried to demonstrate the limitations of the quantity theory of money.[11] Vilar has proposed an interacting rather than a causal model and has introduced additional factors as contributory to the price changes in Spain. But, as he writes in a review of *War and Prices in Spain, 1651–1800*, "After the book of E. J. Hamilton, the Spanish eighteenth century remains to be studied. However, before him it *could not* be studied. This is the highest praise one can give his work." [12] I join in that praise.

Hamilton has also drawn attention to the writings of certain Spanish moralists and economists of the sixteenth century, particularly in Seville and Salamanca, who had observed and tried to interpret some of the phenomena that Hamilton documented so thoroughly. Later Cantillon and Marx, as Vilar has shown, also discussed the relationship between the massive influx of precious metals in the sixteenth century and the general rise in prices; in addition, they considered some problems connected with the relationship between price and wage changes.[13] But Hamilton's great contribution was to provide the quantitative archival data drawn from the records of Spanish hospitals, convents, universities, and palaces, and from the Casa de la Contratación's accounts of gold and silver arriving from the Indies. The series on money, prices, and wages and their relationships led him to offer a revision of the theories of Sombart and Weber on the origins of capitalism and to stress profit inflation—the lag of wages behind prices—as a contributory factor or "chief cause" of industrial progress during the Price Revolution and the Industrial Revolution. As in the case of Max Weber's theories on the relationship of ascetic Protestantism to the origins of capitalism, later critics have raised fundamental questions about the limitations of the data; the importance of other variables, the historical processes involved, and the author's emphasis on the model rather than on the interaction of the variables.

Hamilton would not deny, but probably did not take into account, some of the limitations of his data: the absence from the treasury records of the Casa de la Contratación of the amounts introduced illegally; the differences between the urban prices he used and those of rural markets; the danger of using local prices as indicative of regional prices; the lack of data for areas of Spain with a distinct economy and closer contacts with Europe, notably the Basque country, Navarre, Galicia, and Catalonia; the differences between institutional and private purchasing; the differences between quantities of specie received and specie minted. Hamilton insisted on the richness of institutional price records in Spain and the absence or limited value of market price records (*mercuriales*) preferred by Labrousse for France. Vilar agreed with him and stessed that one or the other type may be preferable in different countries. However, Gonzalo Anes has noted recently that maximum and minimum market prices are also available in Spain, even when a preliminary comparison for Castile with those recorded by Hamilton suggests their interchangeability.[14] The use of calendar years rather than agricultural years, defended by Hamilton, has been questioned by Anes, particularly since it hides seasonal changes that may have provided opportunities to store and hoard, with consequent social tensions. Vilar has also questioned the use of fifty-year periods rather than certain critical dates in much of the analysis.[15]

Basic to Hamilton's thesis is the relationship between the recorded arrivals of gold and silver and the general price level, summarized in a frequently reproduced graph. This relationship was accepted by many historians, notably Braudel.[16] But which stocks of precious metals and which prices need to be related, given the application of even the simplest form of the quantity theory of money? Hammarström stresses the likelihood that much gold and silver disappeared into hoards and religious and lay ornamentation in Spain and, at least to that extent, could not influence the price level. Carande and Simiand show how much newly arrived specie left Spain immediately and hence could not have influenced Spanish price levels.[17] There are also problems of relating time periods of arrivals and of price changes in Spain and other lands.

The application of the quantity theory of money which Hamilton uses requires a study of the other variables in the famous equation $MV = PT$. Hamilton looks only at the M and P; Hammarström argues that increases in the velocity of money and in production in the sixteenth century require consideration.

In his analyses of the effects of price changes, Keynes by the time he published *The General Theory* (1936), came around to repudiating the general price level as too vague for the purposes of causal analysis. In the measurement of price changes, Nadal urges the use of moving averages to relate changes not to a fixed initial point but to preceding periods in each case. To that effect he calculates quinquennial and decennial changes. He also proposes to present data on a logarithmic scale to take account of relative increases, rather than on the arithmetical scale which Hamilton used.[18]

The international comparisons pose additional problems. Nadal proposes that, instead of comparing the Spanish price index for a variety of commodities, the comparison be made for a single important crop, like wheat, in specific areas of Spain and France; this would suggest that sixteenth-century Spanish prices were not higher.[19] The comparison of real wages and the differences between wages and prices in different countries is even more complex. Hamilton's wage data refer to between 50 and 100 occupations, while those for other countries are more limited; his prices are unweighted, while those for other countries are weighted, although he argues that the use of one or the other index makes little difference. Phelps Brown and Hopkins compare real wages for construction workers in southern England, France, and Valencia and conclude that the Spanish worker experienced a progressive loss of income—indeed in some periods a greater loss than his fellow workers abroad.[20] These data led Nadal to question Hamilton's assertion that the smaller gap between wages and prices in Spain excluded those exceptional profits that stimulated capitalism elsewhere.

Vilar, Nadal, and Anes stress that in an ancient, fundamentally agrarian society, the impact of the price revolution has to be studied less in relation to limited industrial activities than to agriculture and particularly land rent. A central point is the relation of agricultural prices, which until 1575 rose faster than industrial prices, to land rent and consequently to the distribution of income between tenant farmers and seigneurial landlords. On this point we find contradictory opinions and limited evidence, except for the data of Vilar on eighteenth-century Catalonia and some data recently collected by Anes. Hamilton thinks that prices rose constantly but that seigneurial rents either remained relatively stable, thus impoverishing the land owners, or else lagged behind prices, allowing the farmer to buy industrial products. Nadal, on the basis of Viñas Mey[21] and Carande's records of the accounts of the time, thinks that land owners, particularly on a large scale, benefited from the price inflation.

Writing from a Marxist perspective, Vilar emphasizes the differential impact of economic changes within a stratified, and in this case rural, society. Anes's analysis of eighteenth-century rural society, *Las crisis agrarias en la España moderna,* stresses that social structure, particularly property structure, prevented an accumulation of commercial capital that could have served as a basis for an industrial revolution in Spain.

Some critics also warn that, in view of the agricultural character of the economy and hence of the importance of nonmonetary transactions, we should not assign too much importance to the fact that the treasury of the Indies was so closely tied with foreign economic relations. Nadal doubts that the relationship between exports from Seville and Andalucian prices, discovered by Chaunu,[22] could compensate for a lack of production indexes. The volume of shipping cannot in his opinion serve to measure Spanish production and business cycles without distinguishing between Spanish and foreign cargoes.

The title of Hamilton's third work—*War and Prices in Spain, 1651–1800*—would suggest that the long and disastrous wars in which Spain was involved were clearly reflected in economic time series. But Hamilton finds that the wars rarely affected Spanish prices and that no consistent relationships comparable to those of the nineteenth and twentieth centuries can be found. Rarely and only locally did war produce scarcity and a consequent rise in prices; colonial wars, in fact, by reducing the import of metals and thereby the monetary circulation, normally led to price drops. Conversely, peace, with its renewed influx of accumulated treasure from the Indies, usually led to inflation. War expenditures contributed to inflation on two occasions: inflation of the *vellón* (copper money) between 1650 and 1680, and the paper money inflation at the end of the eighteenth century. Vilar notes, however, that there was peace during part of the first period and that stabilization after the deflation of 1680 coincided with disastrous wars. The parallels between Spanish prices and those of neutral countries suggest the secondary, temporary, and local relation between war and prices in Spain. Nevertheless, the parallels of the main phases of the price movement; the drop in the seventeenth century, particularly acute in Castile; the stabilization from 1686–89 to 1730–32; the at first slow and then accelerated rise in the last two-thirds of the eighteenth century, corresponding to the phases of Spanish power, decadence, and recovery raise interesting questions. Was the price movement a determining factor or a symptom? Hamilton describes the coincidence between the *vellón* inflation and decadence in classic terms. While the emphasis on Castile, particularly New Castile, is justified for the seventeenth century, the analysis of the recovery in the eighteenth century requires regional analysis. This Hamilton has provided for Valencia, and Vilar has confirmed his conclusions for Catalonia, but other regional analyses are needed, particularly for the Basque country. The contrast between regional economies linked by the sea to other economies, the monetary and fiscal autonomy, the impact of the Indies trade on the Seville monopoly, and the displacement in Spain of precious metals by the *vellón* currency and their export all contribute to Castilian decadence, which is in contrast to the earlier but slower and less extensive decadence of the Spanish Mediterranean kingdoms. The regularity of the secular price movement in Valencia contrasts with the monetary, economic, and psychological chaos in Castile. Hamilton has rightly stressed the long-term implications of regional patterns, and the economic disjunction between Catalonia and the rest of Spain serves as the starting point for Vilar's research on the economic bases of "national structures." This in turn is a starting point for an understanding of the political disjunction between Catalonia and the rest of Spain in the late nineteenth century.[23]

Shipping and Trade

The work of Pierre and Huguette Chaunu, *Seville et l'Atlantique, 1504–1650*, is the most important contribution of quantitative history, both serial and cyclical, to the study of the Spanish economy and an outstanding example of the "new history."[24] Inspired and encouraged by Braudel, it extends to the Atlantic the type of research undertaken by Nina Ellinger Bang and later by Knud Korst for the straits between Sweden and Denmark. The book complements and parallels the price histories studied in such important monographs as those of Simiand, Labrousse, Magalhães Godinho, Beveridge, Posthumus, and Hoszowski, whose research served as a model. The constant references to Hamilton, and especially to his correlations between remittances from the Indies and prices and wages in different parts of Spain, show how the quantification of traffic flows may complement the older study of prices. The two volumes on "conjuncture" —the trade cycles—are rich in methodological contributions and in substantive corrections and confirmations of the work of Hamilton, which the Chaunus praise lavishly.

The Chaunus suggest that traffic flows can serve as an indirect measure of production for which historical data are scarce and unreliable (a point on which Pierre Vilar disagrees). Few works show more clearly how quantitative series reveal the interdependence of economic processes on, for example, the relation between mercury mining in Huancavelica (as established by Guillermo Lohman Villena) and the delivery of silver, shipping, and prices. They point out other relationships, involving the rise in wages and the lag in shipbuilding; gold mining, smuggling, and slave trading. The impact of war and peace and threats of piracy show the interdependence of the economy and politics. Even when analyzed in less detail, developments such as the expulsion of the Moriscos and the decline of the Mexican Indian population, with their subsequent reflection in the Atlantic traffic, show the importance of demographic factors. Here the listings of passengers to the Indies, partly published but largely unanalyzed, require additional research, as the Chaunus point out. The lack of correspondence between certain events and quantitative series is significant; for example, the lack of impact of the Catalan rebellion of 1640 on the Atlantic trade confirms Vilar's stress on the lack of integration among the territories of the Spanish crown, especially the gap between the Spanish Mediterranean and Castilian Atlantic Spain.

The work is based on rich information from the archives (mostly in Seville) and particularly on ship registers, which are the most reliable sources since they are less linked with taxation, on the records of the ad valorem tax on departures (the *averia*) and the *almojarifazgos* in the Indian ports, on the correspondence and accounts of the Casa de la Contratación, and on notarial records. If treated simultaneously, these data, despite their omissions and evasions, permit the reconstruction of the business cycle for most Atlantic shipping—up to 80 percent in the sixteenth century and above 50 percent in the seventeenth. The result required careful analysis of 17,761 crossings—10,438 outbound and 7,323 inbound—over a period of 145 years, with information on each type of ship, tonnage, master and crews, points of departure and arrival, losses due to sea piracy or war, value of the cargo, and so on. Obviously not all these series are equally complete and reliable, and much of the work—particularly the first volume, which is devoted to methodological problems—deals with these difficulties. The

Chaunus devote four volumes to the raw data and two volumes to a statistical summary. In collaboration with Guy Arbellot and Jacques Bertin, the authors present their principal findings in a volume of graphs and maps, a model in its genre, that will provide the interested nonspecialist with the best view of the scope of this monumental work. Another major contribution is the bibliography, which lists archival sources and calls attention as well to many older books containing data of importance to any quantitatively minded historian. The later volumes offer an analytical presentation of the data organized in basic cycles: the first expansion (1504–50), the great midcentury intercyclical recession (1550–59/62), the second long expansion phase (1559/62–92), the high point of the trade (1592–1622), and the great depression (1623–50). Within these periods, various minor cycles are characterized and analyzed. For each phase we are given data on the outbound and inbound traffic in terms of the number of ships and, where possible, tonnage, value, type, and age of ships; covariance with prices; formation of convoys; impact of threats to navigation; and so on. In addition data are given for the traffic with the West Indies, Tierra Firme (the link with the Pacific and Peru), and Mexico, and for the changes through time which in turn mirrored changes in production, demography, etc.

In another volume, Pierre Chaunu presents the geographical setting of Atlantic navigation—the nature of harbors, the process of exploration, and economic expansion (especially of mining)—as well as the shipping technology that provided the structural context for those cyclical fluctuations. Theoretical discussions on the implications of his data for the theses of Hamilton and others concerning the development of the Spanish and the European economy should be noted by historians, whether interested or not in the data that serve as underpinning.

In another work using the same approach, Pierre Chaunu investigates the trans-Pacific trade between Mexico and the Philippines.[25] The statistics on shipping, remittances, taxes, etc. for the years from 1586 to 1790 are based on accounts kept by the Spaniards in Manila and Acapulco and on copies of those preserved in the Archivo de Indias. Chaunu started from a text by Hamilton suggesting that the stagnation (1601–30) and reversal (1631–60) in the trend of treasury funds sent from the Indies to Seville might be due in part to an increase in trade between the Orient and America. The point was called to Chaunu's attention by Braudel, and, although Chaunu did not confirm the hypothesis, his research revealed for the first time a world economic cycle and demonstrated that the cycle for the Philippines was a prolongation of the cycles that he had discovered for the Spanish-American Atlantic of Seville. The detailed tables on shipping entering and leaving Manila, listing origins and destination, offer invaluable information on the relationships between this outpost of the West and China, Japan, and India—relationships important for any future study of the economic cycles of the non-Western world.

The study of shipping has also attracted two Spaniards. Alvaro Castillo Pintado, using the registers of the *peatge de mar* for Valencia under Philip III (1598–1621), demonstrates that Atlantic traffic was limited, since more than half the ships came from Marseilles and much of the shipping was coastal in nature.[26] His statistics, which include cargo information, confirm the broad picture presented by Braudel. Francisco Morales Padrón, on the other hand, studies the traffic between the Canaries and America, providing detailed statistical series on ships, destinations, and cargos; stressing the eighteenth century; and giving very complete data on the connection with Cadiz.[27]

In view of the wealth of information on remittances of public and private treasure, on prices, and on the importance of Seville as an artistic center at the turn of the seventeenth century, it would be tempting for some sociologist-historian of art to explore the relationships between economic changes and the commissioning of works of art. On the cultural side—the building of churches and palaces, the execution of painting and sculpture, the publishing of works of literature and science, university enrollment—we have nothing to compare with the wealth of serial economic history. The relation between the economic base and the culture of Spain's "Golden Age" has not yet been investigated, but research on this subject would certainly give rise to new questions about the interrelations—and perhaps contradictory trends—of political power, economic cycles, and cultural creativity.

In a major older work, Teófilo Guiard y Larrauri studies the Casa de Contratación and the Consulado of Bilbao.[28] He gives us a detailed description not only of its mercantile and maritime institutions but also of the day-by-day operations of the harbor: the ships with their names, masters, origins and destinations (mainly Flanders, the Hanse cities, and the Baltic), cargos, etc. Because this wealth of information is presented principally in the text or in long lists instead of in tables or graphs, it is difficult to apply any systematic quantitative analysis to it or relate the information to research on business cycles, on the various economies, or on shipping between different countries. A reedition of Guiard's work—quantifying much of his data, giving it graphic presentation, and relating it to economic series of later scholars—might be a major contribution. This could be done without further archival research, although I suspect that a new look at many of the original sources would be rewarding if one is to answer the questions asked by historians after Hamilton, the Chaunus, and Vilar. The trade of Hamburg with Spain, important in the study of Guiard, has been the subject of monographic work by German historians Kellenbenz (for 1590–1625) and Pohl (for 1740–1806).[29]

The Social Structure and the Economy

While the scholars just discussed have focused on the international connections of the Spanish economy, others have directed their attention to

Spanish society in the same period. The uprisings in many cities of the kingdom against the authority of Charles I of Spain when he became Emperor Charles V have long been an object of ideological debate among Spaniards. Leopoldo Piles Ros uses archival data to give us a largely quantitative picture of the social bases of the Germania movement that developed in the kingdom of Valencia between 1519 and 1522.[30] The punishment of the culprits has left us with records of their identity and wealth, their confiscated property, and the sums they paid toward the expenses incurred in subduing them. These data, which give the names, occupation, location, and sums paid by individuals and by various artisan guilds and communities, are to be published in detail by Piles.

Noël Salomon's recent work on New Castile is the outstanding monograph on the interactions of the demography, economy, and social structure of rural Spain of the southern Meseta.[31] The author brings tremendous scholarship to his analysis of the quantitative data; his work also reveals the sensitivity of a humanist who had studied the ideology of the treatment of the peasant in the comic theatre at the time of Lope de Vega. The data from two royal questionnaires, circulated in 1575 and 1578, cover 600 population centers and permit a systematic statistical analysis. In the nineteenth century, Fermín Caballero, in his speech of acceptance into the Academy of History, traced the history and the motivations underlying the *Relaciones Topográficas* ordered by Philip II, describing the questionnaire, the difficulties of collecting the data, and the surviving manuscripts.[32] Salomon, by means of well-selected quotations and statistical tables, presents the population, production, and property structure, together with the social relations to be derived. He speaks of the conflict between communal village property and aristocratic and ecclesiastical properties; the complex transitions of "feudal" property with its jurisdictional rights and the "bourgeois" property of nobles and non-nobles; and the "seigneurialization" of peasant property that transformed smallholders into tenants or laborers. A final chapter presents an excellent description of the class structure and the place of the nobility, hidalgos, farmers, artisans, and laborers in that society.

In an interesting though sometimes loosely structured work, José Gentil da Silva skillfully uses data from the *Relaciones* of Philip II and the *Censo de Frutos y Manufacturas* of 1799, as well as material on the gold and silver that went from Seville to other provinces in 1570–71 and on the exchanges between different sectors of the economy.[33] He gives us a complex picture of the Castilian economy, answering some questions pertinent to development and decline and linking his data to theoretical problems. The appendixes by Jacques Bertin provide invaluable graphs of taxes, population, per capita taxes, and wealth of various sorts for selected dates from the middle of the sixteenth century to 1960. Few works better illustrate the way in which the demographic and economic centers of Spain have moved from the interior to the periphery as the stagnation of some areas was offset by the growth of others. This shift from the center has often been neglected in analyses of the background of the problems of national integration.

Content analysis of the replies in the *Relaciones* indicate conditions in each community: insufficient area for cultivation, lack of pasture land or its loss by the community, lack of woods, cultivation of poor land, climate, existence of farm laborers, and so on. Detailed tables breaking down exchanges between Seville and the provinces of the kingdom by economic sectors and different products provide us with a picture of the economy, the functions of different provinces, and the degree and type of internal distribution of the wealth coming from the Indies. The maps and tables show the striking duality between the kingdoms of Castile and Aragon in imperial days. In contrast to most monographic works, da Silva moves back and forth over centuries of Spanish economic life.

Another major monograph making use of quantitative data on the population, economy, society, culture, and values of the sixteenth century is the volume by Bartolomé Bennassar on the city of Valladolid, for a short time the capital of the kingdom.[34] Using information from the 1561 census, Bennassar places Valladolid in the context of five other Castilian cities. Series for baptisms, marriages, and burials over a century contribute to our knowledge of historical demography. The economic base of the city is the tertiary sector: the court, the tribunals, the university, the resident *rentier* nobility, the lawyers, clergymen, and merchants, who set the tone of its life and were more numerous than the artisans. We can follow the debts of the nobility, the interest they paid, and the names of their creditors; we can compare wage series with prices of basic staples between 1499 and 1600. Bennassar describes the style of life, religion, leisure, luxury, and poverty, as well as the cycle of festivals, art, and culture. He ends with a section full of insight on deviant behavior and on social and cultural values as expressed in daily life.

The Moriscos and Their Expulsion: Religion, Politics, Demography, and Socioeconomic Consequences

The fate of the former Moors, mostly converted to Christianity by force but culturally and religiously unassimilated, whose expulsion in 1609 has been likened to that of the French Huguenots, has attracted the attention of several scholars. Lapeyre's *Géographie de l'Espagne Morisque* is a major contribution.[35] The maps and statistics on the places of origin of those expelled as well as on the ports of exit show the quality of records that a monarchy of the seventeenth century was able to keep. The logistics of the expulsion give us indirectly a sense of the bureaucratic and military organization of the state such as no qualitative description alone could. Lapeyre's figures, when related to the population figures of Domínguez Ortiz, show the very different impact of the expulsion on the kingdoms of Aragon and Castile and the misleading nature of national averages, for Aragon lost 12.6

percent of its population and Castile only 1.3, with an overall loss for Spain of 2.2 percent. In Valencia the expulsion affected 26 percent of the population. There, since—contrary to common belief—the land occupied by the Moriscos was poor (with the exception of the orchard area of Gandia), it led to depopulation and abandonment of certain areas and the expansion of large holdings. Because of the demographic weakness of Spain at the time, the abandoned areas were not reoccupied. Jorge Nadal has noted that the expulsion of 88,000 Moriscos from Castile had a limited impact as compared with the half million deaths caused by the plague of 1598–1602 or even with the annual migration of four to five thousand to America. Although Lapeyre's total figure of 272,140 Moriscos expelled has been disputed, his research shows how important quantitative data can be in subjecting ideological interpretations to the test of facts.

Lapeyre depends greatly on an earlier study by Juan Reglá, which analyzes the events leading to the expulsion by means of considerable documentary evidence.[36] He publishes the data from the special census of the Aragonese Moriscos ordered by the viceroy in 1609 before the exodus, recording 14,109 households; multiplied by five, this would represent 70,545 persons or 20 percent of that kingdom's population of 332,450. Lapeyre questions the method of calculation and suggests a lower figure. He not only reproduces Reglá's figures on the number of households, ordering them by the present provinces (while Reglá adds them by region), but records the number of households and persons reported to have left through Navarre and the Mediterranean port of Alfaques. In his appendixes, Reglá lists population centers and the number of old and new Christians and their lords for the kingdom of Valencia, as well as the plans for the concentration of Aragonese Moriscos for expulsion.

The monograph by Tulio Halperin Donghi on the Moriscos of Valencia, which is not used by Lapeyre, has a more limited geographic scope and concentrates less on demographic questions, but it gives us an impressive picture of social relations between Moriscos and other sectors of society.[37] These include their places in the economy and in different social strata and institutions; the theological, moral, and legal debates; and the problems posed by resettlement of depopulated areas. Perhaps Halperin Donghi's greatest achievement is his vivid picture of the life of those men, their hopes and fears—the human side of the exodus and the complex arguments surrounding it before the final decision. His main quantitative contribution is a series of maps and tables on the changes of the population of Valencia (between 1565–72 and 1609 and between 1609 and 1646) in relation to the number of old and new Christians, based on archival sources and the earlier works of Boronat and Danvila. The work of Halperin Donghi and the fascinating book by Julio Caro Baroja on the Moriscos in the kingdom of Granada (they were transferred to other parts of Spain after their rebellion in 1568) give a real feeling for Islam under Christian rule and provide a necessary background for understanding the figures of Lapeyre. But the study of Caro Baroja, like so many brilliant studies, falls outside my focus on quantification.[38]

Historical Demography

I do not intend to review here the increasing number of studies in the field of historical demography that the reader will find briefly but competently reviewed in Jorge Nadal's *La población española (Siglos XVI a XX)*.[39] Among the most important works based on the indispensable parish church archives is Jorge Nadal's research in collaboration with Emilio Giralt on the Catalan population.[40] The demographic history of Catalonia offers special difficulties, since there were no population counts between 1553 and 1717 except for the unreliable census of Aparici in 1708. To reconstruct the demographic changes over 164 years, with a considerable range from the interior and the Pyrenees to the coast, from figures based on from 52,145 to 94,518 households is difficult. It is of considerable interest in view of the seventeenth-century crisis, the repression of the secession attempt in 1640, and the war of succession early in the eighteenth century. The painstaking research based on parish and hospital records for births, marriages, and deaths and the determination of patterns of population change, the ecology of epidemics, and immigration constitute a model for scholars. The central theme of the study is immigration—its causes, its origins in France, its changes over time, and the ages and occupations of the immigrants. The immigration of other foreigners into Catalonia and the comparison of Catalan immigration with that into other regions are additional contributions of the study, as is a thorough analysis of the expulsion of the Moriscos.

Nadal and Giralt were able to use the register of a parish in Gerona, complete from 1511 to 1700, and to find in it the population growth in the sixteenth century up to 1590 as well as information concerning the depression that characterized seventeenth-century Spanish demographic development. They also explored the impact of the years of high mortality, which coincided with years of food shortages or plague. The impact of the cost of living on marriage and birth rates is also explored through correlations of the price of wheat with the baptismal records of the parish of Sant Feliu in Gerona. Incidentally, the *Guía de la Iglesia en España* lists the holdings of the sacramental registers for most of the parishes of Spain, showing the possible scope for this kind of research. Maps and more than 100 pages of tables document the Nadal-Giralt analysis. In their work demography sheds light on political processes such as the emigration of Catalans sympathetic with France and the immigration from Roussillon of Catalans who preferred to live under a Spanish sovereign after the province had been transferred to France. The analysis of internal migrations by regions is particularly fruitful for the understanding of changes in the economy and society.

Bartolemé Bennassar has also contributed a work on epidemics in northern Spain in the sixteenth century which gives special emphasis to sources and methodology.[41]

The Inquisition and the Conversos

The Spanish Inquisition has been the object of extravagant criticism and defense ever since its former secretary, Juan Antonio Llorente, published his four-volume history in 1817–18, with its figures, which modern scholars consider exaggerated, of the number of its victims. A recent work by Henry Kamen indicates the relevant literature and, although it is basically not a quantitative study, gives interesting data on the number of victims. Kamen summarizes the research of Lea, Delgado Merchán, Fita, Rodríguez Moñino, Braunstein, and Birch; he also discusses the research on the persecution of "Lutherans" by Schäfer, the budgets of some tribunals, the expense account of an auto-de-fé, and the confiscation of property. In recent years a number of Inquisition cases have been published, and many more are in the archives. Kamen and Julio Caro Baroja emphasize the interest that a systematic analysis of the details of property confiscation can have for social history.[42] Inevitably the attention of scholars has been attracted more by the famous Inquisition cases of humanists, professors, writers, and highly placed clerics and officials, and by the indexes of forbidden or expurgated books, than by the less illustrious victims. The interest of scholars is likely to shift from the problem of the number of victims to the study of their place in the social structure, their occupation and economic position, their integration into society, and perhaps, through a study of informers, accusers, and witnesses, to the Spanish social milieu that supported the intolerance of alien elements and cultural tendencies after 1481.

Caro Baroja, in his monumental three-volume work on the treatment of Jews in modern Spain, has, without attempting essentially quantitative history, compiled some quantitative series and called the attention of scholars to further opportunities for research on the converted Jews—both the honest new Christians and the crypto-Jews. For example, he gives a statistical graph of cases of *judaizantes* before the Inquisition of Toledo between 1483 and 1800. His study of the families of persecuted *conversos* and their ties is of particular interest. In view of the role of Portuguese Jews—many of whom were of Castilian origin—in the time of Philip IV, his map on new Christians in Portugal in 1631, which comes from the research of Mendes dos Remedios, and his statistical tables based on it are of special interest, as is his detailed study of the great final repression of 1721–25. Other studies which discuss critically the figures for the number of Jews in Spain at the time of their expulsion or forced conversion in 1492 are those of Nicolás

López Martínez and Antonio Domínguez Ortiz.[43] Unfortunately there is no information on the expulsion of the Jews comparable to that on the Moriscos under Philip IV, a fact that seems to reflect the difference in the levels of bureaucratic development at the end of the fifteenth century and the middle of the seventeenth century. Caro Baroja's hypotheses that there were 400,000 Jews in the domains of the Catholic Kings, that 160,000 left Spain, and that 50,000 of those remaining were tried in the first half-century of the Inquisition give us some idea of the number of Jews in Spain—whose total population has been estimated at 7.4 million for 1541.[44] But his research, like that of Domínguez Ortiz, makes the importance of the Jews even clearer by considering the social and economic positions of the converts and their descendants. However, he does not go as far as Américo Castro in his analysis of the unique features brought to Spanish culture and society by the *conversos*—and by the reaction against them and the fetish for purity of blood.[45] The significance of the Jews contrasts with the marginality and disappearance of the Islamic component after the defeat and expulsion of the Moors. Perhaps a more quantitative analysis of the files of the Inquisition and a closer study of the *liber status animorum* could shed further light on elite and mass religious behavior in a society in which religion occupied men as deeply as it did in Spain.

Antonio Domínguez Ortiz's *El estamento eclesiástico*, a historico-sociological study of the church in the seventeenth century, fills a gap well. Without placing special emphasis on quantification, it provides information on the number of clerics, both secular and regular, and on offices and benefices, the finances of the church and its ministers, tithes, holdings, and the contributions to the finances of the state. Its main value is in calling attention to the role of the church, problems for further research, and the type of data and sources available.[46]

Universities and Elites

The importance of university-trained lawyers, clerics, and scholars in the society and government of the monarchy after the fourteenth century makes one regret the scarcity of modern scholarly research on the history of universities and bureaucratic-professional elites. Richard Kagan goes beyond the lengthy descriptive accounts and the publication of documents and matriculation records into an analysis of the published and archival sources and sketches the role played by "imperial" and provincial universities, *colegios mayores,* and Jesuit colleges in Castilian society.[47] His examination of the incomplete and not always reliable records leads him to conclude that there was almost uninterrupted expansion in numbers and size from 1500 to 1600 or, in some cases, 1620; a period of stagnation from the 1620s to approximately 1640; and, after that date, steady decline well into the eighteenth century. With reservations, he estimates that during the last quarter of the sixteenth century there were between 20,000 and 25,000 students enrolled annually in some 20 universities, a figure roughly equal to 2 to 3.7 percent of the male 15-to-24 age group; if the university-level education provided by the Jesuits were to be added, this figure would be even higher. He notes a steady shift, beginning in the middle of the sixteenth century, away from the study of arts and theology to the study of law, particularly canon law, as a gateway to both clerical and secular careers. Kagan links those trends with changes in the social structure and values, the recruitment policies of the bureaucracy, *empleomanía,* and decreasing opportunities, and he notes their impact on cultural life. His data and the sources to which he refers—as well as the records on the politico-administrative, judicial, ecclesiastical, and intellectual elites—should permit quantitative analyses that would add to our understanding of the structure of society and government, elite recruitment and career patterns, and the sociology of bureaucratic empires in general.

José Antonio Escudero's *Los Secretarios de Estado y del Despacho, 1474–1724* is an excellent study of the origins and development of the royal bureaucracy containing some quantitative information on the remuneration of the royal secretaries and on the length of their tenure, which would allow a study of their turnover. I have undertaken a quantitative analysis of biographies of the intellectual elite of the sixteenth and seventeenth centuries and of some of the data collected by the seventeenth-century bibliographer-biographer Nicholas Antonio. This shows differences in intellectual pursuits, education, place of birth, foreign travel, occupation, membership in religious orders, etc. between the two centuries.[48]

THE EIGHTEENTH CENTURY: THE ANCIEN RÉGIME AND ITS REFORMERS

The accession of a grandson of Louis XIV of France to the Spanish throne in 1700 represents much more than a change of dynasty. The last decades of Habsburg rule had been a period of decadence. The new monarchs and their ministers showed a serious concern for the political, administrative, fiscal, economic, and cultural reform of their increasingly centralized kingdom. This was reflected in new efforts to collect accurate information on many aspects of the population, society, and economy. Renewed attempts during this period to revitalize the economy have been the subjects of recent research. However, the main focus of Spanish and foreign scholarship has been, in addition to external history and international relations, the history of ideas: Enlightenment vs. reaction, and the emerging divisions between various reformers that crystallized at the end of the reign of Charles IV. The eighteenth century has long been neglected, perhaps because many historians saw it with a prejudiced eye. It was first seen as a period of Bourbon absolutism and later as one of a loss of authenticity as compared to the golden century, a point of view influenced by Catholic critics like Menéndez Pelayo. The period was influenced by foreign, mainly

French, ideas and institutions, favoring increased secularization or at least a moderate anti-clericalism and Europeanization. These influences are examined in a sympathetic light in the syntheses of Jean Sarrailh and Richard Herr. In Spain, the work of Luis Sánchez Agesta, which centers around the writings of Feijóo and Jovellanos, is another major contribution to the reevaluation of that century.[49]

Social and economic history, despite useful source materials in official censuses, government inquests, and archives, has room for additional monographic research. An older reference work by G. Desdevises du Dezert is still unexcelled, although Antonio Domínguez Ortiz has considerably advanced our knowledge in his *La sociedad española en el siglo XVIII*.[50] The work of Hamilton extends into the eighteenth century and is indispensable, as is the monumental work of Pierre Vilar on Catalonia, to which I have already referred. To these should be added a number of recent monographs, in particular the work of Miguel Artola and his collaborators, which is still in progress. The printing of some basic sources, such as the Catastro de Ensenada and the *Censo de Frutas y Manufacturas,* is probably the first step to a more intensive quantitative approach to the century. A new reading of the authors of the time—government officials and reformers as well as historians, geographers, and travelers such as J. F. de Bourgoing, J. Townsend, and Alexandre de Laborde—in connection with documentary records might serve as a basis for a more comparative, systematic, quantitative, and interpretative analysis of the response of Spain to the crisis in 1700.

The wealth of information on intellectual history might be used for a collective portrait of reforming intellectuals and administrators as well as their traditionalist antagonists. The recent work on the Sociedades Económicas de Amigos del País—associations that gave institutional support to the Enlightenment and numbering fifty-six by 1789—presents another body of useful material at least partly quantifiable, especially with respect to the social composition of their membership. An instance of quantification that could be pushed further—perhaps to include a sociometric network model —is the work of Richard Herr on the social and regional distribution of subscriptions to magazines expressing the ideas of the Enlightenment.[51] In this area of the history of ideas, culture, and science, we may be reaching the point where quantification, particularly in comparative perspective, could add a new dimension to an already rich literature.

The major work in quantitative history, however, will be in the fields of demography, social structure, and economics. Hamilton extended his research on prices and wages up to 1800, and we await the extension of the Chaunus' work on transatlantic shipping and trade—particularly the data on Cadiz, which displaced Seville in the overseas trade until its own monopoly was abolished in 1765. The study of population and production, especially agricultural production, now being written by Gonzalo Anes will give us a necessary base from which to evaluate changes and continuity under the critical conditions of the Napoleonic invasion and the different responses to it.

A few monographs on the eighteenth century make use of quantitative data and information which could be given further quantitative treatment, particularly in regard to statistics collected by the royal officials of the Spanish Bourbons. Pierre Vilar notes that the eighteenth-century Spanish historians (Capmany, Labrada, Cavanilles, Caresman, Larruga, Asso) tend to give figures, but in an unsystematic way; more modern writers such as Carrera Pujal, on the other hand, following a trend initiated by Colmeiro in the nineteenth century, focus their attention on legal and descriptive texts without providing quantitative data.[52] New editions of the earlier works should present in a more systematic and modern fashion the information they collected.[53]

The impact of the Enlightenment after midcentury is reflected in a wealth of censuses and statistics and in the writings of contemporary economists and reformers. Relatively speaking, the earlier decades, the period of transition from Habsburg to Bourbon rule and of institutional discontinuity, and the divisions caused by the War of the Spanish Succession and the subsequent reintegration have only recently been given increased attention—in the works of Pedro Voltes Bou, Joan Mercader i Riba, and Henry Kamen.[54] Pedro Voltes presents considerable statistical information on population, social structure, housing, taxation, banking, etc.; and in the process he directs attention to published and unpublished sources, in particular to José Aparici, a geographer-administrator. Mercader and Kamen present much information on the attempts to restructure the government of the kingdom after the French model in order to achieve the unification and centralization in state building that had been denied to Olivares and Philip IV. Kamen, in addition to writing a general history of the period from 1700 to 1715, has through archival research investigated the war effort—men, suppliers, expenses—in quantitative terms. In his analysis of the political and administrative changes resulting from the dynastic conflict, he deals with the confiscated wealth of the nobility. The wealth of the Indies, taxation in Spain, and government expenditures are studied in detail, and new archival data are presented in many tables including interesting information on prices and population. The institutional, social, and economic aspects of the rebellion against the new sovereign in the eastern parts of the kingdom receive special attention and establish the limits of political integration achieved by Spain before the eighteenth century.

Jorge Nadal and Emilio Giralt give us a good picture of the social and economic structure of Barcelona based on the Catastro of 1717.[55] They provide us with information on age and occupation of the population for the different districts of the city, the condition of housing, and the distribution of income from real estate and other sources based on tax records. The capital of Catalonia stands as a model of preindustrial society. The basic source for the population and economy of the midcentury is the Catastro of the Marquis de la Ensenada. It covers three-fifths of Spain and includes information for each community on cultivated land, cattle, houses and business activities, income for professionals and workers, clergymen and convents, and the poor. For some provinces the original lists on which the inventory was based have been preserved. Matilla Tascón has published a volume of provincial summaries and intends to present a second volume for villages of more than 200 *vecinos*.[56] He traces the history of the census, details the instructions to the enumerators, and shows its connection with attempts at tax reform. Tomás Maza Solano has published the Catastro for the northern coastal region of the Montaña (Santander).[57]

The publication of the Catastro de Ensenada prompted Pierre Vilar to write an excellent article on the social and economic structure of provincial Spain between Galicia and Andalusia.[58] It is difficult to extend this treatment to other parts of Spain, for the data do not cover regions with fiscal autonomy such as the Basque country, Navarre, the kingdoms of the crown of Aragon, nor Madrid. In addition to a methodological critique of the source, Vilar presents basic data on the nobility, the clergy, farmers and farm laborers, and nonagricultural activities. The final section, on the income of different social groups, including the rural-urban wage differentials in various regions, is particularly valuable. Vilar's article emphasizes regional differences and their persistence almost to our own time.

The Catastro of the Marquis de la Ensenada, together with other, mostly contemporary geographical, statistical, and historical sources—and the survey addressed mainly to parish priests by Cardinal Lorenzana around 1787—all have enabled Fernando Jiménez de Gregorio to compile a dictionary of the villages of the province of Toledo.[59] Although the wealth of information remains unanalyzed, statistically or cartographically, it can be helpful to a rural sociologist or anthropologist studying social change in New Castile communities.

The *Censo de Frutos y Manufacturas* of 1799 is one of the most important quantitative sources for Spanish economic and social history, and its recent reprinting should encourage analysis of its data.[60] Based on data requested in 1787, supplied by the *intendentes* in 1799, elaborated by officials in Madrid, and first published in 1803, it gives information for the then 34 provinces. Among the sources for population, society, economy, and, above all, public finances, José Canga Argüelles's *Diccionario de Hacienda*, published in London in 1826, occupies a distinguished place.[61] It is a convenient source for the data of the 1797 census, and the index at the end of the fifth volume facilitates its use.

Pierre Vilar's monumental *La Catalogne dans l'Espagne Moderne*, to which we have already referred, is a masterful contribution to eighteenth-century history.[62] It is a painstaking, critical analysis of the demographic data and sources, compiled from the *Vezindario General* of 1717, the

Relación General of 1718, the census of Floridablanca of 1787, the mid-century data of the "census" of Aranda of 1768, and the *Censo de Frutos y Manufacturas.* The doubling of the population in less than sixty-nine years is an indication of the changes in Catalonia; Vilar analyzes the changes in different regions of the principality in detail. Studying the relationships between population changes, migrations, and economic changes, he presents population data for 1718 and 1787 for each municipality, including the rate of increase and population densities. The *Catalogne* describes in detail the increase in cultivated areas and the intensification of agricultural production, the expansion of irrigation, and the commercialization and specialization of agriculture. It shows price movements for a number of agricultural products, both imported and local, for Barcelona between the 1720s and 1806; and it compares price movements to those for Castile and France, offering a sophisticated analysis of short- and long-term business cycles, price differentials between different types of markets, and political events. The third part focuses on land rents and the process of capital formation over the century, with detailed tables on the revenues of royal farms and the lease of farms. The tables showing types of landholding, occupation and address of the holders and the total area and value of the farms comprise one of the most interesting series of quantitative data. In the analysis, these series are related to price series as well as to data on income of tenants, transportation costs, and wages of agricultural and urban laborers. Vilar carefully notes the consequences for nine different strata in Catalan society from large landlords to farm laborers.

The third volume of the *Catalogne* deals with commercial activities—from small enterprises to large trading companies, from local coastal shipping to the trade with the Indies—particularly after 1778, when the American trade became free. The research on the business cycle is based on five continuous series: (1) the *lezda* as an indicator of the volume of exchanges by sea between Catalan ports and those abroad or in the rest of Spain; (2) the *periage* as an indicator of imports by sea for the capital (both series only for the second half of the century); (3) the *cops* tax, which provides us with a measure for the basic supply of grain for the city and reflects both volume and price; (4) the king's weight, a measure for certain supplies, both foodstuffs and industrial materials, entering the city; (5) the toll of the *barca de St. Boi,* measuring boat traffic on the route to Tarragona-Valencia and part of the traffic to Zaragoza and Madrid. Analysis of these five series, with their correlations and divergences, and comparison of them with similar curves for other countries (i.e., the sales at the fair of Beaucaire) provide us with a unique basis for understanding the development of the Catalan economy.

On the traffic of Barcelona with France between 1782 and 1792, Vilar gives a documented analysis by type of ship, tonnage, origin, products imported and exported, and destination. He gives detailed data for the imports and exports of 1793 and for the trade with the Indies, as well as for the origins of ships arriving between 1804 and 1806. The statistical series are complemented by the "biographies" of shipping enterprises from 1744 to 1808—traffic, time in harbors, time at sea, destinations, shippers, cargo, freight charges, expenses on ship and for repairs, payments to the crew, and profits or losses on each trip for the shareholders—based on archival records for thirteen ships. The *Catalogne* gives a great deal of information about the costs of shipbuilding, wages, shipping charges, composition of invested capital, and pilot training, including the regional origins of the 1077 men attending a school for pilots from 1779 to 1809. One of the most interesting series relates to traffic between Barcelona and the Indies from 1778 to 1788 and the ratio of Catalan ships in the total traffic of 1778.

Account books for a number of enterprises, both small *botigas* and the larger *companyas,* inform us as to their operations, imports, exports, sales, stocks, expenses, profits or losses, and the variety of business operations in which they were engaged. These are seen in the light of the business cycles and the political and military events that affected their activities. The discussion moves back and forth between micro- and macroanalysis, from the level of the enterprise to the level of the Catalan and world economies. Few tables of accounts can give us a better view of the growth of capitalist enterprise or the opportunities and difficulties faced both by independent shopkeepers and by company shareholders. The commercial aspects and the circulation of merchandise are studied as a point of departure of capital, to use a Marxian phrase. The conjunction of micro- and macrodata shows the intensification, specialization, and diversification of economic activities over the eighteenth century, with the volume of profits increasing but not the average rate; data on extraordinary profits and bankruptcies and the responses to those situations allow Vilar to give us a quantitative but also human view, economic but also sociological, of the new society born in Catalonia. His work, which ends with magnificent maps and statistical graphs, leaves us eager to read in a future volume his analysis of industrialization in the eighteenth and nineteenth centuries.

Vilar has also published in the series Affaires et Gens d'Affaires an edition with a lengthy introduction of the manual of the "Companya Nova" of Gibraltar, 1709–23, an important contribution to the history of commercial accounting and the techniques of the financing of trade.[63] This is also a contribution to the main themes of Vilar's work: the duality of the Catalan and Castilian monetary systems, business cycles, and the economic consequences of war. In it he explores further the first Catalan economic revival of 1674–1710, class relations in Catalonia, and the relationship of the bourgeoisie to the nobility and the rural world as well as of Catalonia to the rest of Spain.

A major contribution to the economic history of the century is the work of Miguel Capella and Antonio Matilla Tascón on the five Madrid merchant guilds for: silk, gold, and silver cloth; woolens; linens; spices and drugs; and jewelry.[64] These were given a privileged position in 1686, and in 1763 they constituted a trading company under royal privilege. This company, which in 1777 had 375 members, not only engaged in retail trade in the capital but had representatives in London, Hamburg, Paris, and Morocco. It entered into overseas trade with agents in Mexico, Veracruz, Guatemala, Arequipa, Lima, the Philippines, and California; owned ships; acted as a tax farmer; and controlled supplies for the army and the royal household. As another aspect of its activities it created a number of industrial enterprises, particularly in textiles, in different parts of Spain, and in 1785 was involved in the completion of the Aragon canal as well as in banking operations. Capella and Matilla Tascón's study follows its activities in detail until its dissolution in the 1840s, using figures from its archives and accounts, and reviews the reactions of public opinion and of historians, past and present, to these activities. The detailed account of the crisis it faced as a result of the Napoleonic invasion, together with the loss of the overseas empire and the operations liquidating its assets, is of great interest, since it offers us a glimpse into the disruption of Spain's capitalist development in the first decades of the nineteenth century after the eighteenth-century upsurge.

American scholars, after the pioneering and controversial efforts of E. J. Hamilton, seem to have left the field of Spanish economic history to the French and the Spaniards themselves. La Force's *Development of the Spanish Textile Industry, 1750–1800* and Ringrose's *Transportation and Economic Stagnation in Spain, 1750–1850* are exceptions.[65] La Force uses a wealth of quantitative data but does not seem to be intrigued by the new methods of presentation or of quantitative and graphic analysis. He concentrates on the description of institutional problems, shies away from macroeconomic analysis and from attempts to link social and economic changes, and makes little effort to relate his data to broader problems, as does Pierre Vilar. Ringrose, using quantitative data, mainly from the Catastro of La Ensenada but also from archival sources mostly for the eighteenth century, raises important questions about transportation and economic development. Geographic and economic factors made it difficult to create a transportation system comparable to those of other countries in the interior of Spain before the building of the railroads. The absence of waterways and canals, orography, distances, and the volume of goods made decent roads for carts uneconomical. On the basis of available statistical data, Ringrose estimates supply and demand of transportation and presents data on the cost of transport. In addition, from a variety of sources he constructs maps indicating the patterns of transport activity; these are based on tables of different commodities listing origin and/or destination of the cargo (which have not been included in the book but are available from Rutgers University library).

Agrarian History

Gonzalo Anes views the agricultural growth of the eighteenth century, after the seventeenth-century depression, as a missed opportunity to create a basis for industrialization.[66] He attributes the failure to the persistence of traditional structures in rural society and institutions that prevented the accumulation of commercial capital. This thorough study calls attention to many neglected archival and some published sources, and its tables and graphic appendixes present statistical series on population, production, prices, land rents, market organization, etc. The analysis by region demonstrates the great differences between the economies of the interior and the peripheries, particularly those open to maritime trade. Anes emphasizes the contradictions created by the liberal reforms, such as the free trade of grains in 1765, that were introduced by the state under the stimulation of small and relatively isolated bourgeois centers. The persistence of traditional property and other institutional arrangements and the crisis that preceded the 1808 Napoleonic invasion account for the slow economic development in the nineteenth century. A wealth of information on long-term, cyclical, and seasonal price changes of basic agricultural commodities in different regions and an analysis of their impact on the social structure carry our understanding to the economy beyond the pioneer work of Hamilton and that of Vilar on Catalonia. Unanswered questions raised by the data and the continual references to data open to further analysis offer challenges to economic and social historians. The discussion of sources of price series other than the account books used by Hamilton, particularly of municipal records that give information on market prices and of publications of patriotic economic societies in the later part of the century, and the relations between such price series and those of Hamilton are among the contributions of this important book.

Alain Huetz de Lemps's study of the vineyards of the northwest is an outstanding work by a geographer who has done extensive achival research. It includes tables and maps on aspects of the wine economy of 18 provinces from the Middle Ages to the present, including detailed data from the Catastro de Ensenada. An appendix gives information for each municipality in 1751 (based on 378 volumes in Simancas), in the nineteenth century (from the archives of the Ministry of Agriculture), at present, and, when available, for centuries before the eighteenth. It is an example of the way in which quantitative data can be used in connection with contemporary data (generally 1960–63) to clarify a specific historical problem in a geographical framework. Maps, graphs, tables, an excellent bibliography, and a guide to archival sources enhance the value of this work. Yvette Barbaza's *Le paysage humaine de la Costa Brava* includes an agrarian history of a section of Catalonia, starting from the eighteenth-century sources to the present; it gives data on property, cultivated area, crops, production, and techniques by municipalities. This study, in the tradition of the *géographie humaine,* also includes demographic series from the medieval fogatges to the present and statistics on the cork industry and shipping for the region.[67]

Politico-Administrative Structures. The Nobility and the Military

The administrative structure at the end of the ancien régime and the remnants of seigneurial institutions have been the subject of detailed research by Miguel Artola and his collaborators, who use the Catastro de Ensenada and the *Nomenclator* of Floridablanca and Miñano for population data; the *Memorias* of Larruga, the *Censo de Frutos y Manufacturas* and the *Diccionario de Hacienda* of Canga Argüelles for economic data.[68] Of the eight volumes planned, the two published cover Salamanca and Old Castile, and their tables and maps are invaluable. The objectives are (1) to trace a politico-administrative map of the Spain of the ancien régime, (2) to determine and analyze its demography, and (3) to determine the geographic and social distribution of the seigneurial regime and its diverse modalities. Spain at the time was much more modern in its social-juridical structure than the lands east of the Elbe, and in many ways more so even than France, where serfdom was still the lot of a million and a half people in 1789. Spanish serfdom had disappeared with the Catholic kings, and even the numbers living under seigneurial rather than royal jurisdiction were, according to Artola, already much reduced. However, the areas under seigneurial rule were experiencing population increases. The work gives detailed data on population from censuses and other contemporary sources, with material on age and sex distributions; occupational classifications, particularly in regard to secular and regular clergy; and the rural population of owners, tenants, farm laborers, and shepherds, as well as of those in the various occupations of the secondary and tertiary sectors. It also analyzes the demographic changes over time, in part in relation to the type of rule and the process of urbanization. In the 1797 census, of the 148 cities only seventeen were under secular and seven under ecclesiastical seigneurial rule. This indicates that, despite the importance of that rule in rural Spain, the Crown even in its weakest periods had been able to retain control of the urban areas. Artola and his collaborators also study quantitatively the extinction of the seigneurial regime through the legislation of the Cortes of Cadiz and Ferdinand VII.

So does Salvador de Moxó, in a monograph which focuses more on the legal and ideological battles of the reformers than on a quantitative analysis of the phenomenon.[69] Moxó also provides basic data for the main regions of the kingdom. He rightly notes the differences in attitudes of the reformers toward ecclesiastical and noble rights, punitive in the first case and favorable in the second. This must have been a contributory factor to the absence of aristocratic support for the Carlist, or antiliberal, uprising.

On the nobility there is considerable biographical information appropriate
for historico-sociological analysis. For example, an article by the Marqués
del Saltillo studies 192 individuals in the eighteenth century.[70]

The first two decades of the nineteenth century represent a critical
juncture in Spanish politics and society—partly Ancien Régime, partly the
first steps of the liberal revolution. The outstanding work by Miguel Artola
—*Los orígenes de la España contemporánea*—on the political cleavages resulting from the Napoleonic invasion, the attempts for reform, and the
political philosophy underlying them does not fit readily into an essay on
quantitative history.[71] However, in addition to presenting data on social
structure and the economy, it contains parts of 163 answers from different
sectors of society, from institutions and individuals, to the "Consulta al
país" by the Junta Central in 1809. The material can be compared, on a
more modest scale, to the *cahiers de doléances* addressed to the French
Estates General. Inasmuch as the *cahiers* have been the object of content analysis, it may be possible to analyze the *consulta* in a comparable systematic
and quantitative way. There is a great dearth of studies of the social, demographic, and economic impact of those turbulent years, perhaps because
historians have been more attracted to the politico-ideological cleavages and
the exploits of the people in the war against the Napoleonic invader.

Johann Hellwege has made an interesting contribution to the study of
eighteenth-century society and institutions with his monograph on the
provincial militias, which were conceived largely as a reserve army.[72] It is
rich in information on the ratio between population and the number of
conscripts, including a detailed analysis for all the municipalities in one
district in addition to general data for provinces and regions. Data by
province on the number of men subject to the lottery for conscription
purposes—giving their height and exemptions because of noble status,
physical unfitness, etc.—are of interest to the social historian. The primarily
Castilian *Alistamiento General* of 1762, in accounting for various exemptions of single men between the ages of sixteen and forty, also provides information on some occupational groups by province. In addition, there
is a body of information concerning the officers in command in different
provinces, including birthplace, age, years of service, marital status, noble
or bourgeois origin, performance rating, and private income. In addition
to telling us much about the military organization of the Ancien Régime,
this is another piece in the picture of heterogeneity and uneven development
and national integration which we find in so many of the data.

MODERNIZATION OF SPAIN: THE NINETEENTH AND TWENTIETH CENTURIES

Until recently, research on the nineteenth and twentieth centuries has
had fewer monumental monographs to build on. The quantitative records
for the period were kept less carefully, and those that exist have not been

exploited with much ingenuity. However, two general histories have recently given us challenging syntheses that suggest major problems for research. The work and, even more, the influence of a great teacher and organizer, Jaime Vicens Vives, who unfortunately died just when we could expect his most mature undertaking, have been pathbreaking. Moving from the Renaissance to the nineteenth and twentieth centuries and from Catalonia outward, he was led to the general social and economic history of modern Spain.[73] There is no need to discuss here the broad impact of his work or the determinants of his intellectual evolution, since Stanley Payne had done this in a review article.[74]

Recently, Raymond Carr has contributed to the *Oxford History of Modern Europe* a volume on Spain from 1808 to 1939.[75] These two dramatic and tragic dates encompass the history of a Spain that is far from both the imperial power of the past and the emerging industrial "European" country of the present. Carr's impressive study brings together the available research, ideas, and interpretations from diverse perspectives. Historians who can handle quantitative data may fruitfully explore in depth the hypotheses he advances and the questions he asks but leaves unanswered. In the following pages I hope to point to available data and to approaches that might help historians and social scientists to pursue the areas opened up by Carr and Vicens Vives.

In the nineteenth and twentieth centuries, a great number of problems call for quantitative analysis. If that analysis is not limited to Spain but carried out with a systematic comparative focus, it can contribute enormously to a better understanding of social change in Western society as a whole during the period, increasing our knowledge about such key processes as urbanization, industrialization, mobilization of landed property, extension of education, and the series of changes we term *social mobilization* [76]— extension of the suffrage and membership in parties, participation in interest groups and social movements such as trade unions, lay participation in religious organizations like Catholic Action, military conscription, the acquisition of literacy and secondary and higher education, participation in the economy through product and labor markets, taxation, social security, etc. Recent sociological and historical writings—particularly those of Bendix, Rokkan, Lorwin, Roth, and Lipset, and the earlier ones of Max Weber, T. H. Marshall, and Bull—have stressed the importance of the timing of each of these basic changes in different societies.[77] Some of them can be dated initially by legal enactments, but their implementation and the extent of change must be determined through detailed time series. Only the systematic comparison of such time series for different countries will make it possible to test some of the hypotheses advanced by these authors.

Stein Rokkan and others have stressed the importance of distinguishing between changes at the center of a society—the capital and/or core region—and on the periphery.[78] Areas at the center in one dimension, like political

power, may be on the periphery in another—industrialization, for example
—and vice versa; this is the case with Madrid and Catalonia.[79] The relative
degrees of social, economic, political, or cultural integration within the
boundaries of a state are central to an understanding of the history of any
society. This is particularly true in a society, like that of Spain, experiencing
the conflicts of regions or nationalities. Karl Deutsch has noted the importance of such differences in development in the study of nationalism.[80]

In this area, quantitative data and time series by region could contribute substantially to a better understanding of the unintegrated Spanish
society that was so brilliantly described—though only in qualitative terms
—by Ortega y Gasset.[81] I have developed the methodological problems and
substantive implications of such an approach somewhat further elsewhere.[82]
Obviously a study using different points in time and some type of ecological framework would be most fruitful. Such data would allow us to
place the modernization of Spain in comparative perspective with that of
France, which preceded it; Italy, which in some ways preceded it and in
others lagged behind; or Portugal, which in many respects seemed to trail
behind. This type of comparison between countries sharing many cultural,
social, and institutional characteristics—and of similarly developed regions
within them—can be most fruitful.

Major Themes

Basic problems of Spanish nineteenth-century history that await quantitative comparative analysis might include the following:

1. It is important to account for the slow and generally late industrialization of a European country that had a number of elements favoring modernization accumulated over centuries of political unification, absolute
monarchy and administration, and one that shared Western legal and cultural traditions. This delayed development is particularly striking in view
of the social, cultural, and economic changes Spain underwent in the
eighteenth century, and in view of the destruction of many of the traditional structures by the absolute monarchy, the Napoleonic invasion, and
subsequent liberal reforms.[83] Or, if we compare Spain with Prussia after
the Napoleonic wars, perhaps we should ask whether that weakening of
traditional structures—the nobility, entailment, communal property, guilds
—and even the crisis of the monarchy did not actually make modernization more difficult. To account for the delay in industrialization, and afterwards for the absence of entrepreneurial innovation, would require comparative research of the sort suggested by Kindleberger's comparison of
France and Britain.[84] But that requires many more monographic studies
to begin with.

2. An understanding of social history and its conflicts requires investigation of property and land tenure; productivity; population; and the
changes in population, family structure, inheritance patterns, etc., for

selected areas. The selection of such areas can combine historical and socio-logical interests. We might start with those regions and localities recently studied by Edward Malefakis in which rural social conflicts were most ex-plosive during the Second Republic, or with the magnificent work of Juan Díaz del Moral on Córdoba in the early decades of the century, and go backwards.[85] Or we could start with data from the far past and explore continuities and changes. One could also start with studies of the dis-tribution of land at the Reconquista, such as the work of Julio González on Seville or the studies of Artola and his collaborators on the map of the Ancien Régime.[86] Still another choice would be to begin with data col-lected for certain provinces by the Instituto de Reforma Agraria of the Re-public and in part utilized by Malefakis. It is possible, using the data of the *Censo Agrario* published in recent years and other contemporary sta-tistical publications, to sample types of rural social and economic structure systematically and to trace, even if superficially, the demographic, social, and economic changes over the last two hundred years in order to better understand the rural society and economy—until the 1950s the basis of Spanish society. The explanation of fundamental political and religious problems will not be much advanced without such an effort. Problems such as those that led to different types of *caciquismo,* unrest and violence in the countryside, the strength of Carlism, the emergence of farmer or-ganizations like those of the Catalan *rabassaires* and the Castilian CONCA, the great overseas emigration in the past, and the rural-urban migrations today require such an investigation. Understanding of the vast differences in religiosity in the Spanish countryside ultimately depends on our knowl-edge of agrarian, political, social, and economic history. Without such re-search, the great social and religious consequences of the *desamortización* (the sale of Church lands in the nineteenth century) will remain the object of guesswork and polemics without documentation.

3. A principal objective in the study of Spanish political history is to account for the failure to create a stable democracy. Recent theoretical ef-forts offer many leads to the formulation of questions about the process of incorporation of new strata in the political process. Historical electoral sociology is only in its beginnings, and it alone, using a comparative per-spective, stimulates problem formulations lacking in the hitherto standard literature on the political process. New questions, based on the nature of the two dynastic parties, on the slow mobilization of the new antisystem forces in relation to economic development and the degree of political free-dom, and on the continuity of Carlism and its slow disintegration—which apparently was of benefit to the secular regionalist parties—are raised by the use of such quantitative data as that collected by Miguel Martínez Cuadrado.[87] The study of elections should be combined with the study of political elites, for which there is a wealth of data. The question of democ-ratization requires further attention to material on other forms of social

mobilization, notably trade unions, interest groups, and religious organizations.

Given the importance of the army in Spanish politics, we should not be content with the excellent innovative work of Stanley Payne in *Politics and the Military in Modern Spain;* [88] rather, we should explore further the demographic and social consequences of the civil and colonial wars, the impact of conscription (which may have had, if we remember autobiographical comments of the leaders of protest movements and the perennial issue of the *quintas* in politics, a great deal to do with the radicalization of the lower classes), and the social composition of the officer corps and its changes. Comparison with other European armies might provide clues as to the sources of political intervention and its directions. A more quantitative and sociological analysis of the structure of the officer corps at different times is one of the tasks that Payne has left to the sociologists.

Anyone who has read nineteenth-century Spanish novelists, particularly Galdós, or the critiques of the "reformers" at the turn of the century will be aware of the importance of the administration and of the civil servants in Spanish middle-class society, just as anyone studying the present Spanish elite and power structure will be sensitive to the role of the *cuerpos,* the elite groups in the administration.[89] Quantitative analysis of the contemporary civil service has only begun, but a large number of sources, even aside from archival data, should permit considerable insight into the formation of the Spanish administration.[90] Quantitative data on its performance should help account for the hostility of the periphery (especially Catalonia and the Basque country) to the central government, for the slow growth of social services, and for many of the dissatisfactions of the lower classes.

Recent sociological analyses of democracy have pointed out the importance of a competent administration to support the ruling politicians as well as the dangers of recruiting too large a portion of the political elite from civil servants (a point already made by Max Weber). The taking over of tasks by the central administration from local government, partly as a result of shifts in the tax system, would seem to explain the parochial attitude toward politics in large parts of the country. This attitude is shown in outbursts of political participation and enthusiasm in moments of crisis but has not, outside a few localities, provided for stable participation and pragmatic involvement in politics and administration.

The problems of democracy and political stability continue to confront the historian of Spain. The factors that should have led to the slow but inevitable institutionalization of democracy were the early weakening of predemocratic structures, the openness of the country to foreign ideological influences, the early introduction of universal male suffrage in 1868 and more permanently in 1890, the appearance of the two-party system, and the emergence of a political class from which the government was formed.[91]

In the political and ideological sphere, Spain in the last quarter of the century had conditions more favorable for democracy than Imperial Germany, Austria-Hungary, Imperial Russia, and perhaps some minor countries. But these preconditions were insufficient or soon destroyed, partly by a series of failures that were either real or assumed to be real by intellectual critics of the Restoration.

To explain the failure of democracy, let us not invoke the role of the army, which in this period receded into the background and which was to return to the political arena only much later; nor let us cite the role of the Church, with which Restoration politicians had achieved a modus vivendi assuring a limited clericalism that allowed the beginnings of change within the Church and modernization. There were occasional conflicts, but these might have been solved on the Belgian model, with such a solution suggested by the links between the Liberal party and the academic establishment and the group of the Institución Libre de Enseñanza. If not a Belgian solution, then a French type of peaceful-hostile separation should have been possible. If the clericolaical conflict had taken place within stable constitutional institutions rather than at the installation of a new regime in 1931, during a growing mobilization of lay Catholicism, it would never have led to the "Cruzada" spirit of the Church in the Civil War.

Historians of Spain's attempts at democracy should not assume that its defeat was inevitable. This may seem obvious from the perspective of the 1930s, but it did not seem so in the late nineteenth or early twentieth century. Quantitative data can reveal the social and economic changes that ran counter to the political processes institutionalizing a constitutional democratic government—for example, inflation, leading to the labor unrest and terrorism after World War I that, together with the Moroccan question, made the Primo de Rivera coup of 1923 possible.

Censuses and Statistics

The basic sources for comparative quantitative study are the publications of the statistical offices of each country: population censuses, annual statistical yearbooks, other statistical serial publications, special censuses for industry and agriculture. Italy and Spain have published summary series of many social and economic data which, although they lack the wealth of the *Historical Statistics of the United States, 1789–1945,* cover the periods 1861–1955 and 1900–50.[92] In the case of Spain, three very useful reviews of statistical sources appeared in 1919, 1956, and 1963.[93] In 1834 Moreau de Jonnès published a *Statistique de l'Europe,* which included a *Statistique de l'Espagne.*[94] Despite its limitations, this is a basic accessible summary of quantitative data for the early part of the century. Almost nine decades later another Frenchman, Angel Marvaud, published a widely quoted book containing statistical data: *L'Espagne au XX siècle. Etude politique et économique.*[95]

The series of statistical yearbooks—published first for 1858; then for 1860, 1860–61, 1862–65, and 1866–67; and beginning again in 1912 to run continuously from 1915 to 1935—is indispensable and was reestablished in 1943. Two reviews have appeared of the statistical information available in the national *Reseñas Estadísticas* and in the provincial counterparts after the Civil War.[96] Portugal first published a statistical yearbook in 1877, giving data for 1875, and initiated its regular series with an excellent volume for 1884.[97] Italy began issuing its regular series in 1878 with the *Annuario Statistico Italiano,* each volume of which includes a long introduction on the methods of data collection and the sources of earlier data. Even then, electoral data received considerable attention.[98] The Italian series also attempts to present demographic, economic, and social indicators side by side, with the implicit suggestion of their interdependence.

A systematic elaboration of selected indicators in comparable tables for industrial, semi-industrial, and underdeveloped Spain and Portugal for the same time periods could be the beginning of a comparative study of their modernization. A comparison of northern Italy with France could be another step in the same direction. Such a framework would be useful for work on the history of the modernization of another heterogeneous country such as Brazil.

The description of the population, social structure, and economy of nineteenth-century Spain would not be possible without the works of two geographer–social scientists of the time: Miñano and Pascual Madoz.[99] Madoz was a Progressive party politician, governor of Barcelona in critical times, a cabinet member after the 1854 revolution, and a lobbyist for the protection of Catalan industry. In his introduction he gives us an insight into the motives and intellectual influences that led him to compile statistics on provinces, cities, towns, and villages. He comments favorably on the French Revolution, the genius of Napoleon, and France's success in creating statistical services in 1832 under the leadership of Moreau de Jonnès. However, Madoz reserves his most enthusiastic tribute for the Belgian efforts, particularly those of Quetelet, one of the great founders of quantitative sociology, whom he had met in his political exile. Madoz goes on to mention the Spanish tradition of the gathering of statistical data, from the *Relaciones* of Philip II to the *Censo de Frutos y Manufacturas* of 1799, as well as the *Matrícula Catastral* begun by Ramón Calatrava; and he notes the efforts of the finance minister Mateo Miguel Ayllón to amass statistical data as a basis for public policy. Finally, he includes an extensive bibliography of the works he consulted, as well as a list of public archival sources, particularly the property records in the *Matrículas Catastrales* of 1842.

Regional demographic changes during the nineteenth century have recently attracted the interest of Nicolás Sánchez-Albornoz and have been given graphic representation by F. Vergneault.[100] Massimo Livi Bacci devotes two long scholarly articles to "Fertility and Nuptiality Changes in

Spain from the late eighteenth to the early twentieth century," extending back in time the work of William Leasure on the decline in fertility in the first half of this century.[101] The differential fertility of Catalans and Castilian-speaking immigrants and the Catalan fears for the denationalization of their region aroused the interest of Catalan scholars as early as 1906, and appears particularly in the work of Vandellós, now being carried on by Joaquim Maluquer i Sostres.[102] The volume of internal and external migration led to the important work, *Despoblación y repoblación de España, 1482–1920,* which was followed by modern studies on external migration by Jesús García Fernández, on transoceanic migration by Mariano González Rothvoss, and on internal migration by Alfonso García Barbancho.[103]

Other recent articles provide insights into Spanish society, its regional diversity and processes of change. Heinz Göhring analyzes illegitimacy for selected dates since 1860 by province, capitals, and remaining area and region, showing the continuity of certain cultural patterns.[104] The article by Jesús de Miguel on historical trends in suicide, inspired by the work of Durkheim, contributes to our understanding of the relation between political crisis and stability and suicide; it also poses interesting questions on the impact of the Civil War and its aftermath, on the basis of statistics not originally intended for such analysis.[105]

Quantitative Data Used for Political Arguments

Fernando Garrido, a radical democrat critical of both the *Moderados* and the *Progresistas,* published his *La España contemporánea* on the eve of the 1868 revolution.[106] The work is an excellent example of social and political criticism supported by a wealth of rather inaccessible facts put into comparative perspective and presented chronologically to show change or lack of change resulting from shifts in power and legislation. Statistics on population, production, education, etc. are combined with information on the clergy and the armed forces and a detailed critical analysis of government budgets. An extensive section on Spanish overseas possessions and another that combines data on Spain and Portugal are valuable. A Karl Deutsch would be pleased to see Garrido's use of postal statistics to measure cultural and economic development. Few books give so well organized a view of society in the first half of the nineteenth century and of the Spaniards' critical search for modernity. From 1900 to the late 1960s we find few books of this type, perhaps because the critical-progressive optimism of the midcentury was abandoned after 1898 for a historicist and aesthetic pessimism that questioned the essence of Spain as a unique culture.

A polemic book on the Catalan question by Guillermo Graell, secretary of the Fomento del Trabajo Nacional (lobby of the Catalan industrialists) and a leader in the fight for protectionism, written early in the century was as rich in quantitative data as in insight into their use in respect to political conflicts.[107] The uneven economic development of Spain and its social and political heterogeneity make quantitative data a part of the political struggle. In other countries such data—on, for example, the birthplaces of elites or the language used in death notices—might interest only sociologists. The work is rich in information on tax revenues and government expenditures, areas fruitful for cross-national comparisons of intranational differences. Miguel Beltrán has explored the same problem more recently from the perspective of an underdeveloped region, Andalusia.[108] His is the sort of research which sheds light on a modern state's functions of redistribution among its territorial components.

Government Structure and Activities

For governmental organization and activities, the historian may use quantitative data either previously collected or easily quantifiable. Outstanding among sources of the first type is the publication of the annual national budget, which summarizes both receipts and expenditures in exhaustive detail.[109] The budget is published in the *Gaceta de Madrid,* the *Boletín Oficial del Estado,* or publications of the legislature under any of several names, but the most detailed form is issued by the Ministry of Finance. One of its most interesting sets of data relates to the structure of the bureaucracy, civil and military, as well as to the police force—its number, rank, and (less reliably) pay scale. In countries that lack a separation of Church and State, such as Spain in all but the Republican periods, the budget also reveals the structure of the secular clergy. It can very often be used to contrast the government's policy declarations with actual performance.[110] Often we can get some sense of the activity of a government by the way it affects different regions of a country—for example, when universities, secondary schools, hospitals, and so on are budgeted for particular locations. Data from the budget can often be supplemented with those from the annual *Memorias* of the Ministry of Finance on receipts and expenditures and from special *memorias* on various taxes.[111] For the period 1850–1907, the two volumes of the *Estadística de los presupuestos generales del Estado y de los resultados que ha ofrecido su liquidación* give complete series of planned budgets and their actual accounting as well as information on the public debt, foreign trade, etc.[112] Miguel Beltrán is completing a monograph on the relation between the swings of the political pendulum in the nineteenth century and the changes in expenditures for different purposes.

La reforma fiscal de Villaverde, 1899–1900, by Gabriel Solé Villalonga, is one of the few monographs on public finance and taxation in the nineteenth and twentieth centuries, except for the more general works of J. Sarda and J. M. Tallada.[113] It provides us with useful quantitative series on budgets, deficits, the public debt and its service expenditures, and various taxes and their yields and monetary policy for the years between 1890 and

1908. It is particularly informative on the cost of the colonial wars and their impact on the public debt. This study helps us to understand why the political formula of the Restoration, not an unsuccessful one, was ultimately unable to provide the efficient services of a modern state or to contribute to the solution of the social problems that erupted in working-class discontent.

While the *Presupuesto* gives us the organization chart of the government, other sources allow us to fill the positions with the names of individuals, which are essential for any study of elites. Sometimes sources that would have provided considerable information may have been lost or destroyed, so that a great effort is needed to collect them. Some basic ones, however—particularly the invaluable *Guía Oficial,* published annually with government support [114]—can be found relatively easily. Under different names and with a somewhat changing content, the *Guía* was issued from 1723 to 1935. This publication was founded by the Marqués de Miraval, an ambassador and member of the royal cabinet. For a long time it was called *Guía de Forasteros,* and often the king was consulted about matters of protocol and content; sometimes he even corrected some of the listings personally. In 1872/73 its name was changed to *Guía Oficial de España.* A few years earlier it had added an alphabetical index of names, including two last names, facilitating the identification of brothers and even of cousins and descendants. The series of the *Guía Oficial,* continuous until 1929, was interrupted with the coming of the Republic, and only one—for the year 1935—has been published since. Unfortunately no such publication exists for the Franco regime. Privately published commercial publications, such as *Heráldica* and *Anuario Español del Gran Mundo,* serve as inaccurate substitutes. The useful *Fichero de Altos Cargos* (FAC) has been published since 1939 on 5 x 8 cards which list both political and administrative officials, but nowhere is it collected for the whole period.[115] The *Guía Oficial* is indispensable, for example, to a study of the evolution of the aristocracy, the diplomatic service, the army, the legislatures, and the educational establishment. In addition, since 1772 the government has published an *Estado Militar,* first as a part of the *Guía* and later as the *Anuario Militar.*[116] There are also years for which there is a *Guía Eclesiástica.*[117]

The nobility is another elite whose members can be identified and counted, and the *Guía Oficial* under the Monarchy makes it possible to locate them among other elites.[118] The *escalafones* of the various "Cuerpos" of the higher civil service or of publicly licensed and privileged occupations, such as that of notary, are an invaluable source because they give names, birth dates, often birthplaces, dates of entry into the occupation, location of activity, and often career data. In the case of professions like law or medicine that require membership in a professional association, listings serve both for studies of elites and for studies of social structure.[119] Often the payment of taxes through the *colegio* meant that the association determined the tax categories, which are indicated in the *Guía* for individuals. Any quantitative analysis of the size, location, continuities, and discontinuities in elites must therefore start with the *Guía* and similar sources.

Parliaments and Elections

For parliamentary personnel, excellent information is available in a series of volumes with biographies of senators and deputies for the legislatures of 1869, 1879, 1885, 1907, 1910, and 1914.[120] Similar data exist for the Primo de Rivera corporative chamber, the Asamblea Nacional of 1927.[121] Whatever shortcomings such data have in quality, particularly for the less well-known members (a bias that weights indirectly the importance of men in quantitative analysis), they allow comparisons with studies of parliamentary elites in Germany, France, Great Britain, Italy, Turkey, and the United States. Unfortunately there is no easily accessible biographical source on the legislators of the Republic (1931–36), except for their occupations or on the members of the corporative Cortes created by Franco in 1943, except for the file prepared by DATA on the 1968 legislature.[122]

For data on elections, the sources are not always easily available, nor is their accuracy undisputed.[123] Quantitative analysis has to be combined with critical historical analysis, as in Robert W. Kern's work on the significance of elections, which derives principally from the famous inquest of the Ateneo directed by Joaquín Costa.[124] However, the quantitative data, as I have attempted to show in a paper on elections in Spain in 1907, 1910, and 1914, can identify indirectly the meaning of the vote, the cases of undue influence, the different types of *caciquismo*, etc.[125] The main series of data I am interested in are eligible voters and their relationship to the population, social characteristics of the voters (particularly under taxpaying or other property qualifications for suffrage, or when we have, as in Spain early in this century, data on literate and illiterate eligible voters), rates of participation, invalid votes, votes cast for candidates with a chance for election, scattered votes, votes by party, and electoral contests and incidents (cases taken before the legislature or, after the 1907 election law, before the Supreme Court) as indicators of the honesty of the elections or of civic consciousness. I have attempted to analyze the elections of 1907, 1910, and 1914 (for which Modesto Sánchez de los Santos and his collaborators have published excellent data),[126] using the available information, converting it into percentages, and making the corresponding electoral maps. A similar analysis would be possible for 1885. Less detailed data, consisting only of the names of the elected candidate and his party, are available for the remaining elections between 1900 and 1923 (Primo de Rivera) from the *Año Político*, published by Soldevilla.[127]

The most important study of elections published to date is Miguel M. Cuadrado's two-volume work on elections and parties from 1868 to 1931.[128] Using official statistical publications, the official listing of members of the legislature, newspaper reports, and the volumes of Sánchez Ortiz y Berástagui and Modesto Sánchez de los Santos, Cuadrado has brought together election returns, including participation and votes for different parties as well as number of seats, for the country and for some fifty provinces; he presents these in maps and percentages, giving absolute figures for each electoral district. The elections covered are those under universal male suffrage preceding the establishment of the Republic and those under the restored monarchy with restricted suffrage and after 1890 with universal male suffrage up to the 1931 municipal election that brought the Second Republic. Cuadrado was able to give results from the provincial capitals (almost the only urban centers) and from the surrounding countryside for the 1872 election and for those after 1876, separately for the multimember districts (the larger cities), other provincial capitals, and rural single-member districts. Data on the seats by party are more complete than those on the number of votes by candidates; the latter are missing for many earlier elections, and particularly for districts rather than provinces. This naturally limits the ecological correlations and permits only a descriptive location of the areas of strength for different parties. The size of the provinces and the heterogeneity of their social structure are also obstacles to an ecological-sociological analysis. Relating the electoral data for single-member rural districts to data on occupation, literacy, property, and tenancy patterns remains a task for future research. Nineteenth-century census data by *partidos judiciales* would in this respect be more useful than those of the twentieth century, which give the information only by provinces and provincial capitals. The great scholarly effort of Cuadrado in making the data accessible, in giving the politico-historical setting of each election, and in describing the political tendencies and mapping (in the tradition of Goguel) the participation and political orientation of each province has been a decisive step for Spanish electoral sociology. It is to be hoped that it will be followed by more monographic efforts linking social structure and political behavior.

Javier Tusell, in *Sociología electoral de Madrid, 1903–1931*, has compiled election statistics by district for the capital, relating them to social indicators such as the rents paid for housing and the social, economic, and political changes over the period (using indicators such as price indices and strike statistics).[129] He also uses the data to explore the significance of electoral fraud. Another important addition to the systematic study of elections is Tusell's work on three parliamentary elections and electors for the presidency in Madrid under the Republic (1931–36), based on data in the *Boletines Oficiales de la Provincia de Madrid* and newspapers by districts of the city.[130] This work documents the relation of the electoral system to the polarization that led to the Civil War and the preference of the voters in 1936 for the more moderate leaders in both coalitions. It combines quantitative data, the analysis of which could be pushed somewhat further, with an excellent account of the campaigns and of public opinion as reflected in the press.

The data for the three parliamentary elections of the Republic as well as for the municipal elections, regional parliamentary elections, and referenda on regional autonomy can be found in part in the Statistical Yearbooks, the official *Boletines* of the provinces, the newspapers, and different historical monographs. Jean Becarud has brought these materials together and attempted an interpretation of the elections. Javier Tusell, in *Las elecciones del Frente Popular,* has undertaken the arduous task of analyzing the controversial February 1936 election that preceded the Civil War. Before this we had to rely on polemic sources: writings by the republican José Venegas and the pro-Franco publications, particularly the official *Dictamen de la Comisión sobre ilegitimidad de poderes actuantes en 18 de julio de 1936.* In that 1936 election, the electoral system in most provinces pitted the Popular Front—from Communists to leftist republicans—against a right slightly in disarray. The tensions subsequent to the October 1934 revolution and its repression and the anarcho-syndicalists giving up their traditional abstentionism raised participation to 72 percent and led to a bitter campaign. Tusell, in addition to describing the electoral platforms, the agreements in the formation of coalition slates, and the campaign in different districts, provides us with a careful statistical analysis of participation; votes, including those for minor parties, specifically the Falangists, who are often neglected; correlations between 1933–36 votes; and number of candidates per seat and per party. He uses primary sources not used before and comes up with the most reliable estimate of the national returns available: 34.3 percent of eligible voters for the Popular Front, 5.4 percent for the Basque Nationalists and independent center candidacies, and 33.2 percent for the Right and Right-Center coalitions. He also analyzes the main attempts to interpret the election and the statistical summaries of other authors.[131]

The first study that furnishes information on party membership by province for a party on the right under the Republic is the monograph by R. A. H. Robinson on *Acción Nacional* or *Acción Popular* and later the CEDA.[132] But Robinson makes no effort to relate these admittedly fragmentary figures to social structure, religiosity, or electorate for the right in those provinces. Robinson also presents data on the occupations of deputies by party for 1933 and 1936.

The Labor Movement and Protest

Elections, however, are not the only form of political participation, particularly in a country in which a significant part of the working class follows the anarcho-syndicalist line of rejection of bourgeois parliamentary democracy. Membership in trade unions and the activities of the unions, especially in the case of strikes, are therefore especially important indicators of the politics of Spain on the Left.[133]

Few scholarly efforts are as rich in primary data as Max Nettlau's labor of love, *La Première Internationale en Espagne, 1868–1888*.[134] But few works illustrate better the need for systematic secondary analysis of quantitative data for a contribution to historico-sociological interpretation. The great anarchist historian, who personally knew most of the leaders of the movement, brought together records that would otherwise have been lost forever or buried in libraries or in archives such as the Biblioteca Pública Arús in Barcelona or the Institut International d'Histoire Sociale in Amsterdam. Many of Nettlau's sources have been destroyed by the Civil War. Throughout his pages we find a wealth of quantitative or quantifiable data on working-class organizations, their membership and social composition, the occupations of delegates at congresses, subscription figures of anarchist publications, social conflicts and their repression, generally with indications of locale—regions, provinces, smaller sociogeographic areas, and very often municipalities. These would provide extremely interesting ecological and trend studies if they were to be related to the social characteristics of the localities and to political and economic trend data. Used in that way, and in comparative international perspective, they could reveal the social bases of anarchism and thus the unique history of the Spanish labor movement. Without such an effort, the sheer quantity of information makes it difficult to ask the right questions, even for the reader familiar with Spanish social structure and history. The editor of the posthumous work, Renée Lamberet, contributed an excellent index of names; statistical tables for the periods 1870–74 and 1881–84, including the population of the localities in 1877; and maps for both periods; as well as an introduction and notes on the location of sources, recent monographic research, and publications in progress.

For the early history of the labor movement and the condition of the working class, the recent publication by Seco Serrano of the minutes of the Spanish region of the International Workingmen's Association (1870–74), which includes an introduction on the relation between bourgeois politics (moderates and progressives) and labor, provides a wealth of quantitative and quantifiable information about organizations, wages, working hours, and strikes.[135] Some of these data have been prepared by Renée Lamberet and presented in tables and maps in an appendix to the work of Nettlau.

Fortunately there are reasonably detailed and apparently accurate data on the number of federations and sections (often by occupation and by province although unfortunately not both simultaneously) of the UGT (Unión General de Trabajadores, the Socialist trade union federation, founded in 1882) and for the Socialist Party (PSOE, Partido Socialista Obrero Español, founded in 1879). The data given by the union and the party have been published regularly in the *Anuarios Estadísticos*.

Few sources are so rich for the quantitative historian or sociologist as the reports on the activities of the Socialist party and its affiliated organizations.[136] They include information not only on membership, elections at all levels of government, party finances, and bureaucracy (a really small one), but on propaganda activities, circulation of the party press, speeches and rallies, copies of works of different authors, special contributions, co-operatives and mutual-aid societies, and lay schools. The votes at party congresses are indispensable for an understanding of the party internal life and of the regional basis of the PSOE and the Communists after the split. The biographies of leaders and activists provide insight into the social bases of the cadres. Only a thorough analysis of a complete series of these *memorias* can document the slow growth (compared to the movement in Italy) of the Spanish socialist movement before the thirties and the continuing appeal of the anarcho-syndicalist movement that was so significant for Spanish labor and democracy.

The situation for the CNT (Confederación Nacional del Trabajo, the anarcho-syndicalist organization founded in 1911) is less fortunate—naturally, given its organizational philosophy. Here we have information from a number of histories of the movement, but only about the membership represented at various congresses.[137]

The best source in English on the labor movement from the end of the nineteenth century to its defeat in 1939 is Stanley G. Payne's *The Spanish Revolution*.[138] This work does not attempt a quantitative history of working-class parties and trade unions, as does the excellent monograph on the French CGT by Annie Kriegel, but it contributes many data on membership over time, on political violence in 1917–20 and during the thirties, on the ideological-organizational composition of the units fighting against Franco, and on the size of forces fighting in the Civil War at different times. Some of these data come from Russian publications. Guy Hermet has brought together the limited quantitative data on membership votes, finances, and other activities of the Spanish Communist party, but his monograph deals mainly with the contemporary period.

The work by David Ruiz on the mining region of Asturias, where labor conflicts took on special intensity, gives quantitative information on the number of workers, trade union affiliations, strikes and strikers, wages, and cost of living. It is an example of the sort of regional monograph that is badly needed.[139]

The Instituto de Reformas Sociales (founded in 1903) has collected a large body of strike statistics, particularly for the period 1904–22, and has made reports on specific crises in a statistical series continued by the Ministry of Labor.[140] Unfortunately the data for the Republican period cover only 1931–35; those for 1936 can be found only in the press and are not reliable.[141] Such strike statistics permit the testing of a number of hypotheses concerning the nature of the labor movement in different regions, the relationship between economic conditions and social unrest, the impact of the Russian Revolution, and changes in government or regimes. Interestingly enough, they suggest common trends with Italy.

Strikes are of course not the only indicators of social or political unrest. We also have data about terrorist acts, violence (numbers of dead and wounded), burning of crops, and anticlerical violence. Malefakis collected and used much information on agrarian unrest in the Second Republic.[142] The coding and analysis of such information should aid the analysis of the connections between social structures and social tensions. For example, some of the more simple hypotheses about rural discontent and property structure would seem to be doubtful in light of these data. It is in these areas that systematic comparison with Italy would be particularly rewarding.

The work by Fernanda Romeu Alfaro on the condition of the working classes in Spain from 1898 to 1930 brings together a great deal of statistical information, particularly on wages and costs of living, and cites useful sources: libraries and publications of the Instituto de Reformas Sociales and reports in newspaper articles and books.[143] But it fails to push its analysis far enough.

The most important source for the quantitative study of labor problems under the Republic is Mariano González-Rothvoss's *Anuario español de política social, 1934–35*.[144] The editor was a distinguished civil servant of the Instituto de Reformas Sociales from the time of its foundation and later of the Ministry of Labor. His work contains statistical data on the labor movement and on the interest groups of business and agriculture. It reproduces government statistics on strikes and state welfare activities and policies; reprints the *bases de trabajo* (collective agreements or government-dictated labor regulations); and presents invaluable data on wages, working conditions, and living costs. It gives the names of officials of trade unions, interest groups, and joint worker-employer organizations, as well as of civil servants of the Ministry of Labor. All this material would be useful for studies of various elites, among other things.

Judicial and Police Statistics

Another area in which statistical data throw light on political processes is that of judicial statistics, which contain information on political crimes. The best quantitative source on the social unrest, particularly in Barcelona, that contributed so much to the crisis of the constitutional monarchy before 1923 is the work by José María Farré Moregó.[145] Often we have data by province, occupation, and age that permit definition of the areas of tension in the social system. We also have detailed records on the number of draft dodgers by province. It would be possible, even if arduous, to study the problems of social conformity as opposed to the deviance of the peasantry and the business classes after the 1936–39 Civil War by tabulating the fines and penalties imposed by the Fiscalía Superior de Tasas, as published in the *Boletín Oficial* and other official publications. However, such data might not be rewarding if they reflected not so much violations as administrative practices, as has been the case with the sanctions by labor inspectors. The ways in which the authorities handled various trangressions may reveal much about the political climate. This might be the case with the statistics on arrests of poachers and unauthorized users of grazing land, published regularly by the Guardia Civil.[146] The *Anuario Militar* gives information on the deployment of the Guardia Civil across the nation, permitting us to explore one reaction of the State to internal conflict.

The Church and Religiosity

The relationship of religion and politics has been a problem central to the history of many European nations, perhaps nowhere more than in modern Spain. Of the quantitative data essential to religious and Church history, few have been systematically collected, in contrast to the excellent work done in France.[147] It should be possible to develop adequate indicators of religiosity and the character of Church organization, secular and regular, as well as of the slow mobilization of the laity in church-sponsored organizations.[148]

An important starting point would be a systematic sampling (by villages for selected time periods) of data in the *Liber Status Animorum,* in which priests were required, after the Council of Trent, to keep records of their parishioners as well as of canonical visits by the bishops.[149] Such data might clarify the reasons for the differences in religiosity found even in the nineteenth century and for the success of Carlism in regions that, although no longer Carlist, continue to this day to be the most religious in Spain. For example, was the border between the Carlist and non-Carlist areas a function of previous religiosity, or was religious sentiment reinforced and maintained by political dissidence? [150]

The links between the sale of Church lands in the nineteenth century and changes in religiosity also deserve quantitative study, perhaps by the use of data from Madoz on religious institutions in different communities.[151] The number of priests at different points in time and in different areas is an obvious indicator of changes in Spanish society. In 1769 there was one priest for every 141 inhabitants; by 1859, only one for every 401. Analysis is possible for priestly vocations, through use of the data on the number of seminarians. The maps for the number of priests per 10,000 inhabitants prepared by R. Duocastella for the years 1769, 1859, 1947, and 1957 show interesting patterns of continuity and discontinuity and could be completed for other census years.[152] Because priests were not likely to move from the dioceses of their ordination, the high level of religiosity along the inner fringe of the Pyrenees, the northern border of the Castilian and Leonese *meseta* (but not the coast), the border of Aragon and Levante, and in the Balearic Islands was perceptible at an early date. Until the middle of the nineteenth century there was a southeastern and western Andalusian nucleus with a high number of priests, but this is no longer true of these areas today. The weaknesses in the New Castilian area, long controlled by the Ordenes Militares, and in the southeast and in parts of the coast of Galicia seem to have been long-standing. The percentages of clergy assassinated in Republican areas in the course of the Civil War suggest that some of the provincial differences might be related to the patterns of religiosity.[153] Data on the number of priests as well as the ratio of secular and regular clergy and the number of seminarians, religious schools, and other institutions per unit of population may be obtained, at least in an approximate way, for selected dates for most of the rest of Catholic Europe as well as Spain.[154] Such data would be basic for the comparative study of Church-State relations, anticlericalism, voting patterns, and so on.

For modern times, it is possible to follow quantitatively the growth and strength of Catholic lay organizations, like Catholic Action, and of Catholic functional organizations, like the large farmers' federation (with credit cooperatives, etc.) of the CONCA (Confederación Nacional Católico Agraria), founded in 1911. Their analysis in comparative perspective might account for the late founding of a Demochristian party and, indirectly, for the strong reliance of the Spanish Church on the State.[155]

It would be more difficult to quantify militant religious dissidence, in particular the spread of Masonic lodges, but electoral maps of the anticlerical parties and maps of the anarcho-syndicalist labor movement would indicate the strength of the modern break with traditional Catholicism. Data on secular burials, published in recent years in the Statistical Yearbook of the Catholic Church, could probably be used as well. A recent sociological study of contemporary Spanish Protestantism suggests the past of the religious minority.[156]

An example of the kind of research possible is the study of anticlericalism in the province of Huelva by Juan Ordóñez Márquez.[157] He uses the *Liber Status Animorum* and the documents from a *visita ad limina* through the province of Huelva by Cardinal Ilundain in 1928–32, together with a post–Civil War inquiry into religious persecution and election data. If many such monographs were published, the quantitative historian could turn to the ecological study of religious conflict.

The Military and Wars

The important role of the army in Spain's modern history, the prolonged periods of unrest and civil war, and the costly and unrewarding colonial conflicts are well known. Officers and their careers, soldiers and *matériel*, conscription and casualties, garrisons and troop movements are all quantifiable, and often the data on these social realities are relatively easy to come by. Stanley Payne has made use of such data, but more could be done with them if they were related systematically to other quantitative data in a long time series, especially if international comparisons were made.[158] The qualities that were unique in the Spanish army and those that were similar to other countries in both structure and performance would become more apparent. In addition, the implementation of certain policies and their consequences would be better understood. A few random examples come to mind. The peace of Vergara in 1839 between the Liberals and the Carlists established that Carlist officers had a right to commissions in the regular army if they so desired. A comparison of the *Estado Militar* before and after the peace would allow one to identify such officers, and it would be interesting to follow their later careers. An Azaña decree instituted eleven days after the inception of the Second Republic allowed all generals and most officers to accept complete retirement from all duties with full pay, provided that they asked to do so within thirty days; within a year approximately half the Officer Corps took advantage of the offer. Who were these officers, and what was their subsequent role in Spanish life? Again publications such as the army rank lists could give interesting answers.

Stanley Payne has brought together much quantitative data on the army and war in modern Spain, including the number of generals from 1792 to 1888, the number of officers, changes in average tenure of a minister of war between 1814 and 1868, recruitment and draft policies, age of retirement of officers, size of police forces, expulsions from the army by the Republic for participation in the 1936 uprising, casualties for various wars, losses by the Falangists and Carlists in 1937–39, army suicide rates, military expenditures for 1922–26 and 1931–35, and salary levels for various years between 1918 and 1956. Such data might be enriched by taking the pay scales by rank and comparing them for similar periods with those in the armies of other countries in order to determine the extent of salary inequities in Spain. Comparison could also be made with the inequities of salaries within the civil service at the same time. Political changes over time could be related to changes in civil service salaries or changes in general wage levels or per capita incomes.

The inequities connected with the *quintas* (military levies) provoked continuous protest from the radical parties, the working-class movements, and military reformers in the nineteenth century. A more systematic study of the social impact of conscription, especially in respect to the regional and class differentiation of the casualties in various campaigns, would clarify the reasons for the alienation of important sectors of the population from society. Data on the numbers eligible for draft, on draft dodgers, and on the unfit and exempted for the period 1912–20 have been compiled by Payne. A preliminary analysis of the provinces with the largest numbers of draft evaders suggests that the governing factor was emigration, overseas or trans-Mediterranean, rather than political attitudes. This, together with the physical fitness requirements, led to a paradoxical situation. The highest number of recruits came from the separatist regions, which were socially and economically the most progressive. That localization had political repercussions at the time of the *Semana Trágica* in 1909 and may be related to the political climate of those regions and the antimilitarism of the labor movement.[159] The Italian situation in this period offers many opportunities for comparison and shows similar differences in regional development, in high rates of overseas migration, in colonial ventures sometimes leading to disaster, and in labor movement hostility to the military.

Jorge Nadal notes the absence of studies on the demographic impact of the wars; he cites only one, a local study for Tarragona, on the impact of the Peninsular War. The aftermath of the Civil War produced a monograph by Jesús Villar Salinas, which has been generally ignored in the literature on the war. Gabriel Jackson estimates "Deaths Attributable to the Civil War" in an appendix to his history of the Republic, but his analysis cannot satisfy the demographer. He refers to the decrease in population calculated for 1940 by Villar Salinas, extrapolating the increase in previous years, and assumes that the difference was due to death or emigration, forgetting that population loss may be due to a lower birth rate.[160]

Education and Culture

Quantification would be invaluable in the fields of culture and mass media, but it would present difficulties, except in the case of educational statistics.[161] It would be necessary to know the numbers of newspapers and magazines, with figures on their circulation and distribution, as well as the numbers and types of books with the size of their printings, in order to understand the penetration of ideas into Spain and the diffusion of political and religious ideologies. For recent years many sources—albeit rather inaccurate ones—are available for the mass media, both secular and clerical, but for the past correct estimates would be more difficult to obtain. A statistical survey of the press early in the century does exist, however, and various sources give some idea of the importance of the role played by the press at the time. We may recall the complaints of Maura, the great Conservative leader, about the part that the newspaper "trust" played in his defeat. Gonzalo Redondo's *Las empresas políticas de José Ortega y Gasset. "El Sol," "Crisol," "Luz" (1917-1934)* is one of the rare sources on readership over time and the impact of changes in editorial policies in critical moments on number of copies as well as on the finances of newspapers, government subsidies, advertising revenues, etc. Such statistical data for other newspapers would be highly desirable. For other publications, data from the copyright registers, even if incomplete, might be of help, and the statistical yearbooks contain some relevant information. Even more important but difficult to estimate would be the volume and impact of the propaganda of working-class movements, in particular the anarchist and anarcho-syndicalist movements.[162]

Rural Economic and Social Structure

Until 1940, more than half the active males in Spain were engaged in agriculture. Good or bad crops determined Spain's economic cycles, and exports of agricultural products were a major part of her foreign trade. Quantitative data on the economic and social structures of rural Spain and their changes over time; on the attitudes and behavior of the rural population; on property, land and tenure systems, and their stability or change in different parts of the country are therefore of signal importance.

The rural economic and social structure has been decisively shaped by two historical events that need the intensive monographic study now being undertaken: the *Reconquista* from the Moors and the settlement and legal status that followed it in the Middle Ages; and the *desamortización* in the nineteenth century. Malefakis, in his outstanding *Agrarian Reform and Peasant Revolution,* has briefly sketched the interaction between geographic conditions and the historical process, making critical reference to the relevant literature; for the *Reconquista* he relies heavily on the symposium edited by José María Lacarra, the work of Ignacio de la Concha, and the exhaustive study of central Andalusia by Julio González entitled *Repartimiento de Sevilla.* He rightly notes that the *desamortización* "remains the least studied of all pivotal events in Spanish history," although considerable information is available in publications and archives. The early studies by J. M. Antequera and Carmelo Viñas y Mey are totally inadequate, and it is only recently that investigation of the problem has been undertaken in local monographs.[163]

Francisco Simón Segura has contributed two detailed statistical analyses of the ecclesiastical *desamortización* in Madrid and Gerona, community by community and month by month as well as by area, type of property, and value.[164] The information on the occupations and names of buyers permits a better understanding of the social revolution represented by the sales. Perhaps further research will make clear the links between political elites and the landowning classes and the continuity or discontinuity in the rural oligarchy from 1836 to the present. It is to be hoped that similar volumes will appear on latifundio Spain. The specific evidence and the analysis of the processes involved, in addition to the demographic, religious, economic, political, and other consequences of that social "revolution," still need to be explored.

The political importance of the tenancy conflicts concerning the *rabassa morta* in the Catalan vineyards and the connection between these conflicts and phylloxera and foreign trade have been the subjects of monographic research by Catalan historians.[165]

Happily, Malefakis has discussed the sources of information on land tenure with detailed reference to their publication and to archival resources.[166] Even more important, he has described the categories used and the procedures employed to collect the data, which he evaluates. He describes the *Catastro de la riqueza rústica en España,* which was begun in 1906, carried out for the most part between 1919 and 1925, and completed—except for a few scattered northern counties—as late as 1953–59. He analyzes some causes of the slow and discontinuous collection of data and their incomplete and irregular publication as well as the difficulties that these factors have made in their use. A principal difficulty is the tendency to overstate the number of owners and to understate the average area and income each one controlled, because every owner is counted in each of the several municipalities in which he owned property. The failure to distinguish between municipal and individual ownership tends to overemphasize the importance of large landholdings. There is a failure to separate irrigated from dry land or cultivated land from pasture and forest.

The other two sources discussed in detail are the *Encuestas Agropecuarias* of the *Junta Nacional de Hermandades* of the *Sindicatos* (National Corporative Organization), compiled in 1953, and the 1962 *Censo Agrario,* prepared and published by the Instituto Nacional de Estadística. The first of these rates a very critical judgment. The second, which deals more with land tenure and exploitation than with property, does not take the place of the Catastro, but it is a basic source for the study of many additional aspects of agriculture.

Finally, Malefakis discusses the *Registro de la Propiedad Expropiable del Instituto de Reforma Agraria,* based on the declarations of those owners whose lands were subject to expropriation under the Agrarian Reform Law of September 1932, which consequently deals more with owners than with units of exploitation or units of land in a single *municipio.* He considers that the principal advantages of this register are as follows:

1. It transcends municipal and provincial boundaries.
2. It informs us as to whether or not the owner held a title of nobility.
3. It makes possible, by giving the names of owners, investigation of the overlap between the landowning class and other elites or occupations.
4. It gives certain indications, by specifying place of birth, of absenteeism or ties with regions outside an estate's location.
5. It gives information on various categories of expropriable land: long leaseholds, land not irrigated despite a legal obligation to do so, etc.
6. It specifies the manner of acquisition and thus conveys a sense of the land market.
7. It gives information on mortgages.

Another attraction of the *Registro* is that it is located in a single archive, although it is not easy to use. Malefakis has made use of these data for six Southern provinces; they could be extensively exploited by scholars only if sufficient funds were available.

Some studies of local communities by anthropologists such as Lisón Tolosana or geographers such as the Dutchman Jan Hinderink make use of historical data from local archives, published sources, or national censuses. Such studies allow us to trace processes of social change in a defined ecological context. Hinderink's thesis on the Sierra de Gata, an isolated area close to the Portuguese border between Caceres and Salamanca, uses the Catastro of the Marqués de la Ensenada and contrasts its data with contemporary records, putting special emphasis on demographic trends as well as on the crops cultivated in 1752 and 1955.[167] An excellent example of a detailed cartographic study of rural settlement, property distribution, and crop areas—with a historical dimension—is that of the French geographer Michel Drain on the municipality of Utrera in western Andalusia.[168]

Economic Development: Finances, Prices, Industrialization, and Agriculture

The literature on economic development in the nineteenth and early twentieth centuries is scant, and many studies, even the best, make little or unsystematic use of quantitative data. J. Vicens Vives and J. Nadal in their *Economic History of Spain* devote 607 pages to the period before 1808 and only 140 to "the impact of the industrial revolution." [169] Nevertheless, many of the recent works on the economic structure of contemporary Spain contain retrospective quantitative series and incidentally discuss the historical origins of present institutions and problems.[170] Only for recent decades can we find the wealth of reports from international agencies, government bodies, interest groups, and big banks about the annual economic situation which a quantitative historian needs for research. There are, of course, a number of important government reports for earlier periods: descriptive overviews like *La riqueza y el progreso de España,* published in 1920 and 1924 by the Banco Urquijo; in addition to the series published by the statistical offices, in financial journals, and in the annual reports of important companies.[171] It is beyond the scope of this chapter to list most of those publications. By no accident one of the most useful sources, *Historia económica, financiera y política de España en el siglo XX,* is the work of the editor of a financial journal and the only one attempting to cover the first thirty years of this century. The *Anuario financiero y de sociedades anónimas de España,* founded in 1915, and the *Anuario financiero que comprende el historial de los valores públicos y de sociedades anónimas de España,* founded in 1914, are indispensable for financial statements of banks; reports of many business firms; data on date of founding, capital, dividends, and officers of most corporations and many other enterprises.[172] An index of last names (compiled in 1932) facilitates a study of elite interconnections as well as of interlocking directorates and financial groups. The *Anuario oficial de valores de las bolsas de Madrid y Barcelona,* initiated in 1912, is the basic source on the stock exchange; the *Anuario de minería y metalurgia,* published since 1949, provides similar information for its two sectors.[173]

Unfortunately there are no similar sources for the agricultural sector. Company histories with more or less scholarly pretensions, which serve as such important sources for German economic history, are unfortunately rare for Spain.[174] There has been no effort to assemble company archives, and I fear that such materials are being lost every day. The late emergence, outside the peripheral industrial regions, of major national interest organizations and the impact of the Civil War on these organizations deprive the historian of another potential source of information.[175] However, the provincial Cámaras de Comercio e Industria (y Navegación, in the maritime cities) have published annually their more or less extensive *Memorias,* which contain much information that cannot be found elsewhere and are indispensable for any regional economic history.[176] With a natural emphasis on trade, the consular reports, published or in the archives, are another continuous source used by modern historians like Nicolás Sánchez-Albornoz.[177] Since 1920 the British Department of Overseas Trade has, with more or less regularity, published the *Report on the Industries and Commerce of Spain* prepared by the commercial secretary of the United Kingdom Embassy in Madrid.[178] All these are, of course, only the raw materials for quantitative analysis, not substitutes for scholarly research.

Some overviews of modern economic history are Vicens Vives's work in collaboration with Jorge Nadal and his *Cataluña en el siglo XIX,* a general history of the most industrial region of Spain in which we find intertwined political, economic, social, and cultural history, including some quantitative data. A much more detailed study is Jaime Carrera Pujal's work on the nineteenth century Catalan economy, a companion to his political history of the same period.[179] Carrera Pujal's books are rich in information, referring to archival sources, but they are less interpretative than Vicens Vives's works; the text is scattered with figures, but Carrera Pujal does not present continuous series or bring to his analysis theoretical problems or modern methods. Nor are we better served for the Basque country, the other leading industrial region—there we have to rely on a brief descriptive sketch by José F. de Lequerica, a short Basque nationalist tract, and a centennial volume edited by the Banco de Bilbao.[180] Only the unfinished history of the steel industry by Francisco Sánchez Ramos fills some of the gap, because of the importance of that sector in the economy of Vizcaya.[181] Antoni Jutglar's *La era industrial en España* is another synthesis, looking at the economic history from the perspective of the social consequences with some quantitative information.[182] The critical analysis by Juan Velarde Fuertes of the different attempts since the late nineteenth century to estimate national wealth provides us with historical information and an important bibliography.[183]

The research department of the Bank of Spain has brought together a number of scholars who studied different aspects of the mid-nineteenth century economy with a quantitative approach, offering time series, price comparisons, and other systematic data.[184] Several of the studies link the financial system, particularly banks and foreign investment, with the key sectors of railroads, mining, and industry. The interest of foreign and national promoters and investors in railroads probably deflected capital from industrialization, particularly since the Spanish iron and steel industry could not compete with foreign producers in supplying railroads. The latter did not prove very profitable for private investors, but it did benefit their promoters and indirectly the foreign industries with which they were connected rather than a nascent Spanish heavy industry. The time series on railroad construction and on the production and import of iron and steel products, particularly railroad and public works materials, prove this important thesis.[185] The study also sheds light on how locational factors and price differentials contributed to the failure of the Andalusian iron and steel industry and led to its displacement by northern mills. The chapter on agriculture shows the factors limiting the impact of institutional changes conducive to modernization. The effort to make the import of cereals unnecessary led to an expansion of grain production, mostly through the extension of cultivated area, but not to major technological changes. The appendixes of the volume on privileged banks, the money market, and railroad expansion are a major contribution to economic history.

Much interesting work on the nineteenth century, relating economic, demographic, and political cycles, is contained in the studies of Nicolás Sánchez-Albornoz, which are among the few we can really call quantitative history. His *España hace un siglo* focuses on the dual character of the economy: premodern agriculture and incipient capitalism.[186] Expansion was due more to an increase in cultivated area, characteristically using marginal land, than to intensification of cultivation and technical innovation. Wheat, very dependent on weather in its yields, continued to be the basic crop. This structure, combined with an underdeveloped transportation system and the geographic barriers between regions or even communities, led to great price differentials between interior, Mediterranean, and Atlantic coast markets and even adjacent provinces. Provincial data collected by the governors and consular reports make possible a detailed study of periods around the crisis years of 1857 and 1868. The price differentials and changes, resulting from crop failures and transportation difficulties, are correlated with basic demographic series of nuptiality, births, infant mortality, epidemics, and deaths. Sánchez-Albornoz, however, goes beyond the national framework to discover the parallels between the Spanish cycles and those of other Mediterranean countries, particularly Algeria. These parallels reflect in part the impact of a European production crisis and of the Crimean War. The *España hace un siglo* is also the first systematic effort to link data on the economic cycle with those on political crisis and turmoil, particularly the 1868 revolution, both at the national level and in the context of a commercial maritime city like Cadiz.[187] Sánchez-Albornoz does not ignore, however, the links between developments in finance, mining, and industry and the premodern agrarian economy; for example, he analyzes how the 1866 financial crisis in Barcelona preceded the agricultural crisis and helped aggravate it. The research is extended into two aspects of incipient capitalism: (1) mining, mainly for export, between 1850 and 1875, and the factors that limited its impact on overall, particularly industrial, economic growth; (2) the role of the Crédito Mobiliario Español, 1856–1902.[188] The study focuses on the changes in control of this Spanish offshoot in the French creation of the Pereire brothers; its activities, particularly in the railroad field; its profits; and its connections with the political elite. Sánchez-Albornoz's monographs and essays constitute the most comprehensive and seriously researched view of the dual economy of Spain as it confronted modern capitalism and industrialization. The dual Spain shown by the economic and demographic data which he marshals so well is as important for the historian as the "two Spains" which until recently occupied the politico-cultural-religious interpretations of history.

Business cycles are also studied by Juan Sardá, but from the perspective of government monetary policies, budgets, banking and foreign investments, and balance of trade rather than that of production and population changes. He supplies important time series on money, debt, trade, and prices and a useful appendix and article on a price index for the century.[189] For price indexes in the twentieth century, so necessary for reducing data in current pesetas (in budgets, salaries and wages, etc.) to constant pesetas, see the work of Paris Eguilaz, who has also brought together data on national income, investment, and consumption.[190]

Juan Velarde analyzes the financial and economic policies of the Primo de Rivera dictatorship, particularly the great effort in public works, with a wealth of quantitative information. He examines many of the problems of Spanish economic development in the context of his study of Flores de Lemus, an outstanding economist and formulator of policies in the first decades of the century.[191]

Unfortunately there is no scholarly study of the economic situation of Spain from the fall of Primo de Rivera to the onset of the Civil War—the years of the great worldwide depression—a study that would perhaps contribute to our understanding of the tensions that led to the breakdown of the Republic (even though there are in the time series indications that political factors might have operated independently of, or even run counter to, the economic ones). Such an investigation would also tell us more about the character of the new regime and its specific policies in relation to different social and economic groups. On the financing of the Civil War, particularly the deposit of the gold of the central bank in the USSR, there is the interesting study by Juan Sardá. The Catalan economy and economic policy-collectivization during the Civil War have been studied by José

María Bricall and Albert Pérez Baró. Contemporary studies by Spanish economists might serve as a starting point.[192]

Throughout the nineteenth and twentieth centuries, public finances and monetary policies have been the object of government reports, public debates, and scholarly studies. Here we can only highlight some of them. The Seminario de Historia Moderna of the University of Navarre, under the direction of Federico Suárez and as part of a revisionist study of the reign of Ferdinand VII, has published a number of documents, particularly the plans of the finance minister Martín Garay and those connected with the public debt.[193] For midcentury we have the study of Fernández Pulgar and R. Anes Alvarez on the development of the monetary system between 1847 and 1868; there are also contemporary analyses of the 1864 monetary crisis, and late in the century Ortí y Brull published his study of monetary policy.[194] In the twentieth century we have the *Dictamen* on the introduction of the gold standard (attributed to Flores de Lemus), the contributions of the Catalan finance minister and politician Cambó, and a review of monetary policy by Luis Olariaga. Recently Solé Villalonga has added a study on public debt and the capital market.[195]

Banking is perhaps the sector that has attracted most attention, with works by Canosa, Galvarriato, and Gabriel Tortella, whose monograph on the national bank between 1829 and 1929 is eagerly awaited.[196] The role of the French investment banks in Spanish economic development has received considerable attention by Rondo E. Cameron and more recently by Sánchez-Albornoz.[197] Foreign investment during 1855–80 has been studied by Rafael Anes Alvarez.[198] Foreign investment in the initial stages of economic growth and the process by which later in the twentieth century many foreign firms became "nationalized" as ownership and control passed into Spanish hands would be the subject for a monograph that could have interesting implications for the semideveloped countries of the third world evolving in a capitalist or mixed economy framework. That process—with some important exceptions like petroleum distribution, telephones, and, in part, railroads—took place without government action.

Studies of Catalan banking by Voltes Bou and by Francesc Cabana contribute to our understanding of the economic infrastructure of the tension between regional nationalism and the Spanish state.[199] Cabana, unfortunately without scholarly apparatus, gives figures on the activities of leading Catalan banks, on the Banco de España in Catalonia, and on the circumstances leading to the bankruptcy in 1921 and 1931 of two of the largest Catalan banks. Information on the Catalan capital market and on participation in activities outside the region is of special interest. Catalan particularism contrasts with the national scope of Madrid and Basque banking. There are also useful histories of particular banks, but the role of large banks in Spanish economic and particularly industrial development still has not found its historian.[200]

Only a few sectors of the economy—railroads, textiles, iron and steel, electrical manufacturing—have been the object of historical study; however, even in those sectors, a rich field awaits the scholar.[201] Sánchez Ramos presents considerable quantitative data in his unfinished study of the steel industry; but most of the studies use quantitative information haphazardly, and many sectors have not found even a mediocre historian, to say nothing of investigators using modern economic analysis and a comparative perspective.

There are a number of studies of foreign trade and protectionism, but no general history.[202] The same is true for agriculture, even though Vicens Vives mentions an unpublished manuscript, and G. Anes has recently outlined the main problems for the first half of the century.[203] For a part of the agricultural sector, important in exports, we have a study of cork and its cultivation, commercialization, and industrialization.[204] The wealth of information on particular crops and agricultural regions together with many statistical sources, newspaper reports of agricultural prices, and publications of interest organizations would all be of help in writing either an agrarian history or studies of some of its parts. The monumental bibliography by José Muñoz Pérez and Juan Benito Arranz, *Guía bibliográfica para una geografía agraria de España,* has prepared the ground for the investigator.[205] The attention centered on the inequities in the distribution of landed property and its social and political consequences has probably detracted from the interest in the history of production, technological innovation, prices, and the internal and foreign commerce in agricultural products in the context of the development of the economy, which, as we should not forget, was basically agrarian until only a few decades ago.[206] Some of the publications of the Junta Consultiva Agronómica in the first decades of the century would be useful points of departure.[207] Alain Huetz de Lemps's work on the wine economy of Northwestern Spain deals with all the aspects enumerated on a broad historical canvas from the Middle Ages to the present and includes rich quantitative data on modern times.[208] Unfortunately this outstanding work does not deal with the more important southern, central, and Catalan wine-producing areas. Historical climatology would benefit from quantitative treatment, which could provide important information to agrarian history.[209] Broad overviews will have to be supplemented and tested through local monographs like that of Fernández Marco on Sobradiel, a community in the vega of Zaragoza.[210] Economist Torres Martínez has contributed a study of the regional economy of Valencia, rich in historical data; he has also written a major study on the wheat economy so central to agrarian Spain.[211] Such economic studies, dealing mostly with production and market fluctuations, are a new dimension to the structural analysis of agrarian, social, and political crises, which sociologists and historians tend to see more in the light of land tenure and property structure.

A team comprised of agronomic engineers and an economist has studied rural seasonal unemployment and its relationship to the dominance of single crops (particularly olives) in different provinces, the labor needs for various crops in different months, the degree of mechanization, and related phenomena.[212] Their study also describes the impact of agricultural prices on labor. This data should be taken into account in any study of agrarian unrest, electoral swings, etc. in the countryside, adding an economic structural-cyclical dimension to those derived from property and land-tenure relations.

The more sociological microanalysis of Martínez Alier confronts us with the economic and ideological responses of employers and workers in Andalusian (Córdoba) agriculture to structural determinants.[213] He analyzes a wealth of quantitative economic and social data for different dates and extremely interesting information on agricultural products, wages, farm accounts, types of entrepreneurial mentality, and considerations about alternative forms of socioeconomic organization. Considerable attention has been paid to the organization of protesting farm laborers and peasants, but unfortunately little concern has been given to equivalent conservative, catholic, or moderate organizations. Official statistics and data on CONCA (Confederación Nacional Católica Agraria) suggest the need for a history of the mobilization of the peasantry, mainly north of Madrid, for economic and political purposes.[214]

In recent years, Spanish economists have developed basic tools for macroanalysis: estimates of national income and its provincial distribution, input-output tables, national accounts, studies of concentration, monopoly and interlocking directorates, and relationships with other economies as entry into the Common Market came to be considered.[215] The analysis of the policy-making process by Charles W. Anderson can serve as an introduction to this literature.[216] Monographic issues of *Información Comercial Española* on different economic sectors or regions—often containing historical articles—give us a contemporary picture.[217] I would like to argue that in the case of Spain it might be a fruitful strategy for the historian to begin retrospectively with contemporary problems and ask how they evolved, rather than start in the past and analyze from there the process of development. The comparison of the present with the past at critical dates might be a particularly good way to identify problems for research.

Reality and Perception

In recent Spanish history, the scholar finds two types of data. One was produced at the time by different participants and sources with partisan motives and is subject to ignorance and misconceptions; the other consists, it is to be hoped, of data resulting from serious research, in part sifted and evaluated by the historian from partisan sources. The temptation is to consider the second set of data the main factor for the quantitative historian—to consider it history "as it actually happened," to use Ranke's injunction, ignoring, except for uncomplimentary comments, the other sets of data, which tend to be confusing if not maddening. However, for an understanding of the climate of opinion at any given time, the unreliable and distorted data circulated in the press, in books, and in speeches are as important as the reality, if not more so. If we want to understand the crisis of the Spanish republic, we must construct a "fever curve" of disorder and violence: the number and extent of strikes; fights; murders; burning of crops, churches, or union headquarters; newspapers censored; rapes by Foreign Legion or Moorish troops in Asturias; arrests; casualties of the repressive forces or the revolutionaries; the ousting of farmers from their land; or the occupation of farms by farm laborers.

We shall never know the truth as an absolutely neutral, omnipresent, omniscient observer would have given it to us, but we can learn how the two opposite sides in the conflict, as well as the somewhat more objective middle forces, were perceiving events by turning to their speeches and, best of all, their newspapers. The day-by-day accounts of the same events in the Communist, Anarcho-syndicalist, Socialist, Left-bourgeois, Center Catholic, and Monarchist press are of great interest. The averages for different periods, based on such painstaking accounting, would be most helpful in understanding the processes of polarization that led to the Civil War. The same is true of the figures of casualties and deaths, prisoners, victims of assassinations, and foreign volunteers during the Civil War, and of victims of various sanctions after the war. But, for example, which figures of the victims of religious persecution in the Civil War are more important: the figures of 4,184 secular priests and seminarians, 2,365 regular clergy, and 283 nuns (a total of 6,832 persons) identified as victims of the religious persecution in Antonio Montero Moreno's work of 1961;[218] or the contemporary figures, issued in authoritative statements like the Collective Letter of the Spanish bishops of 1937, of some 6,000 priests said to be victims among the secular clergy alone; or the figures, given in books, of 25,000 religious persons? To base our analysis of the attitude of the religious sector toward the Civil War on the objective facts alone would be as misleading as to take contemporary estimates for the facts.

Let us not forget the dictum of the sociologist W. I. Thomas, "If men define situations as real, they are real in their consequences." The practitioners of scholarly quantification will not forget that there is also a popular quantification. Men have always loved the roundness of numbers above their exactitude in their accounts of historical events. And they have inflated or deflated those numbers as their loyalties and their antipathies have moved them.

NOTES

1 Juan Reglá, "La época de los tres primeros Austrias," *Historia social y económica de España y América*, vol. 3, ed. J. Vicens Vives (Barcelona: Teide, 1957); Jaime Vicens Vives, *An Economic History of Spain*, in collaboration with Jorge Nadal Oller, trans. Frances M. López-Morillas (Princeton: Princeton University Press, 1969); Jacob van Klaveren, *Europäische Wirtschaftsgeschichte Spaniens im 16. und 17. Jahrhundert*, Forschungen zur Sozial- und Wirtschaftsgeschichte, 2, ed. Friedrich Lütge (Stuttgart: Fischer, 1960); Jaime Carrera Pujal, *Historia de la economía española*, 5 vols. (Barcelona: Bosch, 1947); idem, *Historia política y económica de Cataluña*, 4 vols. (Barcelona: Bosch, 1947); Antonio Domínguez Ortiz, *La sociedad española en el siglo XVII* (Madrid: CSIC [Consejo Superior de Investigaciones Científicas], Instituto Balmes de Sociología, Departamento de Historia Social, 1963); idem, *La sociedad española en el siglo XVIII* (Madrid: CSIC, Instituto Balmes de Sociología, Departamento de Historia Social, 1955).

2 Fernand Braudel, *La Méditerranée et le monde méditerraneen à l'époque de Philippe II*, 2 vols., 2d ed. (Paris: Colin, 1966).

3 Ramón Carande [Thobar], *Carlos V y sus banqueros. La vida económica en Castilla, 1516–1556* (Madrid: Sociedad de Estudios y Publicaciones, 1965)—a much revised version of his *Carlos V y sus banqueros. La vida económica de España en una fase de su hegemonía, 1516–1556* (Madrid: Revista de Occidente, 1943); idem, *Carlos V y sus banqueros. La hacienda real de Castilla* (Madrid: Sociedad de Estudios y Publicaciones, 1959); and idem, *Carlos V y sus banqueros. Los caminos del oro y de la plata. (Deuda exterior y tesoros ultramarinos)* (Madrid: Sociedad de Estudios y Publicaciones, 1967).

4 Modesto Ulloa, *La hacienda real de Castilla en el reinado de Felipe II* (Rome: Librería Sforzini, Centro del Libro Español, 1963); Antonio Domínguez Ortiz, *Política y hacienda de Felipe IV* (Madrid: Editorial de Derecho Financiero, 1960).

5 Henri Lapeyre, *Simón Ruiz et les "Asientos" de Philippe II* (Paris: SEVPEN [Société d'Éditions et Vente des Publications de l'Éducation Nationale], 1953); idem, *Une famille des marchands, les Ruiz: Contribution a l'étude du commerce entre la France et l'Espagne au temps de Philippe II* (Paris: SEVPEN, 1955). See also the monograph on another merchant-banker family: Guillermo Lohmann Villena, *Les Espinosa: Une famille d'hommes d'affaires en Espagne et aux Indes à l'époque de la colonisation*, Ecole Pratique des Hautes Etudes, VIe section, Affaires et Gens d'Affaires, 21 (Paris: SEVPEN, 1968).

6 F. Ruiz Martín, *Lettres marchandes échangées entre Florence et Medina del Campo*, Ecole Pratique des Hautes Etudes, VIe section, Centre de Recherches Historiques, Affaires et Gens d'Affaires, 25 (Paris: SEVPEN, 1965); José Gentil da Silva, ed., *Lettres de Lisbonne, 1563–1578*, 2 vols., Ecole Pratique des Hautes Etudes, VIe section, Affaires et Gens d'Affaires, 14 (Paris: SEVPEN, 1959, 1961); Valentín Vázquez de Prada, ed., *Lettres marchandes d'Anvers*, 4 vols., Ecole Pratique des Hautes Etudes, VIe section, Affaires et Gens d'Affaires, 18 (Paris: SEVPEN, n.d.).

7 Earl J. Hamilton, "American Treasure and Andalusian Prices, 1503–1660," *Journal of Economic and Business History* 1 (1928): 1–35; idem, "Wages and Subsistence on Spanish Treasure Ships, 1503–1660," *Journal of Political Economy* 37 (1929): 430–50; idem, "American Treasure nad the Rise of Capitalism. 1500–1700," *Economica*, Nov. 1929, pp. 338–57. These three articles have been published in a Spanish translation entitled *El florecimiente del capitalismo y otros ensayos* (Madrid: Revista de Occidente, 1948). See also Hamilton's *American Treasure and the Price Revolution in Spain, 1501–1650*, Harvard Economic Studies, 43 (Cambridge, Mass.: Harvard University Press, 1934); and *Money, Prices, and Wages in Valencia, Aragon, and Navarre, 1351–1500* (Cambridge, Mass.: Harvard University Press, 1936). For a listing of most of the relevant articles by Hamilton, consult the bibliography listings under

his name in *Cambridge Economic History of Europe* (Cambridge: Cambridge University Press, 1967), 4:609–10. These listings form part of a valuable 10-page bibliography for the article in that volume by Braudel and F. Spooner, "Prices in Europe from 1450 to 1750," pp. 374–486, of which pp. 457–86 are maps, tables, and graphs.

8 Pierre Vilar's many articles on Spanish economic history, theory, and methodology are collected in his *Crecimiento y desarrollo, economía e historia. Reflexiones sobre el caso español* (Barcelona: Ariel, 1964); for his polemic with Hamilton, see esp. pp. 23–248. See also his *Oro y moneda en la historia, 1450–1920* (Barcelona: Ariel, 1969). David Felix, "Profit Inflation and Industrial Growth. The Historic Record and Contemporary Analogies," *Quarterly Journal of Economics* 70 (1956): 441–63; John U. Nef, "Prices and Industrial Capitalism in France and England, 1540–1640," *Economic History Review* 7 (1937): 155–85; Ingrid Hammarström, "The 'Price Revolution' of the Sixteenth Century: Some Swedish Evidence," *Scandinavian Economic History Review*, vol. 5, no. 1 (1957), pp. 118–54. The importance of Hammarström's article for us is its critique both of the simple quantity theory of money and its use by Hamilton and others and of Hamilton's lack of attention to the historic processes whereby specie inflows might have influenced price levels. The scope of the article goes well beyond its title; the Swedish evidence is actually a rather minor part. Jorge Nadal Oller, "La revolución de los precios españoles en el siglo XVI. Estado actual de la cuestión," *Hispania. Revista Española de Historia*, vol. 19, no. 77 (1959), pp. 503–29. See also G. Pinarello, M. Randisi, G. Salini, G. Digioacchino, and D. Cantarelli, "Il movimento dei prezzi in Spagna dal 1695 al 1755," *Giornale degli economisti e annali di economia*, vol. 24, nos. 3–4 (1965), pp. 287–307 and graphs; Tiber Wittman, "Apuntes sobre los métodos de investigación de la decadencia castellana (siglos XVI–XVII)," *Nouvelles études historiques publiées à l'occasion du XIIᵉ Congrès International des Sciences Historiques par la Commission Nationale des Historiens Hongrois*, 2 vols. (Budapest, 1965), 1:243–59. Fernando Ugorri Casado, "Ideas sobre el gobierno de España en el siglo XVII. La crisis de 1627, la moneda de vellón y el intento de fundación de un banco," *Revista de la Biblioteca. Archivo y Museo del Ayuntamiento de Madrid*, vol. 19, nos. 1–2 (1950), pp. 123–230.

9 Earl J. Hamilton, "Prices and Progress," *Journal of Economic History* 12 (Fall 1952): 325–49; idem, "Profit Inflation in the Industrial Revolution," *Quarterly Journal of Economics* 56 (1942): 265–66; idem, *War and Prices in Spain, 1651–1800*, Harvard Economic Studies, 81 (Cambridge, Mass.: Harvard University Press, 1947).

10 Nadal Oller, "La revolución de los precios españoles," p. 528.

11 Gonzalo Anes Alvarez, *Las crisis agrarias en la España moderna* (Madrid: Taurus, 1970), including 88 graphs.

12 Vilar, *Crecimiento y desarrollo*, p. 237.

13 Pierre Vilar, "Los primitivos españoles del pensamiento económico: 'Cuantitativismo' y 'Bullonismo,'" ibid., pp. 175–207 (also in French, in *Mélanges Marcel Bataillon, Bulletin Hispanique*, 1962, pp. 261–84); idem, "El problema de la formación del capitalismo," ibid., pp. 139–74, esp. pp. 156–74 (also in *Past and Present*, Nov. 1956, pp. 15–38).

14 Gonzalo Anes and Jean-Paul Le Flem, "Las crisis del siglo XVII: producción agrícola precios e ingresos en tierras de Segovia," *Moneda y Crédito* 93 (June 1965): 3–55, and 9 graphs.

15 Pierre Vilar, "Historia de los precios, historia general. (Un nuevo libro de E. J. Hamilton)," *Crecimiento y desarrollo*, pp. 209–37 (also in *Annales, Économies, Sociétés, Civilisations*, 1949, pp. 29–46).

16 Hamilton, *American Treasure and the Price Revolution in Spain*, p. 301; Fernand Braudel, preface to C. M. Cipolla, *Mouvement monétaires dans l'état de Milan* (Paris: Colin, 1952), p. 8.

17 François Simiand, *Le salaire, l'évolution sociale et la monnaie*, 3 vols. (Paris: Alcan, 1932).

18 Nadal Oller, "La revolución de los precios españoles," pp. 511–14.

19 Ibid., pp. 520–21.

20 E. H. Phelps Brown and S. V. Hopkins, "Builders' Wage-rates, Prices, and Population: Some Further Evidence," *Economica* 101 (Feb. 1959): 18–36.

21 Carmelo Viñas Mey, *El problema de la tierra en la España de los siglos XVI–XVII* (Madrid: CSIC, Instituto Jerónimo Zurita, 1941).

22 See n. 24 below.

23 Pierre Vilar, *La Catalogne dans l'Espagne moderne. Recherches sur les fondements économiques des structures nationales*, 3 vols., Bibliothèque Générale de l'Ecole Pratique des Hautes Etudes, VIᵉ section (Paris: SEVPEN, 1962), pp. 11–38. Vilar's list of sources (pp. 39–129), primary as well as secondary, is the most complete in the field; it includes general works and even many not directly relevant to his monograph. I strongly urge the reader to use this bibliography in any work on Spanish history he may wish to undertake.

24 Huguette and Pierre Chaunu, *Seville et l'Atlantique, 1504–1650*, Ports-Routes-Trafics, 6 (Paris: Colin, 1955). The work is in two parts: vols. 1–7, *Partie statistique;* vol. 8, 1 and 2, *Partie interprétative: Structures et conjoncture de l'Atlantique espagnol et hispanoaméricain, 1504–1650*. The maps and graphs are in vol. 7. In discussing the work of the Chaunus, one should also cite two classic works that opened this field for research: Clarence H. Haring, *Trade and Navigation between Spain and the Indies in the Time of the Hapsburgs*, Harvard Economic Studies, 19 (Cambridge, Mass.: Harvard University Press, 1918); Gervasio de Artíñano y de Galdácano, *Historia del comercio con las Indias durante el dominio de los Austrias* (Barcelona: Talleres de Oliva de Vilanova, 1917).

25 Pierre Chaunu, *Les Philippines et le Pacifique des Ibériques (XVIᵉ, XVIIᵉ, XVIIIᵉ siecles). Introduction méthodologique et indices d'activité*, Ports-Routes-Trafics, 11, Ecole Pratique des Hautes Etudes, VIᵉ section, Centre de Recherches Historiques (Paris: SEVPEN, 1960).

26 Alvaro Castillo Pintado, *Tráfico marítimo y comercio de importación en Valencia a comienzos del siglo XVII* (Madrid: Seminario de Historia Social y Económica de la Facultad de Filosofia y Letras, Universidad de Madrid, 1967).

27 Francisco Morales Padrón, *El comercio canario-americano. (Siglos XVI, XVII y XVIII)* (Seville: Escuela de Estudios Hispano-Americanos, 1955).

28 Teófilo Guiard y Larrauri, *Historia del Consulado y Casa de Contratación de Bilbao*, 2 vols. (Bilbao: Cámara Oficial de Comercio, Industria y Navegación, 1913–14).

29 Hermann Kellenbenz, *Unternehmerkräfte im Hamburger Portugal und Spanien-handel, 1590–1625* (Hamburg: Veröffentlichungen der Wirtschaftgeschichtlichen Forschungstelle, Verlag der Hamburgischen Bücherei, 1954). See, for the Bourbon period, Hans Pohl, *Die Beziehungen Hamburgs zu Spanien und dem spanischen Amerika in der Zeit von 1740 bis 1808*, Vierteljahrschrift für Sozial- und Wirtschaftsgeschichte, Beiheft 45 (Wiesbaden: Franz Steiner, 1963).

30 Leopoldo Piles Ros, "Aspectos sociales de la germanía de Valencia," *Estudios de Historia Social de España* (Madrid: CSIC, Instituto Balmes de Sociología, 1952) 2:429–78.

31 Noël Salomon, *La campagne de nouvelle Castille à la fin du XVIᵉ siècle, d'après les Relaciones Topográficas*, Ecole Pratique des Hautes Etudes, VIᵉ section, Les Hommes et la Terre, 9 (Paris: SEVPEN, 1964).

32 Fermín Caballero, *Discurso de recepción en la Real Academia de la Historia: Relaciones geográficas escritas en tiempo de Felipe II* (Madrid, 1866). For information on the existing copies of the *Relaciones*, see also Anselmo Sanz Serrano, *Resumen histórico de la estadística en España* (Madrid: Instituto Nacional de Estadística, 1956); Juan Ortega Rubio, *Relaciones topográficas de los pueblos de España. Lo más interesante de ellas* (Madrid: Sociedad Española de Artes Gráficas, 1918). For editions of the *Relaciones* and other analyses based on them, see Carmelo Viñas Mey and Ramón Paz, *Relaciones de los pueblos de España ordenadas por Felipe II*, vol. 1, *Provincia de Madrid*, vol. 2, *Reino de Toledo* (Madrid: CSIC, Instituto Balmes de Sociología e Instituto Juan Sebastián Elcano de Geografía, 1949); *Relaciones Topográficas de España. Relaciones de pueblos que pertenecen hoy a la provincia de Guadalajara*, vols. 1–3 ("Memorial Histórico Español," vols. 41–43), ed. Juan Catalina García (Madrid, 1903–05); vols. 4–6 ("Memorial Histórico Español," vols. 45–47), ed. Manuel Pérez Villamil (Madrid, 1912–15); Julián Zarco Cuevas, *Relaciones de pueblos del obispado de Cuenca hechas por orden de Felipe II*, 2 vols. (Cuenca: Biblioteca

diocesana conquense, 1927); Michel Terrasse, "La region de Madrid d'après les Relaciones Topográficas," *Mélanges de la Casa de Velázquez* (Paris) 4 (1968): 143–72, with maps and charts; Esther Jimeno, "La ciudad de Soria y su término en 1752," *Celtiberia* (Soria, 1956), vol. 6, no. 12, pp. 243–76.

33 José Gentil da Silva, *En Espagne, développement économique, subsistance, déclin,* graphic work by Jacques Bertin (Paris: Mouton, 1965).

34 Bartolomé Bennassar, *Valladolid au siècle d'or. Une ville de Castille et sa campagne au XVIe siècle,* Ecole Pratique des Hautes Etudes, VIe section, Civilisations et Sociétés, 4 (Paris: Mouton, 1967).

35 Henri Lapeyre, *Géographie de l'Espagne morisque,* Démographie et sociétés (Paris: SEVPEN, 1959). The work contains an extended bibliography of ancient and modern works as well as a listing of archival sources in Simancas, Madrid, and Valencia. It also refers to the important work of the 19th century archivist, Tomás González— *Censo de población de las provincias y partidos de la Corona de Castilla en el siglo XVI* (Madrid, 1829)—which includes materials since then lost and attempts a calculation of the number expelled from Granada in 1570.

36 Juan Reglá, "La expulsión de los moriscos y sus consecuencias," *Hispania, Revista Española de Historia,* vol. 13, no. 51, pp. 215–67; idem, "La cuestión morisca y la coyuntura internacional durante la época de Felipe II," *Estudios de Historia Moderna* 3 (1953): 217–34; idem, *Estudios sobre los moriscos,* Anales de la Universidad de Valencia, 37 (Valencia, 1964).

37 Tulio Halperin Donghi, "Un conflicto nacional: moriscos y cristianos viejos en Valencia," *Cuadernos de Historia de España,* Ministerio de Educación, Universidad de Buenos Aires, Facultad de Filosofía y Letras, Instituto de Historia de España, vols. 23–24 (Buenos Aires, 1955), pp. 5–115; vols. 25–26 (Buenos Aires, 1957), pp. 83–250.

38 Julio Caro Baroja, *Los moriscos del Reino de Granada* (Madrid: Instituto de Estudios Políticos, 1957). For additional studies with quantitative data, see Jean-Paul Le Flem, "Les morisques du Nord-Ouest de l'Espagne en 1594," *Mélanges de la Casa de Velázquez* (Paris, 1965), 1:223–40; Claude and Jean-Paul Le Flem, "Un censo de moriscos en Segovia y su provincia en 1594," *Estudios Segovianos* 17 (1964): 5–36, and graphs; Bonifacio de Echegaray, "¿Se establecieron los moriscos en el país vasco de Francia?" *Bulletin Hispanique* 47 (1945): 92–102. For a review of the main studies, see Ramón Carande, "Los moriscos de Henri Lapeyre, los de Julio Caro y algún morisco más," *Moneda y Crédito* 78 (Sept. 1961): 9–26.

39 Jorge Nadal Oller, *La población española, siglos XVI a XVII* (Barcelona: Ariel, 1966). This basic work gives critical bibliographical references. An older, classic work, based in part on lost archives, is Tomás González's *Censo de la población de las provincias y partidos de la Corona de Castilla en el siglo XVI* (Madrid, 1829).

40 Georges Nadal Oller and Emile Giralt, *La population catalane de 1553 à 1717* (Paris: SEVPEN, 1960); idem, "Ensayo metodológico para el estudio de la población catalana, de 1553 a 1717," *Estudios de Historia Moderna* 3 (1953): 237–84. See also Josep Iglésies, *Distribució comarcal de la població catalana a la primera meitat del segle XVI* (Barcelona: Institut d'Estudis Catalans, 1957); Emilio Giralt and Jorge Nadal Oller, "Inmigración francesa y problemas monetarios en la Cataluña de los siglos XVI y XVII," *Riassunti delle comunicazioni, Xº Congresso Internazionale di Scienze Storiche Roma, 1955,* vol. 2 (Florence, 1955); Emilio Giralt, "La colonia mercantil francesa de Barcelona a mediados del siglo XVII," *Estudios de Historia Moderna* 6 (1960).

41 Bartolomé Bennassar, *Recherches sur les grandes épidémies dans le nord de l'Espagne à la fin du XVIe siècle,* Ecole Pratique des Hautes Etudes, VIe section, Centre de Recherches Historiques, Démographie et Sociétés, 12 (Paris: SEVPEN, 1969). See also José María Ibáñez Claris, "Estudio demográfico-médico acerca de la gran epidemia de 1589, en Igualada," *Anales de la cultura igualadina,* 1954, pp. 5–9.

42 Henry Kamen, *The Spanish Inquisition* (London: Weidenfeld and Nicolson, 1965), pp. 150–54, 243–44; Julio Caro Baroja, *Los judíos en la España moderna y contemporánea,* 3 vols. (Madrid: Arión, 1961), 2:97–102.

43 Caro Baroja, *Los judíos en la España moderna y contemporánea,* 1:349–57; Joaquim

Mendes dos Remedios, *Os judeus em Portugal*, 2 vols. (Coimbra: Ff. Amado, 1895, 1922); see esp. 2:150–51. The statistical data are reprinted in Caro Baroja, 3:322–24, 1:56 (map). Nicolás López Martínez, *Los judaizantes castellanos y la Inquisición en el tiempo de Isabel la Católica* (Burgos: Seminario Metropolitano de Burgos, 1954), pp. 353–70; Antonio Domínguez Ortiz, *La clase social de los conversos en Castilla en la edad moderna*, Estudios de Historia Social de España, vol. 3 (Madrid: CSIC, Instituto Balmes de Sociología, 1955), pp. 17–23, 25–29.

44 Caro Baroja, *Los judíos en la España moderna y contemporánea*, 1:182–89.

45 Américo Castro, *The Structure of Spanish History* (Princeton: Princeton University Press, 1954); idem, *De la edad conflictiva. El drama de la honra en España y en su literatura* (Madrid: Taurus, 1961).

46 Antonio Domínguez Ortiz, *La sociedad española en el siglo XVII*, vol. 2, El estamento eclesiástico (Madrid: CSIC, Instituto Balmes de Sociología, 1970).

47 Richard Kagan, "Universities in Castile, 1500–1700," *Past and Present* 49 (Nov. 1970); idem, "Education and the State in Habsburg Spain" (Ph.D. diss., Cambridge University, 1968). In a personal communication to this author, Kagan gave the revised estimate of 3.7 rather than the 2.5 given in the article. On universities, the best general account is C. María Ajo G. y Sáinz de Zúñiga, *Historia de las universidades hispanoamericanas. Orígenes y desarrollo desde su aparición hasta nuestros días*, 4 vols. (Madrid: La Normal, 1957–66), which includes an extensive bibliography (on cover: Avila, Centro de Estudios e Investigaciones Alonso de Madrigal). Vicente de la Fuente, *Historia de las universidades, colegios y establecimientos de enseñanza*, 4 vols. (Madrid: Viuda e hija de Fuentenebro, 1884–89), is still useful. For examples of recent publications of matriculation books that could be used in elite studies, see Santiago Nogaledo Alvarez, *El Colegio Menor de "Pan y Carbón," primero de los colegios universitarios de Salamanca, 1386–1780*, Acta Salmanticensia, Historia de la Universidad, vol. 1, no. 3 [sic] (Salamanca: Universidad de Salamanca, 1958); Luis Ferrer Ezquerra and Higinio Misol García, *Catálogo de colegiales del Colegio Mayor de Santiago el Cebedeo, del Arzobispo, de Salamanca*, Acta Salmanticensia, Historia de la Universidad, vol. 1, no. 3 (Salamanca: Universidad de Salamanca, 1956); José de Rújula y de Ochotorena (Marqués de Ciadoncha), *Indice de los colegiales del Mayor de San Ildefonso y Menores de Alcalá* (Madrid: CSIC, Instituto Jerónimo Zurita, 1946), comprising an index of 21,342 names with reference to the documents in which they appear and to genealogical records, place of birth, offices held; Filemón Arribas Arranz, ed., *Relaciones y justificantes de méritos y servicios de Catedráticos, Profesores y Opositores a cátedras. Catálogo* (Valladolid: Universidad de Valladolid, 1963), listing of professors of the 17th and 18th centuries with biographical data.

48 José Antonio Escudero, *Los Secretarios de Estado y del Despacho, 1474–1724*, 4 vols. (Madrid: Instituto de Estudios Administrativos, 1969); Juan J. Linz, "Intellectual Roles in Sixteenth and Seventeenth Century Spain," *Daedalus* (forthcoming).

49 Jean Sarrailh, *L'Espagne éclairée de la seconde moitié du XVIIIe siècle* (Paris: Imprimerie Nationale, 1954); Richard Herr, *The Eighteenth Century Revolution in Spain* (Princeton: Princeton University Press, 1958); Luis Sánchez Agesta, *El pensamiento político del despotismo ilustrado* (Madrid: Instituto de Estudios Políticos, 1953).

50 Georges N. Desdevises du Dezert's *L'Espagne de l'ancien régime*, 3 vols. (Paris, 1897–1904), is a major synthesis of social and economic with political and cultural history; it does not present quantitative data systematically but refers frequently to them in the text and cites the relevant sources. Antonio Domínguez Ortiz, *La sociedad española en el siglo XVIII* (Madrid: CSIC, Instituto Balmes de Sociología, Departamento de Historia Social, 1955).

51 Herr, *Eighteenth Century Revolution in Spain*, pp. 194–200.

52 Vilar, *Crecimiento y desarrollo*, p. 214; Pujal, *Historia de la economía española*.

53 Ignacio Jordán de Asso y del Río, *Historia de la economía política de Aragón* (Zaragoza, 1798), Prólogo y edición de José Manuel Casas Torres (Zaragoza: CSIC, Estación de Estudios Pirenaicos, 1947); Jaime Caresmar, *Discurso sobre la Agricultura, Comercio e Industria, con inclusión de la consistencia y estado en que se halle cada partido, o veguerío de los que componen el Principado de Cataluña* (1780), ms. 143,

Biblioteca Central de Barcelona, Archives of the Junta Particular de Comercio; Antonio Joseph Cavanilles, *Observaciones sobre la historia natural, geografía, agricultura, población y frutos del Reino de Valencia* (Madrid, 1795–97; Zaragoza: CSIC, Departamento de Geografía Aplicada del Instituto Sebastián Elcano, 1958), 2d ed. prepared by J. M. Casas Torres. See also *Relaciones geográficas, topográficas e históricas del Reino de Valencia hechas en el siglo XVIII a ruego de D. Tomás López*, ed. Vicente Castañeda y Alcover (Madrid: Revista de Archivos, Bibliotecas y Museos, 1919); Miguel Generes, *Reflexiones políticas y económicas sobre la población, agricultura, artes, fábricas y comercio del reino de Aragón* (Madrid, 1793); José Lucas Labrada, *Descripción económica del Reino de Galicia por la Junta de Gobierno del Consulado de La Coruña* (Ferrel, 1804); Eugenio Larruga, *Memorias políticas y económicas sobre les frutos, comercio, fábricas y minas de España, con inclusiones de los reales decretos, órdenes, cédulas, aranceles y ordenanzas expedidas para su gobierno y fomento* (Madrid: Imprenta B. Cano, 1787–1800).

54 Pedro Voltes Bou, *Barcelona durante el gobierno del Archiduque Carlos de Austria, 1705–1714* (Barcelona: CSIC, Instituto Municipal de Historia, 1963), vols. 1, 2, 11; Joan Mercader i Riba, *Felip V i Catalunya* (Barcelona: Edicions 62, 1968); Henry Kamen, *The War of Succession in Spain, 1700–1715* (London: Weidenfeld and Nicolson, 1969).

55 Jorge Nadal and Emilio Giralt, "Barcelona en 1717–1718. Un modelo de sociedad pre-industrial," in *Homenaje a Don Ramón Carande* (Madrid: Sociedad de Estudios y publicaciones, 1963), pp. 277–305. This includes data on the age and social composition of the population (with comparisons with 1516) and on income distribution.

56 Antonio Matilla Tascón, *La única contribución y el catastro de la Ensenada*, (Madrid: Servicio de Estudios de la Inspeccion General del Ministerio de Hacienda, 1947).

57 Tomás Maza Solano, *Nobleza, hidalguía, profesiones y oficios en la Montaña, según los padrones del Catastro del marqués de la Ensenada*, 5 vols. (Santander: Centro de Estudios Montañeses [cantabria], 1956–57).

58 Pierre Vilar, "Structures de la société espagnole vers 1750. Quelques leçons du Cadastre de la Ensenada," in *Mélanges à la mémoire de Jean Sarrailh* (Paris: Centre de Recherches de l'Institut d'Etudes Hispaniques, 1966), 2:425–47.

59 Fernando Jiménez de Gregorio, *Diccionario de los pueblos de la provincia de Toledo hasta finalizer el siglo XVIII. Población, sociedad, economía, e historia*, 2 vols. (Toledo: Biblioteca Toledo, 1962).

60 *Censo de la riqueza territorial e industrial de España en el año de 1799 formado de orden superior* (Madrid: Ministerio de Hacienda, Secretaría General Técnica, 1960), from the original 1803 edition of the Imprenta Real. The new edition has an introductory essay entitled "La economía española según el censo de frutos y manufacturas de 1799," by Juan Plaza Prieto, which compares the 1799 data with contemporary data. The title of the original 1803 edition was *Censo de frutos y manufacturas de España e islas adyacentes, ordenado sobre los datos dirigidos por los intendentes . . . baxo la dirección de su xefe D. Marcos Martin, por el oficial D. Juan Polo y Catalina*. See also José Fontana Lázaro, "El censo de frutos y manufacturas de 1799; un análisis crítico," *Moneda y Crédito* 101 (June 1967): 54–68.

61 José Canga Argüelles, *Diccionario de hacienda para el uso de los encargados de la suprema dirección de ella*, 5 vols. (London: Imp. Española de M. Calero, 1826). Volume 5 includes Argüelles's *Memoria sobre nivelar en tiempo de paz los ingresos y los gastos del erario español, escrita de orden superior en 1802*.

62 Vilar, *La Catalogne dans l'Espagne moderne*, vol. 3.

63 Pierre Vilar, *Le "Manual de la Companya Nova" de Gibraltar, 1709–1723* (Paris: SEVPEN, 1962). The first 107 pages are an analysis of the text and its significance, pp. 111–82 contain the text itself, and pp. 185–233 give a tabular reconstruction of the "Llibre Major" accounts.

64 Miguel Capella and Antonio Matilla Tascón, *Los Cinco Gremios Mayores de Madrid* (Madrid: Cámara de Comercio, 1957).

65 James Clayburn La Force, Jr., *The Development of the Spanish Textile Industry*,

1750–1800 (Berkeley: University of California Press, 1965). See also David R. Ringrose, *Transportation and Economic Stagnation in Spain, 1750–1850* (Durham, N.C.: Duke University Press, 1970).

66 Gonzalo Anes Alvarez, *Las crisis agrarias.* See also, on the grain trade and storage, idem, "Los Pósitos en la España del siglo XVIII," *Moneda y Crédito* 105 (June 1968): 39–69; idem, "Las fluctuaciones de los precios del trigo, de la cebada y del aceite en España, 1788–1808: un contraste regional," *Moneda y Crédito* 97 (June 1966): 96–102, plus graphs; Pierre Ponset, "En Andalousie occidentale. Les fluctuations de la production du blé sous l'Ancien Régime," *Etudes rurales* 34 (1969): 97–112.

67 Alain Huetz de Lemps, *Vignobles et vins du nord-ouest de l'Espagne,* 2 vols. (Bordeaux: Les Impressions Bellenef, 1967); Yvette Barbaza, *Le paysage humaine de la Costa Brava* (Paris: Colin, 1966).

68 María Dolores Mateos, *La España del Antiguo Régimen. Salamanca,* in the collection Estudios Históricos, fasc. O, directed by Miguel Artola, Acta Salmanticensia, Filsofía y Letras, 52 (Salamanca: Universidad de Salamanca, 1966), with numerous maps; María Pilar Calonge Matellanes, Eugenio García Zarza, and María Elena Rodríguez Sánchez, *La España del Antiguo Régimen. Castilla la Vieja,* in the collection Estudios Históricos, fasc. 3, ed. by Miguel Artola, Acta Salmanticensia, Filosofía y Letras, 55 (Salamanca: Universidad de Salamanca, 1967).

69 Salvador de Moxó, *La disolución del régimen señorial en España* (Madrid: CSIC, Escuela de Historia Moderna, 1965). See also Rafael García Ormaechea, *Supervivencias feudales en España. Estudios de legislacion y jurisprudencia sobre señorios,* Biblioteca de la "Revista de Legislación y Jurisprudencia," vol. 52 (Madrid, 1932).

70 Marqués del Saltillo (Miguel Lasso de la Vega), "La nobleza española en el siglo VXIII," *Revista de Archivos, Bibliotecas y Museos* 60 (1954): 417–49. See also idem, *Historia nobiliaria española (contribución a su estudio),* 2 vols. (Madrid, 1953); Manuel García Pelayo, "El estamento de la nobleza en el despotismo ilustrado," *Moneda y Crédito* 17 (1946): 37–59.

71 Miguel Artola, *Los orígenes de la España contemporánea* (Madrid: Instituto de Estudios Políticos, 1959).

72 Johann Hellwege, *Die spanischen Provinzialmilizen im 18 Jahrhundert* (Boppard a/R: Harold Boldt, 1969).

73 See the following works by Jaime Vicens Vives: *Historia social y económica de España y América,* written with the collaboration of 14 historians (Barcelona: Teide, 1957–59), vol. 4, *Burguesía, industrialización, obrerismo,* written in collaboration with Jorge Nadal, Rosa Ortega Canadell, Mario Hernández Sánchez-Barba; *Cataluña en el siglo XIX* (Madrid: Rialp, S.A., 1961); *Coyuntura económica y reformismo burgués y otros estudios de historia de España,* ed. José Fontana Lázaro (Barcelona: Ariel, 1969), including five of Vicens Vives's papers, some of them using quantitative series; Jaime Vicens Vives, *Obra dispersa,* vol. 1, *Catalunya ahir i avui,* vol. 2, *España, América, Europa* (Barcelona: Editorial Vicens-Vives, 1967)—a collection of articles, essays, book reviews. Last but not least, I want to stress Vicens Vives's contribution as editor of the *Estudios de Historia Moderna* (since 1951), which became a Spanish counterpart to *Annales,* and of the *Indice histórico español* (since 1953), a kind of historical abstract. The impact of Vicens Vives on Spanish history is reflected in the two-volume memorial work, with contributions by friends and disciples—Universidad de Barcelona, Facultad de Filosofía y Letras, *Homenaje a Jaime Vicens Vives* (Barcelona, 1965). This includes a detailed bibliography of his publications (pp. xix–xxxv).

74 Stanley G. Payne, "Jaime Vicens Vives and the writing of Spanish history," *The Journal of Modern History* 34 (1962): 119–34. This discusses Vicens, the man and his work, in the context of a Spain divided by the Civil War; it also gives bibliographic references for his many writings.

75 Raymond Carr, *Spain, 1808–1939* (Oxford: Oxford University Press, Clarendon Press, 1966).

76 For the concept of social mobilization, see Karl Deutsch, "Social Mobilization and Political Development," *American Political Science Review* 55 (1961): 493–514.

77 Reinhard Bendix, *Nation-Building and Citizenship. Studies of Our Changing Social Order* (New York: Wiley, 1964), see esp. chap. 3, "Transformations of Western Society since the Eighteenth Century," pp. 55–104, written in collaboration with Stein Rokkan; Stein Rokkan, "Electoral Mobilization, Party Competition, and National Integration," in *Political Parties and Political Development*, ed. Joseph LaPalombara and Myron Weiner (Princeton: Princeton University Press, 1966), pp. 241–65; Val R. Lorwin, "Working-Class Politics and Economic Development in Western Europe," *American Historical Review*, vol. 53, no. 2 (January 1958), pp. 338–51; idem, "Segmented Pluralism: Ideological Cleavages and Political Cohesion in the Smaller European Democracies," *Comparative Politics*, vol. 3, no. 2 (January 1971), pp. 141–75; Guenther Roth, *The Social Democrats in Imperial Germany* (Totowa, N.J.: Bedminster Press, 1963); Seymour M. Lipset and Stein Rokkan, "Cleavage Structures, Party Systems, and Voter Alignments: An Introduction," in *Party Systems and Voter Alignments: Cross-National Perspectives*, ed. Lipset and Rokkan (New York: Free Press, 1967), pp. 1–64; T. H. Marshall, *Class, Citizenship, and Social Development* (Garden City, N.Y.: Doubleday, 1964); E. Bull, *Arbeiderklassen i Norsk Historie* (Oslo: Tilden, 1948).

78 Stein Rokkan and Henry Valen, "Regional Contrasts in Norwegian Politics," in *Mass Politics. Studies in Political Sociology*, ed. E. Allardt and Stein Rokkan (New York: Free Press, 1970), pp. 190–247. See also Rokkan's collected essays in *Citizens, Elections, Parties: Approaches to the Comparative Study of the Processes of Development* (New York: McKay; Oslo: Universitetsforlaget, 1970).

79 Juan J. Linz and Amando de Miguel, "Within Nation Differences and Comparisons: The Eight Spains," *Comparing Nations, The Use of Quantitative Data in Cross-National Research*, ed. Richard L. Merritt and Stein Rokkan (New Haven: Yale University Press, 1966), pp. 267–319; Amando de Miguel and Juan Linz, "El papel de Barcelona en la estructura social española," Diputación Provincial de Barcelona, *Estudios sobre la Provincia, Dimensiones económica, informativa y sociológica* (Barcelona, 1966), pp. 243–54.

80 Karl Deutsch, *Nationalism and Social Communication*, 2d ed. (Cambridge, Mass.: MIT Press, 1965).

81 José Ortega y Gasset, *España invertebrada* (Madrid: Revista de Occidente, 1921).

82 Linz and de Miguel, "Within Nation Differences and Comparisons"; Juan J. Linz, "Ecological Analysis and Survey Research," in *Quantitative Ecological Analysis in the Social Sciences*, ed. Mattei Dogan and Stein Rokkan (Cambridge, Mass.: MIT Press, 1969), pp. 91–131.

83 Richard Herr, in "Good, Evil, and Spain's Rising against Napoleon," *Ideas in History*, 1965, pp. 157–81, has rightly stressed the importance of the crisis undergone by Spain and its monarchy at the time of the Napoleonic invasion and the elements of internal conflict in the struggle against the invader. Unfortunately the history of the Peninsular War has been written mostly as military history, without much attention to the demographic, economic, social, and other consequences. Recently research has started at a local level on some of these aspects.

84 Charles P. Kindleberger, *Economic Growth in France and Britain, 1851–1950* (Cambridge, Mass.: Harvard University Press, 1964).

85 Edward E. Malefakis, *Agrarian Reform and Peasant Revolution in Spain. Origins of the Civil War* (New Haven: Yale University Press, 1970). Juan Díaz del Moral, *Historia de las agitaciones campesinas andaluzas—Córdoba* (Madrid: Revista de Derecho Privado, 1929); a paperback edition was published by Alianza Editorial in Madrid in 1967, which, however, does not include the appendixes and therefore the invaluable quantitative data on the number of workers and farmers affiliated with the labor movement in the different villages.

86 Julio González, *Repartimiento de Sevilla. Estudio y Edición Preparada*, 2 vols. (Madrid: CSIC, 1951). This is one of the most important sources for the social and economic history of the Middle Ages, based on the manuscripts of the Repartimiento, a document with the assignation of land after the Christian conquest of the area.

87 Miguel Martínez Cuadrado, *Elecciones y partidos políticos de España, 1868–1931*, 2 vols. (Madrid: Taurus, 1969).

88 Stanley G. Payne, *Politics and the Military in Modern Spain* (Stanford, Calif.: Stanford University Press, 1967).

89 Under the sponsorship of the Escuela Nacional de Administración Pública (ENAP), a group of social scientists and civil servants at DATA, S. A. (a private social science research organization) has carried out a survey study of higher civil servants in Madrid. The first papers based on the study, presented at the Semana de Estudios Sociales at the Valle de los Caídos (1967), will soon be published. The director of ENAP, José de la Oliva, and his collaborators are working on the history of Spanish administration, making use of available quantitative data.

90 Miguel Beltrán Villalba's "Datos para el estudio de los funcionarios públicos en España," *Boletín del Centro de Estudios Sociales del Valle de los Caídos*, vol. 4, no. 3, pp. 5–31 (also published in Documentación Administrativa, vol. 83, November 1964), is a pioneer effort.

91 Juan J. Linz, "The Party System of Spain: Past and Future," in *Party Systems and Voter Alignments*, ed. Lipset and Rokkan, pp. 197–282, with an extensive bibliography on parties and elections. See also Richard Herr's interesting review of Raymond Carr's *Spain, 1808–1930*, in *English Historical Review* 82 (July 1967): 580–85, which tries to build a model of the factors involved in the "failure of liberal revolution in Spain."

92 Instituto Nacional de Estadística (dependence of the Presidencia del Gobierno), *Principales actividades de la vida española en la primera mitad del siglo XX. Síntesis estadística* (Madrid: INE, 1962), p. 194; Istituto Centrale di Statistica (Italy), *Sommario di Statistiche Storiche Italiane 1861–1955* (Rome: ISTAT, 1958), p. 233. For a review of Italian statistics for this period, see Istituto Centrale di Statistica, "Le Rilevazioni Statistiche in Italia dal 1861 al 1956," in *Annali di Statistica*, ser. 8 vols. 5 and 6, describing the organization and method of official statistics as well as of the censuses.

93 Francisco de A. Rodón, *Organización de la Estadística en España. Contribución al estudio de las publicaciones estadísticas de la Administración Central* (Barcelona: Estudio, 1919), also in the journal *Estudio*. This excellent review includes detailed, carefully edited footnotes listing government publications containing statistical information; not all these publications are mentioned here. For an earlier review of Spanish statistics, see D. Pazos García, *Reseña de la organización y trabajos de la estadística oficial en España* (Madrid: Imprenta del Asilo de Huérfanos del Sagrado Corazón de Jesús, 1898), which describes the organization of statistical services in different government dependencies and makes reference to their publications and collections of data. Anselmo Sanz Serrano's *Resumen histórico de la estadística en España* (Madrid: Instituto Nacional de Estadística, 1956) is a centennial volume of the official statistical department. It includes a reference to statistical efforts throughout Spanish history, from the *Relaciones Topográfico-estadísticas* of Philip II to the organization of statistical activities in the 19th and 20th centuries, quoting legal texts, questionnaires used, etc. Juan Antonio Lacomba, "Fuentes para la geografía de España. Las estadísticas de la Restauración," *Estudios Geográficos*, vol. 29, no. 90 (February 1963), pp. 39–55; the bibliography also gives information on the libraries of Madrid where the works can be found and includes most of the serial publications of different government agencies initiated in the 19th century.

94 Alexandre Moreau de Jonnès, *Statistique de l'Espagne. Territoire, population, agriculture, industrie, commerce, navigation, colonies, finances* (Paris: Imprimerie de Cosson, 1834); the Spanish translation is *Estadística de España, escrita en francés por Moreau de Jonnès*, trans. Pascual Madoz e Ibáñez (Barcelona, 1835).

95 Angel Marvaud, *L'Espagne au XX siècle. Étude politique et économique* (Paris: Colin, 1922).

96 The two most important officially published sources for quantitative data for the 19th and early 20th centuries, before the regular publication of the annual *Anuario Estadístico de España* (since 1912), are the *Reseña geográfica y estadística de España, 1888* (Madrid: Instituto Geográfico y Estadístico, 1888) and the *Reseña geográfica y estadística de España, 1912*, 2 vols. (Madrid: Instituto Geográfico y Estadístico, 1912). These contain data on territory, administrative divisions, population, migration,

strikes and social problems, the church, the military establishment, justice, and prisons. They also include many maps, graphs, and detailed time series. For a description of the population censuses, see Amando Melón, "Los censos de población en España, 1857–1940," *Estudios Geográficos* 43 (1951): 203–82. Melón summarizes the content and classifications used in each census and the corresponding nomenclature (list of population centers, both municipalities and smaller nuclei without administrative autonomy, with some basic information on them) and reproduces the occupational classifications used in 1860 (first to include such data) which unfortunately were simplified in the 1877 census. The 1887 census gives data by occupation and age; the census of 1900 adopts the classification proposed by the International Statistical Institute, with 91 categories. The data by province and provincial capitals are given for 33 occupational groups. In 1920 this report, concerned with a drop in the birth rate, was the first to give number of children live or deceased for married and widowed women by age. In the case of the professions, it distinguishes self-employed and employed among the farm population and in industry, a classification given up from 1930 until the 1950 census. Amando Melón y Ruiz de Gordejuela, *Los modernos nomenclatores de España, 1857–1950* (Madrid: Real Academia de la Historia, 1958), Discurso leído en la recepción pública el 19 de octubre de 1958 por el Excmo. Sr. D. Amando Melón y R. de Gordejuela.

97 The Portuguese *Annuario Estadistico de Portugal,* ed. Reparticao de Estadistica, Ministero das Obras Publicas, Commercio e Industria (Lisbon: Imprenta Nacional, 1886–), initiated its series with the year 1884. The initial volume contains a wealth of information and seems of high quality; this and the earlier starting point of the series gives Portugal an advantage over Spain.

98 The Italian *Annuario Statistico Italiano,* ed. Direzione Generale di Statistica, Ministero dell'Interno, starts its series with the year 1878. An indispensable source of quantitative data on southern Italy, in comparison with the northern and central regions, is the publication of the SVIMEZ (Associazione per lo Sviluppo dell'Industria nel Mezzogiorno), *Statistiche sul Mezzogiorno d'Italia, 1861–1953* (Roma, 1954). This publication brings together materials from a great number of sources—not only official statistics—on demography, economy, labor and social problems, finance of local governments, education, justice, and elections. The convenient summaries for northern, central, and southern Italy and the islands are of great value for the international comparisons of similarly developed or underdeveloped regions in different countries, which we have advocated in the study of social change (see Linz and de Miguel, "Within Nation Differences and Comparisons," p. 270).

99 Sebastián Miñano, *Diccionario Geográfico-Estadístico de España y Portugal,* 11 vols. (Madrid: Imprenta Pierrat-Peralta, 1826–29); Pascual Madoz, *Diccionario Geográfico-Estadistico-Histórico de España y sus posesiones de Ultramar* (Madrid, 1845), 16 vols.

100 Nicolás Sánchez-Albornoz, "La modernisation démographique de l'Espagne: Le cycle vital annuel, 1863–1900"; F. Vergneault, "Essai d'interprétation graphique des données," *Annales, Économies, Sociétés, Civilisations,* vols. 24, no. 6 (Nov.–Dec. 1969), pp. 1407–22.

101 Massimo Livi Bacci, "Fertility and Nuptiality. Changes in Spain from the late 18th to the early 20th Century," *Population Studies,* vol. 22, no. 1 (March 1968), pp. 83–102; no. 2 (July 1968), pp. 211–34, with detailed critical bibliography of statistical sources. J. William Leasure, "Factors involved in the Decline of Fertility in Spain, 1900–1950," *Population Studies* 16 (1962–63): 271–85.

102 Josep A. Vandellós i Solà, *La immigració a Catalunya* (Barcelona: Concursos Patxot i Ferrer, Estudis Historics, Politics i Socials, 1935); idem, *Catalunya, poble decadent* (Barcelona: Llibreria Catalana d'Autors Independents, 1935); Joaquim Maluquer i Sostres, *Població i societat a l'àrea catalana* (Barcelona: Edit. A. C., Col. Cara i Creu, 1965), foreword by Jordi Nadal i Oller and references to many journal articles.

103 Ministerio de Trabajo y Previsión. Dirección General de Acción Social y Emigración, *Despoblación y Repoblación de España, 1482–1920* (Madrid, 1929); Jesús García Fernández, *La emigración exterior de España* (Barcelona: Ariel, 1965). See also Antonio L. Fernández Flórez, "Argelia y los españoles," *Boletín de Emigración,* vol. 1, nos. 2–3, (1929–30); vol. 2, nos. 1–2 (1930–31), Instituto de Reformas Sociales,

Información sobre emigración española a los países de Europa durante la guerra (Madrid: IRS Publicaciones, no. 44, 1919); Mariano González-Rothvoss y Gil, *Los problemas actuales de la emigración española* (Madrid: Instituto de Estudios Políticos, 1949); idem, "La emigración española a Iberoamérica," *Revista Internacional de Sociología*, 1944, pp. 97–116, 179–211; Alfonso García Barbancho, *Las migraciones interiores de España. Estudio cuantitativo desde 1900* (Madrid: Instituto de Desarrollo Económico, 1967).

104 Heinz Göhring, "Konstanz und Wandel: Uneheliche Geburten in Spanien, 1860–1962," *Entwicklung und Fortschritt. Soziologische und Ethnologische Aspekte des sozialen und kulturellen Wandels. W. E. Mühlmann zum 65. Geburtstag* (Tübingen, 1969).

105 Jesús M. de Miguel, "El suicidio en España," *Revista Española de la Opinión Pública* 18 (Oct.–Dec. 1969): 3–41.

106 Fernando Garrido, *La España contemporánea, sus progresos morales y materiales en el siglo XIX*, 2 vols. (Barcelona: Salvador Manero, 1865), first published in French and revised for the Spanish edition.

107 Guillermo Graell, *La cuestión catalana* (Barcelona: A. López Robert, 1902).

108 Miguel Beltrán Villalba, "Andalucía: el presupuesto y la redistribución de la renta," *Anales de Sociología* 4–5 (1968–69): 17–31.

109 On budgets, see José Canga Argüelles, *Memoria presentada a las Cortes sobre las rentas y gastos de la Corona* (Cadiz: Imprenta Real, 1811), and other writings by the same author. The annual *Guía o Estado de la Real Hacienda de España*, published in the early part of the 19th century, I was unable to consult. The detailed publications of the budget for the period 1821–60 (in the library of the Ministry of Finance in Madrid) are *Presupuesto de los gastos de todos los ministerios, 1821* (Madrid: Imprenta Nacional, 1820); *Presupuestos generales para 1837, redactados por la Comisión especial nombrada en el Real Decreto de 2 de septiembre de 1836* (n.p., n.d.); *Presupuesto General para el año de 1840, memorias y proyectos de Ley con que lo presenta a las Cortes el Ministerio de Hacienda en cumplimiento del Artículo 72 de la Constitución* (Madrid: Imprenta Nacional, 1840). The budgets for 1842 and 1844 are available only in manuscript form. Ministerio de Hacienda, *Presupuesto General de los gastos del Estado para el presente año de 1845. Presupuesto General de ingresos del Estado para el corriente año de 1845* (n.p., n.d.); *Proyecto de Ley del Presupuesto de gastos e ingresos para el año de 1849* (n.p., n.d.); *Presupuestos Generales de gastos e ingresos para el año de 1850* (Madrid: Imprenta de la Viuda de Burgos, 1850); *Presupuestos para 1851* (n.p., n.d.); *Presupuestos Generales de gastos e ingresos para el año de 1852* (Madrid: Imprenta de J. M. Ducazcal, 1852); *Presupuestos Generales de gastos e ingresos para el año de 1853* (Madrid: Imprenta Nacional, 1853); *Presupuestos Generales del Estado para el año de 1854* (Madrid: Imprenta y Estereotipia de D. J. M. Alonso, 1854); *Presupuestos Generales del Estado para el año de 1855* (Madrid: Imprenta del Semanario Pintoresco y de la Ilustración, 1855); *Presupuestos Generales del estado para el año de 1856 y los seis primeros meses de 1857* (Madrid: Imprenta Nacional, 1856); *Presupuestos Generales del Estado para el año de 1857* (Madrid: Imprenta de Luis García, 1857). Budgets for the years 1858, 1859, and 1860 were published every year under the title *Presupuestos Generales del Estado para el año de . . .* by the Imprenta Nacional; under the Restoration Monarchy and the Republic, this title was *Presupuestos Generales del Estado para el Ejercicio Económico*. That for 1930, for example, has 1,063 pages.

110 See, e.g., the findings of Edward Malefakis, *Agrarian Reform and Peasant Revolution*, p. 346, about the amount of land distributed under the agrarian reform enacted by the Republic under the Left governments and those of the Right after the election of 1933. Stanley G. Payne, in *Politics and the Military in Modern Spain* (Stanford: Stanford University Press, 1967), p. 307, discusses the military budgets of the last Azaña government and those for 1934 and 1935 of the "bienio negro.'

111 *Información Estadística del Ministerio de Hacienda*, published in recent years by the Secretaría General Técnica, contains the actual results of the budget, the distribution of income from different taxes and expenditures by province and month, and a host of other economic indicators.

112   Intervención General de la Administración del Estado, *Estadística de los Presupuestos Generales del Estado y de los resultados que ha ofrecido su liquidación. Años 1850–1890.* In addition to statistical material, this contains well-written introductions and a long section on the national debt. Another volume from the same source with the same title (Madrid, 1909) covers the years 1890/91–1907.

113   Gabriel Solé Villalonga, *La reforma fiscal de Villaverde, 1899–1900* (Madrid: Editorial de Derecho Financiero, 1967); Juan Sardá, *La política monetaria y las fluctuaciones de la economía española en el siglo XIX* (Madrid: CSIC Instituto Sancho de Moncada de Economía, 1948). José María Tallada's *Historia de las finanzas españolas del siglo XIX* (Madrid: Espasa Calpe, 1946) is mainly an analysis of the fiscal reforms of Mon and Villaverde.

114   For a detailed history of the *Guía Oficial de España* and the *Guía de Forasteros* which preceded it, see the *Guía Oficial de España, 1935* (Madrid: Sucesores de Rivadeneyra, 1935) the only one for the Second Republic and the last one, to my knowledge, to be published— The section by Juan Pérez de Guzmán y Gallo of the Royal Academy of History (pp. 753–89) gives the changing names of the publication and a detailed reference of the libraries which have more or less complete collections. The Italian equivalent, also officially published by the Ministero del Interno, is the *Calendario Generale,* whose publication was initiated in 1862; this also includes an alphabetical index of last names, the rank lists of the Army and Navy (which in Spain are given in the same detail in the *Anuario Militar*), and the names of legislators with their occupations and legislatures to which they have been elected previously. And for each ministry it gives the names and dates in which different persons have held offices.

115   *Heráldica. Guía de Sociedad* (Madrid: Ediciones M. More, various years); I have seen those for 1951 to 1958. A publication which preceded this and is useful for the first years after the Civil War (1940–) is the *Guía del Gran Mundo*. However, the quality and reliability of these publications are very low. For the early years of the Franco regime, a publication by Clyde L. Clark, *The Evolution of the Franco Regime,* 3 vols. (n.p., n.d.), apparently sponsored but not published officially by the Department of State, is very useful for locating office holders. It also includes statistical data and all the basic legal texts in English. The *Who's Who in Spain,* ed. S. Olives Canals and Stephen S. Taylor (Barcelona: Intercontinental Book and Publishing Co., Ltd., and Editorial Herder, 1963)—a biographical dictionary containing about 6,000 biographies of prominent people in and of Spain and 1,400 organizations—is very incomplete, and its selection is far from adequate. For a sociological analysis of those listed, see Salustiano del Campo Urbano, "Análisis sociológico de un grupo de la elite española," *La promoción social en España* (Madrid: Anales de Moral Social y Económica, Centro de Estudios Sociales de la Santa Cruz del Valle de los Caídos, 1966), pp. 111–28. The FAC—*Fichero de Altos Cargos,* ed. Angel Estirado Pérez (Madrid: FAC, Blasco de Garay, 69)—is a permanently renewed card file of office holders, divided in two sections for political and administrative offices. Published at least since the end of the Civil War, it is indispensable for any study of elite circulation.

116   The *Anuario Militar de España* was published yearly by the Estado Mayor Central del Ejército, Ministerio de la Guerra, under the monarchy, apparently since 1780. The last volume—and the only one published under the Republic—came out in 1935. Since the Civil War, equivalent sources are the *Escalillas* by branches of the army (infantry, artillery, etc.), published by the Dirección General de Reclutamiento y Personal of the Ministerio del Ejército, and their equivalents published by the Navy and the Air Force ministries.

117   In 1782 a *Kalendario Manual y Guía del Estado Eclesiástico de España* was authorized; it began publication in 1788 and was published until 1868, with the exceptions of 1809–13, 1836–47, 1851–52, 1855–57, 1859–61, and 1863–67.

118   Nobles legally entitled to use certain titles and styles (after some legal procedures and the payment of taxes) are listed in *Grandezas y Títulos del Reino, Guía Oficial* (Madrid: Ministerio de Justicia, 1959–60 and succeeding years); this comes after the semiofficial *Guía Oficial Nobiliaria* (1956, 1958), which has an alphabetical list of names, the titles and names of their holders, their addresses, and the date of conces-

sion of the title. It includes 2,366 titles held by 1,796 persons. This list and those in the *Guía Oficial* under the monarchy allow an easy check of the presence of the nobility in any elite as well as a study of the places of residency of the aristocracy.

119   The *escalafones* are rank lists for all occupations, mostly for civil servants, recruited by competitive examinations ("oposiciones"). They are official or semiofficial publications published at regular intervals. Engineers trained at the various *Escuelas Especiales* (comparable in some respects to the *grands écoles* in France) had a right to enter the service of the state with the seniority of their date of entry and their class rank, even when many of them opted to leave it for private practice. The *escalafones* include those not in public service as "excedentes," something which allows a good description of whole groups of professionals of high prestige. In recent years, the Instituto de Ingenieros Civiles has published a list of all Spanish engineers in its *Anuario,* though with less detailed information than the old *escalafones.* See, e.g., Ilustre Colegio de Abogados de Madrid, *Guía Oficial. Listas de los Colegios de Abogados, Notarios, Procuradores y Secretarios Judiciales de Madrid y Guía Judicial para 1950,* which also lists 268 members of the legal profession who died on the nationalist side in the Civil War. In a study of legislative elites from 1907 to 1914, I was able to use one for the year 1912.

120   Sources for the collective biography of parliamentary and cabinet elites are *Lista de los señores diputados de las Cortes generales y extraordinarias de la nación española* (Cádiz, 1811); Raúl Morodo and Elías Díaz, "Tendencias y grupos políticos en las Cortes de Cádiz y en las de 1820," *Cuadernos Hispanoamericanos* (Madrid) 201 (1966), which relates the background with roll-call votes; DAFG, *Verdaderas y genuinas semblanzas de los Padres de la Patria para la legislatura de 1820 y 21* (Madrid, 1821); *Condiciones y semblanzas de los diputados a Cortes para la legislatura de 1820 y 1821* (Madrid, 1821); *Impugnación joco-seria al folleto titulado "Condiciones y semblanzas de los diputados a Cortes para la legislatura de 1820 y 1821"* (Madrid, 1821); Fermín Caballero, *Fisonomía natural y política de los procuradores en las Cortes de 1834, 1835, y 1836, por un asistente diario a las tribunas* (Madrid, 1836). An essential source for the study of cabinets and legislatures that would allow a quantitative description of the "political class" from 1834 to 1907 and facilitate the study of its relations to other elites is *Estadística del personal y vicisitudes de las Cortes y de los ministerios de España desde 29 de septiembre de 1833 en que falleció el rey D. Fernando VII hasta el 24 de diciembre de 1879 en que se suspendieron las sesiones* (Madrid: Imprenta y fundición de la viuda e hijos de J. A. García, 1880). *Estadística del personal y vicisitudes de las Cortes y de los ministerios de España. Apéndice primero que comprende desde el 24 de diciembre de 1879 hasta el 29 de diciembre de 1890* (Madrid: Imprenta de los hijos de J. A. García, 1892); *Estadística del personal . . . Apéndice segundo que comprende desde el 29 de diciembre de 1890 hasta el 30 de marzo de 1907* (Madrid: Imprenta de los hijos de J. A. García, 1907); *Historia de las Cortes, de las Armas, de la Letras, y Artes Españolas, o sea, biografías de los senadores, diputados, militares, literatos y artistas contemporáneos,* ed. Manuel Ovilo y Otero (Madrid, Imprenta Baltasar González, 1848); Juan Rico y Amat, *El libro de los diputados y senadores* (Madrid, 1862); Angel Fernández de los Ríos, ed., *La Asamblea Constituyente de 1869: biografías de todos los representantes de la nación* (Madrid, 1869); *Los ministros de España desde 1800 a 1869. Historia contemporánea por uno que siendo español no cobra del presupuesto* (Madrid, 1870); Ciriaco Miguel Vigil, *Cuadro comprensivo de señores senadores y diputados a Cortes, diputados provinciales, Comisión permanente de la Diputación, consejeros provinciales y jefes superiores civiles de la provincia* (Oviedo, 1885); *Los diputados pintados por sus hechos. Colección de estudios biográficos sobre los elegidos por el sufragio universal en las Constituyentes de 1869,* 3 vols. (Madrid, 1869–70); Modesto Sánchez Ortiz and Fermín Berástegui, *Las primeras cámaras de la Regencia* (Madrid: Imprenta de Enrique Rubiños, 1887); Modesto Sánchez de los Santos, *Las Cortes Españolas, las de 1907* (Madrid: A. Marzo, 1908); idem, in collaboration with Simón de la Redondela, *Las Cortes Españolas, las de 1910* (Madrid: A. Marzo, 1910); idem, *Las Cortes Españolas, las de 1914* (Madrid: A. Marzo, 1914). These last three volumes also contain electoral maps and statistics

invaluable for any research on this period. Another source of data on legislators, quoted by V. G. Kiernan in his *The Revolution of 1854 in Spanish History* (Oxford: Oxford University Press, Clarendon Press, 1966), p. 107, is B. Moratilla, ed., *Estadistica del personal y vicisitudes de la Cortes y de los Ministerios de España* (Madrid, 1858). The data Kiernan quotes show the great discontinuities in parliamentary personnel in that period—a pattern we find again in the transition from the Restoration to Primo de Rivera and the Republic in the 20th century, since of 380 men entering the Constituent Assembly of 1854, only 31 had sat in the last Cortes; only 27 would be elected to the Moderado-dominated chamber in 1857; no more than 36 were successful candidates at any one of the four general elections of 1850, 1851, 1853, 1857; and only four were successful in all four elections. Systematic comparisons between countries of the continuity or discontinuity of parliamentary personnel in the period of institutionalization of constitutional and democratic government or after changes of regime would certainly help in understanding the nature of the political process and the development of a consensus (or lack of it) on the rules of the game, as well as the competence of legislatures to deal with specific problems.

121 For biographical data on the members of the Asamblea Nacional created by the dictatorship of Primo de Rivera and composed of representatives of the state, culture, production, labor, commerce, and other activities, the provincial "diputaciones," the municipalities, as well as the Unión Patriótica (the improvised single party), see *La Asamblea Nacional, Biografías y retratos de los 400 asambleístas y numerosos datos del mayor interés*, 2 vols. (Madrid: Publicaciones Patrióticas, 1927). For the Republican Cortes, the *Lista de los Señores Diputados*, officially published by the legislature, is an indispensable source, even where it gives little information. The list for the constituent assembly of 1931 (published Dec. 1932) gives only names, addresses, districts represented, and committee memberships, but not party affiliations —which is understandable, given the number of party labels. The list published in June 1936, however, does give party affiliations. Two publications—one published in exile by José Venegas, *Las elecciones del Frente Popular* (Buenos Aires: Cuadernos de Cultura Española, Patronato Hispano-Argentino de Cultura, 1942), and another by a pro-Franco author, José Gutiérrez Rave, *Las Cortes del Frente Popular* (Madrid: Editora Nacional, 1953)—give more or less accurate information on the fate, mostly tragic, of these parliamentarians in and after the Civil War. The *Boletín de información bibliográfica y parlamentaria de España y del extranjero*, vol. 1, no. 6 (Nov.–Dec. 1933), pp. 930–36, 1054–71; vol. 4, no. 2 (March–April 1936), pp. 440–63; and passim throughout the entire series gives some basic information on deputies. For biographies of the Left Catalan leadership early this century, see Emilio Navarro, *Historia crítica de los hombres del republicanismo catalán en la última década, 1905–14. Resúmenes históricos por Emiliano Iglesias y Juan Andrés Barjol* (Barcelona, 1915). For Catalan elites, two biographical dictionaries are in the process of publication: Carles Soldevila, *Figures de Catalunya* (Barcelona: Aedos, 1955–62); and *Diccionari Biogràfic* (Barcelona: Alberti Editor, n.d.).

122 Equipo DATA, "Quién es quién en las Cortes," *Cuadernos para el Diálogo*, Madrid, Suplementos, 7, 1969. For cabinets, see Equipo Mundo, *Los 90 ministros de Franco* (Barcelona: Dopesa, 1970). I am preparing a study of parliamentary and cabinet elites from the Restoration (1874) to the present, based on IBM cards including the information from the above-mentioned and other sources. For a comparison of the turnover and social background of the cabinets of Portugal, 1900–32, see the articles by A. H. Oliveira Marques, "Estudos sobre Portugal no seculo XX," *O Tempo e o Modo* 47–48, 54–55 (1967); 62–63 (1968); 71–72 (1969).

123 Unfortunately, the historian or sociologist working with Spanish election data finds no equivalent to two important Italian publications on the period from the Risorgimento to Fascism, one official and the other by a private scholar. The *Compendio dell Statistiche Elettorali Italiane dal 1848 al 1934*, vol. 1, *Elettori Politici e Circoscrizioni Elettorali* (Rome: Istituto Centrale di Statistica e Ministero per la Costituente, 1946), has an excellent description of the electoral systems, the number of eligible voters and actual voters, the bases of their eligibility, etc., largely by province and larger cities; this is essential for any study of the "thresholds" of entry

into politics. The volume by Ugo Giusti, *Le correnti politische italiane attraverso due riformi elettorali dal 1909 al 1921* (Florence: Unione statistica delle città italiane, Monografie e Studi, 3, 1923), is very valuable, since it gives the votes by party for the general elections of 1919 and 1921, the 1920 administrative elections for electoral districts and municipalities, and some information on votes by party in 1909 and 1913. The *Compendio* lists on the inside cover 28 publications on elections by the statistical offices from 1867 to 1946.

Working on Spain, we have to turn to the recent work of scholars and isolated detailed contemporary publications. See, on the first direct elections in July and August 1836, Joaquín Tomás Villarroya, "Las primeras elecciones directas en España," *Anales de la Universidad de Valencia* 28 (curso 1964–65), cuaderno II, Derecho, pp. 7–56; idem, "El cuerpo electoral en la ley de 1837," *Revista del Instituto de Ciencias Sociales de la Diputación Provincial de Barcelona*, 1965, pp. 157–205; idem, *El sistema político del Estatuto Real, 1834–1836* (Madrid: Instituto de Estudios Políticos, 1968). See also the pamphlet by the contemporary scholar and politician Fermín Caballero, "Resultado de las últimas elecciones para diputados y senadores" (1837). The work of this early statistician–geographer–electoral sociologist has been studied by Carlos Marichal in his "The Politics of Fermín Caballero" (Harvard College, honors thesis, 1970).

Recent works on nineteenth century history—such as V. G. Kiernan, *The Revolution of 1854 in Spanish History* (Oxford: Oxford University Press, Clarendon Press, 1966); and C. A. M. Hennessy, *The Federal Republic in Spain, Pi y Margall and the Federal Republican Movement 1868–1874* (Oxford: Oxford University Press, Clarendon Press, 1962)—make only passing reference to the elections. Kiernan refers to the restricted censitary suffrage that gave the vote to 695,110 (5% of the population) in the 1854 election, a figure which represented a fivefold increase over 1851 (p. 95); but he otherwise limits himself to giving the number of seats to be filled with a comment that "the total number of candidates prodigiously exceeded that of seats," and he only refers to the fact that single-member constituencies had been abandoned for a single list of candidates for each province (p. 101). Kiernan concludes by giving us the total participation, the vote in Madrid and Málaga, and the names of some important figures elected in provincial districts (pp. 104–05). These data are obviously insufficient. The size of the electorate looks less narrow when compared to other countries: for example, in the kingdom of Sardinia the year before, only 2.1% of the population was entitled to vote, and in the unified kingdom of Italy in 1861 the figure was 1.9%, compared with 4.8% in Spain in 1854. Under the July Monarchy in France, the proportion of eligible voters was even lower—0.68% in 1844.

Hennessy devotes much more attention to the elections, including municipal voting, and tries to account for some of the patterns observed, but much of his information is unsystematically given in footnotes. The article by Miguel M. Cuadrado, "La elección general para las Cortes Constituyentes de 1869," *Revista de Estudios Políticos* 132 (Nov.–Dec. 1963): 65–102, is more detailed for the same period.

There are no local studies of parties, elections, and elites, although some are being prepared for Catalonia. Although not meant as a scholarly study, Javier de Ybarra y Berge's *Política nacional en Vizcaya* (Madrid: Instituto de Estudios Políticos, 1948) contains a wealth of information on national, provincial, and municipal elections in this industrial province. The data are not systematic or complete, but they do allow considerable analysis. Preliminary analysis suggests that the shift from the Liberal Party to the Conservatives was not unrelated to their economic policies, an additional indication that two-party politics was not as undifferentiated as the Regenerationist critics of the Restoration "system" would have us believe.

124 Joaquín Costa, *Oligarquía y caciquismo como la forma actual de gobierno en España. Urgencia y modo de cambiarla. Información en el Ateneo Científico y Literario de Madrid sobre dicho tema*, publícalo la Sección de Ciencias Históricas del Ateneo (Madrid: Imprenta de los Hijos de M. G. Hernández, 1902); Robert W. Kern, *Caciquismo vs. Self-Government: The Crisis of Liberalism and Local Government in Spain, 1858–1910* (University of Chicago, Ph.D. diss., 1966). See also Esteban Mestre,

"Los delitos electorales en España. Reflexiones en torno al tratamiento sociológico del sistema electoral," *Revista Española de la Opinión Pública* 20 (April–June 1970): 125–71, which offers a useful summary of electoral legislation since 1837 and particularly of the sanctions against electoral fraud.

125 A first analysis of this information, *Parties, Elections, and Elites under the Restoration Monarchy in Spain, 1875–1923*, was presented by this author at the Seventh World Congress of the International Political Science Association, Brussels, 1967. See also Javier Tusell Gómez, "Para la sociología política de la España contemporánea: el impacto de la Ley de 1907 en el comportamiento electoral," *Hispania, Revista Española de Historia* 30 (1970): 571–632.

126 See n. 120 above.

127 Fernando Soldevilla, *El año político . . .* , 1901–27 (annually).

128 Miguel Martínez Cuadrado, *Elecciones y partidos políticos de España, 1868–1931* (Madrid: Taurus, 1969).

129 Javier Tusell Gómez, *Sociología electoral de Madrid* (Madrid: Ed. Cuadernos para el Diálogo [Edicusa], 1969).

130 Idem, *La segunda República en Madrid, Elecciones y partidos políticos* (Madrid: Tecnos, 1970).

131 Javier Tusell Gómez, *Las elecciones del Frente Popular en España*, 2 vols. (Madrid: Edicusa, 1971); Jean Bécarud, *La deuxième République espagnole, 1931–1936. Essai d'interprétation* (Paris: Fondation Nationale des Sciences Politiques, serie C, Recherches 7, October 1962); Spanish edition, *La segunda República Española* (Madrid: Taurus, 1967); José Venegas, *Las elecciones del Frente Popular*. Estado Español, Ministerio de la Gobernación, *Dictamen de la Comisión sobre la ilegitimidad de los poderes actuantes el 18 de julio de 1936*, 2 vols. (Madrid: Editora Nacional, 1939), vol. 1, Dictamen, vol. 2, Apéndice al Dictamen; vol. 2 contains most of the controversial election data. It should be noted, however, that often the differences between pro- and anti-Franco sources are not great in terms of absolute numbers or percentages of votes, even when those differences were of great importance for electoral outcomes, because the electoral law gave the winning coalition a great advantage in the number of seats. In any event, such differences between the sources are not too disturbing for sociological purposes.

132 Richard A. H. Robinson, *The Origins of Franco's Spain. The Right, the Republic, and Revolution, 1931–1936* (Newton Abbot: David & Charles, 1970), see pp. 415–24.

133 The basic bibliographic reference work is Renée Lamberet's *Mouvements ouvriers et socialistes, chronologie et bibliographie. L'Espagne, 1750–1936* (Paris: Editions Ouvrières, 1953). For a chronology, see Emili Giralt, Albert Balcells, and Josep Termes, *Els moviments socials a Catalunya, país valencià i les illes. Cronologia, 1800–1939* (Barcelona: Lavínia, 1967).

134 Max Nettlau, *La première internationale en Espagne, 1868–1888*, ed. Renée Lamberet, 2 vols. (Dordrecht: D. Reidel, 1969).

135 Asociación Internacional de los Trabajadores, *Actas de los Consejos y Comisión Federal de la Región Española, 1870–1874*, Transcripción y estudio preliminar por Carlos Seco Serrano, Colección de Documentos para el estudio de los movimientos obreros en España en la época contemporánea, Publicaciones de la Cátedra de Historia General de España, Facultad de Filosofía y Letras, Universidad de Barcelona, 1969, vol. 1.

136 See, for example, Partido Socialista Obrero Español, *Convocatoria y Orden del Día para el XII Congreso Ordinario del Partido y memorias reglamentarias de la Comisión Ejecutiva, subdirección y administración de "El Socialista," de la minoría parlamentaria y de la gráfica socialista, con un breve resumen de la actividad obrera en sus diversos aspectos desde abril 1921 a diciembre de 1927* (Madrid: Gráfica Socialista, 1927).

Few data can be more revealing about the Socialist Labor movement in Spain—in comparison with those of other European countries—than those given by an opponent (probably a Communist), Juan de Andrade, in his *La burocracia reformista en el movimiento obrero* (Madrid: Gleba, 1935), which discusses the paid personnel and the budgets of the PSOE and the UGT. Andrade's information is taken from the *Memoria del XII Congreso Ordinario del Partido Socialista*, the *Memoria y Orden del Día del XII Congreso de la Unión General de Trabajadores* (1932), and the *Memoria de la Junta Administrativa de la Casa del Pueblo* (de Madrid) for 1934. To give one example, this organization, the pride of the Madrid working class and headquarters of one of the most powerful labor organizations in the country in 1934, had only 19 paid white collar and service employees (including cleaning women). The Mutualidad Obrera, according to the *Memoria de la Federación de Cooperativas de España, IV Congreso, 1934*, had 162 employees (Cooperativa Socialista Madrileña, 36), the Madrid Federación Local de Obreros de la Edificación (construction workers' federation) had 7 employees, etc. This source is important because it reveals the wealth of quantitative information on finances of trade unions in different official union publications. Andrade's conclusion, that there was one paid person for every 1,000 members, can be compared with data on other socialist labor movements.

137 Notably, José Peirats, *La CNT en la revolución española*, 3 vols. (Toulouse: Ediciones CNT, 1953).

138 Stanley G. Payne, *The Spanish Revolution* (New York: Norton, 1970); see bibliography for additional references, some of which contain scattered quantitative information. On the Communists, see Eduardo Comín Colomer, *Historia del partido comunista de España* (Madrid: Editora Nacional, 1967); Guy Hermet, *Les communistes en Espagne. Étude d'un mouvement politique clandestin* (Paris: Colin, Fondation Nationale des Sciences Politiques, 1971). The data on the Catholic trade union movement can be found in the *Anuario Social de España, 1929*, and in the brief history by Juan N. García Nieto, *El sindicalismo cristiano en España* Bilbao: Instituto de Estudios Económico-Sociales, Universidad de Deusto, 1960), esp. pp. 22, 70–71, 74, 106, 119–22, 138, 156, 159.

139 David Ruiz González, *El movimiento obrero en Asturias: de la industrialización a la segunda República* (Oviedo: Amigos de Asturias, 1968).

140 For a listing of early reports, see Fernanda Romeu Alfaro, *Las clases trabajadoras en España, 1898–1930* (Madrid: Taurus, 1970), pp. 218–21. Some reports are now being reprinted in the *Revista de Trabajo*.

141 Jaime Vicens Vives, Jorge Nadal Oller, and Casimiro Martí, "Les mouvements ouvriers en Espagne en temps de dépression économique, 1929–39. Leurs conséquences d'ordre politique et social," in *Mouvements Ouvriers et Dépression Economique de 1929 à 1939*, ed. Denise Fauvel-Rouif, International Commission on the History of Social Movements and Social Structures, Publications on Social History, International Institute of Social History (Assen: Van Gorcum, 1966), pp. 103–23.

On strikes, see the study by Manuel Ramírez Jiménez, "Las huelgas durante la segunda República," *Anales de Sociología* (Barcelona) 1 (1966): 76–87. For a study of labor conflicts in recent years, related to the political orientation of different regions under the Republic, see José María Maravall, *El desarrollo económico y la clase obrera* (Barcelona: Ariel, 1970).

142 Malefakis, *Agrarian Reform and Peasant Revolution*.

143 Fernanda Romeu Alfaro, *Las clases trabajadoras en España, 1898–1930* (Madrid: Taurus, 1970). See also Juan Antonio Lacomba Avellán, *La crisis española de 1917* (Madrid: Ciencia Nueva, 1970). This descriptive study does not integrate the social and economic indicators, particularly on the condition of the working class, into the analysis, but presents them in an appendix (pp. 363–85). Manuel Tuñón de Lara, *Variaciones del nivel de vida en España* (Madrid: Península, 1965); Antonio Jutglar, "En torno a la condición obrera en Barcelona, entre 1900 y 1920," *Anales de Sociología* (Madrid), vol. 1, no. 1 (June 1966), pp. 88–107; Pierre Conard and Albert Lovett, "Problèmes de l'évaluation du coût de la vie en Espagne. I: Le prix du pain depuis le milieu du XIXᵉ siècle: Une source nouvelle," *Mélanges de la Casa de Velázquez* (Paris) 5 (1969): 411–41; Práxedes Zancada, *El obrero en España (notas para su historia política y social)*, foreword by Canalejas (Barcelona: Casa Editorial Maucci, 1902).

For early reports on the condition of the urban working classes, see Ildefonso Cerdá, *Teoría general de la urbanización y aplicación de sus principios y doctrinas a la reforma y ensanche de Barcelona* (Madrid: Imprenta Española, 1867), of which the appendix to volume 2 has been reprinted in *Anales de Sociología* (Madrid), vol. 1, no. 1 (June 1966), pp. 189–214; *Información oral y escrita sobre el estado y las necesidades de la clase obrera, 1884–1889, practicada en virtud de la Real Orden de 1° de diciembre de 1883*, 3 vols., Instituto de Reformas Sociales, reprinted in *Revista de Trabajo* 25 (1968): 159–493; José Ubeda y Correal, *El presupuesto de una familia obrera* (Madrid: Publicaciones de la Dirección General de Sanidad, 1902); Julio Puyol y Alonso, Eduardo Sanz Escartín, and Rafael Salillas, *Informe referente a las minas de Vizcaya*, Instituto de Reformas Sociales, vol. 5 (1904), reprinted in *Revista de Trabajo* 19 (1967): 179–301, 20 (1967): 169–297; Instituto de Reformas Sociales, *Informe de los Inspectores de Trabajo sobre la influencia de la guerra europea en las industrias españolas, 1917–1918* (Madrid: IRS, 1918), vol. 41, no. 3; Instituto de Estadística y Política Social, Ayuntamiento de Barcelona, *Monografía estadística de la clase obrera* (Barcelona, 1921).

144 Mariano González-Rothvoss y Gil, *Anuario español de política social, 1934–35* (Madrid: Rivadeneira, 1934); the bibliography (pp. 1745–63) lists a large number of publications on labor and social problems, including those of the Instituto de Reformas Sociales, statistical reports for the period 1904–23 (214 titles), and those of the Instituto Nacional de Previsión or Social Security Administration (423 titles).

145 Ministerio de Gracia y Justicia, *Estadística de la administración de Justicia en lo civil en la península e islas adyacentes*, 1880, 1887–98, 1900–03, and 1905 for the older civil series; idem, *Estadística de la administración de justicia en lo criminal en la península e islas adyacentes*, 1884–88, 1890–91, 1897, and 1904 for the older criminal series; Dirección de Penales, *Anuario penitenciario, administrativo y estadístico, año 1888* (Madrid, 1889); José María Farré Moregó, *Los atentados sociales en España: estudio sociológico, jurídico y estadístico de los cometidos desde 1° de enero de 1917 hasta 1° de enero de 1922, especialmente los cometidos en Barcelona desde 1° de enero de 1910 hasta 1° de enero de 1922*, preface by Dr. Quintiliano Saldaña (Madrid: Faure, 1922).

146 *Anuario Estadístico de España*, Año XIX (Madrid: Dirección General del Instituto Geográfico, Catastral y de Estadística, 1934), pp. 678–79.

147 Works like Fernand Boulard's *Introduction to Religious Sociology* (London: Darton, Longman and Todd, 1960) and Michael P. Fogarty's *Christian Democracy in Western Europe, 1820–1953* (Notre Dame, Ind.: University of Notre Dame Press, 1957) contain many of the relevant data and extensive bibliographies. An excellent example of quantitative research on past religious behavior using documentary and archival data is Christianne Marcilhacy's *Le Diocèse d'Orleans sous l'épiscopat de Mgr. Dupanloup, 1849–1878. Sociologie religieuse et mentalités collectives* (Paris: Plon, 1962).

148 For the quantitative study of the Spanish church in the first 30 years of the 20th century—particularly after the mobilization of the laity was initiated around 1910—the work edited by Juan Soler de Morell, S.J., *Anuario Social de España, 1929* (Madrid: Fomento Social, Estudios y Acción Social Católica, 1929), is an excellent source. I have been unable to consult the *Anuario Social de España, 1916*, published and edited by Acción Social Popular, and I am not certain if any similar publication appeared under the Republic. The 1929 edition contains a statistical and descriptive summary of the social welfare activities of the State and different public bodies; data on labor problems (social security, strikes, wages, labor inspection, etc.); and, in a second part, a wealth of statistics on the Church—secular and regular clergy—and the "sponsored organizations" (to use the term coined by Gianfranco Poggi in his study of Italian Catholic Action), from Catholic Action to various pious associations and such functional organizations as trade unions and the farmers' CONCA). It also gives circulation figures for many Catholic publications and, in addition to statistical data, gives a brief history of all these organizations, summarizes their bylaws, and lists their officers. Few sources can give us a better sense of the belated but sudden start of Catholic mobilization; its growing impetus; its initial localization in the northern periphery, some areas on the Mediterranean, and Old Castile; its mixture of traditionalism and modernity; and its disproportionate involvement of women as compared to men. The resurgent anti-

clericalism and its style in the thirties, the ties between clericalism and Basque nationalism, etc. can be much better understood in the light of these data.

149 One study using such archival data for recent centuries is Carmelo Lisón Tolosana's *Belmonte de los Caballeros. A Sociological Study of a Spanish Town* (Oxford: Oxford University Press, Clarendon Press, 1966).

150 The continuities and discontinuities in religiosity of different dioceses as "indicated" by the number of priests per population and the number of vocations are revealing in this respect. Unfortunately, except for some late electoral data, we do not have quantitative studies of the Carlist appeal. On the number of priests in 1769, 1859, 1947, and 1957, see Rogelio Duocastella, Jesús A. Marcos-Alonso, J. M. Díaz Mozaz, and P. Almerich, *Análisis sociológico del catolicismo español* (Barcelona: Nova Terra and Instituto de Sociología y Pastoral Aplicadas, 1967), p. 28. Fernando Garrido's *La España contemporánea,* perhaps because of the anticlericalism of the author, is particularly rich in information on the Church, especially on the number of convents, parishes, friars, nuns, priests, and state expenditures for the Church, many of them by province. For official data at the turn of the century, see Instituto Geográfico y Estadístico, *Comunidades religiosas existentes en España en 31 de diciembre de 1900* (Madrid, 1902). For more recent periods, the historian will find much relevant statistical information on the Church, its activities, and its organizations, as well as on the clerical and lay elites staffing them, social origins of the seminarians, contributions to collections, educational activities, etc. in the publication of the Oficina General de Información y Estadística de la Iglesia en España, *Guía de la Iglesia en España,* first published in 1954, with appendixes for 1955, 1956, 1957, 1958, and new volumes for succeeding years. This also contains considerable information on religious practice. One of the most helpful items is the information ordered by dioceses for each parish with the dates for which the oldest baptismal, confirmation, marriage, and death registration is available and the date from which the books are complete to the present, as well as archival losses due to the Civil War. However, Bartolomé Bennassar, in *Recherches sur les grandes épidémies dans le nord de l'Espagne à la fin du XVIe siècle,* pp. 16–17, cautions us against expecting completeness of the sources reported there as extant. The *Guía* also gives information on the existence of local civil cemeteries for the burial of non-Catholics (see the 1960 volume, pp. 419–701, 885–927; and pp. 36–143 of the 1955 *Suplemento*). I have been unable to consult the *Anuario Subirana,* published between 1917 and 1936, apparently a directory without statistical data.

151 Madoz, *Diccionario Geográfico-Estadístico-Histórico de España y sus posesiones de Ultramar* (Madrid, 1845).

152 Duocastella et al., *Análisis sociológico del catolicismo español,* p. 28. For the Second Republic and the early years of the Franco regime, see the data collected by the Catholic sociologist and social reformer Severino Aznar in *La revolución española y las vocaciones eclesiásticas* (Madrid: Instituto de Estudios Políticos, 1949) on the social origin of the secular clergy and of a number of religious orders, including the Jesuits. Since then, the *Guía de la Iglesia en España* has published further data on social origins of the clergy.

153 See data in Antonio Montero Moreno's *Historia de la persecución religiosa en España, 1936–1939* (Madrid: Biblioteca de Autores Cristianos, 1961).

154 For a review of contemporary quantitative sociology of religion in Spain, with some references to more historical materials, see Rogelio Duocastella, "Géographie de la pratique religieuse en Espagne," *Social Compass* 12 (1965): 253–302, with detailed bibliographic references; reprinted in Duocastella et al., *Análisis sociológico del catolicismo español.* There the reader will find, for example, a curve of the number of priests and seminarians per population from 1767 to the present. A bibliographic essay by P. Almerich, "The Present Position of Religious Sociology in Spain," *Social Compass* 12 (1965): 312–20, lists some of the articles and books published in the 1930s that first called attention to secularization, particularly in the cities and among the working class. For a study of religious practice in a suburban industrial city near Barcelona with data covering this century, see Rogelio Duocastella, *Sociología religiosa de una ciudad industrial: Mataró* (Barcelona: Nova Terra, 1965); in

a Basque industrial town, J. M. Larrañaga and R. Iruretagoyena, *Hernani, 1962* (Zarauz, 1964). See also Fundación FOESSA (Fomento de Estudios Sociales y de Sociología Aplicada), *Informe sobre la situación social de España, 1970* (Madrid: Euramerica, 1970), chap. 6, pp. 433–70.

155   See Linz, "The Party System of Spain: Past and Future," pp. 228–31.

156   Juan Estruch, *Los protestantes españoles* (Barcelona: Nova Terra, 1968).

157   Juan Ordóñez Márquez, *La apostasía de las masas y la persecución religiosa en la provincia de Huelva, 1931–1936* (Madrid: CSIC, Instituto Enrique Flórez, 1968).

158   Stanley G. Payne, *Politics and the Military in Modern Spain* (Stanford: Stanford University Press, 1967). See also E. Christiansen, *The Origins of Military Power in Spain, 1800–1854* (London, Oxford University Press, 1967). The work of a sociologist, Julio Busquets Bragulat, *El militar de carrera en España* (2d rev. ed. Barcelona: Ariel, 1971), presents quantitative data on the officers of the Spanish Army, entrants into the Academia General Militar, and the General Staff, particularly on social and regional origins. The Spanish military historical archive in Segovia has complete personnel records on army officers over more than a century, which could be a mine of information for monographic work. Santiago Otero Enríquez, *La nobleza en el ejército: estudio histórico de legislación nobiliaria militar, 1500–1865* (Madrid, 1915); see p. 33 on presence of nobility in different branches. For data that could be used for "collective biography," see *Galería Militar Contemporánea, colección de biografías y de retratos de los generales que más celebridad han conseguido en los ejércitos liberal y carlista,* 2 vols. (1846); P. Chamorro y Baquerizo, *Estado Mayor General del Ejército Español. Historia del ilustre buerpo* [sic] *de oficiales generales formada con las biografías de los que más se han distinguido e ilustrada con los retratos de cuerpo entero,* 3 vols. (1851); E. Fernández San Román, *Statistique, organization et institutions militaires de l'armée espagnole* (1852); A. Carrasco y Sayz, *Icono-biografía del generalato español* (1901). For the artillery, Jorge Vigón's 3-volume *Historia de la Artilleria española* (Madrid: CSIC, Instituto Jeronimo Zurita, 1947) is a basic source. For detailed data on conscription, draft evasion, exemptions by payment and other causes, and the physical and educational characteristics of conscripts by province and with some international comparisons, see Ministerio de Instrucción Pública y Bellas Artes, Dirección General del Instituto Geográfico y Estadístico, *Estadística del reclutamiento y reemplazo del Ejército, Trienio 1912–1914* (Madrid, 1915).

159   On the antiwar and antimilitary origin of the "Semana Trágica," see Joan Connelly Ullman, *Tragic Week, A Study of Anti-Clericalism in Spain, 1875–1912* (Cambridge: Harvard University Press, 1968).

160   Jorge Nadal Oller, "Les grandes mortalités des années 1793–1812: Effets à long terme sur la démographie catalane," in *Problèmes de mortalité. Méthodes, sources et bibliographie en démographie historique* (Liège, 1965), pp. 409–21; José María Recaséns Comes, "La población de la ciudad de Tarragona durante la guerra de Independencia," *II Congreso Histórico Internacional de la Guerra de Independencia y su Epoca* (Zaragoza, 1964), 1:467–87; Jesús Villar Salinas, *Repercusiones demográficas de la última guerra civil española. Problemas que plantean y soluciones posibles* (Madrid: Academia de Ciencias Morales y Políticas, 1942); Gabriel Jackson, *The Spanish Republic and the Civil War, 1931–1939* (Princeton, Princeton University Press, 1965).

161   There is no history of Spanish education which makes use of the quantitative information available in the Anuarios Estadísticos, special statistics published by the Ministerio de Instrucción Pública y Bellas Artes—*Estadística escolar de España en 1908* and *Anuario Estadístico de Instrucción Pública correspondiente al curso de 1909–1910 y matrícula oficial de 1900–1911* are two examples. There has been no systematic use of the data on literacy of military recruits, on voters' literacy from the electoral censuses, on the number of people able to sign their names on marriage licenses, etc., nor of the data from the *Presupuestos* and the *Guía Oficial.* Chapter 24 of Fernando Garrido's, *La España contemporánea* (Madrid: J. Cosano, 1926) presents some basic data for 1797, 1855, 1859, and 1860, with ratios for population changes over time calculated for all levels of education. For a nineteenth century

history, see Antonio Gil de Zárate, *De la instrucción pública en España,* 3 vols. (Madrid, 1855). The best source on Spanish education in the late 19th century is Yvonne Turin, *L'éducation et l'école en Espagne de 1874 à 1902. Liberalisme et tradition* (Paris: Presses Universitaires de France, 1959), see pp. 100–05 for some basic statistical data; the bibliography is an excellent starting point for work in this field.

On literacy in the early part of the 20th century, see the interesting monograph by Lorenzo Luzuriaga, *El analfabetismo en España* (Madrid: Museo Pedagógico Nacional, 1926), with an excellent map by Partidos Judiciales. Luzuriaga also collected the basic documentary-legal information for the 2-volume *Documentos para la historia escolar de España* (Madrid: Junta de Ampliación de Estudios e Investigaciones Científicas, 1917), covering from the Middle Ages to 1825.

The statistical yearbooks contain the basic information on education for modern times. In recent years, separate statistics on education have been published: Instituto Nacional de Estadística, Servicio de Estadísticas Culturales, *Estadística de la Enseñanza en España,* curso 1946–47 (Madrid: INE, 1949), which had been preceeded by *Estadística de los establecimientos de enseñanza* and *Estadística de la enseñanza oficial,* mentioned in the foreword to the new publication without reference to dates. For the present, see Ministerio de Educación y Ciencia, *La Educación en España. Bases para una política educativa* (Madrid, 1969), called "Libro Blanco"; also Fundación FOESSA, *Informe sociológico sobre la situación social de España, 1970* (Madrid: Euramérica, 1970), chap. 14, pp. 835–1050, on education. The Organization for Economic Cooperation and Development (Paris) has published a number of country reports on *Education and Development* as part of *The Mediterranean Regional Project;* the 1965 volume on Spain brings together much of the available information in systematic and comparative perspective. The FERE (Federación de Religiosos de la Enseñanza) has initiated the publication of an annual statistical yearbook: *Guía de Centros de Enseñanza Media de la Iglesia 1964* (Madrid, 1965, with supplements for later years).

Data now available on the social origins of university students in Spain, France, and Italy, compiled by university faculties for various dates, make possible significant comparisons. It should be possible to prepare a comparative statistical study of the history of educational expansion and its determinants—social, economic, political—of almost all European nations which, including higher education and the major professions, would give us fundamental information on certain elites and the educated middle classes.

For the history of Spanish intellectual life, the contact with the international scientific community, and the flows of influence, areas of inquiry, for a considerable length of time may be selected through the annual reports of the Junta de Ampliación de Estudios, *Memoria,* and the *Boletín de la Institución Libre de Enseñanza,* first published in 1877; and, for recent years, the *Memorias,* with listing of collaborators, of the CSIC, as well as a publication of the Fundación Juan March which lists all its fellowship holders. Once more the *Guía Oficial de España* and the *Escalafones* of the university professors, secondary school teachers (catedráticos de instituto), etc. would allow us to describe statistically the evolution of education, the continuities and discontinuities in academic personnel, the presence of academics in other elites and their career lines. The *Escalafón de Catedráticos de Universidad* gives information on birthplace, year of birth, date of entry into State service, etc. With those data, I have analyzed the contribution of different provinces to the academic elite, showing the disproportionate importance of those universities that are located in nonindustrial areas, a finding that coincides with data available for the place of birth of Italian university professors.

162   Dirección General de Seguridad, *Estadística de la prensa periódica,* for 1887, 1891, 1892, and 1900, mentioned by Francisco A. de Rodón, who is critical of their quality. In the last two years there was no information on circulation. Afterwards, see Ministerio de Instrucción Pública y Bellas Artes, D. G. del Instituto Geográfico y Estadístico, *Estadística de la prensa periódica de España referida al 1 de abril del año 1913* (Madrid, 1914). Gonzalo Redondo, *Las empresas políticas de José Ortega y Gasset. "El Sol," "Crisol," "Luz" (1917–1934),* 2 vols. (Madrid: Rialp, 1970). The

Memorias of the PSOE give considerable information on the Socialist press, the copies of books published, and propaganda meetings held.

163   The standard 19th century Catholic source is José María Antequera, *La desamortización eclesiástica considerada en sus distintos aspectos y relaciones* (Madrid: Imprenta de A. Pérez Dubrull, 1885), containing some statistical data. For a recent nonquantitative summary, see Francisco Tomás y Valiente, *El marco político de la desamortización en España* (Barcelona: Ariel, 1971). Richard Herr is doing research on *desamortización* initiated by the regalistic monarchy before the Napoleonic invasion. For the properties expropriated by the legislation first enacted in 1812, reinstated and extended in 1820, and developed and applied after the legislation introduced by Mendizábal in 1837, see the data in Vicens Vives's *Historia social y económica de España y América*, 4:92, taken from work in preparation by José Fontana using the figures given in the *Diccionario Geográfico-Estadístico-Histórico* of Pascual Madoz. The table gives the valuation of the land put up for sale, the price obtained, the land remaining then unsold. The valuations of the land put up for sale—by provinces—already allow interesting conclusions. There are also data on the sales made between 1855 and 1856 after the 1854 revolution. On the ecclesiastical *desamortización*, see Manuel González Ruiz, "Vicisitudes de la propiedad eclesiástica en Epaña," *Revista Española de Derecho Canónico* 1 (1946). The *Anuario Estadístico* for 1859, pp. 570–71, also gives figures on the land sold by the *desamortización* in its second wave as well as for unsold properties in 1857 (pp. 551 ff.), as well as a statistical digest for the period 1836–56 (pp. 574–75).

164   Francisco Simón Segura, *Contribución al estudio de la desamortización en España. La desamortización de Mendizábal en la provincia de Gerona* (Madrid: Instituto de Estudios Fiscales, 1969): idem, *Contribución al estudio de la desamortización en España. La desamortización de Mendizábal en la provincia de Madrid* (Madrid: Instituto de Estudios Fiscales, 1969); idem., "La desamortización de 1855. Valencia," *Cuadernos Residencia del Campo Español* (Valencia, 1964), pp. 65–67, also in *Economía Financiera Española* 19–20 (1967): 72–126; idem., "La desamortización de Mendizábal en la provincia de Barcelona," *Moneda'y Crédito* 98 (Sept. 1966): 121–44. See also Alfonso Lazo, "La desamortización eclesiástica en la provincia de Sevilla: estudio de las fuentes," *Moneda y Crédito* 100 (March 1967): 91–103; idem, *La desamortización eclesiástica de las tierras de la Iglesia en la provincia de Sevilla, 1835–1845* (Seville, 1970); Julio Porres Martín-Cleto, *La desamortización del siglo XIX en Toledo* (Toledo: Diputación Provincial, Publicaciones del Instituto Provincial de Investigaciones y Estudios Toledanos, Serie Tercera, vol. 2, Patronato José María Quadrado, CSIC, 1966); Fernando Jiménez de Gregorio, "La población en la Jara toledana," *Estudios Geográficos* 14 (1954): 527–82; Francisco Quirós Linares, "La desamortización, factor condicionante de la estructura de la propiedad agraria en el Valle de Alcudia y Campo de Calatrava. Estudio de Geografía Social," *Estudios Geográficos* 96 (1964): 367–407; V. Cámara Urraca and D. Sánchez Zurro, "El impacto de los capitales urbanos en la explotación rural: Las grandes fincas de los alrededores de Valladolid," *Estudios Geográficos* 97 (1964): 535–612.
The sale of public, especially municipal, lands also deserves research. For a local monograph, see Alfredo Floristán Samanes, "La desamortización de bienes pertenecientes a corporaciones civiles y al Estado en Navarra," in *Homenaje al Excmo. Sr. D. Amando Melón* (Zaragoza: CSIC, Instituto de Estudios Pirenaicos-Instituto Juan Sebastián Elcano de Geografía, 1966), pp. 109–16.

165   Albert Balcells, *El problema agrari a Catalunya, 1890–1936. La qüestió rabassaire* (Barcelona: Nova Terra, 1968), with some statistical series of prices, court cases, and bibliographic references; Josep Iglésies, *La crisi agrària de 1879–1900. La fil-loxera a Catalunya* (Barcelona: Edicions 62, 1968); Emilio Giralt i Raventós, "Evolució de l'agricultura al Penedès. Del cadastre de 1717 a l'època actual," in *Actas y comunicaciones de la I Asamblea Intercomarcal de investigadores del Penedès y Conca d'Odena* (Martorell, 1950), pp. 166–76.

166   Malefakis, *Agrarian Reform and Peasant Revolution*, apps. A-D, pp. 400–24, 442–51.

167   Jan Hinderink, *The Sierra de Gata. A Geographical Study of a Rural Mountain Area in Spain* (Groningen: J. B. Wolters, 1963).

168 Michel Drain, "Carte des paysages et structures agraires de l'Andalousie occidentale (feuille d'Utrera)," in *Mélanges de la Casa de Velázquez* (Paris, 1968), 4:371–86.

169 Vicens Vives, *Economic History of Spain*.

170 Juan Antonio Lacomba, *Introducción a la historia económica de la España contemporánea* (Madrid: Guadiana, 1962), an elementary textbook with some statistical series; Ramón Tamames, *Estructura económica de España* (Madrid: Sociedad de Esudios y Publicaciones, 1960; 5th ed. Guadiana); idem, *Introducción a la economía española* (Madrid: Alianza Editorial, 1967); idem, *Los centros de gravedad de la economía española* (Madrid: Guadiana, 1968); Jesús Prados Ararte, *La economía española en los próximos veinte años* (Madrid: Sopec, 1958); Román Perpiñá, *De estructura económica y economía hispana* (Madrid: Rialp, 1952); idem, *Corologia estructural y estructurante de la población de España, 1900–1950* (Madrid: CSIC, 1954); The International Bank for Reconstruction and Development, Report of the Mission organized at the request of the Government of Spain, *The Economic Development of Spain* (Baltimore: Johns Hopkins, 1963). For a critique, see Enrique Fuentes Quintana, ed., *El desarrollo económico de España. Juicio crítico del Informe del Banco Mundial* (Madrid: Revista de Occidente, 1963). See also Horst Hans Hergel, *Industrialisierungspolitik in Spanien seit Ende des Bürgerkrieges. Auswirkungen des staatlichen Wirtschaftsinterventionismus auf das Wirtschaftswachstum* (Köln and Opladen: Westdeutscher Verlag, 1963); Fundación FOESSA, *Informe sociológico sobre la situación social de España, 1970*, of which, while fundamentally sociological, a number of chapters deal with the economic structure and include time series. For an earlier survey of the Spanish economy, see Antonio de Miguel, *El potencial económico de España* (Madrid: Gráfica Administrativa, 1935).

171 For example, *Dictamen de la comisión nombrada por Real Orden de 9 de enero para el estudio de la implantación del patrón-oro* (Madrid: Consejo Superior Bancario, 1929), reprinted in *Documentación Económica*, vol. 1, nos. 3–5, with a foreword by J. Vergara and synthesis by A. Ullastres. The Ullastres' comments have been reprinted in *Información Comercial Española* 318 (1960), with corrections and additional graphs. This report was published anonymously but is attributed to Flores de Lemus. Banco Urquijo de Madrid, *La riqueza y el progreso de España* (Madrid: Banco Urquijo [not for sale], 1920, 1924). Much economic information is contained in the *Gaceta de Madrid* and the *Boletín Oficial del Ministerio de Fomento*. Among the private magazines are *El Economista*, first published in Madrid in 1857; *El Financiero*, founded in 1901, *España Económica y Financiera;* and *Economía Española*, for the 2d Republic.

172 José G. Ceballos Teresí, *La realidad económica y financiera de España en los treinta años del presente siglo*, vols. 1–3; vols. 4–8 are entitled *Historia económica, financiera y política de España en el siglo XX* (Madrid: El Financiero, 1931). Volume 8 covers the year 1931 and has no date of publication. This is a basic source that reprints many statistics, reports, laws, government declarations, etc.; it is absolutely indispensable. *Anuario Financiero y de Sociedades Anónimas de España*, founded by Daniel Ríu y Periquet in 1915 and published annually; *Anuario Financiero que comprende el historial de valores públicos y de sociedades anónimas de España*, founded by Guillermo Ibáñez in 1914 and published annually. Both these yearbooks are often referred to by the names of their founders, Ríu and Ibáñez.

173 *Anuario Oficial de valores de las bolsas de Madrid y Barcelona, publicado por los Colegios de Agentes de Cambio y Bolsa de ambas plazas*, published since 1918; *Anuario de minería y metalurgia* (Madrid: n.p., first published 1949).

174 As examples we may quote *Real Compañía Asturiana de Minas, 1853 a 1953* (Brussels, Paris, and Madrid: Real Compañía, 1953); Alberto del Castillo, *La Maquinista Terrestre-Marítima, personaje histórico, 1855–1955* (Barcelona: Maquinista, [not for sale] n.d.) For a critical review, see Juan Velarde, "Lo que enseña la historia de la Maquinista Terrestre y Marítima," *Sobre la decadencia económica de España* (Madrid: Tecnos, 1967), pp. 287–92; Francisco de Cossío, *Cien años de vida sobre el mar, La Compañía Transatlántica, 1850–1950* (Madrid, 1950).

175 On the history of interest groups, see Juan J. Linz and Amando de Miguel, *Los empresarios ante el poder público* (Madrid: Instituto de Estudios Políticos, 1967),

pp. 25–30, for additional references; Manuel Ramírez Jiménez, *Los grupos de presión en la segunda República española* (Madrid: Tecnos, 1969), pp. 112–41.

176   The Cámaras exist in all provincial capitals and a number of important cities. Their publications are often very detailed and give information not found elsewhere. They generally publish an annual *Memoria* and a journal, which constitute an indispensable instrument for local or regional economic history.

177   See Nicolás Sánchez-Albornoz, "Cádiz, capital revolucionaria en la encrucijada económica," in *La revolución de 1868. Historia, pensamiento, literatura*, ed. Clara E. Lida and Iris M. Zavala (New York: Las Américas, 1970), pp. 80–108, for an example of the use of the *Correspondence Commerciale* by the French consul. Some of those reports were published in *Annales du Commerce Extérieur, Espagne, Faits commerciaux* (Paris: Département de l'Agriculture, du Commrce et des Travaux Publics).

178   United Kingdom, Department of Overseas Trade, *Report* [by the commercial secretary of the embassy in Madrid] *on the Industries and Commerce of Spain* (London: His Majesty's Stationery Office, 1920–); later vols. have been published, somewhat irregularly, for the Board of Trade, Commercial Relations and Exports Department, in the series *Overseas Economic Surveys*.

179   J. Vicens Vives, *Cataluña en el siglo XIX* (Madrid: Rialp, 1961), translation of his Catalan *Industrials i politics del segle XIX* (Barcelona: Teide, 1958). The Catalan edition includes a number of biographies by Montserrat Llorens. Jaime Carrera Pujal, *La economía de Cataluña en el siglo XIX*, vol. 1, La cuestión arancelaria, vol. 2, Agricultura, artesanía, industria, vol. 3, Comercio, moneda, banca, bolsa y tributos, vol. 4, Marina mercante, puertos, carreteras y ferrocarriles (Barcelona: Bosch, 1961); idem, *Historia política de Cataluña en el siglo XIX*, 7 vols. (Barcelona: Bosch, [1957–58]).

180   José F. de Lequerica, *La actividad económica de Vizcaya en la vida nacional* (Madrid: Academia de Ciencias Morales y Políticas, 1956); Andoni de Soraluze, *Riqueza y economía del país vasco* (Buenos Aires: Editorial Vasca Ekin, 1945). Banco de Bilbao, *Un siglo en la vida del Banco de Bilbao. Primer centenario, 1857–1957* (Bilbao: Banco de Bilbao, 1957).

181   Francisco Sánchez Ramos, *La economía siderúrgica española. Estudio crítico de la historia industrial de España hasta 1900* (Madrid: CSIC, Instituto Sancho de Moncada, 1945).

182   Antoni Jutglar, *La era industrial en España*, (aproximación a la historia social de la España contemporánea) (Barcelona: Nova Terra, 1963), expanded version of a Catalan edition of 1962.

183   Juan Velarde Fuertes, "Crítica de distintas estimaciones efectuadas sobre la riqueza nacional de España," *Riqueza nacional de España*, Estudio conmemorativo del cincuentenario de la Universidad Comercial de Deusto, by a committee under the direction of José Angel Sánchez Asiain, 5 vols. (Bilbao: n.p., 1968), 1:263–327.

184   Servicios de Estudios del Banco de España, *Ensayos sobre la economía española a mediados del siglo XIX*, with contributions by G. Tortella, J. Nadal, G. Anes, R. Anes, and C. Fernández Pulgar (Madrid: [Ariel], 1970). The companion volume—El Banco de España, ed., *Una historia económica* (Madrid: El Banco de España, 1970)— is a major work with contributions by F. Ruiz Martín, E. J. Hamilton, G. Anes, G. Tortellá, J. Nadal, and J. Sardá that has come to my attention too late to be considered. Even though most chapters deal with the history of banking and of the central bank, they include a wealth of information on other aspects, much of it quantitative.

185   Jordi Nadal Oller, "Los comienzos de la industrialización española, 1832–1868: La industria siderúrgica," in servicio de Estudios del Banco de España, *Ensayos*, pp. 203–33; see also pp. 210, 212, 214, 299–311 (tables).

186   See the following works by Nicolás Sánchez-Albornoz: *España hace un siglo: una economía dual* (Barcelona: Península, 1968); *Las crisis de subsistencias de España en el siglo XIX*, Colección de Estudios y Monografías, serie C, no. 1 (Rosario, Argentina: Instituto de Investigaciones Históricas, Universidad Nacional del Litoral, Facultad de Filosofía y Letras, 1963), pp. 46–112, reprinted in *España hace un siglo: una economía dual;* "La crisis de 1866 en Madrid: la Caja de Depósitos, las sociedades

de crédito y la Bolsa," *Moneda y Crédito* 100 (March 1967): 3–40; "El trasfondo económico de la Revolución," in Lida and Zavala, *La Revolución de 1868*, pp. 64–79, also in *Revista de Occidente* 67 (October 1968): 39–63; "Los bancos y las sociedades de crédito en provincias, 1856–1868," *Moneda y Crédito* 104 (March 1968): 39–68.

187 Nicolás Sánchez-Albornoz, "Cádiz, capital revolucionaria, en la encrucijada económica," in Lida and Zavala, *La Revolución de 1868*.

188 Sánchez-Albornoz, *España hace un siglo*, pp. 179–218.

189 Juan Sardá, *La política monetaria y las fluctuaciones de la economía española en el siglo XIX* (Madrid: CSIC, Instituto Sancho de Moncada, 1948); see also idem, "Spanish prices in the 19th century," *Quarterly Journal of Economics* 62 (Nov. 1948): 143–59.

190 Higinio Paris Eguilaz, *El movimiento de precios en España. Su importancia para una política de intervención* (Madrid: CSIC, Instituto Sancho de Moncada, 1943). This book includes average wholesale price index and wholesale prices for a series of products as well as cost of living indexes for capital cities and other economic series for the period 1913–42. See also idem, *Renta nacional, inversión y consumo en España, 1939–1959* (Madrid, 1960); "Precios al por mayor y números índices, 1913–1941," *Boletín de Estadística*, número extraordinario (Madrid: Ministerio de Trabajo, Dirección General de Estadística, 1952).

191 Juan Velarde Fuertes, *Política económica de la Dictadura* (Madrid: Guadiana, 1968). For many quantitative data for that period, see also José Calvo Sotelo, *Mis servicios al Estado* (Madrid: Imprenta Clásica Española, 1931). Juan Velarde Fuertes, *Flores de Lemus ante la economía española* (Madrid: Instituto de Estudios Políticos, 1968).

192 Juan Sardá, "El Banco de España, 1931–1962," in Banco de España, *Una historia económica*, pp. 419–79. Josep Maria Bricall, *Política económica de la Generalitat (1936–1939), evolució i formes de la producció industrial* (Barcelona: Edicions 62, 1970). See also Albert Pérez Baro, *Trenta mesos de colectivisme a Catalunya* (Barcelona: Ariel, 1970).

193 Luis Olariaga, "España y la situación económica del mundo," *Economía Española*, vol. 1, no. 6 (June 1933), pp. 95–118, in "Folletos de paginación independiente"; Olegario Fernández Baños, "La crisis económica española en relación con la mundial," *El Financiero* 1717 (May 11, 1934): 646 ff.

194 *Martín Garay y la reforma de la Hacienda, 1817*, and *Real Caja de Amortización*, both in *Documentos del reinado de Fernando VII*, ed. Seminario de Historia Moderna, Universidad de Navarra, intro. and notes by Federico Suárez, 2 vols. (Pamplona: Universidad de Navarra and CSIC, 1967); Carlos Fernández Pulgar and Rafael Anes Alvarez, "La creación de la peseta en la evolución del sistema monetario de 1847 a 1868," in Servicio de Estudios del Banco de España, *Ensayos sobre la economía española a mediados del siglo XIX*, pp. 147–86; Manuel Colmeiro, "De la crisis monetaria en 1864," and Laureano Figuerola, "De la crisis monetaria en 1864," both in *Memorias de la Real Academia de Ciencias Morales y Políticas* (Madrid, 1884), vol. 5. See also Nicolás Sánchez–Albornoz, "La crisis financiera de 1866 en Barcelona," *España hace un siglo*, pp. 153–78; idem, "La crisis de 1866 en Madrid," *Moneda y Credito* 100 (March 1967): 3–40. Vicente Ortí y Brull, *La cuestión monetaria* (Madrid, 1893).

195 See n. 171 above. Francisco Cambó, *La valoración de la peseta* (Madrid: Aguilar, n.d., but possibly 1932); see also idem, "Proyecto de Ley sobre régimen ulterior de la banca de emisión y de la banca privada," *Ordenación Bancaria de España* (Madrid: Ministerio de Hacienda, 1921). Luis Olariaga, *La política monetaria en España* (Madrid: Victoriano Suárez, 1933); see also Olegario Fernández Baños, "Aplicación del análisis estadístico a un problema económico. Análisis del cambio y paridad económica de la peseta respecto al franco francés a partir de Enero de 1913," *Economía Española*, vol. 1, nos. 10–12 (Oct.–Dec. 1933), pp. 1–16. Gabriel Solé Villalonga, *La deuda pública española y el mercado de capitales* (Madrid: Instituto de Estudios Fiscales, 1964).

196 Ramón Canosa, *Un siglo de banca privada, 1845–1945* (Madrid: Nuevas Gráficas, 1945); Juan Antonio Galvarriato, *El Banco de España, su historia en la centuria 1829–1929* (Madrid: Banco de España, 1932), also quoted as *El Banco de España*.

Constitución, historia, vicisitudes y principales episodios en el primer siglo de su existencia; Gabriel Tortella Casares, "'La evolución del sistema financiero español de 1856 a 1868," in Servicio de Estudios del Banco de España, *Ensayos sobre la economía española a mediados del siglo XIX,* pp. 17–146; idem, "El Banco de España entre 1829–1929. La formación de un banco central," in Banco de España, *Una historia económica,* pp. 261–313 (includes data on monetary circulation); idem, "Banking, Railroads, and Industry in Spain, 1843–1875" (Ph.D. diss., University of Wisconsin, 1971). For a contemporary account, see Ramón de Santillán, *Memoria histórica sobre los Bancos Nacionales de San Carlos, Español de San Fernando, Isabel II, Nuevo de San Fernando y de España,* 2 vols. (Madrid: Establecimiento Tipográfico de T. Fortanet, 1865); Sánchez-Albornoz, "Los bancos y las sociedades de crédito en provincias, 1856–1868."

197   Rondo E. Cameron, *France and the Economic Development of Europe, 1800–1914* (Princeton, N.J.: Princeton University Press, 1961), chaps. 8–9 passim; Nicolás Sánchez-Albornoz, "De los orígenes del capital financiero: el crédito mobiliario español, 1856–1902," in his *España hace un siglo: una economía dual,* pp. 179–218.

198   Rafael Anes Alvarez, "Las inversiones extranjeras en España de 1855–1880," in Servicio de Estudios del Banco de España, *Ensayos sobre la economía española a mediados del siglo XIX,* pp. 187–202. See also Manuel Campillo, *Las inversiones extranjeras en España, 1850–1950* (Madrid, 1963).

199   Pedro Voltes Bou, *La banca barcelonesa de 1840 a 1920* (Barcelona: Ayuntamiento de Barcelona, Instituto Municipal de Historia, Documentos y Estudios, 1963); Francesc Cabana, *La banca a Catalunya. Apunts per una historia,* foreword by Juan Sardà i Dexeux (Barcelona: Edicions 62, 1965).

200   Banco Hispano Americano, *El primer siglo de su historia* (Madrid, 1951); also Banco de Barcelona, *Banco de Barcelona, quincuagésimo aniversario de su creación* (Barcelona, 1894). For the most recent period, see Ildefonso Cuesta Garrigós, "Los grandes bancos españoles. Su evolución, 1922–1943", *Moneda y Crédito* 11 (Dec. 1944): 36–57; and the annual reports of the leading banks which in the last decades have served as excellent reviews of the Spanish economy.

201   Jorge Nadal Oller's "La economía española, 1829–1931," in Banco de España, *Una historia económica,* pp. 315–417, is an excellent synthesis with quantitative data on those sectors with bibliographic references. Francisco Waiss San Martín, *Historia general de los ferrocarriles españoles, 1830–1941* (Madrid, Editora Nacional, 1967); RENFE (Red Nacional de Ferrocarriles Españoles), *Los ferrocarriles en España, 1848–1958* (Madrid: RENFE, 1958); Gabriel Tortella Casares, "Ferrocarriles, economía y revolución," in Lida and Zavala, *La Revolución de 1868,* pp. 126–37. For the 19th century, *Gaceta de los Caminos de Hierro, Industria, Minas, Seguros y Sociedades de Crédito* is particularly useful for railroad history. The Compañía de los Caminos de Hierro del Norte de España published *1858–1939: Historia, actuación, concesiones, ingresos, gastos y balance* (Madrid: Espasa Calpe, 1940). The "Norte" was one of the two largest railroads. An important government report is *Memoria sobre las Obras Públicas en 1867, 1868 y 1869, comprendiendo lo relativo a ferrocarriles, presentada al Exemo. Sr. Ministro de Fomento por la Dirección General de Obras Públicas* (Madrid, 1870). See also anonymous, *El problema de los ferrocarriles españoles. Antecedentes, datos, soluciones* (Madrid, 1931). An example of the kind of source likely to be neglected but fruitful for the social historian is: Patronato Nacional del Turismo, *Guia general de líneas exclusivas de transporte en automóviles para viajeros, equipajes y mercancias en toda España* (Madrid: Imprenta del Patronato de Huérfanos de los Cuerpos de Intendencia e Intervención Militares, 1929). This timetable gives distances, travel time, and fares and therefore allows us to determine the degree of communication or isolation in rural Spain, information that may be important for research on migration, diffusion of ideologies, etc. Lucas Beltrán Flórez, *La industria algodonera española* (Barcelona, 1943); Nadal, "Los comienzos de la industrialización española, 1832–1868: La industria siderúrgica," in Servicio de Estudios del Banco de Espana, *Ensayos sobre la economía española a mediados del siglo XIX,* pp. 203–33; Sánchez Ramos, *La economía siderúrgica española.* For some additional references, particularly on the contemporary period, see Ronald H. Chilcote, *Spain's Iron and*

Steel Industry (Austin: Bureau of Business Research, University of Texas, 1968). José Luis Martín Rodríguez and José María Ollé Rumeu, *Orígenes de la industria eléctrica catalana*, Documentos y estudios, vol. 10 (Barcelona: Instituto Municipal de Historia del Ayuntamiento de Barcelona, 1961).

202 Manuel Pugés, *Como triunfó el proteccionismo en España. La formación de la política arancelaria española* (Barcelona: Juventud, 1931). José Acisclo Castedo y Hernández de Padilla's *Referencias históricas y comentarios sobre la economía arancelaria española* (Madrid, 1958) is not a scholarly work but the contribution of a civil servant with a wealth of information. See also Elli Lindner, *El derecho arancelario español. Defensa de la producción y nacionalismo económico bajo tres regímenes: Hasta la postguerra, durante la Dictadura y con la República* (Barcelona: Bosch, 1934); José María Tallada, "La política comercial y arancelaria española en el siglo XIX," *Anales de Economía*, vol. 3, no. 9 (Jan.–March 1943), pp. 47–71. The many pitfalls of foreign trade statistics are noted by Valentín Andrés Alvarez, "Las balanzas de nuestro comercio exterior," *Revista de Economía Política* 1 (Feb. 1945): 73–94. For a statistical summary, see Instituto Nacional de Estadística, *Comercio exterior de España, 1901–1956* (Madrid, INE, 1958); and for fuller details, Dirección General de Aduanas, *Estadística general del comercio exterior de España* (Madrid, 1860–1909), containing complete series for 1858–1908. The Dirección General de Aduanas has published a number of other series on coastal shipping, wheat trade from 1870 to 1894, tonnage tax, etc. On the trade with Portugal, see José Miguel Ruiz Morales, *La economía del bloque hispano-portugués* (Madrid: Instituto de Estudios Políticos, 1946). On Spanish mineral exports, see M. W. Flinn, "British Steel and Spanish Ore, 1871–1914," *The Economic History Review*, 2d ser., vol. 8, no. 1 (August 1955), pp. 84–90.

203 Salvador Millet, "Historia de l'agricultura espanyola durante else segles XIX i XX," an unpublished manuscript awarded a prize by the Institut d'Estudis Catalans and frequently quoted by Vicens Vives; Gonzalo Anes Alvarez, "La agricultura española desde comienzos del siglo XIX hasta 1868: algunos problemas," in Servicio de Estudios del Banco de España, *Ensayos sobre la economía española a mediados del siglo XIX*, pp. 235–63. See also the works on the *desamortización* and Sánchez-Albornoz's *España hace un siglo*. For an elementary introduction with tables and charts but incomplete references, see José López de Sebastián, *Política agraria en España, 1920–1970* (Madrid: Guadiana, 1970); pp. 19–123 cover the period 1920–56. For the most important theoretical analysis of Spanish agrarian economy by an economist, see Antonio Flores de Lemus, *Sobre una dirección fundamental de la producción rural española* (Madrid: Sucesores de Rivadeneyra, 1926), reprinted in *Moneda y Crédito* 36 (March 1951): 141–68.

204 Ramiro Medir, *Historia del gremio corchero* (Madrid: Alhambra, 1952).

205 José Muñoz Pérez and Juan Benito Arranz, *Guía bibliográfica para una geografía agraria de España*, foreword by Amando Melón y Ruiz de Gordejuela (Madrid: CSIC, Instituto Juan Sebastián Elcano de Geografía, 1961), including 6,375 titles, many with brief comments and references to critical reviews. The handy indexes by author, subject matter, and place name make this a basic bibliographic source not only for rural geography—as the title would suggest—but for agricultural history, government publications, censuses and statistics, bibliographies, etc.; it goes far beyond agriculture. A second part is organized by region and province and is indispensable for the local historian, often quoting 19th and early 20th century statistical, demographic, and economic studies of local scope otherwise ignored in the literature.

206 See, for example, Manuel de Terán, "Santander, puerto de embarque para las harinas de Castilla," *Estudios Geográficos* (Madrid), vol. 8, no. 29 (1947), pp. 746–58.

207 Pérez and Arranz, *Guía bibliográfica para una geografía agraria de España*—see nos. 1724, 1732, 2156, 2276, 2287, and 2288 for statistical reports on agricultural and husbandry production around 1910 by province; no. 720 on irrigation; and no. 779 on use of fertilizers by province.

208 I have already referred to the work of Alain Huetz de Lemps, *Vignobles et vins du nord-ouest de l'Espagne,* in my section on the 18th century, but this work covers the history of vineyards in northwestern Spain to the present day.

209 Manuel Rico y Sinobas, *Memorias sobre las causas metereológico-físicas que producen las constantes sequías de Murcia y Almería, señalando los medios de atenuar sus efectos* (Madrid, 1851); idem, "Estudio sobre la marcha de las cosechas de la vid en Valladolid durante el siglo XVIII," *Boletín Oficial del Ministerio de Fomento* (Madrid) 1 (1852): 179–91, reprinted in Gonzalo Anes Alvarez, "La tradición de los estudios de climatología retrospectiva en España," *Estudios Geográficos* 28 (April 1967): 243–263.

210 Juan I. Fernández Marco, *Sobradiel. Un municipio de la vega de Zaragoza* (Zaragoza: CSIC, Departamento de Geografía Aplicada del Instituto Sebastián Elcano, 1955).

211 Manuel de Torres Martínez, *Una contribución al estudio de la economía valenciana* (Valencia: Diario de Valencia, 1930), a study of the agrarian regional economy, 1900–29. See also idem, *El problema triguero y otras cuestiones fundamentales de la agricultura española. Una investigación estadística sobre la economía agraria de España* (Madrid: CSIC, Instituto Sancho de Moncada, 1944), which gives a thorough picture of the wheat economy from 1906 to 1935 (and at times to 1942). Incidentally, the newspaper *El Norte de Castilla* (Valladolid) published regularly data on prices of wheat, the most important Spanish crop, and an annual report on the wheat economy. On the wheat market, see the important monograph with policy implications by José Larraz, *El ordenamiento del mercado triguero en España* (Madrid: Centro de Estudios Universitarios, 1935).

212 Sindicato Vertical del Olivo, under the authorship of Dionisio Martín Sanz et al., *El paro estacional campesino* (Madrid: Sindicato Vertical del Olivo, 1946).

213 Juan Martínez Alier, *La estabilidad del latifundismo. Análisis de la interdependencia entre relaciones de producción y conciencia social en la agricultura latifundista de la Campiña de Córdoba* ([Paris]: Ruedo Ibérico, 1968).

214 Ministerio de Agricultura, *Censo estadístico de sindicatos agrícolas y comunidades de labradores* (Madrid, 1934).

215 *La renta nacional de España en . . . y avance de . . .* (Madrid: Comisión de la renta nacional of the Consejo de Economía Nacional, 1946–), published annually; *La renta nacional de España, 1940–1964* (Madrid: Comisión de la renta nacional of the Consejo de Economía Nacional, 1965). See also n. 183 above for earlier evaluation and methodology. Banco de Bilbao, *Renta nacional de España y su distribución provincial. Año . . .* (Bilbao: Servicio de Estudios del Banco de Bilbao, 1957, 1959, 1962, 1965), referring, respectively, to the years 1955, 1957, 1960, and 1962; Instituto de Estudios Políticos, under the authorship of A. Alcaide, G. Begué, J. Fernández Castañeda, and A. Santos, *Estructura de la economía española. Tabla input-output (de 1954)*, foreword by V. Andrés Alvarez, epilogue by M. de Torres (Madrid: Instituto de Estudios Políticos, 1958); Ministerio de Hacienda, Secretaría General Técnica, *Contabilidad nacional de España, Años 1954, 1955, y 1956* (Madrid: Fábrica Nacional de Moneda y Timbre, 1959); idem, *Contabilidad nacional de España* (Madrid: Fábrica Nacional de Moneda y Timbre, 1960); idem, *Contabilidad nacional de España, Años 1954 a 1960* (Madrid: Fábrica Nacional de Moneda y Timbre, 1964); Ramón Tamames, *La lucha contra los monopolios* (Madrid: Tecnos, 1961), chap. 5, pp. 177–257; Fermín de la Sierra, *La concentración económica en las industrias básicas españolas* (Madrid, 1953), reprinted from articles in *Revista de Estudios Políticos* and *Revista de Economía;* José Larraz, *La integración económica europea y España* (Madrid: Espasa Calpe, 1962); idem, *Estudios sobre la unidad económica de Europa,* 9 vols. (Madrid: Sociedad Estudios Económicos Españoles y Europeos, 1951–61); Santiago García Echevarría, *Wirtschaftsentwicklung Spaniens unter dem Einfluss der europäischen Integration* (Köln and Opladen: Westdeutscher Verlag, 1964).

216 Charles W. Anderson, *The Political Economy of Modern Spain* (Madison: University of Wisconsin Press, 1970).

217 Servicio de Estudios del Ministerio de Comercio, *Información comercial española,* published monthly since 1946; the journal took on its present character in 1958.

218 Moreno, *Historia de la persecución religiosa en España:* "Apéndice Estadístico," pp. 758–68; and the list of names, offices, locales, and dates, pp. 769–883.

6

HISTORICAL STATISTICS IN
THE NORDIC COUNTRIES

by Birgitta Odén

INTRODUCTION

A sporadic interest in historical statistics among scholars can be traced in the Nordic countries back to the eighteenth century. It is related to the general intellectual climate during that time: the emphasis on rational thinking and the promotion of industry and commerce. Examples of this are the large group of parish historical descriptions published in Finland, often based on extensive demographic material, and the more scientific statistical works published in Denmark by scholars in political science. The real breakthrough of statistical source material in historical research, however, came much later. In Sweden, the historian-politician Hans Forssell was a pioneer. His *Sverige 1571* [Sweden in 1571] (Stockholm: P. A. Norstedt, 1872) endeavored to describe Sweden (excluding Finland and Estonia) from an administrative-statistical point of view. The work was based on fiscal material, mainly detailed registers of a property valuation made in 1571 as the basis for a tax whose object was to redeem the Swedish fortress Älvsborg from the Danes. Forssell reported, in the form of tables, the number of farms, the stock of cattle, money, bullion, precious metals, and the total value of personal property. From another source he added the two-thirds of that year's grain tithe that went to the Crown. The information covered practically the whole country, but with weaknesses common to all the early statistical material based on tax data.

In 1884 Forssell published another work based on extensive use of statistical material, *Anteckningar om Sveriges jordbruksnäring i sextonde seklet* [Notes on Swedish agriculture in the sixteenth century] (Stockholm: Kongl. Vitterhets, Historie och Antiquitets Akademien, 1884). Using cadastres, tithe accounts, tax returns, and farm records, Forssell skillfully mapped the structure of Swedish agriculture and social conditions in the latter part of the sixteenth century. Thereafter politics absorbed all Forssell's energy, and his scholarly production ceased.

The breakthrough in the historical use of statistical material in Denmark came with the statistician-historian Marcus Rubin's research in demographic and economic history. His pioneering work, *Folketal og fødselhyppighed, historisk-statistisk belyst* [Number of inhabitants and birth rates, in the light of historical statistics], was published in Copenhagen in *Dansk Historisk Tidsskrift,* ser. 7, no. 3 (1900–02), pp. 1–54. Another milestone was the Danish historian Nina Ellinger Bang's 1906 publication of her famous tables containing inexhaustible information from the Sound Toll registers of shipping activity and the movement of goods through the Sound.

In Finland and Norway it is more difficult to point to specific breakthroughs in historical statistics. Interest in the subject awakened later there than in Sweden or Denmark, but since the 1920s many scholars have used statistical material in their research. In Norway the earlier economically and statistically orientated research dealt primarily with two problems: Norwegian foreign trade, consisting mainly of timber exports; and socioeconomic conditions of the Middle Ages. In Finland, the breakthrough of quantitative history is associated with regional research in economic and social history, carried out notably by V. Voionmaa, P. Renvall, and E. Jutikkala. One of Jutikkala's works, *Suomen historian kartasto* [Atlas of Finnish history] (Helsinki: Suomalainen tiedeakatemia, 1949), is unique for Scandinavian conditions and is based largely on statistical source material.

In Denmark, modern economic-historical research took on a distinct quantitative orientation with the thesis of A. Olsen, *Studier over den danske finanslov, 1850–1864* [Studies of the state and requirements of the treasury in Denmark, 1850–1864] (Copenhagen: Koppel, 1930). This research has, in later years, been strongly concentrated on international rather than national problems. The international emphasis is a distinguishing characteristic of the Danish tradition of historical research.

Today Sweden carries on the most extensive research in economic history of any of the Scandinavian countries. Eli F. Heckscher, the economist of international fame, was the chief founder of its research tradition. Sture Bolin, a well-known scholar in numismatics, introduced sophisticated mathematical analysis into historical research. Later, special economic-historical institutes were founded at each of the five universities. Social history, on the other hand, has not been allotted any special professorships; it is carried on within institutes of political or economic history.

Interest in quantitative methods has also been keen among historians without special economic orientation. A Nordic historians' discussion of quantitative problems at a symposium in Oslo in 1966 gave rise to a report published as *Studier i Historisk metode, 2* [Studies in historical method, vol. 2] ed. O. Dahl (Oslo: Universitetsforlaget, 1967), in which Stein Rokkan, Aksel E. Christensen, Sven Lundkvist, and I deal with different aspects of "cliometrics."

A common organ for Nordic research is the *Scandinavian Economic History Review,* published (in English) since 1953; its editor since 1962 has been Professor Kristof Glamann of Copenhagen. Articles can also be found in the historical-statistical and economic reviews of the various countries and in the Nordic-oriented journal *Scandia,* edited in Lund by J. Weibull. *Scandia* is written mostly in Swedish, but some of its articles are in English and German. The annual review, *Economy and History,* edited in Lund by O. Bjurling, contains, among other things, a selected bibliography of works on economic history.

My object in this chapter is to survey the most important spheres of historical-statistical source material, primarily in the fields of social and economic history. I will also consider problems in the character and reliability of the source material relevant to their use in research. The limited size of the chapter gives no scope for exhaustive treatment. My selection is necessarily subjective, but those interested can, with the aid of the bibliographical material presented, further explore the problems and form their own opinions.

THE ADMINISTRATIVE FRAMEWORK FOR THE PRODUCTION OF STATISTICS

In terms of their origins, three different types of statistical data can be discussed: officially produced data, privately produced data, and research-produced data. In a sweeping generalization, it can be said that officially produced data are the earliest and most extensive, privately produced data belong primarily to industrialized society (from the 1850s on), and research-produced data have been produced mainly during the most recent decades. Nevertheless, modern researchers, delving deeply into source materials, have in some fields been able to reach back beyond the first large bodies of official statistics and establish significant bodies of data for pre-statistical times.

Central and local government administrative organs early began to show an interest in using statistical information. Some of the earliest data we have consist of summaries of exports and imports compiled in Stockholm during the latter part of the sixteenth century to provide information for the king and the Privy Council on the balance of trade. An intense interest in population statistics dates from the end of the seventeenth and first half of the eighteenth century. Sweden-Finland in 1749 was the first country in western Europe to have an independent administrative organ for statistics, the famous *Kungliga Kommissionen för Tabellverket* (Royal statistical commission). At the end of the eighteenth century, an office for collecting population statistics was also founded in Denmark-Norway. The statistical office had a relatively stronger position in Sweden-Finland, where the four estates of the Riksdag initiated the collection of independent sources of information, than in the absolute monarchy of Denmark-Norway, where royal ministers collected the data and kept the results secret.

Economic statistics, in the form of data collected by departments and commissions, began to develop in all the Nordic countries at the end of the eighteenth century. The years 1830–60 saw the collection of statistics organized and institutionalized. These measures were related to the growing influence of the representative bodies and their increased need for information. Denmark, after several attempts, founded a Central Bureau of Statistics in 1849. In 1858, one was organized in Sweden; in 1861, the Norwegian statistics office became operational; in 1865, Finland founded a provisional bureau of statistics. Iceland had no special bureau until 1914, but as early as the 1850s Icelandic statistics were published. They were, however, published privately, as a manifestation of nationalist sentiment against Danish rule of the island.

This institutionalization encouraged an effort to make the official statistics of the Nordic countries comparable. Both the Swedish and the Finnish central bureaus were created after study tours in the other countries and on the continent. The 1850s were a time of growing international cooperation in the field of statistics. In 1853, the Congrès International de Statistique was founded to promote international comparability of data. Conscious cooperation among the Nordic countries is most demonstrable in the union of Sweden and Norway. The Norwegian sociologist Eilert Sundt pleaded repeatedly for Swedish and Norwegian statistics to be collected and published in comparable form.

In this spirit, there was much practical cooperation among officials dealing with data compilation, although official cooperation only began in 1899 at a meeting in Kristiania (now Oslo). Since World War II, cooperation has been intensified, with the aim of making the Nordic official statistics more and more comparable. As a part of this attempt, statisticians often undertake a critical appraisal of the sources of historical statistics. The statistical publications of the Nordic countries therefore frequently contain articles about the sources and compilation of data extremely valuable for historians.

Historical data have been assembled by Nordic statisticians into long time series. In the three-volume *Historisk statistik för Sverige* [Historical statistics of Sweden], volume 1 (2d ed. 1969) covers population (1720–1967); volume 2 (1959) discusses climate, land surveys, agriculture, forestry, and fisheries; and volume 3 (1960) is a statistical survey. Four volumes of the *Statistiske Oversikter* [Statistical surveys] have appeared in Norway, of which that for 1948 (*Norges officielle Statistikk* [Norway's official statistics], ser. 10, no. 178) is the most valuable for information about the basic data. Recently a *Historisk statistikk* [Historical statistics] (*Norges officielle Statistikk,* ser.

12, no. 245 [1969]) has been published for 1968, corresponding to the Swedish volumes. In Denmark, *Folketal, areal og klima, 1901–1960* [Population, land surveys, and climate] (*Statistiske Undersøgelser,* vol. 10) was published in 1964. In Iceland and Finland, though, modern volumes of historical statistics are still lacking.

POPULATION STATISTICS

Many Nordic researchers—especially at the end of the nineteenth century—tried to estimate the early population of their countries with the aid of papal accounts of income from these areas, such as Peter's Pence. All such attempts are considered to have failed, because the original accounts give only fiscal amounts. The intended relation between amounts of taxes and numbers of persons is regarded as largely fictional; therefore population figures cannot be calculated from such revenue data alone.

In modern time, interest in demographic research has largely moved from absolute population figures to investigations of the geographical distribution of population and its relative density in different areas. Here, among other things, a retrospective method has attempted to derive earlier population estimates from records from the sixteenth and seventeenth centuries. Asgaut Steinnes and Andreas Holmsen in Norway have pioneered in this field. In Sweden and Finland, also, problems of population distribution are being tackled eagerly. The source materials for these studies are mainly the public accounts of taxes paid on farms. In these accounts, however, the public administration did not have any primary goal of population enumeration.

Since the state first manifested an interest in the size of the population for purposes of taxation and military service, the earliest records of population were of a fiscal nature. In Sweden-Finland the national registration of the population for taxation is associated with the so-called *mantals-längderna* (poll-tax lists), first regularly compiled during the 1620s in connection with intensified taxation. According to the instructions, all men and women between the ages of twelve and sixty-three had to register. Those who were unable to pay the tax on account of poverty were at first excluded, but from 1672 on they too had to be registered. To avoid tax evasion, the local clergyman had to be present at the enumeration and, guided by his parish registers, testify to the correctness of the registration.

Poll-tax lists in Sweden and Finland have been compiled annually until our own times. In duration, their coverage is unique. But the question remains, What reality do the poll-tax registers reflect? The first to deal with this problem was Heckscher. In *Ekonomisk-historiska studier* [Studies in economic history] (Stockholm: Albert Bonniers, 1936) he based his investigations on the total figures of the poll-tax lists for each county and found them to fluctuate greatly from year to year. Heckscher concluded that this must have been the result of variations in the manner of registration in different years. In years of famine, the recorders did not register those too poor to pay the tax. Therefore, the population registers were measures not so much of population change as of change in levels of living standards.

Recent investigators have shifted their analysis from the total figures to those for small districts. Thereby, attention has been directed primarily on technical factors of registration—for example, changes of clerks and new rules for registration. Eino Jutikkala's investigations into the Finnish poll-tax lists enabled him to establish that some of those lists are good sources for population studies, whereas others are useless. He reported on this research in an article, "Can the Population of Finland in the Seventeenth Century be Calculated?" in *Scandinavian Economic History Review* 5 (1957): 155–72.

In Sweden the poll-tax lists have most recently been treated by Gösta Lext in *Mantalsskrivningen i Sverige* [The poll-tax registration in Sweden] (Gothenburg: Ekonomiskhistoriska institutionen, 1968). From a detailed analysis of the registration process, he finds that the natural increase and decrease of the population are of primary significance when the fluctuations in the data are to be interpreted. This is a significant change of emphasis from that of Heckscher, who had argued that changes in the conduct and reporting of registration by the registrars—e.g., fuller registration by an ambitious man or less complete registration by a man anxious to shield the poor—were of primary importance. Lext established that administrative behavior could not have been responsible for all the changes in the growth of population, as Heckscher had argued, but that changes must have been largely a result of natural increase or decrease in the population. Thus the data on taxpayers indicates changes in population rather than in the standard of living.

Geographical researchers have also dealt with poll-tax lists in regional studies. David Hannerberg's *Närkes landsbygd 1600–1820: Folkmängd och befolkningsrörelse, åkerbruk och spannmålsproduktion* [The countryside of Närke, 1600–1820: population and population movements, agriculture and grain production] (Gothenburg: Göteborgs högskolas geografiska institution, 1941), and Nils Friberg's *Dalarnas befolkning på 1600-talet* [The population of Dalecarlia in the seventeenth century] (Stockholm: Nordiska bokhandeln, 1954) have found that approximately 40 percent of the population was registered in the seventeenth century poll-tax lists. Underrepresented groups were women, unmarried sons of farmers, and small holders.

In Denmark-Norway in the seventeenth century, fiscal population registration did not take place annually but only during certain years. The registers of 1645 and those from the 1660s have been most often used in research; in both countries, research workers consider the data to be comparatively reliable. The material is not annual and thus does not permit serial or trend studies of the kind carried out in Sweden; however, it has been used for regional comparisons. The most recent work utilizing this material is Aksel Lassen's *Fald og fremgang: Traek af befolkningsudvik-lingen i Danmark, 1645–1960* [Decline and progress: population trends in Denmark, 1645–1960] (Aarhus: Universitetsforlaget, 1965). In Denmark, extra taxation registers were introduced fairly regularly during the latter part of the eighteenth century, but the information is believed to be un-reliable because of widespread tax evasion. In Norway, the most detailed information comes from the first decade of the eighteenth century and from the 1740s. This extensive material, collected in the Norwegian Na-tional Record Office, has not yet been given a thorough critical examina-tion.

Besides the fiscal material, other data relevant for population statistics are *kyrkoböcker* (church registers), which have been kept since the seven-teenth century. Originally, the methods of church registration were an internal parish matter, but the state's interest was rapidly aroused as it saw the potential value of such records for checking on fiscal registration. Church registers in Denmark and Norway recorded weddings, baptisms, and burials. However, no register recorded the entire population of the parish.

Church registers are found in Denmark from 1621, and more frequently from 1645; in Norway they date from 1623, but they are not comprehen-sively preserved until the later decades of the seventeenth century. As early as the 1680s, attempts were made to centralize the information pro-duced in the various parishes: for Denmark, there exist a few summary tables from this early time. In Norway and Iceland, systematic collection did not begin until the 1730s. The demographic material of the eighteenth century for Denmark and Norway, although held secret by the monarchy, was published in part and perhaps with considerable errors by A. C. Gas-pari in *Materialien zur Statistik der Dänischen Staaten*, part 2 (Flensburg and Leipzig, 1786). The data in this private publication are still used ex-tensively. But they must be corrected in the light of the original returns, as shown by Michael Drake in an appendix to his article, "The Growth of Population in Norway, 1735–1855," in *Scandinavian Economic History Re-view* 13 (1965): 97–142. For Denmark, a survey of population in the nine-teenth century was published in *Statistisk Tabelvaerk*, (1905), ser. 5, letter A, no. 5, and for Norway a similar survey was published in *Norges offisielle statistikk, Ny Raekke* (1876), ser. C, vol. 1.

In Sweden-Finland, church registration was developed under strong pressure from the state. The earliest church register in Sweden dates from 1607; in Finland, from 1648. But church registration was not effective and systematized until the 1750s. Unfortunately many church archives have been destroyed, especially in Finland. The Swedish-Finnish church registers differ somewhat from the Danish-Norwegian. The clergy were instructed to keep—in addition to the records of weddings, baptisms, and burials—registers of the entire population of the parish, called *"husförhörslängder* (parish catechetical meeting registers) or, later, *församlingslängder* (parish residents' registers). Before the 1750s only those who were confirmed were registered, but after that time all were registered, including young children. The parsons also kept registers of those moving in or out of their parishes. Since different types of registers were kept, they could be used to check each other. A control of that kind occurred in connection with lists of data being sent in to the authorities and also when lists were summed up. The Swedish-Finnish data thus were subject to a central control and verification lacking in the vital statistics collected by parishes in most other countries. The survival of such data and their utilization have given Sweden (with Finland) a unique position as a model country of demographic statistics.

Not until the 1730s did it occur to the Swedish authorities that records ought to be required and used as a basis for statistical compilations and calculations. After a few tentative attempts, the plan was put forward in 1748; the next year the *Kungliga Kommissionen för Tabellverket* started its activity. The collection of data was to be retroactive to 1721, but that part of the project was never completed. The commission published its compilations periodically until the middle of the following century. Some scholars, notably Sundbärg, later attempted corrections of the early published accounts, but a number of historians have preferred to go back to the original unprocessed data.

The parochial registration of marriages, christenings, and burials has forced both statisticians and historians to wonder about the reliability and comparability of this information. For Denmark, the problem was first raised by Gustav Bang in his *Kirkebogsstudier* [Studies in church registers] (Aarhus: Gyldendal, 1906). Bang found that the clergy did not register about 5 percent of all births, since neither stillborns nor infants who died soon after birth were christened. His observations have recently been confirmed by Aksel Lassen in "The Population of Denmark, 1660–1960," *Scandinavian Economic History Review* 14 (1966): 134–57. For Norway, the most recently published work is Michael Drake's *Population and Society in Norway, 1735–1865* (Cambridge: Cambridge University Press, 1969), a critical analysis of Norwegian demographic material. Drake concludes that 5 percent of the deaths, too, were not registered in the lists of burials, particularly in the more remote parts of the country. Jutikkala deals with the first half of the eighteenth century in Finland in his large work, *Die Bevölkerung Finnlands in den Jahren, 1721–1749* (Helsinki: Suomalainen tiedeakatemian toin., 1945). The reliability of population statistics is analyzed for Sweden by Heckscher in an article, "Sveriges befolkning från det stora nordiska krigets slut till tabellverkets början" [The population of Sweden from the end of the great northern war to the beginning of the official population statistics], included in his *Ekonomisk-historiska studier*.

Heckscher's calculations have been criticized recently by the economic historian Gustav Utterström in "Some Population Problems in Preindustrial Sweden," *Scandinavian Economic History Review* 2 (1954): 103–65.

During the eighteenth century, the state's interest in statistics was developed in all the Nordic countries. As elsewhere in Europe, interest in this field was concerned mainly with the possibilities of a population census. The first census offers a natural boundary between the prestatistical and statistical periods. Research into the time before the first census can partially reconstruct the size of the population in prestatistical periods, thanks to the church registration data. In Finland, Sweden, and Denmark, attempts have been made to reconstruct population figures back to the seventeenth century. This has been possible only for smaller regions, where the material has been preserved until our times. The research has been published in the works by Jutikkala, Hannerberg, Friberg, and Lassen discussed above.

Iceland had the very first census. It was taken in 1703, with the aid of enumeration lists worked out by the Icelandic Professor Árni Magnusson. (He was a professor at Copenhagen, since Iceland had no university then.) The method was direct, and everyone residing on the island at the time was counted.

In Denmark, the first census was taken in 1769, the second in 1787, and the third in 1801. The first census was not nominative—for fear of frightening the population—whereas the other two were. The censuses were similar to those in Iceland, with the resident population recorded on official forms. In Norway, too, the first census was taken in 1769; however, the second was not until 1801. As in Denmark, the censuses were carried out by the "direct method" and were intended to count the resident population. Plans have been made to process the 1801 nominative census for Norway by computer to extract new results for regional studies.

In Sweden-Finland, the first census took place in 1749. It was based entirely on data summarized from the parish residents' registers. The material is preserved in the form of parish tables, ruridecanal tables, diocesan (or county) tables, and, finally, nationwide tables. At first, the censuses were supposed to be taken annually. However, in 1751 it was decided that they be taken every third year; in 1772, every fifth year; and during the nineteenth century, every tenth year. They were carried out by the "indirect method," counting those who administratively and juridically belonged to a church unit. Only in Stockholm was the counting done de facto by the "direct method." In Finland, the regular censuses of the larger towns in the nineteenth century were also based on the de facto principle.

Up to modern times, the nationwide censuses have, in principle, been carried out in the indirect manner in Sweden and Finland. The difference between the two countries is chiefly that since 1860 the Swedish censuses have been centralized and based on nominative information, which is open to verification, whereas the Finnish, up to 1930, were based on tables submitted by parish clergymen.

More recently, alterations in methods have increased comparability between the censuses of the Nordic countries. For instance, a partial census based on the direct method and the de facto principle was carried out in Sweden in 1936. In Norway and Denmark, an attempt has been made to disaggregate de jure population by distinguishing between those actually present and those "domiciled" in an area. This distinction could be achieved only after Denmark (in 1924) and Norway (in 1946) created civil population registers.

The reliability of the population figures of the statistical period has been discussed by both statisticians and historians. Utterström, in a paper in D. V. Glass and D. E. C. Eversley, eds., *Population in History* (London: Edward Arnold, 1965), pp. 523–48, summarizes the literature and the present state of the problem for Sweden. For Norway and Denmark, Drake and Lassen have given the most recent accounts of critical aspects of the older census material.

In Danish historical research, population of towns has attracted special interest, perhaps chiefly because Danish towns even in olden times were larger and received more immigrants than other Nordic cities. The town population of the seventeenth century has been studied by H. Fussing in *Bybefolkningen, 1600–1660. Erhvervsfordelning, ambulans, indtjeningsevne* [Urban population, 1600–1660. Distribution of occupations, migration, incomes] (Aarhus: Universitetsforlaget, 1957) on the basis of three groups of sources: the parish registers, the records and accounts of the town recorders, and the trade license registers. A later period is treated by A. Olsen in *Bybefolkningen i Danmark paa Merkantilismens Tid* [The Urban population of Denmark in the era of mercantilism] (Aarhus: Universitetsforlaget, 1932).

Changes in the spatial distribution of population are affected not only by variations in local birth and death rates but also by migration. Using compilations from different sources, it has been possible to establish that the transfer of people, even prior to industrialization, was much greater in extent than we have hitherto imagined. Lassen could thus demonstrate that a mass migration took place in Denmark during the 1660s after some districts were depopulated by war and plague, which induced young families to move to where land was cheap and houses empty. During the eighteenth century, labor shortages were an economic and political problem, which in the absolute monarchy of Denmark led to the introduction of *Stavnsbaand* (agrarian bondage) to prevent the migration of rural workers. In Sweden, talk of similar labor shortages led to anxious discussions in the Riksdag about the risks which emigration posed for the country and to the setting up of investigating committees. It soon turned out that the whole problem was exaggerated, although in Sweden, as elsewhere, there must have been considerable internal migration of agricultural laborers and servants. But no extensive studies of this migration have yet been published.

The possibilities of analyzing modern migration statistically are very limited in Iceland, Denmark, and Norway but better in the other two Nordic countries. In Sweden-Finland, the clergy were obliged to keep registers of both in-migration and out-migration. Some of these have been preserved, at least from the beginning of the nineteenth century. But this local information was not utilized by the central authorities in Sweden until after 1860, when clergymen were required to send to the central statistical office a summary of information concerning migration. In Finland, such summary information is found from 1878 on.

In Norway, the clergy were not expected to keep registers of newcomers (except during a few decades of the nineteenth century), and only as late as 1947 did administrative practice permit a continuous follow-up of migration through information on individuals. In Denmark, this can be done only for the years since 1923. Comparative historical studies of migration within and among the Nordic countries in earlier periods are therefore difficult to carry out.

Historical research based on migration statistics of the statistical period has not been extensive. Much of the existing research in this sphere has, moreover, been undertaken by investigators in geography, sociology, or economic science whose interests have been enlarged to include the historical background of contemporary phenomena. Because of the availability of sources, migration has been dealt with most intensively in Sweden and Finland.

A pioneering work was Heikki Waris's *Työläisyhteiskunnan syntyminen Helsingin pitkänsillan pohjoispuolelle* [The rise of a workingman's community on the north side of the long bridge of Helsinki] (Helsinki: Historiallisia tutkimuksia, 16, 1932–34). In it, the Finnish sociologist investigated migration to a certain area in Helsinki and the resulting structural peculiarities in its demography and occupational pattern. Another study of migration within Finland during the era of industrialization (1878–1939) was Reino Lento's *Maassamuutto ja siihen vaikuttaneet tekijät Suomessa vuosina, 1878–1939* [Internal migration in Finland and factors affecting it, 1878–1939] (Helsinki: Tekijä, 1951). E. Jutikkala's review, "Internal Migration and Industrialization in Finland, 1878–1939," in *Scandinavian Economic History Review* 1 (1953): 247–51, gives some idea of the main result of Lento's important work.

Migration in Finland in earlier periods has been analyzed by Antti Rosenberg in his work on the county of Nyland in 1821–80: *Muuttoliike Uudenmaan läänissä esiindustrialistisen kauden lopulla, 1821–1880* [The mobility in the county of Uusimaa during the last part of the preindustrial era,

1821–1880] (Helsinki: Historiallisia tutkimuksia, 70, 1966); and "Mobility of Population in the Finnish County of Uusimaa (Nyland), 1821–1880," in *Scandinavian Economic History Review* 14 (1966): 39–59.

At the Institute for Social Science of the University of Stockholm, two migration investigations with a historical background have been completed under the auspices of Gunnar Myrdal. The first, the American demographer Dorothy Swaine Thomas's *Social and Economic Aspects of Swedish Population Movements* (Stockholm: Norstedt, 1941), subjected the period 1895–1933 to intensive analysis. The other was the work of a team headed by Svend Riemer, *Population Movements and Industrialization. Swedish Counties, 1895–1930* (Stockholm: Norstedt, 1941). More recently, several geographers have dealt with these problems, especially through studies of birthplace areas and migration patterns. The report of a conference, *Migration in Sweden*, edited by D. Hannerberg, T. Hägerstrand, and B. Odeving (Lund: Gleerup, 1957), gave an account of current research in this field.

In economic history, the problem of migration has been treated most recently by S. Martinius in *Befolkningsrörlighet under industrialismens inledningsskede i Sverige* [Population mobility in the initial period of industrialism in Sweden] (Gothenburg: Ekonomiskhistoriska institutionen vid Göteborgs universitet, 1967). This treats, among other subjects, the errors in population statistics that are revealed in a comparison with private accounts from factories and estates.

Ethnography, too, deals with migration and with more temporary movements of workers called *arbetsvandringar* (short-term migrations without the family)—a historically interesting type of migration. The most recent work of this type is Göran Rosander's *Herrarbete. Dalfolkets säsongvisa arbetsvandringar i jämförande belysning* [Seasonal migrations of workers from Dalecarlia. A comparison] (Uppsala: Lundequistska bokhandeln, 1967). He uses statistical information based on the voluntary registrations of work certificates by the clergy in some parts of Sweden during the seventeenth and eighteenth centuries.

In Denmark and Norway, the study of migration is considerably more hazardous, because the demographic source material is less extensive. The birthplace information in the censuses, however, provides some data, as does the statistically calculated net migration. T. Agersnap, in his *Studier over indre vandringer i Danmark* [Studies on internal migration in Denmark] (Aarhus: Universitetsforlaget, 1952), deals mainly with migration after 1931. In Norway, migration prior to 1947 can be studied primarily in the form of trends of migration gains or losses and analysis of birthplace areas. This is done, for instance, in a work by Ø. Rødevand, *Nordmenn på flyttefot. Studier over den geografiske mobilitet innem Norges befolkning i vårt århundre* [Norwegians on the move. Studies in geographical mobility in Norway in the twentieth century] (Oslo: Universitetsforlaget, 1959). Difficulties in a more intensive analysis of the migration of earlier centuries are illustrated in a brief article by P. Mathiesen, "Lokalmigrasjon eller tømmernomadisme, 1769–1865" [Local migration or nomadism of timber workers], in *Heimen* 14 (1967).

Modern researchers have been greatly interested in the study of emigration to foreign countries, especially to the United States. Nordic emigration to the United States began in Norway, but it soon became a significant and much-debated social phenomenon in Sweden. The need for a statistical measurement of the development grew. After tentative attempts to measure it in various ways, Sweden had its first official emigration statistics in 1865 (with reconstruction retroactively to 1860); Norway, in 1869. Because of the differences in the structures of national registration, reconstruction had to be done with different materials as bases. In Sweden, those who reported to the parish their intention to leave the country were recorded in the emigration registers. In Norway, those who held emigration certificates and were recorded in the journals of the harbor police were registered. Sweden, too, kept such police journals, but they have been considered less reliable for registration of emigrants and therefore have been less utilized than in Norway. The sources of error in these two types of emigration statistics were quite different. The errors have limited effect on the information on a large scale, but various systematic errors can appear in detailed analyses.

In Denmark, emigration was less important, and no official emigration statistics for the whole country were collected for a long time. From 1868, the police in Copenhagen kept a continuous record of those leaving the country from that city. The material was the basis for statistical compilations published in the annual reports of the chief commissioner of police. Kristian Hvidt is now carrying out a large-scale computer analysis of personal data in the Danish emigration statistics. He describes some of his interesting problems in "Danish Emigration Prior to 1914: Trends and Problems", *Scandinavian Economic History Review* 14 (1966): 158–78.

Finnish emigration did not begin seriously until the 1890s, and there was no comprehensive registration until 1893. Here the passport journals of the county administrations that were used to obtain information about emigration present new problems of reliability.

Swedish emigration statistics, unlike those of the other Nordic countries, also cover nontransoceanic movements such as the sometimes large emigration to Germany and to other Nordic countries. Emigration from Sweden was dealt with for the first time in a large public survey at the beginning of the present century, *Emigrationsutredningen* [The emigration survey] (Stockholm: Nordiska bokhandeln, 1908–13), for which the statistician Gustav Sundbärg was mainly responsible. A few American and English scholars have studied the subject, but with insufficient criticism of the basic statistical material. Renewed investigations in Sweden are now probing more deeply into the history of migration within the nation and to other nations; the results have not yet been published.

In Norway, emigration has been dealt with by the historian Ingrid

Semmingsen in a large two-volume work, *Veien mot vest* [The road to the west] (Oslo: Aschehoug, 1941, 1950). A corresponding investigation for Finland was carried out by Anna-Leena Toivonen in *Etelä-Pohjanamaan valtamerentakainen siirtolaisuus, 1867–1930* [The emigration from Ostrobothnia to the United States, 1867–1930] (Helsinki: Helsingin yliopisto, 1963). A survey of current Nordic research represented in published works is given in my article on "Emigrationen från Norden till Nordamerika under 1800-talet. Aktuella forskningsuppgifter" [Emigration from Scandinavia to North America during the nineteenth century. Problems in recent research] in *Historisk tidskrift*, 1964, pp. 261–77.

Historical demography has thus already provided some interesting results in the Nordic countries, but the research so far shows a rather scattered and unsystematic picture. It is to be hoped that the attempts to found a common Nordic research institute will gain the approval and support of the authorities, to make possible a closer cooperation among statisticians, sociologists, geographers, economists, and historians.

SOURCES FOR SOCIAL HISTORY

If we use the word *social* in a wide sense to embrace the circumstances related to man's conditions in society, a large number and variety of statistical data are available. First, we have data related to the social variables in the life of the individual—notably language, education, family status, income, and wealth. Second, there are data related to the socially oriented services of the state or community: public health and provision of medical care, public relief, schools, and courts. Third, we have data related to society in its socioeconomic function—for instance, wages, hours, working conditions, consumption, levels of living, and housing. Statistical registration of these phenomena in the Nordic countries came fairly late. It is impossible here to account for the development of all these forms of statistics. Instead, I want to call attention to some lines of development and to illustrate the value of the available materials.

Up to the end of the eighteenth century, the authorities in the Nordic countries do not appear to have compiled much statistical information about social conditions. The information that exists today is the result of laborious research, and much work must still be done to produce the statistical data of social history for these early periods. But much could be extracted, for instance, from the accounts of the churches and the local administrations or from the states' registers of the poor and the sick who were unable to pay taxes.

In the 1780s and at the beginning of the nineteenth century, the interest in social information increased. Statistics on poor relief in Denmark began to be collected during the 1780s in order to provide information for a poor relief committee, which was set up in 1787 to investigate destitution.

Statistics on schools were also accumulated more or less regularly from this time on. The first volume of data on alcoholism in Denmark was published in 1834. In Sweden, the poor relief committee of 1837 collected information throughout the country. Statistics were gathered in Norway on the social and economic conditions of the largest group of agricultural workers, *husmaend* (crofters). Some medical statistics go back as far as the eighteenth century and were published in medically oriented magazines. In Norway, medical statistics were officially published from 1835 on. Moreover, the economic statistics summarized from the 1820s to the 1830s often included social data.

The big breakthrough, however, came in Norway, where during the 1850s and 1860s, the clergyman-sociologist Eilert Sundt made himself the spokesman for the need for considerably enlarged social statistics. He dedicated his life to the collection of data and the investigation of social conditions in Norway. One of his earliest works treated the wandering bands of gypsies and tinkers. Another discussed alcoholism on the basis of a questionnaire sent to all primary school teachers throughout the country to which more than 2,000 of the 2,400 replied. In 1858 he also carried out a detailed interview investigation into the home conditions of school children in an area of in-migration on the outskirts of Oslo.

Sundt's program for enlarged social statistics was only partly realized. Continuous school statistics exist in Norway from 1861, official crime statistics from 1860, and modern public relief statistics from 1866. However, other demands—for housing data, for instance—met with no immediate response. In Sweden, too, it was in the 1860s that some branches of social statistics were shaped, primarily those of public relief, crime, and education.

A critical examination of this information in Sweden was made by Per Hultqvist in "Kommunernas fattigvård och finanser, 1874–1917" [Official statistics concerning public relief, 1874–1917], *Scandia* 31 (1965): 247–87. He showed in these earlier public relief statistics a number of short-comings that are difficult to remedy or eliminate without detailed studies of the raw data remaining in each local community. As often happens in early statistics, the reporting forms were imprecise, difficult to interpret, and were changed time after time, so that the opportunity for comparability between various periods was lost. Apparent increases of public relief expenditures are often not actual increases but only reflections of improved methods of data collection. In Denmark, no poor relief statistics existed other than the listing of the poor in the information about occupations in the census lists. But this information is very unsatisfactory as Richard Willerslev has pointed out in *Studier i dansk Industrihistorie, 1850–1880* [Studies in Danish industrial development, 1850–1880] (Copenhagen: Harck, 1952). As the archives of the Danish communes are not well preserved, early poor relief in Denmark can hardly be studied directly through quantitative material.

Denmark paid prompt attention to statistical information about working conditions. As early as 1874, the Danish Home Office in Copenhagen published *Oplysninger over Arbejdernes Økonomiske Kaar i Kongeriget Danmark i Aaret 1872* [Notes on the socioeconomic situation of workers in Denmark in the year 1872]. Danish trade unions began to collect data on wages and consumer habits. In Norway, a parliamentary commission on working conditions gathered statistical data in 1885, and in Finland the following year a Helsinki trade union initiated the collection of data concerning industrial working conditions. In Sweden in 1889, a committee collected data on workers' insurance.

A new period of creative activity in social statistics in Scandinavia came around the turn of the twentieth century. Statistical series on working conditions, labor disputes, and unemployment were then started, to fill the need for information in relation to the demands for social legislation advanced with increasing intensity under the influence of repeated labor conflicts and of the socialist movement. Impulses from German social policy can also be noted. Statistical publications were produced on wages and working conditions, unemployment, and social insurance. In Finland, Hans Gebhard headed an investigation, the results of which filled several volumes, dealing with the social situation of landless agricultural workers in 1901. Annual publications treating social conditions and the labor market began to be issued.

Unemployment and marketing problems during the 1920s and the depression in the 1930s increased and dramatized the need for social statistics. Statistics on consumption and labor increased in Sweden. The household budget investigation of 1933 and the housing count of that year exposed social evils. Alva and Gunnar Myrdal's *Kris i befolknings-frågan* [Crisis in Swedish population trends] (Stockholm: Bonnier, 1934) pointed out other social problems. These studies led to increased socio-political activity. In Finland, social and political needs brought about the collection of social statistics in 1936–37 concerning child protection and the treatment of vagrants and alcoholics. In Denmark, social welfare statistics were radically reorganized after the big social reform of 1933. Norway developed increased information about the needs for public aid to invalids and the physically handicapped in connection with the 1935 committee on social legislation. And statistics on housing were rapidly developed as a result of new theories about public responsibility for housing.

During the 1930s, the Nordic countries were affected by a serious university crisis, which increased demands for statistics on the influx of students and on the results of examinations. Such information naturally existed far back in time in the registers and the matriculation records of the various universities, but now university statistics were included in the official statistics for the first time. In Sweden, an expansion of university statistics took place with the objective of creating a predictive instrument for the academic labor market and an instrument for testing the effectiveness of academic teaching. The statistics can at the same time be used to measure some of the social effects of educational policy. Technical shortcomings in techniques for measuring teaching, however, still make it difficult to utilize these data.

Statistics concerning research and development are a late phenomenon in the Nordic countries. The subject became of topical interest during the 1960s, as research policy developed into an important and much discussed element in the welfare state. But measuring techniques are complicated and as yet hardly shaped into useful tools. The first volume in this field—*Forskningsstatistik* [Research statistics] (Stockholm: Statistiska meddelanden, 1965), vol. 1, letter 5, no. 21—appeared in Sweden in 1965; it was a survey conducted mainly in accordance with the recommendations of a manual of the Organization for Economic Cooperation and Development (OECD).

The gradual building up of the welfare state in all the Nordic countries during the twentieth century has thus produced an increasingly refined and differentiated system of social statistics, whose various branches are reported in general statistical reference works and therefore need not be discussed in detail here. A retrogression in time of modern statistical series is possible to some extent but will demand extensive historical research, which so far has hardly advanced past the planning stage. Historians and sociologists in Scandinavia are at present at work on a program of collecting historical series of various types of social data under the guidance of the Norwegian political sociologist Stein Rokkan of the University of Bergen.

Before leaving the social statistics of the earlier history of the Nordic countries, I shall touch briefly upon two subjects vitally associated with the social situation of the individual and with social and political cleavages and solidarities: language and occupation.

Each of the Nordic countries is largely uniform in language but nevertheless has some language problems. Modern Norway, for example, has one official language and many local variants. The distribution of these variants has not been recorded statistically except in data on languages of instruction in the schools. There is a general account of this problem in E. Haugen's *Language Conflict and Language Planning: The Case of Modern Norwegian* (Cambridge, Mass.: Harvard University Press, 1966), giving some figures from the 1930s and onward.

Finland and Denmark have politically important linguistic minorities. Since the Middle Ages, Finland has had a Swedish linguistic minority, living mainly in the coastal districts. Information about the use of languages in Finland was collected as early as 1845, but it was cursory, without benefit of proper inquiry or fixed criteria of language use. Moreover, the reporting depended on the political and linguistic attitudes of the individual reporting clergymen. The information is therefore impaired by a systematic bias in favor of Swedish at the expense of Finnish. Not until the 1880 census was information collected more systematically. A partially quantitative analysis of the Finnish linguistic situation can be found in M. Klövekorn's *Die sprachliche Struktur Finnlands, 1880–1950* Helsinki: Finska vetenskaps-societen, 1960).

A small German minority lives in the Danish border area between Denmark and Germany. The Danish censuses do not report the use of language. Instead, the determination of nationality groupings of German and Danish in the border area, has been made by indirect and related criteria, primarily by election results and referenda. Moreover, German censuses and a German language count in 1905 have been used for the present Danish areas which before 1918 lay within the German Empire.

Sweden and Norway have small Lappish and Finnish minorities, primarily in their northern areas, which have been registered by the censuses. In Norway, the information is based on questions connected with registration; in Sweden, the clergy's opinions of the language of the persons in question are decisive. Unfortunately, the information is accumulated according to different principles in Norway and Sweden and therefore is not commensurate. In Sweden in the 1960s, a shortage of workers has brought new language minorities into the country, registered in official statistics but not yet studied as a historical phenomenon.

A central question in all social history is the determination and classification of occupations and social positions. Such information comes primarily from the censuses. In Sweden-Finland, the occupational information was reported by clergy in the parish registers. This form of reporting did not record people's changes of occupation or double employment. In Denmark-Norway, the information concerning occupation was more up-to-date, but on the other hand it was unconfirmed because given personally to the census enumerator. Richard Willerslev's critical investigation has shown that the occupational information of the nineteenth century census in Denmark is useless for historical studies (*Studier i dansk Industrihistorie*, p. 21). Also, in the other Nordic countries much criticism has been directed at the occupational information in the older censuses. An interesting, semantically oriented analysis of the changed significance of occupational designations during the last century has been made by Sten Carlsson in the collective work, *Samhälle och riksdag* [Society and the Riksdag], vol. 1, ed. A. Thomson (Stockholm: Almqvist & Wiksell, 1966).

Classification into occupational groups in Sweden-Finland was made as early as the eighteenth century in so-called *ståndstabeller* (tables of the classes or estates), broken down into some sixty groups; Denmark-Norway at the same time used only eight groups. In the statistical reorganizations during the mid-nineteenth century, the classifications became more alike. The subject was for a long time a matter for debate at the Scandinavian statisticians' meetings, and it was not until very recently that a first solution, for an inter-Nordic classification system, was agreed upon; see *Nordisk yrkesklassificering* [Nordic occupational classification] (2d ed. Stockholm: Nordiska bokhandeln, 1967).

Social history in the Nordic countries is still in its infancy. Most of the published works treat social legislation and social ideology rather than social structures, and they do not use quantified data. An example of this type of research is the investigation into the history of the working class in Denmark published by P. Engelstoft, H. Jensen, and H. Bruun during the 1930s. A quantitative approach is used in Edvard Bull's pioneering research concerning the working milieus of the woodpulp, paper, and timber industries in southeast Norway during the late nineteenth and early twentieth century. His main work—*Arbeidermiljö under det industrielle gjennembrudd* [The working milieu during the industrial breakthrough] (Oslo: Universitetsforlaget, 1958)—is based partly on "oral history," extensive interviews with older workers who themselves lived through some of the profound changes of Norway's industrial revolution early in this century. Professor Bull (not to be confused with his father, the labor historian of the same name) has described his methods in "Autobiographies of Industrial Workers: Sources of Norwegian History," *International Review of Social History*, vol. 1, part 2 (1956); he gives some of his findings in an article entitled "Industrial Workers and Their Employers in Norway circa 1900," in *Scandinavian Economic History Review* 3 (1955): 64–84.

The same subject has been investigated by Bo Gustafson in *Den norrländska sågverksindustrins arbetare, 1890–1913* [The workers in the sawmills of northern Sweden, 1890–1913] (Uppsala: Almqvist & Wiksell, 1965). To some extent, the large Swedish series *Den svenska arbetarklassens historia* [The history of the Swedish working class] (Stockholm: Tiden 1941–57) is also based on statistical data in its treatment of craftsmen, miners, workers in urban industries, and agricultural workers from various sociohistorical perspectives.

More extensive quantification, primarily for social mobility, has been done from biographical registers of government personnel, university students, the liberal professions, etc., and from biographies. The pioneering work of Sten Carlsson, *Ståndssamhälle och ståndspersoner* [Estate society and persons of rank] (Lund: Gleerup, 1949), shows that the nobility in Sweden at the beginning of the eighteenth century dominated the higher positions in the bureaucracy and the military service, whereas a century later they no longer dominated either. Intermarriages between nobles and commoners increased, and landed property, which in the seventeenth century had belonged exclusively to noblemen, was to a large extent transferred to commoners.

Gösta Carlsson has used data from modern times to treat social mobility from a sociological point of view in his *Social Mobility and Class Structure* (Lund: Gleerup, 1958). Similar problems in Denmark have been analyzed by Svend Aage Hansen in *Adelsvaeldens grundlag* [The basis for the political power of the aristocracy] (Copenhagen: Gad, 1964); in it he reworks data on demographic, economic, and social conditions from the late Middle Ages to the eighteenth century.

Other occupational groups have also been analyzed statistically: the burgher elite in Denmark during the seventeenth century by S. Larsen, the clergy in Norway during the nineteenth century by D. Mannsåker, civil servants in Sweden during the eighteenth and twentieth centuries by I. Elmroth and S. S. Landström, and military groups in Finland by K. Wirilander. An example of the modern combination of sociological analysis and historical data is an essay by G. Carlsson and K. Svalastoga, "Social Stratification and Social Mobility in Scandinavia," *Sociological Inquiry* 31 (1961), which gives an account of historical studies of mobility in the Nordic countries.

There has been much debate on the significance of education for social mobility. It has been analyzed in a number of works in the Finnish language. Professor Sven-Erik Åström of Helsinki has discussed the role of the universities as a means of social mobility during the eighteenth century in *Universitetsbesöken som socialt fenomen i Österbotten, 1722–1808* [University attendance as a social phenomenon in Ostrobothnia, 1722–1808] (Helsinki: Finska vetenskaps-societen, 1950). Sociohistorical studies of mobility among intellectuals have been made in Denmark by T. Geiger and in Sweden by S. Moberg, C. E. Quensel, and J. Weibull. In Norway, the academic professions in society have been analyzed by several researchers, who give an account of their data in *The Professions in Norwegian Social Structure*, ed. V. Aubert, vols. 1–2 (mimeographed) (Oslo: Institute for Social Research, 1961–62). A project of great importance has been in progress for some years at Uppsala University under the title *Folkrörelserna* (the popular movements). Its purpose is to trace the grass roots history of mass movements, above all the temperance and labor movements, and their roles in the processes of democratization in Sweden. C. G. Andrae and S. Lundkvist report on this research in "Folkrörelserna och den svenska demokratiseringsprocessen" [Popular movements and the process of democratization in Sweden], *Historisk tidskrift*, 1969: 197–214.

The development of sociohistorical statistics has thus been intimately connected with changes in the structure of society in the Nordic countries. The materials have still been only partially utilized in historical research. Attractive research projects lie ahead for social historians in these countries.

ECONOMIC STATISTICS

Quantitative data on economic conditions in the Nordic countries can be obtained for a considerably earlier period than data on social conditions. During the late Middle Ages, *jordeböcker* (land registers) were often kept of the number of farms and the incomes derived from them. Land registers, primarily for property complexes belonging to the church but also for some property complexes belonging to the higher nobility, are preserved. This material has been used to study the agrarian crisis in the Nordic countries in the late Middle Ages: the increase in the number of deserted farms and the reduction in *avraden* (land rents) from *landbönderna* (tenants). From a comparative standpoint, the problem has been discussed in a collective report, "Ödegårder og ny bosetning i de nordiske land i senmiddelalderen" [Deserted farms and new settlements in the Nordic countries in the late Middle Ages], in *Problemer i nordisk historieforskning* (Oslo: Universitetsforlaget, 1964).

Land registers had a legally binding function and were therefore preserved for posterity. Estate accounts, however, have only been preserved in exceptional cases, so that we are more poorly informed about the management of the property complexes.

Economic data from the sixteenth and seventeenth centuries make it possible to illustrate agricultural conditions. It is primarily records from the public administration that have been preserved in large numbers: in Sweden-Finland from the 1540s; in Denmark-Norway from the latter part of the sixteenth century. Broadly speaking, the following types of relevant agricultural source material are available:

1. Accounts of the state's incomes from taxes
2. Land registers and other registers, which record the number of farms, acreage, and charges
3. Cattle lists
4. Tithe records, intended to record the harvest each year, but which have a tendency to stagnate into fixed tithe setting
5. Accounts of the management of farms belonging to the Crown

This large body of material has as yet scarcely been utilized for quantitative investigations. Many regional studies, however, in all the Nordic countries have analyzed the value of the fiscal material as sources for economic history. A penetrating investigation of the value of the Danish agricultural statistics, for instance, is F. Skrubbeltrang's "Nogle Kilder till aeldre dansk landbrugsstatistik" [Some sources of earlier Danish agricultural statistics], *Dansk Historisk Tidskrift*, ser. 11, no. 1 (1944–46), p. 245, in which the cattle tax registers are checked against deeds of inheritance (distribution) from the same district. This research indicated that a significant number of animals were concealed from the tax collectors.

For Iceland, a register exists from 1683 for the land belonging to the Danish Crown. There are more extensive land registers of hired cattle, rents, and tax values of farms from 1686 and from 1695/96. Later land registers or lists are found from 1753/54 and from the 1840s. These Icelandic sources are examined critically by B. Láruson in *The Old Icelandic*

Land Registers (Lund: Ekonomisk-historiska föreningen i Lund, 1967).
Agricultural information in the eighteenth century was still produced
mainly for fiscal reasons. However, other reasons began to make themselves
felt in private and official descriptions and reports. For Denmark and
Norway, an extensive agrarian statistical inventory was made in 1743 by
Erik Jessen, justice of the supreme court, in order to obtain a basis for
an economic description of the whole country. The material has not
yet been published. G. Utterström, among others, comments on administrative reports from Sweden in his large work, *Jordbrukets arbetare* [Agricultural workers] (Stockholm: Tiden, 1955).

The statistical period for agricultural data began in the Scandinavian
countries around the end of the eighteenth century. But for some decades
the information was often unsystematically collected, the reporters sometimes unqualified, and the collection managed by people completely lacking
in statistical training; thus this material merits little confidence.

New arrangements for official agricultural data collection were made in
the period 1830–65. During the latter part of the nineteenth century and in
the present century, statistical collection methods have developed and
improved. To the earlier information about holdings, sowing, crop
statistics, and livestock have been added, notably, distribution of arable
land, number of agricultural workers, and number of machines.

The value of these official agricultural statistics in their earlier forms in
Sweden has been questioned in a significant investigation by the economic
historian Jörn Svensson, *Jordbruk och depression, 1870–1900* [Agriculture
and depression, 1870–1900] (Lund: Ekonomisk-historiska föreningen i Lund,
1965). Svensson subjects the official statistics to a minute analysis by
breaking down averages for large units (counties) to a considerably lower
level of aggregation. Thus he can establish that changed and/or improved
data collection methods, not an actual expansion in agriculture, are
responsible for the growth in some of the time series that are fundamental
for Swedish agricultural history. The investigation reminds historians that
not even the broad lines of development, let alone details, can be followed
confidently in time series in which changed methods of collection or
compilation of the raw data have made successive figures incommensurable.
Because such changes were often made successively in one small area after
the other, the suspected interruptions of continuity in the series were
smoothed over at higher levels of aggregation. Moreover, they were often
carried out without any change in the external framework of data collection.
Svensson might have employed more advanced statistical methods and
aimed at reconstruction of the official statistics as well as showing the
various sources of error therein. A proposal in that direction has been made
by L. Jörberg in a review of Svensson's thesis in *Historisk tidskrift,* 1967.

Industry (including handicrafts during earlier periods) is another important area in which we need quantitative data. The earliest information concerns mining production; there are series of accounts for some of the mines as early as the sixteenth century. During the seventeenth century, the state began to demand statistical information about production in different parts of Norway and Sweden, both of which possessed important mines. The production of iron and copper as well as trade in these ores and metals became an increasingly more complicated procedure through the centuries, as is reflected in the records of business companies, central and local administration, and interest groups. In Sweden especially, this material has been much utilized in economic-historical research. The Stora Kopparbergs Bergslag Company (Falun) has archival material preserved since the Middle Ages and abundant since the sixteenth century. This data has been subjected to extensive analysis in recently published studies by B. Boëthius, K. G. Hildebrand, S. Lindroth, and myself. The history of the Swedish iron industry has been dealt with in the three-volume *Fagerstabrukens historia* [The history of the Fagersta mines] (Stockholm: Almqvist & Wiksell, 1957–58) by A. Attman, K. G. Hildebrand, and E. Söderlund. The statistical material which research can produce on the conditions in the capital market for the iron industry has been subjected to a penetrating analysis by Rolf Adamson, who gives a summary of his results in "Finance and Marketing in the Swedish Iron Industry, 1800–1860," *Scandinavian Economic History Review* 16 (1968): 47–101.

All the Nordic countries have some scattered information about manufactures and handicrafts as early as the eighteenth century. Modern industrial statistics, including those for production, have been produced in Sweden since 1863 and in Finland since 1884.

A critical examination of Swedish industrial statistics is Lennart Jörberg's *Growth and fluctuations of Swedish Industry, 1869–1912* (Stockholm: Almqvist & Wiksell, 1961). By comparing the official statistics and the accounts of individual enterprises for selected years, Jörberg demonstrates both faults and merits in the official material. He concludes that both long-term and cyclical variations can be studied in the data but that some changes in collection methods impair comparability in time.

Critical observations on the industrial statistics for Finland have been made by Lauri Korpelainen in "Trends and Cyclical Movements in Industrial Employment in Finland, 1885–1952," *Scandinavian Economic History Review* 5 (1957): 26–48. A number of monographs relating to branches of industry or to specific companies also offer criticism of modern industrial statistics.

Denmark and Norway had no annual statistics of industrial production for a very long time. In Denmark an investigation of industrial enterprises and employed workers was carried through for some selected years (1847, 1855, 1872); Willerslev discusses its value in his *Studier i dansk Industrihistorie*. P. Bagge examines Willerslev's thesis critically in *Historisk tidsskrift* (Copenhagen, 1953–56), p. 105. A three-volume history of Danish industry—*Industriens historie i Danmark* [The history of industry in Denmark], ed. A. Nielsen (Copenhagen: Gad, 1933–44)—covers the period until 1870.

In Norway, annual statistics on industial enterprises and employed workers began to be gathered in 1870, but it was not until 1908 that statistics on production were first taken into account—four years earlier than the corresponding information was compiled in Denmark. Research in Norway has been concentrated on the production of timber, the country's most important industry in the 1840s and 1850s. The latest contribution is Francis Sejerstad's "Aspects of the Norwegian Timber Trade in the 1840s and 1850s," in *Scandinavian Economic History Review* 16 (1968): 136–54.

Statistics of foreign trade are among the earliest data collected by the state, because import and export information functioned as checks on customs revenues. From as early as the sixteenth century, there are port books kept regularly in Swedish and Finnish ports; from the seventeenth century, the Danish and Norwegian ports were also held liable for information on exports and imports. Ledgers of imports and exports were bulky, however, and the authorities, rapidly losing interest in them, frequently sorted them out and destroyed much of the material. Often only the sum totals—*extrakten* (extracts)—remain, making it impossible to verify the reliability of the aggregate data. The information preserved in Sweden from the seventeenth century was published by Bertil Boëthius and Eli F. Heckscher in *Svensk handelsstatistik, 1637–1737* [Swedish statistics of foreign trade, 1637–1737] (Stockholm: Thule, 1938).

Nordic historians have regarded the information in the customs declarations with a certain skepticism, suggesting that the extent of smuggling makes them fundamentally useless. For the sixteenth century, this unreliability is shown in my case study of "A Netherlands Merchant in Stockholm in the Reign of Erik XIV," in *Scandinavian Economic History Review* 10 (1962): 1–37. A stimulating investigation by Steinar Kjaerheim, "Norwegian Timber Exports in the Eighteenth Century: A Comparison of Port Books and Private Accounts," in *Scandinavian Economic History Review* 5 (1957): 188–201, shows certain Norwegian export records from the latter part of the eighteenth century to be notoriously faulty. Smuggling was in this case caused less by fear of customs duties than by a wish to escape production limitations, which were checked by the authorities in connection with exports. For Sweden, comparisons with English port books have been made by Sven-Erik Åström in *From Cloth to Iron*, vols. 1–2 (Helsinki: Commentationes humanarum litteratum, 1963–65).

Official shipping statistics were not kept before the eighteenth century. In Sweden-Finland they are gathered in the Royal Board of Trade from 1738; in Denmark-Norway, in the treasury from 1750. Most of the original records are now lost, but the data is preserved in the so-called trade-balance statements. Two valuable recent works deal with the origin of this material and its potential utilization for Sweden: R. Vallerö's *Svensk handels-och sjöfartsstatistik, 1637–1813* [Swedish foreign trade and shipping statistics, 1637–1813] (Stockholm: Beckman, 1969); and S. Högberg's *Utrikes-handel och sjöfart på 1700 talet* [Foreign trade and shipping in the eighteenth century] (Stockholm: Bonnier, 1969).

For even earlier periods, the historian must go back to accounts of those customs and other duties that rested upon shipping. An ingenious study of this type by Oscar Bjurling—*Skånes utrikessjöfart, 1660–1720* [Foreign shipping of Scania, 1660–1720] (Lund: Gleerup, 1945)—utilizes various communal port charges to obtain quantitative data on merchant shipping. Some idea of his working methods can be gained from the essay "Sweden's Foreign Trade and Shipping around the Year 1700," in *Economy and History* 4 (1961): 3–33. For Norway, there is an investigation carried out by Stein Tveite, *Engelsk-Norsk trelasthandel, 1640–1710* [The Norwegian timber trade between Norway and England in the seventeenth century] (Bergen: Universitetsforlaget, 1961). S. Kjaerheim offers a critical analysis of the material utilized by Tveite in "The Norwegian Timber Trade in the Seventeenth Century," in *Scandinavian Economic History Review* 12 (1964): 91–95.

For commerce and shipping, the statistical period in all the Nordic countries goes back to the mid-nineteenth century. I. Hammarström has examined the source material critically in "Svensk transocean handel och sjöfart under 1800–talet" [Swedish transoceanic trade and shipping in the nineteenth century], *Historisk tidskrift*, 1962, pp. 377–431. A number of monographs give useful criticism of the value of the statistical material on exports of specific commodities; two such studies are G. Fridlizius's *Swedish Corn Export in the Free Trade Era* (Lund: Gleerup, 1957) and his "Sweden's Exports, 1850–1960. A Study in Perspective," in *Economy and History* 6 (1963): 3–100. For Denmark, B. N. Thomsen and Brinley Thomas's "Dansk-engelsk samhandel, 1661–1963" [Anglo-Danish trade, 1661–1963], in *Erhvervshistorisk årbog*, 1965, is noteworthy.

The Sound Dues, or duties on shipping and goods passing through the Öresund (Sound), which Denmark collected from the 1430s to 1857, have naturally received special attention. Registers for ships passing in and out of the Baltic and for dutiable goods have been preserved annually and almost continuously from the 1560s, until the duties were abolished under the influence of free-trade ideas. As I already mentioned (see p. 264 above), this enormous body of material has been arranged and published by Nina Ellinger Bang and K. Korst (1906–50). Their work has aroused lengthy discussion about the value of both the original material and the manner of its publication. Leading Nordic and other scholars have taken part in the discussion: Heckscher in *Historisk tidskrift* (Stockholm, 1942), p. 170;

Astrid Friis in *Scandia* 8 (1935): 9, and in *Historisk tidsskrift,* ser. 9, no. 4 (1925), p. 109; Aksel E. Christensen in *Hansische Geschichtsblätter* 59 (1934): 28, and in *Dutch Trade to the Baltic about 1600* (Copenhagen and The Hague: E. Munksgaard and M. Nijhoff, 1941); Pierre Jeannin in "Les Comptes du Sund comme sources pour la construction d'indices généraux de l'activité économique en Europe," *Revue historique,* 1964, pp. 55, 307; and James Dow in "A Comparative Note on the Sound Toll Registers, Stockholm Customs Accounts, and Dundee Shipping Lists, 1589, 1613–1622," *Scandinavian Economic History Review* 2 (1964): 79.

The analyses have utilized control materials in the ports of import and export. The most important conclusions are that the accounting system and eventually the system of control were considerably improved after 1618; that the number of ships is given correctly in the main; and that the quantities of goods shown are too low, partly on account of smuggling and partly on account of duty-free goods. The most recent investigation— Marianne Nilsson's *Öresundstullräkenskaperna som källa för fraktfarten genom Öresund under perioden 1690–1709* [The accounts of the sound dues as sources for the shipping trade through the Öresund during the period 1690–1709] (Gothenburg: Ekonomiskhistoriska institutionen vid Göteborgs universitet, 1962)—checks the sound toll registers with the aid of customs records from some ports in the eastern Baltic.

Price and wage data are a classical field for research. Scandinavian scholars were very interested in Sir William Beveridge's ambitious plan of the 1930s for international price history. Of the plans then presented by Nordic scholars, only the Danes have carried out their program. In 1958, Astrid Friis and Kristof Glamann published *A History of Prices and Wages in Denmark, 1660–1800* (London, New York, and Toronto: Longmans, Green, 1958). In Norway, some information was collected, but the raw material remains unpublished in the School of Economics in Bergen. In Sweden and Finland, the major task remains to be done; a price history for Sweden by Lennart Jörberg has been promised for 1972.

Individual researchers have made significant contributions to the study of price and wage changes. Among these are, for Sweden, two works in the series of Stockholm Economic Studies: G. Bagge, E. Lundberg, and I. Svennilson, *Wages in Sweden, 1860–1930* (Stockholm: Stockholm University, Institute of Social Science, 1933, 1935); and G. Myrdal, *The Cost of Living in Sweden, 1830–1930* (Stockholm: Stockholm University, Institute of Social Science, 1933). For Denmark there is J. Pedersen and O. Petersen's *An Analysis of Price Behaviour during the Period 1855–1913* (Copenhagen: Institutet for Historie og Samfundsøkonomi, 1938); for Finland, H. Björkqvist's *Prisrörelser och penningvärde i Finland, 1878–1913* [Price movements and the value of money in Finland, 1878–1913] (Helsinki: Finlands banks institut för ekonomisk forskning, 1958). No modern investigation has been made of price history in Norway, but prices play an important part in a recently published general economic analysis by J. Bjerke entitled *Langtidslinjer i norsk økonomi, 1865–1960* [Trends in the Norwegian economy, 1865–1960] (Oslo: Statistisk sentralbyrå, 1966).

Governments made attempts to get periodic surveys of the economic situation as a whole. In Sweden-Finland, as early as the end of the seventeenth century the Crown tried to obtain information about the economic situation in the country by demanding reports from the governors. These reports were, of course, essentially narrative, but they did contain some numerical information. During the period in the eighteenth century when the Riksdag had power in Sweden, it continued along this path and demanded regular reports. In the 1820s, the reporting was systematized by fixed formulas. The quinquennial report of the Swedish provincial governor occupied a central place in official statistics during the whole of the nineteenth century, while the Central Bureau of Statistics prepared summaries for the entire country. After the separation from Sweden, Finland continued the old reporting system and even followed changes in Swedish procedure, although under Russian suzerainty. In Denmark-Norway, some secret reporting by local government officials occurred during the eighteenth century, but a fixed tradition never came into being. After Norway was joined in union with Sweden in 1814, its governors (*amtmaendene*), possibly under the influence of Swedish practice, made quinquennial reports along lines that were at least formally similar to those of the Swedish provincial governors. No such official reports were published in Denmark.

The Swedish quinquennial reports were often cursory and unreliable, but some use has been made of them. When the archives of the county administrations are examined, they often show extensive and ambitious statistical collection by the governor's staff before the summarizing reports were written. This local material—which exists in Denmark as well, where it was collected for local administrative purposes—ought to be critically examined and more extensively utilized.

The quinquennial reports by the Swedish governors were to serve as bases for government and Riksdag political decisions. As the demands for statistics grew, however, responsibility for their collection was transferred from the governors to special organs with greater expert knowledge. Therefore this form of summary statistical description was discontinued in the Nordic countries at the beginning of the twentieth century. But the need for an informative survey of the economic situation remained, and it increased under the influence of changes in economic theory and the growing importance of fiscal and other economic decisions.

In all the Nordic countries, current national accounts were beginning to be worked out during the 1930s. The interest in long-term trends resulted in the reconstruction of earlier national accounts series. For Sweden, the reconstruction has gone back as far as 1860; for Norway, 1865; for Finland, 1926; and for Denmark, 1870, with scattered information for the years 1818–60.

The state early had need of data of its revenues and expenditures. Some rough estimates of income were made as long ago as the Middle Ages in the Nordic countries. Later these rough estimates acquired greater scope and precision.

In Sweden-Finland, two rough estimates were made of revenue and expenditure in 1573 and 1582. In Denmark-Norway, there are some corresponding rough estimates from the first decades of the seventeenth century. I have analyzed the Swedish financial statistics from the sixteenth century in *Rikets uppbörd och utgift* [Survey of royal revenue and expenditure] (Lund: Gleerup, 1955), with the aid of recovered papers and calculations which originated in the "budget work" of the King's Chamber. The rough estimates are a kind of compromise between budget and account, which enabled the sovereigns to estimate their future income and expenditure. During the reign of Gustavus Adolphus, the keeping of accounts in Sweden was reorganized, so that from 1620 on there exist both budget and accounts.

In Denmark, it was suspected that Sweden's political and military expansion was rooted in a better financial administration, and the Danes therefore reorganized their keeping of accounts according to the Swedish pattern in the 1660s. Extensive research has been carried out on public finances in Denmark during the absolute monarchy, most recently by J. Boisen Schmidt in *Studier over Statshusholdningen i kong Frederik IV's regeringstid, 1660–1699* [Studies in the king's finances in Denmark, 1660–1699] (Copenhagen: Gyldendal, 1967). This work is critically analyzed by H. C. Johansen in *Historie* 8 (1968). An awkward situation in the use of the financial material is that none of the countries had a fiscal unity or a centralized accounting system.

Financial statistics were for a long time state secrets. But after the constitutional reforms and statistical breakthroughs of the mid-nineteenth century, they were systematically published in the Nordic countries. Among modern works on the public finances of the last hundred years is Gisli Blöndal of Reykjavik's "The Growth of Public Expenditure in Iceland," in *Scandinavian Economic History Review* 17 (1969): 1–22; in it Blöndal analyzes the great increase in the public expenditure of the industrial and welfare state, using statistical materials for the years 1876–1960.

A problem related to the increase in public revenues is the extent to which tax statistics can illustrate the distribution of incomes and wealth after taxation during the nineteenth century began to be based on these considerations. Several investigations have been made without any great historical perspective; an exception is Lee Soltow's interesting study, *To-*

ward Income Equality in Norway (Milwaukee and Madison: University of Wisconsin Press, 1965).

During recent years, economic-historical research has been so extensive that I cannot give an account here of even most of the significant published works based on quantitative data. Reviews and surveys in the *Scandinavian Economic History Review* and in *Economy and History* give the interested reader an insight into the orientation and results of such research.

POLITICAL STATISTICS

The Nordic countries offer a great wealth of quantitative or easily quantifiable data on political developments. So far only a few projects of quantitative analysis have been undertaken by political historians, but political scientists and sociologists have helped to stimulate increasing interest in the potentialities of the extraordinary mass of data at hand in the five countries.

In an international perspective, the nation-states of the North stand out as a privileged area for systematic comparative analysis: they offer great masses of comparable time-series data and at the same time differ markedly from each other in the developments of their central institutions. There is first of all the clear-cut contrast between the two old-established powers of the North: the strength and continuity of the representative institutions in Sweden, the protracted period of absolutism and sudden transition to mass suffrage in Denmark. There are also intriguing differences among the three newer nations: the cumulation of linguistic, religious, and rural-urban cleavages and the late class polarization in Norway; the more sudden and much more violent polarization on class lines in Finland; and the slower process of national mobilization in Iceland.

So far these differences have been analyzed largely in qualitative terms. S. Rokkan and H. Valen's article in *Politische Forschung*, ed. O. Stammer (Cologne: Westdeutsches Verlag, 1960), presents a review of comparative analysis up to 1960. An example of one possible approach is Rokkan's comparison of Denmark and Sweden in *Scandinavian Political Studies* 5 (1970). But with the proliferation of efforts to generate computer-readable files of electoral statistics and biographical data, it will soon be possible to push on toward detailed quantitative comparisons. What follows is a quick review of the most likely sources of data for such analyses and a discussion of some of the more interesting of the single-nation studies carried out on the basis of such data.

Of the five countries, Sweden can boast the longest continuous history of representative rule. There was, however, no legal provision for the col-

---

This section, "Political Statistics," has been contributed by Stein Rokkan.

lection of electoral data before the great reform of 1866. The records of the elections to the four Estates were not aggregated by any national agency but are still available in archives. The first steps toward a national system of electoral accounting were taken in the 1840s: the King's Council set up a committee to collect data from all tax registers to determine the probable sizes of the national electorate under different franchise criteria. Such "suffrage counts" preceded the introduction of regular electoral bookkeeping in Norway and Finland: in Norway there were two highly detailed counts across all parishes in 1868 and 1876; in Finland, estimates were published in 1899 of the proportions of the population enfranchised under the rules of the four estates for all provinces, cities, and rural communes. These statistical records of the transition from restricted suffrage to mass democracy deserve detailed scrutiny in a comparative perspective. A first attempt in this direction has been made in Norway through the establishment of a historical-ecological data archive for the period 1868–1903, from the first suffrage count until the first elections under manhood suffrage. This is discussed in S. Rokkan and F. Aarebrot's article, "The Norwegian Archive of Historical Ecological Data," in *Social Science Information* 8 (1969) as well as in their paper for the World Congress of the International Political Science Association held in Munich in September 1970—"Nation-Building, Democratization, and Mass Mobilization."

The Danes were the first to establish a regular series of electoral tabulations. The first such summary appeared in 1851 and covered the data on enfranchisement and electoral participation in the first election under near-manhood suffrage in a Northern country, the one held in 1849. The Swedes followed suit in 1873, when the Central Bureau of Statistics published the first regular volume of electoral statistics. This covered the election of 1872, the third of the elections to the bicameral Riksdag instituted in 1866—the election of 1867 had been only partially covered by the bureau, and the one in 1869 can be documented only from newspapers. In Norway there was little pressure to organize electoral statistics before the great constitutional struggles of the 1870s and 1880s. A member of the Central Bureau of Statistics, J. N. Mohn, published a first account of the elections from 1815 to 1874 just before he organized the second suffrage count in 1875. The first regular tabulations of electoral results came after the election of 1882, the last election before the extension of the suffrage. Interestingly, the records for the early period of politicization were published in two series: one by the Central Bureau, giving details on the electorate and on turnout; the other at first privately and later by parliament, giving a breakdown by the parties of the candidates. The two series were not unified until 1906: at this time the entire responsibility for production of the statistics was given to the office of the *Storting*. The final institution of electoral bookkeeping took even longer in Finland and in Iceland. The Finns published only a few scattered tables on the electoral bases of the four-estate Diet. The first regular volume of electoral statistics came out in 1909, two years after the first election under universal suffrage. In Iceland no official statistics were published until 1912: the first installment covers all the elections during the *régime censitaire* from 1874 to 1903, the next deals with the elections of 1908 and 1914, and the later ones treat one election at a time. Volume 1 of the *International Guide to Electoral Statistics,* ed. S. Rokkan and J. Meyriat (Paris: Mouton, 1969), includes chapters on the five Nordic countries and gives bibliographical details of the statistics of the early elections.

These early attempts at statistical bookkeeping were paralleled by a scattering of analytical efforts—some by academic scholars; others by experts in the central administration, the parties, and the press. A variety of subjects was covered in these analyses, but three themes seem to have attracted more attention than any others: the electoral behavior of the peasantry, the working class, and women. These themes are still of central importance in academic studies of the processes of mass democratization. Work on the early phases of political and social mobilization has gone farthest in Sweden. Gunnar Wallin analyzed the early electoral statistics in considerable detail in his *Valrörelser och valresultat: Andrakammarvalen i Sverige, 1866–1884* [Electoral campaigns and results: the elections to the Second Chamber, 1866–1884] (Stockholm: Christophers, 1961) which includes an interesting chapter on selected local results for the elections for the burgher and the peasant Estates immediately prior to the great reform. A brilliant analysis of the elections from 1890 to 1902 has been carried out by the historian Sten Carlsson in *Lantmanna politiken och industria-lismen* [The politics of the peasant party and the industrial breakthrough] (Lund: Gleerup, 1953); this is particularly important for its effort to group the candidates and the votes by party factions. Much more detailed analyses will be carried out once these early data have been made computer-readable. A major project of computerization for the data since 1887 has recently been completed at Uppsala under the direction of Leif Lewin. The data at hand do not allow parallel analyses for the early phase of mobilization in Finland. Probably the best analytical treatment of the available records is Jutikkala's detailed account, in volume 5 of the official history of the Finnish parliament, of the differences between the regions in the character of the recruitment to the Estates and in the strength of the early "counter-cultural" parties.

Parallel work is under way in Denmark and Norway. The Danish elections from 1849 to 1901 offer particularly interesting opportunities for analysis: the elections were open, and in many cases it is still possible to analyze electoral behavior directly from the individual records. Erik Høgh has recently completed a thesis based on such individual-level data for selected districts: "Dansk vælgeradfærd, 1850–1901" [Danish electoral behavior, 1850–1901] (Ph.D. diss., University of Copenhagen, 1970). This goes further in analytical detail than the corresponding study of English data from the elections before the introduction of the secret ballot, John Vincent's *Poll Books: How Victorians Voted, 1830–1872* (Cambridge: Cambridge University Press, 1966). The historian Vagn Dybdahl has used data similar to Høgh's in a study of the economic basis of the Conservative party *entitled Partier og erhverv, 1880–1913* [Parties and occupations, 1880–1913] (Aarhus: Universitetsforlaget, 1969); this goes beyond the period of open voting and covers all the elections from 1880 to 1913, the last election before proportional representation. In Norway, the archive of historical-ecological data established at the University of Bergen will allow similar analyses of the correlations between time-series data on economic, cultural, and political mobilization during this early period. So far analyses have been published at the provincial and regional levels only; see the chapter by Stein Rokkan, "Geography, Religion, and Social Class," in *Party Systems and Voter Alignments*, ed. S. M. Lipset and S. Rokkan (New York: Free Press, 1967), pp. 376–444. But a number of detailed analyses at the parish level are under way, with reports expected by 1972.

The next phases in the process of democratization, the mobilization of workers and of women, have been studied mainly by sociologists and political scientists. Much of this work has been inspired by the Norwegian historian Edvard Bull, who focuses on the impact of rapid industrialization on the radicalization of the working class and sets forth a number of hypotheses about the factors making for differences in levels of radicalization in Denmark, Sweden, and Norway in "Die Entwicklung der Arbeiterbewegung in den drei skandinavischen Ländern," *Arch. Ges. d. Sozialismus* 10 (1922): 329–61. Bull's hypotheses have recently been subjected to detailed scrutiny in a comparative analysis of data on industrialization and the response of labor by William Lafferty: *Industrialization and the Response of Labour* (Oslo: Universitetsforlaget, 1971).

Conditions for detailed research on these developments are better in Sweden than in any other country. The Swedish electoral statistics from 1909 to 1945 were organized by social groups, details on which are given in E. Janson's chapter on Sweden in volume 1 of *International Guide to Electoral Statistics*. This allows thorough analyses of turnout for men and women in the working class and makes it possible to characterize even very small electoral districts by class composition. Much remains to be done to tap the potentialities of these data. Herbert Tingsten uses only a very small part of the data in his pioneering work on *Political Behavior* (London: King, 1937; reprinted Totowa, N.J.: Bedminster, 1963). Perhaps the most sophisticated work on these time-series data has been carried out by the sociologist Gösta Carlsson in his analysis of the socioeconomic conditions for the growth of the Social Democratic party after 1909, "Partiförskjutningar som tillväxtprocesser," in *Statsvetenskaplig Tidskrift*, vol. 66, nos. 2–3 (1963), pp. 177–213. This model has been developed in greater statistical detail by Leif Lewin et al. in *Den svenska valmanskåren, 1887–1968* [The Swedish electorate, 1887–1968] (Uppsala: Institute of Political Science, 1971), but so far only at the level of the *län* (province). Attempts have recently been made to apply the Carlsson model to ecological time-series data for Denmark, Sweden, and Norway, but it will take some time before the results can be published.

In Finland, Hannu Soikkanen has carried out a very detailed study of the Socialist upsurge in 1907. Erik Allardt's factor analysis of time-series data from 1910 to 1950, summarized in his chapter with Pertti Pesonen in *Party Systems and Voter Alignments* (pp. 325–66); Onni Rantala's chapter in the same book; and Vilja Rasila's work on the rural proletariat in *Scandinavian Economic History Review* 17 (1969): 115–35 all look into a variety of factors affecting the deep splits in the Finnish working-class movement before and after the civil war. Rantala's extensive collection of tables and analyses across all elections from 1907 to 1958 in *Suomen poliittiset alueet* (Turku: Institute of Political Science, 1965) is of particular importance in this context; worthwhile, too, is his article in *Scandinavian Political Studies* 2 (1967): 117–40. Once all these data have been made machine-readable and linked with the available social, economic, and cultural statistics, they will allow far-reaching comparisons with the similar time-series files for Denmark, Norway, and Sweden. Much remains to be done to standardize these files and make them available for cooperative research; these problems will be taken up in the near future at the Nordic level and within the recently established European Consortium for Political Research.

BIBLIOGRAPHY

To the bibliographical material in the chapter itself I shall add here only some bibliographical works, some works in English, and some recently published works with comprehensive bibliographies. For additional information, see B. Schiller and B. Odén. *Statistik för historiker* (Stockholm: Almqvist & Wiksell, 1970).

HISTORIOGRAPHY

DENMARK: *Dansk historisk bibliografi.* Completed to 1947. Copenhagen: H. Hagerupsforlag, 1956.

FINLAND: *Suomen historiallinen bibliografia.* Completed to 1960. Helsinki, 1968.

ICELAND: *Ritaukaskrá landsbøkasafnsins.* Completed to 1943. Reykjavik: Rikisprentsmidjan Gutenberg, 1944.

NORWAY: *Bibliografi til Norges historie.* Published annually from 1926. Oslo: Den norske historiske forening.

SWEDEN: *Svensk historisk bibliografi.* Carried through to 1960. 1968. Later published annually. Stockholm: Svenska historiska föreningen.

STATISTICAL PUBLICATIONS

SCANDINAVIA: *Nordic Statistical Journal.* 1929–32.
Nordisk statistisk årsbok. Published since 1962.
Nordisk statistisk skriftserie. Published since 1954.
Nordisk udredningsserie. Published since 1960.
DENMARK: *Statistisk Årbog.* Includes an annual publication list of the official statistics in Denmark.
Statistiske Meddelelser.
Statistiske Undersøgelser.
Statistisk Tabelvaerk.
FINLAND: *Finlands officiella statistik.* Published in Swedish and Finnish.
Statistisk årsbok för Finland. Includes a publication list of the official statistics in Finland.
ICELAND: *Hagskýrslur Íslands.* Published since 1914.
Hagtiðindi. Published since 1916.
Statistical Bulletin. Published since 1932.
NORWAY: *Guide to Norwegian Statistics.* Oslo: Statistisk sentralbyrå, 1969.
Historisk statistikk, 1968. Oslo, 1969. Oslo: Statistisk sentralbyrå, 1969.
Norges offisielle statistikk. A publication list is included in ser. 11, vol. 63 (1951).
SWEDEN: Guinchard, J., ed. *Sweden: Historical and Statistical Handbook.* Stockholm: Norstedt, 1914.
Hofsten, E. *Vägvisare i svensk statistik.* 5th ed. Stockholm: Rabén & Sjögren, 1965.
Sveriges officiella statistik. Indexes are included in *Sveriges offentliga utredningar,* ser. 1922, no. 15, and in *Officiella statistiska publikationer.* Stockholm, 1964.

INSTITUTIONAL CONDITIONS

SCANDINAVIA: *Archivum* 8 (1958). Paris: Presses Universitaires de France, 1959.
Jörgensen, H. *Nordiske arkiver.* Copenhagen, 1968.: Arkivar-foreningen, 1968.
DENMARK: Jensen, A. "La statistique au Danemark." In *Monographies sur l'organisation de la statistique administrative dans différents pays,* 1:111–35. Paris: Institut internationale des sciences administratives, 1933.
"Samfundet og statistiken. Et historisk rids, 1769–1950." *Statistiske meddelelser* (Copenhagen), ser. 4, vol. 139, no. 1 (1949).
FINLAND: Kovero, M. "La statistique officielle de la Finlande." In *Monographies sur l'organisation de la statistique administrative dans différent pays,* 1:87–107. Paris: Institut internationale des sciences administratives, 1933.
Lindberg, V. "En reformplan för statistiken i Finland." *Statistisk tidskrift.* Stockholm, 1956.
ICELAND: Thorsteinsson, T. "Den islandske Statistiks Omfang og Vilkaar." *Statistiske Meddelelser* (Copenhagen), ser. 4, no. 64, fasc. 3 (1921).
NORWAY: "Statistisk sentralbyrå gjennom 75 år." *Norges offisielle statistik,* ser. 11, no. 65. Oslo, 1951.

SWEDEN: Arosenius, E. "The History and Organization of Swedish Official Statistics." In *The History of Statistics, their Development and Progress in Many Countries*, edited by J. Koren. New York: Macmillan, 1918.

Ottervik, G.; Möhlenbrock, S.; and Andersson, I. *Libraries and Archives in Sweden*. Stockholm: The Swedish Institute Forum, 1954.

Statistiska centralbyrån 100 år. Stockholm: Statistiska centralbyrån, 1959.

POPULATION STATISTICS

SCANDINAVIA: Gille, H. "The Demographic History of the Northern Countries in the Eighteenth Century." *Population Studies* 3 (1949–50).

Jensen, A. "Befolkningsforhold i de nordiske Lande i det 18 Aarhundrede." *Nationaløkonomisk tidsskrift* 73 (1935).

DENMARK: Agersnap, T. *Studier over indre Vandringer i Danmark*. Aarhus: Universitetsforlaget, 1952.

"Folketal, areal og klima, 1901–1960." *Statistiske undersøgelser* 10 (1960).

Lassen, A. "The Population of Denmark, 1660–1960." *Scandinavian Economic History Review* 14 (1968).

FINLAND: Jutikkala, E. "Finland's Population Movement in the Eighteenth Century." In *Population in History*, edited by D. V. Glass and D. E. C. Eversley. London: Edward Arnold, 1965.

Strömmer, A. *Väestöllinen muuntuminen Suomessa*. Helsinki: Väestöpoliittisen tutkimuslaitoksen julk, 1969.

ICELAND: "Manntalid, 1703." *Hagskýrslur Íslands*, ser. 2, no. 21 (1960).

Thorsteinsson, T. "The Census of Iceland in 1703." *Nordic Statistical Journal* 8 (1929).

NORWAY: Backer, J. E. "Population Statistics and Population Registration in Norway." *Population Studies* 1 (1948); 2 (1949).

Myklebost, H. *Norges tettbygde steder, 1875–1950*. Oslo and Bergen: Ad novas, 1960.

Sogner, S. "Historical Demography in Norway Today." *Congrès et colloques de l'Université de Liège* 33 (1965).

SWEDEN: Ahlberg, G. "Population Trends and Urbanization in Sweden, 1911–1950." *Lund Studies in Geography*, ser. B, 16. Lund, 1956.

Hyrenius, H. "Reproduction and Replacement. A Methodological Study of Swedish Population Changes during 200 Years." *Population Studies* 4 (1951).

Quensel, C. E. "Tillförlitligheten i de äldsta befintliga befolkningsdata." In *Minnesskrift med anledning av den svenska befolkningsstatistikens 200-åriga bestånd*. Stockholm: Statistiska centralbyrån, 1949.

SOCIOHISTORICAL STATISTICS

SCANDINAVIA: Carlsson, G., and Svalastoga, K. "Social Stratification and Social Mobility in Scandinavia." *Sociological Inquiry* 31 (1961).

DENMARK: Geiger, T. *Soziale Umschichtungen in einer dänischen Mittelstadt*. Aarhus: Universitetsforlagen; Copenhagen: Munksgaard, 1951.

FINLAND: Åström, S. E. "Literature on Social Mobility and Social Stratification in

Finland: Some Bibliographic Notes." *Transactions of the Westermarck Society* 2 (1953).

Holm, T. W., and Immonen, E. J. "Bibliography on Finnish Sociology." *Transactions of the Westermarck Society* 13 (1966).

Rasila, V. "The Finnish Civil War and Land Lease Problems." *Scandinavian Economic History Review* 17 (1969).

NORWAY: Allwood, M. S. *Eilert Sundt. A Pioneer in Sociology and Social Anthropology.* Oslo: Norli, 1957.

Arctander, S. "Socialstatistikkens historie i Norge gjennom hundre år, 1850–1950." *Norges offisielle statistikk*, ser. 11, no. 113. Oslo, 1952.

SWEDEN: Hofsten, E. "Socialstatistik—ett föråldrat begrepp." *Sociala meddelanden* 7–8 (1962).

Nordström, O. "Population and Labour Problems in Sweden's Depopulated Districts." *Economy and History* 5 (1962).

ECONOMIC STATISTICS AND ECONOMIC HISTORY

SCANDINAVIA: Jörberg, L. "The Industrial Revolution in Scandinavia, 1850–1914." In *The Fontana Economic History of Europe*, vol. 4. London: Collins, 1970.

Heckscher, Eli F. et al. *Sweden, Norway, Denmark, and Iceland in the World War.* New Haven: Yale University Press, 1930.

DENMARK: Bjerke, K., and Ussing, N. *Studier over Danmarks National-produkt, 1870–1950.* Copenhagen: Gad, 1958.

Milhøj, P. *Lønudviklingen i Danmark, 1914–1950.* Copenhagen: Munksgaard, 1954.

Olsen E. *Danmarks økonomiske historie siden 1750.* Copenhagen: Gad, 1962.

Pedersen, J. *Arbejdslønnen i Danmark under skiftende Konjunkturer i perioden ca. 1850–1913.* Copenhagen: Gyldendal, 1930.

Technical and Economic Changes in Danish Farming. 40 Years of Farm Records, 1917–1957. Copenhagen: Landhusholdnings-selskabet, 1959.

FINLAND: Björkqvist, H. *Exchange Rate Policy and Empirical Research Concerning Economic Growth.* Åbo: Nationalekonomiska institutionen vid Handelshögskolan, 1968.

Lindberg, V. *Suomen kansantulo vuosina, 1926–1938.* Helsinki: Akatuminen kirjakauppa, 1943.

NORWAY: "Nasjonalregnskap, 1865–1960." *Norges offisielle statistikk,* ser. 12, vol. 163. Oslo, 1968.

Steen, S. *Det gamle samfunn.* Oslo: Cappelen, 1957.

SWEDEN: Attman, A. "Ekonomisk historia." In *20 års samhällsforskning.* Stockholm: Norstedt, 1969.

Heckscher, E. F. *An Economic History of Sweden.* Cambridge, Mass.: Harvard University Press, 1954. Translated from the Swedish and abridged.

Höijer, E. "Källorna til den ekonomiska statistiken". *Statistisk tidskrift,* 1966.

Lindahl, E.; Dahlgren, E.; and Kock, K. *National Income of Sweden, 1861–1930.* Stockholm: Norstedt, 1937.

Samuelsson, K. *From Great Power to Welfare State. 300 Years of Swedish Social Development.* London: Allen and Unwin, 1968.

Söderlund, E., ed. *Swedish Timber Exports, 1850–1950.* Stockholm and London: Almqvist & Wiksell, 1952.

The Swedish Journal of Economics. Published in English since 1965.

Industrins utredningsinstitut has recently published a series of investigations on economic trends in Sweden from 1870 to 1970, conducted by Professor Ragnar Bentzel, Uppsala (Stockholm: Almqvist & Wiksell).

7

QUANTIFICATION IN THE STUDY

OF MODERN GERMAN

SOCIAL AND POLITICAL HISTORY

by James J. Sheehan

In 1916 an observer of quantitative research in Germany reported that "serious statisticians are looking with great concern on the growing 'cemetery of numbers' and the considerable overproduction of statistical data, and are demanding a further sociological penetration of the numerical mass observations." [1] A survey of the situation in 1970 suggests that there is still cause for concern. The student of German social and political history confronts an extraordinary abundance of quantitative data, but he finds a relative scarcity of sociological or historical penetrations of this material. My purpose in this chapter is to suggest some of the data available and to discuss the ways in which scholars have used these data to analyze social and political change in nineteenth- and twentieth-century Germany. At the same time, I will try to point out problems which seem particularly appropriate for quantitative research.

INTRODUCTION

The evolution of statistical inquiry in Germany is an important historical problem in itself. It is hoped that some day a study of this evolution will be undertaken that will not only facilitate research but also illuminate some important themes in German intellectual and political history. [2] At the moment it is possible only to sketch the two separate but frequently overlapping traditions within which quantitative research evolved. The

Sandra Christenson, Robert Neuman, James Roth, and Heinz Schwinge assisted me in the preparation of this chapter. It is a pleasure to be able to express my gratitude for their aid.

first tradition was developed by those academicians who gradually asserted the superiority of numerical analysis over the descriptive form of statistics popular in the eighteenth century. By the second half of the nineteenth century, statistics as an essentially quantitative enterprise was an established academic discipline, and its practitioners had begun to pick up institutional support from groups like the *Verein für Sozialpolitik*.[3] The second tradition was shaped by men within the bureaucracy who adopted statistical techniques in order to increase the state's knowledge about, and therefore its control over, social resources. This tradition naturally tended to follow the evolution of the state apparatus as a whole. In the seventeenth and eighteenth centuries, officials collected (but rarely published) data to serve their monarchs' desire for power. In the early nineteenth century the collection of data became much more systematic when special statistical bureaus were established in the most important German states. Finally, by the end of the century, the collection of statistics was carried on by a wide range of bureaucratic agencies at the national, state, and local levels.

Although the renowned assiduity of Germany's scholars and the almost notorious efficiency of her bureaucrats have generated a large amount of data, two aspects of German history have somewhat attenuated the usefulness of these materials. First, at the dramatic turning points in Germany's recent past—1871, 1918, 1933, 1945—discontinuities in the data have often been produced by shifts in the categories within which they were ordered or in the standards under which they were collected. Second, the political fragmentation of preimperial Germany and the persistence of federalism after 1871 have meant that data were compiled by a wide array of agencies; ordered according to a diverse set of categories; and stored in a number of different archives or published in a variety of periodicals, yearbooks, and special collections. The effects of this discontinuity and fragmentation limit the duration of time series and the geographical scope which are desirable for certain kinds of statistical study.

These considerations also make the location of material a difficult task. A convenient guide to the development of the various statistical agencies and a list of their publications can be found in the articles on statistics which appeared in the third edition of the *Handwörterbuch der Staatswissenschaften*.[4] For a more detailed account of the various governmental statistical offices, it is necessary to turn to their own publications and, when available, to the historical accounts of these institutions. The most distinguished of these histories are the two works on the administration of Prussian statistics by E. Blenck.[5] There is not yet a German equivalent to the compilations of historical statistics available for Britain and the United States, although the publications by Viebahn, Dieterici, Mayr, and, most recently, Hoffmann are useful collections, especially for economic data.[6] Finally, mention should be made of three general guides to statistical research compiled by Friedrich Zahn, Friedrich Burgdörfer, and Charlotte

Lorenz, which contain a great deal of information on the history, methodology, and organization of quantitative inquiry in Germany.[7]

POLITICAL BEHAVIOR

Voting behavior is the most appropriate subject with which to begin a discussion of quantitative research in political history. For those of us who must work in periods before the advent of systematically gathered survey data, election returns provide an imperfect but indispensable clue to popular attitudes. Unfortunately there has not been the kind of intensive research on German elections that has been carried on with such success in France and the United States. German historiography's traditional concern for diplomacy and intellectual trends tended to inhibit the development of electoral studies, an inhibition which was reinforced by the rather low regard for party politics long prevalent in academic circles. There are now signs that this neglect is beginning to be replaced by a new interest among German historians in parties, parliaments, and elections.[8] It is to be hoped that this interest will produce a more rigorous application of quantitative methods and a more intensive exploitation of the materials available.

Although there were representative institutions throughout Germany in the first half of the nineteenth century, there are very few quantitative data available for elections held during this period. This is not only because the records have been lost over the years but also because the conception and implementation of the electoral process tended to deemphasize its quantitative character. Indirect voting, for example, put the crucial decision-making power into the hands of a small group of electors whose face-to-face negotiations were usually not recorded.[9] This situation continued through the first national elections, held during the revolution of 1848. Theodore Hamerow has made a careful study of these elections and has pointed out both the diverse character of the supposedly equal suffrage and the scarcity of evidence on the election results. After a careful search, Hamerow was able to locate statistical evidence for only about 10 percent of the constituencies.[10]

Given the complexity and the scarcity of the evidence, it is not surprising that the most successful analyses of the 1848 elections have focused on a limited geographical area. Perhaps the most impressive of these studies is Konrad Repgen's work on the Rhineland.[11] Repgen was able to assemble a great deal of interesting information on the character of political life during the revolution, but his efforts also underscore the problems of undertaking quantitative work in this period. He found it impossible, for example, to discover the ratio of voters to representatives which was used to establish the districts for the elections to the Frankfurt Assembly. Moreover, the indistinct nature of political cleavages at the time and the significance of the candidates' personality and status combined to make it very difficult for Repgen to gauge the political meaning of the records he did uncover.

The role of personal loyalties and social status in elections continued to be important throughout the middle third of the nineteenth century, and therefore the political meaning of voting behavior—especially in elections to the electoral college in an indirect suffrage system—is often almost impossible to interpret. In Prussia, historical analysis of voting in the 1850s is further complicated by the sparseness of evidence and by the government's habit of redrawing the constituency boundaries before each election. Almost all the electoral research which does exist on the 1850s is concerned with the Rhineland; this region has been the geographical focus for a very useful series of dissertations written by students of Max Braubach at the University of Bonn.[12] As these dissertations make clear, a shift in the character of political life and in the quality of the evidence was produced by the constitutional conflict in Prussia during the early 1860s: political alignments tended to be more visible, and, as electoral activity intensified, electoral data in newspapers and government sources became relatively more available.[13] The best source for electoral behavior in Prussia during the early 1860s is Eugene Anderson's publication of the statistics gathered by the Ministry of the Interior on the elections of 1862 and 1863.[14] These data give a complete breakdown on party alignments at the county (*Kreis*) level, although their value is impaired by the rather clumsy and ill-informed manner in which many local officials reported the returns from their districts. In any event, Anderson's compilation is the best evidence available for Prussian elections until the government began publishing fairly complete results at the end of the 1890s.[15]

Although evidence on elections in Prussia and the other states is fragmentary for almost all the nineteenth century, the data on the national parliament established in 1867–71 are relatively complete and easily available.[16] When using the imperial Reichstag data, however, it is necessary to bear in mind two aspects of the system that tended to blur the accuracy with which these elections mirrored political opinion. First, the district boundaries drawn in 1867–71 were not altered to take into account the massive shifts of population to industrial regions that occurred after the formation of the Reich. Since urban areas were greatly underrepresented, the Reichstag membership only imperfectly reflected the political preferences of the nation.[17] Second, the national totals for votes received by the parties in an election are somewhat misleading indications of their relative strength, because some parties did not enter candidates in districts where their chances of winning were small, while others (especially the Social Democrats) attempted to have someone on the ballot in every district.

A more serious difficulty in working with the Reichstag data is that the parliamentary districts during the imperial era were not congruent with other governmental units. As a result, the social and economic data gathered for these units cannot be correlated with voting data. Berlin, for example, was divided into six Reichstag constituencies; none of these correspond to other governmental units, nor did the six together make up the officially defined *Stadtgebiet* Berlin, which included pieces of two other constituencies as well.[18] Perhaps archival research will uncover unpublished data on smaller electoral or administrative units which can then be aggregated. Without such data, however, quantitative work on the social basis of imperial politics is severely hampered.

Despite the difficulties inherent in the use of pre-1914 election data, these materials deserve a good deal more scholarly attention than they have thus far received. At present we have only a number of very general surveys,[19] some local studies (as for the earlier period, largely concerned with the Rhineland),[20] and a few more specialized inquiries into individual issues. In this last category, the most interesting work has been done on the origins and significance of the dramatic electoral growth of Social Democracy in the years after 1890. We are still very far from having a satisfactory statistical analysis of this problem, but the contemporary studies by Eitner on the role of religion and Blank on the social basis of the SPD suggest possible approaches to the question.[21] The most important recent historical account of the SPD which has attempted to follow some of these leads is G. A. Ritter's admirable work on the Wilhelmian labor movement.[22]

The social basis of the SPD is also a central theme of R. A. Comfort's important book on Hamburg politics during the early years of the Weimar Republic. Comfort is concerned with the Socialists' inability "to integrate the bulk of the working classes into some orderly movement favoring the continuation of the Republic." Since he was able to use congruent occupational and electoral data from archival sources, the author could employ a Spearman rank-order correlation to trace the social basis of voter participation and party alignment. He was therefore able to demonstrate the manner in which certain important social groups shifted away from the SPD into either apathy or antirepublicanism.[23]

Very few of the electoral studies on the 1920s have either the data base or the methodological sophistication which distinguishes Comfort's monograph. In addition to the usual general surveys, there are a few notable but brief analyses of the roles of women, young people, and nonvoters in Weimar elections.[24] The most impressive cluster of studies on republican voting behavior is devoted to the National Socialists' rapid rise in electoral strength during the three years before the establishment of Hitler's government in 1933. These efforts to explain the Nazis' growing support have usually emphasized their ability to attract voters from the middle classes, the youth, and the previously apolitical.[25] The most precise dissections of Nazi support can be found in books which concentrate on a single region, such as W. S. Allen's study of a Hanoverian town and G. Franz's analysis of Lower Saxony.[26] R. Heberle's work on Schleswig-Holstein deserves mention because of the way in which he combines intimate knowledge of a region with statistical expertise. Like Comfort, Heberle was able to work with unpublished data on rather small geographical units and could therefore correlate election returns with social data in order to uncover those elements within the population most responsive to the Nazis' appeals.[27]

One of the most promising approaches to the still unresolved problems of German electoral behavior is provided by the examination of local elections. In the first place, the study of elections to local bodies often makes it possible to ascertain the role of regional issues and traditions in voting, considerations of particular importance for Germany before 1945.[28] Second, a comparison of the returns for local and national elections frequently uncovers new means of measuring the origins and continuity of political alignments. This is especially true for the period before 1914, when local and national elections were carried out under different suffrage regulations.[29] Finally, the class-oriented character of the suffrage for many local parliaments created categories of voters that allow the historian to plot with some precision the social basis of political action.[30]

In addition to voting data, there is a wide range of other evidence on political behavior that is appropriate for quantitative analysis. For example, Konrad Repgen's excellent article on the political role of the Rhenish clergy in 1848 analyzes the petitions circulated during the revolution as indications of political involvement.[31] Police records are another potential mine of information which has been only infrequently exploited by historians for data on political parties, revolutionary movements, and resistance groups.[32] Moreover, party records and newspapers, protocols, and other publications often contain material on the size and composition of political organizations.[33] Robert Michels' article on the Social Democrats in 1906 is a brilliant example of the ways in which such material can be used.[34] Another example can be found in Hans Gerth's famous essay on the Nazi Party, which is a model of the use of quantitative data in an analysis of political phenomena.[35] In addition to party records, there is evidence available on the nature and composition of interest groups, which became an important source of political expression in the late nineteenth century.[36]

Finally, valuable material on the development of political attitudes and behavior can be found in the history of journalism. Unfortunately, there are very few statistical studies of newspaper circulation, although this problem is obviously a fruitful one for quantitative examination.[37] Similarly, quantitative studies are needed on the profession of journalism, its role in the formation of opinion, and the ways in which its evolution reflected changes in the character of the reading public. Rolf Engelsing's work on the press in Bremen is a suggestive start in this direction.[38]

ELITES

Traditionally, German historians have been more interested in elites than in voting behavior or political organizations. Many historical analyses of elites, however, have not attempted to use quantitative methods, even when these methods seemed most appropriate. Take for example the study of Rhenish entrepreneurs by Friedrich Zunkel, in which the author continually refers to "many," "some," or "a few" entrepreneurs but does not tell us either numerical absolute or relative ranges of these words or the basis on which he made the essentially quantitative distinctions among them.[39] A more striking example is Fritz Peters's recent work on the Bremen Senate. Peters presents a chronologically arranged list of 134 senators with a brief résumé of their social origins, careers, and political affiliations. He does not, however, present any aggregative tabulations. Without such tabulations the reader has no way to ascertain the social character of the group and the lines of its historical change. As anything other than a chatty collective biography, therefore, Peters's book is useless.[40]

Quantification is an important element in the study of elites, not only because it can give precision and order to the data, but also because it enables historians to penetrate and exploit the extraordinarily abundant supply of evidence on social and political leaders in the nineteenth and twentieth centuries. Some of this evidence—e.g., personnel records, business files, and police records—is difficult to obtain. But a great deal of material is readily available in various reference works and source collections. I will mention some of these sources in my discussion of various elite groups. Of general interest are works like Wilhelm Kosch's *Biographisches Staats-handbuch* (1959–), the *Neue deutsche Biographie* (1952–), and a number of series devoted to famous men from particular regions.[41] A rather inexpensive way of encouraging quantitative analysis of social and political history would be to put the information from these works in machine-readable form and to make them available in a data archive, which could then serve as a depository for evidence on elites collected by other scholars.[42]

The persistence of the sociopolitical power of the aristocracy is one of the central facts of modern German history, and it has been a subject of importance for both contemporaries and historians. Although the quantity of the material available still overshadows the amount of historical research, there have been some important studies of the nobility's role in German social, economic, and political life.[43] A great deal of fascinating statistical material on the changing position of the eighteenth century aristocracy can be found in the older monographs of Johannes Ziekursch and Fritz Martiny and in the more recent study of Prussia by Reinhart Koselleck,

Preussen zwischen Reform und Revolution.[44] For the nineteenth century, one can turn to the contemporary analyses by Max Weber and Johannes Conrad, whose points of departure were established by the political controversy surrounding entailed estates at the turn of the century.[45]

Another subject of both political controversy and scholarly concern has been the role of the aristocracy in the bureaucratic and military apparatus. This problem is examined for eighteenth-century Hanover by Joachim Lampe, who provides quantitative data on the administration and on the taxonomy of the Hanoverian nobility.[46] Walter Schärl has traced the participation of the aristocracy in the bureaucracy of nineteenth-century Bavaria.[47] In *Preussen zwischen Reform und Revolution,* Koselleck suggests the range and depth of the data available by his statistical analysis of the early-nineteenth-century Prussian administration and the function of a bureaucratic career as a means of attaining aristocratic status.[48] A somewhat more detailed analysis of these themes in the years 1794–1806 can be found in a recent article by Henning von Bonin.[49] For the later period there are a number of monographs on administrative institutions, many of which provide brief statistical summaries of the officials' social origins and status.[50] The best data on the aristocracy in the army are to be found in Karl Demeter's classic account of the officer corps, which can be supplemented with a few more specialized studies.[51]

The two most extensive analyses of the aristocracy in the pre-1914 state apparatus are Lysbeth Muncy's *The Junker in the Prussian Administration under William II, 1888–1914* (Providence, R.I.: Brown University Press, 1944) and Nikolaus von Preradovich's *Die Führungsschichten in Österreich und Preussen, 1804–1918* (Wiesbaden: Steiner, 1955). Muncy has studied 1,500 officeholders from over 600 "Junker" families and thereby succeeds in providing statistical data on career patterns, landholding, and marriage and family relationships from an unusually wide sample. Preradovich, on the other hand, is interested in the position of the aristocracy in top-level leadership posts for selected years betwen 1804 and 1918. Although his work is far less illuminating than Muncy's in most ways, Preradovich does demonstrate the advantage of a comparative dimension for isolating and evaluating the most salient features of an elite group.

The most valuable recent studies of the bureaucracy as an institution have focused on the development of the administration in a particular region; examples of these are F. Schaer's study of Aurich, D. Wegmann's of Westphalia, August Klein's of Cologne, Peter Letkemann's of Danzig, and K. Rehfeld and Irene Berger's of Bromberg.[52] All these books contain some statistical material, but they are much more concerned with providing biographical narratives on the best-known officials in their districts. It is a measure of the lack of methodological progress in much of German historiography that none of these authors goes beyond the kind of analysis offered by Johannes Ziekursch in his 1907 study of Silesian officials.[53]

Of somewhat greater methodological interest are the studies of the impact on the bureaucracy of the great political unheavals in 1918, 1933, and 1945. Wolfgang Zapf's work on German *Führungsgruppen* since 1919 has some stimulating insights concerning long-run trends in the evolution of the administration.[54] The impact of the abortive revolution of 1918 on the state machinery is examined in recent works by Wolfgang Runge and Hans-Karl Behrend.[55] Hans Gerth's article on the Nazi party contains some remarks on the leadership of this regime, whereas Lewis Edinger has examined continuities and changes in the social background and political character of decision makers after the collapse of the Third Reich.[56] Also of interest on political elites in twentieth-century Germany is Daniel Lerner's study of the 1934 *Führerlexikon*.[57] Lerner is quite resourceful in suggesting correlations from his data. Unfortunately, the usefulness of his conclusions is diminished by two important difficulties: the *Führerlexikon* is a very poor data base, since it is by no means a list of the "Nazi elite"; and Lerner employs a number of categories in ordering his material ("plebians," "middle income skill groups," etc.) which have little meaning for German social history.

Until now most studies of the army and the bureaucracy have tended to emphasize the social composition and political behavior of those at the top. It is to be hoped that soon more attention will be paid to lower-ranking officials, subalterns, and noncommissioned officers. These men might have been less colorful figures than their superiors, but they played key roles in their institutions, roles we know almost nothing about. Otto Most's fascinating study of an imperial administrative district is one of the few examples of an attempt to probe into the social and economic position of the bureaucracy's lower ranks.[58] Closely related to the problems of secondary leadership groups is the question of the growth of governmental institutions in both size and social relevance. Two recent works on the development of government employment and expenditure open up new and highly significant areas for research.[59]

There is more evidence on the men elected to representative institutions in the first half of the nineteenth century than there is on the elections themselves. Koselleck, for example, was able to assemble statistics on the role of officials in the Prussian provincial Landtag during the 1830s and in the United Landtag of 1847.[60] Some data are also available on the parliamentarians in other German states during the Vormärz era.[61] More extensive, if by no means complete, information can be established for the social composition of the revolutionary parliaments and for the most important state Landtage in the preimperial period.[62] It is also possible to get some notion of the dynamics of political leadership on the local level by considering occupational data on the electoral colleges compiled in the local voting studies cited above.[63]

For the period after 1871 the quantity of evidence increases significantly. These data have been exploited in a number of monographic studies of the imperial era which are largely concerned with the changing occupational composition of the Reichstag.[64] These studies illustrate the kinds of problems involved in using the data available on parliamentary elites: first, most of the authors use the parliamentarian's own designation of his occupation, even though this designation frequently gave only the individual's most prestigious or politically useful role, not his main occupation; second, most authors make no provision for multiple occupations, even though some combinations (official and landowner, for example) are highly significant; finally, and most important, the authors do not provide precise definitions of the categories they employ, nor do they make clear the bases of these assignments of various individuals to certain categories. As a result of these difficulties, most of the Reichstag studies have gone over the same evidence for essentially the same purpose but have come up with different results. Take for example the following figures on the percentage of businessmen in the Reichstag of 1893: [65]

Rosenbaum	16.2
Borell	16.2
Kremer	12.1
Molt	11.5
Jaeger	22.8

The best examples of works which confront and to some degree overcome these difficulties are provided by the more specialized studies of individual parties such as Lenore O'Boyle's articles on the Liberals and Erich Matthias and Eberhard Pikart's discussion of the Socialists' Reichstag delegation.[66]

A great deal more work needs to be done on the social composition of German representative institutions. The members' social origins (as opposed to their occupations) are rarely discussed in the literature, but knowledge of those origins would be useful in considering the problem of political channels for upward social mobility. Moreover, there has been no sustained work done on the Weimar parliaments, despite the existence of a great deal of appropriate evidence.[67] Finally, there is a need for studies of parliamentary elites in local representative assemblies, which would illuminate both the political makeup of regions, and the relationship between political power and the communities' social, economic, and religious character.[68]

Business leaders have not received the kind of historical attention given to aristocrats, officials, or even parliamentarians. In the last few years, however, there are signs that historians are becoming more concerned about the economic elites. The creation of a periodical (*Tradition*) devoted primarily to the exploits of entrepreneurs and the publication of a number of biographical collections testify to the scholarly interest now commanded by this group.[69] Unfortunately, little of this new research utilizes the abundant data available for quantitative analysis. For example, the *Adressbuch der Direktoren und Aufsichtsratsmitglieder der Aktiengesellschaften*, which began publication in 1898, is a rich source of information on business leaders that could best be analysed in a machine-readable edition. Such an edition would have the added advantage of being easily supplemented with material from other business handbooks, yearly publications, and the like.[70]

Further possibilities for research on business leaders can be suggested by considering a few studies which do employ quantitative methods for an analysis of the economic elite. Horst Beau has studied 400 early-nineteenth-century entrepreneurs from the Rhineland in order to ascertain the relationship between their theoretical training and their practical experience, a problem of considerable importance for understanding the role of education and technology in economic development and the position of the entrepreneur in society.[71] It would be most useful to have an analysis carrying Beau's themes beyond the end of the nineteenth century. Another problem of immediate importance concerns the distinctions which must be made within the business community. Helga Nussbaum's monograph on the opposition to monopolization among businessmen is a suggestive beginning which demonstrates how even the crude data in the occupational censuses can be fruitful used.[72] The complexity of the business community in Germany also emerges in Hans Jaeger's work on entrepreneurs' political activity during the Wilhelmian era,[73] a book which is especially useful for the statistics it presents on the role of economic leaders in representative institutions between 1890 and 1918.

Jürgen Kocka's study of the Siemens' firm is without question the most important contribution to our understanding of economic leadership to be published since 1945.[74] Kocka studied not only the leading members of the managerial elite in this firm but also analyzed the evolution of an industrial bureaucracy. His data on their social backgrounds, wages, education, and working habits are of great interest to anyone interested in the social history of industrial societies.

One of the features of German society is the importance of education as a cultural norm and as an agent of social stratification. Studies of educational leaders, therefore, take us into an area close to the heart of the German social and value systems. Recent works by Fritz Ringer and Wolfgang Zorn provide helpful introductions to the elite of *Bildung* and summarize some of the most important statistical data about them.[75] A more detailed collection of data on the social origins of German professors can be obtained in the recent work of Christian von Ferber. Information on social origins as well as on career patterns is provided in the fascinating statistical analyses of the lower ranks of the academic profession by Franz Eulenburg and Alexander Busch.[76]

Not only the professors but also the students can be analyzed with the statistical material at hand.[77] However, even the best of the works which use this material, such as Albert Rienhardt's study of university students in Württemberg,[78] do little more than compile and organize the data. Additional analysis of these materials is necessary to uncover the significance of the changes they record for German intellectual life as well as for patterns of stratification in German society.[79] At the same time, it is to be hoped that scholars will pursue in more detail the relationship between the social and economic position of university students and their political behavior, a problem of particular importance for the interwar period.[80]

In the study of elites, as in the study of political behavior, we need to know a great deal more about the character of specific groups and regions. In both problem areas, however, it is necessary to place specific studies within as wide a perspective as possible. Just as voting in a single region can be fully understood only if seen in relationship to a wider pattern of voting behavior, so various segments of the German leadership must be seen in relationship to one another. For example, the changing role of ascriptive status, of wealth, and of education in the acquisition of political power can best be seen if we have a means of comparing the development of the aristocratic, economic, and educational elites. I have already suggested that the creation of a data bank might be one way of facilitating cooperative efforts at closing the gap between micro- and macroanalysis. Equally important is the definition of those variables which are most relevant for understanding elites. In this regard it seems to me that the work by Wolfgang Zapf cited above is especially relevant.[81] Unlike the overwhelming majority of those who study elites, Zapf tries systematically and explicitly to formulate categories necessary for analysis of the relationship of elites to one another and to the social structure.

QUANTITATIVE DATA ON SOCIAL HISTORY

The quantitative research on the nature and relationships of social groups in modern German history is much more difficult to summarize than the comparable material on political behavior and elites. This discussion of "social data," therefore, must necessarily be more impressionistic and less inclusive than the preceding sections. I will make no effort to survey a field where the literature is as diffuse as the subject itself; rather, I will call attention to a few interpretations which suggest important sources of data or point to significant areas for future research.

We can begin by considering the quantitative work on stratification.

The obvious difficulty here, which no work on the subject fully overcomes, is that a number of the agents of stratification—status, tradition, influence—are simply not susceptible to quantitative measurements. Thus one must try to construct from evidence on taxes, voting qualifications, and occupations a social hierarchy of which these data are at best an imperfect reflection. Added to this basic problem is the fact that the existing data are often fragmentary and therefore reliable only for a rather narrow chronological or spatial unit. So it is not surprising that the most successful efforts at establishing a rough quantitative picture of social hierarchies focus on a limited region. Notable among these are Pierre Ayçoberry's recent article on Cologne and Wolfgang Köllmann's monograph on Barmen, studies which combine an intimate knowledge of local conditions with a sure grasp of methodological problems posed by the data.[82] The availability of evidence on stratification for other parts of Germany is discussed in some of the electoral studies of the Rhineland cited above and in the sociological monographs recently published by G. Wurzbacher, R. Pflaum, E. W. Buchholz, Helmuth Croon, and K. Utermann.[83]

The evidential and methodological problems involved in the quantitative study of stratification are especially intractable for the twentieth century, when the complexity of society seems to defy accurate measurement. These problems emerge clearly in Theodor Geiger's classic, *Die soziale Schichtung des deutschen Volkes* (Stuttgart: Enke, 1932), perhaps the most ambitious effort to provide a statistical analysis of the German social structure.[84] Geiger based his work on the 1925 occupational census, which proved to be a rather unsatisfactory foundation. In the first place, the occupational categories used in 1925 were so different from those in earlier censuses that a developmental analysis was impossible. Second and more important, Geiger was not able to determine from the occupational categories a picture of social hierarchies, because the categories did not yield complete information on the distribution of wealth and status, the two most important indicators of social position. As a result, Geiger's ingenious calculations remain unconvincing. His book is filled with suggestive insights, but in the end they are not organically related to the quantitative analysis.

Although the census data may not be sufficient to support a project as ambitious as Geiger's, they are extremely useful in tackling other problems in social history.[85] Karl Heinrich Rieker, for example, has provided some interesting material on the changing structure of German industry after 1875 by comparing census data on the size and number of enterprises in the industrial sector.[86] Some fascinating technical and conceptual questions of comparative social and economic history are suggested by the discussion of census materials in the well-known exchange between Alexander Gerschenkron and David Landes on social values and economic growth.[87] E. A. Wrigley's excellent monograph on economic change and population growth in northwestern Europe provides an all-too-rare example of the value of using census and demographic data from more than one nation to illuminate transnational regional problems of great substantive and methodological import.[88]

Probably the most extensive use of the census material for German social history has been concerned with the movement of the population from rural to urban areas, from the agricultural to the industrial sector. Notable here are Wolfgang Köllmann's analysis of the 1907 census, which focuses on the pattern of movement to German cities, and Peter Quante's study of the decline of the numbers of agricultural workers.[89] Quante's monograph is especially useful for its discussion of early-nineteenth-century data and for its stimulating treatment of the general methodological problems involved in the study of demography and migration. Population growth and movement are also treated in Rudolf Heberle and F. Meyer's study of urbanization, which provides a valuable analysis of the *Meldestatistiken,* another important source of information on population shifts.[90]

Unfortunately, historical demography in Germany does not have the institutional support provided by either the Institut National d'Etudes Demographiques in France or the Cambridge Group for the History of Population and Social Structure in Britain.[91] Nevertheless, Köllmann and a few other scholars are making some progress in this vital field.[92] For the demography of the precensus era, Hans Mauersberg, in a recent set of urban studies, analyzes some of the evidential problems.[93] Some pioneering work on nineteenth-century demography has recently been published by John Knodel, who studied the consequences of legislative restrictions on marriage and of infant mortality on fertility and population growth.[94] Also relevant for the problem of legislation and population are David Glass and Dudley Kirk's accounts of the National Socialists' pronatalist policies.[95] Another aspect of the general problem of population growth and movement is emigration. Although there are some important difficulties involved in using emigration data—one cannot, for example, ascertain how many people went illegally and therefore were unrecorded, or how many registered to go but did not leave—a good deal of quantitative evidence does exist.[96] Mack Walker's monograph on the emigration and German society from 1816 to 1885 suggests the way in which these data can provide insights on broader patterns of social and political change.[97]

We can now turn to a consideration of the uses of quantitative data in the study of various social groups. Here the material is especially fragmentary and the need for further work acute. As the following paragraphs will suggest, we now have enough research to expose the emptiness of the old clichés about German social history but not to form the basis for a great many new generalizations. The following discussion will also make clear how much of our knowledge is derived from the research of contemporaries in the pre-1933 period and how relatively little use has been made of this work recently.[98]

Scholars interested in quantitative research on the evolution of rural social groups must still look back to such classic studies as that of Georg Friedrich Knapp, whose work first illuminated the changes produced in peasant life by social, economic, and political developments during the early nineteenth century.[99] Similarly, work on the latter half of the century must begin by considering the statistical material gathered during the imperial period by Theodor von der Goltz, Gottlieb Schnapper-Arndt, and those researchers whose monographs were published under the auspices of the *Verein für Sozialpolitik*.[100] More recent work on nineteenth-century rural life has been done by Hans Linde, who examines the crisis of the village community created by the demographic and economic pressures of an industrial society. This crisis is also the subject of an excellent monograph by Ernst Buchholz, who uses statistical data on Braunschweig as the basis for his analysis of social relationships in the countryside during the early nineteenth century.[101]

For the social history of artisans and factory workers during the nineteenth century, we must mine the data in classics like Gustav Schmoller's analysis, a century ago, of the Württemberg statistics.[102] For these groups, as for the peasantry, the *Verein für Sozialpolitik* monographs contain a wealth of valuable quantitative data.[103] A useful guide to the archival evidence on artisans and workers can be found in Horst Krüger's monograph on manufacturing in Prussia and in Karl Erich Born's most recent work on the evolution of governmental policy toward the so-called *Soziale Frage* before 1914.[104]

Much of the recent research on the urban lower classes has been concerned with wages and living costs. Antje Kraus, for example, has studied the income and expenses of the lower classes in Hamburg from the 1780s to the 1840s; she concludes that approximately 80 percent of that city's population lived close to the margin of survival.[105] In addition to studies of wages and levels of living, there has been some recent quantitative research concerning labor unrest, especially strikes and lockouts. For these subjects the data are fairly extensive but sometimes quite unreliable. We badly need, therefore, a critical edition of strike and lockout statistics in which the official material—frequently gathered by the police—is checked with other sources.[106] It is much more difficult to acquire statistical evidence on other aspects of industrial relations such as the rates of turnover, promotion, work loads, and the like. Only for the mining industry do we have a cluster of research which provides us with some insights into these important human interactions in German industry.[107]

During the 1920s two other issues became of great contemporary concern and thereby received some highly useful quantitative attention. The first of these was the rise and plight of the so-called new middle class of white collar employees, whose political mobilization in the twenties helped to sustain right-wing movements opposed to the Republic.[108] The second issue was that of social ascent and descent, a subject whose popularity reflected the generally restless and unstable social context of the Weimar era.[109]

For the period from 1933 to 1945, one is faced with the absence of those contemporary social inquiries which so illuminate nineteenth- and early-twentieth-century social history. Moreover, the character of the regime does not inspire confidence in the reliability of official statistics, whose value is further compromised by the frequent shifts in the meaning of statistical categories after 1933. Nevertheless, a large amount of potentially useful information does exist on German social history during the Nazi era. We are now fortunate to have David Schoenbaum's study of *Hitler's Social Revolution,* which points up a number of important problems in the social history of the period and also cites some of the most important evidence available for future research.[110]

DATA ON SUICIDE, CRIME, SEXUAL BEHAVIOR, AND RELIGION

During the nineteenth century, suicide, crime, and sexual behavior were among the problems most frequently studied by statisticians, who hoped to formulate a numerical science of moral life.[111] Unfortunately, historians have shown little interest in either the data or the problems which fascinated these "moral statisticians" before 1914. Perhaps a new concern for the quantitative study of social history will engender a willingness to examine historically these usually ignored facets of life.

Historians who seek to study these issues quantitatively must confront a fact frequently overlooked by the practitioners of moral statistics: the study of suicide, crime, and sexual behavior requires the use of public statistics to explore the most private regions of human experience. The difficulties involved in this enterprise can be illustrated by considering the problem of suicide, a subject of great interest to scholars like Emile Durkheim and Ferdinand Tönnies, who were convinced that suicide was a social phenomenon which could be correlated with data on other aspects of social life.[112] These correlations, they believed, could then be used to provide quantitative measurements of the differences in the quality of life among various social groups. More specifically, both Tönnies and Durkheim argued that suicide rates would uncover the damaging psychological effects of urbanization. Unfortunately, the data were not appropriate for this kind of theorizing. For example, the long-time series on suicide in Germany created from the official statistics by Durkheim rests upon his mistaken assumption that changes in the rate reflect changes in the frequency of the phenomenon; in fact, the most dramatic changes were caused by shifts in the methods of collecting the data.[113] Moreover, it is impossible to establish whether the differences in the suicide rate between the city and the countryside reflect differences in the rates of occurrence or in the pressures and opportunities for concealment of the occurrence.[114] Many similar difficulties can be found in the use of crime statistics, which are also highly subject to problems of concealment and categorization. Thus fluctuations in the crime rate may merely record changes in the efficiency of the recording mechanism, not changes in the volume of criminal activity.[115]

The character of the evidence on suicide and crime certainly makes the ambitious efforts of the early moral statisticians less than convincing. The quality of the data does not, however, preclude more limited and cautious research. Mortiz Liepmann, for example, shows great care in dealing with the statistics on wartime criminality, which he used as the basis for some highly interesting hypotheses on the character of social relationships in Germany between 1914 and 1918.[116] There is enough of value in Liepmann's monograph to inspire hope that we will have similar studies for comparable periods in German history.

Data on sexual behavior—or, more accurately, on sexual misbehavior, since this is what is usually measured—are of course beset by the same problems as the material on suicide and crime. Indeed, in dealing with subjects like illegitimacy, prostitution, and venereal disease, the pressure and possibility for concealment and the dangers of inappropriate categorization are probably greater than in any other field of social statistics.[117] Nevertheless, there is a great deal of evidence on these matters, including a few primitive surveys, which could be expressed in quantitative form.[118] Surely if one recognizes the importance of sexual behavior as a subject of historical research, these data—with all their faults—are less misleading than the scattered literary references which are customarily employed to discuss changes in the so-called moral climate.

Despite the obvious importance of religion for German social and cultural life during the period under consideration, historians have paid very little attention to the evolution of religious practice or to the functions of churches as social institutions. We do not know, for example, how the frequency or intensity of religious practice changed over time, nor how it varied from one region to another and from one social group to another. The evidential problems here are great, but data do exist. For some regions, at least, there are scattered statistics on the numbers of communicants. Moreover, there are indications that archival research might be able to take advantage of the government's interest in the ratio between births and baptisms and between civil marriages and church weddings.[119]

Although there are a few older studies of the religious behavior of social groups—especially factory workers [120]—most of the research devoted to a statistical study of religion has concerned the relationship between religious affiliation and education, occupation, and political orientation. One of the earliest of such efforts is Martin Offenbacher's analysis of the religious statistics of Baden, which served as a point of departure for Max Weber's famous thesis on the relationship of capitalism and ascetic Protestantism.[121] More recently, Annemarie Burger has published a valuable but rather uncritical synthesis of the data available on religion, occupation, political behavior, and so on.[122] Her bibliography is the best place to look for a guide to this literature.

It is unnecessary to conclude this chapter with a prolonged appeal for a wider use of quantitative data by students of German political and social history. There are signs that such an appeal would be both redundant and superfluous; even that bastion of conventional historiography, the *Historische Zeitschrift,* has recently published an essay on the value of the computer in historical research.[123] This essay will have performed its function if it succeeds in demonstrating the wealth of data available, not only for the analysis of traditional historical problems, but also for the illumination of facets of the human experience that have been too long ignored by historians.

NOTES

1   Quoted in A. Oberschall, *Empirical Social Research in Germany, 1848–1914* (The Hague: Mouton, 1965), p. 141.
2   A very suggestive sketch of the intellectual origins of statistical investigation is given in P. F. Lazarsfeld, "Notes on the History of Quantification in Sociology—Trends, Sources, and Problems," *Isis* 52 (1961): 277–333. For German developments, see the still useful classic by August Meitzen, *History, Theory, and Technique of Statistics* (Philadelphia: American Academy, 1891); this was translated from a work published in 1886.
3   The best guide to statistical work in the eighteenth and early nineteenth century is Magdalene Humpert, *Bibliographie der Kameralwissenschaften* (Cologne: K. Schroeder, 1937), esp. pp. 991–1005. On the later period see the remarks in Oberschall, *Empirical Social Research.*
4   *Handwörterbuch der Staatswissenschaften,* 3d ed. (Jena: Fischer, 1906), esp. 7:824–58. See also the useful article by Carl Reichel, "Die Statistik des Deutschen Reiches und der grösseren Staaten desselben," *Schmollers Jahrbuch* 1 (1877): 339–62, on the Reich, 537–76, on Prussia; 2 (1878): 142–215, on Bavaria, Saxony, Württemberg, Baden, Hesse, Alsace-Lorraine.
5   E. Blenck, *Das königliche statistische Bureau in Berlin beim Eintritte in sein neuntes Jahrzehnt* (Berlin: Königliches Statistisches Bureau, 1885); idem, *Das königliche statistische Bureau, 1885–1896* (Berlin: Königliches Statistisches Bureau, 1898). See also Blenck's *Festschrift des königlichen Preussischen statistischen Bureaus,* 2 vols. (Berlin: Königliches Statistisches Bureau, 1905). For Prussian statistics before 1805, see Otto Behre, *Geschichte der Statistik in Brandenburg-Preussen bis zur Gründung des königlichen statistischen Bureaus* (Berlin: C. Heymann, 1905). For the latter half of the nineteenth century, important Prussian data appeared in the

Bureau's *Zeitschrift*, which has an index covering 1861–1912 following vol. 56 (1916). Most other states and some major cities had both a periodical publication and a centennial history.

In addition to these guides, each region of Germany has its own bibliographical compilation. Most of the works cited in these compilations are concerned with the earlier periods of local history, and most are rather narrow in scope. The guides are worth checking, however, for some problems of social and political history. A complete list of these local bibliographies can be found in R. Oberschelp, *Die Bibliographien zur deutschen Landesgeschichte und Landeskunde im 19. und 20. Jahrhundert* (Frankfurt: Klostermann, 1967).

For the period after 1871 the most important single source of quantitative data is the imperial statistical series, which contains electoral and census material as well as routinely published statistics on trade, population, emigration, and crime. The most convenient way to use this series is with the index published in the Imperial Statistical Office's *Jahrbuch*. Since the index is cumulative, the most complete one for the pre-1945 era appeared in the *Jahrbuch* for 1941–42 (p. xix–xlx). Sometimes there are also interesting statistics in the official publications of the various governmental agencies. See, for example, *Ministerialblatt für die gesammte innere Verwaltung in den königlich preussichen Staaten* (1840–); *Verwaltungsberichte des Ministers für Handel, Gewerbe, und öffentliche Arbeiten* (1855–).

6   G. von Viebahn, *Statistik des zollvereinten und nördlichen Deutschlands* (Berlin: Reimer, 1858–68); C. F. W. Dieterici, *Statistische Übersicht der wichtigsten Gegenstände des Verkehrs und Verbrauchs im Preussischen Staate und im Deutschen Zollverbande in dem Zeitraume von 1831 bis 1836* (with 5 supplements to 1853) (Berlin, Posen, Bromberg: E. Mittler, 1838–57) (on Dieterici, see the remarks in D. Rohr, *The Origins of Social Liberalism in Germany* [Chicago and London: University of Chicago Press, 1963], pp. 72 ff.); G. von Mayr, *Statistik und Gesellschaftslehre*, 3 vols. (Freiburg: J. C. B. Mohr, 1895–1917) (on von Mayr, see Oberschall, *Empirical Social Research*, pp. 51 f.); W. Hoffmann, *Das Wachstum der deutschen Wirtschaft seit der Mitte des 19. Jahrhunderts* (Berlin, Heidelberg, New York: Springer, 1965).

7   F. Zahn, ed., *Die Statistik in Deutschland nach ihrem heutigen Stand*, 2 vols. (Munich and Berlin: J. Schweitzer, 1911); F. Burgdörfer, ed. *Die Statistik in Deutschland nach ihrem heutigen Stand. Ehrengabe für Friedrich Zahn*, 2 vols. (Berlin: P. Schmidt, 1940); C. Lorenz, *Forschungslehre der Sozialstatistik*, 3 vols. (Berlin: Duncker and Humblot, 1951–64). See also Lorenz's article in the tenth edition of Dahlmann-Waitz, *Quellenkunde der deutschen Geschichte*, part 23 (1968).

8   See W. Abendroth, "Aufgaben und Methoden einer deutschen historischen Wahlsoziologie," *Vierteljahreshefte für Zeitgeschichte* 3 (1957); W. Conze, "Wahlsoziologie und Parteigeschichte," *Aus Geschichte und Politik* (Düsseldorf: Droste, 1954); N. Diederich, *Empirische Wahlforschung: Konzeptionen und Methoden* (Cologne and Opladen: Westdeutscher Verlag, 1965). The most recent guide to election data is Jean Meyriat and Stein Rokkan, eds., *International Guide to Electoral Statistics* (The Hague: Mouton, 1969), vol. 1. Also of value is B. Vogel, D. Nohlen, and R.-O. Schultze, *Wahlen in Deutschland. Theorie, Geschichte, Dokumente, 1848–1970* (Berlin: de Gruyter, 1971).

9   For a discussion of the conception of the suffrage in this era, see H. Boberach, *Wahlrechtsfrage im Vormärz: Die Wahlrechtsanschauung im Rheinland 1815–1849 und die Entstehung des Dreiklassenwahlrechts* (Düsseldorf: Droste, 1959).

10 T. Hamerow, "The Election to the Frankfurt Parliament," *Journal of Modern History* 33 (1961): 15–32. See also Frank Eyck, *The Frankfurt Parliament* (London: Macmillan, 1968), pp. 57 ff.

11 K. Repgen, *Märzbewegung und Maiwahlen des Revolutionsjahres 1848 im Rheinland* (Bonn: Röhrscheid, 1955). For electoral data on the revolutionary period, see also W. Hütterman, *Parteipolitisches Leben in Westfalen vom Beginn der Märzbewegung 1848 bis zum Einsetzen der Reaktion 1849* (diss., Münster, 1910); H. Kessler, *Politische Bewegungen in Nördlingen und dem bayerischen Ries während der deutschen Revolution 1848/49*, Münchener historische Abhandlungen, Erste Reihe, no. 15 (1939); R. Noack, *Die Revolutionsbewegung von 1848/49 in der Saargegend* (diss., Frankfurt,

1929); H. Pahl, *Hamburg und das Problem einer deutschen Wirtschaftseinheit im Frankfurter Parlament, 1848–49* (Hamburg: Broscheck, 1930); J. Philippson, *Über den Ursprung und die Einführung des allgemeinen gleichen Wahlrechts in Deutschland mit besonderer Berücksichtigung der Wahlen zum Frankfurt Parlament im Grossherzogtum Baden* (Baden and Leipzig: W. Rothschild, 1913); V. Valentin, *Frankfurt-am-Main und die Revolution von 1848–49* (Stuttgart and Berlin: Cotta, 1908).

12 Three works by Max Braubach's students have recently been published: R. Kaiser, *Die politischen Strömungen in den Kreisen Bonn und Rheinbach, 1848–1878* (Bonn: Röhrscheid, 1963); O. Röttges, *Die politischen Wahlen in den linksrheinischen Kreisen des Regierungsbezirkes Düsseldorf, 1848–1867* (Kempen/Niederrhein: Landkreis Kempen-Krefeld, 1964); and H. Schierbaum, *Die politischen Wahlen in den Eifel-und Moselkreisen des Regierungsbezirkes Trier, 1849–1867* (Düsseldorf: Droste, 1960). A guide to the unpublished dissertations and other electoral studies of the Rhineland can be found in K. Müller, "Das Rheinland als Gegenstand der historischen Wahlsoziologie," *Annalen des historischen Vereins für den Niederrhein* 9 (1965): 124–42.

13 Röttges, pp. 275–76; Schierbaum, p. 179.

14 E. N. Anderson, *The Prussian Election Statistics, 1862 and 1863* (Lincoln, Nebr.: University of Nebraska Press, 1954). Some of the problems involved in using these data are suggested by Anderson's discovery that "the number of electors given in the manuscripts [from the Ministry files] does not agree in about one-third of the instances with that of the published tables" (p. xi).

15 The best guide to the location and the contents of the Prussian electoral data is the summary published with the results of the elections of 1908 in *Zeitschrift des königlichen Preussischen statistischen Landesamts*, Ergänzungsheft 30 (1909).

16 Imperial election data are published with the Reich statistics (see n. 5 above). Data are given for each constituency on the number of eligible voters, votes cast, party alignments, and religion. A breakdown on urban and rural regions is also given. A summary of these data up to 1907 can be found in F. Specht and P. Schwabe, *Die Reichstagswahlen, 1867–1907*, 3d ed. (Berlin: C. Heymann, 1908).

17 In 1912, for example, one delegate represented a district with about 19,000 voters, another a district with 329,000.

18 See the remarks on this problem in A. Braun, "Die Elemente der Statistik der deutschen Reichstagswahlen," *Neue Zeit* 21 (1903): 412–14.

19 The most recent general analysis is an essay by Peter Molt on elections since 1871, which is published in E. Faul, ed., *Wahlen und Wähler in Westdeutschland* (Villingen: Ring, 1960). Notable among the older works are A. Böck, *Die Berufsgliederung der Reichstagswahlkrise* (Meiningen: Th. Otto, 1911), which provides a useful list of Reichstag districts; A. Dix, *Die deutschen Reichstagswahlen 1871–1930 und die Wandlungen der Volksgliederung* (Tübingen: J. C. B. Mohr, 1930); H. Gabler, *Die Entwicklung der deutschen Parteien auf landschaftlicher Grundlage von 1871–1912* (diss., Berlin, 1934). The two best studies of individual elections contain a summary of the results but are basically only descriptive in form and content; these are G. Crothers's *The German Elections of 1907* (New York: Columbia University Press, 1941) and J. Bertram's *Die Wahlen zum Deutschen Reichstag vom Jahre 1912* (Düsseldorf: Droste, 1964). For a briefer but more statistically oriented analysis of two elections, see the article by A. Braun, "Die Reichstagswahlen von 1898 und 1903," *Archiv für soziale Gesetzgebung und Statistik* 18 (1903): 539–63. Some interesting insights on the elections of 1903 and 1907 can be found in E. Würzburger, "Die Partei der Nichtwähler," *Jahrbücher für Nationalökonomie und Statistik*, 3d ser. 33 (1907): 381–89. A. Blaustein provides some statistics on liberal voters in *Von der Uneinigkeit der Liberalen bei den Reichstagswahlen, 1867–1910* (Munich: Nationalverein, 1911).

20 A summary of work on the Rhineland can be found in Müller, "Das Rheinland als Gegenstand der historischen Wahlsoziologie." The best of the local electoral studies on the imperial era is B. Ehrenfeuchter, "Politische Willensbildung in Niedersachsen zur Zeit des Kaiserreiches," (unpubl. diss., Göttingen, 1951). Less useful are R. Frank,

Der Brandenburger als Reichstagswähler (diss., Berlin, 1934); G. Franz, *Die politischen Wahlen in Niedersachsen, 1867–1949*, 3d ed. (Bremen: W. Dorn, 1953); H. Graf, *Die Entwicklung der Wahlen und politischen Parteien in Gross Dortmund* (Marburg: Goedel, 1958); and A. Hess, *Die Landtags- und Reichstagswahlen im Grossherzogtum Hessen, 1865–1871* (Oberursel: Ahkönig, 1958). B. Vogel and P. Haungs's *Wahlkampf und Wählertradition. Eine Studie zur Bundestagswahl von 1961* (Cologne and Opladen: Westdeutscher Verlag, 1965) is mainly concerned with recent elections in Baden, but its introduction (pp. 58–93) covers the period before 1914.

21 O. Eitner, "Die Stärke der Protestanten und Katholiken in den einzelnen Reichstagswahlkreisen und die Sozialdemokratie," *Historisch-Politische Blätter* 149 (1912): 687–93. On the political significance of religion, see also A. Klöcker, *Die Konfession der sozialdemokratischen Wählerschaft* (München-Gladbach: Volksverein, 1923), based on the election of 1907; J. Schauff, *Die deutschen Katholiken und die Zentrumspartei. Eine politisch-statistische Untersuchung der Reichstagswahlen seit 1871* (Cologne: J. P. Bachem, 1928); R. Blank, "Die soziale Zusammensetzung der sozialdemokratischen Wählerschaft Deutschlands," *Archiv für Sozialwissenschaft* 20 (1905): 507–50. See also A. Neumann-Hofer, *Die Entwicklung der Sozialdemokratie bei den Wahlen zum deutschen Reichstage, 1871–1903* (Berlin, 1903); and the excellent contemporary analysis of the SPD and the election of 1907 in Saxony, Bavaria, and East Prussia published in *Neue Zeit* 25 (1907): 668–82.

22 G. A. Ritter, *Die Arbeiterbewegung im Wilhelminischen Reich* (Berlin-Dahlem: Colloquium Verlag, 1963); see especially pp. 77–78, n. 136 on Blank's article, "Die soziale Zusammensetzung der sozialdemokratischen Wählerschaft Deutschlands." Also worth noting are three recent local studies of the SPD: E. Schneider, "Die Anfänge der sozialistischen Arbeiterbewegung in der Rheinpfalz, 1864–1899" (diss., Mainz, 1956); H. Eckert, *Liberal- oder Sozialdemokratie. Frühgeschichte der Nürnberger Arbeiterbewegung* (Stuttgart: Klett, 1968); H. Regling, *Die Anfänge des Sozialismus in Schleswig-Holstein* (Neumünster: Wachholtz, 1965).

23 R. A. Comfort, *Revolutionary Hamburg: Labor Politics in the Early Weimar Republic* (Stanford: Stanford University Press, 1966), pp. 148 ff., app. 1.

24 The best overall guide to Weimar elections is A. Milatz's *Wähler und Wahlen in der Weimarer Republik* (Bonn: Bundeszentrale für Politische Bildung, 1965). See also M. Hagmann, *Der Weg ins Verhängnis. Reichstagswahlergebnisse 1919 bis 1933, besonders aus Bayern* (Munich: Beckstein, 1946). Some interesting contemporary analysis can be found in H. Gosnell, *Why Europe Votes* (Chicago: University of Chicago Press, 1930), pp. 69–96; and H. Tingsten, *Political Behavior* (London: P. S. King, 1937), pp. 83 ff. Finally, for an excellent analysis of the relationship between political behavior in the empire and the republic, see G. A. Ritter, "Kontinuität und Umformung des deutschen Parteisystems, 1918–1920," in *Entstehung und Wandel der modernen Gesellschaft. Festschrift für Hans Rosenberg* (Berlin: de Gruyter, 1970), pp. 342–84.

25 A. Milatz, "Das Ende der Parteien im Spiegel der Wahlen 1930 bis 1933," in *Das Ende der Parteien*, ed. E. Matthias and R. Morsey (Düsseldorf: Droste, 1960); S. Nilson, "Wahlsoziologische Probleme des Nationalsozialismus," *Zeitschrift für die gesamte Staatswissenschaft* 110 (1954): 279–311; R. Bendix, "Social Stratification and Political Power," *American Political Science Review* 46 (1952): 357–75 (pp. 367 ff. on National Socialism): S. M. Lipset, "Fascism—Left, Right, and Center," in *Political Man* (Garden City, N.Y.: Doubleday, 1963), pp. 127–79 (pp. 138 ff. on the rise of National Socialism); and K. O'Lessker, "Who Voted for Hitler? A New Look at the Class Basis of Nazism," *American Journal of Sociology*, vol. 74, no. 1 (1968), pp. 63–69.

26 W. S. Allen, *The Nazi Seizure of Power. The Experience of a Single German Town, 1930–1935* (Chicago: Quadrangle, 1965); Franz, *Die politischen Wahlen in Niedersachsen.*

27 R. Heberle, *From Democracy to Nazism. A Regional Case Study on Political Parties in Germany* (Baton Rouge: Louisiana State University Press, 1945). The complete German edition has recently been published under the title *Landbevölkerung und Nationalsozialismus. Eine soziologische Untersuchung der politischen Willensbildung in Schleswig-Holstein, 1918 bis 1932* (Stuttgart, 1963). Heberle correlated his voting

and social data with a formula developed by F. Tönnies and H. Streifler; when he checked his results with the Spearman method he found no significant difference (pp. 105–07). For analyses of the problem which parallel Heberle's, see J. K. Pollack, "An Area Study of the German Electorate, 1930–1933," *American Political Science Review* 38 (1944); C. Loomis and A. Beegle, "The Spread of German Nazism in Rural Areas," *American Sociological Review* 11 (1946): 724–34.

28 On this point, see the general remarks in S. Rokkan's excellent article, "The Comparative Study of Political Participation: Notes towards a Perspective on Current Research," in *Essays on the Behavioral Study of Politics*, ed. A. Ranney (Urbana, Ill.: University of Illinois Press, 1962), pp. 47–90.

29 Some recent work underlines the value of this approach: W. Hofmann, *Die Bielefelder Stadtverordneten. Ein Beitrag zu bürgerlicher Selbstverwaltung und sozialem Wandel, 1850–1914* (Lübeck: Matthiesen, 1964); and W. Köllmann, *Sozialgeschichte der Stadt Barmen im 19. Jahrhundert* (Tübingen: J. C. B. Mohr, 1960).

30 A useful survey of the suffrage systems in various German cities (and some valuable data on urban political life in general) can be found in the *Schriften des Vereins für Sozialpolitik*, vols. 117–20. Valuable insights into the Rhineland and Westphalia are provided by Helmuth Croon's *Die gesellschaftliche Auswirkungen des Gemeindewahlrechts in den Gemeinden und Kreisen des Rheinlandes und Westfalen* (Cologne: Westdeutscher Verlag, 1960) and "Die Städtevertretung von Krefeld und Bochum im 19. Jahrhundert," *Forschungen zu Staat und Verfassung. Festgabe für Fritz Hartung* (Berlin: Duncker and Humblot, 1958), pp. 289–306. Croon's excellent article in the *Archiv für Kommunalwissenschaft* 5 (1966): 125–34 surveys the recent historical literature on German cities. For a guide to the older works, see E. Keyser, ed., *Bibliographie zur Städtegeschichte Deutschlands* (Cologne, 1969). Unfortunately most of this older literature on urban developments is anecdotal and of interest only to hometown historians. An exception to this is Johannes Ziekursch's splendid *Das Ergebnis der friderizianischen Städteverwaltung und die Städteordnung Steins (am Beispiel der schlesischen Städte dargestellt)* (Jena: H. Costenoble, 1908). I have discussed in some detail the relationship between urban and national politics in my article, "Liberalism and the City in Nineteenth Century Germany," *Past and Present*, no. 51 (1971), pp. 116–37.

31 K. Repgen, "Klerus und Politik 1848," *Aus Geschichte und Landeskunde* (Steinbach Festschrift) (Bonn: Röhrscheid, 1960). Along these same lines is Edward Shorter's analysis of the 656 answers to a royal essay contest in Bavaria: "Middle Class Anxiety in the German Revolution of 1848," *Journal of Social History*, vol. 2, no. 3 (1969), pp. 189–216.

32 Some examples of recent research using police records are E. Süss, *Pfälzer im Schwarzen Buch. Ein personengeschichtlicher Beitrag zur Geschichte des Hambacher Festes, des frühen pfälzischen, und deutschen Liberalismus* (Heidelberg: C. Winter, 1956); G. Seeber, *Zwischen Bebel und Bismarck. Zur Geschichte des Linksliberalismus in Deutschland, 1871–1893* (Berlin: Akademie Verlag, 1965); R. Hoppe and J. Kuczynski, "Eine Berufs- bzw. auch Klassen- und Schichtanalyse der Märzgefallenen 1848 in Berlin," *Jahrbuch für Wirtschaftsgeschichte*, 1964, pp. 200–76; and B. Puchert and H. Handke, "Politische Gefangene des Naziregimes im Zuchthaus Brandenburg. Eine soziologische Untersuchung," ibid., 1967, pp. 37–76. There is nothing in German historiography to compare with the work of this sort done on France by A. Soboul, G. Rudé, and others. Professor Richard Tilly of the University of Münster is now engaged in a very promising study of collective violence in nineteenth-century Germany which should add a great deal to our knowledge of usually ignored kinds of political behavior. See Tilly's article, "Popular Disorders in Nineteenth-Century Germany: A Preliminary Survey," *Journal of Social History*, vol. 4, no. 1 (Fall 1970), pp. 1–40.

33 An indispensible guide to the study of political organization is given in D. Fricke et al., *Die bürgerlichen Parteien in Deutschland*, 2 vols. (Leipzig: VEB Institut, 1968–70). The various contributors often give a brief summary of membership statistics for the groups discussed. Also of value for the development of organizations in the early twentieth century are the data on *Die Verbände der Arbeitgeber,*

Angestellten, und Arbeiter, published as a *Sonderheft* of the *Reichsarbeitsblatt* (Berlin, 1913–).

34 R. Michels, "Die deutsche Sozialdemokratie, I: Parteimitgliederschaft und soziale Zusammensetzung," *Archiv für Sozialwissenschaft und Sozialpolitik* 23 (1906): 471–556. An ambitious and highly successful attempt to follow up some of the insights in Michels's article is J. Siemann's "Die sozialdemokratische Arbeiterführer in der Zeit der Weimarer Republik" (unpubl. diss., Göttingen, 1955). Siemann studied 1,838 leaders from all parts of the labor movement. It is very unfortunate that his work, like many of the best dissertations of the fifties, has not been published.

35 H. Gerth, "The Nazi Party: Its Leadership and Composition," *American Journal of Sociology* 45 (1940): 517–41. There are some data on the pre-1933 Nazi leadership in D. Orlow, *The History of the Nazi Party* (Pittsburgh: University of Pittsburgh Press, 1969), vol. 1.

36 H.-J. Puhle has some excellent data on the leadership of the *Bund der Landwirte* in *Agrarische Interessenpolitik und preussischer Konservatismus im wilhelminischen Reich, 1893–1914* (Hanover: Verlag für Literatur und Zeitgeschehen, 1967): see also the information on the CVDI in H. Kaelble, *Industrielle Interessenpolitik in der wilhelminischen Gesellschaft: Centralverband Deutscher Industrieller, 1895–1914* (Berlin: Walter de Gruyter, 1967).

In addition to the well-known interest groups studied by Puhle and Kaelble, there were a wide range of other organizations that often had considerable political importance. For an example of the variety of such institutions, see the fascinating material in Heinz Schmitt's *Das Vereinsleben der Stadt Weinheim* (Weinheim: Stadt Weinheim, 1963). Also worth mentioning is Hansjoachim Henning, "Kriegervereine in den preussischen Westprovinzen. Ein Beitrag zur preussischen Innenpolitik zwischen 1860 und 1914," *Rheinische Vierteljahrsblätter* 32 (1968): 430–75.

37 For some statistics on newspapers in the nineteenth century, see H. Schacht, "Statistische Untersuchungen über die Presse Deutschlands," *Jahrbücher für Nationalökonomie und Statistik* 70 (1898): 503–25; M. Wittwer, *Das deutsche Zeitungswesen in seiner neueren Entwicklung* (diss., Halle, 1914); G. Muser, *Statistische Untersuchungen über die Zeitungen Deutschlands* (Leipzig: Reinicke, 1918).

38 Engelsing, *Massenpublikum und Journalistentum im 19. Jahrhundert in Nordwestdeutschland* (Berlin: Duncker and Humblot, 1966). See also the interesting data on the social origins of the contributors to selected eighteenth-century periodicals in J. Schultze, *Die Auseinandersetzung zwischen Zeitschriften der letzten drei Jahrzehnten des 18. Jahrhunderts* (Berlin: E. Ebering, 1925).

39 F. Zunkel, *Der Rheinische–westfälische Unternehmer, 1834–1879* (Cologne: Westdeutscher Verlag, 1962).

40 F. Peters, "Über die Herkunft der bremischen Senatoren von der Verkündung der ersten demokratischen Verfassung bis zur Gegenwart, 1849–1955," *Jahrbuch der bremischen Wissenschaft* 1 (1955): 189–240.

41 A convenient guide to these biographical collections can be found in three review articles by H. Rogge in *Blätter für deutsche Landesgeschichte* 94 (1958): 227–36; 96 (1960): 272–92; and 98 (1962): 337–49. An early study based on the *Allgemeine deutsche Biographie*—F. Maas's "Über die Herkunftsbedingungen der geistigen Führer," *Archiv für Sozialwissenschaft und Sozialpolitik* 41 (1916): 144–86—suggests some of the possibilities and limitations of these data.

42 The University of Oregon's Bundestag-Volkskammer Study provides one example of a coding system appropriate for this kind of elite data bank. I am grateful to Professor Arthur Hanhardt for sending me the draft code for this study.

43 The following is a sample of the handbooks and collections which contain readily available and highly useful data on the aristocracy: *Handbuch über den königlich Preussischen Hof und Staat* (Berlin, 1794–); K. F. Rauer, *Hand-Matrikel der in sämtlichen Kreisen des preussischen Staates auf Kreis- und Landtagen vertretenen Rittergüter* (Berlin: Rikühn, 1857); *Handbuch des Grundbesitzes im deutschen Reiche*, 10 vols. (Berlin: Nicolai, 1888–1912); *Jahrbuch des deutschen Adels*, 3 vols. (Berlin: Bruer, 1896–99); M. Gritzner, *Chronologische Matrikel der Brandenburgisch-Preussischen Standeserhöhungen und Gnadeacte* (Görlitz: Starke, 1874),

covering the period from 1600; and A. O. M. von Houwald, *Brandenburg-Preussische Standeserhöhungen und Gnadeacten für die Zeit, 1873–1918* (Berlin, 1939). These sources form the basis for Lamar Cecil's interesting new article on "The Creation of Nobles in Prussia, 1871–1918," *American Historical Review*, vol. 75, no. 3 (1970), pp. 757–95.

44 J. Ziekursch, *Hundert Jahre schlesischer Agrargeschichte* (Berlin: F. Hirt, 1927); F. Martiny, *Die Adelsfrage in Preussen vor 1806 als politisches und soziales Problem* (Stuttgart and Berlin: Kohlhammer, 1938); R. Koselleck, *Preussen zwischen Reform und Revolution. Allgemeines Landrecht, Verwaltung, und soziale Bewegung von 1791 bis 1848* (Stuttgart: Klett, 1967).

45 M. Weber's "Agrarstatistische und sozialpolitische Betrachtungen zur Fideikommissfrage in Preussen" was first written in 1904 and reprinted in *Gesammelte Aufsätze zur Soziologie und Sozialpolitik* (Tübingen: J. C. Mohr, 1924). J. Conrad's research appeared in a series of articles in the *Jahrbücher für Nationalökonomie und Statistik*, 2d ser. 16 (1888): 121–70; 3d ser. 2 (1891): 817–44, 3 (1892): 481–95, 6 (1893): 516–42, 10 (1895): 706–39, 15 (1898): 705–29. On entailment, see also F. Lenz, "Beiträge zur Fideikommissstatistik," ibid., 3d ser. 39 (1910): 353–61. The problem of working with the relevant statistics is discussed on pp. 353–54.

46 J. Lampe, *Aristokratie, Hofadel, und Staatspatrizrat in Kurhannover . . . 1714–1760*, 2 vols. (Göttingen: Vandenhoeck and Ruprecht, 1963).

47 W. Schärl, *Die Zusammensetzung der bayerischen Beamtenschaft von 1806 bis 1918* (Kallmünz: M. Lassleben, 1955).

48 Koselleck, *Preussen zwischen Reform und Revolution*, esp. pp. 434–37, 676 ff. There are also data on nobles and state offices in Martiny's *Die Adelsfrage in Preussen*.

49 H. von Bonin, "Adel und Bürgertum in der höheren Beamtenschaft der preussischen Monarchie, 1794–1806," *Jahrbuch für die Geschichte Mittel- und Ostdeutschlands* 15 (1966): 139–74.

50 J. Gillis, *The Prussian Bureaucracy in Crisis, 1840–1860* (Stanford: Stanford University Press, 1971); R. Morsey, *Die oberste Reichsverwaltung unter Bismarck, 1867–1890* (Münster: Aschendorff, 1957); J. C. G. Röhl, "Higher Civil Servants in Germany, 1890–1900," *Journal of Contemporary History* 2 (1967): 101–21; F. von Schulte, "Adel im deutschen Offizier- und Beamtenstand," *Deutsche Revue* 21 (1896): 181–92.

51 K. Demeter, *Das deutsche Offizierskorps in Gesellschaft und Staat, 1650–1945* (Frankfurt: Bernard and Graefe, 1962); there is an incomplete English translation of this book, published in New York in 1965 as *The German Officer Corps*. The social composition of a few selected regiments in the early nineteenth century is given in P. Paret, *Yorck and the Era of Prussian Reform, 1807–1815* (Princeton: Princeton University Press, 1966), pp. 265–66. A large quantity and variety of data on the army are given in C. Jany, *Geschichte der königlich preussischen Armee*, 4 vols., 2d ed. (Osnabrück: Biblio Verlag, 1967). On the navy, see J. Steinberg, "The Kaiser's Navy and German Society," *Past and Present*, no. 28 (1964), pp. 102–10.

52 F. W. Schaer, *Die Stadt Aurich und ihre Beamtenschaft im 19. Jahrhundert* (Göttingen: Vandenhoeck and Ruprecht, 1963); D. Wegmann, *Die leitenden staatlichen Verwaltungsbeamten der Provinz Westfalen, 1815–1918* (Münster: Aschendorff, 1969); A. Klein, *Die Personalpolitik der Hohenzollernmonarchie bei der Kölner Regierung* (Düsseldorf: Schwann, 1967); P. Letkemann, *Die preussische Verwaltung des Regierungsbezirks Danzig, 1815–1870* (Marburg: Herder, 1967); Irene Berger, *Die preussische Verwaltung des Regierungsbezirks Bromberg, 1815–1847* (Cologne and Berlin: Grote, 1966); K. H. Rehfeld, *Die preussische Verwaltung des Regierungsbezirks Bromberg, 1848–1871* (Cologne and Berlin: Grote, 1968).

53 J. Ziekursch, *Beiträge zur Charakteristik der preussischen Verwaltungsbeamten in Schlesien bis zum Untergange des friderizianischen Staates* (Breslau: Wohlfarth, 1907).

54 W. Zapf, *Wandlungen der deutschen Elite, 1919–1961* (Munich: Piper, 1965). See also the essays edited by Zapf, *Beiträge zur Analyse der deutschen Oberschicht* (Munich: Piper, 1965).

55 W. Runge, *Politik und Beamtentum im Parteienstaat. Die Demokratisierung der politischen Beamten in Preussen zwischen 1918 und 1933* (Stuttgart: Klett, 1965);

H.-K. Behrend, "Zur Personalpolitik des preussischen Ministeriums des Innern. Die Besetzung der Landratstellen in den östlichen Provinzen, 1919–1933," *Jahrbuch für die Geschichte Mittel- und Ostdeutschlands* 6 (1957): 173–214. See also the brief study on the highest offices in the Reich by M. Knight, *The German Executive, 1890–1933* (Stanford; Hoover Institute, 1952).

56 Gerth, "The Nazi Party"; L. Edinger, "Continuity and Change in the Background of German Decision Makers," *Western Political Quarterly* 14 (1961). Valuable data on the Nazi leadership can be found in the four-volume *Parteistatistik 1935* (n.p., 1935).

57 D. Lerner, "The Nazi Elite," first published in 1951 and reprinted in *World Revolutionary Elites*, ed. H. Lasswell and D. Lerner (Cambridge, Mass.: The MIT Press, 1966), pp. 194–318.

58 O. Most, "Zur Wirtschafts- und Sozialstatistik der höheren Beamten in Preussen," *Schmollers Jahrbuch* 39 (1915): 181–218. Most's article provides some valuable material on living expenses; this is also treated in G. Hermes, "Ein preussischer Beamtenhaushalt, 1859–1890," *Zeitschrift für die gesamte Staatswissenschaft* 76 (1921). Valuable raw data on noncommissioned officers in the army can be found in G. Evert, "Die Herkunft der deutschen Unteroffiziere und Soldaten am 1. Dezember 1906," *Zeitschrift des königlichen preussischen statistischen Landesamtes, Ergänzungsheft* 28 (Berlin, 1908).

59 J. Cullity, "The Growth of Governmental Employment in Germany, 1882–1950," *Zeitschrift für die gesamte Staatswissenschaft*, vol. 123, no. 2 (April 1967), pp. 201–17, based on Cullity's Ph.D. dissertation (Columbia University, 1964); S. Andic and J. Veverka, "The Growth of Government Expenditure in Germany since the Unification," *Finanzarchiv* 23 (1964): 169–278. On similar issues, see the fine new monograph by Peter Witt, *Die Finanzpolitik des Deutschen Reiches, 1903–1913* (Lübeck and Hamburg: Matthiesen, 1969).

60 Koselleck, *Preussen zwischen Reform und Revolution*, pp. 691–96.

61 See, for example, W. Fischer, "Staat und Gesellschaft Badens im deutschen Vormarz," in *Staat und Gesellschaft im deutschen Vormarz, 1815–1848*, ed. W. Conze (Stuttgart: Klett, 1962), p. 149.

62 On the social composition of the parliaments in 1848, see G. Schilfert, *Sieg und Niederlage des demokratischen Wahlrechts in der deutschen Revolution, 1848/49* (Berlin: Rütten and Loening, 1952); Eyck, *Frankfurt Parliament*, pp. 93 ff. For the preimperial period, the most complete analysis of a representative body is A. Hess's study of the 1862 Prussian Landtag: *Das Parlament das Bismarck widerstrebte* (Cologne and Opladen: Westdeutscher Verlag, 1964). Hess is able to sketch the main outlines of the Landtag's social makeup, but his account reflects the limits on precision imposed by the data. He could not, for example, establish the year of birth for almost half the delegates. See pp. 51–72, 138–50.

63 See, for example, Kaiser, *Die politischen Strömungen*, p. 403.

64 A. Borell, *Die soziologische Gliederung des Reichsparlaments als Spiegelung der politischen und ökonomischen Konstellationen* (diss., Giessen, 1933); K. Demeter, "Die soziale Schichtung des deutschen Parlaments seit 1848: Ein Spiegelbild der Strukturwandlung des Volkes," *Vierteljahrsschrift für Sozial- und Wirtschaftsgeschichte* 39 (1952): 1–29; G. Franz, "Der Parlamentarismus," *Jahrbuch der Rankegesellschaft* 3 (1957): 85–99; W. Kamm, *Abgeordnetenberufe und Parlament. Ein Beitrag zur Soziologie des Parlamentarismus* (Karlsruhe: G. Braun, 1927); W. Kremer, *Der soziale Aufbau der Parteien des deutschen Reichstages von 1871–1918* (diss., Cologne, 1934); E. Maschke, "Die Industrialisierung Deutschlands im Spiegel der Parlamentszusammensetzungen von 1848 bis heute," *Tradition*, nos. 5–6 (1965), pp. 230–45; L. Rosenbaum, "Beruf und Herkunft der Abgeordneten zu den deutschen und preussischen Parlamenten, 1847–1919," in *Die Paulskirche* (Frankfurt, 1923). In many ways the most sophisticated recent work on the sociology of the imperial parliament is Peter Molt's *Der Reichstag vor der improvisierten Revolution* (Cologne and Opladen: Westdeutscher Verlag, 1963). See also my article, "Political Leadership in the German Reichstag, 1871–1918," *AHR* 74 (1968): 511–28. A useful handbook

on German parliamentarians has been prepared by M. Schwarz, *M d R. Biographisches Handbuch der Reichstage* (Hanover: Verlag für Literatur und Zeitgeschehen, 1965).

65 This table is based on Hans Jaeger's *Unternehmer in der deutschen Politik, 1890–1918* (Bonn: Röhrscheid Verlag, 1967), p. 48.

66 L. O'Boyle, "Liberal Political Leadership in Germany, 1867–1884," *Journal of Modern History*, vol. 28, no. 4 (Dec. 1956), pp. 338–52; E. Matthias and E. Pikart, eds., *Die Reichstagsfraktion der deutschen Sozialdemokratie, 1898 bis 1918*, 2 vols. (Düsseldorf: Droste, 1966).

67 See, for example, the very interesting survey of the delegates to the Weimar Assembly carried out by G. Maas in *Die Verfassungsgebende Deutsche Nationalversammlung* (Charlottenburg: P. Baumann, 1919).

68 See Hofmann, *Die Bielefelder Stadtverordneten;* Köllmann, *Sozialgeschichte der Stadt Barmen.* Helmuth Croon has done some very valuable work on local elites in western Germany; see, for example, his *Die gesellschaftliche Auswirkungen des Gemeindewahlrechts.*

69 The most important biographical collections on entrepreneurs are discussed Rogge's articles, cited in n. 41 above.

70 The usefulness of the *Adressbuch* is discussed in H. Radandt's *"Adressbuch der Direktoren und Aufsichträte,* Hilfsmittel für Strukturuntersuchungen von personellen Beziehungen zwischen kapitalistischen Unternehmern in Deutschland im 20. Jahrhundert," *Jahrbuch für Wirtschaftsgeschichte*, 1966, 241–57.

71 H. Beau, *Das Leistungswesen der frühindustriellen Unternehmertums in Rheinland-Westfalen* (Cologne: Rheinisch-Westfälisches Wirtschaftsarchiv, 1959). See also W. Huschke, *Forschungen über die Herkunft der thüringischen Unternehmerschicht des 19. Jahrhunderts* (Baden-Baden: A. Lutzeyer, 1962).

72 H. Nussbaum, *Unternehmer gegen Monopole. Über Struktur und Aktionen antimonopolistischer bürgerlicher Gruppen* (Berlin: Akademie, 1966), see esp. pp. 19 ff.

73 Jaeger, *Unternehmer in der deutschen Politik.*

74 J. Kocka, *Unternehmensverwaltung und Angestelltenschaft am Beispiel Siemens, 1847–1914* (Stuttgart: Klett, 1969).

75 F. Ringer, "Higher Education in Germany in the Nineteenth Century," *The Journal of Contemporary History* 2 (1967): 123–38; idem, *The Decline of the German Mandarins. The German Academic Community, 1890–1933* (Cambridge, Mass.: Harvard University Press, 1969); W. Zorn, "Hochschule und höhere Schule in der deutschen Sozialgeschichte der Neuzeit," in *Spiegel der Geschichte (Braubach Festschrift)* (Münster: Aschendorff, 1964), pp. 321–39.

76 C. von Ferber, "The Social Background of German University and College Professors since 1864," *Transactions of the Third World Congress of Sociology*, 1956, pp. 239–44; idem, *Die Entwicklung des Lehrkörpers der deutschen Universitäten und Hochschulen, 1864–1954*, vol. 3 of *Untersuchungen zur Lage der deutschen Hochschullehrer*, ed. H. Plessner (Göttingen: Vandenhoeck and Ruprecht, 1956); F. Eulenburg, *Der akademische Nachwuchs. Eine Untersuchung über die Lage und die Aufgaben der Extraordinarien und Privatdozenten* (Leipzig and Berlin: Teubner, 1908); A. Busch, *Die Geschichte des Privatdozenten. Eine soziologische Studie zur grossbetrieblichen Entwicklung der deutschen Universitäten* (Stuttgart: Enke, 1959). There is some interesting new material on the professors in Helene Tompert's *Lebensformen und Denkweisen der akademischen Welt Heidelbergs im wilhelminischen Zeitalter* (Lübeck and Hamburg: Matthiesen, 1969).

77 See the following collections of data on university study: C. F. W. Dieterici, *Geschichtliche und statistische Nachrichten über die Universitäten im preussischen Staate* (Berlin: Duncker and Humblot, 1836); J. Conrad, "Einige Ergebnisse der deutschen Universitätsstatistik," *Jahrbücher für Nationalökonomie und Statistik*, 3d ser. 32 (1906): 433–92; F. Eulenburg, *Die Frequenz der deutschen Universitäten von ihrer Gründung bis in die Gegenwart* (Leipzig: Teubner, 1904); *Die deutsche Hochschulstatistik* (Berlin, 1928–35, published biannually); C. Lorenz, *Zehnjahres-Statistik des Hochschulbesuchs und der Abschlussprüfungen* (Berlin, 1943). Valuable information is also to be found in publications on various universities; see, for

example, F. Lenz, "Statistik der Universität," in M. Lenz, *Geschichte der königlichen Friedrich-Wilhelms Universität zu Berlin* (Halle: Buchhandlung des Waisenhauses, 1910), 3:483–536.

78 A. Rienhardt, *Das Universitätsstudium der Württemberger seit der Reichsgründung* (Tübingen: J. C. B. Mohr, 1918).

79 See, for example, the interesting remarks on education and mobility in S. Riemer, "Sozialer Aufstieg und Klassenschichtung," *Archiv für Sozialwissenschaft und Sozialpolitik* 67 (1932): 531–60.

80 There is some useful information on this subject in W. Kotschnig's *Unemployment in the Learned Professions* (London: Oxford University Press, 1937), pp. 117–23.

81 See n. 54 above.

82 Köllmann, *Sozialgeschichte der Stadt Barmen*. See also Köllmann's analysis of the Westphalian social structure in *Friedrich Harkort*, vol. 1, *1793–1838* (Düsseldorf: Droste, 1964), pp. 190–97. The Ayçoberry article is "Probleme der Sozialschichtung in Köln im Zeitalter der Frühindustrialisierung," in *Wirtschafts- und Sozialgeschichtliche Probleme der Frühindustrialisierung*, ed. W. Fischer (Berlin: De Gruyter, 1968). Also worth noting is H. Mauersberg, *Die Wirtschaft und Gesellschaft Fuldas in neuer Zeit* (Göttingen: Vandenhoeck and Ruprecht, 1969).

83 For an example of the data on social structure given in the local electoral studies, see Kaiser, *Die politischen Strömungen*, pp. 9 ff. See also G. Wurzbacher, *Das Dorf im Spannungsfeld industrieller Entwicklung*, 2d ed. (Stuttgart: Enke, 1961); E. W. Buchholz, *Ländliche Bevölkerung an der Schwelle des Industriezeitalters. Der Raum Braunschweig als Beispiel* (Stuttgart: G. Fischer, 1966), pp. 42 ff.; H. Croon and K. Utermann, *Zeche und Gemeinde. Untersuchungen über den Strukturwandel einer Zechengemeinde im nördlichen Ruhrgebiet* (Tübingen: J. C. B. Mohr, 1958), esp. pp. 288 ff.; R. Pflaum, *Soziale Schichtung und sozialer Wandel in einer Industriegemeinde* (Stuttgart: Klett, 1958).

84 See also Geiger's two articles: "Statistische Analyse der wirtschaftlich Selbstständigen," *Archiv für Sozialwissenschaft und Sozialpolitik* 69 (1933): 407–39; "Soziale Gliederung der deutschen Arbeitnehmer," ibid., pp. 151–88.

85 For a general introduction to the census data, see Lorenz, *Forschungslehre der Sozialstatistik*, 3:4 ff. See also the analysis of the censuses of 1882, 1895, and 1907 in G. Neuhaus, "Die berufliche und soziale Gliederung der Bevölkerung im Zeitalter des Kapitalismus," *Grundriss der Sozialökonomik* (Tübingen: J. C. B. Mohr), vol. 9, no. 1 (1926), pp. 360–434. For a guide to the material published after 1918, see U.S. Library of Congress, *National Censuses and Vital Statistics in Europe, 1918–1939: An Annotated Bibliography* (Washington, D.C.: Government Printing Office, 1948).

86 K.-H. Rieker, "Die Konzentrationsentwicklung in der gewerblichen Wirtschaft. Eine Auswertung der deutschen Betriebszählungen von 1875–1950," *Tradition* 5 (1960): 116–31.

87 "Social Attitudes, Entrepreneurship, and Economic Development," *Explorations in Entrepreneurial History* 6 (1953–54): 1–19, 245–72; 7 (1954–55): 111–20.

88 E. A. Wrigley, *Industrial Growth and Population Change. A Regional Study of the Coalfield Areas of Northwest Europe in the later Nineteenth Century* (Cambridge: Cambridge University Press, 1961).

89 W. Köllmann, "Industrialisierung, Binnenwanderung, und 'Soziale Frage' (Zur Entstehungsgeschichte der deutschen Industriegrossstadt im 19. Jahrhundert)," *Vierteljahrschrift für Sozial- und Wirtschaftsgeschichte* 46 (1959): 45–70; idem, "Binnenwanderung und Bevölkerungsstrukturen der Ruhrgebietsgrossstädte im Jahre 1907," *Soziale Welt* 9 (1958): 219–33; P. Quante, *Die Abwanderung aus der Landwirtschaft* (Kiel: Institut für Weltwirtschaft, 1958). See also M. Hainisch, *Die Landflucht* (Jena: G. Fischer, 1924); and the critique of Hainisch by Quante, pp. 31 ff. For a brief but interesting treatment of a specific region, see H. Wirth, "Die Wanderung von der Landwirtschaft in die gewerbliche Wirtschaft in den letzten 74 Jahren in Baden-Württemberg," *Berichte über Landwirtschaft*, new ser. 34 (1956): 80–89.

Two recent articles on minorities in the Reich—H. Linde's "Die soziale Problematik der masurischen Agrargesellschaft und die masurische Einwanderung in das Emscherrevier" and H.-U. Wehler's "Die Polen im Ruhrgebiet bis 1918"—also illuminate geographical and occupational shifts. Both are reprinted in a collection edited by Wehler, *Moderne deutsche Sozialgeschichte* (Cologne and Berlin: Kiepenheuer und Witsch, 1966), pp. 437–55, 456–70.

90   R. Heberle and F. Meyer, *Die Grossstädte im Strome der Binnenwanderung* (Leipzig: S. Hirzel, 1937). Other useful material on urbanization can be found in R. Kuczynski, *Der Zug nach der Stadt. Statistische Studien über Vorgänge der Bevölkerungsbewegung im deutschen Reiche* (Stuttgart: Cotta, 1897); and S. Schott, *Die grossstädtischen Agglomerationen des deutschen Reiches, 1871–1910* (Breslau: W. G. Korn, 1912).

91   On these institutions and the present state of "Historical Population Studies," see the Spring 1968 issue of *Daedalus* which is devoted to this subject. Also useful as an introduction to historical demography are the essays in part 1 of D. V. Glass and D. E. C. Eversley, eds., *Population in History* (London: E. Arnold, 1965).

92   A great deal of the relevant literature is cited in W. Köllmann, "Grundzüge der Bevölkerungsgeschichte Deutschlands im 19. und 20. Jahrhundert," *Studium Generale* 12 (1959): 391–92. See also Köllmann's recent article on "Bevölkerung und Arbeitskräftepotential in Deutschland, 1815–1865," *Jahrbuch des Landesamts für Forschung, Nordrhein-Westfalen*, 1968, pp. 209–54.

93   H. Mauersberg, *Wirtschafts- und Sozialgeschichte zentraleuropäischer Städte in neuerer Zeit. Dargestellt an den Beispielen von Basel, Frankfurt a.M., Hamburg, Hannover, und München* (Göttingen: Vandenhoeck and Ruprecht, 1960).

94   See the following articles by J. Knodel: "Law, Marriage, and Illegitimacy in Nineteenth-Century Germany," *Population Studies* 20 (1967): 279–94; "Infant Mortality and Fertility in Three Bavarian Villages: An Analysis of Family Histories from the Nineteenth Century," ibid. 22 (1968): 297–318; "Aussichten für die historische demographische Forschung," *Mitteilungen der deutschen Gesellschaft für Bevölkerungswissenschaft* 38 (1968): 33–37.

95   D. Kirk, "The Relation of Employment Levels to Births in Germany," *Milbank Memorial Fund Quarterly* 20 (1942): 126–38; D. V. Glass, *Population Policies and Movements in Europe* (London: Oxford University Press, 1940), pp. 269–313.

96   Emigration data for the Reich were published regularly in the *Statistik des deutschen Reiches*. See also the information on the various German states collected in *Auswanderung und Auswanderungspolitik in Deutschland. Schriften des Vereins für Sozialpolitik* 52 (1892). The kind of data available for intensive regional studies is suggested in W.-H. Struck, *Die Auswanderung aus dem Herzogtum Nassau, 1806–1866. Ein Kapital der modernen politischen und sozialen Entwicklung* (Wiesbaden: F. Steiner, 1966).

97   M. Walker, *Germany and the Emigration, 1816–1885* (Cambridge, Mass.: Harvard University Press, 1964).

98   For signs of new interest in German social history, see the introductory essays and the fine bibliography in Wehler, *Moderne deutsche Sozialgeschichte*.

99   G. F. Knapp, *Die Bauernbefreiung und der Ursprung der Landarbeiter*, 2 vols. (Leipzig: Dunker and Humblot, 1887); see pp. 256–73 for a discussion of statistical data on the period.

100 Theodor von der Glotz, *Die Lage der ländlichen Arbeiter im deutschen Reich* (Berlin: Wiegandt, Hempel, and Parey, 1875); G. Schnapper-Arndt, *Fünf Dorfgemeinden auf dem Hohen Taunus. Staats- und Sozialwissenschaftliche Forschungen* (Leipzig: Duncker and Humblot, 1883), vol. 16; *Schriften des Vereins*: vols. 22–24, *Bäuerliche Zustände in Deutschland* (1883), vols. 53–54, *Die Verhältnisse der Landarbeiter in Deutschland* (1892). Also of note on rural conditions are a number of the monographs in the *Münchner Volkswirtschaftliche Abhandlungen* series, edited by Lujo Brentano and W. Lotz, and the *Staats- und Sozialwissenschaftliche Forschungen* series, edited by Gustav Schmoller. For some useful insights into the history of research on rural society before 1914, see Oberschall, *Empirical Social Research in Germany*.

101 Hans Linde, *Preussischer Landesausbau. Ein Beitrag zur Geschichte der ländlichen Gesellschaft in Südostpreussen am Beispiel des Dorfes Piasutten, Krs. Orgelsburg* (Leipzig: Hirzel, 1939); E. Buchholz, *Ländliche Bevölkerung an der Schwelle des*

Industriezeitalters. There are some valuable insights on rural developments in a recent collection of essays entitled *Beiträge zur deutschen Wirtschafts- und Sozialgeschichte im 18. und 19. Jahrhundert* (Berlin: Akademie, 1962). See also F. Wunderlich, *Farm Labor in Germany, 1810–1945* (Princeton: Princeton University Press, 1961), which emphasizes the post-1918 period.

102 G. Schmoller, *Zur Geschichte der deutschen Kleingewerbe im 19. Jahrhundert* (Halle: Buchhandlung des Waisenhauses, 1870). On Schmoller's use of statistics, see Lorenz, *Forschungslehre der Sozialstatistik,* 1:33–34.

103 On artisans and *Heimarbeiter* see the following *Schriften des Vereins:* vols. 39–42, 48, *Die deutsche Hausindustrie* (1889–); vols. 62–70, *Untersuchungen über die Lage des Handwerks in Deutschland* (1895–97), esp. 70:629–70, for an account of the censuses of 1882–95; vols. 84–87, *Hausindustrie und Heimarbeit in Deutschland und Österreich* (1899). On factory workers see the data in vols. 133–35, *Auslese und Anpassung der Arbeiterschaft der geschlossenen Grossindustrie.* On this project, see Oberschall, *Empirical Social Research,* pp. 113 ff.; for a guide to other surveys on factory workers, see esp. pp. 79 ff., 94 ff.

104 H. Krüger, *Zur Geschichte der Manufakturen und der Manufakturarbeiter in Preussen* (Berlin: Rütten and Loening, 1958), esp. pp. 21 ff.; K. E. Born et al., *Quellensammlung zur Geschichte der deutschen Sozialpolitik 1867 bis 1914* (Wiesbaden: Steiner, 1966). For the earlier period, see the excellent bibliography in C. Jantke and D. Hilger's *Die Eigentumslosen* (Munich: K. Alber, 1965) and the insightful review article by F. Marquardt in *Central European History,* vol. 2, no. 1 (March 1969), pp. 77–88.

105 A. Kraus, *Die Unterschichten Hamburgs in der ersten Hälfte des 19. Jahrhundert* (Stuttgart: G. Fischer, 1965). See also A. Desai, *Real Wages in Germany, 1871–1913;* L. Schneider, *Der Arbeiterhaushalt im 18. und 19 Jahrhundert* (Berlin: Duncker and Humblot, 1967); G. Bry, *Wages in Germany, 1871–1945* (Princeton: Princeton University Press, 1960); E. H. Phelps Brown and Margaret Browne, *A Century of Pay: The Course of Pay and Production in France, Germany, Sweden, the United Kingdom, and the United States, 1860–1960* (London: Macmillan, 1968); and R. Engelsing, "Lebenshaltungen und Lebenshaltungskosten im 18. und 19. Jahrhundert in den Hansestädten Bremen und Hamburg," *International Review of Social History* 11 (1966): 73–107. There is a great deal of material of uneven quality in J. Kuczynski's massive work, *Die Geschichte der Lage der Arbeiter unter dem Kapitalismus,* part 1, *Die Geschichte der Lage der Arbeiter in Deutschland von 1789 bis zur Gegenwart;* vols. 1–6 (Berlin: Akademie, 1961–64) concern the years 1789–1945. Among the older works on these issues, see especially P. Ballin, *Der Haushalt der arbeitenden Klassen* (Berlin: Münnich, 1881); E. Conrad, *Lebensführung von 22 Arbeiterfamilien Münchens* (Munich: Lindauer, 1909); H. Mehner, "Der Haushalt und die Lebenshaltung einer Leipziger Arbeiterfamilie," *Schmollers Jahrbuch,* 2d ser. 1 (1887): 304–34.

106 On the collection of strike statistics in the pre-1914 period, see C. Heiss, "Die deutsche Streikstatistik," *Archiv für soziale Gesetzgebung und Statistik* 17 (1902): 150–68; M. Meyer, "Zur Reform der Streikstatistik," *Jahrbücher für Nationalökonomie und Statistik,* 3d ser. 37 (1909): 204–18. J. Kuczynski, in "Für den Aufbau einer zuverlässigen Streikstatistik für die Jahre 1880 bis 1945," *Jahrbuch für Wirtschaftsgeschichte* 2 (1961): 297–302, discusses the statistical problems, placing particular emphasis on 1914–18. There are some useful data on strikes in G. Frey, *Die Streikbewegung in Deutschland 1900 bis 1910* (diss., Erlangen, 1927); and, in more detail, in H. Seidel, *Streikkämpfe der mittel- und ostdeutschen Braunkohlenbergarbeiter von 1890 bis 1914* (Leipzig, 1964), which emphasizes the mass strikes of 1906–07. Finally, mention should be made of W. Steglich's efforts to compile data on the years before the imperial statistical publication of strike statistics: "Eine Streiktabelle für Deutschland 1864 bis 1880," *Jahrbuch für Wirtschaftsgeschichte* 2 (1960): 235–83.

107 See especially G. Adelmann, *Die soziale Betriebsverfassung des Ruhrbergbaus vom Anfang des 19. Jahrhunderts bis zum ersten Weltkrieg* (Bonn: Röhrscheid, 1962); E. Wächtler, *Bergarbeit zur Kaiserzeit. Die Geschichte der Lage der Bergarbeiter im*

sächsischen Steinkohlenrevier Lugau-Oelsnitz in den Jahren 1889 bis 1914 (Berlin: Tribüne, 1962); M. Koch, *Die Bergarbeiterbewegung im Ruhrgebiet zur Zeit Wilhelms II* (Düsseldorf: Droste, 1954); W. Döhler, *Die ökonomische Lage der Zwickauer Bergarbeiter im vorigen Jahrhundert* (Leipzig: Deutscher Verlag für Grundstoffindustrie, 1963). There is some information on the miners' organizations in J. Fritsch, *Eindringen und Ausbreitung der Revisionismus im deutschen Bergarbeiterverband (bis 1914)* (Leipzig: Deutscher Verlag für Grundstoffindustrie, 1967). For titles on other branches of German industry, see Wehler, *Moderne deutsche Sozialgeschichte.*

108 On the growth of officials and white-collar workers, see the comparison of the censuses of 1907 and 1925 in P. Krische, "Die soziale Schichtung der Erwerbstätigen im Zeitalter der Dampfmaschine und des Kapitalismus," *Zeitschrift für Völkerpsychologie und Soziologie* 4 (1928): 11 ff. On the "new middle class" before and after World War I, see E. Lederer, *Die Privatangestellten in der modernen Wirtschaftsentwicklung* (Tübingen: J. C. B. Mohr, 1926), pp. 120–41; R. Jaeckel, *Statistik über die Lage der Technischen Privatbeamten in Gross Berlin* (Jena: G. Fischer, 1908); F. Croner, *Soziologie der Angestellten* (Cologne and Berlin: Kiepenheuer and Witsch, 1962). Rolf Engelsing's recent article—"Die wirtschaftliche und soziale Differenzierung der deutschen kaufmännischen Angestellten," *Zeitschrift für die gesamte Staatswissenschaft* 123 (1967): 347–80, 482–514—puts the problems of one sector of this group into historical perspective. Kocka's *Unternehmensverwaltung und Angestelltenschaft am Beispiel Siemens* illuminates the entire range of issues associated with this social group and is especially useful for the managerial bureaucracy.

109 See, for example, J. Nothass, "Sozialer Auf- und Abstieg im deutschen Volk," *Beiträge zur Statistik Bayerns*, no. 117 (Munich, 1930). The literature on mobility in Germany is discussed in P. Sorokin, *Social and Cultural Mobility* (Glencoe, Ill.: The Free Press, 1959); and in S. M. Lipset and R. Bendix, *Social Mobility in Industrial Society* (Berkeley and Los Angeles: University of California Press, 1959), esp. pp. 34–36, 43. See also Riemer, "Sozialer Aufstieg und Klassenschichtung."

110 D. Schoenbaum, *Hitler's Social Revolution: Class and Status in Nazi Germany, 1933–1939* (New York: Doubleday, Anchor books, 1967).

111 On "moral statistics" in Germany, see the remarks in Oberschall, *Empirical Social Research*, pp. 45 ff. For some examples of this kind of research, see A. Wagner, *Die Gesetzmässigkeit in den scheinbar willkürlichen menschlichen Handlungen* (Hamburg: Boyes and Geisler, 1864); A. von Oettingen, *Die Moralstatistik in ihrer Bedeutung für eine Sozialethik*, 3d ed. (Erlangen, Deichert, 1882); and F. Prinzing, *Trunksucht und Selbstmord* (Leipzig: J. E. Hinrichs, 1895).

112 E. Durkheim, *Suicide: A Study in Sociology* (New York: Free Press, 1951); F. Tönnies, "Der Selbstmord in Schleswig-Holstein," *Veröffentlichungen der Schleswig-Holsteinschen Universitätsgesellschaft* 9 (1927). See also S. J. Krose, *Der Selbstmord im 19. Jahrhundert nach seiner Verteilung auf Staaten und Verwaltungsbezirke* (Freiburg i. B.: Herder, 1906); and the rather macabre *Bibliographie des Selbstmords*, compiled by Hans Rost (Augsburg: Haas and Grabherr, 1927). On Tönnies's statistical research, consult A. Bellebaum, *Das soziologische System von Ferdinand Tönnies unter besonderer Berücksichtigung seiner soziographischen Untersuchungen* (Meisenheim-am-Glan; A. Hain, 1966). The best introduction to the general problem of research on suicide is Jack Douglas's *The Social Meaning of Suicide* (Princeton: Princeton University Press, 1967).

113 Durkheim, *Suicide*, pp. 192 ff.

114 Ibid., pp. 203 ff.

115 For some very useful remarks on statistical problems in the study of deviance and crime, see J. I. Kitsuse and A. V. Cicourel, "A Note on the Official Use of Statistics," *Social Problems* 11 (1963): 131–39. The availability and nature of crime statistics for Germany are discussed in G. Lindenberg, "Die Ergebnisse der deutschen Kriminalstatistik, 1882–1892," *Jahrbücher für Nationalökonomie und Statistik*, 3d ser. 8 (1894): 588–99, 714–29. A guide to comparative data in the nineteenth century is K. Reichel's "Die Statistik der Strafrechtspflege in den Staaten Europas und in den Staaten des deutschen Reichs," *Schmollers Jahrbuch* 4 (1880): 379–414. Tönnies's

study of Schleswig-Holstein—"Verbrechertum in Schleswig-Holstein," *Archiv für Sozialwissenschaft und Sozialpolitik* 52 (1924): 761–805; 57 (1927): 608–28; 61 (1929): 322–59—is one of the few efforts at a close study of crime in a particular region. See the critique of Tönnies in Oberschall, *Empirical Social Research*, pp. 52 ff.

116 M. Liepmann, *Krieg und Kriminalität in Deutschland* (Stuttgart, Berlin, Leipzig: Deutsche Verlagsanstalt, 1930). On statistical problems see p. 5 ff.

117 The best introduction to the limits of sexual statistics is R. Michels, "Altes und Neues zum Problem der Moralstatistik (Kritik der Geschlechtsmoralstatistik)," *Archiv für Sozialwissenschaft und Sozialpolitik* 57 (1927): 417–69, 701–45. A useful guide to the published data is provided by the annotated bibliography, *Die Frauenfrage in Deutschland . . . 1790–1930*, ed. H. Sveistrup and A. von Zahn-Harnack (Burg bei München: Hopfer, 1934).

118 The following is a sample of the data collected on sexual behavior: F. Prinzing, *Handbuch der medizinischen Statistik* (Jena: G. Fischer, 1906), on illegitimacy, venereal disease, prostitution; Dr. Meyer, "Statistik der Geschlechtskranken," *Jahrbücher für Nationalökonomie und Statistik*, 3d ser. 63 (1922): 351–66, on results of a 1921 survey of physicians; C. Wagner, *Die geschlechtlichsittlichen Verhältnisse der evangelischen Landbewohner im deutschen Rieche*, 2 vols. (Leipzig: R. Werther, 1895–96), giving results of a survey of Protestant pastors in Germany on the sexual behavior of their congregations. Also of interest are C. Schneider's classic, *Die Prostituierte und die Gesellschaft* (Leipzig: J. A. Barth, 1908); and F. Lindner, *Die unehelichen Geburten als Sozialphänomen. Ein Beitrag zur Statistik der Bevölkerungsbewegung in Königreich Bayern* (Leipzig: Deichert, 1900). Shorter's "Middle Class Anxiety" and Knodel's "Law, Marriage, and Illegitimacy" are both relevant to an understanding of the social significance of illegitimacy. For Shorter's recent work on these matters, see his two forthcoming articles: "Sexual Change and Illegitimacy: The European Experience," in *New Directions in European Social History*, ed. Robert J. Bezucha (Boston: D. C. Heath, 1972); and "The Sexual Consequences of Social Change," *Journal of Interdisciplinary History*, [October 1971].

119 See E. Rolffs, *Das kirchliche Leben der evangelische Kirchen in Niedersachsen* (Tübingen: J. C. B. Mohr, 1917). For a hint of the data gathered by the government, see the statistics on "Das Verhältnis der Taufen zu den Geburten und der kirchlichen Trauungen zu den bürgerlichen Eheschliessungen bei den evangelischen Gemeinden der älterern preussischen Provinzen im 4. Quartel 1874, in *Ministerialblatt für die gesamte innere Verwaltung in den königlich preussischen Staaten* 37 (1876): 43–44.

120 Günther Dehn, *Proletarische Jugend* (Berlin, 1923); P. Piechowski, *Proletarischer Glaube* (Berlin: Furche, 1927). On these and other works, see Oberschall, *Empirical Social Research*, pp. 33 ff.

121 M. Offenbacher, *Konfession und soziale Schichtung. Eine Studie über die wirtschaftliche Lage der Katholiken und Protestanten in Baden* (Tübingen and Leipzig: J. C. B. Mohr, 1901). Offenbacher has come under attack by the critics of the Weber thesis. See especially K. Samuelsson, *Religion and Economic Action. A Critique of Max Weber* (New York and Evanston, Ill.: Harper Torchbooks, 1964), pp. 137–47.

122 A. Burger, *Religionszugehörigkeit und soziales Verhalten. Untersuchungen und Statistiken der neueren Zeit in Deutschland* (Göttingen: Vandenhoeck and Ruprecht, 1964).

123 Carl August Lückerath, "Prolegomena zur elektronischen Datenverarbeitung im Bereich der Geschichtswissenshaft," *Historische Zeitschrift*, vol. 207, no. 2 (1968), pp. 265–96.

8

A DATA ARCHIVE FOR MODERN
BRITISH POLITICAL HISTORY

by William O. Aydelotte

Over the last several decades there has been a rapidly developing interest in the study of British political history by quantitative means. Scholars have come increasingly to realize that the collection of large amounts of data and their presentation in tabular form may be used to advance the discussion of certain types of problems that could not properly be dealt with in other ways. Yet, though significant work has already been done, scholars in this area have been under a handicap. Assembling information for such investigations is immensely laborious, and the lack of readily available collections of quantitative data in a suitable form has placed limitations on research and has made it difficult to follow up certain promising lines of investigation. In this respect students of British history are at a disadvantage as compared to students of American history. Vigorous efforts have been made in the United States to meet these needs with various collections of information, the most notable of which is the immense collection of materials now being assembled by the Inter-University Consortium for Political Research at Ann Arbor, Michigan. I wish to raise the question of whether it would be possible to attempt a similar enterprise for Great Britain: to collect, for British political history in the nineteenth and twentieth centuries, data in machine-readable form comparable, as far as circumstances permit, to the data for American political history in the same period which are now being gathered by the consortium.

The consortium, in addition to providing special information for in-

I wish to express my thanks to William J. Marland, my research assistant, for help in assembling these materials, and to Jerome M. Clubb, director of the Historical Archive of the Inter-University Consortium for Political Research, for providing me with information about the operation and plans of the consortium. I am also indebted to colleagues both in the United States and in England who have read the chapter and made a number of extremely useful suggestions. This chapter is also appearing as chapter 4 in my book, *Quantification in History* (Reading, Mass.: Addison-Wesley, 1971).

dividual projects, has undertaken three large general programs: the collection of electoral, roll-call, and demographic data. First, it is gathering and processing county-level returns for elections to the four offices of president, governor, and United States senator and representative. These county returns will be summed to constituency totals. Plans are also being considered for assembling information on selected state referenda—it is estimated that there have been between 15,000 and 20,000 of these [1]—and on primary elections in southern states. Second, the consortium is recording and processing the votes of all individuals in all roll calls in both houses of Congress, from the Continental Congresses to the present. Finally, it is assembling data on demographic conditions from the published United States census reports from 1790 to the present and will, presumably, try to obtain such information from other sources as well. These data, which are mostly at the county level, will be summed to the congressional district level and the state level.

To follow this example for Great Britain would be an immense undertaking. Even so, it would be restricted: this is only one of a number of lines that the collection of quantitative data could take. In the first place, such an enterprise, with its focus on political history, would make only limited contributions to social and economic history, two areas of British studies where a good deal of active quantifying is already going on.[2] Nor would it embrace all the possibilities for the collection of quantitative data even in political history. Local authority elections in Britain have attracted the attention of several scholars and are clearly of great interest,[3] though their incorporation in the present scheme would constitute an almost unmanageably large addition to an already huge project. Possibly use could be made, for electoral data, of information in the surviving pollbooks. Votes in Parliament, particularly since party discipline has increased, are not always revealing and might be supplemented by other types of information that would yield more direct clues to the opinions of members. Punch cards could also be used to record information about the personal backgrounds of members of Parliament and could serve, in this way, as the basis for analyses of the composition of Parliament, collective biographies of its members, in different periods. On this last point a good deal of interesting work has already been done, though not always with punch cards.

It seems essential, however, in any program for the collection of quantitative data, to impose restrictions. Efforts to collect such materials are more likely to be successful if directed toward limited objectives, and a program that is too broad or too ambitious may be self-defeating. Although the possibilities of quantitative research in social and economic history are by no means exhausted, the need for assembling materials in political history is also great. It is true that a significant start has been made and that valuable data have been collected by several English scholars, including David Butler, Henry Pelling, B. R. Mitchell, Richard Rose, Hugh Berrington, and others. If the project suggested here is undertaken, every effort should be made to take advantage of the knowledge and experience of these individuals and of any assistance that they are willing to give. The other side of the picture, however, is that work along these lines has been impeded by the lack of a large and readily available collection of basic data and that, for this reason, those who have pioneered in the field have been operating under difficulties.

Though the field of political history offers various possibilities for data collection, there are arguments for attempting to follow the precedent of the consortium that appear to have some weight. The limits this precedent sets are not in any case stringent: this program is in itself so large that there may be a real question whether it can ever be carried through. Also, whatever other types of information might be considered for inclusion, there can be little question that the three kinds of data now being assembled by the consortium are central to the study and understanding of any parliamentary system. It is an additional consideration that following the precedent of the consortium might make possible some interesting comparisons. The complaint is frequently made, and it is well justified, that historians working on similar problems in different fields or in different periods do not ask the same questions; as a result, their findings cannot be compared, and the gain in cumulative knowledge that might have been expected does not occur. The value of comparative studies, when circumstances permit them, has been increasingly appreciated; indeed, a journal devoted to such studies has been established and is now being published from Ann Arbor. Following the example of the consortium would also make it possible to benefit from what those associated with that enterprise have learned during the six years in which it has been in operation. The consortium, though its work is far from complete, has already advanced so far that it can scarcely avoid being regarded, to some extent at least, as a model by those engaged in similar enterprises. Its staff has, in fact, been increasingly drawn into an advisory function, into the work of providing technical suggestions to other organizations on the full range of problems of data handling, and has come to regard this work as part of its normal task.[4]

ELECTORAL DATA

In any democratic or parliamentary system, elections are presumed to constitute the principal machinery through which the nation at large is able to exert control over those who govern it. Though it is now clear that this control is more complex in nature and more ambiguous in impact than was once believed, it is still in a sense true that information about elections forms the basic data of political history. Students of national politics or of legislative behavior naturally wish to know something of the local circumstances in the constituencies where the elections took place. They will be concerned about such matters as, for example, whether a contest occurred, the nature of the party competition, the extent of malapportionment, and the degree of participation by the electorate.

Of the various categories of elections on which the consortium is gathering data for the United States—the elections of president, governor, senator, and so forth—all but one are irrelevant for British politics. There is no presidential election in Great Britain, since the prime minister is chosen by the sovereign with the approval of Parliament. There is nothing to correspond to the election of a governor, since there is no local office of comparable importance. There is nothing similar to the election of a senator, since the House of Lords is not elective. American state referenda and primary elections do not have significant parallels in Great Britain. The only elections in Great Britain that can be studied in this way are those to the House of Commons. Scholars concerned with British electoral data need to study only one set of elections, not four or more, and this constitutes an initial simplification of the task.

Furthermore, information on how many votes were cast for each candidate in each local election is usually, though not always, easy to get. It can be obtained from a number of convenient sources that can, when necessary, be checked against each other.[5] Information about by-elections does not always appear in such sources; it is often, however, reported in the newspapers. B. R. Mitchell and Klaus Boehm, in their survey of electoral results since 1950, were able to obtain additional information about by-elections from the librarian of the London *Times* and from the electoral registration officers of a number of constituencies. It is also an advantage that for British elections the consortium's problem of summing county-level returns to constituency totals does not arise; it is the constituency totals that are given in the first place.

There seems no reason at present to expect unusual difficulties in processing this information. It might be supposed that party labels would be troublesome, since a good many different ones have appeared in British politics over the last two centuries and, in addition, a number of candidates have claimed to be independent. A conscientious scholar might find himself burdened with an uncomfortably large number of party categories. It turns out, however, that the consortium is now working with well over eight hundred individual party labels and with many unaffiliated candidates as well. (Candidates are, of course, recorded by name as well as by party.) If such a variety can be managed for American political history, presumably it can be for British political history too. There might also be a question about the feasibility of processing, in addition to the results of general elections, the results of by-elections occurring at irregular times. On this point, too, the experience of the consortium is reassuring. I am informed that, though there has been some difficulty in recovering data for by-elections, including this information, once it is obtained, in the data archive has created no special problems.

The difficulties of handling British electoral statistics are quite different. They do not relate to finding and tabulating the information, which appear to be relatively easy matters. They arise, rather, from the character of the British electoral system, which is, or at least has been, different from the American one in important respects. As a result of these differences, electoral information cannot be used for scholarly purposes in quite the same way, and some of the things commonly done with American data cannot be done with British data. Problems develop particularly when an attempt is made to appraise the general or national political situation.

There are, first, the matters of the "multiple vote" and the "plural vote." In multiple-member constituencies, until 1867, each elector had as many votes as there were members for the constituency. In 1867 multiple voting was reduced though not eliminated: voters in three-member constituencies, for example, were now allowed only two votes instead of three. Multiple voting almost disappeared in 1885, when single-member constituencies were made nearly universal. Yet eighteen two-member constituencies, and even one three-member constituency (the Scottish Universities), survived until the legislation of 1948, so that the first general election in which there was no multiple voting whatsoever was that of 1950. This feature of the British electoral system makes it difficult, for most of the nineteenth century, to get any clear idea of the total number of individuals supporting a particular party. One cannot simply add the votes in the various constituencies, since a vote might represent one elector, half an elector, or even one-third or one-fourth of an elector. The number of votes cast will in any case be much greater than the number of electors who voted. Furthermore, the number of votes cast in a constituency with two or more members is not even a multiple of the number of electors who voted, because of the practice of "plumping" which enabled an elector to give one of his votes to a candidate while withholding his other vote or votes. In other words, although an elector could not cast more than one vote for a single candidate, he was at liberty to refrain from exercising his privilege to vote for anyone else, and it was of course advantageous to the candidate of his choice that he should do so. In some elections in some constituencies the number of plumpers is known from contemporary sources such as pollbooks that have survived, and D. C. Moore and J. R. Vincent have done interesting work with this kind of material.[6] When such information is not available, it is difficult to determine the number of electors who supported either side. This in turn makes it difficult to determine the extent of participation by the electorate. Furthermore, the system frequently resulted in the return of candidates of opposite political persuasions from the same constituency, often without a contest,[7] making the party loyalty or political affiliation of the constituency an ambiguous matter.

It was also possible for a single individual to vote in more than one constituency. Plural voting, in the sense of the business vote and the university vote, did not altogether disappear until 1948. In certain circumstances, a man with a home in one constituency and a business establishment in another could vote in both. Also, some of those who voted in the constituencies in which they lived could vote in university constituencies as well, provided that they were graduates of the universities concerned who had kept their names in the universities' registers. Since the incidence of plural voting is not easy to calculate, this is another factor that can distort regional or national summations.

The most serious problem, however, is that of elections which were uncontested or not fully contested. It is often not possible to say what was the vote in a given constituency in a given general election because there was no vote: only one candidate presented himself for each seat, he was returned unopposed, and no contest occurred. The problem here is not that the data are difficult to recover but that they do not exist: the events that could have generated them never took place. Since there is no point to setting up a large project to collect nonexistent information, the question of the exact incidence of contests in the period since 1832 is crucial. This information is presented in table 8.1. Norman Gash has pointed out that "it is surprisingly difficult to get agreed figures of contested elections" for the period 1832–47,[8] and this is true also for the succeeding decades. The figures it proved possible to assemble from the available sources do not invariably coincide with those presented by other students, who indeed often do not agree with each other, but the differences are in all cases small, and the general picture stands out clearly enough.[9]

From table 8.1 it appears that, until the election of 1880, the proportion of uncontested seats was always more than one-fourth, and that in the 1840s and 1850s it was often more than one-half. After the mid-nineteenth century, the proportion of uncontested seats gradually decreased, but, with the exceptions of the elections of 1885 and 1892, it remained considerable until after the First World War. Since then, 90 percent or more of the seats have generally been contested, though the first election in British history in which contests took place in every constituency was that of 1955; a fact that attracted some attention at the time. These figures do not, however, tell the whole story, and actually the number of seats effectively contested by the two major parties was, during a considerable part of the nineteenth century, even less. As H. J. Hanham has pointed out, some seats were contested only by rival candidates of the same party, while others in two-member constituencies were virtually uncontested because the weaker party put up only one candidate. Also, the development of the Home Rule movement put an end to contests in Ireland between Liberals and Conservatives, except in the smallest boroughs and in Ulster, since one party usually withdrew and left the other to fight the Home Rulers. Hanham estimates, on the basis of some figures he has presented in a table, that "about half the 650-odd seats were either absolutely uncontested or virtually uncontested in 1868 and 1874, and about two-fifths of them in 1880."[10] It is extremely difficult to make reliable estimates of the total national support for either party before the

Table 8.1

Uncontested Seats, 1832–1964

Year of general election	Number of uncontested seats	Total number of seats	Percentage of seats uncontested
1832	189	658	28.7
1835	271	658	41.2
1837	234	658	35.6
1841	336	658	51.1
1847	368	656	56.1
1852	257	654	39.3
1857	330	654	50.5
1859	379	654	58.0
1865	301	658	45.7
1868	210	658	31.9
1874	187	652	28.7
1880	108	652	16.6
1885	44	670	6.6
1886	224	670	33.4
1892	63	670	9.4
1895	188	670	28.1
1900	243	670	36.3
1906	113	670	16.9
1910 (Jan.)	75	670	11.2
1910 (Dec.)	162	670	24.2
1918	107	707	15.1
1922	57	615	9.3
1923	50	615	8.1
1924	32	615	5.2
1929	7	615	1.1
1931	65	615	10.6
1935	40	615	6.5
1945	3	640	0.5
1950	2	625	0.3
1951	4	625	0.6
1955	0	630	0.0
1959	0	630	0.0
1964	0	630	0.0

SOURCE: These figures are based primarily on the following sources: *Returns of Election Expenses* in *Parliamentary Papers;* the successive volumes of Dod's *Parliamentary Companion;* idem, *Electoral Facts;* McCalmont, *Parliamentary Poll Book* (see p. 357 n. 5 below). See p. 357 n. 9 for the explanation of the small variations in the total number of seats before 1885.

First World War. Hanham has argued persuasively that nineteenth-century elections bear only superficial resemblances to twentieth-century ones and that comparisons between the two are largely meaningless. This is not only because election registers and election results were more carelessly prepared or recorded in the last century; it is principally because general elections in the period he discusses were not general, since only about half the seats were contested by both parties. Such comparisons, according to Hanham, can be made only for the limited number of constituencies that were, in the nineteenth century, contested at every election by enough candidates to make it clear that the contest was a party one as well as a local one.[11]

Students of British politics have of course turned their attention to these problems, and statistical devices have been worked out to deal with them and to make appropriate corrections in the total figures. Yet an element of uncertainty, the exact size of which is difficult to calculate, still remains.[12] This feature of the situation, the inevitable incompleteness of British electoral data, may well raise some question as to how far an expensive program of assembling such data for the nineteenth and twentieth centuries can be justified.

The other side of the argument, however, is that, for any subject or for any period of history, one must make do with what one has. Although a realistic assessment of the difficulties should be made at the outset, the question should also be asked whether the materials at hand are still sufficiently abundant to furnish some solid basis for study. The answer to this question is clearly in the affirmative, as indeed Hanham's own suggestive manipulations of nineteenth-century election figures go far to show. It should not be forgotten that the lack of a contest in a given constituency is itself a significant datum, and that even contests between candidates of the same party are often worth studying.

Consideration should also be given to including in the data archive types of electoral information that are peculiar to British politics and that it would not be appropriate to collect for the United States. One feature of great interest is the extent of electoral influence, but this, though its existence and importance are indubitable, is so various in its manifestations and so difficult to appraise exactly that it would be almost impossible to quantify. Figures on the size of the electorate and the size of the population for each constituency, on the other hand, are easy to get and could be included. From these figures some interesting ratios could readily be derived which perhaps should be calculated—a simple matter—and incorporated in the data. The ratio of the electorate to the number of seats and the ratio of the population to the number of seats, for each constituency, would make useful crude indexes of malapportionment. The ratio of the population to the electorate would give an indication of the impact of the differing franchise requirements in different types of constituencies and, for constituencies of the same type, would give some indication of how large a segment of the population could meet these requirements—in the mid-nineteenth century this was a far smaller segment in southern Ireland, for example, than in other parts of the United Kingdom. Figures on these three points for the entire country are shown for illustrative purposes in table 8.2. They could

Table 8.2

Variations in Relationships Between Size of Electorate,
Size of Population, and Number of Seats in
House of Commons, 1832–1964

Year	Ratio of electorate to number of seats	Ratio of population to number of seats	Ratio of population to electorate
1832	1,230	37,132	30.19
1835	1,277	38,198	29.92
1837	1,465	38,983	26.62
1841	1,594	40,592	25.47
1847	1,728	42,640	24.67
1852	1,810	41,970	23.18
1857	1,843	43,100	23.39
1859	1,936	43,717	22.59
1865	2,063	45,479	22.04
1868	3,764	46,641	12.39
1874	4,327	49,849	11.52
1880	4,617	53,103	11.50
1885	8,219	53,755	6.54
1886	8,462	54,199	6.41
1892	9,185	56,916	6.20
1895	9,451	58,539	6.19
1900	10,046	61,425	6.11
1906	10,843	64,718	5.97
1910 (Jan.)	11,485	67,039	5.84
1910 (Dec.)	11,507	67,564	5.87
1918	30,258	61,229	2.02
1922	34,354	72,150	2.10
1923	34,604	72,515	2.10
1924	35,335	73,034	2.07
1929	46,912	74,263	1.58
1931	48,717	74,919	1.54
1935	51,023	76,210	1.49
1945	51,307	76,847	1.50
1950	54,832	80,986	1.48
1951	55,433	80,360	1.45
1955	55,331	80,902	1.45
1959	56,186	82,517	1.47
1964	56,972	85,238	1.50

NOTE: The figures in this table cannot be accepted as entirely exact, partly because it is known that there were many inaccuracies in the returns of the numbers of registered electors, and partly because general elections often do not coincide with census years—when this is the case, it is necessary to rely on contemporary estimates of the size of the population.

easily be prepared for individual constituencies, and this should be done, since local variations at any one time could be extensive.

For the study of the attitudes and opinions of the British political elite, the division lists, though they have hitherto been surprisingly little exploited for research purposes, are an extraordinarily rich source. They relate to major questions of the day; they are voluminous and give ample and repeatedly corroborated information; they are remarkably accurate and reliable, as historical sources go; and they give comparable information for a large number of individuals, the members of the House of Commons. Their possible value was suggested many years ago by A. Lawrence Lowell in a monograph published in the annual report of the American Historical Association for 1901.[13] His study, though crude by present-day standards, was imaginative and forward-looking and anticipated in an interesting way some of the trends of modern research. Yet Lowell's work was not extensively followed up, and only comparatively recently have scholars again begun to address themselves to the kinds of questions that could be answered with such information. Historians now have more powerful analytical tools, largely supplied by workers in other disciplines, with which to come to terms with these great masses of material. They also have the aid of computers, if they want them and are willing to learn how to use them. What they do not have is the information itself, which is so voluminous and so difficult to collect that a single individual, working with limited time and money, can scarcely hope to assemble even all the evidence relevant to his own subject of study.

Information on the divisions is easily available, at least from 1836, when the House of Commons commenced publication of its own division lists. Hansard also gives division lists, but its information for the early nineteenth century is incomplete. For 1836, for example, the first year of publication of the official lists, Hansard gives 128 divisions, and of these only 110 were recorded entire; for 18 the votes on only one side were listed. The official published list, on the other hand, gives 187 divisions for 1836.[14] There is a copy of the published lists of divisions in the House of Commons, from 22 February 1836 through August 1897, in the Library of the Institute of Historical Research in London, of which I have had a microfilm made for the University of Iowa Library. I have used these lists in preparing this report, but, for the period after 1897—when Hansard, so far as I have been able to check it, appears to be much more complete—I have used only Hansard.

It might be best to begin the tabulation of divisions in the House of Commons with 1836, the first year of the publication of the official lists. Professor Donald Ginter of Duke University is collecting information on early divisions in the House of Commons, and he intends to bring his survey down at least through the general election of 1830, and possibly further. The present project should, in any case, be set up so as to mesh with his and to avoid leaving a no-man's-land in between. If the years 1830–35 are not to be included in his project, then they could be incorporated into this one. It does not make much difference, since there are only a limited number of divisions in these years for which information can be obtained, and including them would not involve a large addition to the task. Arrangements should be made so that the materials before and after 1830 are placed in the same data collection and punched in such a way that they can be mechanically compared. Presumably these matters can be worked out, since Professor Ginter is already in touch with the consortium about his plans.

The technical problems of recording and punching information on the division lists are not serious. On this point I can speak from experience, since I have, for my own research, tabulated nearly 200 divisions and found few difficulties. The kind of problem that occurs is, for example, that of differentiating between men of similar names who were recorded in the same way in the division lists, but these matters can generally be puzzled out, and such ambiguities usually involve relatively small numbers. It would be premature to discuss here matters of detail—how far, for example, the ten voting categories set up by the consortium for the United States, or some adaptation of them, can be used for Great Britain—but the formats and procedures already worked out by the consortium for handling roll calls would provide at least some hints and guidelines for tabulating divisions in the House of Commons.

I have tried to make some estimate of the size of the task. The division lists for 1836–97 in the library of the Institute of Historical Research, according to my count, include 14,824 divisions. The divisions in Hansard from 1898 to 25 November 1966 amount to 19,839. This produces a total of 34,663. (The numbers of divisions for each year are shown in Table 8.3) Even if the divisions in Hansard for 1830–35 were added, the total would be only slightly over 35,000. This is a much smaller enterprise than that proposed by the consortium for the United States. Though the exact figure is not yet known, the best present estimate appears to be that the consortium will record, for both houses of Congress, from 1775 to the present, in the neighborhood of 60,000 roll calls. This is, of course, for a period about sixty years longer than that suggested for Great Britain, and for two houses instead of one. This last point raises the question of the divisions in the House of Lords, which will be discussed presently. For the House of Commons, at least, the task suggested for Great Britain would be decidedly smaller than what is being attempted for the United States. The consortium hopes to add data for future Congresses as well, and this would doubtless also be possible for Great Britain.

The most serious problem in the use of data on the division lists is neither

Table 8.3

Number of Divisions in House of Commons Each Year, 1836–1966

Year	Number of divisions	Year	Number of divisions	Year	Number of divisions
1836	187	1882	405	1926	563
1837	185	1883	314	1927	482
1837/38	294	1884	216	1928	366
1839	250	1884/85	289	1928/29	300
1840	256	1886 (Session 1)	143	1929/30	484
1841 (Session 1)	109	1886 (Session 2)	46	1930/31	521
1841 (Session 2)	12	1887	485	1931/32	366
1842	237	1888	357	1932/33	311
1843	220	1889	360	1933/34	414
1844	156	1890	262	1934/35	308
1845	170	1890/91	416	1935/36	326
1846	106	1892 (Session 1)	196	1936/37	322
1847	128	1892 (Session 2)	1	1937/38	329
1847/48	255	1893/94	450	1938/39	308
1849	219	1894	246	1939/40	70
1850	329	1895 (Session 1)	140	1940/41	21
1851	242	1895 (Session 2)	38	1941/42	24
1852	127	1896	413	1942/43	29
1852/53	257	1897	367	1943/44	45
1854	240	1898	310	1944/45	22
1854/55	213	1899 (Session 1)	363	1945/46	294
1856	197	1899 (Session 2)	18	1946/47	383
1857 (Session 1)	15	1900 (Session 1)	290	1947/48	278
1857 (Session 2)	162	1900 (Session 2)	8	1948 (14 Sept.–25 Oct.)	10
1857/58	185	1901	482	1948/49	310
1859 (Session 1)	41	1902	648	1950 (Mar.–Oct.)	65
1859 (Session 2)	59	1903	263		
1860	265	1904	341		
1861	187	1905	364	1950/51	170
1862	222	1906	501	1951/52	245
1863	188	1907	466	1952/53	227
1864	156	1908	463	1953/54	230
1865	104	1909	920	1954/55 (Nov.–May)	61
1866	80	1910	159		
1867	164	1911	451	1955/56	298
1867/68	168	1912	604	1956/57	180
1868/69	160	1913	17	1957/58	206
1870	244	1914	214	1958/59	177
1871	270	1914/15	34	1959/60	156
1872	287	1916	67	1960/61	269
1873	226	1917	157	1961/62	261
1874	162	1918	95	1962/63	183
1875	248	1919	166	1963/64	148
1876	242	1920	460	1964/65	276
1877	314	1921 (Session 1)	367	1965/66 (Nov.–Mar.)	39
1878	278	1921 (Session 2)	1		
1878/79	237	1922	272	1966/67 (to 25 Nov. 1966)	209
1880 (Session 1)	47	1923	345		
1880 (Session 2)	169	1924	201		
1881	411	1924/25	506	Total	34,663

the accessibility of the information nor its bulk; rather, it is the astonishingly low level of participation in voting in the House of Commons until quite recent times. The largest division on record is said to be that of 11 August 1892, when, on a motion expressing lack of confidence in the government, the vote was 350 to 310.[15] The size of the House at that time was 670, so that participation in this division was extremely high, particularly if one counts the four tellers. So large a vote was, however, altogether exceptional, as appears from table 8.4, which gives figures on participation every tenth year from 1836 to the present. (I have used the year 1964/65

Table 8.4

Extent of Participation in Voting in Divisions in the House
of Commons, Selected Years, 1836–1964/65

Year	Total number of divisions	Extent of Participation in Voting			
		Under 100	100–99	200–99	300 or more
1836	187	36.9	43.3	11.8	8.0
1846	106	41.5	32.1	17.0	9.4
1856	197	14.2	46.7	30.0	9.1
1866	80	28.8	26.2	10.0	35.0
1876	242	16.5	29.8	30.2	23.5
1886	189	4.8	25.9	39.1	30.2
1896	413	0.2	21.8	37.3	40.7
1906	501	0.0	4.8	20.2	75.0
1916	67	16.4	46.3	32.8	4.5
1926	563	0.4	5.1	27.0	67.5
1935/36	326	0.0	7.1	23.3	69.6
1945/46	294	0.0	2.7	18.0	79.3
1955/56	298	0.7	3.0	11.1	85.2
1964/65	276	1.1	3.2	17.4	78.3

NOTE: The figures in the last four columns show, for each year, as a percentage, the proportion of divisions in which the number indicated at the top of the column participated. Thus, in 1836, the proportion of the divisions in which fewer than 100 men participated was 36.9%; in 1964/65, this proportion was 1.1%.

instead of 1965/66, since the information available to me for 1965/66 was not complete.) If the decennial samples in this table are a reliable guide—and the consistency of the figures suggests that some confidence may be placed in them—participation was extremely low until the twentieth century. The proportion of divisions in which at least 300 men participated, in a House that always included well over 600 members, appears to have been under one-tenth until the end of the 1850s, and well under one-half until the end of the nineteenth century. In the twentieth century, except in time of war, participation was greater, though still far from approaching completeness. For the division lists, as for electoral data, the difficulty is not that the information is hard to get but, rather, that much of the desired information—the opinions of many members of Parliament on many subjects—does not exist, since the events that would have produced it did not occur.

This brings up an issue of policy. The question may legitimately be raised of how useful it is to tabulate these very small divisions, which are particularly numerous in the earlier period. The purpose of recording votes in the divisions is presumably to provide information about the opinions of members of Parliament on issues of the day. These tiny divisions, however, reveal the opinions of only a few men, and are not of much help in judging the temper of Parliament as a whole. They also impose a restriction on the correlation of votes in Parliament with other kinds of information, such as the personal circumstances of members of Parliament or the kinds of constituencies they represented. One cannot make these comparisons for members who did not vote and it is always an open question how far the patterns emerging from the study of small divisions can be used to characterize the entire body.

It might be asked, then, whether a certain number of divisions, those below a stipulated minimum size, might not be omitted from the tabulations. Certainly this would result in a considerable saving of labor. Certainly, also, scholars working alone, with limited resources of time and money, have often followed the policy of disregarding roll calls in which the turnout did not reach a certain proportion of the total membership of the legislative body, say 50 percent or even 80 percent. In my own research on the House of Commons in the 1840s, when participation was low, I shall probably examine less than one-fifth of the divisions that took place in the Parliament I am studying and shall make a disproportionately larger use of the big divisions than of the small ones. The consortium is recording all roll calls, regardless of the degree of turnout or the degree of unanimity, but on this point the American example may not be relevant, since those dealing with American roll-call data, I have been told, are not faced with the problem of nonparticipation on anything like the same scale.

On the other hand, omitting divisions below a certain size might involve losing valuable information. Questions dealt with in such divisions may have an interest for modern scholars that they apparently did not have for contemporaries. In view of what came of these matters later, it is interesting to trace their early development. It is also useful to learn what kinds of legislation slipped through the House of Commons with few or no divisions. Further, a study of the small divisions can reveal which members of Parliament were regular attenders and participants, and on what subjects. Besides, there were periods when divisions were small for special reasons— as they apparently were in wartime, to judge from the figures in the table for 1916—and it would be undesirable to lose these by the general application of a cutoff point. It is also relevant that the use of certain techniques of analysis that are now available, such as scaling, may enable the student to extract more information from the small divisions than originally appeared possible.

For the most recent period of British history, there is a problem of quite another kind. With the growth of party discipline, votes have tended more to follow party lines, and the division lists for the twentieth century, even though participation has been high, may be of less value as indicators of opinion than those of the nineteenth century when participation was low. There is a real question whether the division lists in the most recent period reveal enough additional information to be worth recording.

Here again there is another side to the argument. Party discipline in the present age, though it is presumed to be strong, has not been subject to controlled observation, and it would be interesting to learn how far the general impression that obtains about it is sustained by the facts. More important, we do not yet know when straight or almost straight party voting started. It is sometimes assumed to be a twentieth-century phenomenon, but I have recently seen, in the research findings of some of my former students, evidence of strong correlations between party and vote in the second half of the nineteenth century.[16] On the other hand, there have been notorious deviations from straight party voting in the twentieth century. The story of the development of the relation between party and vote in the House of Commons is not yet known, and it is worth investigating.

There are also more general arguments for tabulating all divisions. A policy of comprehensiveness seems more justifiable for a permanent archive, to be used by different scholars for different purposes, than it would be for a project undertaken by a single individual. If all the data were included, individual scholars could, as they do with data from the consortium, develop and use their own definitions of significance and exclude by mechanical means—an easy matter with the aid of computers—the classes of items they did not want. The policy of punching everything also means that complications of selection are avoided. If there is reasonable doubt about an item, it may be better to include it than to exclude it, to avoid the trouble of having to retrace one's steps later. To cover everything while the machinery is in operation may be more economical of time in the long run. In addition, a rigid commitment to a certain criterion might result in the exclusion of items that, in the light of further knowledge, could prove significant. It is hard to lay down in advance a general rule that will cover all contingencies; if certain classes of items were omitted, one could never be sure how much distortion the omissions had produced. For all these reasons, the case for punching everything may be stronger than the case for attempting to make a selection.

Some thought should be given to the possibility of recording divisions in the House of Lords as well. The situation here was very different. There were far fewer divisions, and the extent of participation, in relation to the total size of the House, was even less. Even for the nineteenth century there were relatively few divisions in which half the House participated, and, in the decennial sample I have examined, for the twentieth century there were none. The House of Lords is one legislative body in which participation in voting has, over the last century, decreased rather than increased. This is no doubt due in part to its enormous growth in size: it has more than doubled in the period since 1836 and has in fact doubled in the ninety years since 1876. The figures in table 8.5 give some information about the number of divisions in the Lords and the size of the turnout. To get a rough estimate of the extent of this task, I have had a count made of the number of divisions in Hansard, taking one year in each decade from 1836 to 1966. For these fourteen years there was a total of 216 divisions, an average of 15.43 divisions a year. This figure, extrapolated for the entire 131-year period, yields an estimate of 2,021 divisions. Though this estimate is extremely rough, it will serve to give a general idea of the amount of work involved. It seems clear that the addition of perhaps 2,000 divisions in the Lords to the 35,000 divisions in the Commons, making a total of 37,000, would not be an enterprise of great magnitude.

Table 8.5

Extent of Participation in Voting in the House of Lords, Selected Years, 1836–1965/66

Year	Total number of divisions	Size of divisions (proxies, when stated, included)					Total membership of House
		1–49	50–99	100–99	200–99	300–99	
1836	22	3	12	4	1	2	435
1846	3	1	0	0	1	1	459
1856	7	1	2	2	2	0	455
1866	12	2	8	2	0	0	460
1876	5	0	2	1	2	0	501
1886	7	0	1	4	2	0	544
1896	15	1	2	11	1	0	575
1906	38	1	4	26	7	0	613
1916	2	1	1	0	0	0	659
1926	30	3	15	11	1	0	720
1935/36	22	6	14	2	0	0	750
1945/46	10	0	10	0	0	0	810
1955/56	26	5	19	1	0	1	844
1965/66	17	2	9	6	0	0	1,013

Whether this is worth doing is another question. Political attitudes could not be correlated with electoral and demographic data for the Lords, though this would be possible for the Commons, since members of the Upper House, unlike those of the Lower, were neither elected nor politically tied to constituencies, even though some of them had deep local roots. However, patterns of political attitudes could be worked out from the division lists, as far as the information reaches, and the correlations of these patterns with party membership could be examined. Also, voting patterns in the House of Lords might be interesting on other grounds: in the nineteenth century, because of the still great power and influence of the Upper House and the frequent location of party leadership there; in the twentieth century, because of the special tone of the House that has developed, in contrast with the Commons, involving the more leisurely and extended examination of issues in debate and the rather different configurations of parties and other political groups. Though the divisions in the Lords are less important than those in the Commons, they have an interest of their own, and this relatively small addition to the total task might be well worth undertaking.

DEMOGRAPHIC DATA

Information on economic and social conditions in the constituencies is not always easy to get, but there can be little doubt about its theoretical interest in view of the accumulated findings showing its relation to the political attitudes of members of a legislature.[17] Some recent research has indeed suggested that demographic data may ultimately prove more significant than electoral data in the study of legislative behavior.[18] What has been discovered for the United States and other countries in the mid-twentieth century does not, of course, necessarily hold for Great Britain in the nineteenth century, but the questions that have been raised in some of the studies of the contemporary scene are so interesting and their implications so broad that it would be a pity not to investigate them so far as possible for earlier periods as well.

This discussion of demographic data is only tentative, since I am not qualified as a demographer and have done little research that involves the use of the census or similar materials. In planning this phase of the project it would be essential to seek the aid of those who have special experience with such matters: demographers and social and economic historians. This is particularly desirable since the incorporation of demographic information will, as has been pointed out,[19] make the data archive of interest to a wider group than political historians, and those who will use it for other purposes should be consulted as to what kinds of data should be gathered.

The example of the consortium is less helpful in this field than in the areas of electoral and roll-call data, since its program of collecting demographic data is still in a relatively early stage, and it is not yet clear what categories of data it will be able to process. I have been referred, for general guidance, to the report of a conference on historical demographic data held at the University of Pennsylvania on 16 October 1964, which recommended the tabulation of eleven classes of information.[20] I have used these eleven categories, plus five others kindly furnished me by the director of data recovery at the consortium, to make some preliminary comparisons.

It might be interesting, as a tentative first step, to see how far such material can be found in the reports of the British census. The pamphlet describing the British census from 1801 to 1931, which is one of the *Guides to Official Sources* published by Her Majesty's Stationery Office,[21] can serve as a general guide for this trial run. Table 8.6 shows to what extent information on each of the sixteen categories, or the nearest thing to it, is listed as available for Great Britain. I have reason to suppose that the table does not tell the whole story, since I have found, in looking over individual census reports for different dates, considerably more material than is here indicated. Yet table 8.6, however incomplete, suggests that information for Great Britain can be obtained for a substantial number of the points on which the consortium is considering collecting information for the United States, though not always quite the same information and not for all years. There is at least something to show for ten of the sixteen categories.

Also, a number of the gaps can probably be filled in quite easily. Figures are scattered throughout the *Parliamentary Papers* on the area of constituencies [22] and on the numbers of illiterates at elections (items 4 and 12).[23] In regard to the value of land and buildings (item 9), Dod's *Parliamentary Companion* gives the "Number of 10£ Houses" for each constituency up to 1885, and McCalmont's *Parliamentary Poll Book* gives a figure for the value of "Property." On industrial and agricultural production (items 10 and 15), Mitchell and Deane give gross national figures and occasionally regional figures. It may be possible to extract further information from the handbooks, from *Parliamentary Papers*, from local histories,[24] or from local guides and directories.

Yet the collection of such materials, even on a national basis, may not be easy. The British census was, in the early nineteenth century, a beginning enterprise. Although the first United States census was taken in 1790, the first for Britain was in 1801 and the first for Ireland in 1821. In Britain, as in the United States, the census inquiries changed in scope so that certain types of information are available only for a restricted number of years. On the whole the early census reports are less complete, and for some classes of data there is adequate information only from the middle or the end of the nineteenth century. There may be similar problems with other sources: I have noticed that many of the time series in Mitchell and Deane start late and do not cover the whole nineteenth century. There have also occurred, in successive census reports, so many changes in definition and in methods of classification that, for some important categories such as occupation, it is hard to get comparable figures for any extended period.[25]

The greatest difficulty, however, appears to be that of getting demographic information at the constituency level, the form in which it would be most useful for the study of political history. Even on the elementary point of population, the figures in the census may not yield everything that is needed.[26] For other kinds of information the task may be even more formidable, in view of the variety of local jurisdictions. The subdivisions of Britain used for ecclesiastical purposes; local government; parliamentary representation; the administration of justice; and the registration of births, deaths, and marriages differed from one another to such an extent as to bring the compilers of the census to a state of frustration. In the general report of the 1901 census for England and Wales there appears the following statement: "The whole of England and Wales has been divided at different

Table 8.6

Demographic Information

Column 1	*Column 2*
Points on which the consortium is considering collecting information for the United States	*Years for which information on subjects in column 1 or on related matters is available from the British census*
1. Nativity	⎱ Birthplace and nationality, 1841–
2. Race	⎰
3. Religion	1851
4. Area (sq. mi.)	—
5. Total population	1801–
6. Age distribution	1821, 1841–
7. Sex	1801–
8. Percentage urban, in different sized categories	—
9. Value of land and buildings, both rural and urban	—
10. Value of manufactured products	—
11. Occupation	Personal occupation, 1801, 1841– Family occupation, 1811–31 Whether employer or employed, 1841–
12. Literacy rates	—
13. School attendance	1851–1921, but apparently not for 1931; 1891 and 1901 for Scotland only
14. Family size	Condition as to marriage 1851– Children of present marriage, 1911 Number of children under 16, 1921
15. Agricultural production (general categories rather than specific commodities)	—
16. Home and farm ownership and indebtedness	Number of houses inhabited, 1801– Number of families occupying house, 1801–31, 1911–31 Houses being built, 1811–1921; not 1931 Houses uninhabited, 1801– Number of rooms in household, 1891– (England and Wales only)

times into various administrative areas with so little regard for previously existing divisions that, at the present time, the serious overlappings of boundaries render the work both of the Census Office and local Officials, in ascertaining the precise limits of the several divisions to be separately distinguished in the Tables, laborious and extremely complicated." [27] These difficulties are heightened, of course, by the fact that the boundaries of parliamentary constituencies were altered by legislation at various times during the nineteenth and twentieth centuries.

The past failure of the census to provide information on a constituency basis is apparently a major impediment to the kind of research envisaged in this chapter. I am not sufficiently experienced to estimate the extent of this difficulty, but I have consulted those better informed and find that, for the most part, they tend to take a pessimistic view. I have also been told that there seems no way of obtaining this information retrospectively and that the ingenious efforts to get around this problem by various means have not proved entirely adequate. Though the first and second parts of the project seem quite feasible for England, the collection of demographic data in a form useful for political analysis presents considerable difficulties. It may turn out that this part of the project, if it is carried through, can be handled only in a less precise and less satisfactory manner.

However, there are certainly a great deal of demographic data, and if they can be incorporated their richness and diversity will make necessary some difficult decisions about what classes of information should be included or excluded and what arrangements of the information will be most useful for research purposes. I understand from my friends at the consortium that they anticipate that demographic data may present more severe processing problems than either of the other two types of material: that the large and varied body of demographic data available for the United States makes the choice of categories a complicated one, that the bulk of the material to be handled is expected to be enormous, and that the number of variables involved will present serious technical problems. Similar difficulties can probably be expected for Great Britain.

In any case, this phase of the enterprise, if it proves feasible, would clearly depend far more than the other two upon the cooperation of scholars in England. Though a good deal of the work on electoral and roll-call data could be done in the United States, many of the sources of demographic information are available only in Britain. Help will be needed from British scholars not only in supervising the work but also in planning it and in deciding what categories of materials should be assembled.

CONCLUSIONS

It seems clear, then, that for electoral and roll-call data there exists, for Great Britain in the nineteenth and twentieth centuries, a large body of relevant and useful information which is readily accessible in a form convenient for tabulating. This record is, however, less complete for Britain than for the United States, because of the frequency of uncontested elections and the relatively low rate of participation in divisions until recent times as well as the absence of official published division lists until 1836. Despite this, the materials available on both elections and divisions are enormous and sufficiently informative to be well worth recording. Furthermore, the size of the job is not a major obstacle, since, at least for these two classes of data, the task is smaller for Great Britain than for the United States: one type of election as compared with four; 37,000 roll calls as compared with 60,000.

For demographic materials the situation is less clear, and it is not possible to speak with such assurance. There is reason to suppose that much information is available that would be of great value for political history. What is not certain is the extent to which the information can be gathered on a constituency basis. This may prove a real stumbling block, and on this point parallel studies between Great Britain and the United States may be more difficult.

There is also a technical problem which need not be discussed at length here but which should be identified so that it will not be lost from sight. Making the collected materials available in machine-readable form to scholars both in Great Britain and in the United States will require special arrangements, since, to a considerable degree, different kinds of machines are in use in the two countries. It will be necessary to settle at the outset on policies for the transferral of information, so that data recorded in one country can immediately be put on cards or tape usable in the other. The details will have to be worked out by specialists in computer work who are acquainted with the procedures in both countries. I have been told by those who know more about these matters than I do that the problem, though aggravating, is by no means insurmountable.

The special interest of the data collection project described in this chapter is that it relates closely to two major and to some extent connected phases of present-day scholarship: the extensive interest in parliamentary history that has developed over the last several decades, and the active contemporary experimentation with quantitative methods in the study of political history. For the history of Parliament this project would make a distinctive contribution of a kind that has not yet been attempted, at least on this scale. For quantitative research it would provide a body of basic and important data that would serve, if the American experience can be taken as a guide, as an effective aid and stimulus.

One of the most significant results of the recent concern with parliamentary history has been the setting up of the History of Parliament Trust, which operates under an annual grant placed at its disposal by the British government in 1951.[28] Its program is an immense one, comparable in bulk to that of the consortium, though in other respects these are very dissimilar enterprises. The trust is undertaking to publish biographies of all men who sat in the House of Commons up to 1901, together with certain other information about the history of Parliament. The first installment, a three-volume work by Sir Lewis Namier and John Brooke covering the period 1754–90, appeared in 1964; the two volumes by Romney Sedgwick, covering the period 1715–54, were published in 1970. The History of Parliament will present not only biographies of individuals, which of course is not a part of the consortium's program, but also other information more closely related to the concerns of the consortium. I am informed that it is intended, as far as the evidence permits, to state how many votes were cast for individual candidates at contested elections, to describe the voting records of members of Parliament, and to say something about the political structure and behavior of constituencies at different times.

This sounds, at first, so similar to the program proposed here as to raise the question of duplication of effort. If there is any likelihood of this, my suggested project should not be undertaken. Every effort should be made to leave the trust a clear field in the area that it has marked out for itself. I believe, however, that the two enterprises are entirely different and that no problem of duplication may be expected to arise.

The trust, as far as I know, does not propose to set up a data archive. The information it collects will be stored in books, not in machines. The difference is not a trivial one. For the kind of research that has been assumed as an objective throughout this chapter, which requires the manipulation and comparison of large amounts of different kinds of data, it is essential that the data be "so ordered and stored as to be retrievable in almost any subset or combination of subsets." Furthermore, the exceptionally rich possibilities for such research "can be realized only through the use of a high-speed computer for storage, retrieval and data processing." [29] To present in book form all the information that could be stored and used in this way would be an unprofitable undertaking for the trust or for anyone else. A given individual sitting in Parliament in the nineteenth or the twentieth century might have the opportunity to vote in several thousand divisions. To publish his votes or abstentions in all of these, and to do the same for every other individual in Parliament, would be an inefficient use of space. Such information is too voluminous and, by itself, too unimportant to be worth printing, although if punched on cards and manipulated by machines it can be used for research in a constructive fashion. Even if all these materials were printed they would eventually have to be put on cards or tape to make it possible to work with them effectively. To proceed otherwise, in the present state of research techniques, would involve a waste of time that could only be described as calamitous. For electoral data similar considerations apply. It would be possible to gather and print the votes for individual candidates in each contested election, but, if correlations and other work with these materials were to be attempted on any extensive scale, the matter could not be left there—it would be necessary to punch the information as well. The same argument applies to demographic information, with which, however, I gather that the trust is less concerned.

This project would, then, be supplementary to the work of the trust and would make a different kind of contribution to parliamentary history. There seems no serious danger of an overlap, even when the work of the trust is extended into the nineteenth century, as I hope it eventually will be. It seems highly desirable, on the other hand, that the officials of the History of Parliament Trust be consulted and kept informed in regard to plans, and that full use be made of any cooperation they are willing to provide. Their experience and knowledge could be of great assistance for this project, and it is fortunate that they have already expressed a benevolent interest in it.

For historians interested in quantitative research, and their numbers seem to be fast increasing,[30] an archive of basic political data would have great value. Research of this kind, when an individual is working alone, requires much intensive and uninteresting labor at the outset. It takes a long time before the preliminary tasks are completed and the results begin to show, as I have learned from my own experience. The ready accessibility of the necessary information, or a substantial amount of it, would make a great difference. The availability of such data changes the character of the research problem: it is no longer a matter of trying to reach the stage where the materials have been gathered; one can take this as a starting point and go on from there. A collection of data in this form would greatly facilitate the work of scholars now engaged in such studies, as well as making further such enterprises possible or at least more feasible than they would be in present circumstances.

The value of quantitative research is, of course, still debated in some quarters. I have said elsewhere what I have to say on the subject,[31] and I need not repeat myself here. It may be enough to point out here that, though the published studies are unequal in value, it seems clear already that substantial results have been achieved. Accepted theories have been refuted, former assumptions about the character of the representative process have been called into question, general issues have been clarified and their discussion placed on a firmer basis, and new and interesting questions have been raised. The accomplishments along this line are already so considerable, the lines of inquiry that have been opened up so promising, and the interest of scholars so active that a good case can be made for supporting this work on a considerable scale.

Such a project would not only serve present research but would also be guided by it and, in this manner, benefit from it. Those in charge of collecting quantitative data on modern British political history would not be flying blind. They would, on the contrary, have excellent indications as to the kinds of materials it would be most useful to gather and the purposes they could serve. The study of representative institutions in Britain and America has raised questions on which these materials would bear and, in so doing, has laid out some fairly clear paths for the assembling of further information. Neither of the two great data-collecting programs in the two countries would duplicate this effort, but both could furnish guidance for it. The History of Parliament Trust, though its labors are directed to a somewhat different purpose, could provide background and assistance. The work of the consortium, though its example should not be slavishly followed, can still serve in certain important respects as a precedent.

These data would enable historians to study, with more convenience and precision, the general trends in each of these three subject areas: the changes in the patterns of electoral behavior and the strength of the various party groups at different times in different kinds of constituencies; the patterns of voting in Parliament and what they reveal about the thinking of contemporaries on the subjects under consideration, as well as the relation, at different times, of votes to party affiliation; [32] and finally, if it proves feasible to handle demographic data, the kinds of demographic conditions prevailing in different types of constituencies. Even more interesting would be the correlation of these types of information: the study of the relation of demographic conditions to what happened in the elections, making due allowance for the "ecological fallacy," [33] and the study of the relation of both these variables to the political attitudes and behavior of members of Parliament. These points could be further elaborated, but perhaps enough has been said to indicate that, with proper materials and tools, it might be possible to raise some fairly basic questions about the nature of legislative behavior and the motives of political action and to go some distance toward clarifying these subjects, limiting the number of hypotheses that could be considered, and placing the discussion on a more solid foundation.

NOTES

1 Inter-University Consortium for Political Research, *Annual Report, 1964–1965* (Ann Arbor, Mich., 1965), p. 13.

2 Economic history is the basic emphasis of the indispensable collection of materials assembled by B. R. Mitchell and Phyllis Deane; quantitative materials have been used for social history with impressive results by, among others, Lawrence Stone, Peter Laslett, E. A. Wrigley, and R. S. Schofield.

3 See, for further details on local elections, David Butler and Jennie Freeman, *British Political Facts, 1900–1960* (London: Macmillan, 1963), pp. 189, 192–93.

4 Consortium, *Annual Report, 1964–1965*, p. 15.

5 In addition to the information in the Parliamentary or Sessional Papers, convenient summaries of election figures can be found in a variety of readily accessible handbooks or similar sources. For the nineteenth century there are the successive volumes of

Charles Roger Phipps Dod, *Parliamentary Companion* (London: Whittaker, 1832–); idem, *Electoral Facts, from 1832–1853, Impartially Stated, Constituting a Complete Political Gazeteer*, 2d ed. (London: Whittaker, 1853), which covers the years 1832–52; Frederick Haynes McCalmont, *The Parliamentary Poll Book of All Elections from the Reform Act of 1832 to February, 1910 (Inclusive)*, 7th ed. (London and Nottingham: E. Stanford, 1910); and the *Times* (London) and other newspapers. Some information can also be gleaned from the *Annual Register* and Whitaker's *Almanac*. For the twentieth century, especially the most recent period, the convenient secondary sources are even more ample. Brian R. Mitchell and Klaus Boehm present detailed figures for the five elections in the years 1950–64 in *British Parliamentary Election Results, 1950–1964* (Cambridge: Cambridge University Press, 1966). Their sources include, in addition to the material in the Sessional Papers, the successive books of *The House of Commons* published after each general election by the London *Times*, and also the Press Association's *List of Candidates*, which was made available to them by the Press Association, Ltd. Further sources for electoral data are listed in Butler and Freeman, *British Political Facts*, p. 131.

6 D. C. Moore, "Social Structure, Political Structure, and Public Opinion in Mid-Victorian England," in *Ideas and Institutions of Victorian Britain: Essays in Honour of George Kitson Clark*, ed. Robert Robson (London: Bell, 1967), pp. 20–57; John Richard Vincent, *Pollbooks: How Victorians Voted* (Cambridge: Cambridge University Press, 1967).

7 H. J. Hanham, *Elections and Party Management: Politics in the Time of Disraeli and Gladstone* (London: Longmans, 1959), p. 199. See also Trevor Lloyd, "Uncontested Seats in British General Elections, 1852–1910," *Historical Journal*, vol. 7, no. 2 (1965), pp. 260–65.

8 Norman Gash, *Politics in the Age of Peel: A Study in the Technique of Parliamentary Representation, 1830–1850* (London: Longmans, 1953), p. 440.

9 The incidence of election contests for various parts of this period has been discussed by Lloyd, Hanham, and Gash; it has also been dealt with by James Frederick Stanley Ross in *Elections and Electors: Studies in Democratic Representation* (London: Eyre & Spottiswoode, 1955). Gash's figures are for uncontested constituencies, not uncontested seats. The figures in table 8.1 do not always agree exactly with those presented by the other writers, but I prefer to keep my own figures until I have seen evidence that they need to be changed. Most of the discrepancies are, in any case, small. A special problem in calculating the proportion of uncontested seats in each election is that there were slight changes from time to time in the size of the House of Commons. Sudbury (2 seats) was disfranchised in 1844, reducing the number of seats in 1847 to 656, and St. Albans (2 seats) was disfranchised in 1852, so that only 654 seats were available in the elections of 1852, 1857, and 1859; these four seats were reassigned in 1861. Lancaster (2 seats), Reigate (1), Totnes (2), and Great Yarmouth (2) were disfranchised in 1867, but their seats were reassigned for the general election of 1868, and their disfranchisement does not affect the figures. Beverly (2 seats), Bridgewater (2), Cashel (1), and Sligo (1) were disfranchised in 1870, reducing to 652 the number of seats in 1874 and 1880, the two elections between 1870 and the general redistribution of 1885.

10 Hanham, pp. 191, 197–98.

11 Ibid., pp. 191–92.

12 "Election figures suffer much more from being inherently confusing than from being inaccurately reported. The complications that arise from unopposed returns, from plural voting, from two-member seats, and, above all, from variations in the number of candidates put up by each party are the really serious hazards in psephological interpretation" (Butler and Freeman, *British Political Facts*, p. 121). Some of these problems have also been discussed by other writers. See especially Henry Pelling's *Social Geography of British Elections, 1885–1910* (London: Macmillan, 1967).

13 Abbott Lawrence Lowell, "The Influence of Party Upon Legislation in England and America," *Annual Report of the American Historical Association for the Year 1901* (Washington, D.C.: Government Printing Office, 1902), 1:321–542.

14 The published division lists, however, though they give the names of the tellers, do not list the pairs; for these it is necessary to consult Hansard.

15 Norman Wilding and Philip Laundy, *An Encyclopaedia of Parliament* (London: Cassell, 1958), p. 154.

16 John Robert Bylsma, "Political Issues and Party Unity in the House of Commons, 1852–1857: A Scalogram Analysis" (Ph.D. diss., University of Iowa, 1968); James Cook Hamilton, "Parties and Voting Patterns in the Parliament of 1874–1880," (Ph.D. diss., University of Iowa, 1968).

17 This appears, for the twentieth century, in a variety of studies. I have presented some evidence on the subject for the mid-nineteenth century in "The Country Gentlemen and the Repeal of the Corn Laws," *English Historical Review* 82 (January 1967): 54–55, 60.

18 A number of these findings, and the challenges to accepted views that they present, have been discussed by John C. Wahlke in an unpublished paper, "Public Policy and Representative Government: The Role of the Represented," presented at the Seventh World Congress of the International Political Science Association in Brussels, September 1967; see pp. 26–29.

19 Report by Samuel P. Hays on the conference on historical demographic data on 16 October 1964, in Consortium, *Annual Report, 1964–1965,* p. 34.

20 Ibid., p. 36.

21 *Census Reports of Great Britain, 1801–1931,* Inter-departmental Committee on Social and Economic Research, Guides to Official Sources, no. 2 (London: His Majesty's Stationary Office, 1931).

22 For example, in *Parliamentary Papers* (1883), 54:369 ff.

23 *Return of Number of Illiterates at Elections in the United Kingdom,* published at various dates such as, for example, 1890–91, 1892, 1893–94, 1896.

24 Charles Gross's famous bibliography of local history, now over 70 years old, has recently been revised and brought up to date: Charles Gross, *A Bibliography of British Municipal History, Including Gilds and Parliamentary Representation,* 2d ed., with a preface by G. H. Martin (Leicester: Leicester University Press, 1966).

25 The difficulties and hazards of using census data, particularly for the early part of the nineteenth century, have been more extensively discussed by George Kitson Clark in *The Critical Historian* (New York: Basic Books, 1967), pp. 182 ff.

26 The populations of parliamentary cities, boroughs, and districts of boroughs in England and Wales were first given in 1841, the addition of this information apparently being considered necessary after the reform legislation of 1832 had destroyed the previous identity between municipal and parliamentary boroughs. It was not until 1851, however, that population figures were given for the 21 burghs and districts of burghs in Scotland entitled to send members to Parliament, or for parliamentary counties and parliamentary county divisions (*Census Reports of Great Britain, 1801–1931,* pp. 7, 98–101).

27 Ibid., p. 95.

28 I wish to thank E. L. C. Mullins, the secretary of the editorial board of the History of Parliament Trust, for supplying me with certain information about the operations and plans of the trust.

29 Consortium, *Annual Report, 1964–1965,* pp. 14–15.

30 For recent summaries see Allan G. Bogue, "United States: The 'New' Political History," *Journal of Contemporary History,* vol. 3, no. 1 (January 1968), pp. 5–27; Samuel P. Hays, "Computers and Historical Research," in *Computers in Humanistic Research: Readings and Perspectives,* ed. Edmund A. Bowles (Englewood Cliffs, N.J.: Prentice-Hall, 1967); Robert P. Swierenga, "Clio and Computers: A Survey of Computerized Research in History," *Computers and the Humanities,* vol. 5, no. 1 (September 1970), pp. 1–21.

31 William O. Aydelotte, "Quantification in History," *American Historical Review,* vol. 71, no. 3 (April 1966), pp. 803–25.

32 I have tried to show how this could be done in "Voting Patterns in the British House of Commons in the 1840s," *Comparative Studies in Society and History,* vol. 5, no. 2

(January 1963), pp. 134–63; and in "Parties and Issues in Early Victorian England," *Journal of British Studies,* vol. 5, no. 2 (May 1966), pp. 95–114.

33 W. S. Robinson, "Ecological Correlations and the Behavior of Individuals," *American Sociological Review,* vol. 15, no. 3 (June 1950), pp. 351–57. See also Leo A. Goodman, "Some Alternatives to Ecological Correlation," *American Sociological Review,* vol. 24, no. 6 (May 1959), pp. 610–25.

9

QUANTITATIVE DATA FOR THE STUDY OF RUSSIAN HISTORY

by Arcadius Kahan

INTRODUCTION

Anyone superficially acquainted with Russian history would assume the existence of ample quantitative data for its study, at least since the beginning of the eighteenth century. A centralized state apparatus controlling the daily lives and destinies of the Russian people must have left vast documentary evidence of its efforts. The normal assumption is that a fiscally motivated, mercantilistically oriented government that taxed everything from beards to coffins (if diapers had been in use, they too would have been taxed) would leave a rich legacy of quantitative data bearing on the relationship between the government and the economy as a whole, or at least the areas affected by government operations.

Indeed, for Russian history before the nineteenth century, most of the surviving documents concern activities in one way or another connected with the government rather than private contractual relationships or other dealings among the citizens themselves. The public or semipublic nature of the surviving documents tends to slant our understanding of social and economic processes and activities in Russia. To paraphrase a remark by the Russian historian M. N. Pokrovsky, we know, therefore, much more and in greater detail about Russian cannons than about Russian pots and pans.

There are relatively few private collections of documents that would provide quantitative materials for historical studies. The surviving documents pertain mostly to large landed estates and, for the nineteenth century, to business firms. There is a conspicuous scarcity of documentation left by social groups, by the urban merchants and artisans, and by the peasants who "wrote only with the plough on the soil." Peasant petitions, litigation, and government investigations involving peasants have been documented. But the quantitative data for the study of Russian history may still be compared to an iceberg, with the published items constituting the visible tip. Most of the data are available only in unpublished sources in the archives of the Soviet Union and abroad.

A few factors will help explain this phenomenon. First, since much of the data were collected and accumulated by various government agencies, the publication of data was selective, depending upon various turns of government policies and in particular upon what the ruling elite or the not-very-enlightened bureaucracy considered, at each point in time, to be in the national interest. Second, the publication of documents involved expenditures which particular branches of the administration had to justify to those holding the purse strings. Third, the majority of Russian historians prior to the revolution were interested less in social and economic history than in intellectual and general political history. Even those who were concerned with social and economic history did not consider it necessary to find or provide empirical proof for their hypotheses. Thus there was little demand on the part of historians for extensive publication of quantitative data.

During the early Soviet period, a massive effort was started to publish documents of social and economic history. During the Stalinist period, however, the secret police administered the state archives, and the publication of documents was highly selective. As a result, the output decreased drastically in quality as well as in quantity. It is only during the 1960s that both the use and publication of quantitative data pertaining to Russian history started to grow and constitute an integral part of the revival of published historical scholarship in the USSR.

Extensive bibliographies and descriptions of available archival collections, published recently, provide the historian with an insight into the wealth of untouched primary sources. The state of the primary sources is such that in all probability in the near future we may expect a whole series of "finds" of significant sources, as yet unknown or hardly utilized, for the quantitative study of various periods in the history of Russia.

Valuable materials containing quantitative data concerning Russia are available in the major archives and libraries of Europe and the United States. Many of the diplomatic papers and much of the correspondence concerning Russia were published either abroad or by the Russian Historical Society (RIO) prior to the revolution. But consular reports, economic intelligence reports, and travel reports dealing with nonpolitical matters such as population problems, agriculture, commerce, and industry are still dispersed in the British Museum, Public Record Office (London), Bodleian (Oxford), and in the archives of Paris, Amsterdam, The Hague, Stockholm, Istanbul, and even the United States. And these archives have not been sufficiently tapped for Russian data.

THE TSARIST PERIOD

Population Data

Prior to the eighteenth century, population data for Russia were available indirectly through household counts, which were carried out occasionally for the purposes of military service (in the case of the nobility and service population) or fiscal policies. But although the data of the household counts for various regions provide a basis of comparisons in time, they suffer from a lack of the precision that would be needed to assess population changes reflected in the size of households rather than their sheer number. A major change took place early in the eighteenth century at the time of Peter the Great, when the head count of the male population, which became the new unit for the poll tax, replaced the previous unit of the household as a basis for both taxation and population estimates.

From the first quarter of the eighteenth century until the revolution, Russia had ten censuslike counts of the male population (*revizii*) [1] and one modern population census. The revizii had the following shortcomings from the point of view of population statistics:

1. Irregularity. The revizii were not conducted at regular intervals, their dates depending upon fiscal considerations (levying of taxes) or military and political considerations (assessment of the aftermath of the Napoleonic War or the Crimean War).
2. Lack of uniformity of territorial coverage. Due to the territorial expansion of Russia on the one hand and to territorial changes of the administrative units on the other, it is difficult to establish the changes either in total population or in the population of particular regions.
3. Insufficient coverage and exemption of some population groups. This is probably the major shortcoming of the revizii, since the *revizia* was a count of the male population and not of the total population. Moreover, it was for all practical purposes a count of the taxable male population rather than of the total male population. A relatively large portion of the population, including whole groups and large geographical areas, was exempt from the revizia. These categories included the members of the nobility and gentry, the clergy, those employed in state service, some groups in military service (the Cossacks), people having academic degrees, teachers, the Bashkirs, the Kirgiz, the inhabitants of the Caucasus, the autochthons of Siberia, the inhabitants of the Polish Kingdom and Finland, and a number of other categories embracing smaller population groups.
4. The notorious underestimation of even the taxable population groups by the revizii. This can be attributed to the largely fiscal and military service goals of the revizii, which gave people an incentive to underreport their

numbers. The additional counts following each revizia could only partially remedy this shortcoming. Still another cause of underreporting was confusion resulting from the complexity of primary documents and the low level of literacy of both local officials and officials sent from the center to conduct the revizia or to check upon its accuracy.

In spite of all the shortcomings of the revizii when viewed either as substitutes for population censuses or as near-substitutes for current vital statistics, they are useful sources for historians. The few available publications based upon the revizia data, starting with those of the statisticians of the early nineteenth century, provide us with a wealth of indispensable information. Modern historians will deplore most, not the qualitative shortcomings of the data, but the relative paucity of studies providing the information that could be extracted from the revizii by skillful historical demographers.

During the first half of the nineteenth century, three vital statistics systems were established:

1. Civil records (*Spiski po Sostoianiiam*), separate for the gentry, the clergy, and the urban estates
2. Fiscal records, separate for homeowners, urban taxpayers, and rural taxpayers
3. Police records, exclusively for urban areas, with differing coverage and scope

On the basis of these three types of records, the district (*gubernia*) statistical authorities were obliged, beginning in 1857, to record and submit the population estimates for their districts, including the counties (*uyezdy*) and cities, to the Central Statistical Committee. Given the imperfection of the primary data, confidence in the district or total estimates was not very great. Nevertheless, it signified progress and improvement over the system of irregular revizii.

A major change was introduced by the first general population census of the Russian empire. A number of foreign censuses were used as models for this, which was conducted on 28 January 1897 of the Julian calendar (9 February). The questionnaire included the following information: (1) last and first name, including patronymic, as well as information on physical inadequacies (blindness, deafness, muteness, and mental illness); (2) family status (single, married, widow, etc.); (3) relationship to head of household; (4) sex; (5) age; (6) membership in an estate, rank, and (for foreigners) nationality; (7) religion; (8) birthplace; (9) permanent address; (10) place of registered habitat; (11) remarks about temporary presence and temporary absence; (12) mother tongue; (13) literacy; (14) employment, craft, or profession.

For a while the census, despite its inadequacies, provided a much more solid base for population estimates than had previously been available. In fact, it helped to revise previous population estimates and was used to refine subsequent ones. However, since the machinery for generating current population data was not changed—the parishes continued to act as offices of vital statistics, supplying their registrations of marriages, deaths, births, and baptisms to the district statistical committees—the discrepancies between the estimates of the Central Statistical Committee and other estimates grew, particularly in the absence of further population censuses between 1897 and 1913.

The significance of the 1897 census was that for the first time the whole population of the empire was covered (although the count in some regions on its fringes was probably not exact), and a number of interesting demographic data were made available for the first time.

Land and Agricultural Data

Data reflecting landholdings by institutions and individuals were collected and recorded in Russia as early as the period of Mongol supremacy. During the centuries of Moscow's rise to a position of dominating power in Russia, land redistributions and grants of various kinds were recorded. The rivalry between the service gentry and the old nobility, which was as much a rivalry for land and peasants as for political power within the state, produced more land data.

The late sixteenth and the seventeenth centuries provide us with landholding estimates for institutions (churches and monasteries) as well as for the members of the nobility. Although the descriptions occasionally provide a breakdown of arable land or plowland, it was not until the middle and second half of the eighteenth century, and in some regions not until the early nineteenth century, that land titles were established based upon a primitive version of a cadastre.[2] But even this cadastre did not always draw a distinction between meadows, pasture, forests, and wasteland, so that an accurate distribution of the different kinds of land by use is not available until the present. We still operate in this area with various kinds of estimates; the most accurate, or rather the least inaccurate, might be estimates of the area of plowland, but even those are more or less educated guesses rather than accurate measurements.

One of the curious results of the lack of a cadastre was the inability of the Soviet government to supply a reliable figure of the total land confiscated under the terms of its agrarian reform. Since the first agricultural census was conducted during World War I (in 1916) for a smaller territory than the Russian prewar empire, comparisons of the available data of an earlier period have to be treated with caution. Land data first became important around the time of the emancipation of the serfs, in connection with the size of transferred landholdings to be held in communal ownership by the former serfs. For most districts, we know the distribution of landholdings by ownership, since, after the liberation of the serfs in 1861, special studies of land ownership were conducted in 1877/78, 1895/96, and 1905. Nevertheless, the data are not very helpful in the assessment of the value of the landholdings unless they can be adjusted for the differing qualities of land.

Scattered data on grain yields are available for some regions for the eighteenth century, collected either in conjunction with the cadastre or by district governors at the command of the central authorities. Demands for grain-yield reports to be sent to St. Petersburg by the district governors were usually prompted by the frequent droughts and famines in Russia. During the eighteenth century the records of yield estimates—reported in terms of output-seed ratios—were spotty and probably inaccurate. The system of reporting did not improve much during the first half of the nineteenth century. It was only with the establishment of district statistical offices that the Ministry of the Interior started to collect yield data. During the second half of the nineteenth century, at least in the districts of European Russia, yield data were collected and published by two more authorities besides the Central Statistical Committee, namely by the Chief Authority of Land Settlement and Agriculture (GUZIZ), later superseded by the Department of Rural Economy and Agricultural Statistics of the Ministry of Agriculture, and by the regional authorities of the organs of local self-government known as *zemstvos.*

In addition to the inaccuracy of the land-use data, resulting apparently in a systematic underreporting of the planted area, the following criticisms of the agricultural statistics may be made:

1. The system of collection of agricultural data by the Central Statistical Committee, which relied upon the reports of local administrative officials, was imperfect and did not reflect accurately the level of yields. To the extent that the conflicting tendencies to underreport (on the part of the producers) and overestimate (on the part of the officials) tended to cancel each other out, and in the absence of a prevailing bias in one direction, the data covering a large territory (district) were more accurate than the county data, and the long-term averages reflected the long-term trend quite accurately (although at a level of estimated yields lower than the reality).

2. The reports by the various departments of the Ministry of Agriculture were the least reliable, because of the relatively small, unrepresentative group of correspondents they used.

3. The zemstvo data were the most accurate for yearly levels of yields and for yield differentials between regions; however, they were inferior in reflecting the changes of yields over time.[3] Thus the current yield (and output) statistics suffered from a number of fallacious methods of data collecting and aggregating, and the service of providing prognoses of yield levels (to the trade or transportation sectors of the economy) was poorly organized.

A major shortcoming was the exclusion of the fringes of the empire—

Siberia, the Caucasus, and Central Asia—whose share of agricultural output was growing, from the total crop output statistics until the beginning of the twentieth century.

In spite of these and other shortcomings of the crop yield and output data, they can be used (since we know their bias) much more readily than the data pertaining to the livestock and work stock herds and to livestock output. Since the veterinary service was subordinated to the military authorities, who were also interested in horse breeding and the acquisition of horses for the army, livestock estimates were provided primarily by the military; from the 1880s on a survey of livestock known as the Military-Horse Count was conducted. The agricultural census of 1916 revealed the inadequacy of the previous estimates.

Price data were generated by some of the authorities who produced the agricultural estimates. The first stimulus came from the state, which demanded prices prevailing during famines and grain shortages in order to decide whether to prohibit grain exports, to impose price controls, or to provide famine relief in various other forms. The data were spotty and did not lend themselves to the construction of price indexes. More consistent were the price data reported by the army quartermaster of payments for food and forage and the wholesale food prices collected after the 1830s by the Trade and Manufacturing Department of the Ministry of Finance. The most reliable wholesale price data for agricultural products started to appear after the 1890s, in the form of information given to the government by the commodity exchanges. The lack of continuity and reliable documentation by public or private institutions (hospitals, schools, etc.) deprives us of some price-data collections of types available for earlier periods in western European countries. As in other areas of social and economic activity, data were reported primarily by central government authorities, even in agriculture. The major exception is constituted by the zemstvo statistics.

The Zemstvo Statistics

Among the most useful sources of data for the social history of Russia are the various works published by the zemstvos. The zemstvos had the authority to collect taxes, primarily on land, for local needs. Hence determining the ability to pay was of major concern to them. Out of fiscal considerations arose the need to collect data pertaining to the economic and social situation of the largest social stratum, the peasantry.

This led to a spontaneous process of collecting data by the late 1860s and to the establishment of statistical offices at the *gubernia* level by the early 1870s.[4] Subsequently the results of these studies began to appear in print. The basic forms of study were both the one-time censuslike questionnaire and the continuing observation of selected households. The unit chosen was invariably the peasant household. These studies expanded constantly both in territorial coverage and in scope of the questionnaire, which included an increasing number of questions pertaining to different aspects of production, income, consumption, education, etc. The censuslike household studies varied in coverage from a general census of households of a particular district to a more or less representative sample of households or farm groups. The continuing, usually annual observations involved selected households or correspondents which were used as a sample for the study of the changes in peasant agriculture over time, rather than cross-sectionally.

The zemstvo statisticians constantly introduced changes and improvements in the techniques of data collection and analysis. One curious check upon the accuracy of the primary data was introduced very early in the data-collecting process by conducting the interviews during the meetings of the village assembly, thus having the potential or actual reaction of knowledgeable neighbors to the data supplied. However, in spite of their best intentions, the statisticians never eliminated some basic deficiencies. The major one, from the point of view of an aggregate analysis of peasant agriculture, was the lack of uniformity of program, procedure, and techniques among the various districts and provinces. Thus, even had the zemstvo statistics covered all Russia, the aggregation of the data would not have produced a full picture. In addition, changes in procedure, scope, and emphasis prevent us from building continuous series even for the particular localities.[5]

These criticisms of the zemstvo statistics, however pertinent to economic analysis, ought not to deter the historian interested in cross-sectional data. Particularly for the period 1880–1913, the zemstvo statistics represent a wealth of materials on a number of subjects. Among the pioneering efforts of the zemstvo statisticians are the attempts to study peasant budgets, which provided interesting insights not only into the role of peasant households as farm producers, but also into the behavior of households as consumer units. The peasant budgets, published for various localities beginning in the 1880s, reflect the adjustment of agriculture and the agricultural population to changes in prices, supply of factors of production, technology, etc. Before the revolution, about 11,500 peasant household budgets were studied for purposes of research and publication.[6]

Another area of broad interest was the work of the zemstvo statisticians on educational levels of the rural population. This included data on schools and schooling in the various provinces and, in some cases, library facilities, adult education, etc. This area of the zemstvo statistics was moving toward a uniform program of classification, which was recommended by the all-zemstvo conference on school statistics in 1913, when the war upset all such plans.

The zemstvo statistics pioneered in other fields as well, notably health. They constitute an indispensable source for the social history of Russia of the postemancipation period.

Industry

One of the basic problems of industrial statistics in Russia was that of defining an industrial enterprise. For better or worse, the definitions did not change much from the beginning of the eighteenth to nearly the end of the nineteenth century. Even the definition of an industrial establishment provided by the Statute of Industry of 1893 [7] did not deviate substantially from the earlier statutes of 1723 and 1820. But matters were complicated by ambiguities in the definition, particularly pertaining to size, distinction between large and small industry, and handicrafts.

The two major problems affecting the quality of the data on the industrial sector of the economy were the divisions between the various governmental departments that collected and processed the data and the reporting of the data by the enterprises themselves. The data pertaining to industry were collected, by and large, by three government agencies, all under the Ministry of Finance: data for the mining and ferrous metal industries were collected by the Mining Department; those for industries subject to the excise tax, by the Revenue Department; and those for all other industries, by the Trade and Industry Department (later the Ministry of Trade and Industry). Although these agencies were all under the same ministry (except for the period when state-owned enterprises reported to the Ministry of State Estates), each agency collected and reported on its own basis, using a different methodology and internal classification of output, labor force, and description of technology. This made it very difficult to assemble data for the whole industrial sector.

The reporting during the eighteenth century was largely sporadic, except for a few attempts to conduct a quasi-censuslike review of mining and manufacturing. The first official attempts to regulate reporting to the government agencies were made by a decree of 30 June 1804. Additional rules for reporting were published in 1830, 1834, 1835, 1862, 1867 and 1893. The decrees, however, did not assure coverage, promptness, or accuracy of the reports. Furthermore, the district administrations had no incentive, except in the cases where revenue was involved, to check upon the accuracy of the reported data. Thus the yearly reports of the performance of the industrial sector, including the published reports, were inadequate.

The best sources for the industrial sector during the period 1900–13 are the publications of the censuslike studies for 1900, 1908, and 1910–12. Conducted by the statistician V. E. Varzar for the government, these studies utilized some of the experience of the zemstvo statistics. Although the data were reported by the owners of the enterprises, there were some built-in checks of consistency that gave the factory inspectors a greater measure of control over the primary data than was possible for the district administrations.

Of the three censuslike studies, that of 1900 was least inclusive in terms of geographic coverage, and it excluded state enterprises, as well as mines and ferrous metallurgy. But it was most comprehensive in its scope of information. The studies provided information on quantity of output, use of inputs (raw materials, labor, and machinery), energy supply, capital stock, number of days worked, length of working day, etc. Although the study of 1910–12 was conducted on an abbreviated questionnaire, its reporting of three consecutive years nevertheless provided continuous data for the same enterprises, thus revealing some of the dynamics of industrial development in Russia which could not be obtained from sporadic studies.

The information collected for the periods between the censuslike studies was inferior. Checks for consistency are necessary if that information is to be used at all. For the specific problems of industrial output, the most widely used estimates pertaining to large-scale industry were worked out during the 1920s by the Russian economist Kondratiev. The Kondratiev index has a number of shortcomings that were pointed out by Raymond Goldsmith in *Economic Development and Cultural Change,* 1961; Goldsmith also suggested some corrections.

Transportation and Communication

The availability of transportation and communication data varied with the historical period, but in general it improved over time. The following types of data are available:

1. Among the oldest records are those related to maritime shipping of the different ports. Such data for the eighteenth century can be checked against foreign records and, although incomplete for certain years, are generally reliable. The nineteenth-century data are quite adequate.

2. The documents related to shipping over the internal waterways (particularly the various canal systems) were not completely preserved until the nineteenth century. They provide information about ships, tonnage of freight (mostly in terms of type and tonnage of the ship itself), and in some cases the commodity composition of freight. From the 1830s on, data on internal waterway transportation were published annually. Special emphasis was given to the transportation of food grains, and during the navigation season such data were collected on a monthly basis.

3. Railroad transportation statistics originated and were processed in two ministries, those of finance and communications (*Putei Soobshchenia*). The railway department of the Ministry of Finance was interested both in railway construction and in freight rates. The statistics department of the Ministry of Communications was interested chiefly in the technical and financial aspects of railroad operation. As a result of these divergent interests, two parallel sets of data were produced in the form of monthly and annual reports by the two ministries.

4. In addition to data on railways and railroad transportation, the Ministry of Communications published data on roads of different kinds under

its jurisdiction, specifying their length and classification and also the amounts of tolls collected on the roads, bridges, etc. These reports provide some information on goods traffic.

5. Both the Ministry of Finance and the Ministry of the Interior, in their respective yearbooks, published data on the performance of the post office, telephone, and telegraph systems. Most of the data were provided by the respective administrative departments themselves.

Within this general classification, the best data are those for the railroads, in terms of both coverage and methodology. The data of the Ministry of Finance on railroad freight cover up to 400 commodities and indicate their points of loading and destination, thus providing information on interregional movements of goods and lengths of haul. The data of the Ministry of Communications are very helpful in assessing the costs of transportation and fuel consumption by the railroads. The statistical yearbooks of the two ministries provide the final data, with lags of up to three years. But for historical research this is now no drawback, and the yearbooks tend to be more accurate than the preliminary current transportation statistics used for operations control by the government departments of transportation and communication.

Labor Force, Wages, and the Standard of Living

Quantitative data pertaining to the labor force as a whole were not collected in Russia. Given the deficiencies of population statistics, the estimates of the agricultural labor force can be treated only as guesses. But even for the nonagricultural labor force, the estimates are based upon incomplete primary data collected by various institutions and by different methods. Within the nonagricultural sector, the best data are those of railroad employment. The data on government employment are very incomplete for the simple reason that they were never collected or classified as a single category and are therefore difficult to arrange. For the industrial labor force, the data are mostly scattered. During the existence of serfdom, the industrial labor force data, collected by the government as a by-product of industry surveys conducted among employers in the various districts, did not make a sufficiently clear distinction between free and serf labor. In addition, serf labor was often counted not in numbers but in service equivalent units. The uneven coverage caused by unsystematic reporting renders the data for the period of serfdom almost useless for measuring short-term changes in industrial employment.

Some improvement in data collection occurred after 1861. But even during the subsequent period no uniform methods were employed, and data were collected primarily for European Russia. The labor force data were collected separately for mining and metallurgy, for enterprises paying the excise tax (alcohol, tobacco, salt, petroleum), and for enterprises not paying the excise tax. Depending upon the degree of government control, enterprises often reported their labor force without distinguishing between full-time and part-time workers and in most cases chose an arbitrary date for reporting.

A valuable source of data on labor and wages was the collection of reports by the factory inspectors, published regularly from the 1890s. Located in the districts, the factory inspectors provided data for the industrial firms subject to factory inspection. Exempt from the inspection were small-size and cottage industry, metallurgy, and industry upon which the excise tax was levied.

Ancillary data pertaining to the labor force can be found in the reports of municipal governments and of employer associations and similar institutions, but they all suffer from a lack of uniformity and continuity. Two collections of data on factory employees, for the years 1900 and 1908, were published by the Ministry of Trade and Industry under V. E. Varzar's editorship. Those collections, together with the 1897 population census, provide the best data that we have for the composition of the industrial labor force. The works by G. A. Rashin and A. K. Pazhitnov published during the Soviet period provide some useful estimates for particular industry branches.

Wage data were, naturally, collected even less frequently. For the agricultural sector they comprise, by district, averages of payments to field hands. Distinctions are made between the sexes; among permanent, seasonal, and day laborers; and often between money wages and wages inclusive of food and shelter. Such data were published in the yearbooks of the Ministry of Agriculture and occasionally in the publications of the Ministry of Finance. Studies of agricultural wages can also be found in the zemstvo statistics. For urban industrial wages, one has to rely upon the data of the factory inspectors and the yearbooks of the Ministry of Transportation. The studies by Varzar provide an additional useful source for wage data for the two years they cover, 1900 and 1908. The archives of some large industrial firms contain wage data that could be used for the construction of wage indexes. Few of the archives, however, have been utilized; and of those that have been consulted for writing the history of firms, the wage data have not been published.

To study the changes in the standard of living of various groups, income data have to be developed from wage and price statistics. The sources for such data can be found in the publications of the Ministry of Finance. Price series for 1890–1913 for different regions are available from data collected from commodity exchanges. The number of commodities represented in the series increased over time, until by 1913 it reached about 150. The price indexes (being arithmetic averages of wholesale prices with a 1890–1900 base) were published periodically by the Ministry of Finance and after 1905 by the Ministry of Trade and Industry.[8] Wholesale prices were published by the *Torgovo-Promyshlennaia Gazeta,* and local agricultural prices by the Ministry of Agriculture. Retail prices were published for agricultural areas (local rural markets) by the district zemstvos and for urban markets by some municipalities.

The availability of some wage and price data does not solve the problem of standard-of-living changes, since earnings and income statistics as such were not collected. Materials that can be used in the absence of income estimates for Russia, at least for a few years, include the Ministry of Finance publication on incomes of the top income group (over 1,000 rubles per year) for the early part of the twentieth century and the budget studies of industrial workers and peasants in various parts of the country (sponsored by the zemstvos in the case of the peasants and privately in the case of industrial workers). Imperfect as such substitutes are, they nevertheless indicate the general trend in incomes and standards of living in the late nineteenth and early twentieth centuries.

Trade

Foreign trade produced some of the most thorough collections of data. Prior to the eighteenth century the government participated actively in foreign trade, at various periods monopolizing whole branches that appeared advantageous. Not only in the fur trade, but even in the grain and timber trades, the government occasionally monopolized exports. Thus government records concerning certain branches of foreign trade, particularly some of the traditional exports, were relatively abundant. Although the government remained a major exporter of some commodities (iron and timber) during the eighteenth century, nevertheless the import records became more plentiful and of a higher quality than the export records.

Government records pertaining to foreign trade and particularly to imports were kept more meticulously than other government records. This was perhaps due to the importance of customs revenues in total state revenue, the protective features of the Russian tariff, and the fact that for long periods of the Russian ruble's inconvertibility import duties were paid in silver.

Given the fiscal motives, the available data for imports were relatively more reliable. The foreign trade data included primarily customs information, registering largely imports and some exports subject to export tax. The major shortcomings of the foreign trade statistics, which were almost entirely supplied by the customs offices, were twofold: the relative inferiority of the export data, particularly for the exports that passed duty-free; and the absence of estimates of foreign trade that did not pass through customs. Merchandise that did not pass through customs was considered smuggled goods. Although data for confiscated smuggled goods were published annually from the 1830s, the data are too crude to yield estimates of total smuggling.

In spite of the shortcomings and variations in the degree of accuracy of the customs data, it is possible to reconstruct the patterns of commodity composition and changes in foreign trade, using averages for five-year periods or decades. Year-to-year estimates would be much less reliable. Thus the task of modern research in the area of the relatively abundant Russian foreign trade data is to compare them with available data on Russia's exports found in the trade statistics of her major trading partners. Given the relative concentration of Russian exports within a narrow range of commodities, the trade data could serve (in the absence of violent fluctuations in foreign demand) as indicators of the growth of domestic output of such commodities.

The area of domestic trade, in the absence of collected data, is terra incognita. For the period before 1753, there were occasional estimates of internal customs receipts that can be used as rough approximations in calculating interregional domestic trade. With the abolition of the internal custom zones and duties in 1753, even this very inaccurate source for estimating the value of domestic trade disappeared, with the exception of the data pertaining to goods whose sale was monopolized at various points in time by the government (namely, alcohol, salt, matches, etc.). Those data are clearly inadequate for estimating domestic trade as a whole. Two sets of data have occasionally been used as substitutes for direct internal trade data. The first set is that of the trade tax (*promyslovyi nalog*).

For fiscal purposes trade establishments were classified into five major groups: (1) large wholesale and purchasing firms, banks, credit institutions and insurance companies, grain elevators, hotels; (2) retail firms and medium-size wholesale firms, small hotels, baths; (3) small-size retail shops, bars, saloons, furnished rooming houses; (4) market-stalls, tea-houses; (5) carrying trade and peddling in rural areas. Within each category, the number of firms and their employees were recorded, and their trade turnover was calculated. The data were reported for counties and districts, separated for rural and urban areas, and finally published by the Ministry of Finance. The latest publication covers the year 1912.

The data collected and published in conjunction with the trade tax (which supposedly reflected total trade turnover) had a number of shortcomings that prevent their use as approximations for internal trade estimates. On the one hand, they are not sufficiently comprehensive, since they omit joint stock companies, consumer cooperatives (in other words, the trading firms under the obligation of public accountancy), and government trading. In addition, since the trade tax was not paid in Siberia and Central Asia, the data do not cover those territories. On the other hand, since the data on total turnover of the listed firms also include various financial transactions, credit operations not necessarily of a mercantile nature, insurance, and some other services, the raw data cannot be used in their reported form to reflect trade turnover. An additional adjustment would be required to separate wholesale from retail trade operations.

Nevertheless, given the available data from the trading tax, the sales data of the government monopolies, data on sales of particular raw materials and products manufactured by joint-stock companies and other private corporations, and production data by major industries combined with some export data for the same products, it is possible to arrive at estimates of retail trade for years for which reliable price data are available.[9] Yearly estimates of domestic retail trade thus determined would not be very reliable, and changes reflected by such estimates would not be quite accurate. But estimates arrived at by such methods of utilizing available raw data can be utilized in conjunction with other economic data to reflect long-range trends in the Russian economy. The only serious attempts at estimating the volume and changes in total domestic trade turnover to date have been those of the Soviet economist S. G. Strumilin, who calculated the total domestic trade turnover for the years 1899–1913.[10]

The second set of data for estimating short- and long-term changes in the volume of retail trade, frequently used by economic historians of Russia, are the data on the volume of transactions at the Nizhnyi-Novgorod (previously Makarievskaia) annual fair. This fair, the most important of the many fairs in Russia, provides estimates on the volume of transactions calculated uniformly over time since 1817. However, indiscriminate use of the data supplied by a single fair (even the most important one) can lead to serious errors of judgment if generalized for short-term changes in the total of retail sales. But the Nizhnyi-Novgorod data can be combined with available data for other fairs and sources of domestic trade to produce more reliable estimates. The scattered data on the domestic trade of Russia require a strenuous effort to provide regional or national estimates.

STATISTICS OF THE SOVIET PERIOD

Separating the treatment of quantitative data for the Soviet period from that of earlier periods of Russian history is essential for several reasons.

1. Opinions concerning the use of statistics underwent a fundamental change after the revolution. An official Soviet definition of *statistics* supports this contention: "Statistics is a social science, with its theory based upon the principles of historical materialism and the Marxist-Leninist political economy. Based upon the laws of these scientific disciplines, statistics illuminate the quantitative changes in concrete social mass phenomena and processes and explain the regularities which they exhibit or represent." [11]

2. The collection and publication of quantitative data became nationalized with the gradual elimination of private individuals and voluntary associations from this activity, and later the monopoly of designated governmental institutions was established. Norms of behavior for such institutions were drawn up, and the scope and direction of their activities prescribed. Lenin played a pioneering role in controlling the institutions of data

gathering. He wrote: "The Central Statistical Authority ought not to be an 'academic' or 'independent' organ, which, following the old bourgeois habit, it is even today nine-tenths [of the time], but an organ of socialist construction, re-evaluation, control, accounting, [in the areas] of what it is necessary that the socialist state ought to know right now. The resistance of old habits will unavoidably be very stubborn, and the more insistent ought to be the fight [against it]." [12] This view had an impact upon the criteria of selection of the phenomena to be recorded and studied, and it gave a definite "practical" slant to the collection and publication of the data.

3. The monopoly of the state institutions in the gathering of quantitative data was the first step toward the subjection of the use and interpretation of such data to censorship and later to rationing the data among research institutions and trusted scholars. In addition, at any moment the state agencies could impose a veto on the publication of data for lengthy periods of time.[13]

4. During the early period of Soviet rule, the collected quantitative data could conceivably have served as a basis for public policy discussions. But subsequently the demand for data became increasingly a demand by the state administration for a service to help it perform its functions and ultimately to provide the ex post facto confirmation of the correctness of its previous decisions. Thus the data-collecting institutions gravitated gradually from a position of information gathering to one of supporting the policy arms of the government.

5. This trend of integration of the functions of data gathering and processing into the executive branch of the government was congruent with the development of economic and social planning from a system of general forecasting to a system of rigid centralized planning and plan execution. To the extent that execution and control became intertwined with planning, data collecting in many areas assumed the role of a control measure and as such became increasingly the domain of the administrators rather than the scholars or the public.[14] The role of the Central Statistical Authority, the agency of centralized data gathering, was defined by a leading authority on this subject as follows:

The main objective of the TsSU SSSR (Central Statistical Authority) is the processing, analysis and timely presentation to the government of reliable, scientifically based statistical data, reflecting the degree of fulfillment of the state plans, the relationships in the development of various sectors of the economy, the growth of the national economy and culture, the growth of national welfare, and the availability, distribution and utilization of labor and material resources in the national economy. An important goal of the TsSU is also to introduce proposals about the elimination of existing shortcomings in the utilization of reserves for the purpose of overfulfillment of the plans.[15]

It is thus clear that, in the area of collection and processing of quantitative data, the discontinuities between the prerevolutionary and Soviet periods warrant treating the Soviet period separately. And within the Soviet period, changes in the quantity and methods of collection, processing, and publishing of the data, as well as in their accuracy and reliability, are closely related to changes in political, social, and economic institutions.

One of the sources of the massive growth of data collection and publication during the 1920s was the belief in the need for information as a prerequisite for the social engineering undertaken by the government and by various social institutions. A vast data-gathering and data-processing apparatus was set up, within which various institutions were originally competing with the Central Statistical Authority, with some overlapping work in several government agencies—for example, in the Ministries of Labor, Agriculture, Finance, and Trade. The centralization process and concentration of statistical work within the Central Statistical Authority, which was not done for reasons of efficiency, reduced sharply the number of sponsors but not immediately the volume or scope of data collection and publication.

An exaggerated respect for quantitative data, which provided arguments and positions with the aura of the "scientifically sound" or the "empirically tested" in the Soviet Union during the 1920s; is typical of current attitudes in many developing countries. Data were collected and published not only in areas of social research and history, but also in areas where there was no intellectual advantage to the use of such data for analysis or presentation.[16]

The period of intensive data collecting coincided with the development of Marxian sociology in historical research and with the beginning of broad sociological studies and some pioneering efforts in selected areas of macroeconomic analysis, economic forecasting, and economic planning. The development of such scholarly interests, the reevaluation of the historical record, and the juxtaposition of the present with the past in the areas of social relations created an intensified demand for quantitative data, while the supply of such data was feeding and supporting a growing literature in these areas. In order to satisfy the curiosity of scholars and institutions, resources were made available to allow data collection on whole populations even where statistical sampling would have been sufficient.

Apart from the rapid growth of data collection, another positive development during this early period of Soviet rule was the standardization of methods in data processing. This was a significant improvement over the prerevolutionary period, when methods changed frequently in some areas, but, most important, when almost each government institution adhered to its own methods of treating and processing the statistical data it gathered. Later standardization and uniformity, when combined with a lack of choice about what to study or how to change the standards, would result in a straitjacket for statistical research, but this possibility did not yet appear to trouble most of the producers or consumers of the quantitative data.

One of the first basic tasks of Soviet statisticians was to establish the continuity and comparability of the quantitative data for the Soviet Union with those of prerevolutionary Russia, to take account of both the territorial changes after World War I and the revolutionary changes in social relations within the territory of the Soviet Union.[17] In view of the rapidity of change and the instability in a number of areas, the prerevolutionary quantitative indicators were chosen as a base or yardstick, at least for the first postrevolutionary decade. Therefore the range of the prewar indicators was broadened and their accuracy improved, so that to a considerable extent the basic continuity of the quantitative indicators was preserved for a while at least.

Population

The new regime made one of its first objectives the establishment of a regularized and uniform procedure of civil registration which would provide continuous data for population statistics. The new arrangement was a logical result of the separation of church and state, which was decreed on 23 January 1918. During the prerevolutionary period the registration of baptisms, marriages, and burials was handled by the clergy of the various religious denominations, who served in the capacity of civil servants acting in a decentralized manner. But only the Greek Orthodox Church, through the Holy Synod, its central authority, was able to provide summary data on population changes. Current population data always presented a major problem for the statistical authorities in the prerevolutionary period.

After the revolution, the function of providing current population statistics was taken over by the newly created offices of Documentary Registration of Civil Status (*Zags-Zapisi Aktov Grazhdanskogo Sostoiania*). Copies of the civil documents transferred to the statistical authorities could be used to determine short-term changes in the size, civil status, and territorial distribution of the population. It took about five or six years before the registration of births, marriages, divorces, and deaths became uniform and effective as a source of pertinent information. Even by 1926, about 13.7 percent of the population, mainly in the areas of Central Asia and the Caucasus, was outside the registration area.

The first Soviet population census was carried out on 28 August 1920, but the territory then under Soviet rule did not include some regions of the Ukraine and Siberia nor all of the Crimea, Central Asia, and Transcaucasia. The territory covered accounted for about 70 percent of the population of the country. For the missing regions, until the subsequent population census of 1926, the materials of the agricultural census of 1916, as corrected by the agricultural surveys of 1921–24, were used as a basis for rural population data; an urban population count in the spring of 1923 provided urban demographic data. The second Soviet population census took place chiefly in December 1926. But in the Tadzhik Republic, part of the Turkmen Republic, and the extreme northern regions, the census was conducted during the summer of 1927.

The census data, together with the data of current population registration, provided a basis for the construction of mortality tables, general demographic indicators, estimates of patterns of migration, etc. Beginning with the period of the five-year plans, the demographic data were used extensively not only for economic forecasting and manpower planning but also for the formulation of social and educational policies. During the 1930s the strengthening of political and social controls played an increasingly important role in both the gathering of information and its use. The censuses of 1937 (whose materials were discarded and never published) and of 1939 exhibited these tendencies.

During the immediate post–World War II period, when the withholding of information from the public reached its peak, lists of eligible voters combined with surveys of lower-age brackets were used as substitutes for internal information on population size and mobility. During the 1950s the greatest effort in this field went into the improvement of the current population registration in order to shorten the informational lag. By the time of the postwar population census of January 1959, it was reported that the divergence between the current population estimates for the total population (including its sex distribution), on the one hand, and the census results, on the other, was within one half of one percent. While the combination of current civil registration data and the census data of 1959 was sufficient to predict a serious decline in manpower increase for the early 1960s and a rise in the rate of population growth due to a relatively high birth rate, the ensuing decrease in the birth rate was a surprise even to Soviet demographers. The census data of 1970 would therefore serve as an important check upon the reliability of the basic methods used in collecting and evaluating short-term changes in the size and composition of the Soviet population.

Statistics of GNP and National Income

Except for a few attempts during the Tsarist years, serious efforts to estimate GNP and national income in Russia did not begin until the post-revolutionary period. As in so many other areas of economic thought and quantitative measurement, the groundwork was laid during the 1920s, prior to the complete bureaucratization of statistical and economic studies.

During the mid-1920s, when some of the outstanding Russian economists were interested in macroeconomic data, when the problems of economic forecasting were hotly debated prior to the establishment of rigid centralized planning, when work on interindustry balances (an early and perhaps primitive form of input-output analysis) was under way and macroeconomic mathematical models were debated, the first two estimates of national income were discussed and published. One of the major problems was that of definition. Most of the Russian and Soviet economists (such as S. M. Prokopovich, the author of the estimates of national income of Russia for 1900 and 1913) were in favor of a Marxist definition of GNP and national income that included only the goods and services created in the sphere of material production—a definition more restricted than the one generally used outside the Soviet Union, which includes the total of goods and services.[18] The one Russian statistician to use a non-Marxian definition of national income was L. N. Litoshenko in 1925.

Beginning with the work on the interindustry table for the USSR for 1923/24, prepared under the editorship of P. I. Popov, and continuing with the work by S. G. Strumilin and V. I. Kats, who provided estimates for the national income of the USSR for 1925/26, a Marxist definition of national income was the basis for calculations. In 1928 the State Planning Committee published its estimates of national income for the year 1926/27, but without much explanation of its statistical methodology. The end of the 1920s signaled the end of publications of detailed calculations of national income.

We are still in the dark as to the reasons for the discontinuation of these publications. Some sources allude to a Stalin directive to discontinue such studies;[19] others point out that until around 1931 there were still studies under way in Gosplan concerned with the calculation of national income in current and 1928 prices, studies published in part for internal use.[20] Whatever the reason, even though studies were no longer being published and hardly any work inside the Statistical Authority (apart from purely methodological papers for internal consumption) was going on in the area of national income research, a summary figure for USSR national income was published for almost every year up to 1940. These were the famous national income data, calculated in 1926/27 constant prices. It is now common knowledge, with semiofficial acknowledgment, that these national income figures bore very little resemblance to the dynamics of real national income. There is a vast literature on the "enigma wrapped in a mystery" of the 1926/27 prices, to which interested readers can turn.[21] The official estimates of national income before World War II are nearly worthless as a guide for students of Soviet national income. The only reliable sources are studies by American scholars for some selected time periods.[22]

Beginning with the late 1950s the Soviet statistical handbooks started to publish a series of estimates of the size of national income, originally in the form of index numbers and later in absolute figures as well. The relationship between the series for 1950–61 and the base year 1913 is clearly wrong. But the series for 1950–69, with 1950 as the base year, reflects a much greater uniformity in the methodology used and consistency in the calculation of the components of the national income totals. Despite valid grounds for criticism, the work has to be treated seriously by students interested in a very general indicator of economic activity in the Soviet Union for this period.

The Soviet official publications gradually become more specific about definitions and concepts, and about methods of information gathering and data processing for estimating the national income. There is not much point, except for specialists, in tracing the intricacies of the process, which is obviously little more than an exercise in semantics. It is more useful to present some of the more important concepts and methods used, according to the most recent definitions available.[23] The two concepts most widely used by Soviet economists and statisticians are gross social product and national income; the latter, when translated into Western national accounting terms, corresponds to the concept of net material product.

Official Soviet statistics, as I have said, include in the calculation of the national income only the branches of the national economy which belong to the sphere of so-called material production, as distinct from the service sector of the economy, which is usually referred to in the Soviet literature as the nonmaterial sphere.[24] To be clear about this distinction, the following branches of the national economy are considered to be within the material production sphere: industry, agriculture, forestry, irrigation, freight transportation, communications serving producing units, construction, geological explorations involving deep boring for ore and natural gas, trade and public dining, material technical supply, government procurement of agricultural products, and a miscellaneous category.[25]

The nonmaterial sphere, according to the most recent definition, includes the following branches of the national economy: housing, municipal, and other services to the population; passenger transportation; communications utilized by nonproducing units and the general population; general geological explorations; health, physical education, and social security services; education; culture and art; science and scientific services; credit operations and government insurance; public administration; party and social organizations.

Even the most recently published definitions and descriptions of methods leave much to be desired in illuminating a methodology which still exhibits some obscure and somewhat inconsistent procedures. It is, for example, unclear whether the procedures yield an estimate of domestic national income or total national income.[26]

The published estimates of national income are at present calculated either for the country as a whole or for the major administrative units, the Union republics. The estimates of national income are broken down for five major branches of the economy: (1) industry, (2) construction, (3) agriculture, (4) transportation and communication, and (5) other branches.[27] But there are no comparable GNP estimates for the same branches of the economy that indicate the relationship between gross output and net production for these branches. Thus the size of the material outlays (or the difference between the estimates of the social product and the national income) in a particular branch is not revealed and can only be roughly estimated by the use of data of the Soviet input-output tables on interindustry flow. As a result, we have an incomplete notion of the contribution by particular branches of the economy to the national income.

Since "the gross social product is calculated in prices of sales inclusive of the turnover tax," [28] one would assume that national income is calculated in the same prices. Thus, the determinations of price, including the turnover tax, have a profound impact upon the reported relative shares of the various industries or branches of the economy in the national income. A prime example is the share of agriculture in the official estimates of Soviet national income; this is clearly underestimated, since the taxes on foods and textiles are levied either at the level of industrial processing or within the trade network. The official Soviet data on national income provide important information. But they have to be used with great caution, in the light of what they actually do and do not represent.

Price Statistics

Government collection of price statistics following the October Revolution was a result of the need to cope with the galloping inflation, rising prices, and short supplies of food and manufactured consumer goods which the new government had inherited from the previous regimes and which had contributed to the discontent which facilitated the Bolsheviks' seizure of power. Though the Soviet government was committed ideologically to a system of direct distribution of goods and services by noneconomic criteria, the civil war necessitated the imposition of a system of rationing designed primarily to support the military effort. The bulk of the population had to satisfy its needs through channels of semilegal and illegal markets in which prices reflected the existing scarcities. During the period of War Communism (1918–21), the collected price information had very little impact upon policies, but the data were collected and later published, so that one can analyze the information in order to draw conclusions about such matters as the differences between market prices and official prices.

Price statistics as a source of information and as a basis for the formation of government policies became prominent during the period of the NEP (New Economic Policy, 1921–27), which legalized free markets for most consumer goods and services and allowed some measure of individual initiative in the areas of small industry and trade. The price statistics gathered extensively during this period provided a clear view of the so-called scissors crisis (the divergent trends of industrial and agricultural prices at the expense of the farm population) and were helpful to the government in its intervention in the economy and in its setting of prices for the government sector.

The collection of price data in the sectors of state, cooperative, and private trade assumed greater importance after the monetary reform of 1924, when inflationary pressures abated for a while and the government began to gradually eliminate private middlemen and increase the state and cooperative sectors of internal trade. The work of collecting price statistics during the 1920s was decentralized. Retail prices were collected primarily by the TsSU (Central Statistical Authority) and the People's Commissariat for Trade; wholesale prices were collected by the Gosplan; industrial prices by the VSNKh (Supreme Council of National Economy); prices of commodities making up the family "market basket" by the PC (People's Commissariat) of Labor; prices for rural cost-of-living indexes by the Institute of Business Fluctuations of the PC of Finance. The decentralization of collection, processing, analysis, and publication resulted in a certain amount of duplication, differences in coverage and methodology, and perhaps omission of some areas. But whatever its inefficiencies, this decentralized system of data collection at least provided much raw data for multifaceted economic analyses.

By 1930 the price data began to reflect the rapid inflation resulting from the forced industrialization and the sharply changed priorities between capital goods and consumer goods of the First Five-Year Plan. The publication of price data was discontinued and their collection modified. Under conditions of direct planning of production in physical quantities, price data lost most of their usefulness, except as indicators of inflation and as propaganda devices. These are practically the only purposes for which price data were used in the three decades following 1930.

The government set wholesale and retail prices as well as prices for procurement of agricultural commodities from collective and state farms. Data pertaining to the dual or triple price systems were used to derive indexes for retail, wholesale, or procurement prices with little effort at verification of actual prices by sampling or other verifying procedures. The only area in which sampling was conducted was that of prices in the collective farm market. Thus the unpublished price statistics were reduced to a calculation of the impact of decreed price changes of various commodities upon the official indexes of retail prices in the state and cooperative trade networks, without much concern for the actual weights of commodities in the total trade turnover.

This inadequate system of collecting and calculating price data during the Stalin era was disastrous for any rational price policy during the post-Stalin period, when increasing prices for agricultural products became the accepted form of income incentives to that sector and when retail price changes for consumer goods became increasingly important with a broader range of consumer goods on the market.

The range of price statistics in the Soviet economy is much broader than those of goods and services in the trade and distribution sector. Prices are used for interenterprise transactions, for calculation of the growth rate of

sectors of the economy, and for national income accounting. The concepts
of prices as an aid to planning and as a means of accounting of course
differ considerably from the concepts of prices in the West. Though Soviet
prices are theoretically determined by social costs, in practice the setting of
prices very often appears to be arbitrary.

During the 1960s the government started to publish price statistics and
to develop an improved system of collecting and processing them. But
Soviet statisticians found it difficult to reproduce the necessary data for
earlier decades to provide continuity between the 1920s and the 1960s.

Industrial Production

The first attempt to estimate the volume of industrial production in
Soviet Russia was a count of the existing industrial enterprises in the
territory controlled by the Soviets in 1918. Included in the count were the
so-called census enterprises (enterprises with mechanical motive power employing at least 16 workers and enterprises without motive power employing
at least 30 workers) of manufacturing industries, all mining enterprises, and
enterprises whose production had been taxed by the Tsarist or Provisional
Government (alcoholic beverages, sugar, cigarettes, matches, etc.). The goal
of the count was not only to estimate the current output and productive
capacity of the existing enterprises for policy purposes, but also to learn
about experiences during the years 1913–18—the size of the existing capital
stock, the skilled labor force, and the levels of costs and prices. The practical results of the enterprise census were meager (Siberia, the Urals,
Ukraine, and Caucasus had to be left out), and the detailed information
was not published until many years later. But the learning experience of
this census provided Soviet statisticians with data and with unresolved
methodological problems for the organization of a flow of current statistical
information and of accounting or reporting at less frequent intervals. In
1919, the TsSU (Central Statistical Authority) and the VSNKh (Supreme
Council of the National Economy) organized a system of current reporting
of industrial production. In 1920 there was another census of industrial
enterprises, which covered a larger territory than that of 1918 and included
not only census enterprises but also small-scale industrial enterprises. Given
the detailed reports and the relatively long period of processing the data
of both the first and second censuses of industrial enterprises, the impact of
these censuses was limited to methodology rather than policy.

During the early 1920s the problems of definitions of industrial output
and their inclusiveness were discussed, while in practice various reporting
units used apparently different definitions and methods of calculating output. The choices available were: (1) a concept of "gross turnover," which
included a double count of semifinished goods (first as goods produced by
enterprises and then as components of finished goods produced by other
enterprises); (2) the prerevolutionary concept of commercial final output,

which was more restricted than the concept of gross product of the industry; (3) gross output of final goods, which did not include semifinished products. The definition of gross output which was finally recommended by the statisticians corresponded to the concept of commercial final output by the enterprise, but including the output of semi-finished goods produced by the enterprises. This definition and accounting method, termed the "enterprise method," led to the calculation of industrial output which was by and large the sum of gross output of the various enterprises. This method was not fully adapted by the statistical agencies until 1936, a delay due in part to the fact that in many branches industrial output was calculated and reported not by the individual enterprises but by branch associations (called "trusts") which did not report all their interenterprise transactions. While the uniformity of reporting in the industrial sector was important for future accounting periods, it probably contributed in 1936 to an unwarranted leap forward of the industrial production index, for reasons discussed later.

Apart from the definition of industrial production, which was basically the concept of a gross value of output arrived at as a sum of the gross output of the various enterprises, Soviet statisticians tried to use the concept of net output of industry to measure the share of industry in the national income. The term "net output" is used in this case because the Soviet concept of national income is one of net material production.

The statistical studies of industrial output have of course other purposes than the construction of indexes. Of much greater importance was the task of providing the planners and policy makers with data on the size and composition of industrial output and the degree of fulfillment of the various short-term and long-term plans, to reflect the costs of production and reveal the bottlenecks of rapid industrialization. Industry, being the sector of highest priority in the economy, had to provide a multitude of data. After 1929/30 the monthly, quarterly, and yearly reports of enterprises became the chief sources of information on output of the enterprises, industry branches, and the industrial sector as a whole. The yearly reports contained the accounts for the statistical agencies of the size and composition of output, along with the bookkeeping (financial) and technical information. For most of industry (with the exception of small-scale industry) the yearly reports are still the primary source of data on output in physical terms. This obviously required the elaboration of reporting standards for products (in terms of quality as well as assortment) and the establishment of technical coefficients for various types of production and various levels of technology.

Construction of time series of industrial production required the use of constant prices for the physical output data. Thus, apart from the use of actual prices of the current year, prices of a chosen year had to be assumed as a base to measure the past and future changes in the size of industrial output. The first set of "comparable" or constant prices to be used were the average prices of 1912, which were preferable to later prices under conditions of inflation. But by 1927/28 the Soviet prejudice against the use of prerevolutionary data won out, and the 1926/27 constant prices were introduced as a deflator of the production series.

The use of the 1926/27 prices became a notorious problem, with Soviet economists insisting that they were perfectly good, and economists outside the Soviet Union arguing that the so-called 1926/27 prices helped to inflate the Soviet index of industrial production because they deviated from even the original 1926/27 prices. To the extent that one can determine, the 1926/27 prices were at the beginning not uniform or average prices of that year, but product sales prices of the output of each particular enterprise. Enterprises founded after 1926/27 used to establish their own "1926/27 prices," and new products were priced for 1926/27 by analogies which were often questionable (tractors by locomotive prices, for example). Given rapid inflation accompanying the early phases of Soviet industrialization, the product prices thus retroactively created and used as weights for the index introduced an upward bias in the total production index. The index reflected not only the real growth of output but also the relationship between various products within the product mix, depending upon the time when the various products were introduced. In 1936 the use of one uniform set of 1926/27 prices was made obligatory for all enterprises for the products introduced prior to 1936.[29]

The introduction of uniformity in the set of 1926/27 prices did not provide a remedy for the future nor correct the official index of industrial production, with the exception that it produced for 1936 a rate of growth which exceeded previous ones. The production of small-scale industry (local industries and industrial cooperatives) was priced and entered the index according to the prices of 1932. Thus using the prices of 1926/27 resulted in making the index of industrial production of the 1930s more one of current prices than of constant prices. The use of the 1926/27 price weights until 1950 became increasingly difficult and burdensome and reflected no form of reality, neither current economic relations between enterprises (which were conducted in current prices) nor the cost structure or levels of costs, which by definition of the Soviet planners had to be approximated by industrial wholesale prices.

Thus a price reform was imminent, but it had to wait until the completion of the Fourth Five-Year Plan in the immediate post–World War II period of reconstruction, 1946–50. While the wholesale prices of 1949 were used in 1951, they were soon superseded by 1952 wholesale prices, and during 1956–68 by wholesale prices of 1 July 1955, which were used for the statistical purpose of measuring industrial production and for planning. Since 1969 the wholesale prices of 1 July 1967 have been used as weights for the index of industrial output.

Since the wholesale prices at which enterprises sell their output to the distribution network do not include the turnover tax, it is important for nonspecialized students of the Soviet data to distinguish those indexes of industrial production which use as weights the wholesale prices of the enterprises from those indexes which use as weights the wholesale prices of industry. The wholesale prices of industry include the turnover tax; the index numbers using them as weights are centrally calculated by the Central Statistical Authority.

For reasons of ideology as well as propaganda, the indexes of industrial output were considered by the Soviet policy makers and planners the "success indicators" of the Soviet system. This in itself would both explain and justify the caution with which such indexes are treated by students outside the Soviet Union. The prevailing view among serious and objective scholars of the growth of industrial production in the Soviet Union is that in spite of methodological shortcomings the indexes pertaining to the recent period (10–15 years) are a good approximation to the rate of growth of the industrial sector. One is, however, warned against accepting uncritically the indexes of particular industry branches even for the recent period, on the one hand, and the series related to the 1930s and 1940s, on the other. This lack of confidence in the data of the early period of Soviet industrialization makes it very difficult to study the continuity between industrialization under the tsars and industrialization under the Soviets.

Agricultural Production

The area of agricultural production is one in which the collection of quantitative data presents a clear continuity between the Tsarist and Soviet periods. This is due chiefly to two factors: (1) the continuity of statistical work between the old zemstvos and the local offices of agricultural statistics created by the Soviet government; and (2) the fact that the first revolutionary agrarian reform, which confiscated large and also some middle-sized landholdings, allowed peasant landownership to continue. Thus there is more of a qualitative break in the data at the time of the forced collectivization of the early 1930s than in the years immediately following the revolution.

The major components of agricultural production data are those of crops and of livestock, and the chief problems in the development of these data are the methods of calculating and evaluating crops and livestock production and combining or integrating the two. Gross crop output data were derived primarily by multiplying the data on the areas planted (or actually harvested) in particular crops (or groups of crops which were approximately homogeneous) by the yield of the crops during a specified period (usually one year). Since the statistics of planted areas are discussed separately, it is the derivation of yield data which concerns us here.

During the prerevolutionary and early postrevolutionary periods, the yields were determined largely by using a network of correspondents who had to approximate a representative sample of farm producers in various regions. The data received from the correspondents prior to and after the harvest were used to determine the average size of yields and were interpreted by a committee of experts who applied appropriate correction factors to the reported data. Such corrections dealt with underreporting, inadequate representativeness of the sample, short-run shifts in planted areas, and the impact of weather conditions, to the extent that such elements were insufficiently reflected in the reports by the correspondents. The sample of correspondent farms was about 20,000, a relatively small sample for the estimation of crop yields given the extent of territory, regional differences, and diversity of farming methods. Therefore the Statistical Authority attempted to utilize in addition the taxation data provided by the People's Commissariat of Finance. The taxation data were derived (for taxable farms) from two questionnaires per year, one during spring involving about 10 percent of the taxable farms, and one during late autumn (post-harvest and winter crop planting), involving about 3–5 percent of the taxable farms. Such information was used for correcting the estimates of yields, until in the second half of the 1920s a special 3 percent sample of farms in designated regions assumed to be more typical than the previous samples was established.

Rapid collectivization necessitated a basic reconstruction of the data-gathering apparatus. The reports of the collective and state farms, coupled with the family budget samples of rural dwellers, provided the necessary information. But the drastic decrease in the number of farm units, as one immediate result of collectivization, did not automatically assure an improvement in the reporting or estimation of crop yields. There was no prima facie incentive to report accurately the size of agricultural output. The authorities resorted to a device previously used to determine biological yield (the yield of ripening grain prior to the harvest, before harvesting losses) —that is, the use of spot checks in representative fields by counting the grain on one square meter (called in popular speech the *metrovka* device). This device became one of the chief instruments in the reporting of the yield and in determining the amount of taxation in kind.

Beginning with 1933, data on the reported yield of the grain crops and then of other crops were not on the actual yield or barn yield (representing the output which was collected and storable) but on biological yield, which represented the maximum of attainable yield while exceeding the actual yield by as much as one third or more. This phenomenon of Soviet agricultural statistics was known and described by Western economists. After Stalin's death, Soviet leaders (Khrushchev in particular) denounced the use of a biological yield measure. The definition of yield that has prevailed since then is the so-called "bunker yield," which represents the grain (and sunflower seed) harvested by the combine harvesters. It still differs from the barn yield by the extent of impurities or higher-than-normal moisture content in the grain.

Among the most accurate data on the usable output of crops are those for industrial crops, which can be checked against the data on raw material supplies of the textile and food industries. Among the least accurate are the data for vegetables, potatoes, fruits, and succulent feeds. Their lack of accuracy is due to the high share of total output which comes from the private plots and to the fact that most feed is consumed on the farm itself and thus escapes the controls on marketed commodities.

The problems of methodology in calculating and reporting crop output in physical terms had their counterparts in the calculation and reporting of livestock output. During the 1920s the data included the output of livestock products and changes in values of herds. But during the 1930s, apart from the output of milk, wool, and eggs, the meat increase of the total herd —instead of the meat increase of animals slaughtered—became the basis of meat output estimates. The transition from private to socialized agriculture was accompanied by a dramatic decrease of livestock and also of yields, facts too conspicuous to be entirely hidden but whose extent could be in part hidden by changing definitions of production. Therefore, during the 1930s milk consumed by calves was included in milk output, meat by-products were included in meat output, and manure was included in livestock output. As in the case of crop production, more clarity as to the components of livestock output and uniformity of reporting were introduced during the post-Stalin period. The accuracy of reported gross output of livestock products in physical terms is somewhere between that of the grain crop and that of vegetable and fruit crops, because a high share of livestock output is still privately produced by farm households and consumed either by these households or on the farms.

A gross output measure of the various branches of agricultural production exceeds the net output available for consumption or for industrial processing by a number of components, of which the most important are the seed and feed used up on the farm in the production process. The data on such uses are probably available from the yearly farm reports which break down the production data by their uses (taxes, sales, carryover reserves, seed, feed, distribution to the farm labor force, spoilage, losses, etc.); these were used by planners to construct balances between production and utilization of agricultural products. But the publication of such balances was discontinued in 1929 and has never been resumed by the statistical agencies. This fact makes it very difficult to calculate independently, or to reconstruct, the Soviet measures of net output of agriculture or the contribution of agriculture to the national income.

The most general measure of agricultural production reported by the Soviet Statistical Authority is the output of agriculture (also reported separately as crop output and livestock output) in money terms, published either in index numbers or in actual figures. This measure is calculated in current prices and in constant prices (at the beginning, 1913 prices). During the 1920s, both these figures were published; during the 1930s and 1940s only data on output in constant prices were published; and by the mid-1950s and 1960s either one or sometimes both figures were published. One of the major difficulties in calculating a price index for agricultural output was the multipricing system for agricultural products. To use just one example, that of grain prices, there were different sets of prices to be considered for (1) obligatory deliveries from collective farms, (2) above-plan deliveries, (3) purchases from state farms, and (4) collective farm market sales. These were the major sales prices, apart from the calculated costs of the share of production which was consumed on the farm, and still more were possible. In addition, attempts to simplify the multiprice system led to the establishment of regional price differentials.

At this point, the calculation of the value of agricultural output in current prices requires that the production be calculated separately for each type of producer—for the state farms, collective farms, and auxiliary private farm plots. Commercial output is calculated in average prices of actual sales for each sector for each product. Average prices therefore may deviate from the actual prices received by particular farms, but they represent prices for the total marketed output. For the nonmarketed output, the state farms use the actual cost of each farm, and the collective farms use average calculated costs. For the private output consumed by the producers' households, they use the average of sales prices of commercial output of collective farms and private plot sales.

The calculation of value in constant prices uses average prices for the base year. Prices for the base year are calculated as weighted averages of the prices of commercial output and noncommercial output of that year. As base years for constant prices after collectivization, the following years have been taken: until 1952, 1926/27; from 1952 to 1956, 1951; from 1956 to 1958, 1956; from 1958 to 1967, 1958; and from 1968 on, 1965.

Not all the necessary information is available with which to calculate net output in constant prices. We know, for example, that grain and potatoes used as feed are calculated at a lower-than-average price for the calculations of gross output. We know also that there is a special price index to relate the current-price index for industrial goods expenditures by farms to the prices of the base year to obtain constant prices. But the details are not revealed and thus do not allow us to reconstruct the Soviet data. Only by a reading of both Soviet sources and non-Soviet studies can the scholar develop the basis for critical use of the available sources for agricultural output.

Planted Areas

A combination and comparison of the data of the 1916 agricultural census and the all-Russian land investigation of 1922 served as the basic sources for the statistics of planted areas by region, crop, and type of farm for the 1920s. These sources enabled the statistical offices of the People's

Commissariats of Agriculture and of Finance to set up clusters of sample farms providing the direct data on planted areas that could later be converted into national data. But because of the inadequacy of the sample and the incompleteness of the fiscal data, the estimating procedure had to be supplemented by additional spring and autumn sampling. The spring sample included about 10 percent of all agricultural households; the autumn sample, between 3 and 5 percent of the households. The view that the pre–World War I statistics of the planted area had a built-in underestimation bias (held by such experts as Ivantsov) could probably be applied to the period of the 1920s when it was in the interest of the peasants, for fiscal reasons, to underestimate their planted area. The new conditions created by collectivization and the drastic reduction in the number of farm units made it relatively easy to derive more accurate information on the size of the planted area. Since the total number of socialized farms was smaller than the number in the previous samples, one would have expected a marked improvement in the quality and flow of information. This was not necessarily the case because of institutional factors whose examination is beyond our scope here. The fact that the reporting was done for a long time—not by the farms themselves but by the Machine Tractor Stations, a government institution with goals different from the goals of the farms—contributed to inaccuracies. The poor quality of farm reports (which reflected the quality of farm management), the need to adjust to frequently changing directives from above, and the lack of proper crop rotation all contributed to the sore state of reporting and aggregating information.

The foremost reason for the absence of reliable data, however, was the lack of a land cadastre, which would have been of enormous help both to farm management and to the statistics of land use in general and of the planted area in particular. It is only during the last two or three years that work on a land cadastre has started, and therefore there is hope within the near future of a real breakthrough in the quality of the planted area statistics. One may hope that in the future the data on the planted area will reflect not only the area originally planted but, in the case of grains, also the area of winter kill, the area of replanting, and finally the area actually harvested. Given the climatic conditions of the Soviet Union and the frequency of winter kills, sandstorms, and droughts, this type of information is useful for any appraisal of the conditions of agricultural production.

There is still another area of deficiency in reporting data, namely the breakdown of planted areas under crops located in areas of irrigation and drainage. Not only is irrigated land a prerequisite for the location of such crops as cotton or rice in the Soviet Union, but irrigation and drainage play an important role in the expansion of other crops in areas of insufficient or excessive precipitation. This information has been made available only recently, and we have no published data for the earlier period. The release of data on crop distribution in irrigated and drained lands (if they exist) would fill an important gap in our knowledge and understanding of the intent of the Soviet policy makers and of actual crop production in the Soviet Union during the past 30–40 years.

The accuracy of the data on the planted area reported by the farms to the statistical agencies was a major concern of the policy makers in agriculture, and that concern was among the motives to discontinue the typical Stalinist policy of a system of taxation based upon the size of the reported or planned planted area. Thus a significant source and motive to distort the accuracy of the data was removed. By granting more autonomy to the farms in planning the utilization of land, the policy makers might further reduce the distortion of data on the planted areas.

Livestock Statistics

The basic data on the livestock population inherited by the Soviet regime were collected in the agricultural censuses of 1916 and 1917, conducted under war conditions and on a territory smaller than that of the whole Russian Empire. Given the experiences of World War I, the civil war and the famine that followed it, and the boundary changes, the livestock census data were of little use as a benchmark for subsequent data collection. The data collection of the period 1918–29 therefore reverted to the traditional prewar "military horse-counts," which had an obvious downward bias. Such counts were carried out in 1919–20 and during 1923–25. They were organized by the People's Commissariat of Agriculture and by the Central Statistical Authority and the Ministry of Finance for taxpaying households on the basis of samples, correspondents' reports, and various estimating procedures. Thus for the 1920s we are dealing with estimates, the accuracy of which varied from case to case, not with censuses.

The first Soviet livestock census took place on 1 February 1932. That was in the latter part of the agricultural collectivization drive, in the midst of the slaughtering of livestock herds which accompanied the protests against forced collectivization. The census reports included data on the size of herds and their age distribution and, for the socialized sector of agriculture, on the various breeds. Both the 1932 livestock census and the following one, that of 1 January 1934, were incomplete and were to be supplemented by an on-the-spot control check of about 10 percent of the livestock-owning households. From 1935 until 1941 (with the exception of 1939), yearly counts recorded the changes in the size and basic characteristics of livestock herds. While the war necessarily curtailed the extent of information sought, the postwar period saw a return to prewar procedures of data collection. The accumulation of documentation about livestock herds, in both the socialized and private sectors and over a longer period of relative stability, made it easier to count the livestock, to check the results against the inventory data, and when necessary to verify by on-the-spot checks.

One of the characteristics of Soviet agriculture and, by analogy, of other branches of economic and social life is the impact of statistics and data-gathering procedures upon the behavior of institutions and individuals. Observers and students outside the Soviet Union may readily understand the impact of environmental conditions upon the quality of the information supplied or the biases to be expected from such information. But it is much more difficult to understand how reporting procedures influence behavior. That a livestock count fixed for the first of January of each year should influence the size of the herd and the cost of producing livestock products is not clear unless we are informed that the production plans for livestock numbers and procurement plans for livestock products are also tied to the calendar year. Thus every slaughtering of livestock prior to 1 January might put the farm at a disadvantage in plan fulfillment in terms of livestock numbers. On the other hand, keeping livestock until 1 January might help fulfill the livestock plan in terms of numbers but increase the cost of production per unit of the final output of meat, hides, and so forth.

It was not until 1953 that the connection between the statistical counts of livestock (in terms of heads or number) and the procurement plan of livestock output was discontinued, and that plan fulfillment in numbers was pushed back three months. Needless to say, this new arrangement saved a substantial volume of feed, which previously was spent for maintenance at constant weight rather than for weight increase of the livestock.

The livestock statistics within the socialized sector still retain their significance as a basis for the production goals and procurement plans of livestock output. Although their usefulness as a policy or control tool tended to diminish over time, the emphasis upon the quality of the statistical data and their reliability was on the rise. If there is a legitimate complaint about the published livestock data, it pertains to the lack of information on pedigreed cattle. Students of Soviet agriculture have somehow reconciled themselves to the idea that there is in most cases no distinction between dairy cattle and beef cattle, and it is usually assumed that the category "large horned cattle" excluding the category "cows" represents the main resource for beef production. We lack information on pedigreed cattle of the different breeds as a share in the total cattle herd, or on the distribution of the sheep herd according to the various breeds. These are serious omissions in our knowledge of the quality of livestock. The relatively low productivity of livestock in the Soviet Union is usually blamed upon the insufficiency of feed, but the reported high feed-output ratios point also to the low quality of livestock breeding as an additional explanatory factor. Without data, however, one remains in the realm of opinions instead of knowledge.

The Labor Force

The history of the organization of data collection and processing in the area of labor is typical of its development in many areas. We can distinguish the following phases: (1) an early proliferation of data-collecting agencies, stimulated by the interest in quantitative data in general and in labor in particular; (2) attempts to centralize data collection and, where desirable, to standardize data processing, still preserving the multitude of agencies but with a clearer division of labor and hierarchy of tasks; (3) centralization combined with strict control of the collecting, processing, and dissemination of information; (4) preservation of a centralized structure but a somewhat liberalized policy on publication of collected data.

In time periods, the first postrevolutionary years coincided with the first phase, when data were collected, processed, and published by the People's Commissariat of Labor (NKTrud), the Supreme Council of the National Economy (VSNKh), and the All-Union Central Council of Trade Unions (VTsSPS), in addition to the Central Statistical Authority (TsSU). The second half of the 1920s coincided with the second phase. The early 1930s showed the tendencies leading to the third phase—that is, the period between 1936 and 1953, when almost no data were published. Subsequently a gradual liberalization set in, comprising phase four. By 1967 a special statistical handbook on labor modeled upon the handbooks of the early 1930s was published. The political reasons for the virtual blackout of labor statistics are clear. The data were sensitive, for they not only showed demographic changes but provided insights into the industrial structure, conditions of life, and standards of living of the society. Therefore only cumulative data and the most general aggregates were published, such as the total labor force and its sex composition.

Very early in the development of labor statistics, the distribution of the labor force by major industry groups and its breakdown by size of enterprises were singled out as important indicators. The main interest was focused upon large-scale industry, thus confirming the policy makers' bias in favor of large-scale production. To the extent that policies promoted large-scale industry at the expense of small-scale industry, the labor statistics focusing on large-scale enterprises became increasingly representative of all industrial labor.

Data on sex and age distribution for the labor force as a whole were collected by sporadically organized surveys of varying frequency. But industrial labor force data were gathered on a more systematic basis, from the yearly reports of the industrial enterprises or summary reports of defined industry branches. Their consistency was occasionally tested by specially organized surveys, at dates related to the specific purposes of the test—seasonality, migration, turnover, and so forth.

The use of the regular industrial enterprise reports for the study of the utilization of labor time was a routine operation. But it proved insufficient during periods of statutory changes in the length of the industrial work-day: in 1927/28, in connection with the shift from an 8-hour to a 7-hour workday; in 1939/40, while shifting back to an 8-hour day; and in the 1960s, when the 7-hour day was being reestablished. During such periods special surveys were conducted to provide more accurate information on the actual length of the workday and on the utilization of statutory work time, thereby providing a basis for estimating the probable effects of the statutory work-time change upon the level of output, upon the productivity of different categories of labor, or upon the composition of the labor force under conditions of relatively free labor mobility. During periods of limited labor mobility (1940–54/55), surveys of the utilization of labor time, supplemented by studies of the size and composition of the labor force, could have been used to test the relative effectiveness of government restrictions upon labor mobility.

Of primary importance to labor policy in a centralized planned economy is the information on labor force distribution by occupations and within the occupations by skill levels. This type of information presumably was a basis for the planning of training programs for new entrants into the labor force and for retraining programs for other workers in order to meet demands for various occupations, specialties, and skills under conditions of rapidly expanding industrial output. One of the usual difficulties in obtaining the necessary information within a situation of both inflated demand for labor and rapid technological change is that of changing definitions of occupations and skill categories. The distinctions between the different occupational categories kept changing and becoming more refined, so that the number of categories grew constantly. The distinctions among different skill levels within particular occupations were drawn from the data on occupational distribution according to wage scales (on the assumption that the wage-scale distribution was a substitute for skill-level distribution, an assumption very close to that of a competitive labor market).

The study of wage-scale distribution borders on, or is often a part of, the study of wages and labor earnings. The latter is an area of methodological complexity as well as political sensitivity. The difficulties were less a function of the data-collection process than of the processing and interpretation of the data. Given the periods of inflation and of price controls and rationing, the derivation of real wage data as compared with nominal (money) wage data presents problems which cannot be resolved exclusively by index numbers solutions. For times when payments in kind made up a major part of the wage, or for times when double- or triple-pricing systems were in operation, the averages of nominal wages are of doubtful meaning or usefulness. During such periods, studies of the prices of "baskets" of consumables and family budget studies had to supplement the conventional wage statistics.

Wage statistics were at times of dubious importance as policy guides for the government, especially when they were at variance with other government policy indicators or when they simply confirmed the impression of the inability of the central authorities to enforce a particular wage policy, especially one that would curb wage inflation. The effectiveness of an enforced wage policy could not be tested by the use of wage statistics alone. Price data of consumer goods and services had to be combined with wage data, just as price policies in those areas had to be synchronized with the setting of wage rates for the different types of labor according to skill, occupation, and productivity. Needless to say, the wage rates were closely tied to technical output norms per unit of time or of output.

Apart from the data on nominal and real wages actually paid out, wage statistics encompassed a number of categories of what is defined as the "social wage." These categories include various subsidies and payments as well as implied costs of education, health, and—for purposes of comparison or propaganda—in some cases benefits of full employment. The usefulness of the social wage data can conceivably be defended by distinguishing, primarily for decision making, between private and social consumption of goods and services. Major studies of wage statistics were usually tied to an overhaul of wage rates, including significant changes in the differentials among skill categories.

Under normal circumstances, the current reports and accounts of the various enterprises are used as the main source of wage data. Wage data were collected and processed but rarely published between 1936 and 1966, so that no consistent, reliable, and continuous time series of official wage data for any category of labor are available. Thus, while labor statistics of varying scope and quality can be found for the study of various aspects of the recent social and economic history of Russia, they are generally scarcer and in many respects inferior to the data available for other developed countries. The USSR still offers the paradox of a regime which has claimed to put labor at the center of its social policies but which provides insufficient data for any serious evaluation of its labor policies.

Technical Manpower

The organization of statistics on technical manpower in the Soviet Union was instituted in part as a carryover of measures (not very effective ones) taken by the tsarist government in its war effort. For the Soviet regime a registration of available technical manpower was to serve the needs of both defense and economic and social development. Thus, its decrees of 19 December 1918 and 18 February 1919 created a Chief Bureau of Registration and Distribution of Technical Manpower and required registration of technical specialists of both sexes and all ages. They could be called upon (mobilized) to serve in their capacities as technical specialists according to the directives of the state authorities. The following categories were subject to registration:

1. All graduates of physics-mathematics departments of Russian and foreign universities
2. Students of the last four semesters of all technical institutions of higher learning
3. Graduates of special technical schools with a program above secondary school levels
4. Technical managers of industrial, transportation, and agricultural enterprises without formal technical training, but with at least two years of managerial experience

Thus a filing system of personal data about the members of the country's technical-managerial elite became the chief source of information on the country's most valuable human resource. The results of the registration, combined with a special effort to obtain more detailed information about the technical specialists in agriculture during 1922, were reported for 1922/23. This was a period of early reconstruction in both industry and agriculture connected with "New Economic Policy" (NEP). The data on technical manpower were used to provide guidelines and to set priorities in the field of technical education and training. At the time of the preliminary preparatory work on the First Five-Year Plan, a decree of the Council of People's Commissars of 9 July 1926 ordered a new survey of technical specialists and agronomists to be conducted by 1 January 1927. At the outset of forced-draft industrialization, by the decree of 23 May 1928, the personal registration of technical specialists had to be brought up to date.

The expansion of industrial construction and output and the collectivization of agriculture increased the immediate demand for technical specialists, and both allocation and redistribution of technical manpower necessitated a special registration by 1 March 1930. This registration coincided with the beginning of a policy to replace the older technical elite by a younger one, educated and technically trained under Soviet rule and thereby presumably more reliable politically.

During the subsequent period, there was less reliance upon a central file of technical manpower based upon personal registration. As a result of the growth in numbers of such personnel, the information was decentralized. It was collected and utilized by the various governmental agencies (such as the industrial ministries and ministries of agriculture and transportation), and special surveys were conducted by the central statistical agencies (TsUNKhU, TsSU) at dates significant for the development of the economy, e.g., preparation of new five-year plans and postwar reconstruction. The significance attached to the information on technical manpower reflected the intensive effort at expanding technical education to increase the quantity and improve the quality of highly skilled personnel for the Soviet economy.

Statistics of Education

In popular literature, the data on education, including one of its most spectacular indicators—the level of literacy—are usually treated in terms of comparisons of the Soviet population census data of 1926, 1939, or 1959 with the data of the tsarist population census of 1897. But such comparisons ignore the considerable progress of Russia during the two decades 1897–1917, unless one also takes into account the school censuses of 1905 and 1911. From the point of view of historical continuity, the returns of the 1920 population census (albeit incomplete in its territorial coverage) are very important.

As far as literacy and educational levels are concerned, the population census has served during the Soviet period as the main source of information. The most valuable sources of current information for enrollment in schools of various types have been the yearly reports of the Ministry of Education, combined with the reports of the department of educational statistics of the Central Statistical Authority, which cover not only enrollment but also teacher employment, physical plant, and equipment of the schools.

In harmony with the policy of preferential treatment for working-class children in school enrollment, data on the social origin or social position of students became available in the statistical reports; these reflected the relative successes or failures of government attempts to change the social recruitment of students for secondary and higher education. The statistical sources also provided data which enable us to study government policy on the types of education and training during various periods. From the data, one can distinguish the periods when more emphasis was placed upon elementary rather than secondary education, or on technical training rather than general education on the secondary school level. Information is available about the numbers of technicians and engineers trained as compared to specialists in other areas of the sciences, humanities, or social sciences; the numbers of students in professional-technical schools as compared to young workers trained on the job; and the numbers of full-time as compared to part-time students.

Universal seven-year elementary education was introduced by law in cities and citylike settlements in 1930, but it was only shortly before 1950 that such an educational goal was also established for rural areas. Thus the rural-urban educational differential at the elementary level was continued as a matter of policy until the 1950s. In the 1950s the government redefined elementary education as eight years of schooling (instead of seven) and set the goal of a ten-year schooling period (secondary schools) primarily for the urban centers. During the early 1960s, in connection with a demographically determined labor shortage, the last two years of secondary school were combined for many students with on-the-job training or employment; however, a loosening of the labor market led to the abandonment of this practice.

The statistics of education provide an interesting insight into an area in which the Soviet regime has made sizable investments and achieved impressive results. For the general discussion of sources of economic growth or patterns of modernization, the Soviet data on education and schooling are of great interest. The data enable one to test a whole series of hypotheses and estimate the rate of economic returns on Soviet investments in education.

In addition to data on education at various levels, the Soviet statistical publications also contain data on scientific institutions and research establishments and their scientific and technical personnel. It is, however, difficult to establish the relation of the data on scientific research in educational institutions to the data on scientific research in industry, agriculture, or other sectors of the economy.

The network of public libraries in the Soviet Union is considered a part of the educational network. The data for libraries and their services provide information on some aspects of adult education, including the reading habits of the public. Adult education is still an important element of the total educational network, but it was particularly significant in the past for the older generation.

The quantitative data for the educational system, in spite of shortcomings during some time periods, serve an important function for the study of the cultural and educational progress of Soviet society.

TRADE STATISTICS

Soviet trade is defined as the distribution of goods in the retail trade network; thus by definition it excludes most of the transactions between enterprises, industrial or agricultural. The development of domestic trade statistics has been similar to that of labor statistics: institutional changes have had a strong impact upon the choice of data to be collected and published. Consequently, the nature of trade statistics has followed closely the changes in the institutional arrangements and major policies in domestic trade. In addition, to the extent that statistics of internal trade revealed economic conditions of the population and results of governmental social and economic policies (the total quantities and distribution of goods and services for the consumer sector), they were considered sensitive information by the political decision makers.

Like other statistics directly related to social and economic conditions, the history of trade statistics can be divided into periods. During the earliest period, trade statistics tended to provide the maximum information, over and above what was necessary for both policy decisions and directly pertinent economic research. During the subsequent period, trade statistics directly served the planners and policy makers, while the information accessible to the public was censored and limited primarily to what was of propaganda value. This was followed by a blackout of information, which, during the post-Stalin period, changed into a phase of controlled information accessible to the public.

The Soviet statistics on internal trade consist of three major subsets: (1) data on physical quantities of goods distributed through various channels of the trade network; (2) retail prices for various markets and various categories of commodities; (3) quantitative data on the organization and performance of the trade network and its institutions. The first and second subsets have a great deal in common, namely, the organization and classification of data collection, processing, and publication according to the institutional arrangements of the markets (channels of trade, forms of distribution, etc.). The most meaningful distinction for the historical development of Soviet retail trade is that among state trade, cooperative trade, and private (including collective farm market) trade. In the state sector, the trade in urban areas is of the greatest significance, but special distribution institutions for selected population groups or for special arrangements (sales for gold or foreign exchange), sales to institutions of a limited volume of capital goods, etc. are also included. The network of the trade cooperatives was for most of the period equivalent to the organization of the supply of goods for the rural, and primarily the agricultural, population.

Private trade was carried on until 1930 by private traders in both agricultural products and manufactured consumer goods. It was prohibited in 1930 and revived in 1932, but only as a market for agricultural products in which collective farmers could sell their surpluses. In fact, the only market in which sellers were relatively free to seek a market level of prices was the above-mentioned private market or, later, the collective farm market. In all other markets or trading institutions, prices were set by the state. Because of government determination of both prices and quantities to be sold in the state and cooperative sectors, much of the data, even when available, are of limited interest to the researcher. Moreover, between 1930 and 1935 and between 1941 and 1947 most consumer goods were rationed. The periods during which the data reflect either income changes or the elasticities of demand for particular goods are therefore very limited. Nevertheless, the Soviet trade statistics which are being published are of considerable interest for the study of consumption patterns, urban-rural income differentials, the performance of the distributive apparatus for consumer goods, and many other topics.

The data provided on physical quantities of goods in retail trade are considered by experts more reliable than the retail price indexes. The latter, for many categories, involve the problems of appropriate weights, and the procedure of constructing the overall indexes leaves much to be desired at the level of aggregation. Lack of reliability of the retail price index should make students of Soviet society cautious in using it as an exclusive deflator to arrive at figures of real wages or real incomes.

Not only do prices (except for the collective farm market) fail to reflect the levels at which the market is actually being cleared, but changes in the quality of products are reflected to only a minor extent or not at all. Other evidence indicates the existence of a large percentage of substandard goods (in terms of the officially established quality standards), but official trade statistics, for all practical purposes, ignore the quality problem. This is a shortcoming of which the policy makers are as much aware as the consumers, but one for which the Soviet system has as yet devised no remedy.

The statistical data that deal with the performance of the trade network are primarily of interest for the study of how government policies, often using dysfunctional criteria of success, are being translated into success indicators. One example: the government, in trying to decrease the costs of distribution, may decrease the number of retail clerks. At a constant total volume of sales, this measure will result in a higher indicator of clerks' productivity (volume of sales per clerk). But such a policy will probably result in a decrease in the number and quality of services provided to the public, a cost that will not appear in the statistics, that will be borne by consumers. In the absence of data reflecting the nature and availability of services, most of the performance indicators for services are not of much value to the student of Soviet society.

Family Budget Studies

The research, compilation, and study of family budgets can be traced back to the beginnings of the development of the zemstvo statistics of the late 1870s and 1880s. The prevailing tendency among the zemstvo statisticians and other students of the conditions of rural life was to use peasant family budget data to provide a profile of the agricultural economy. Thus the emphasis was more upon the farm as a production and consumption unit than upon the family as an earning and spending unit. During the first decade of the twentieth century, studies of family budgets of urban dwellers, industrial workers, and employees of various localities and branches of industry were added to the growing literature on this subject.

After the revolution, increasing emphasis was given to the family budget studies. For this there were a number of reasons:

1. The policy of war communism and the ensuing hyperinflation made rationing and direct food supply the prevailing form of wage and income payments.

2. Food requisitions from the peasants became a substitute for other forms of direct and indirect taxation.

3. Data on patterns of family expenditures were helpful in the construction of "balances in kind" between production and consumption of various basic commodities in agriculture, food, and other branches of industry.
4. During the early period of the New Economic Policy (NEP), the problems of the marketable share of agricultural output and the purchasing power of various social groups could be studied from family budget data, and some extrapolation for the future could be derived from such data.
5. Family budget data were helpful in studying the problems of social differentiation within the agrarian sector and gave useful insight into the areas of employment and labor productivity on the one hand and the impact of the market upon the peasant economy on the other.

The interest in family budget studies resulted in increasing the scope of coverage as well as of the details and characteristics of family backgrounds and economic behavior. By the middle and late 1920s the family budgets were organized on a year-round basis and covered a larger and more representative sample. The beginning of the industrialization drive and collectivization of agriculture, with the accompanying vast institutional changes and economic dislocations, slowed down for a time the process of broadening the family budget studies. But by the end of the 1930s the official reports indicated the existence of a sample of about 20,000 urban families and an approximately equal number of collective farm families that constituted the basis for the budget studies. Although this sample was decreased during the war (probably as a result of Nazi occupation of Soviet territories), it was restored afterward. The growth of the state farm sector necessitated a state farm workers' sample, which was introduced by 1957. In October 1958 a study of 240,000 urban families was conducted, perhaps as a check against the data of the yearly samples.

Although the family budget samples, according to the official pronouncements, are considered to be representative, there exist many doubts on this account. The major reason for doubt is that after the 1920s the studies were never published; thus they constitute an unknown entity even to most Soviet economists or historians. The sporadic data that were occasionally released as based upon the budget studies exhibited substantial discrepancies with the published internal trade statistics, food industry statistics, etc. The family budget data in the past were cited to support the most excessive claims about high incomes and consumption levels ever made in the Soviet press or other publications. For outsiders, it is impossible to determine the extent of bias in the family budget studies. The studies are in the domain of the Central Statistical Authority, an agency known in the past for its leanings toward a monopoly of information.

During the early 1930s and 1940s, when rationing prevailed, the family budget data were useful for purposes of income and distribution policy. Their present usefulness for planners of the consumer goods sector ought not to be minimized. That such data can help furnish estimates of income elasticities for a number of commodities is beyond dispute; they can be of major assistance in carrying out some of the economic reforms to which the Soviet leadership has committed itself. However, as long as access to the data is restricted to a small group of high-ranked planners and decision makers, social scientists and historians will be deprived of a valuable source of information that could tell much of the human story of social and economic development of the Soviet Union during the last fifty years.

Tax Data

The old tsarist tradition of a huge administrative apparatus geared toward the collection of direct and indirect taxes has influenced the organization and flow of information about Soviet taxation. State taxation was a powerful tool of national and social policy in tsarist Russia and has remained preeminent since.

Taxation policies have been dominated by various tendencies during successive stages of Soviet rule. The major tendency during the period of war communism was to assure the minimum resources (mostly in kind) for the survival of the urban population; a secondary aim was to appropriate some of the accumulated wealth of the members of the social classes that were to be expropriated. During the period of the NEP, taxation policy was adjusted to provide some incentives for private initiative and to siphon off some of the current incomes of particular social groups for both government investment and income redistribution. The policies of the period of rapid industrialization were in part at least based upon a system of indirect and direct taxation that kept consumption levels of the population relatively low and allowed for a smoother policy of capital accumulation. Taxation, combined with wage and price policies, had to help establish a balance between personal disposable incomes and the volume of consumer goods at existing price levels. In view of the strong inflationary tendencies, taxation policies had a primarily anti-inflationary bias. Their effectiveness was to be measured both by the efficiency of tax collection and by the minimizing of psychological impact upon the population.

The taxation data available for the 1920s reflect the many varieties of taxes paid by the state-owned industrial and trade organizations. They reflect a cumbersome taxation system requiring much information about the economic activities of the taxable units. In this respect the Soviet system was even more complicated than the tsarist system. The tax reform of 2 September 1930 simplified the system by abolishing some of the taxes, consolidating others, and introducing basically two tax items—first the tax on profits of the enterprises, and second the turnover or sales tax levied primarily upon consumer goods. This simplified both tax collection and information gathering. Before the 1930 tax reform, the People's Commissariat of Finance was the largest depository of economic information. After the reform, not only the state planning agencies and statistical authorities but many others exceeded the institutions of public finance as sources and collectors of economic information. The People's Commissariat of Finance began to specialize in the state budget and its fulfillment rather than in the initiation of tax policies.

Since the bulk of taxes were indirect (sales taxes added to the wholesale prices), the impact of the direct money taxes throughout the economy was limited. The targets of personal taxation most affected by the system during the 1920s were the private small-scale industrial and agricultural producers and middlemen and afterward the collective farm members, in other words the "private sector." Thus, while the data on indirect taxation can help to measure the overall success of the policies of resource allocation by the state, the data on direct taxation can help determine the direction and effect of government policies upon the private sector. After the death of Stalin and the end of rigid taxation policies toward the private sector, subsequent measures have indicated a greater sensitivity and flexibility in the application of personal taxation. The effects of the various turns of taxation policy upon the incomes and productivity of those affected by the policies of the last 15 years can be studied from indirect evidence rather than from the direct evidence that was provided during the 1920s.

Money and Banking

Although according to the Soviet classification the statistics of money and banking are lumped together with taxation data in the broad category of "financial statistics," it is more appropriate here to separate the two in accordance with Western classifications. The Soviet convention is probably based upon the sharp distinction between "real" and "financial" assets, but this has little meaning in the context of a Western analysis.

The data on money were important during the first decade of Soviet rule, but they declined in importance with the advent of the industrialization drive. The monetary data were considered important during the period of post-World-War-I inflation and hyperinflation and during the subsequent period of relative monetary stability. When it became clear that the process of rapid industrialization produced inflationary pressures which could hardly be controlled by the government, the data disappeared from the public eye. The reason apparently was that the government could not admit its inability to control inflation, while the industrialization process was fed not only by budget revenues but also by an increase of the volume of money in circulation.

During the 1920s the published data on the money supply included information not only on currency in circulation but also on bank reserves, velocity of money in circulation, purchasing power of the currency, etc. The combination of the monetary and price data can produce interesting studies on the patterns of development of the Soviet economy. The inflation of the

1930s resulted in a dearth of monetary data, to such an extent that from the mid-1930s on scholars are deprived of even the most general figures of currency in circulation.

The data on credit and banking started to appear in the early 1920s and originated primarily with the State Bank. While the data on bank credit were forthcoming, the data on other forms of credit, particularly the credit provided by one enterprise to another, were not very reliable. The credit reform of January 1930 prohibited enterprises from crediting one another and made the state the exclusive creditor for the socialized sector of the economy in the most direct sense, enabling the State Bank to interfere even in credit transfers from account to account. But this reform did not produce data on the total credit flow in the economy, although by definition the credit flow was equated with the short-term credit operations of the State Bank and with long-term credits by the State Bank and the five specialized banking institutions that financed particular branches of the economy.

The centralization of credit operations became so entrenched that it survived all subsequent attempts to decentralize other areas of decision-making. Whether policy makers prefer the centralized system of credit operations because of its efficiency or because of its features of control is a question that cannot be answered with any certainty, since the control function of economic institutions is high on the preference list of the policy makers in determining the role of particular institutions. Thus the banking system was entrusted not only with the routine function of crediting planned expansion of output and with the control function of adjusting the volume of credits to the actual plan performance, but also with some discretionary power to use the credit mechanism as a policy tool to discriminate against or bestow favors upon particular enterprises in areas of the wage fund, capital construction (investment), and current operations. This made the banking system one of the "gray eminences" of the Soviet apparatus of economic and social policies. While monetary policy (with respect to the currency) was largely determined and prescribed for the banking system by the highest state authorities, in its credit operations the banking system maintained a modicum of autonomy. In view of the absence of detailed published data, it is difficult to determine the effect of such autonomy, because only a comparison of series of planned and actual indicators would enable one to pass judgment.

After the publishing of data on money supply and the credit flow was discontinued, the only available data that occasionally appeared in print were the ones on some credits outstanding by the end of the year (for particular institutions or economic sectors) and also on the end-of-the-year balances of personal savings in the savings banks. Thus the bulk of quantitative data absolutely essential for an analysis of economic performance that were collected in one of the most vital and sensitive economic institutions—the State Bank—remained unavailable even to Soviet scholars. The opening of the archives of the State Bank in the Soviet Union to historians and economists would enable them to study aspects of economic and social behavior that remain terra incognita at present.

NOTES

1   The *revizii* were conducted in 1718, 1742, 1762, 1781, 1794, 1811, 1815, 1833, 1850, 1857. The dates are not very meaningful, since in every case the corrections and revisions in the population counts continued almost until the new revizia.
2   The process of compiling such a cadastre and providing the owners with titles of ownership was known as *generalnoe mezhevanie*.
3   The peasant sector reports to the zemstvos were more accurate than those of the landed estates. Some of the shortcomings in the long-term averages might be due to the changing weights of the landed estate sector in total output.
4   The first data were collected in the Podol'e and Kherson zemstvos in 1869. The first statistical offices were set up in 1871 in Kazan and Tver. By the beginning of the 1880s, statistical offices of various size and quality were functioning in all zemstvos.
5   The best treatment of content, methodology, and methodological deficiencies is to be found in N. A. Svavitskii, *Zemskie Podvornye Perepisi* (Moscow: Gosstatizdat, 1961).
6   The total includes different numbers for particular districts, collected for different time periods, so that they can hardly be compared. Collection started in Voronezh province (*gubernia*) with 230 budgets (1887–96); in Kaluga, with 2,417 (1887–97); Zabaikal'e, 885 (1897); Perm, 666 (1899–1901); and Viatka, 1,987 (1900).
7   *Statute of Industry*, 11:2 (St. Petersburg, 1893).
8   Ministerstud Torgovli i Promyshlennosti, *Svod Tovarnykh Tsen na Glavnykh Russkikh i Inostrannykh Rynkakh*.
9   See pp. 367, 372–73, above.
10 The Strumilin estimates were calculated and published in the 1920s. A convenient source for the estimates, together with additional information, is G. A. Dikhtiar's *Vnutrennaia Torgovlia v Dorevolutsionnoi Rossii* (Moscow: Akademia Nauk SSSR, 1960).
11 *Istoria Sovetskoi Gosudarstvennoi Statistiki*, Sbornik Statei (Moscow: Gosstatizdat, 1960), pp. 67–68.
12 V. I. Lenin, *Collected Works*, 33:303, 4th ed. (Moscow, 1965).
13 For example, no statistical handbooks of the Soviet Union were published between 1936 and 1955.
14 During the period 1930–48 the Central Statistical Authority was not only subordinated to, but virtually a department of, the State Planning Commission. This arrangement made clear that the statistical   work performed would be limited to the problems of short- and middle-range economic planning and determined by the preferences of the economic administrative authorities.
15 A. I. Ezhov, "Gosudarstvennaia Statistika, ee Razvitie i Organizatsia," in *Istoria Sovietskoi Gosudarstvennoi Statisiki*, Sbornik Statei (Moscow: Gosstatizdat, 1960), p. 71.
16 Such titles as "The Communist Party in Figures," "The Communist International and Its Decisions in Figures," or "Nationality Policies in Figures and Diagrams" are a few examples of such excesses of the quantitative approach.
17 A similar task had to be carried out after World War II as a result of the boundary changes of 1939–45. The task for the latter period was easier because of the greater availability and reliability of data for the interwar period collected in Poland and the Baltic countries. In the earlier adjustments, 1913 was taken as a base; in the second case, a modified 1940 base was established.
18 "The Soviet concept of national income is in line with the classical tradition, in distinguishing between 'productive' and 'unproductive' activities, only the former being

considered as generating a real product. As in Adam Smith, civil servants, soldiers, teachers, doctors, 'opera singers and opera dancers', etc., are deemed to be unproductive" (Alec Nove, *The Soviet Economy*, 2d ed. [New York: A. F. Praeger, 1969] p. 284).

19 G. Sorokin, "Vydaiushiisia Deiatel' Leninskoi Partii," in *Pravda*, 1 December 1963.

20 *Materialy po Balansu Narodnogo Khoziaistva SSSR za 1928, 1929 i 1930 gg* (Moscow: TsUNKHU, 1932).

21 Albert L. Vainshtein, *Narodnyi Dokhod Rossii i SSSR* (Moscow: Nauka, 1969); Alexander Gerschenkron, *A Dollar Index of Soviet Machinery Output* (Santa Monica: Rand Corporation, 1951); Abram Bergson, *Soviet National Income and Product in 1937* (New York: Columbia University Press, 1953).

22 A. Becker, *Soviet National Income, 1958–64* (Berkeley: University of California Press, 1969). Other non-Soviet students who have published excellent work on Soviet national income include Naum Jasny and Oleg Hoeffding.

23 Gosplan SSR, *Metodicheskie Ukazania k Sostavleniiu Gosudarstvennogo Plana Razvitiia Narodnogo Khoziaistva SSSR* (Moscow: Ekonomika, 1969).

24 This classification is produced from *Metodicheskie Ukazania*, p. 699, which is more exhaustive than the lists published in the statistical handbooks.

25 The category "miscellaneous" includes the following types of activities: (1) publishing; (2) movie production; (3) procurement and primary processing of scrap metal; (4) procurement and primary processing of junk; (5) collection of firewood, the production of forestry products, hunting, fishing; (6) handicrafts (*Methodicheskie Ukazania*, p. 558).

26 This is pointed out by Vainshtein in *Narodnyi Dokhod Rossii i SSSR*. Vainshtein leans toward the view that the calculation of national income in use represents total national income in which the net foreign trade balance is included.

27 "The national income is calculated as the sum of net production of separate branches of material production. The net production of separate branches is calculated as the difference between the gross output and material production outlays" (TsSU SSSR, *Narodnoe Khoziaistvo SSSR v 1959 godu* [Moscow, 1960], p. 829).

28 TsSU SSSR, *Narodnoe Khoziaistvo SSSR v 1961 godu* (Moscow, 1962), p. 787.

29 A. I. Ezhov, *Sistema i Metodologia Pokazatelei Sovietskoi Statistiki* (Moscow: Statistika, 1965), p. 80.

BIBLIOGRAPHY

ABBREVIATIONS

Akad. Nauk	Akademia Nauk SSSR (Academy of Sciences of the USSR)
CSC	Tsentral'nyi Statisticheskii Komitet (Central Statistical Committee)
GK	Geologicheskii Komitet (Geological Committee)
Gosbank	Gosudarstvennyi Bank (State Central Bank)
Gosplan	Gosudarstvennyi Planovoi Komitet (State Planning Committee)
GUZUZ	Glavnoe Upravlenie Zemleustroistva i Zemledelia (Chief Administration of Land Settlement and Agriculture)
IRGO	Imperatorskoe Russkoe Geograficheskoe Obshchestvo (Royal Russian Geographical Society)
IVEO	Imperatorskoe Vol'noe Economicheskoe Obshchestvo (Royal Free Economic Society)
KZag	Komitet Zagotovok (Committee of Procurement)
MF	Ministerstvo Finansov (Ministry of Finance)
MGI	Ministerstvo Gosudarstvennykh Imushchestv (Ministry of Government Estates)

Min Zag Ministerstvo Zagotovok (**Ministry of Procurement**)

MMF Ministerstvo Morskogo Flota (Ministry of the Navy, when pertaining to a prerevolutionary publication; Ministry of the Merchant Marine, when pertaining to a post-World War II publication)

MNP Ministerstvo Narodnogo Prosveshchenia (Ministry of Public Education)

MPS Ministerstvo Putei Soobshchenia (Ministry of Ways of Communication)

MRF Ministerstvo Rechnogo Flota (Ministry of the River Marine)

MS Ministerstvo Sviazi (Ministry of Communications)

MT Ministerstvo Torgovli (Ministry of Trade)

MTP Ministerstvo Torgovli i Promyshlennosti (Ministry of Trade and Industry)

MVD Ministerstvo Vnutrennykh Del (Ministry of the Interior)

MVT Ministerstvo Vneshnei Torgovli (Ministry of Foreign Trade)

MYu Ministerstvo Yustitsii (Ministry of Justice)

MZ Ministerstvo Zemledelia (Ministry of Agriculture)

NKFin Narodnyi Komissariat Finansov (People's Commissariat of Finance)

NKMF Narodnyi Komissariat Morskogo Flota (People's Commissariat of the Merchant Marine)

NKP Narodnyi Komissariat po Prodovol'stviiu (People's Commissariat of Food Supply)

NKPS Narodnyi Komissariat Putei Soobchcheniia (People's Commissariat of Ways of Communication)

NKRF Narodnyi Komissariat Rechnogo Flota (People's Commissariat of the River Fleet)

NKRKI Narodnyi Komissariat Raboche-Krestianskoi Inspektsii (People's Commissariat of Workers-Peasant Inspection)

NKS Narodnyi Komissariat Sviazi (People's Commissariat of Communications)

NK Torg Narodnyi Komissariat Torgovli (People's Commissariat of Trade)

NK Trud Narodnyi Komissariat Truda (People's Commissariat of Labor)

NK Vneshtorg Narodnyi Komissariat Vneshnei Torgovli (People's Commissariat of Foreign Trade)

NKZ Narodnyi Komissariat Zemledelia (People's Commissariat of Agriculture)

NKZdrav Narodnyi Komissariat Zdravokhranenia (People's Commissariat of Health)

RIO Russkoe Istoricheskoe Obshchestvo (Russian Historical Society)

RSFSR Rossiiskaia Sovietskaia Federativnaia Sotsialisticheskaia Respublika (Russian Federative Socialist Republic)

SNK Soviet Narodnykh Komissarov (Council of People's Commissars)

TsSU Tsentral'noe Statisticheskoe Upravlenie (Central Statistical Authority)

TsUNKhU Tsentral'noe Upravlenie Narodno-Khoziaistvennogo Ucheta (Central Authority for National-Economic Accounting)

VSNKh Vyzhsyi Soviet Narodnogo Khoziaistva (Supreme Council of the National Economy)

VTsSPS   Vsesoiuznyi Tsentral'nyi Soviet Professional'nykh Soiuzov (Central Council of Trade Unions)

THE TSARIST PERIOD

Periodicals

Artilleriiskii Zhurnal. 1825–.

Gornyi Zhurnal. 1825–1917.

Narodnoe Khoziaistvo v. . . godu. MF, 1914–16. Petrograd, 1915–18.

Rossiiskii Morskoi Kalendar'. 1804–.

St. Petersburgskii Zhurnal. St. Petersburg: MVD, 1805–09.

Sel'skoe Khoziaistvo i Lesovodstvo. Zhurnal Ministerstva Zemledeliia i Gosudarst·vennykh Imushchestv. St. Petersburg, 1865–1905.

Statisticheskii Zhurnal. St. Petersburg, 1806–08.

Trudy Imperatorskogo Vol'nogo Ekonomicheskogo Obshchestva. St. Petersburg, 1766–1917.

Vestnik Finansov, Promyshelennosti i Torgovli (weekly). St. Petersburg: MF, 1885–1915.

Voenno-Meditsinskii Zhurnal. St. Petersburg, 1882–1914.

Zapiski Imperatorskogo Russkogo Geograficheskogo Obshchestva po Otdeleniu Statistiki. St. Petersburg, 1886–1916.

Zhurnal Glavnogo Upravleniia Putei Soobshcheniia i Publichnykh Zdanii. St. Petersburg, 1845–65.

Zhurnal Manufaktury i Torgovli. 1825–.

Zhurnal Ministerstva Gosudarstvennykh Imushchestv. St. Petersburg, 1841–64.

Zhurnal Ministerstva Narodnogo Prosveshcheniia. St. Petersburg, 1803, 1834–1917.

Zhurnal Ministerstva Putei Soobshcheniia. 1886–1917.

Zhurnal Ministerstva Vnutrennikh Del. St. Petersburg, 1829–61.

Zhurnal Putei Soobshcheniia. 1826–43.

General Sources

Before 1825

Polnoe Sobranie Zakonov Rosiiskoi Imperii. St. Petersburg, 1830.

Kotoshikhin, G. K. *O Rossii, v Tsarstvovanie Alekseia Mikhailovicha.* St. Petersburg, 1906.

Kryzhanich, Iu. G. *Russkoe Gosudarstvo v Polovine XVII Veka.* Moscow, 1859–60.

Kirilov, V. I. *Tsvetushchee Sostoianie Vserossiiskogo Gosudarstva . . .* Moscow, 1831.

Tatishchev, V. N. *Izbrannye Trudy po Geografii Rossii.* Moscow, 1950.

De Gennin, Vil'lem. *Opisanie Ural'skikh i Sibirskikh Zavodov.* Moscow, 1937.

Krasheninnikov, S. *Opisanie Zemli Kamchatki.* St. Petersburg, 1755.

Orenburgskaia Guberniia . . . St. Petersburg, 1762.

Rychkov, P. I. *Vvedenie v Astrakhanskuiu Topografiiiu . . .* Moscow, 1774.

[Schlotzer, A. L.] *Neuveraendertes Russland . . .* Vols. 1–2. Riga, Mitau, Leipzig. 1767, 1772.

Geograficheskii Leksikon Rossiiskogo Gosudarstva ili Slovar' . . . Moscow, 1773.

Chebotarev, Kh. A. *Geograficheskoe Metodicheskoe Opisanie Rossiiskoi Imperii.* Moscow, 1776.

Georgi, J. G. *Opisanie Vsekh, Obitaiushchikh v Rossiiskom Gosudarstve Narodov.* St. Petersburg, 1776.

Shcherbatov, M. M. *Statistika v Razsuzhdenii Rossii.* Moscow, 1859.

Maksimovich, L. M. *Putevoditel' k Drevnostiam i Dostopamiatnostiam Moskovskim.* Moscow, 1782.

Topograficheskoe Opisanie Kaluzhskogo Namestnichestva. St. Petersburg, 1785.

Kraft, M. Essai sur les Tables des Mariages, des Naissances, et des Morts de la Ville de St. Petersbourg . . . In *Acta Academia Scientiarum Imp. Petropolitanea.* St. Petersburg, 1786.

Istoricheskoe i Topograficheskoe Opisanie Gorodov Moskovskoi Gubernii . . . Moscow, 1787.

Novyi i Polnyi Geograficheskii Slovar' Rossiiskago Gosudarstva ili Leksikon. Moscow, 1788.

Chulkov, M. D. *Istoricheskoe Opisanie Rossiiskoi Komertsii, pri Vsekh Portakh i Granitskah.* Vols. 1–7. St. Petersburg, 1781–88.

Chulkov, M. D. *Slovar' Uchrezhdennykh v Rossii Iarmarok i Torgov.* 1788.

Pleshcheev, S. I. *Obozrenie Rossiiskoi Imperii v Nyneshnem ee Novoustroennom Sostoianii.* St. Petersburg, 1786.

Herman, B. F. J. *Statistische Schilderung von Russland . . . St. Petersburg,* 1790.

Topograficheskoe Opisanie Zavodov Lezhashchikh v Ufimskom Namestnichestve. 1791.

Georgi, J. G. *Opisaniie Rossiisko-Imperatorskogo Stolichnogo Goroda Sankt-Peterburga.* St. Petersburg, 1794.

Recueil sur la Russie du XVIII siècle. Vol. 4, Planches, cartes, Mélanges Statistiques . . . St. Petersburg.

Maksimovich, L. M., and Shchekotov, A. M. *Geograficheskii Slovar' Rosiiskogo Gosudarstva Sochinennyi v Nastoiashchem Vide.* Vols. 1–4. Moscow, 1801–09.

Storch, H. *Historisch-Statistisches Gemälde des Russischen Reichs.* Riga-Leipzig, 1797–1803.

Bakhturin, A. N. *Kratkoe Opisanie Vnutrennego Rossiskoi Imperii Vodokhodstva . . .* St. Petersburg, 1802.

Golitsyn, I. A. *Statisticheskie Tablitsy Vserossiiskoi Imperii . . .* Moscow, 1807.

Ziablovskii, E. F. *Noveishee Zemleopisanie Rossiiskoi Imperii.* 2 vols. St. Petersburg, 1807.

Ziablovskii, E. F. *Statisticheskoe Opisanie Rossiiskoi Imperii v Nyneshnem ee Sostoianii,* St. Petersburg, 1808.

Ziablovskii, E. F. *Zemleopisanie Rossiiskoi Imperii . . .* St. Petersburg, 1810.

Khvostov, V. *O Tomskoi Gubernii i O Naselenii Bol'shoi Sibirskoi Dorogi do Irkustkoi Granitsi.* St. Petersburg, 1809.

German, Ivan. *Istoricheskoe Nachertanie Gornogo Proizvodstva v Rossiiskoi Imperii.* Ekaterinburg, 1810.

Vsevolozhskii, N. S. *Dictionnaire géographique et historique de l'empire de Russie . . .* Moscow, 1813.

Arseniev, K. I. *Nachertanie Statistiki Rossiiskogo Gosudarstva.* St. Petersburg, 1818–19.

German, K. *Statisticheskoe Issledovanie Otnositel'no Rossiiskoi Imperii.* St. Petersburg, 1819.

1825–1855
Lecointre de Laveau. *Opisanie Nizhnego Novgoroda i Ezhegodno Byvaiushchei v Nem Iarmarki.* Moscow, 1829.
Androssov, V. *Statisticheskaia Zapiska o Moskve.* Moscow: S. Selivanskii, 1832.
Pel'chinskii, V. *O Sostoianii Promyshlennykh Sil Rossii do 1832 g.* St. Petersburg: Akad. Nauk., 1833.
Evetskii, Orest. *Statisticheskoe Opisanie Zakavkazskogo Kraia s Prisovokupleniem Statii: Politicheskoe Sostoianie Zakavkazskogo Kraia v Ishode XVII v. i Sravnenie Onogo s Nyneshnim.* St. Petersburg, 1835.
Bulgarin, F. *Rossiia v Istoricheskom, Statisticheskom, Geograficheskom, i Literaturnom Otnosheniiakh.* 2 vols. St. Petersburg, 1837.
Banki i Drugie Kreditnye Ustanovleniia v Rossii i v Innostrannykh Zemliakh. St. Petersburg, 1840.
Obozrenie Glavnykh Vodianykh Soobshchenii v Rossi St. Petersburg, 1841.
Fuks, F. *Kazanskie Tatary v Statisticheskom i Etnograficheskom Otnosheniiakh.* 1844.
Obozrenie Glavnykh Otraslei Manufakturnoi Promyshlennosti v Rossii. St. Petersburg, 1845.
Levshin, A. I. *Description des hordes et des steppes des Kirghiz-Kazaks ou Kirghiz-Kaissaks.*
Zhuravskii, D. P. *Ob Istochnikakh i Upotreblenii Statisticheskikh Svedenii.* 1846.
Veselovskii, K. L. *Opyty Nravstvennoi Statistiki Rossii.* St. Petersburg, 1847.
Arseniev, K. I. *Statisticheskie Ocherki Rossii.* St. Petersburg, 1848.

1855–1914
Materialy Dlia Statistiki Rossii Sobrannye po Vedomstvu Ministerstva Gosudarstvennyh Imushchestv. St. Petersburg, 1858.
Materialy Dlia Geografii i Statistiki Rossii Sobrannye Ofitserami General'nogo Shtaba. Vols. 1–29. St. Petersburg, 1860.
Geograficheskii Slovar' Rossiiskoi Imperii. St. Petersburg, 1863.
Aperçu statistique des forces productives de la Russie. Paris, 1867.
Voenno-Statisticheskii Sbornik. St. Petersburg, 1871.
Voennyi Statisticheskii Sbornik Rossii. Atlas. Prilozheniie k IV Vypusku. St. Petersburg, 1871.
Livron, V. de. *Statisticheskoe Obozrenie Rossiiskoi Imperii.* St. Petersburg, 1874.
Vseobshchaia Statistika Rossiiskogo Gosudarstva. Moscow, 1880.
Sbornik Svedenii po Evropeiskoi Rossii za 1882 g. St. Petersburg, 1884.
Sbornik Svedenii po Rossii za 1883 g. St. Petersburg: CSC, 1886.
Sbornik Svedenii po Rossii za 1884–85 gg. St. Petersburg, 1887.
Ukazatel' Izmenenii i Raspredelenii Administrativnyh Edinits i Granits Imperii s 1860 po 1887 g. St. Petersburg: CSC, 1887.
Supplément à l'annuaire statistique de la Russie, 1884–85. St. Petersburg: CSC, 1888.
Sbornik Svedenii po Rossii za 1890 g. St. Petersburg: CSC, 1890.
Relevé général des tableaux de l'annuaire statistique de la Russie, 1896. St. Petersburg: CSC, 1897.

Sbornik Svedenii po Rossii za 1896 g. St. Petersburg: CSC, 1897.
Ezegodnik Rossii. St. Petersburg: CSC, 1904–1916.
Semenov Tian-Shanskii, Veniamin. *Gorod i Derevnia v Evropeiskoi Rossii.* St. Petersburg, 1910.
Statisticheskii Ezhegodnik na . . . god. Edited by V. I. Sharyii. St. Petersburg, 1913–14.
Aziatskaia Rossiia. St. Petersburg: GUZIZ, 1914.

Population Censuses

Pervaia Vseobshchaia Perepis' Naseleniia Rossiiskoi Imperii, 1897. Edited by N. A. Troinitskii. Vol. 120. St. Petersburg: CSC, 1899–1905.
Pervaia Vseobshchaia Perepis' Naseleniia Rossiiskoi Imperii, 1897. Raspredeknie Naselennyh Mest Rossiiskoi Imperii po Chislennosti v nih Naseleniia. St. Petersburg: CSC, 1902.
Pervaia Vseobshchaia Perepis' Naseleniia Rossiiskoi Imperii, 1897. Obshchii Svod po Imperii Resultatov Razrabotki Dannyh Pervoi Vseobschei Perepisi Naseleniia, 28/1/1897. St. Petersburg: CSC, 1905.
Dvizhenie Naseleniia v Evropeiskoi Rossii za. 1867 g. [*–1902 g.*].24 vols. St. Petersburg: MVD, CSC, 1872–1909.
Giliarovskii, F. V. *Issledovanie o Rozhdenii i Smertnosti Detei v Novgorodskoi Gubernii.* St. Petersburg, 1866.
Prostranstvo i Naselenie Evropeiskoi Rossii. St. Petersburg: MVD, CSC, 1871.
Nalichnoe Naselenie Rossiiskoi Imperii za 1870 g. Edited by L. Karashunskii. St. Petersburg, 1875.
Statisticheskie Svedeniia o Nasil'stvennyh Smertiakh v 1870–1874 gg. St. Petersburg: MVD, CSC, 1882.
Evreiskoe Naselenie i Zemlevladenie v Jugozapadnyh Guberniiakh Evropeiskoi Rossii. Edited by V. Alenitzyn. St. Petersburg: MVD, CSC, 1884.
Nombre d'enfants, 1867–1881. St. Petersburg, 1889.
Statisticheskie Dannye o Razvodah i Nedeistvitel'nyh Brakakh za 1867–1886. Edited by P. Bechanov. St. Petersburg, 1893.
Umershie Nasil'stvenno i Vnezapno v Rossiiskoi Imperii v 1875–1887 g. St. Petersburg, 1894.
Umershie Nasil'stvenno i Vnezapno v Rossiiskoi Imperii v 1888–1893 g. St. Petersburg, 1897.
Svod Statisticheskih Materialov Kasaiushchikhsia Ekonomicheskogo Polozheniia Sel' skogo Naseleniia Evropeiskoi Rossii. St. Petersburg, 1894.
Statisticheskie Dannye po Pereselencheskomu Delu v Sibiri za 1897 g. St. Petersburg.
Glavneishie Dannye po Statistike Naseleniia Krainego Vostoka Sibiri, Primorskoi i Amurskoi Oblasti i Ostrova Sakhalin. Edited by S. Patkanov. St. Petersburg, 1903.
Goroda v Rossii v 1904 g. St. Petersburg: CSC, 1906.
Goroda v Rossii v 1910 g. St. Petersburg: CSC, 1912.
Patkanov, S. K. *Statisticheskie Dannye Pokazyvaiushchie Sostav Naseleniia Sibiri.* St. Petersburg, 1911–12.
Novosel'skii, S. A. *Smertnost 'i Prodolzhitel'nost Zhizni v Rossii.* Petrograd, 1916.
Novosel'skii, S. A., and Paevskii, V. V. *Smertnost' i Prodolzhitel'nost' Zhizni Naseleniia SSSR.* Moscow, 1930.

Rashin, A. G. *Naselenie Rossii za 100 let.* Moscow, 1959.
Statisticheskii Obzor o Sostoianii Narodnogo Zdravia i Organizatsii Meditsinskoi Pomoshchi v Rossii. Edited by S. A. Novosel'skii. St. Petersburg, 1903–14 annually.

Agriculture

Svedeniia o Poseve i Sbore Khlebov i Kartofelia v 1870–1872 g. i Chislennosti Skota v 1870 g. v Evropeiskoi Rossii. Edited by G. Ershov. St. Petersburg, 1875.
Materialy po Statistike Khlebnoi Proizvoditel'nosti v Evropeiskoi Rossii, 1870–1874. St. Petersburg, 1880.
Urozhai v Evropeiskoi Rossii. 1883–85 annually. St. Petersburg: CSC, 1884–86.
Zverinskii, V. *Urozhai v Evropeiskoi Rossii. Obshchie Vyvody.* St. Petersburg: CSC, 1884.
Srednii Urozhai v Evropeiskoi Rossii za 1883–1887 gg. St. Petersburg: CSC, 1888.
Glavnye Resultaty Urozhaia . . . 1889–92 annually. St. Petersburg, 1890–93.
Urozhai Khlebov v Pudakh s Desiatiny po Pokazaniiam Krestian Starozhilov. St. Petersburg, 1893.
Srednii Sbor Khlebov i Kartofelia za Desiatiletie 1883–1892 v 60 Guberniiakh Evropeiskoi Rossii. St. Petersburg, 1894.
Posevnye Ploshchadi po 50 Gub. Evropeiskoi Rossii, 1881–1887 i 1893–1899. St. Petersburg, 1901.
Srednii Posev i Srednii Sbor Zernovykh Khlebov i Kartofelia za Piatiletie 1896–1900. St. Petersburg, 1902.
Urozhai v . . . *godu.* 1901–07 annually excluding 1906. St. Petersburg, 1902–06, 1908.
Urozhai . . . *v Evropeiskoi i Aziatskoi Rossii.* 1909–12 annually. St. Petersburg, 1910–13.
Sel'skokhoziaistvennye i Statisticheskie Svedniia po Materialam Poluchennym ot Khozaiev. Vols. 1–11. Ministerstvo Zemledliia, 1884–1903.
. . . *god v Sel'skokhoziaistvennom Otnoshenii po Otvetam, Poluchennym ot Khoziaev.* St. Petersburg, 1894–1916.
Predvaritel'nye Dannye o Sbore, Posevakh i Ostatke Khlebov v . . . *g.* St. Petersburg: CSC, 1902–10.
Résultats généraux de la récolte de 1895 céréales d'hiver et d'été comparée aux récoltes de 1890–1894. St. Petersburg: MVD, CSC, 1896.
Résultats généraux de la récolte de 1896 céréales d'hiver et d'été comparée aux récoltes de 1891–1895. St. Petersburg: MVD, CSC, 1897.
Résultats généraux de la récolte de 1897 céréales d'hiver et d'été comparée aux récoltes de 1892–1896. St. Petersburg: MVD, CSC, 1898.
Résultats généraux de la récolte de 1898 céréales d'hiver et d'été comparée aux récoltes de 1893–1896. St. Petersburg: MVD, CSC, 1899.
Résultats généraux de la récolte en Russie-années 1895–1907. 1899–1907 annually. St. Petersburg: MVD, CSC, 1900–08.
Svod Statisticheskikh Svedenii po Sel'skomu Khoziaistvu Rossii k Kontsu XIX Veka. Vols. 1–2. St. Petersburg, 1902–03.
Sbornik Statistichesko-Ekonomicheskikh Svedenii po Sel'skomu Khoziaistvu Rossii i Inostrannykh Gosudarstv. Vols. 1–10. Glavnoe Upravlenie Zemledeliia i Zem-leustroistva. St. Petersburg, 1906–16.

Chuprov, A. I. *Vliianie Uroszhaev i Khlebnykh Tsen na Raznye Storony Ekono-micheskoi Zhizni.* St. Petersburg, 1897.

Ivanstov, D. N. *K Kritike Russkoi Urozhainoi Statistiki. Zapiski IRGO po otd. Statistiki XIV.* St. Petersburg, 1915.

Ezhegodnik Glavnogo Upravlenii Zemleustroistva i Zemledelii. St. Petersburg: GUZIZ, 1907–15.

Itogi Ekonomicheskogo Issledovaniia Rossii po Dannym Zemskoi Statistiki. Moscow, 1892. Vol. 1. *Obshchii Obzor Zemskoi Statistiki Krest'ianskogo Khoziaistva.* Edited by A. Fortunatov. Vol. 2. *Krest'ianskie Vnenadel'nye Arendy.* Edited by N. Karyshev.

Spravochnye Svedeniia o Deiatel'nosti Zemstv po Sel'skomu Khoziaistvu po Dannym na . . . g. 1897–1913. St. Petersburg, 1899–1915.

Veselovskii, B. B. i Frenkel'. *Iubileinyi Zemskii Sbornik, 1864–1914.* St. Petersburg, 1914.

Sbornik Materialov Dlia Izucheniia Sel'skoi Pozemel'noi Obshchiny. St. Petersburg, 1880.

Pozemel'naia Sobstvennost' v Evropeiskoi Rossii v 1877 i 1878 gg. Edited by G. Ershov. St. Petersburg: MVD, CSC, 1886.

Raspredelenie Zemel' po Ugodiiam i Pakhotnykh po Raznogo Roda Posevam v Evropeiskoi Rossii. Edited by P. Struve. St. Petersburg: MVD, CSC, 1884.

Svedeniia o Zemlevadenii v Privislanskikh Guberniiah. Edited by I. I. Kaufman. St. Petersburg: MVD, CSC, 1886.

Glavneiskhie Dannye Pozemel'noi Statistiki po Obsledovaniiu 1886 g. (po Guberniiam). Nos. 1–47. St. Petersburg, 1893–1901.

Materialy po Statistike Dvizheniia Zemlevladeniia v Rossii. Vols. 1–24. St. Petersburg: MF, 1896–1915.

Statistika Zemlevladeniia v 1905 g. Svod Dannykh po 50 Guberniiam Ev. Rossii. St. Petersburg: CSC, 1907.

Blagoveshchenskii, N. A. *Svodnyi Statisticheskii Sbornik Khoziaistvennykh Svedenii po Zemskim Podvornym Perepisiam.* Vol. 1. Moscow, 1893.

Svavitskii, Z. M. *Zemskie Povdvornye Perepisi 1880–1913. Pouiezdnye Itogi.* Moscow: CSU, 1926.

Ovtsevodstvo v Rossii . . . Edited by S. P. Shepnin. St. Petersburg, 1869.

Issledovanie Sovremennogo Sostoianiia Ovtsevodstva v Rossii. Vols. 1–4, 5–7. 1882–86.

Voenno-Konskaia Perepis' za . . . 1891–1914. St. Petersburg, 1894–1915.

Opyt Rascheta Stoimosti Pshenitsy, Rzhi, Ovsa i Iachmenia v Proizvodstve. St. Petersburg, 1889.

Materialy po Voprosu Stoimosti Obrabotki Zemli v Evropeiskoi Rossii. St. Petersburg, 1889.

Stoimost' Proizvodstva Glavnykh Khlebov. Statisticheskie Svedeniia po Materialam Poluchennym ot Khoziaev. Petrograd, 1915.

Tseny na Zemliu v Evropeiskoi Rossii po Prodazham Sdelannym v 1882 i 1887 gg. St. Petersburg, 1889.

Tseny na Pshenitsu, Rozh, Oves i Iachmen' v Evropeiskoi Rossii v 1881–1887 g. po Mestnym Svedeniiam. St. Petersburg, 1889.

Tseny na Proviant i Furazh po Svedeniiam Intendantskogo Vedomstva. St. Petersburg, 1889.

Svod Tovarnykh Tsen na Glavnykh Russkikh i Inortrannykh Rynkakh za . . . g.
Materialy Dlia Torgovo-Promyshlennoi. Statistiki, 1890–1914. Vol. 1, 1890–95;
vol. 2, 1890–96; annual 1897–1914. St. Petersburg, 1891–1915.

Sel'sko-Khoziaistvennye Mashiny i Orudiia v Evropeiskoi i Aziatskoi Rossii v 1910 g.
St. Petersburg, 1913.

Predvaritel'nye Dannye Vserossiiskoi Sel'skokhoziaistvennoi Perepisi 1916 g. Oso-
boye Sovieshchanie Dlia Obsuzhdeniia i Obiedineniia Meropriiatii po Prodo-
vol'stvennomu Delu. Petrograd, 1916.

Schcherbina, F. A. *Krestianskie Biudzhety.* Voronezh, 1900.

Industry

Obzor Razlichnykh Otraslei Manufakturnoi Promyshlennosti Rossii. Vols. 1–2. St.
Petersburg, 1862, 1863.

Materialy Dlia Statistiki Zavodskoi Fabrichnoi Promyshlennosti v Evropeiskoi
Rossii za 1868 g. Edited by I. Bok. St. Petersburg: MVD, CSC, 1872.

Skalkovskii, K. A. *Tableaux Statistiques de l'Industrie des Mines en Russie en*
1868–1876. St. Petersburg, 1878.

———. *Tableaux Statistiques de l'Industrie des Mines en Russie en 1871.* St.
Petersburg, 1873.

Orlov, P. A. *Ukazatel' Fabrik i Zavodov Evropeiskoi Rossii s Tsarstvom Pol'skim*
i Vel. Kn. Finlandskim (1879). St. Petersburg, 1887.

———. *Ukazatel' Fabrik i Zavodov Evropeiskoi Rossii i Tsarstva Pol'skogo (1884).*
St. Petersburg, 1887.

Ukazatel' Fabrik i Zavodov Evropeiskoi Rossii. Edited by P. A. Orlov and I. G.
Budagov. 3d ed. St. Petersburg, 1894.

Timiriazev, D. A. *Istoriko-Statisticheskii Obzor Promyshlennosti Rossii.* Vols. 1–2.
St. Petersburg, 1883, 1886.

The Industries of Russia. Vols. 1–4. Prepared for the 1893 World's Columbian
Exposition at Chicago. St. Petersburg: MF, 1893.

Gornozavodskaia Promyshlennost' Rossii. St. Petersburg, 1893.

Fabrichno-Zavodskaia Promyshlennost' i Torgovlia Rossii. St. Petersburg: MF, 1893;
2d ed. 1896.

Russia, Its Industries and Trade. Glasgow: MF, 1901.

Svod Dannykh Fabrichno-Zavodskoi Promyshlennosti v Rossii za 1897 g. St. Petersburg, 1900.

Torgovlia i Promyshlennost' Evropeiskoi Rossii po Raionam. Vols. 1–13. St. Petersburg: MTP, 1902–11.

Nisselovich, L. N. *Istoria Zavodsko-Fabrichnogo Zakonodatel'stva Rossiiskoi Im-*
perii. Vols. 1–2. St. Petersburg, 1883.

Pazhitnov, K. A. *Ocherki Istorii Tekstil'noi Promyshlennosti Dorevolutsionnoi*
Rossii. 2 vols. Moscow, 1955, 1958.

Fokin, L. F. *Obzor Khimicheskoi Promyshlennosti v Rossii.* Vols. 1–2. Petrograd,
1920.

Lukianov, P. M. *Istoria Khimicheskikh Promyslov i Khimicheskoi Promyshlennosti*
Rossii. Vols. 1–5. Moscow, 1954–61.

Strumilin, S. G. *Istoria Chernoi Metallurgii SSSR.* Moscow, 1954; 2d ed. 1967.

Sbornik Statisticheskikh Svedenii o Gornozavodskoi Promyshlennosti Rossii v . . .
Zavodskom godu. Gornyi Uchenyi Komitet 1859–1911. St. Petersburg, 1861–1913.

Varzar, V. E. *Statisticheskie Svedenia po Obrabatyvaiushchei Fabrichnozavodskoi Promyshlennosti Rossiiskoi Imperii za 1900 g.* St. Petersburg: MTP, 1902.

————. *Statisticheskie Svedenia po Obrabatyvaiushchei Fabrichnozavodskoi Promyshlennosti Rossiiskoi Imperii za 1900 g.* St. Petersburg: MTP, 1902.

Statistika Neschastnykh Sluchaev s Rabochimi v Promyshlennykh Zavedeniiakh za . . . god. St. Petersburg: MTP, 1912–14.

Svod Otchetov Fabrichnikh Inspektorov za . . . god 1900–1914. St. Petersburg: MTP, 1902–15.

Varzar, V. E. *Statisticheskie Svedeniia o Stachkakh Rabochikh na Fabrikakh i Zavodakh za Desiatiletie 1895–1904.* St. Petersburg, 1905.

————. *Statistika Stachek Rabochikh na Fabrikakh i Zavodakh za 1905.* St. Petersburg: MTP, 1908.

Dannye o Prodolzhitel'nosti Rabochego Vremeni za . . . god. St. Petersburg: MTP, 1904–05.

Materialy Dlia Izucheniia Kustarnoi Promyshlennosti i Ruchnogo Truda v Rossii. St. Petersburg: MVD, CSC, 1872.

Sbornik Materialov ob Arteliakh v Rossii. St. Petersburg, 1874.

Otchet Gornogo Departmenta za . . . go. 1891–1911 annually. St. Petersburg: MTP, 1892–1913.

Statisticheskie Tablitsy po Obrabatyvaiushchei Fabrichnozavodskoi, Dobyvaiushchei Gornoi i Gornozavodskoi Promyshlennosti Rossii 1892–1900. St. Petersburg: MF, 1901.

Materialy Dlia Statistiki Khlopchatobumazhnogo Proizvodstva v Rossii. St. Petersburg: MF, 1901.

Statistika Bumagopriadil'nogo i Tkatskogo Proizvodstva za 1900–1910 gg. St. Petersburg: MTP, 1911.

Transportation and Communication

Statisticheskii Sbornik Ministerstva Putei Soobshcheniia. Vols. 1–144. St. Petersburg: MPS, 1877–1917.

Materialy Dlia Statistiki Rechnogo Sudokhodstva v Evropeiskoi Rossii. Edited by V. Zverinskii. St. Petersburg: MVD, CSC, 1872.

Materialy po Razrabotke Tarifov Rossiiskikh Zheleznykh Dorog. St. Petersburg: MF, 1889.

Statisticheskii Obzor Zheleznykh Dorog i Vnutrennikh Vodnykh Putei. St. Petersburg, 1893.

Statistika Sluzhashchick na Zheleznykh Dorogakh, Uchastnikov Pensionnykh i Sberegatel'no-Vspomogatel'nykh Kass. Vols. 1–4. St. Petersburg, 1896, 1906–08.

Ruskoe Tekhnicheskoe Obshchestvo: Aperçu des chemins de fer Russes depuits l'origine jusqu'ee 1892. Vols. 1–3. Brussels: P. Weissenbruch, 1897.

Aperçu statistique des chemins de fer et des voies navigables de la Russie. Section de la statistique et de la cartographie. St. Petersburg: MPS, 1900.

Volga. Voies navigables du bassin du Volga . . . Moscow: MPS, 1908.

Rossia v Dorozhnom Otnoshenii. Edited by V. F. Meien. Vols. 1–3. St. Petersburg: MVD, 1902.

Obshchii Obzor Pochtovoi Deiatel'nosti v Imperii za 10 let, 1857–1866. St. Petersburg: MVD, CSC, 1868.

Obshchii Obzor Telegrafnoi Deiatel'nosti, 1860–1866. St. Petersburg: MVD, CSC, 1868.

Pochtovaia Statistika, 1875–1914. St. Petersburg: MVD, 1876–1915.

Trade

Obzor Vneshnei Torgovli Rossii po Evropeiskoi i Aziatskoi Granitsam za . . . g. St. Petersburg: MF, Departament Tamozhennykh Sborov, 1860–1915.

Svedeniia o Vneshnei Torgovle po Evropeiskoi Granitse za . . . Mesiats . . . g. 1884–1917 monthly. St. Petersburg: MF, Departament Tamozhennykh Sborov, 1884–1917.

Vneshniaia Torgovlia Rossii, Predvaritel'nye Svedeniia. St. Petersburg: MF, Departament Tamozhennykh Sborov, 1893, 1897.

Kratkie Svedeniia o Vneshnei Torgovle Rossii za . . . g. St. Petersburg: MF, Departament Tamozhennykh Sborov, 1895, 1896.

Tableaux statistiques du commerce exterieur de la Russie. Edited by V. I. Pokrovskii. St. Petersburg, 1896.

Sbornik Svedenii po Istorii i Statistike Vneshnei Torgovli Rossii. Edited by V. I. Pokrovskii. St. Petersburg: MF, Departament Tamozhennykh Soborov, 1902.

Svod Statisticheskikh Dannykh o Privoze Tovarov . . . za 1898–1908 gody. Edited by V. I. Pokrovskii. St. Petersburg: MTP, 1909.

Statisticheskie Svedeniia o Torgovle Rossii s Kitaem. St. Petersburg: MF, 1909.

Vyvoz Rossiiskikh Tovarov Zagranitsei: Svod Dannykh Russkoi Statistiki Vneshnei Torgovli za 1900–1911 gg. Materialy k Peresmotru Torgovogo Dogovora s Germaniei. St. Petersburg: MF, Departament Tamozhennykh Sborov, 1913.

Eksport Zagranitsu Produktov Gornoi i Gornozavodskoi Promyshlennosti Yuga Rossii. Edited by N. F. von Ditmar. Vols. 1–5. Kharkov, 1911–13.

Vyvoz i Privoz Glaveneishikh Tovarov po Vneshnei Torgovle Rossii . . . Svod Dannykh Russkoi Statistiki za 1908–1912 g. St. Petersburg: MF, Departament Tamozhennykh Sborov, 1914.

Statistika Privoza Inostrannykh Tovarov . . . v Rossii za 1910–1912 gg. Petrograd, 1916.

Trudy Ekspeditsii, Snariazhennoi IVEO i IRGO, Dlia Issledovaniia Khlebnoi Torgovli i Proizvoditel'nosti Rossii. Vols. 1–4. St. Petersburg, 1870–74.

Lodyzhenskii, K. N. *Istoriia Russkogo Tamozhennogo Tarifa.* St. Petersburg, 1886.

Sobolev, M. N. *Tamozhennaia Politika Rossii vo Vtoroi Polovine XIX Veka.* Tomsk, 1911.

Dikhtiar, G. A. *Vnutrennaia Torgovlia v Dorevolutsionnoi Rossii.* Moscow, 1960.

Money and Banking

Gosudarstvennyi Bank. *Gosudarstvennyi Bank. Otchet za . . . god. 1860–1916.* Vols. 1–57. St. Petersburg, 1861–1917.

Gosudarstvennye Sberegatel'nye Kassy. *Otchety Gosudarstvennykh Sberegatel'nykh Kass po Sberegatel'noi Operatsii za . . . god, 1907–1915.* St. Petersburg, 1908–16.

Kaufman, I. I. *Statistika Russkikh Bankov.* Vols. 1–2. St. Petersburg: CSC, MVD, 1872, 1875.

———. *Statistika Gorodskikh Sberegatel'nykh Kass.* St. Petersburg: CSC, MVD, 1875.

Reforma Donezhnogo Obrashcheniia v Rossii. St. Petersburg: IVEO, 1896.

Russkie Banki. Spravochnye i Statisticheskie Svedeniia o Vsekh Deistvuiushchikh v Rossii Gosudarstvennykh, Chastnykh i Obshchestvennykh Kreditnykh Uchrezhdeniiakh. Edited by A. K. Golubev. Vols. 1–4. 1896, 1897, 1899, 1908.

Kovanko, A. *Les caisses d'epargne en Russie, 1841–1902.* St. Petersburg: CSC, 1903.

Statistika Dolgosrochnogo Kredita v Rossii. Edited by A. K. Golubev. St. Petersburg, 1903–12 annually.

Migulin, P. *Nasha Bankovaia Politika.* Kharkov, 1904.

Ministerstvo Finansov, *Russkii Denezhnyi Rynok, 1908–1912.* St. Petersburg: MF, 1908–12.

Katsenellenbaum, S. S. *Kommerchekie Banki i Ikh Torgovo-Kommissionnye Operatsii.* Moscow, 1912.

Borovoi, S. I. *Kredit i Banki v Rossii.* Moscow, 1958.

Gindin, I. F. *Russkie Kommercheskie Banki.* Moscow, 1948.

———. *Gosudarstvennyi Bank i Ekonomicheskaia Politika Tsarkogo Pravitel'stva.* Moscow, 1960.

Government Finance

Ziablovskii-Desiatovskii, A. *Obozrenie Gosudarstvennykh Dokhodov Rossii.* St. Petersburg, 1868.

Gosudarstvennye Dokhody Rossii, Ikh Klassifikatsiia, Nyneshnee Sostoianie i Dvizhenie 1866–1872. Edited by V. P. Bezobrazov. St. Petersburg: MVD, CSC, 1872.

Kaufman, I. I. *Statistika Gosudarstvennykh Finansov Rossii v 1862–1884 gg.* St. Petersburg: MVD, CSC, 1886.

Ponizhenie Vykupnogo Platezha po Ukazu 28/12/1881 g. Edited by G. Ershov. St. Petersburg: MVD, CSC, 1885.

Svod Dannykh o Postuplenii Okladnykh Sborov po Imperii za . . . 1888–1893. Vols. 1–2. St. Petersburg: MF, 1891, 1894.

Svod Danykh o Postuplenii Kazennykh Okladnykh Sborov po Imperii za . . . g. St. Petersburg: MF, 1894–1913.

Postuplenie Okladnykh Sborov v Kaznu s Sel'skikh Soslovii za 1888–1892. St. Petersburg: MF, 1894.

Svod Dannykh o Postuplenii Kazennykh i Zemskikh Okladnykh Sborov a Takzhe Otsenochnogo Sbora s Gorodskikh Nedvizhimykh Imushchestv va 1888–1892. St. Petersburg, 1895.

Svod Svedenii o Rezul'tatakh i Oborotakh po Kazennoi Vinnoi Operatsii za 1897–1901 gg. St. Petersburg: MF, 1902.

Proekt Gosudarstvennoi Rospisi Dokhodov i Raskhodov s Obiasnitel'noi Zapiskoi Ministra Finansov. St. Petersburg: MF, 1901–16 annually.

Gosudarstvennye Raskhody po Glavnym Predmetam Naznacheniia v 1907–1912 gg. St. Petersburg: MF, 1914.

Statistika Dokhodov i Raskhodov Gorodov Evropeiskoi Rossii s Privislanskimi Guberniiami s 1870 po 1884 g. St. Petersburg: MVD, CSC, 1887.

Mirskie Raskhody i Dokhody za 1891 g. v 50 Guberniiakh Evropeiskoi Rossii. St. Petersburg, 1895.

Mirskie Dokhody i Raskhody za 1892–1894 gg. v 50 Guberniiakh Evropeiskoi Rossii. St. Petersburg, 1897.

Gminnye Dokhody i Raskhody za 1892–1894 g. v 10 Privislanskikh Guberniiakh. St. Petersburg, 1898.

Mirskie Dokhody i Raskhody 1894 g. v 50 Guberniiakh Evropeiskoi Rossii. St. Petersburg, 1909.

Raskhody Zemstv 34 Gubernii po Smetam na 1895 g. St. Petersburg: MF, 1896.

Dokhody Zemstv 34 Gubernii po Smetam na 1896 g. St. Petersburg: MF, 1897.

O Zadolzhennosti Zemlevladeniia v Sviazi s Statisticheskimi Dannymi . . . St. Petersburg: CSC, 1888.

Ministerstvo Finansov. *Ministerstvo Finansov, 1802–1902.* St. Petersburg, 1902.

————. Ministerstvo Finansov, 1904–1913. St. Petersburg, 1914.

————. *Proekt Gosudarstvennoi Rospisi Dokhodov i Raskhodov na . . . god.* St. Petersburg, 1862–1916 annually.

————. *Sbornik Svedenii i Materialov po Vedomstvu Ministerstva Finansov.* 1865–68.

————. *Ezhegodnik Ministerstva Finansov.* 1869–1916 annually.

Gosudarstvennaia Kontrol. *Otchet Gosudarstvennogo Kontrola po Ispolneniu Gosudarstvennoi Rospisi i Finansovykh Smet, 1866–1914.* St. Petersburg, 1867–1915.

Ministerstvo Finansov. *Kassovyi Otchet Ministra Finansov 1870–1914.* St. Petersburg, 1870–1914.

Bliokh, I. C. *Finansy Rossii XIX Stoletia.* Vols. 1–4. St. Petersburg, 1882.

Pecherin, Ya. I. *Istoricheskii Obzor Rospisei Gosudarstvennykh Dokhodov i Raskhodov.* St. Petersburg, 1896, 1898.

Migulin, P. P. *Russkii Gosudarstvennyi Kredit, 1769–1899.* Vols. 1–3. Kharkov, 1899–1902.

Petit, P. *La dette publique de la Russie.* Poitiers, 1912.

Education

Svedeniia po Statistike Narodnogo Obrazovaniia v Evropeiskoi Rossii, 1872–1874. Edited by A. Dubrovskii. St. Petersburg: MVD, CSC, 1872.

Obiasnitel'nyi Tekst k Karte Narodnogo Obrazovaniia v Rossii 1876 g. St. Petersburg: MNP, 1880.

Statisticheskie Svedeniia o Sel'skikh Uchilischchakh v Evropeiskoi Rossii i Privislanskikh Guberniiakh . . . Obsledovanie 20/3/1880 g. Edited by A. Dubrovskii. St. Petersburg: MVD, CSC, 1884.

Universitety i Srednie Uchebnye Zavedeniia v 50ti Gub. Evropeiskoi Rossii i 10ti Privislanskikh po Perepisi 20/3/1880. Edited by A. Dubrovskii. St. Petersburg, 1888.

Spetsailnye Uchebnye Zavedeniia Muzhskie i Zhenskie v 50ti Guberniakh Evropeiskoi Rossii 10ti Privislenskikh gub. po Perepisi 20/3/1880 g. St. Petersburg, 1890.

Fal'bork i Charnolusskii. *Nachal'noe Narodnoe Obrazovanie v Rossii po Obslevdovaniau IVEO. Yanvar' 1895.* Vols. 1–4. St. Petersburg: IVEO, 1900–05.

Statisticheskie Svedennia po Nachal'nomu Obrazovaniiu v Rossiskoi Imperii. St. Petersburg: MNP, 1902.

Pokrovskii, V. I. *Odnodnevnaia Perepis' Nachal'nykh Shkol Rossiiskoi Imperii, 1911.* St. Petersburg, 1913.

Miscellaneous

Statisticheskie Svedeniia o Pozharakh v Rossii v 1870–1874 gg. Edited by V. V.
Zverinskii. St. Petersburg, 1882.
Pozhary v Rossii, 1875–1882. St. Petersburg: MVD, CSC, 1887.
Pozhary v Rossiiskoi Imperii v 1883–1887 gg. i svod za 28 let 1860–1887. St.
Petersburg: MVD, CSC, 1889.
Statistika Pozharov v Rossiiskoi Imperii za 1895–1910 gg. Vol. 1, *63 gub.*
Evropeiskoi Rossii. Vol. 2, *Gubernii i Oblasti Aziatskoi Rossii.* St. Petersburg,
1912.
Vzaimnoe Strakhovanie ot Ognia, Gubernskoe, Zemskoe i Gorodskoe, 1889–1892.
St. Petersburg, 1893.
Obshchaia Stalistika Aktsionernykh Strakhovykh (ot ognia) Obskchestv. Izdanie
1906 goda. Vols. 1–2: 1900–04. St. Petersburg, 1906. *Izdanie 1911 goda.* Vols. 1–2:
1900–09. St. Petersburg, 1911.
Aktsionernye Strakhovye Obshchestva (Tarifnyi Otdel): Aktsionernoe Strakhovanie
ot Ognia v Rossii, 1827–1910 gg. St. Petersburg, 1912.

THE SOVIET PERIOD

Periodicals

Vestnik Statistiki (Courier of Statistics). Moscow: TsSU, 1919–29, 1949–.
Narodnoe Khoziaistvo (National Economy). Moscow: VSNKh RSFSR, 1918–22.
Sotsialisticheskoe Khoziaistvo (Socialist Economy). Moscow: RANION, 1923–30.
Problemy Ekonomiki (Problems of Economics). Moscow: Akad. Nauk, 1929–41.
Voprosy Ekonomiki (Questions of Economics). Moscow: Akad. Nauk, 1948–.
Izvestia Akademii Nauk SSSR (News of the Academy of Sciences). Moscow and
Leningrad: Otdelenie Ekonomiki i Prava (Branch of Economics and Law), 1917–.
Ekonomicheskoe Obozrenie (Economic Review). Moscow, 1923–30.
Planovoe Khoziaistvo (Planned Economy). Moscow: Gosplan, 1923–41, 1944–.
Vedomosti Verkhovnogo Soveta SSSR (Records of the Supreme Council of the
USSR). Moscow, 1936–.
Biulleten TsSU (Bulletin of the Central Statistical Authority). Moscow: TsSU,
1919–26.
Vneshnaia Torgovlia (Foreign Trade). Moscow: NK Vneshtorg, 1922–26, 1928–29,
1931–.
Statistika Vneshnei Torgovli SSSR (Foreign Trade Statistics). Moscow: NK
Vneshtorg, 1924–38.
Vestnik Promyshlennosti, Torgovli, i Transporta (Courier of Industry, Trade, and
Transportation). Moscow: NK Torg, 1922–26.
Sovietskaia Torgovlia (Soviet Trade). Moscow: NK Torg, 1926–31, 1932–41.
Voprosy Torgovli (Questions of Trade). Moscow: NK Torg, 1927–30.
Organizatsiia i Tekhnika Sovietskoi Torgovli (Organization and Technique of
Soviet Trade). Moscow: NK Torg, 1933–37.
Khlebnoe, Mukomol'noe, i Elevatornoe Delo SSSR (Grain, Flourmilling, and
Elevators Business of the USSR). Moscow: NK Torg, 1925–27.

Zagotovki Sel'skokhoziaistvennykh Produktov (Procurement of Agricultural Commodities). Moscow: KZag, 1927–42, 1949–62.

Zakupki Sel'skokhoziaistvennykh Produktov (Purchases of Agricultural Commodities). Moscow Min Zag, 1963–.

Voprosy Truda (Questions of Labor). Moscow: NK Trud, 1923–33.

Na Trudovom Fronte (On the Labor Front). Moscow: NK Trud, 1930–33.

Sotsialisticheskii Trud (Socialist Labor). Moscow: NK Trud, 1922–29, 1959–.

Statistika Truda (Labor Statistics). Moscow: NK Trud, 1922–29.

Vestnik Truda (Courier of Labor). Moscow: VTsSPS, 1920–28.

Profsoiuzy SSSR (USSR Trade Unions). Moscow: VTsSPS, 1931–41.

Vestnik Finansov (Courier of Finances). Moscow: NKFin, 1922–30.

V Pomoshch' Finansovomu Rabotniku (Assisting the financial Worker). Moscow: NKFin, 1926–40.

Sovietskie Finansy (Soviet Finances). Moscow: NKFin, 1940–52, 1954–.

Finansy i Kredit SSSR (USSR Finances and Credit). Moscow: MF, Gosbank, 1952–30.

Vestnik Gosudarstvennogo Strakhovaniia (Courier of State Insurance). Moscow: G. P. Gosstrakh NFKin, 1922–30.

Kredit i Planovoe Khoziaistvo (Credit and Planned Economy). Moscow: Gosbank, 1925–30.

Kredit i Khozrazshchet (Credit and Economic Accounting). Moscow: Gosbank, 1932–38.

Dengi i Kredit (Money and Credit). Moscow: Gosbank, 1938–41, 1946–52, 1954–.

Voprosy Pitaniia (Questions of Nutrition). Moscow: NKZdrav, 1932–41, 1952–.

General

SNK. *God Raboty Pravitel'stva*, 1924–25 . . . 1928–29. Moscow, 1926–30.

TsSU. *Itogi Desiatiletia Sovietskoi Vlasti v Tsifrakh, 1917–1927*. Moscow: TsSU, 1928.

TsUNKhU. *20 Let Sovietskoi Vlasti, Statisticheskii Sbornik*. Moscow, 1938.

Mirovoe Khoziaistvo, Statisticheskii Sbornik za 1913–1925. Edited by N. D. Kondratiev. Moscow: NKFin, 1926.

Gosplan. *SSSR i Kapitalisticheskie Strany, Statisticheskii Sbornik za 1917–1937*. Moscow and Leningrad, 1938.

TsSU. *Statisticheskii Sbornik za 1913–1917*. Vols. 1–2. Moscow, 1921–22.

———. *Sbornik Statisticheskikh Svedenii po SSSR za Piat' Let Raboty TsSU, 1918–1923*. Moscow, 1924.

———. *Statisticheskii Ezhegodnik*. Vols. 1–7. Moscow, 1921–26.

NKFin. *Statisticheskii Ezhegodnik za* . . . *1923–24, 1926–27*. Moscow, 1924–28.

TsSU. *Statisticheskii Spravochnik SSSR, 1924* . . . *1928*. Moscow, 1925–29.

TsUNKhU. *Kratkii Statisticheskii Spravochnik, 1935*. Moscow, 1935.

———. *SSSR Strana Sotsializma, Statisticheskii Sbornik*. Moscow, 1936.

———. *SSSR v Tsifrakh, 1934, 1935*. Moscow, 1934–35.

TsSU. *SSSR v Tsifrakh, Statisticheskii Sbornik, 1957* . . . Moscow, 1958–.

———. *Narodnoe Khoziaistvo SSSR v* . . . *godu*. Moscow, 1956–.

Central Statistical Board. *Soviet Union 50 Years*. Moscow, 1969.

Economic Planning

TsSU. *Balans Narodnogo Khoziaistva SSSR za 1923–1924.* Edited by P. I. Popov. Moscow, 1926.

Gosplan. *Kontrol'nye Tsifry Narodnogo Khoziaistva SSSR na . . . 1925–1926, 1926–1927, 1927–1928, 1928–1929, 1929–1930.* Moscow, 1925–30.

———. *Perspektivy Razvertyvaniia Narodnogo Khoziaistva SSSR na 1926/27–1931/32.* Edited by S. G. Strumilin. Moscow, 1927.

———. *Piatiletnii Plan Narodno-Khoziaistvenogo Stroitel'stva SSSR.* Vols. 1–3. Moscow, 1929.

———. *Itogi Vypolneniia Pervogo Piatiletnego Plana Razvitiia Narodnogo Khoziaistva SSSR.* Moscow, 1934.

———. *Proekt Vtorogo Piatiletnego Plana Razvitiia Narodnogo Khoziaistva SSSR, 1933–1937.* Vols. 1–3. Moscow, 1934.

———. *Vtoroi Piatiletnii Plan Razvitiia Narodnogo Khoziaistva SSSR, 1933–1937.* Vols. 1–2. Moscow, 1934.

———. *Narodno-Khoziaistvennyi Plan na 1935 god.* Moscow, 1936.

———. *Narodno-Khoziaistvennyi Plan na 1936 god.* Vols. 1–2. Moscow, 1936.

———. *Narodno-Khoziaistvennyi Plan Soiuza SSR na 1937 g.* Moscow, 1937.

———. *Itogi Vypolneniia Vtorogo Piatiletnego Plana Razvitiia Narodnogo Khoziaistva SSSR.* Moscow, 1939.

———. *Tretii Piatiletnii Plan Razvitiia Narodnogo Khoziaistva SSSR, 1938–1942.* Moscow, 1939.

SNK. *Gosudarstvennyi Plan Razvitiia Narodnogo Khoziaistva SSSR na 1941 g. Prilozhenie k Postanovleniiu SNK SSSR i TsK VKP (b) No. 127 ot 17/1/1941.* American Council of Learned Societies.

Population Censuses

TsSU. *Predvaritel'nye Itogi Perepisi Naseleniia 28/8/1920.* Vols. 1–5. Moscow, 1920–21.

———. *Itogi Perepisi Naseleniia 1920 g.* Moscow, 1928.

———. *Vsesoiuznaia Perepis' Naseleniia 17/12/1926. Predvaritel'nye Itogi.* Vols. 1–3. Moscow, 1927.

———. *Vsesoiuznaia Perepis' Naseleniia 17/12/1926 g. Kratkie Svodki.* Vols. 1–8. Moscow, 1927–29.

———. *Vsesoiuznaia Perepis' Naseleniia 1926 g.* Vols. 1–56. Moscow, 1928–33.

———. *Itogi Vsesoiuznoi Perepisi Naseleniia 1959.* Vols. 1–16. Moscow, 1962.

———. *Vestnik Statistiki,* no. 5, pp. 65–84. Moscow, 1970.

———. *Itogi Vsesoiuznoi Perepisi Naseleniia 1970 g.* Vols. 1–4. Moscow, 1972.

Population

TsSU. *Mezhdunarodnye i Mezhokontinental'nye Migratsii v Dovoennoi Rossii i SSSR.* Edited by V. V. Osinski-Obolenskii. Moscow, 1928.

———. *Estestvennoe Dvizhenie Naseleniia SSSR, 1923–1925.* Moscow, 1926.

———. *Estestvennoe Dvizhenie Naseleniia Soiuza SSR v 1926.* Edited by M. P. Krasilnikov. Moscow, 1929.

Gosplan. *Smertnost' i Prodolzhitel'nost Zhizni Naseleniia SSSR, 1925–1927. Tablitsy Smertnosti.* Moscow and Leningrad, 1930.

Itogi Vserossiiskoi Gorodskoi Perepisi 1923 g. Vols. 1–4. Moscow, 1924–27.
Molodezh SSSR v Tsifrakh. Edited by Schwarz and Zaitsev. Moscow, 1924.
Molodezh SSSR. Statisticheskii Sbornik. Edited by A. V. Kosarev. Moscow, 1936.
TsUNKhU. *Zhenshchina v SSSR. Statisticheskii Sbornik.* Moscow, 1937.
TsSU. *Zhenshchiny i Deti v SSSR. Statisticheskii Sbornik.* Moscow, 1961–.

Agriculture

Sel'skoe Khoziaistvo Rossii v XX veke. Sbornik Statistiko-Ekonomicheskikh Svedenii za 1901–1922 g. Edited by N. P. Oganovskii and N. D. Kondratiev. Moscow, 1923.
TsSU. *Pogubernskie Itogi Vserossiiskoi Sel'skokhoziaistvennoi i Pozemel'noi Perepisi 1917 g. po 52 Guberniiam i Oblastiam.* Moscow, 1921.
————. *Pouezdnye Itogi Vserossiiskoi Sel'skokhoziaistvennoi i Pozemel'noi Perepisi 1917 g. po 57 Guberniiam i Oblastiam.* Moscow, 1923.
————. *Pogubernskie Itogi 10% Vyborochnoi Sel'skokhoziaistvennoi Perepisi Krestianskikh Khoziaistv 1919 g.* Moscow, 1920.
————. *Ekonomicheskoe Rassloenie Krestianstva v 1917 i 1919 g.* Moscow, 1922.
————. *Itogi Vserossiiskoi Sel'skokhoziaistvennoi Perepisi 1920 g. (Pouezdnye Dannye po Guberniiam).* Vols. 1–8. Moscow, 1921–23.
————. *Itogi Razrabotki Sel'skokhoziaistvennoi Perepisi 1920 g po Tipam i Gruppam Khoziaistv.* Vols. 1–6. Moscow, 1924–26.
————. *Gruppovye Itogi Sel'skokhoziaistvennoi Perepisi 1920 g.* Moscow, 1926.
Peresektivy Razvitiia Sel'skogo Khoziaistva SSSR. Edited by N. D. Kondratiev and N. P. Oganovskii. Moscow, 1924.
NKZ. *Trudy Zemplana.* Vols. 1–18. Moscow, 1924–29.
NKFin. *Sel'skoe Khoziaistvo SSSR v . . . 1922, 1923/24, 1924/25, 1925/26, 1926/27.* Moscow, 1923–27.
TsSU. *Sel'skoe Khoziaistvo SSSR, 1925–1929.* Moscow, 1929.
————. *Osnovnye Elementy i Produktsiia Sel'skogo Khoziaistva SSSR za 1925/ 1926–1928/1929 gg. s prilozheniem Khlebofurazhnogo Balansa za 1928–1929 gg.* Moscow, 1929.
NKZ. *Sel'skoe Khoziaistvo SSSR, 1935.* Moscow, 1936.
TsUNKhU. *Sotsialisticheskoe Sel'skoe Khoziaistvo SSSR.* Edited by Sautin. Moscow, 1939.
TsSU. *Sel'skoe Khoziaistvo SSSR.* Moscow, 1960.
————. *Selskoe Khoziaistvo SSSR.* Moscow, 1971.
Gosplan. *Kolkhozy Nakanune XVI Sezda VKP (b).* Moscow, 1930.
————. *Kolkhozy v 1928 g.* Moscow, 1930.
————. *Kolkhozy v 1929 g.* Moscow, 1931.
————. *Kolkhozy v 1930 g.* Moscow, 1931.
TsUNKhU. *Mashiny i Orudia v Sel'skom Khoziaistve SSSR.* Moscow, 1934.
NKZ. *MTS i Kolkhozy v 1936 godu.* Moscow, 1937.
TsUNKhU. *MTS vo Vtoroi Piatiletke.* Moscow, 1939.
————. *Posevnye Ploshchadi SSSR.* Moscow, 1936.
————. *Posevnye Ploshchadi SSSR.* Moscow, 1939.
TsSU. *Posevnye Ploshchadi SSSR.* Vols. 1–2. Moscow, 1957.
————. *Voenno-Konskaia Perepis' (Pereuchet) 1924 g.* Moscow, 1927.
————. *Voenno-Konskaia Perepis' 1924–1925 gg.* Moscow, 1928.

Nifontov, V. P. *Zhivotnovodstvo SSSR v Tsifrakh.* Moscow and Leningrad, 1932.

TsUNKhU. *Chislennost' Skota v 1934 godu.* Moscow, 1935.

————. *Zhivotnovodcheskie Kolkhoznye Fermy SSSR, Itogi Raboty za 1932–1934 gg.* Moscow, 1936.

————. *Itogi Vsesoiuznoi Perepisi Skota na l Ianvaria 1935.* Vols. 1–3. Moscow, 1935–36.

————. *Zhivotnovodstvo v SSSR v Iunie 1936.* Moscow, 1936.

————. *Dinamika Chislennosti Skota. Zhivotnovodstvo v Sovkhozakh, v Kolkhozakh i u Kolkhoznikov.* Moscow, 1937.

Nifontov, V. P. *Produktsiia Zhivotnovodstva.* Moscow, 1937.

TsUNKhU. *Zhivotnovodstvo v SSSR za 1916–1938 gg. Statisticheskii Sbornik.* Moscow, 1940.

TsSU. *Chislennost' Skota v SSSR.* Moscow, 1957.

Jasny, Naum. *The Socialized Agriculture of the USSR.* Stanford: Stanford University Press, 1949.

Volin, Lazar. *A Century of Russian Agriculture.* Cambridge: Harvard University Press, 1970.

Industry

TsSU. *Fabrichno-Zavodskaia Promyshlennost' v Period 1913–1918 gg.* Moscow, 1926.

————. *Spisok Fabrik, Zavodov, i Drugikh Promyshlennykh Predpriiatii . . . po Perepisi 1918 g.* Moscow, 1919–20.

————. *Vserossiiskaia Promyshlennaia i Professional'naia Perepis' Naseleniia 1918 g.* Moscow, 1920.

————. *Vserossiiskaia Promyshlennaia i Professional'naia Perepis' 1918 g.* Moscow, 1926.

Dinamika Rossiiskoi i Sovetskoi Promyshlennosti. Edited by V. E. Varzar and L. B. Kafengauz. Moscow, 1928.

TsSU *Vserossiiskaia Perepis' Promyshlennykh Zavedenii 1920 g.* Vols. 1–15. Moscow, 1921–27.

————. *Dinamika Tsen na Glavneishie Izdeliia Fabrichno-Zavodskoi Promyshlennosti za Period 1913–1918 g.* Moscow, 1926.

————. *Materialy po Tekushchei Promyshlennoi Statistike za 1919 i 1920 g.* Moscow, 1922.

————. *Produktsiia Fabrichno-Zavodskoi Promyshlennosti za 1912, 1920, i 1921 g.* Moscow, 1922.

VSNKh. *Russkaia Promyshlennost' v 1922 g. Materialy k 10-mu S'ezdu Sovetov.* Petrograd, 1922.

TsSU. *Fabrichno-Zavodskaia Promyshlennost' za 1922.* Moscow, 1924–25.

VSNKh. *Russkaia Promyshlennost' v 1923 g.* Moscow, 1923.

TsSU. *Fabrichno-Zavodskaia Promyshlennost' za 1923.* Moscow, 1925. Rev. ed. GK. *Sbornik Statisticheskikh Svedenii po Gornoi i Gornozavodskoi Promyshlennosti SSSR za 1911–1924/25 gg.* Leningrad, 1928.

VSNKh. *Statistika Elektricheskikh Stantsii SSSR 1922–1926.* Moscow, 1927.

TsSU. *Fabrichno-Zavodskaia Promyshlennost' za 1924.* Moscow, 1926.

————. *Fabrichno-Zavodskaia Promyshlennost' za 1924–1925.* Vols. 1–4. Moscow, 1925.

————. *Fabrichno-Zavodskaia Promyshlennost' SSSR v 1925–1926.* Moscow, 1927.

————. *Fabrichno-Zavodskaia Promyshlennost' SSSR. Osnovnye Pokazateli ee Dinamiki za 1924–1925, 1925–1926, 1926–1927.* Moscow, 1929.

VSNKh. *Promyshlennost' SSSR v . . . 1924 . . . 1927–1928, Ezhegodnik.* Moscow, 1925–30.

————. *Gosudarstvennaia Promyshlennost' SSSR za Pervoe Polugodie 1924–1925 Operatsionnogo Goda.* Moscow and Leningrad, 1925.

————. *Promyshlennost' SSSR v 1925–1926 Operatsionnom Godu.* Moscow, 1927.

————. *Promyshlennost' SSSR v 1927–1929 Operatsionnykh Godakh.* Vols. 1–2. Moscow, 1930.

GK. *Sbornik Statisticheskikh Svedenii po Gornoi i Gornozavodskoi Promyshlennosti SSSR za 1925–1926, 1926–1927, 1927–1928.* Leningrad, 1928–30.

TsSU. *Fabrichno-Zavodskaia Promyshlennost' SSSR v Ego Ekonomicheskikh Raionakh.* Moscow, 1928–29.

————. *Fabrichno-Zavodskaia Promyshlennost' SSSR.* Moscow, 1929.

————. *Melkaia i Kustarno-Remeslennaia Promyshlennost' SSSR v 1925.* Moscow, 1926.

TsUNKhU. *Melkaia Promyshlennost' SSSR po Dannym Vsesoiuznoi Perepisi 1929.* Vols. 1–3. Moscow, 1932–33.

————. *Osnovnye Kapitaly Tsenzovoi Promyshlennosti.* Moscow, 1929.

————. *Kontrol'nye Tsifry Piatiletnego Plana Razvitiia Promyshlennosti SSSR, 1927/28–1931/32.* Moscow, 1927.

Kuibyshev, V. V. *Kontrol'nye Tsifry Piatiletnego Plana Promyshlennosti na 1928–29, 1932–33.* Moscow, 1929.

Gosplan. *Energeticheskoe Khoziaistvo SSSR.* Moscow and Leningrad, 1931.

TsUNKhU. *Metaloobrabatyvaiushchie Oborudovanie SSSR.* Moscow, 1933.

————. *Oborudovanie Metaloobrabatyvaiushchei Promyshlennosti.* Vols. 1–5. Moscow, 1935.

TsSU. *Promyshlennost' SSSR, Statisticheskii Sbornik.* Moscow, 1957.

————. *Promyshlennost' SSSR, Statisticheskii Sbornik.* Moscow, 1964.

Transportation and Communication

NKPS. *Statisticheskii Sbornik Narodnogo Komissariata Putei Soobschchenia.* Moscow, 1917–20.

————. *Materialy po Statistike Putei Soobshchenia.* Moscow, 1921–38.

————. *Ezhemesiachnyi Biuleten Transportnoi Statistiki.* Moscow, 1923–31.

————. *Zheleznodorozhnoe Delo.* Moscow, 1924–31.

————. *Sotsialisticheskii Uchet na Zheleznodorozhnom Transporte.* Moscow, 1932–39.

MPS. *Zheleznodorozhnyi Transport.* Moscow, 1941–.

TsSU. *Materialy po Dinamike Gruzooborota . . .* Moscow, 1925, 1927.

————. *Itogi Zheleznodorozhnogo Gruzooborota Krupnykh Tsentrov v 1924–25.* Moscow, 1926.

————. *Itogi Mezhraionnogo Gruzooborota v 1925–1926.* Moscow, 1927.

TsUNKhU. *Mezhraionnyi Gruzooborot na Zh. D. i Vodnykh Putiakh Soobshchenia za 1926/27 i 1927/1928 g.* Moscow, 1930.

————. *Dinamika i Geografia Gruzovogo Dvizhenia na Putiakh Soobshchenia, 1928–1931 gg.* Moscow, 1932.

———. *Tovarnoe Dvizhenie na Vnutrennykh Vodnykh Putiakh Dovoennoi Rossii i Sovetskogo Soiuza.* Moscow, 1929.

———. *Vodnyi Transport, 1928–1934 gg. Statisticheskii Sbornik.* Moscow, 1936.

———. *Transport i Sviaz SSSR v Tsyfrakh.* Moscow, 1936.

TsSU. *Transport i Sviaz SSSR. Statisticheskii Sbornik.* Moscow, 1957.

NKMF and NKRF. *Vodnyi Transport.* Moscow, 1923–40.

MMF. *Morskoi Flot.* Moscow, 1941–.

MRF. *Rechnoi Transport.* Moscow, 1941–.

Ministerstvo Avototransporta RSFSR. *Avtomobil'.* Moscow, 1923–.

NKS. *Tekhnika Sviazi.* Moscow, 1917–, 1924, 1930–38.

———. *Zhizn i Tekhnika Sviazi.* Moscow, 1922–29.

MS. *Master Sviazi.* Moscow, 1939–40.

———. *Vestnik Sviazi.* Moscow, 1941–.

Foreign Trade

Narodnyi Komissariat Vnutrennei i Vneshnei Torgovli. *Vneshniaia Torgovlia Rossii za . . . 1922, 1923.* Moscow, 1922–24.

NK Torg. *Vneshniaia Torgovlia po Evropeiskoi Granitse.* Published monthly.

Vneshtorg. *Vneshniaia Torgovlia SSSR, 1934–1935.*

Krasin, L. B. *Osnovnye Tsifry Vneshnei Torgovli.* Moscow, 1925.

Vneshniaia Torgovlia SSSR za Period 1918–1927/28 gg. Statisticheskii Obzor. Edited by A. P. Vinokur and S. N. Bakulin. Moscow and Leningrad, 1932.

Vneshtorg. *Ezhegodnik Vheshnei Torgovli za 1931.* Moscow and Leningrad, 1932.

Vneshniaia Torgovlia SSSR za Pervuiu Piatiletku. Statisticheskii Obzor. Edited by A. N. Voznesenskii. Moscow, 1933.

Vneshniaia Torgovlia SSSR za 20 let, 1918–1937. Statisticheskii Spravochnik. Edited by S. N. Bakulin. Moscow, 1939.

MVT. *Vneshniaia Torgovlia SSSR za 1955 . . . god.* Moscow, 1956–.

———. *Vneshniaia Torgovlia SSSR, 1918–1940 gg.* Moscow, 1960.

———. *Vneshniaia Torgovlia SSSR za 1955–1959 gody.* Moscow, 1961.

———. *Vneshniaia Torgovlia SSSR za 1959–1963 gody.* Moscow, 1965.

———. *Vneshniaia Torgovlia SSSR, 1918–1966.* Moscow, 1967.

Domestic Trade

NKP. *Vtoroi God Bor'by s Golodom.* Moscow, 1919.

———. *Tri Goda Bor'by s Golodom.* Moscow, 1920.

NK Torg. *Vnutrennaia Torgovlia SSSR v 1922/23 i 1923/24 Operatsionnykh Godakh.* Moscow, 1925.

———. *Materialy po Statistike Vnutrennei Torgovli SSSR, 1923–1926 gg.* Moscow, 1928.

TsSU. *Vnutrennaia Torgovlia SSSR za 1924/25–1925/26 gg.* Moscow, 1928.

———. *Torgovlia SSSR za 1926/27 god . . .* Moscow, 1930.

———. *Materialy po Tekushchei Statistike Obmena.* Moscow, 1928–29.

NK Torg. *Vnutrennaia Torgovlia Soiuza SSR za X let.* Moscow, 1928.

Mikoian, A. I. *Problema Snabzhenia Strany i Rekonstruktsia Narodnogo Khoziaistva.* Moscow, 1929.

Gromyko, E. V., and Riauzov, N. N. *Sovietskaia Torgovlia za 15 let.* Moscow, 1932.

NK Torg. *Sovietskaia Torgovlia Mezhdu XVI i XVII S'ezdami VKP (b).* Moscow, 1934.

———. *Itogi Razvitia Sovietskoi Torgovli ot VI k VII S'ezdu Sovietov SSSR.* Moscow, 1935.

TsUNKhU. *Sovietskaia Torgovlia.* Moscow, 1935.

TsSU. *Sovietskaia Torgovlia. Statisticheskii Sbornik.* Moscow, 1956.

———. *Sovietskaia Torgovlia. Statisticheskii Sbornik.* Moscow, 1964.

MT. *40 let Sovietskoi Torgovli.* Moscow, 1957.

NKRKI. *Sindikaty i Gosudarstvennaia Torgovlia.* Moscow, 1923.

Kantorovich, V. Ia. *Sovietskie Sindikaty.* Moscow, 1928.

NK Torg. *Sindikatnaia Sistema SSSR.* Moscow, 1928.

———. *Sovietskaia Torgovaia Birzha k 1926 g.* Moscow, 1926.

TsUNKhU. *Roznichnaia Torgovaia Set' SSR. Itogi Perepisi 1935 g.* Moscow, 1936.

———. *Kadry Sovietskoi Torgovli.* Moscow, 1936.

Tsentrosoiuz. *Otchet Vserossiiskogo Tsentral'nogo Soiuza Potrebitel'skikh Obshchestv za 1920.* Moscow, 1922.

———. *Otchet o Deiatel'nosti Tsentrosoiuza v 1922 godu.* Moscow, 1923.

———. *Otchet o Deiatel'nosti Tsentrosoiuza v 1923 godu.* Moscow, 1924.

———. *Potrebitel'skaia Kooperatsiia v Narodnom Khoziaistve SSSR v 1923–1924 Khoziaistvennom godu.* Moscow, 1925.

TsSU. *Kooperatsia v 1923–1924 i v 1924–1925.* Moscow, 1928.

Tsentrosoiuz. *Potrebitel'skaia Kooperatsiia za 10 let Sovietskoi Vlasti.* Moscow, 1927.

———. *Potrebitel'skaia Kooperatsiia SSSR. Osnovnye Pokazateli . . .* Moscow, 1928–30.

———. *Potrebitel'skaia Kooperatsiia SSSR za 1929–1933.* Moscow, 1934.

———. *Tri Goda Raboty Potrebitel'skoi Kooperatsii.* Moscow, 1934.

———. *Potrebitel'skaia Kooperatsiia SSSR za . . . 1935, 1936, 1937 g.* Moscow, 1936–38.

TsSU. *Vidimye Khlebnye Zapasy.* Moscow, 1923–26.

———. *Rynochnyi Oborot Krestianskikh Khoziaistv.* Moscow, 1928.

———. *Dvizhenie Tsen na Glavnye Predmety Potrebleniia.* Moscow, 1923–27.

———. *Indeks Roznichnykh Gorodskikh Tsen za . . .* Moscow, 1926.

TsUNKhU. *Kolkhoznaia Torgovlia v 1932–1934 gg.* Moscow, 1935.

———. *Kolkhoznaia Torgovlia.* Moscow, 1935.

———. *Kolkhoznaia i Individualno'-Krestianskaia Torgovlia.* Moscow, 1936.

Labor, Wages, Income

NK Trud. *Materialy po Statistike Truda . . .* Moscow, 1919.

TsSU. *Trudosposobnoe Naselenie 37 Gubernii Evropeiskoi Rossii po Glavneishim Professiiam. Predvaritel'nye Itogi Perepisi Naseleniia 28/8/1920.* Moscow, 1921.

———. *Statistika Truda v Promyshlennykh Zavedeniiakh v 1920 g.* Moscow, 1922.

———. *Statistika Truda v Promyshlennykh Zavedeniiakh v 1921 g.* Moscow, 1923.

Trud v SSSR. *Statistiko-Ekonomicheskii Obzor, 1922–1924.* Edited by A. G. Rashin. Moscow, 1924.

TsSU. *Dinamika Proizvoditel'nosti Truda i ee Vazheishikh Faktorov v 1923/1924 i 1925/1926 gg.* Moscow, 1927.

VTsSPS. *Trud v SSSR. Statisticheskii Spravochnik za 1924–1925 g.* Moscow, 1926.
———. *Trud v SSSR v 1926–1928. Diagramy.* Moscow, 1928.
NK Trud. *Kontrol'nye Tsifry po Trudu na 1928–1929.* Moscow, 1928.
———. *Voprosy Truda v Tsifrakh. Statisticheskii Spravochnik za 1927–1930 k XVI Sezdu VKP (b).* Moscow, 1930.
TsUNKhU. *Podgotovka Kadrov v SSSR, 1927–1931 gg.* Moscow, 1933.
Trud v SSSR. Ekonomiko-Statisticheskii Spravochnik. Edited by Z. L. Mindlin and S. A. Heinman. Moscow and Leningrad, 1932.
TsUNKhU. *Trud v SSSR. Ezhegodnik 1934.* Moscow, 1935.
———. *Trud v SSSR. Statisticheskii Spravochnik 1935.* Moscow and Leningrad, 1936.
TsSU. *Trud v SSSR.* Moscow, 1968.
———. *Materialy Ucheta Professional'nogo Sostava Personala Fabrichnozavodskoi Promyshlennosti SSSR v 1925 g.* Moscow, 1929.
Evreinov, N. N., and Rashin, A. G. *Sostav Fabrichno-Zavodskogo Proletariata SSSR v Diagrammakh i Tablitsakh.* Moscow, 1930.
TsSU. *Rabochii Den' v Fabrichno-Zavodskoi Promyshlennosti v 1928.* Moscow, 1928.
NK Trud. *Statistika Promyshlennogo Travmatizma za 1922–1923, 1924.* Moscow, 1924, 1925.
———. *Naemnyi Trud v Rossii, i na Zapade, 1913–1925.* Moscow, 1926.
———. *Statisticheskie Materialy po Trudu i Sotsial'nomu Strakhovaniiu za 1926–1927 g.* Moscow, 1928.
———. *Sotsial'noe Strakhovanie v 1923–1924.* Moscow, 1925.
———. *Statistika Sotsial'nogo Strakhovaniia za 1924–1925 g.* Moscow, 1927.
———. *Sotsial'noe Strakhovanie v SSSR v 1925–1926.* Moscow, 1927.
TsSU. *Sostoianie Pitaniia Gorodskogo Naseleniia SSSR, 1919–1924.* Moscow, 1926.
———. *Sostoianie Pitaniia Gorodskogo Naseleniia SSSR v 1925/26 S/kh godu.* Moscow, 1927.
———. *Sostoianie Pitaniia Gorodskogo Naseleniia Zakavkazskogo SFSR, Sredneaziatskikh SSR, Dal'nevostochnogo Kraia, Iakutskoi i Kirgizskoi ASSR v 1924/25 i 1925/26 s/kh godakh.* Moscow, 1929.
G. S. Polliak. "Biudzhet Rabochego k Nachalu 1923 g." In *Voprosy Zarabotnoi Platy.* Moscow, 1923.
———. "Zarabotnaia Plata i Potreblenie." In *Statisticheskoe Obozrenie,* 1929, no. 3.
Biudzhety Rabochikh i Sluzhashchikh. Vols. 1–3. Moscow, 1929.
N. Gumilevskii. *Biudzhet Sluzhashchikh v 1922–1926.* Moscow, 1928.
L. E. Mints. *Kak Zhivet Bezrabotnyi.* Moscow, 1927.
S. G. Strumilin. *Rabochyi Byt v Tsifrakh.* Moscow and Leningrad, 1926.
R. D. Gindina. *Biudzhet Turkestanskogo Rabochego i Sluzhashchego.* In *Materialy po Statistike Truda Turkrespubliki.* Tashkent: TsSU Turkrespubliki, 1922.
V. L. Belenkii. *Biudzhet Bakinskogo Neftepromyshlennogo Rabochego v Nachale 1923 g.* Moscow, 1925.
L. P. Pushnova. *Biudzhety Leningradskikh Rabochikh i Sluzhashchikh v 1922–1926 gg.* Leningrad, 1927.
I. N. Dubinskaia. *Biudzhety Rabochikh Semei na Ukraine v 1925–1927 gg.* Kharkov, 1928.
I. Lipkes. *Godovye Biudzhety Kievskikh Rabochikh 1925–1926 gg.* Kiev, 1926.

F. Iu. Aleshina. "Izmeneniia Urovnia Zhizni Rabochikh Semei," in *Sotsiologiia v SSSR*, vol. 2. Moscow, 1965.

I. N. Dubinskaia. "Biudzhet Petrogradskikh Rabochikh." In *Materialy po Statistike Truda Severnoi Oblasti*, vol. 1. Petrograd, 1918.

S. G. Strumilin. "Prozhitochnyi Minimum i Zarabotki Chernorabochikh v Petrograde." In *Statistika Truda*, 1918, nos. 2–3.

———. "Pitanie Petrogradskikh Rabochikh v 1918." In *Novyi Put'*, 1919, nos. 4–5.

A. Stopani. "Biudzhet Moskovskogo Rabochego." In *Statistika Truda*, 1919, nos. 1–4 (10–13).

N. A. Filippova. "Pitanie Gorodskikh Rabochikh v 1918 g." *In Organizatsiia Truda*, 1921, no. 2.

E. O. Kabo. *Pitanie Russkogo Rabochego do i posle voiny*. Moscow, 1926.

Naemnyi Trud v Sel'skom Khoziaistve. Edited by S. G. Strumilin. Moscow, 1926.

TsSU. *Naemnyi Trud v Sel'skom i Lesnom Khoziaistve SSSR v 1926 g.* Moscow, 1928.

NK Trud. *Otkhod Sel'skogo Naseleniia na Zarabotki v SSSR v 1926–1927*. Moscow, 1929.

———. *Batrachestvo i Pastushestvo SSSR*. Moscow, 1929.

TsSU. *Sostoianie Pitaniia Sel'skogo Naseleniia SSSR*. Vols. 1–2. Moscow, 1926–28.

———. *Krestianskie Biudzhety 1922–1923 g. . . . 1925–1926 g.* Vols. 1–4. Moscow, 1923–29.

———. *Itogi Razrabotki Krestianskikh Biudzhetov v Gruppirovkakh po Dokhodu*. Moscow, 1930.

———. *Denezhnyi Oborot v Krestianskikh Khoziaistvakh po Mesiatsam*. Moscow, 1926.

———. *Denezhnyi Oborot v Krestianskikh Khoziaistvakh za 1927 g. po Mesiatsam*. Moscow, 1929.

———. *Denezhnyi Balans Krestianskikh Khoziaistv po Biudzhetnym Zapisiam za 1926/27 g.* Moscow, 1930.

Education

TsSU. *Narodnoe Obrazovanie po Osnovnomu Obsledovaniiu 1920 g.* Vols. 1–2. Moscow, 1922, 1924.

———. *Gramotnost' v Rossii (k X S'ezdu Sovietov)*. Moscow, 1922.

———. *Narodnoe Obrazovanie v SSSR po Dannym Tekushchikh Obsledovanii na 1 Ianvaria 1922, 1923 i 1924 gg.* Moscow, 1926.

———. *Narodnoe Obrazovanie v SSSR po Dannym Tekushchego Obsledovanii na 1 Ianvaria 1925 g.* Moscow, 1926.

———. *Narodnoe Obrazovanie SSSR v 1925–1927 Uchebnom Godu . . .* Moscow, 1927.

TsSU. *Narodnoe Prosveshchenie v SSSR*. Moscow, 1929.

Narodnyi Komissariat Prosveshcheniia RSFSR. *Narodnoe Prosveshchenie v RSFSR k . . . Uchebnomu Godu. 1923–24, 1925–26, 1926–27, 1927–28, 1928–29*. Moscow, 1925–30.

———. *Narodnoe Prosveshchenie v RSFSR. Statisticheskii Sbornik*. Moscow and Leningrad, 1928.

Gosplan. *Vseobshchee Obuchenie. Likvidatsiia Negramotnosti i Podgotovka Kadrov*. Moscow, 1930.

TsUNKhU. *Massovoe Prosveshchenie v SSSR k 15-letiiu Oktiabria.* Moscow and Leningrad, 1932.

————. *Massovoe Prosveshchenie v SSSR. K Itogam Pervoi Piatiletki.* Moscow and Leningrad, 1933.

————. *Kul'turnoe Stroitel'stvo SSSR, 1930–1934.* Moscow, 1935.

————. *Kul'turnoe Stroitel'stvo SSSR v Tsifrakh.* Moscow, 1936.

————. *Kul'turnoe Stroitel'stvo v SSSR.* Moscow and Leningrad, 1940.

TsSU. *Kul'turnoe Stroitel'stvo SSSR. Statisticheskii Sbornik.* Moscow, 1956.

Iatsinskii, N. F. *Knizhnaia Statistika SSSR, 1918–1923.* Moscow, 1925.

Vseoiuznaia Knizhnaia Palata: Tsifry o Pechati SSSR. Moscow, 1939.

Miscellaneous

NKZdrav. *Trudy Komissii po Obsledovaniiu Sanitarnykh Posledstvii Voiny 1914– 1920.* Moscow and Petrograd, 1923.

TsSU. *Aborty v 1925.* Moscow, 1927.

————. *Sostoianie Zdorovia Promyshlennykh Rabochikh i Sluzhashchikh.* Moscow, 1928.

TsUNKhU. *Zdorovie i Zdravookhranenie Trudiashchikhsia SSSR.* Moscow, 1936.

TsSU. *Prestupnost' i Samoubiistvo vo Vremia Voiny i Posle Nee.* Moscow, 1927.

————. *Samoubiistva v SSSR 1922–1925, v 1925 i 1926 gg.* Moscow, 1927, 1929.

NK Trud. *Piat' Let Gosudarstvennogo Strakhovaniia v SSSR, 1921–1922, 1925–1926.* Moscow, 1927.

NK Trud. *Svedeniia o Pozharakh v SSSR. Statisticheskie Tablitsy za . . . Operatsionnyi god, 1925, 1926, 1927.* Moscow, 1927–29.

TsSU. *Statistika Osuzhdennykh v SSSR v 1923–1924.* Moscow, 1927.

————. *Statistika Amnistirovannykh v Oznamenovanie Desiatiletiia Oktiabr'skoi Revoliutsii.* Moscow, 1928.

TsSU. *Itogi Perepisi Vladenii, Stroenii i Kvartir v Gorodakh i Poseleniakh Gorodskogo Tipa.* Vols. 1–3. Moscow, 1924–26.

Gosplan. *Rekonstruktsiia Gorodov SSSR, 1933–1937.* Vols. 1–2. Moscow, 1933–.

10

QUANTIFICATION IN LATIN AMERICAN
COLONIAL HISTORY

by John J. TePaske

Until recently, colonial Hispanic American historians have not been distinguished by their ardor for statistical studies. With a few outstanding exceptions, scholars in the field have not been prone to establish time series from raw data; to take a fresh look at traditional estimates for population, trade, or mining production; to make careful statistical analyses; or to argue historical trends or cycles on the basis of numerical data. Despite the richness of the documentation and the rewards of such work, Latin American colonialists have adhered to more conventional history based on conventional documentary sources—letters, reports, law cases, *residencias,* and the like.

Since World War II this emphasis has begun to change. In response both to the development of a vigorous group of Marxist and neo-Marxist interpreters and to the demonstrated need for reliable quantitative studies to advance interpretation, statistical works have begun to appear in an increasing number in Europe, Latin America, and the United States.[1] The necessity for such research has been argued by a number of scholars in the period since the war. One of the most eloquent appeals came from the Spanish medievalist, the late Jaime Vicens Vives. In the prologue to the second edition of his *Aproximación a la historia de España,* he took historians to task for perpetuating conventional history, to him a "historical jungle" characterized by a romantic foliage that obscured reality. Although recognizing that conventional history might have a rhetorical grandeur or brilliant intuitive insights, Vicens Vives argued that without solid grounding in numerical data for population, prices, wages, trade, industry, and other things which could be counted, history had no clarity, order, or objective reality. The material and spiritual values and priorities of a people or a nation could be documented only with such evidence. Historians failing to use it deprived themselves of one of their best working tools—a tool which could relieve history of its baroque obscurantism and allow it to emerge from the foggy realm of metaphysical speculation.[2]

These are strong words to those of us who wish to preserve history as one of the humanities. Clearly there are many kinds of history which make fundamental contributions to our understanding of the past. To give an overriding priority to quantitative studies is to open a Pandora's box of futile controversy. The purpose here is not to argue the preeminence of statistical research over conventional investigation but to assess the avenues open for research in quantifiable data for the colonial period in Latin America (1492–1810) and provide some guidelines for those who may wish to follow the injunctions of Vicens Vives.

In the past a number of factors mitigated against statistical analyses in colonial Hispanic American history. First, there was no systematic survey of the masses of data available for investigation. Except for statistical materials appearing in an occasional monograph, historians of the colonial epoch were not aware of the immense quantities and many types of raw statistical evidence reposing in the archives of Latin America and Europe. This fact alone has turned many a would-be quantifier to other topics or caused him to shift his focus to conventional types of documentation.

Another problem, at least until ten years ago, was the difficulty in handling large masses of numerical data. The investigator working with statistics often found himself bogged down in a morass of figures demanding an inordinate number of man-hours for meaningful analysis. Now, of course, the computer has resolved this problem. The precision and rapidity with which it can make calculations or store and record data from tape or cards are staggering in their implications. The computer can make correlations, draw graphs, and perform other operations formerly demanding immense amounts of time and effort. In fact, the machine's ramifications as a research tool are just now being realized.

A third impediment to statistical work on the colonial period of Latin America has been the type of historical training given in the field. Most of us were nurtured on a conventional curriculum geared to conventional history. Our preparation in fields outside history was limited to two languages and perhaps some Latin American literature, anthropology, political science, or economics. Without skills in statistical method or mathematics, we simply were not equipped to undertake more than the rudimentary kind of quantification. Now this has begun to change. Recognizing the advantages of computer research and the need for quantitative studies in history, some graduate departments have begun to encourage students to study computer techniques, statistics, economic and demographic analysis, and other subjects involving quantitative data.

A last obstacle to more statistical studies has been the long-standing disdain or rejection of social science by those historians studying Latin America who have preferred to remain in the tradition of William Hickling

Prescott as humanist-littérateurs. They have taken the stand that social science (the word *science* is anathema), statistical analysis, or counting of any sort drains humanity from history and relegates it to an inferior status.[3] But this barrier, too, has begun to crumble. The increased respectability of the social sciences taken up by a new breed of graduate student has changed the direction of historical research. This new student has turned in part to the social sciences to explain his own predicament in a society which he views as mechanistic and deterministic and in which he feels victimized and dehumanized. Yet, paradoxically, he is afflicted by a peculiar fascination for the infernal machine, the symbol of his dehumanization, and is determined to use it, even to the point of letting it determine the choice of his research topic.

DEVELOPMENT OF QUANTITATIVE STUDIES ON COLONIAL HISPANIC AMERICA

One of the contradictions of Latin American colonial history is the small amount of quantitative work carried on in the first half of the twentieth century, despite the tremendous achievements of the groundbreakers in the field, Clarence Haring and Earl J. Hamilton. Solidly based on statistical records from Spanish archives, Haring's works on trade and navigation, buccaneers, treasure, and the Spanish exchequer appeared in the second and third decades of this century and are still classics.[4] Even more detailed, Hamilton's contributions on American treasure and European prices began in the late 1920s and have served both historians and economists ever since.[5] His figures for the importation of American treasure to Europe and its effect on prices were long regarded as unassailable, although recently new research and new interpretations of the data have challenged and modified his findings.[6] The work of both Hamilton and Haring clearly demonstrated the rewards of quantification, yet, oddly enough, neither scholar left a train of younger followers in his wake committed to statistical study.[7] In fact, since 1945 the impetus for quantification in colonial Hispanic American history has come from those not directly influenced by either Haring or Hamilton.

For the sake of convenience, three "schools" can be isolated where use of quantifiable data and application of statistical techniques have gone on in earnest since World War II. One of these, to use Pierre Chaunu's term, is the Berkeley school. At that campus of the University of California, a group of scholars—historians, physiologists, litterateurs, geographers—have made significant breakthroughs in developing demographic patterns for colonial Mexico. Prior to World War II the work of Carl Sauer and Sherburne Cook hinted at the direction of research for the Berkeley school, but the most significant contributions—those of Woodrow Borah, Cook, Lesley Bird Simpson, and the others publishing in the Ibero-

Americana Series—have come since 1945.[8] Their scrupulous, critical reading of fiscal and religious records has permitted these historians to describe and document a demographic disaster for the indigenous population of central Mexico that had profound ramifications for the entire kingdom of New Spain.[9] At the same time, these Berkeley scholars provided detailed explanations of their methodology in dealing with the records, both as guides to researchers anxious to carry on similar work and as points of departure for those who might challenge their conclusions.[10]

The quantitative work on Mexican colonial demography has not been the only achievement of the Berkeley school, for its findings on population have been inextricably related to analysis of other aspects of colonial life. The school has begun developing what might be termed a historical ecology for colonial Mexico by carrying on research which complements and supports its demographic work. Simpson's studies of Indian labor, the *encomienda*, and landholding patterns are directly related to his research on Mexican colonial population.[11] The same is true of Cook's monographs on soil erosion, disease, epidemics, price trends, and ecology.[12] Borah's investigations of silk raising, the Mexican-Peruvian trade, and the seventeenth-century depression in New Spain have given a wider dimension to his research on demography as well. Recently Borah has suggested approaches for analyzing the worldwide effects of the New World demographic disaster.[13] To cast those of the Berkeley school primarily as quantifiers would be an oversimplification: their work in demography has opened up a great many other avenues of research as well. Also to their credit, they have not only carried on a dialogue with the scholarly community outside Berkeley, but they have also carried on a dialogue with one another, revising their population estimates whenever new research or new techniques have led to refinement of their earlier findings.[14]

A second group of scholars deeply committed to the use of quantifiable materials for colonial Latin America centers around Fernand Braudel, the journal *Annales: Économies, Sociétés, Civilisations,* and the VIe section of the École Pratique des Hautes Études in Paris. The most significant contribution of this group so far has been the work of Pierre and Huguette Chaunu, *Séville et l'Atlantique, 1504–1650.* In twelve volumes they have put together a wealth of statistics, charts, graphs, tables, and syntheses. Reconstructed from the *libros de registro* of the Casa de Contratación in Seville, their tables contain information on some 17,967 voyages of Spanish ships into the Atlantic—name and type of vessel, master, owner, tonnage, number in the crew, cargo, destination. Other tables list data on importation of slaves; slave ships; mercury shipments; mercury, silver, and gold production; and commodity trade statistics for such items as cochineal, indigo, dyewoods, sugar, spices, medicinal plants, and textile fibers. The Chaunus have also tallied the number and types of losses incurred by Spanish vessels in the Atlantic. In an attempt at synthesis, Pierre Chaunu develops cyclical patterns of boom and depression which make his statistics more meaningful. Unquestionably this is the most impressive work of quantification yet to appear in the colonial Latin American field, and the Chaunus have promised the same for Cádiz and the Atlantic from 1651 to 1800.

The awesome size and scope of these volumes should not cast a shadow over the achievements of other members of the French group. In content and methodology Frédéric Mauro's *Le Portugal et l'Atlantique au XVIIe siècle (1570–1670)* emulates the work of the Chaunus, although with one volume instead of twelve he has shown more restraint and selectivity. Jean-Pierre Berthe uses quantitative data in his study of New Spain, but he is not as prolific as some of his French colleagues.[15] In her work on Callao and Peruvian trade in the seventeenth century, Marie Helmer demonstrates the French school's reliance on, and sophistication in dealing with, numerical data.[16] Michèle Colin's monograph on Cuzco, 1680–1720, in no way measures up in data or interpretation to the other contributions of the French group, but its conclusions rely in large measure on statistical materials.[17] In sum the French school, like the Berkeley school, has made an indelible mark.

Still a third center for quantification, greatly influenced by the French, is located in Santiago, Chile, at the Centro de Investigaciones de Historia Americana, with Álvaro Jara and Rolando Mellafe of the University of Chile as its prime movers. Jara in economic history and Mellafe in ethnohistory have pioneered in the use of colonial statistics and have been training a new generation of Latin American students in their utilization. Jara's work on mining production in Peru has come to challenge the previously accepted figures of Earl Hamilton. The Chilean scholar has not only calculated gold and silver shipments to Spain on the basis of value rather than weight, but he has also used the Lima accounts (*cartas cuentas*) to revise Hamilton's estimates of the production of precious metals in Peru to 1660.[18] Mellafe's research has focused on Negro slavery, the relationship of mining and agriculture, social structure, and the coca trade, but his still unpublished study of Huánuco in the sixteenth century will be his most important contribution to date.[19] Using sources and methodology similar to those of the Berkeley school, Mellafe's findings will for the first time give us the demographic figures for comparison of the patterns of development in sixteenth-century Peru and New Spain.

To pick out three leading centers of research where quantifiable data are being used on a large scale is to ignore the many contributions of isolated scholars who have worked with statistics in the past. In the United States, Walter Howe. Clement Motten, and R. C. West use statistical materials in their work on Mexican mining.[20] Roland D. Hussey, in his monograph on the Caracas Company, relies in some measure on the financial records of that institution.[21] Robert S. Smith's articles, ranging over a variety of topics including shipping in the port of Vera Cruz, sales taxes in New Spain, and indigo production and prices in Guatemala, are all based on statistical evidence which he uncovered in archives in Latin America and Spain.[22] These works represent contributions of distinguished scholars in the United States to the field, yet contrasted with the Chaunu volumes they are limited in scope.

Until recently, historiography in Latin Ameria proper has not revealed a large number of scholars dedicated to statistical analysis. A few works, however, deserve mention. One of the most impressive is Guillermo Lohmann Villena's study of the mercury mine at Huancavelica with its tables of mercury production for the year 1579–1700.[23] García Chuecos used materials from accounts housed in the Archivo General de Venezuela for his study of the Venezuelan colonial treasury.[24] The statistics of Eduardo Arcila Farías and Manuel Moreyra Paz-Soldán are still other examples of quantitative work of an elementary nature.[25] And in view of his vigorous dispute with the Berkeley school, one cannot ignore the contributions of Ángel Rosenblat. He has spent virtually a lifetime devising population figures for colonial Latin America, but, unlike the Berkeley or Chilean scholars pursuing demographic studies, Rosenblat has not worked extensively or as critically with raw statistical data.[26]

To this list of more seasoned scholars might be added the names of younger investigators beginning to make their mark. Recently the German historian Günter Vollmer completed a thorough study of the population of Peru in 1792 which supersedes all previous estimates.[27] His current project is a demographic study of Puebla de los Angeles for the entire colonial period. For a number of years Peter Boyd-Bowman has been compiling exhaustive lists of Spanish immigrants to the New World, setting down information on them in much the same way as the Chaunus did for Spanish ships.[28]

In Spain, María Encarnación Rodríguez Vicente has directed a team of researchers who have just completed an analysis of the income and outgo of the treasury of Lima for the colonial period.[29] Her colleague, María Lourdes-Díaz Trechuelo Spinola, uses company accounts in a well-received study of the Royal Philippine Company.[30] This work reflects a trend toward quantification on the part of some scholars at the Escuela de Estudios Hispano Americanos. Antonio Domínguez Ortiz focuses his attention primarily upon Spanish history, but his quantitative studies of seventeenth-century Spanish economic policy and of mercury production provide new insights into problems in the Indies as well.[31] At the University of Barcelona, Pedro Voltes and his faculty in the Department of Economic History have also been active in this field.

In the United States, Dauril Alden has begun to break ground on the difficult problems of Brazilian demography; he proposes to use quantitative data for a study of the Jesuits in the New World.[32] Paul Hoffman of the University of Wyoming dissects sixteenth-century accounts in an effort to determine the efficiency or lack of efficiency with which Spain defended the Caribbean. The books of Peter Bakewell and David Brading on mining in colonial Mexico both have a quantitative base. David Cook has made new breakthroughs on Peruvian demography in the sixteenth century, and Bradley Benedict proposes to use numerical data for his study of the Jesuit *temporalidades*. Trent Brady and John Lombardi are using computers to analyze census data for the bishopric of Caracas from 1780 to 1820.[33] Henry Dobyns has also been active in the demographic field.[34] In his book on sixteenth-century Peru, James Lockhart suggests statistical work which might be carried on from notarial records.[35] Fred Bronner of the University of Jerusalem has studied the *union de armas* in Peru in the seventeenth century, and John Elliott has done the same for Spain.[36]

In Latin America, besides the Centro in Santiago, groups of quantifiers have been active in both Argentina and Mexico. In Argentina the leader has been the Instituto de Investigaciones Históricas of the Universidad del Litoral in Rosario, directed by Nicolás Sánchez-Albornoz. Quantitative research in Mexico has centered at El Colegio de México, where the results are just now being published. The recent work of Enrique Florescano on corn prices and agricultural crises in Mexico from 1708 to 1810 is a landmark.[37] The formation of the Comisión de Trabajo de Historia Económica of the Consejo Latinoamericano de Ciencias Sociales (CLACSO) in 1968 was a move to coordinate research in economic history and may well be a boon to quantitative history.

These examples in no way attempt a catalog of work presently under way, but they do suggest some of the types of quantitative research being undertaken, both at the three centers and by smaller groups of individuals on three continents. Now let us turn to possibilities for future research.

AVAILABLE DATA AND SUGGESTIONS FOR RESEARCH

To assess the utility of the raw numerical data available to the scholar in colonial Hispanic American history and to suggest ways to use them are overwhelming tasks. The Spanish were inveterate record keepers, perhaps even more inveterate and proficient than their modern counterparts in Latin America. The types of data still preserved vary in both quantity and quality. As the Chaunu study has so well demonstrated, all sorts of shipping statistics were scrupulously kept in the *libros de registro* of the Casa de Contratación, now reposing in the Archivo de Indias in Seville. For trade there are also figures for the shipping tax (*avería*) and import-export tax (*almojarifazgo*); accounts of the *consulado* (merchant guild); and records of the eighteenth-century monopolistic companies in Caracas, Manila, and Havana. Sales tax receipts kept by tax farmers like the *consulado* or by royal treasury officials could be developed into statistical series which would provide indexes to commercial activity in the major centers of the Spanish empire in

America. Records of specie coined in the Indies are extant for most colonial mints. The raw data for tax receipts from tithe and indulgence payments, tribute, and sale of offices may all be developed into time series for almost all areas of the empire. There were also accounts kept for the royal monopolies—snow, pulque, tobacco, stamped legal paper, and playing cards. Parish records, notarial records, censuses, and a host of other materials survive in published or manuscript form to testify to the work of the record keepers and the concern of administrative officials in Spain for the state of the Empire.

Spanish attempts to exercise tight control over the colonies led to a penchant for scrupulous accounting. Private sectors of economic life such as mining and trade were in many ways part of the public sector as well, scrutinized continually by authorities in Madrid and Seville demanding meticulous records of what was going on in the Indies. The very nature of Spanish imperial control probably makes it easier to reconstruct a statistically based picture for the Spanish empire than for the English colonies, where the private activities of merchants and storekeepers were not as much the business of His Majesty's Government.

One of the most fertile sources of raw statistical data on the economic status of the Spanish empire is the *carta cuenta* or account of income and outgo from the various *cajas* (treasuries) in the Indies. Each major area was divided into a number of fiscal districts where two treasury officials (*oficiales reales*), an accountant and a treasurer, tended to the business of collecting taxes and disbursing monies. (Major cajas like Lima or Mexico usually had more than two officials.) Lima, for example, had within its jurisdiction the cajas of Arequipa, Arica, Cailloma, Carabaya, Carangas, Castrovirreyna, Cuzco, Chachapoyas, Huamanga, Huancavelica, Jauja, Piura y Paita, Puerto de Callao, San Juan de Matacuna, Saña, Trujillo, Vico y Pasco, and Zipagura. Royal treasury officials in these areas kept accounts of income and outgo (*cargo* and *data*) and submitted yearly summaries to the royal officials and the Tribunal of Accounts in Lima for incorporation into the Lima summary and for auditing by the Tribunal.[38] In Peru prior to 1700 the Lima account was normally closed out at the time of the sailing of the Armada del Sur from Callao, sometimes every two or three years; after 1700 the accounts were compiled yearly. (Regional accounts were normally submitted yearly.)

A sample of income entries for the caja of Lima gives some idea of what may be found in a carta cuenta. It includes such items as the royal fifth payment (*quinto* or *diezmo*), the sums sent to Lima from the cajas outside the city (*venido de fuera*), encomienda tribute accruing to the crown (*tributos*), income from the sale of offices (*oficios*), a salary tax on civil officials and the clergy (*media anata* and *mesada*), port tax (*avería*), import-export tax (*almojarifazgo*), sales tax (*alcabala*), income from taxes on stores (*pulperías*), income from seizure of contraband goods (*comisos*), money from vacant clerical offices (*vacantes mayores* and *menores*), tax on the sale of stamped paper (*papel sellado*), and special income (*extraordinario*).

On the expense or *data* side of the ledger are entries for money sent to Spain (*remitido a España*); salaries of civil officials (*salarios*); war expenses (*guerra*); the subsidy for the mercury mine at Huancavelica (*Huancavelica*); expenses for wine and oil assigned to the religious (*limosnas*); monies freed for charitable and educational institutions (*situaciones y mercedes*); subsidies for the garrisons and fortifications at Valdivia, Panama City, and Concepción (Valdivia, Panama, and Chile); special expenses (*extraordinario*); and, less important, expenses for collecting assessments such as *oficios, media anata, comisos, vacantes,* and the like or the allocations made from these sources to pious works. All entries do not appear in every account for every year. During wartime, for example, there might be entries for donations (*donativos*) or for assessments made on the salaries of civil officials (*diez porciento de salarios*). But many of the entries occur in unbroken series for a 100- to 250-year period, with some having continuity from the sixteenth century to the Wars of Independence.

The possibilities for historical research are immediately obvious for analysis of trade and commerce, military activity, the church, mining, Indian policy, the bureaucracy, and many other topics. The fact that most accounts are broken down to indicate the individual paying or the amount paid to him is also significant. By making such a breakdown for the *quinto,* for example, one could approximate the income and economic status of miners for any area or period for which accounts are available. The same is true for the merchant's contribution to the sales tax, at least after it fell into the hands of royal treasury officials. On the data side, a breakdown of war expenses gives clues to the priorities Spanish officials placed on military and naval expenditures—ships, men, artillery, powder, naval stores, and forced labor on fortifications.

The difficulties in dealing with the cartas cuentas should not be underestimated. Entries were made in various types of money—*pesos ensayados, pesos de ocho, pesos de diez reales, ducados, pesos del oro, castellanos del oro* of different *quilates,* and so on ad infinitum. Bullion entries were made by weight in *marcos, granos,* and *onzas.* Values of money and bullion fluctuated greatly during the colonial period and present real problems in standardizing the figures, especially if one wishes to establish reliable time series from the sixteenth to the nineteenth century. Also, many entries were split or combined. For example, in the seventeenth century, income from vacant church offices appears only as *vacantes.* In the eighteenth century, income from vacant bishoprics and archbishoprics becomes *vacantes mayores;* that from lesser church offices, *vacantes menores.* In 1671 in Lima the *unión de armas* was combined with the *avería* and *alcabala.* Some taxes were farmed out, and the income from them remained constant over the period of the *asiento* or contract. Only through analysis of the tax farmer's records—if they are at all accurate—could one arrive at what was actually collected. At the end of the eighteenth century the introduction of double-entry book-keeping also compounds problems.

How complete are the accounts for the major areas of the Spanish empire, Peru, and Mexico? In her study of the Lima caja for the colonial period, María Encarnación Rodríguez is missing data for only three years, 1697–99.[39] For Mexico the problems are far greater, because fire has ravaged many accounts in the Contaduría section of the Archivo de Indias. However, a great many summaries are still legible, and perhaps Jean-Pierre Berthe, who has seen many of them, will salvage some evidence from these charred documents and uncover copies in Mexico of those illegible or missing.

The discussion above has focused primarily upon the opportunities and difficulties in working with the cartas cuentas for major areas of the empire— Peru and Mexico—but a vast number of accounts are extant for the various fiscal districts and corregimientos of the Spanish Indies. Regional accounts exist for the various cajas of Buenos Aires, Caracas, Cuba, Charcas, Chile, Filipinas, Guadalajara, Guatemala, Lima, Luisiana y Florida, Mexico, Panamá, Puerto Rico, Quito, Santa Fé de Bogotá, and Santo Domingo. Accounts for the multitude of corregimientos are not included in this list, but every corregidor or alcalde mayor was supposed to keep financial records, and many of these have survived. From these data it would be possible to develop time series for the areas outside the vital centers of Lima and Mexico and to make meaningful comparisons of economic patterns. For example, for Potosí, the important mining center in upper Peru, a number of accounts are in the Archivo de Indias and the Archivo Nacional, Sección Histórica, in Lima. Still others have been uncovered in Potosí, Sucre, and Buenos Aires.

At this stage it is not possible to estimate how many of these regional or corregimiento accounts have survived. A great number still exist in the Contaduría and Gobierno sections of the Archivo de Indias, but archives throughout Latin America house many more. A brief survey of a general guide to these repositories reveals that most have a royal treasury (real hacienda) section for the colonial period, or perhaps, as in Peru, a separate hacienda archive.[40] In Venezuela there are at least 3,000 volumes in the hacienda section of the Archivo General, most of which are account books. In Quito, the Archivo de la Corte Suprema de Justicia houses accounts for late 1586 and for the eighteenth century. In Lima both the Sección Histórica of the Archivo Nacional and the Archivo Histórico de Hacienda have accounts for various parts of Peru. Álvaro Jara has pointed out that the Archivo General de la Nación in Buenos Aires contains some 2,500 account books for the last half of the eighteenth century.[41] In sum, a concentrated search for such records may well reveal many more regional accounts than we now know of and enable us to develop statistical series for most regions of the empire.

While the cartas cuentas are important sources, other statistical materials are also available for research on a variety of economic topics. Year-by-year listings of the receipts for such items as the sales tax, tribute, tithe, sale of indulgences, stamped paper, pulque, or tobacco often appear in hacienda documents along with the cartas cuentas for the various regions. Officials of colonial mints recorded silver purchased and coined, although not always with the precision desired by administrators in Spain. The merchant guilds of Lima and Mexico kept accounts, as did those established late in the eighteenth century in Buenos Aires, Caracas, Cartagena, Guadalajara, Havana, Manila, Santiago de Chile, and Veracruz. A *consulado* expert points out that not only do these records contain trade statistics and tax collection information (when the *consulado* held the tax farm for the *alcabala*), but also that the documents give statements from individual merchants estimating their total assets. Unfortunately, like the regional cartas cuentas, these are scattered among various archives in Spain and Latin America.[42] The eighteenth-century monopolistic trading companies such as the Caracas, Havana, and Philippine companies also kept accounts of their operations; these show the kind and quantity of trade they carried on and the profitability of these enterprises for investors and the Crown. Annual figures for mercury production at Huancavelica, keys to the production of silver at Potosí and in Peru, have already been published by Guillermo Lohmann Villena, but accounts and reports in archives in Spain and Peru contain data for the eighteenth century to complete his figures. Statistics on land tenure might ultimately be ferreted out of notarial records for land sales, but this type of research demands the most painstaking efforts of a multitude of investigators before meaningful patterns emerge.

The amount of raw statistical data on economic matters for the colonial period in Latin America is staggering, and much needs to be done with the extant materials. True, the ravages of time, fire, natural calamities, and bureaucratic neglect have combined to destroy some documents and to obscure the location of others, but the amount that has survived is more impressive than that which is missing. Despite this wealth of evidence, however, there are gaps in statistical data which prevent more sophisticated analysis of the materials at hand. Perhaps the most gnawing problem is uncovering wage and price information for the establishment of reliable or even semireliable wage-price indexes. Earl Hamilton tried and failed to find such data in various areas of Latin America. Woodrow Borah and Sherburne F. Cook made an attempt to establish price trends in Mexico for a period in the sixteenth century; they and Ruggiero Romano have both pointed out the difficulties involved.[43] Only until this problem is resolved, either by discoveries of new data or by new theoretical constructs which will replace missing documentary evidence, can we use the available statistics to the best advantage.

Social statistics, particularly demographic data, are also plentiful for colonial Hispanic America. Broadly these are of two types—religious and civil documents. Religious records are made up of parish listings of baptisms, burials, and marriages; diocesan counts of population made at the request of the bishop or archbishop; and tithe collection accounts. Civil government records include fiscal counts made for tribute and tax collection or assessment of head taxes; nonfiscal administrative counts made for enrollment of men into the militia or for some other nonfiscal reason; and the census. For the Spanish and Portuguese empires, the census was an innovation of the Enlightenment and came in the last half of the eighteenth century.[44]

Obviously these different types of records demand different modes of analysis. Parish records, for example, require tedious counting that must also take into account the laziness, neglect, or peculiarities of the parish priests who originally kept them. To make estimates of village or regional population from such data is time-consuming. To this type of "microdata" should be added tribute lists and head counts. Diocesan population counts and censuses, however, are documents of a different sort, which give broad, more encompassing figures for larger areas. As Günter Vollmer has indicated, their reliability is often questionable, especially in the sixteenth and seventeenth centuries.[45] In such cases the Berkeley school has tried wherever possible to check the more inclusive census figures with microdata.[46] Where the differences are irreconcilable or inexplicable, the scholar must be discriminating. Fortunately the Berkeley scholars have given us some guidelines.

These demographic materials are scattered widely in various places in Spain and Hispanic America, perhaps even more widely than the economic materials.[47] Once again the Archivo de Indias and the national archives of the various Latin American republics make useful starting points, but from these one must turn to episcopal repositories, individual churches, or provincial archives, especially in countries where a church-state controversy has forced deposit of religious records in the hands of civil authorities. Raw demographic data and research activity are most scanty for the period 1600–1750. The conquest and early colonial epoch have attracted more attention from scholars than the Baroque epoch; for the late eighteenth century, fortunately, the investigator encounters more reliable source materials. Such a wide gap, however, makes it difficult to establish general patterns of economic or social development for land tenure, labor, Indian policy, mining, agriculture, and other important topics. We can only hope that new data and research will begin filling this 150-year gap.

Demographic research has resulted in vital historical controversy. Despite the careful work of the Berkeley school on Central Mexico and of Rolando Mellafe on Huánuco and David Cook on Peru, Ángel Rosenblat's figures still have defenders in the scholarly community. Perhaps controversy is inherent in the difficulties of using such documentary materials for evidence. The failure of some villages or parishes to report population figures, falsifications of lists by administrators or priests to cheat on tribute or tithe payments, loss or destruction of key records, scholars' inability to agree on the average size of a family, difficulties in extrapolation, and inconsistencies in reportage, even for the same census count, all challenge the scholar's ingenuity, integrity, and indefatigability and lay him open to criticism. There are those who would prefer to abandon documents for assessments made on the number of people the land could support at a given point in time or on dietary patterns—something, incidentally, which has interested the Berkeley school. Still, the debates initiated by the findings of that school and its adherents have been among the healthiest and most vigorous of many years in the colonial Latin American field.[48]

To conclude this discussion of the types of quantifiable materials extant for colonial Spanish America, a category might be established for random numerical data, consisting of numerical information from the periodic but irregular reports of civil and religious officials or of occasional visitors in the Indies. For example, letters or reports from colonial religious leaders often contained counts of convents, regular and secular clergy, parishes, missions, church ornaments, and the like. Military and civil officials all over the empire made periodic enumerations of garrison size, artillery, small arms, powder, ships, militia, stores, and a host of other items. Thus the religious records might trace, among other things, the growth or decline of the clerical establishment in certain areas of the empire, the secularization controversy, the growth or decline of mission efforts, and the accumulation of church wealth. In this vein, Michael P. Costeloe has studied the *Juzgado de Capellanías* to determine the extent of church wealth in the Archbishopric of Mexico.[49] From the military reports, a fairly accurate picture might be reconstructed of the defensive posture of Spain in the Indies. In other words, systematic collection, compilation, and comparison of the statistics from these isolated reports would be a further step toward laying down a more substantial numerical base for our studies of Spanish imperial affairs and institutions.

So far this discussion has focused on the Spanish empire in America, with little attention given to colonial Brazil. To assess the Portuguese records in the same way as the Spanish would be an immense task beyond my expertise, but perhaps a few generalizations, however risky, are warranted. Essentially quantitative materials available for research on colonial Brazil seem very similar to those already described in detail for Spanish America. This is clear from a survey of the work of a few contemporary quantifiers— Frédéric Mauro, Eulalia Maria Lahmeyer Lobo, and Manuel Nuñes Dias. All have demonstrated that statistical materials of the type encountered for the Spanish empire may be found in archives in Portugal and Brazil. For his work on Portugal and the Atlantic in the seventeenth century, Mauro consulted documents in some eleven archives in Lisbon; in archives in other Portuguese cities; in repositories in the Madeiras and the Azores; in

Brazilian archives in Bahia, Recife, Rio de Janeiro, and São Paulo; and, finally, in archives in France, Great Britain, Holland, Spain, and the United States. Trade statistics of the type developed by the Chaunus serve as the basis for Mauro's study and indicate the survival of a large amount of data for the Portuguese empire.[50] The same is true for sources used by Eulalia Maria Lahmeyer Lobo and Manuel Nuñes Dias.[51] For the demography of colonial Brazil, Dauril Alden has reviewed the resources available and reveals the existence of data similar to those for the Spanish empire. He points out that although sixteenth- and seventeenth-century materials are sparse, in the eighteenth century they are more extensive since the Portuguese began their census taking in Brazil about the same time the Spaniards did in the Indies.[52]

In some respects economic studies for Brazil seem a bit ahead of those for colonial Spanish America. This lead may come from the publication in 1937 of Roberto Simonsen's two-volume *História econômica do Brasil, 1500–1820*. Although these figures will be modified by further research, this work has provided a point of departure for Celso Furtado's analysis of the Brazilian colonial economy, which depends in large measure on Simonsen's tables for sugar production and mining.[53] A similar work for all Spanish America, Peru, or Mexico would go a long way toward defining research needs more clearly and opening the way for more analyses such as Furtado's for Brazil.

THE FUTURE OF QUANTITATIVE RESEARCH

Although this survey has touched all too briefly on the kinds and quality of numerical data available in the colonial Latin American field, a number of comments and suggestions seem appropriate as points of departure for the future. I would urge first a survey of available quantitative materials in manuscripts and published form. This might be done in stages—first the accounts and censuses for Peru and Mexico, followed by a catalog of statistical materials for less significant areas. For Peru and Mexico, the principal repositories like the Archivo de Indias have manuscript catalogs which reveal what is available. For other archives and the less important regions the task may be more difficult; nevertheless, this is the kind of information needed to move forward more intelligently with quantitative analysis. The young scholar desiring to undertake a study of Quito, for example, has no idea of what accounts are available or where they are located.

Scholars should also give attention to priorities. What sorts of quantitative materials would be most useful for established or aspiring scholars? If funds were available for putting either the accounts of Potosí or of Guadalajara on machine-readable tape, which should take precedence? I am under no illusion that there could be agreement over the priorities, but the important thing is that they be discussed. Once again primacy might be given to the vital centers of empire—Mexico and Peru. From these one could then move outward to accumulate data for New Granada and Buenos Aires, Potosí and Guadalajara, Guatemala and Venezuela, Chile and Panama, and so on. Another possibility would be to put all published materials in machine-readable form first, and only then establish priorities for manuscript materials.

This plea for the establishment of priorities is integrally tied to another suggestion for further activity—immediate establishment of a data bank. Perhaps it might resemble the Inter-University Consortium for Political Research at the University of Michigan, which makes all sorts of machine-readable data on the United States available to interested investigators. The same sort of arrangement could be set up either for Latin American colonialists or for Latin Americanists in general, since many researchers in all fields of Latin American studies are now using computerized data. Scholars, it is hoped, would contribute their data to the bank for processing as soon as (or, if possible, even before) their individual need for the data was fulfilled. Once authenticated and put into machine-readable form, these materials could be made available to all scholars. This should be done immediately with María Encarnación Rodríguez's study of the caja of Lima. The same is true for Chaunu's statistics, which, in book form, are not easily retrievable or workable. The data bank could become a virtually new archive for use by all interested scholars and provide a new dimension to the work of many.

There are, of course, a great many difficulties involved in setting up such a bank. First, it demands money for staff and operation. Second, materials must be meticulously checked before being opened to other investigators. Third, it will be difficult to persuade those investigators who have spent long hours compiling data to give them up. Like the *hacendados* they so often criticize in their lectures for retaining proprietary rights over their land, scholars are prone to assume proprietary rights over their research materials, and they are as tenacious as *hacendados* in retaining control. Fourth, the bank must clarify the assumptions under which data were collected. If an investigator sets up artificial accounting years differing from those of the manuscript records, this must be clarified. If his figures are reduced to one kind of currency such as *pesos de ocho* or *maravedís,* his conversion figures at given points in time for the various monies entered in the accounts must be pointed out. For this last problem, however, one might invoke the injunction of one quantifier concerning the collection and storing of certain types of data: "The rawer the better."

Establishment of a data bank has another concomitant: a training program for scholars in the use of quantifiable materials. I am inclined to suggest that this be resolved by individual institutions wherever possible rather than by a professional training center, especially since many universities now prepare graduate students and train faculty of an older generation in computer techniques and statistical analysis. However, the data bank directors might operate occasional training sessions. Periodic gatherings of quantifiers might also be useful. As new data are uncovered and new techniques for handling them are developed, scholars need to keep abreast of progress being made.

One can only be impressed by how much needs to be done with quantitative materials for the colonial period in Hispanic America. Other economic historians espousing what they call the "new history" are already propounding or disputing the virtues of counterfactual analysis (comparing what was with what might have been in quantifiable terms) or constructing models to fill in gaps when data are lacking. In the colonial Hispanic American field, however, we have only begun to collect and analyze the rich sources available to us, the first stage for the new economic historians. For counter-factual analysis—if indeed it has rewards—we have a long way to go.

One last word. Quantification is simply another way of getting at historical reality and should not become a fetish. There is a danger of quantifiers setting themselves up as a superior breed whose research has a far more solid basis than that of the traditional historians. This seems implicit in the views of Jaime Vicens Vives. But quantification is not an end in itself. It complements traditional research but can never replace it. In fact, quantitative analysis poses as many new historical problems as it resolves. If the work of the Chaunus has shown cycles of boom and recession, these cannot always be explained in terms of the statistics themselves but demand rigorous examination of conventional sources as well. Quantitative research alone gives no complete answers to vital historical questions; it provides only another important dimension to investigation. For either the quantifiers or those pursuing more conventional research to set themselves apart serves no useful purpose. The noisy claims of some quantifiers about the superiority of their methods and data have no place among scholars.[54] In the same vein the humanist has no reason to disdain those who use statistical data and program a computer. There is too much to do. All types of historical research should be wed in fruitful interdependence. Only through such a union can we have more precise, more enlightened interpretation and come closer to the truth.

NOTES

1   These will be discussed in detail later (see pp. 433–37).
2   Jaime Vicens Vives, *Approaches to the History of Spain,* trans. Joan Connelly Ullman (Berkeley and Los Angeles: University of California Press, 1967), pp. ix–xxv.
3   This attitude may be reflected by the comment of one distinguished Latin American historian. In a conversation I praised the research of two Latin American quantifiers whose work has received considerable attention. While admitting their contributions

to our understanding of the colonial epoch, he said perfunctorily: "They count too much to suit me."

4 Clarence Haring, *The Buccaneers in the West Indies in the XVII Century* (New York: Dutton, 1910); idem, *Trade and Navigation between Spain and the Indies in the Time of the Hapsburgs* (Cambridge, Mass.: Harvard University Press, 1918); idem, "American Gold and Silver Production in the First Half of the Sixteenth Century," *Quarterly Journal of Economics* 29 (May 1915): 433–74; idem, "The Early Spanish Colonial Exchequer," *American Historical Review* 23 (July 1918): 779–96; idem, "Ledgers of the Royal Treasurers in Spanish America in the Sixteenth Century," *Hispanic American Historical Review* 2 (May 1918): 173–87.

5 Earl J. Hamilton, *American Treasure and the Price Revolution in Spain, 1501–1650* (Cambridge, Mass.: Harvard University Press, 1934); idem, *El florecimiento del capitalismo y otros ensayos de historia económica* (Madrid: Revista de Occidente, 1948); idem, *Money, Prices, and Wages in Valencia, Aragon, and Navarre, 1351–1500* (Cambridge, Mass.: Harvard University Press, 1936). idem, *War and Prices in Spain, 1651–1800* (Cambridge, Mass.: Harvard University Press, 1947). Many of the following articles became part of Hamilton's books, but they deserve separate listing to demonstrate his evolution as a quantifier: "American Treasure and Andalusian Prices, 1503–1660," *Journal of Economic and Business History* 1 (Nov. 1928): 1–35; "American Treasure and the Rise of Capitalism, 1500–1700," *Economica* 9 (Nov. 1929): 338–57; "The Decline of Spain," *Economic History Review* 8 (May 1938): 168–79; "En periode de révolution économique. La monnaie en Castille, 1501–1660," *Annales d'Histoire Économique et Sociale,* nos. 14–15 (March–May 1932), pp. 1–24; "Imports of American Gold and Silver into Spain, 1503–1660," *Quarterly Journal of Economics* 43 (May 1929): 436–72; "The Role of Monopoly in the Overseas Expansion and Colonial Trade of Europe before 1800," *American Economic Review, Proceedings* 38 (May 1948): 35–53; "Wages and Subsistence on Spanish Treasure Ships," *Journal of Political Economy* 37 (Aug. 1929): 430–50.

6 Criticism of Hamilton's methods and interpretations may be sampled in P. Vilar, "Problems of the Formation of Capitalism," *Past and Present* 10 (1956): 15–35; Ingrid Hammarström, "The Price Revolution of the Sixteenth Century: Some Swedish Evidence," *Scandinavian Economic History Review* 5 (1957): 118–54; J. D. Gould, "The Price Revolution Reconsidered," *Economic History Review,* 2d ser. 17 (1964): 249–66; D. Felix, "Profit, Inflation, and Industrial Growth," *The Quarterly Journal of Economics* 70 (1956): 441–63; J. U. Nef, "Prices and Industrial Capitalism in France and England, 1540–1640," *Economic History Review* 7 (May 1937): 155–85.

7 Both Haring and Hamilton turned out some students pursuing statistical methods and using numerical data, but neither developed anything resembling a "school" such as that of Fernand Braudel in Paris.

8 See particularly Carl Sauer, *Aboriginal Population of Northwestern Mexico,* Ibero-Americana, 10 (Berkeley: University of California Press, 1935); Sherburne F. Cook, *The Extent and Significance of Disease among the Indians of Baja California, 1697–1773,* Ibero-Americana, 12 (Berkeley: University of California Press, 1937); idem, *Population Trends among the California Mission Indians,* Ibero-Americana, 17 (Berkeley and Los Angeles: University of California Press, 1940). Founded in 1932, the Ibero-Americana Series has served as the principal outlet for the Berkeley school's findings.

9 For the aboriginal population of central Mexico, their findings so far are as follows: 1519—25,200,000; 1532—16,800,000; 1548—6,300,000; 1568—2,650,000; 1580—1,900,000; 1595—1,375,000; 1605—1,075,000.

10 Sherburne F. Cook and Lesley Bird Simpson, *The Population of Central Mexico in the Sixteenth Century,* Ibero-Americana, 31 (Berkeley and Los Angeles: University of California Press, 1948); Woodrow Borah and S. F. Cook, *The Population of Central Mexico in 1548: An Analysis of the Suma de visitas de pueblos,* Ibero-Americana, 43 (Berkeley and Los Angeles: University of California Press, 1960); idem, *The Indian Population of Central Mexico, 1531–1610,* Ibero-Americana, 44 (Berkeley and Los Angeles: University of California Press, 1960); idem, *The Aboriginal Population of Central Mexico on the Eve of the Spanish Conquest,* Ibero-Americana, 45

(Berkeley and Los Angeles: University of California Press, 1963); idem, *The Population of the Mixteca Alta, 1520–1960,* Ibero-Americana, 50 (Berkeley and Los Angeles: University of California Press, 1968); S. F. Cook and Woodrow Borah, *Essays in Population History: Mexico and the Caribbean,* vol. 1 (Berkeley and Los Angeles: 1971).

11 Lesley Bird Simpson, *Studies in the Administration of the Indians in New Spain,* Ibero-Americana, 7 (Berkeley: University of California Press, 1934): vol. 1, *Law of Burgos,* vol. 2, *The Civil Congregation,* Ibero-Americana, 13 (Berkeley: University of California Press, 1938); vol. 3, *The Repartimiento System of Native Labor in New Spain and Guatemala,* Ibero-Americana, 16 (Berkeley and Los Angeles: University of California Press, 1940); vol. 4, *The Emancipation of the Indian Slaves and the Resettlement of the Freedmen, 1548–1553, Exploitation of Land in Central Mexico in the Sixteenth Century,* Ibero-Americana, 36 (Berkeley and Los Angeles: University of California Press, 1952). See also *The Encomienda in New Spain* (Berkeley and Los Angeles: University of California Press, 1966).

12 See n. 8 above; also Sherburne F. Cook, *The Conflict Between the California Indians and White Civilization,* Ibero-Americana, 21–24 (Berkeley and Los Angeles: University of California Press, 1943); idem, *The Historical Demography and Ecology of the Teolalpán,* Ibero-Americana, 33 (Berkeley and Los Angeles: University of California Press, 1949); idem, *Soil Erosion and the Population in Central Mexico,* Ibero-Americana, 34 (Berkeley and Los Angeles: University of California Press, 1949); Sherburne F. Cook and Woodrow Borah, *Price Trends of Some Basic Commodities in Central Mexico, 1531–1570,* Ibero-Americana, 40 (Berkeley and Los Angeles: University of California Press, 1958). Besides these contributions, Cook has written a host of articles. Some examples are "Demographic Consequences of European Contact with Primitive Peoples," *Annals of the American Academy of Political and Social Science* 237 (Jan. 1945): 107–11; "The Incidence and Significance of Disease among the Aztecs and Related Tribes," *Hispanic American Historical Review* 26 (Aug. 1946): 320–35; "Human Sacrifice and Warfare as Factors in the Demography of Pre-Colonial Mexico," *Human Biology* 18 (1946): 81–102.

13 See nn. 10–12 above; also Woodrow Borah, *Silk Raising in Colonial Mexico,* Ibero-Americana, 20 (Berkeley and Los Angeles: University of California Press, 1943); idem, *New Spain's Century of Depression,* Ibero-Americana, 35 (Berkeley and Los Angeles: University of California Press, 1951); idem, *Early Colonial Trade and Navigation between Mexico and Peru,* Ibero-Americana, 38 (Berkeley and Los Angeles: University of California Press, 1954); idem, "Social Welfare and Social Obligation in New Spain: A Tentative Assessment," *XXVI Congresso Internacional de Americanistas* (Seville, 1966), 4 : 45–57; idem, "América como modelo? El impacto demográfico de la expansión europeo sobre el mundo no europeo," *Cuadernos Americanos* 4 (Nov.–Dec. 1962): 176–85.

14 For an example of this type of dialogue resulting in revision of earlier estimates of aboriginal population, see W. Borah and S. F. Cook, *The Aboriginal Population of Central Mexico on the Eve of the Spanish Conquest,* Ibero-Americana, 45 (Berkeley and Los Angeles: University of California Press, 1963), pp. 1–5.

15 See Jean-Pierre Berthe, "El cultivo del 'pastel' en Nueva España," *Historia Mexicana* 9 (Jan.–March 1960): 340–67; idem, "Las minas del oro del Marqués del Valle en Tehuántepec, 1540–1547," *Historia Mexicana* 8 (July–Sept. 1958): 122–31.

16 See, for example, the following articles by Marie Helmer: "Le Callao, 1615–1618," *Jahrbuch für geschichte von Staat, Wirtschaft und Gesellschaft Lateinamerikas* 2 (1965): 145–95; "Economie et société au XVIIe siècle: *un cargador de Indias*," *Jahrbuch für geschichte von Staat, Wirtschaft und Gesellschaft Lateinamerikas* 4 (1967): 399–409; "La vie économique au XVIe siècle sur le haut plateau andin," *Travaux de l'Institut Français d'Études andines* 3 (1951): 115–50; "La visitación de los Yndios Chupachos: Inka et Encomendero," *Travaux de l'Institut Français d' Études andines* 5 (1955–56): 3–50.

17 Michèle Colin, *Le Cuzco à la fin du XVIIe et au début du XVIIIe siècle* (Paris: Institut des Hautes Études de l'Amérique Latine, 1966).

18 See the following works by Álvaro Jara: *Guerre et société au Chili. Essai de sociologie coloniale* (Paris: Institut des Hautes Études de l'Amérique Latine 1961); *Tres*

ensayos sobre economía minera hispanoamericana, Economía minera hispanoamericana, 1 (Santiago: Universidad De Chile, 1966); "Administración de los bienes y censos de las comunidades de indios," *Boletín de la Academia Chilena de la Historia* 58 (1958): 102–35; "Los asientos de trabajo y la provisión de mano de obra para los no-encomenderos en la ciudad de Santiago, 1586–1600," *Revista Chilena de Historia y Geografía* 125 (1957): 21–95; "La estructura económica de Chile durante el siglo XVI," *América Indígena* 20 (Jan. 1960): 53–62; "Importación de trabajadores indígenas en el siglo XVII," *Revista Chilena de Historia y Geografía* 124 (1958): 177–212; *El salario de los indios y los sesmos del oro en la tasa de Santillán* (Santiago: Universidad de Chile, 1961); "La producción de metales preciosos en el Perú en el siglo XVI," *Boletín de la Universidad de Chile* 44 (Nov. 1963): 58–64.

19   Mellafe's best known works are those on slavery. See Rolando Mellafe, *La esclavitud en Hispano América* (Buenos Aires: Eudeba Editorial Universitaria de Buenos Aires, 1964); idem, *La introducción de la esclavitud negra en Chile. Tráfico y rutas* (Santiago: La Universidad de Chile, 1959).

20   Walter Howe, *The Mining Guild of New Spain and its Tribunal General, 1770–1821* (Cambridge, Mass.: Harvard University Press, 1949); Clement Motten, *Mexican Silver and the Enlightenment* (Philadelphia: University of Pennsylvania Press, 1950); Robert C. West, *The Mining Community in Northern New Spain: The Parral Mining District,* Ibero-Americana, 30 (Berkeley and Los Angeles: University of California Press, 1949).

21   Roland D. Hussey, *The Caracas Company, 1728–1784: A Study in the History of Spanish Monopolistic Trade* (Cambridge, Mass.: Harvard University Press, 1934).

22   Robert S. Smith, *The Spanish Guild Merchant, A History of the Consulado, 1250–1700* (Durham, N.C.: Duke University Press, 1940); idem, "Datos estadísticos sobre el comercio de importación en el Perú en los años 1698 y 1699," *Revista Chilena de Historia y Geografía* 113 (1949): 162–77; idem, "Indigo Production and Trade in Colonial Guatemala," *Hispanic American Historical Review* 39 (May 1959): 181–211; idem, "Sales Taxes in New Spain, 1575–1770," *Hispanic American Historical Review* 28 (Feb. 1948): 2–37; idem, "Shipping in the Port of Veracruz, 1790–1821," *Hispanic American Historical Review* 23 (Feb. 1943): 5–20.

23   Guillermo Lohmann Villena, *Las minas de Huancavelica en los siglos XVI y XVII* (Seville: La Escuela de Estudios Hispano-Americanos, 1949).

24   Hector García Chuecos, *Hacienda colonial venezolana: contadores mayores e intendentes de ejército y real hacienda* (Caracas, 1949).

25   Eduardo Arcila Farías, *Comercio entre Venezuela y México en los siglos XVI y XVII* (Mexico: El Colegio de México, 1950); idem, *Economía colonial de Venezuela* (Mexico: Fondo de Cultura Mexicana, 1946); Manuel Moreyra Paz-Soldán, *Estudios sobre el tráfico marítimo en la época colonial* (Lima: Gil, 1944).

26   Ángel Rosenblat, *La población indígena de América desde 1492 hasta la actualidad* (Buenos Aires: Institución Cultural Española, 1945); idem, *La población indígena y el mestizaje en América,* 2 vols. (Buenos Aires: Editorial Nova, 1954); idem, *La población de América en 1492–viejos y nuevos cálculos* (Mexico: El Colegio de México, 1967).

27   Günter Vollmer, *Bevölkerungspolitik und Bevölkerungsstrucktur im Vize-konigreich Peru zur Ende der Kolonialzeit, 1741–1821* (Bad Homburg, Berlin, Zurich, Gehlen, 1967).

28   Peter Boyd-Bowman, *Índice geobiográfico de 40,000 pobladores de América en el siglo XVI,* vol. 1, *La época antillana, 1493–1519* (Bogotá: Instituto Caro y Cuevo, 1964), vol. 2, *1520–1539* (Mexico: Editorial Jus, 1968); idem, "La emigración peninsular a América, 1520–1539," *Historia Mexicana* 13 (Oct.–Dec. 1963): 165–92; idem, "Regional Origins of the Earliest Spanish Colonists of America," *Proceedings of the Modern Language Association* 71 (Dec. 1956): 1157–72.

29   Her findings have not as yet been published.

30   María Lourdes-Díaz Trechuelo Spinola, *La Real Compañía de Filipinas* (Seville: La Escuela de Estudios Hispano-Americanos, 1965).

31   Antonio Domínguez Ortiz, *Orto y ocaso de Sevilla: estudios sobre la prosperidad y decadencia de la cuidad durante los siglos XVI y XVII* (Seville: Junta de Patronato

de la Sección de Publicaciones de la Excma. Diputación Provincial, 1946); idem, *Política y hacienda de Felipe IV* (Madrid: Editorial de Derecho Financiero, 1960); idem, *La sociedad española en el siglo XVII* (Madrid: Consejo Superior de Investigaciones Científicas, 1963); idem, *La sociedad española en el siglo XVIII* (Madrid, 1955). Domínguez Ortiz's study of Almadén should appear in the near future.

32 Dauril Alden, "The Population of Brazil in the Late Eighteenth Century: A Preliminary Survey," *Hispanic American Historical Review* 43 (May 1963): 173–205.

33 Paul Hoffman, "The Computer and the Colonial Treasury Accounts: A Proposal for a Methodology," *Hispanic American Historical Review* 50 (1970): 731–40; Peter Bakewell, *Silver Mining and Society in Colonial Mexico: Zacatecas, 1546–1700* (Cambridge: Cambridge University Press, 1971); David Brading, *Mines and Merchants in Bourbon Mexico, 1763–1810* (Cambridge: Cambridge University Press, 1971). Trent Brady and John Lombardi kindly provided me with a mimeographed paper, "The Application of Computers to the Analysis of Census Data: The Bishopric of Caracas, 1780–1820: A Case Study" (1968).

34 Henry F. Dobyns, "Estimating Aboriginal American Population, I, An Appraisal of Techniques with a New Hemispheric Estimate," *Current Anthropology* 7 (Oct. 1966): 395–460; idem, "An Outline of Andean Epidemic History to 1720," *Bulletin of the History of Medicine* 38 (1963): 493–515.

35 James Lockhart, *Spanish Peru, 1532–1560: A Colonial Society* (Madison: University of Wisconsin Press, 1968).

36 Fred Bronner, "La union de armas en el Perú: Aspectos políticos-legales," *Anuario de Estudios Americanos* 14 (1967): 1133–76. See also John H. Elliott, *The Revolt of the Catalans: A Study in the Decline of Spain, 1598–1640* (Cambridge, 1963), pp. 204–08.

37 See particularly the *Anuario* of the Instituto, vols. 6 and 8 (1963, 1965). For the work of the scholars at El Colegio de México, see *Historia Mexicana* 17 (Jan.–March 1968) and also Enrique Florescano, *Precios del maiz y crisis agricolas en México, 1708–1810* (Mexico: El Colegio de México, 1969).

38 See Guillermo Céspedes del Castillo, "Reorganización de la hacienda virreinal peruana en el siglo XVIII," *Anuario de Historia del Derecho Español* 23 (1953): 329–69; Ismael Sánchez Bella, "La jurisdicción de hacienda en Indias (s. XVI y XVII)," ibid. 29 (1959): 1–50, 225–27; María Encarnación Rodríguez Vicente, "La contabilidad virreinal como fuente histórica," *Anuario de Estudios Americanos* 23 (1966): 1523–42.

39 In a conversation with me in 1968, María Encarnación Rodríguez indicated a ten-year gap in her data for 1690–99, but since then the carta cuenta for 1690–96 has turned up in a published source.

40 See the *Catálogo de la Sección Colonial del Archivo Histórico* (Lima: Imprenta Torres Aguirre, 1944). This is a catalogue for the archives of the Ministerio de Hacienda y Comercio, not the Archivo Nacional, Sección Histórica.

41 Álvaro Jara, *Tres ensayos sobre economia minera hispanoamericana,* Economía Minera Hispanoamericana, 1 (Santiago: Universidad de Chile, 1966), p. 99.

42 For information on the *consulado* accounts I am deeply indebted to Ralph Lee Woodward of Tulane University.

43 Woodrow Borah and Sherburne F. Cook, *Price Trends of Some Basic Commodities in Central Mexico, 1531–1570,* Ibero-Americana, 40 (Berkeley and Los Angeles: University of California Press, 1958); Ruggiero Romano, "Historia de los precios e historia colonial hispanoamericana," in *Temas de historia económica hispanoamericana"* (Paris and The Hague, 1965), pp. 11–21; idem, "Mouvement des prix et développement économique: L'Amérique du Sud au XVIIIᵉ siècle," *Annales. Economies Sociétés, Civilisations,* vol. 18, no. 1 (Jan.–Feb. 1963), pp. 63–74.

44 I am deeply indebted for a great deal of this discussion on demographic materials to Woodrow Borah. He kindly allowed me the use of a mimeographed paper: "The Historical Demography of Latin America: Sources, Techniques, Controversies, Yields" (1968). This has since been published in P. Deprez, ed., *Population and Economics* (Winnipeg: University of Manitoba Press, 1970), pp. 173–205.

45 In the summer of 1966, Vollmer informed me that he had made checks on the counts of 1591, 1615, and 1754 in Peru and found them unreliable.

46 See n. 10 above.

47 For the most part, accounts are located in official archives. Social statistics, however, are more widely scattered—in episcopal archives, churches, convents, and other semi-official or private repositories in addition to the official archives.

48 See, for example, the new book by Ángel Rosenblat, *La población de América en 1492—viejos y nuevos cálculos* (México: El Colegio de México, 1967); the review of this book by Bernardo García Martínez in *Historia Mexicana* 17 (July–Sept. 1967): 147–52; and Bailey Diffie's review of Charles Gibson's *Spain in America* in *American Historical Review* 72 (April 1967): 1068–69.

49 Michael P. Costeloe, *Church Wealth in Mexico: A Study of the 'Juzgado de Capellanías' in the Archbishopric of Mexico, 1800–1856* (Cambridge: Cambridge University Press, 1967).

50 Frédéric Mauro, *Le Portugal et l'Atlantique au XVIIᵉ siècle, 1570–1670*, Ports-Routes-Trafics, 10 (Paris: SEVPEN, 1960).

51 Eulalia Maria Lahmeyer Lobo, *Aspectos da atuacão dos Consulados de Sevilha, Cádiz e da América Hispanica na evolucão economica do século xviii* (Rio de Janeiro, 1965); idem., "As frotas do Brasil," in *Jahrbuch für Geschichte von Staat, Wirtschaft und Gesellschaft Lateinamerikas* 4 (1967): 465–88; Manuel Nuñes Dias, "Fomento e mercantilismo: política portugesa na Baixada Maranhense, 1775–1778," in *Jahrbuch für Geschichte von Staat, Wirtschaft und Gesellschaft Lateinamerikas* 2 (1965): 257–334.

52 See n. 32 above.

53 Celso Furtado, *The Economic Growth of Brazil: A Survey from Colonial to Modern Times*, trans. Ricardo W. de Aguiar and Eric Charles Drysdale (Berkeley and Los Angeles: University of California Press, 1965).

54 In his excellent review of the Chaunu volumes in *Journal of Economic History* 22 (June 1962): 253–59, Robert S. Smith points out a number of these pretentions, particularly the six-decimal figure for the average time of a voyage from Spain to the Indies.

BIBLIOGRAPHY

This is a selective bibliography, aimed primarily at providing a guide to secondary sources useful for those working with quantitative materials for the colonial period in Latin America. Some references are to model studies using statistical data; others give essential background material to complement statistical analysis. I have not included archival guides for the colonial period, which are listed elsewhere, but I would particularly recommend Lino Gómez Canedo's *Los archivos de la historia de América*, vol. 1, *Periódo colonial español* (Mexico: Instituto Panamericano de Geografía y Historia 1961); and Arthur E. Gropp's, "Bibliografía de fuentes archivisticas relacionadas con Ibero-América. Catálogos, guias, índices, inventarios, listas, y publicaciones periódicas," *Anuario de Estudios Americanos* 12 (1965): 919–73. The latter contains 389 entries of significant guides and bibliographical aids to archives for colonial Latin America. I have also omitted published documents containing quantitative data.

ABBREVIATIONS

AESC   *Annales. Economies, Sociétés, Civilisations*

AEA   *Anuario de Estudios Americanos*

AIIH   *Anuario de Instituto de Investigaciones Históricas* (University of Litoral, Rosario, Argentina)

BACH   *Boletín de la Academia Chilena de Historia.*

BAGN   *Boletín del Archivo General de Nación* (Mexico)
HAHR   *Hispanic American Historical Review*
  HM   *Historia Mexicana*
MAMH   *Memorias de la Academia Mexicana de la Historia*
PMLA   *Publications. Modern Language Association*
RCHG   *Revista Chilena de Historia y Geografía*
RANP   *Revista del Archivo Nacional de Perú*
 RHA   *Revista de Historia de América*
  RI   *Revista de Indias*
  TE   *El Trimestre Económico*

GENERAL WORKS

Arcila Farías, Eduardo. *Economía colonial de Venezuela.* Mexico: Fondo de Cultura Económica, 1946.

Arellano Moreno, A. *Origines de la economía venezolana.* Caracas: Ediciones Edimes, 1960.

Bagú, S. *Economía de la sociedad colonial. Ensayo de historia comparada de América Latina.* Buenos Aires: El Ateneo, 1949.

Brito Figuero, Federico. *La estructura económica de Venezuela colonial.* Caracas: Instituto de Investigaciones, Universidad Central de Venezuela, 1963.

Carrera Pujal, Jaime. *Historia de la economía española.* 5 vols. Barcelona: Bosch, 1943–47.

Colin, Michèle. *Le Cuzco à la fin du XVII et au début du XVIIIᵉ siècle.* Paris: Institut des Hautes Études de l'Amérique Latine, 1966.

Colmeiro, M. *Historia de la economía política en España.* 2 vols. Madrid: Taurus, 1965.

Diffie, B. *Latin American Civilization: The Colonial Period.* Harrisburg, Pa.: Stackpole Sons, 1945.

Ely, R. T. *La economía cubana entre las dos Isabeles, 1492–1832* Bogotá: Aedita Editores Ltda., 1962.

Friedlander, H. E. *Historia económica de Cuba.* Havana: J. Montero, 1944.

Gibson, Charles. *The Aztecs under Spanish Rule: A History of the Indians of the Valley of Mexico, 1519–1810.* Stanford: Stanford University Press, 1964.

————. *Tlaxcala in the Sixteenth Century.* New Haven: Yale University Press, 1952.

Gómez de Cervantes, G. *La vida económica y social de Nueva España al finalizar el siglo XVI.* Mexico: Antigua Librería Robredo de J. Porrua e Hijos, 1944.

Haring, C. *The Spanish Empire in America.* New York: Oxford University Press, 1947.

Humboldt, Alexander von. *Political Essay on the Kingdom of New Spain.* 4 vols. London: Longman, Hurst, Rees, Orme, and Brown, 1811–22.

Humphreys, R. A. "Economic Aspects of the Fall of the Spanish American Empire." *RHA,* no. 30 (1950), pp. 450–56.

Levene, R. *Investigaciones acerca de la historia económica del virreinato del Plata.* 2 vols. La Plata: El Ateneo, 1928.

Levillier, R., ed. *Antecedentes de la política económica del Río de la Plata.* 2 vols. Madrid: Tip, "Sucesores de Rivadeneyra," 1915.

Mauro, Frédéric. "México y Brasil: Dos economías coloniales comparadas." *HM* 10 (1961): 571–587.

Parry, J. H. *The Spanish Seaborne Empire.* New York: Knopf, 1966.

Peñaloza, L. *Historia económica de Bolivia.* 2 vols. La Paz, 1953–54.

Pérez G., Juan de. "Situación estadística de Yucatán en 1581." *BAGN* 19 (1948): 399–463; 20 (1949): 127–86, 277–300.

Relaciones estadísticas de la Nueva España de principios de siglo xix. Mexico, 1944.

Sayous, André E. "Les changes de l'Espagne sur l'Amérique au XVIᵉ siècle." *Revue d'Economie Politique,* 41ᵉ année (1927): 1417–43.

Vargas Ugarte, R. "Cuadros estadísticos de los siglos XVIII y XIX." *Boletín de la Sociedad Geográfica de Lima* 71 (1954): 3–17.

Veitia Linaje, José de. *Norte de la contratación de las Indias Occidentales.* Buenos Aires: Comisión Argentina de Fomento Interamericano, 1945.

Vicens Vives, Jamie, ed. *Historia social y económica de España y América.* Vol. 3, *Imperio. Aristocracia. Absolutismo,* by Juan Regla and G. Céspedes Castillo. Barcelona: Editorial Teide, 1957. Vol. 4, *Burguesia. Industrialización,* by J. Mercader, A. Domínguez, and M. Hernández Sánchez-Barba. Barcelona: Editorial Teide, 1958.

Vicens Vives, Jaime. *Manual de historia económica de España.* Barcelona: Editorial Vicens-Vives, 1965.

TRADE AND NAVIGATION

Anuario de Estudios Americanos 25 (1968).

Arcila Farías, E. *Comercio entre Venezuela y México en los siglos XVII y XVIII.* Mexico: El Colegio de México, 1950.

———. "Nueva España en la economía monetaría venezolana." *TE* 15 (1948): 243–71.

———. *El siglo ilustrado en América: reformas económicas del siglo XVIII en Nueva España.* Caracas: Ediciones del Ministerio de Educación, 1955.

Artiñano y de Galdácano, G. de. *Historia del comercio con las Indias durante el dominio de los Austrias.* Barcelona: Talleres de Oliva de Villa Nueva, 1917.

Báncora Cañero, C. "Las remesas de metales preciosas desde El Callao a España en la primera mitad del siglo XVII." *RI* 19 (1959): 35–88.

Bennassar, B. "Facteurs sévillans au XVIᵉ siècle d'après des lettres marchandes." *AESC,* 12ᵉ année (1957): 60–70.

Bernal, Rafael. "México en Filipinas." *HM* 14 (1964): 187–205.

Bernard, G. "La Casa de la Contratación de Sevilla, luego en Cádiz en el siglo XVIII." *AEA* 12 (1955): 253–86.

Borah, W. *Early Colonial Trade and Navigation between Mexico and Peru.* Ibero-Americana, 38. Berkeley and Los Angeles: University of California Press, 1954.

Bromley, Juan. "El Callao, puerto de Lima, 1535–1637." *Revista Histórica* 26 (1962–63): 7–76.

Brown, V. L. "Contraband Trade: A Factor in the Decline of Spain's Empire in America." *HAHR* 8 (1928): 178–89.

Carrera Stampa, M. "Le nao de la China." *HM* 9 (1959): 97–118.

Castro y Bravo, F. *Las naos españolas en la carerra de Indias. Armadas y flotas en la segunda mitad del siglo XVI.* Madrid: Editorial Voluntad, 1927.

Céspedes del Castillo, G. "Lima y Buenos Aires. Repercusiones económicas y políticas de la creación del virreinato de la Plata." *AEA* 3 (1946): 677–874.

Chaunu, Pierre. "Le galion de Manille." *AESC*, 6ᵉ année (1951): 447–62.

———. "Manille et Macao face à la conjuncture des XVIᵉ et XVIIᵉ siècles." *AESC*, 17ᵉ année (1962): 555–80.

———. "Navigation espagnole en Atlantique." *AESC*, 12 année (1957): 71–72.

———. *Les Philippines et le Pacifique des Ibériques (XVI, XVIIᵉ, XVIIIᵉ siècles). Introduction méthodologique et indices d'activité.* Ports-Routes-Trafics, 11. Paris: École Pratique des Hautes Études, VIᵉ section, 1960.

———. "Veracruz en la segunda mitad del siglo XVI y primera del XVII. *HM* 9 (1960): 521–57.

———, and Chaunu, Huguette. "Autour de 1640: politiques et économies atlantiques." *AESC*, 9 année (1954): 44–45.

———. *Séville et l'Atlantique.* 8 vols. in 11, plus *Construction graphique.* Ports-Routes-Trafics, 6. Paris: Colin, 1955–60.

Chevalier, F. "Les cargaisons des flottes de la Nouvelle Espagne vers 1600." *RI* 4 (1943): 323–330.

Christelow, A. "Contraband Trade between Jamaica and the Spanish Main." *HAHR* 22 (1942): 309–43.

Cushner, N. P. "Merchants and Missionaries: A Theologian's View of Clerical Involvement in the Galleon Trade." *HAHR* 47 (1967): 360–69.

Dahlgren, E. W. *Les rélations commerciales entre la France et les côtes de l'océan Pacifique (commencement du XVIIIᵉ siècle).* Vol. 1, *Le commerce de la Mer du Sud jusqu'à la paix d'Utrecht.* Paris: H. Champion, 1909.

Díaz Arenas, Rafael. *Memorias históricas y estadísticas de Filipinas.* Manila: Imprenta del Diario de Manila, 1850.

Díaz-Trechuelo, M. L. "El comercio de Filipinas durante la segunda mitad del siglo XVIII." *RI* 23 (1963): 463–85.

———. "Dos nuevos derroteros del galeón de Manila, 1730–1773." *AEA* 13 (1956): 1–83.

Domínguez Ortiz, A. *Orto y ocaso de Sevilla: Estudio sobre la prosperidad y decadencia de la ciudad durante los siglos XVI y XVII.* Sevilla: Junta de Patronato de la Sección de Publicaciones de la Excma. Diputación Provincial, 1956.

Florescano, Sergio. "La política mercantilista española y sus implicaciones económicas en la Nueva España." *HM* 17 (1968): 455–68.

Garcilla, Policarpo. *Los primeros mercaderios en Chile 1535–1600.* Santiago, 1918.

Girard, Albert. *Le commerce français à Séville et Cadix au temps des Habsbourg. Contribution à l'étude du commerce étranger en Espagne aux XVIᵉ et XVIIᵉ siècles.* Paris: E. de Boccard, 1932.

———. *La rivalité commerciale et maritime entre Séville et Cadix jusqu'à la fin du XVIIIᵉ siècle.* Paris: E. de Boccard, 1932.

Gortari, H. de y Palacios, G. "El comercio novohispano a través de Veracruz, 1802–1810. *HM* 17 (1968): 427–54.

Haring, C. *Trade and Navigation between Spain and the Indies in the Time of the Hapsburgs.* Cambridge, Mass.: Harvard University Press, 1918.

Helmer, Marie. "Le Callao, 1615–1618." In *Jahrbuch für Geschichte von Staat, Wirtschaft und Gesellschaft Lateinamerikas* 2 (1965): 145–95.

————. "Économie et société au XVIIᵉ siècle: *un cargador de Indias.*" In *Jahrbuch für Geschichte von Staat, Wirtschaft und Gesellschaft Lateinamerikas* 4 (1967): 399–409.

Jara, A. "Estructuras de colonización y modalidades del tráfico surhispanoamericano." In *Historia y Cultura: Tres Estudios.* Lima: Museo Nacional de Historia, 1966.

King, James F. "Evolution of the Free Slave Trade Principle in Spanish Colonial Administration." *HAHR* 22 (1942): 34–56.

Kroeber, Clifton. *The Growth of the Shipping Industry in the Rio de la Plata Region, 1794–1860.* Madison: University of Wisconsin Press, 1957.

Lafuente Machain, R. *Los portugeses en Buenos Aires (siglo XVII).* Madrid: Tipografía de Archivos, 1931.

Loosley, A. C. "The Puerto Bello Fairs." *HAHR* 13 (1933): 314–35.

López-Portillo y Weber, J. "El comercio y los caminos en la época colonial." *MAMH* 11 (1952): 84–108.

Lorente Rodrigañez, L. M. "El galeón de Manila." *RI* 5 (1944): 105–20.

MacLachlan, J. O. *Trade and Peace with Old Spain, 1667–1750. A Study of the Influence of Commerce on Anglo-Spanish Diplomacy in the First Half of the Eighteenth Century.* Cambridge: The University Press, 1940.

Manfredini, James M. J. D. "Algunas observaciones sobre el primer comercio de España en América." *MAMH* 3 (1944): 92–112.

Mateu y Llopis, F. "Navios ingleses en el puerto de Vera Cruz en 1762." *RI* 4 (1943): 683–707.

Molina, R. A. "Una historia desconicida sobre los navios de registro arribados a Buenos Aires en el siglo XVII." *Historia* 16 (1959): 11–100.

Morales Padrón, F. "Canarias y Sevilla en el comercio con América." *AEA* 9 (1952): 173–207.

————. *El comercio canario americano (siglos XVI, XVII, XVIII).* Seville: La Escuela de Estudios Hispano-Americanos, 1945.

Moreno, Laudelino. *Los estranjeros y el ejercicio del comercio en Indias.* Madrid: Compañía Ibero-Americana de Publicaciones, 1936.

Moreyra Paz-Soldán, M. *Estudios sobre el tráfico marítimo en la época colonial.* Lima: Gil, 1944.

Muñoz Pérez, José. "El comercio de Indias bajo los Austrias y la crítica del proyectismo del XVI." *AEA* 13 (1956): 85–103.

————. "El comercio de Indias bajo los Austrias y las tratadistas españoles del siglo XVII." *RI* 17 (1957): 209–22.

————. "La publicación del Reglamento de Comercio Libre a Indias de 1778." *AEA* 4 (1947): 615–64.

Nelson, G. H. "Contraband Trade under the Asiento, 1730–1739." *AHR* 51 (1945): 55–67.

Otte, Enrique. "Mercaderes burgaleses en los inicios del comercio con México." *HM* 18 (1968): 108–44.

Pantaleão, Olga. *A pentracão comercial de Inglaterra na América espanhola de de 1713 a 1783.* São Paulo: Universidade Faculdade de Filosofia, Ciências e Letras, 1946.

Pereyra, C. "El Guadalquivir en la historia de América." *RI* 1 (1940): 15–34.

Pereza de Ayala, José. *El régimen comercial de Canarias con las Indias en los siglos XVI, XVII, y XVIII.* La Laguna, 1952.

Pérez Guilhou, M. H. "El comercio rioplatense del siglo XVII." *Historia* 5 (1959): 10–24.

Pérez Tudela, J. *Las armadas de Indias y los origines de la política de colonización, 1498–1505.* Madrid, 1956.

Pike, R. *Enterprise and Adventure: The Genoese in Seville and the Opening of the New World.* Ithaca: Cornell University Press, 1966.

Pulido Rubio, J. *El piloto mayor de la Casa de la Contratación de Sevilla. Pilotos mayores del siglo XVI (datos biográficos).* Seville: Tip Zarzuela, 1923.

Rahola y Trémols, F. *Comercio de Cataluña con América en el siglo XVIII.* Barcelona: Artes Gráficas, S.A., 1931.

Romero, F. "The Slave Trade and the Negro in South America." *HAHR* 24 (1944): 368–86.

Romero Solano, Luis. "La Nueva España y las Filipinas." *HM* 3 (1954): 420–31.

Ross, Agustín. *Reseña histórica del comercio de Chile durante la era colonial.* Santiago, 1894.

Rubio Mañé, J. I. "Egresos de caudales por el puerto de Veracruz, 1784–1804." *BAGN* 25 (1954): 469–518, 661–701; 26 (1955): 53–90, 259–91, 457–86, 665–85; 27 (1956): 101–64.

———. "Necesidades y precios en el mercado de Vera Cruz, año de 1800." *BAGN* 30 (1959): 473–86.

Sayous, André E. "Les débuts du commerce de l'Espagne avec l'Amérique, 1503–1518." *Revue Historique* 174 (1934): 185–215.

Schurz, Wm. L. *The Manila Galleon.* New York: Dutton, 1939.

Silva Herzog, J. "El comercio de México durante la época colonial." *Memoria de El Colegio Nacional* 3 (1956): 43–73.

Smith, Robert S. "Datos estadísticos sobre el comercio de importación en el Perú en los años 1698 y 1699." *RCHG,* no. 113 (1949), pp. 162–77.

———. "Shipping in the Port of Veracruz, 1790–1821." *HAHR* 23 (1943): 5–20.

Szasdi de Nagy, Adam. "El comercio ilícito en la provincia de Honduras." *RI* 17 1957): 271–83.

Torre Revello, José. "Merchandise Brought to America by the Spaniards, 1534–1586." *HAHR* 23 (1943): 273–81.

———. "Puertos habilitados en España en el siglo XVI para comerciar con las Indias Occidentales." *Humanidades* 25 (1936): 353–62.

Usher, A. P. "Spanish Ships and Shipping in the XVIth and XVIIth Century." In *Facts and Factors in Economic History,* pp. 189–213. Cambridge, Mass.: Harvard University Press, 1932.

Velásquez, María del C. "La navegación transpacífica." *HM* 18 (1968): 159–78.

Verlinden, Charles. "Modalités et méthodes du commerce dans l'Empire espagnol au XVI siècle." *RI* 12 (1952): 249–76.

Vignols, Léon. "El asiento francés (1701–1713) e inglés (1713–1750) y el comercio franco-español desde 1700 hasta 1730. Con dos memoriales francescas de 1728 sobre estos asientos." *Anuario de Historia del Derecho Español* 5 (1928): 266–300.

———, and Sée, Henri. "La fin du commerce enterlope français dans l'Amerique espagnole." *Revue d'Histoire Economique et Sociale,* XIII année (1929): 300–13.

Villalobos R., Sergio. "El comercio extranjero a fines de la dominación española." *Journal of Inter American Studies* 4 (1962): 517–44.

————. *Comercio y contrabando en el Río de la Plata y Chile, 1700–1811.* Buenos Aires: Editorial Universitaria de Buenos Aires, 1965.

————. "Contrabando francés en el Pacífico." *RHA,* no. 51 (1961), pp. 49–80.

————. *Tradición y reforma en 1810.* Santiago: Ediciones de la Universidad de Chile, 1961.

TRADING COMPANIES

Amétaga Aresi, Vicente D. *Hombres de la Compañía Guipuzcoana.* Caracas, 1963.

Arcila Farías, E. *El Real Consulado de Caracas.* Caracas: Instituto de Estudios Hispanoamericanos, 1957.

Barras de Aragón, F. "Las sociedades económicas en Indias." *AEA* 12 (1955): 417–47.

Basterra, Ramón de. *Una empresa del siglo XVIII. Los navios de la ilustración. Real Compañía Guipuzcoana de Caracas y su influencia en los destinos de América.* Caracas: Imprenta Bolívar, 1925.

Caplán, Benedicto. "La institución del consulado colonial." *Anuario del Instituto de Derecho Público* 1 (1938): 427–64.

Díaz-Trechuelo, M. L. *La Real Compañía de Filipinas.* Sevilla: La Escuela de Estudios Hispano-Americanos, 1965.

Guice, C. N. "The Consulado of New Spain, 1594–1795." Ph.D. dissertation, University of California, Berkeley, 1952.

Hoff, Hellmut. *Der Niedergang des Konsulats der Kaufleute in der Stadt Mexiko, 1778–1827.* Hamburg, 1955.

Hussey, R. D. "Antecedents of the Spanish Monopolistic Trading Companies, 1624–1728." *HAHR* 9 (1929): 1–30.

————. *The Caracas Company, 1728–1784.* Cambridge: Harvard University Press, 1934.

Lobo, E. M. L. *Aspectos da atuação dos consulados de Sevilha, Cádiz e da América Hispânica na evolução econômica do século XVIII.* Rio de Janeiro, 1965.

Malca Olguin, O. "Gobierno Colonial: Tribunal Mayor del Consulado de la Ciudad de los Reyes." *RANP* 20 (1956): 3–41; 21 (1957): 3–47.

————. "Ordenanzas para el gobierno del Consulado y comercio de Chile." *RANP* 21 (1957): 282–99; 22 (1958): 56–84.

Moreyra Paz-Soldán, M. *El Tribunal del Consulado de Lima.* Vol. 1, *1706–1720;* vol. 2 *1721–1727.* Lima: Publicaciones del Instituto Histórico del Perú, 1956–59.

————. *El Tribunal del Consulado de Lima: sus antecedentes y fundación.* Lima, 1950.

Olguin Mosqueda, S. "El consulado de Guadalajara." *HM* 3 (1953): 127–28.

Pacheco Velez, C. "El Tribunal del Consulado de Lima y la emancipación del Perú." *Cuadernos de Información Bibliográfica* 1 (1957): 6–14.

Ramírez Flores, J. *El Real Consulado de Guadalajara: Notas históricas.* Guadalajara, 1952.

Rodríguez Vicente, M. E. *El Tribunal del Consulado de Lima en la primera mitad del siglo XVII.* Madrid: Ediciones Cultura Hispánica, 1960.

Sayous, André E. "Partnership in the Trade between Spain and America and also in the Spanish Colonies in the Sixteenth Century." *Journal of Economic and Business History* 1 (1929): 282–301.

Schurz, W. L. "The Royal Philippine Company." *HAHR* 3 (1920): 491–508.

Shafer, R. J. *The Economic Societies in the Spanish World, 1763–1821.* Syracuse: Syracuse University Press, 1958.

Smith, R. S. "Antecedentes del Consulado de México, 1590–1594." *RHA,* no. 15 (1942), pp. 299–313.

———. "The Consulado in Santa Fe de Bogotá." *HAHR* 45 (1965): 442–51.

———. "The Institution of the Consulado in New Spain." *HAHR* 24 (1964): 61–83.

———. "Origins of the Consulado of Guatemala." *HAHR* 16 (1946): 150–61.

———. "A Research Report on Consulado History." *Journal of Inter-American Studies* 3 (1961): 41–52.

———. *The Spanish Guild Merchant: A History of the Consulado, 1250–1700.* Durham, N.C.: Duke University Press, 1940.

Soraluce y Zubizarreta, N. de. *Historia de la Real Compañía Guipuscoana de Caracas.* Madrid, 1875.

Vargas Ugarte, R. "Informe del Tribunal del Consulado de Lima, 1790." *Revista Histórica* 22 (1955–56): 266–335.

Villalobos, R. Sergio. *La justicia comercial en el Reino de Chile: notas para su estudio.* Santiago, 1955.

Woodward, R. L., Jr. *Class Privilege and Economic Development: The Consulado de Comercio of Guatemala, 1793–1871.* Chapel Hill, N.C.: University of North Carolina Press, 1966.

FINANCE, TAXATION, ACCOUNTING, CROWN REVENUE

Acevedo, E. O. "Los impuestos al comercio cuyano en el siglo XVIII, 1700–1750." *RCHG* 126 (1958): 34–76; 131 (1963): 75–120.

Aiton, A. S. "Real Hacienda in New Spain under the First Viceroy." *HAHR* 6 (1926): 232–45.

Bermúdez Plata, Cristobal. "Contratos sobre fabricación de naipes en Nueva España." *AEA* 2 (1945): 717–22.

Borah, Woodrow. "The Collection of Tithes in the Bishopric of Oaxaca during the Sixteenth Century." *HAHR* 21 (1941): 386–409.

———. "Tithe Collection in the Bishopric of Oaxaca, 1601–1867." *HAHR* 29 (1949): 498–517.

Bronner, F. "La union de armas en el Perú. Aspectos políticos-legales." *AEA* 14 (1967): 1133–76.

Carande, Ramón. *Carlos V y sus banqueros.* 2 vols. Madrid: Revista de Occidente, 1943, 1949.

Céspedes del Castillo, G. "La renta de tobaco en el virreinato de Perú." *Revista Histórica* 21 (1954): 138–63.

———. "Reorganización de la hacienda virreinal peruana en el siglo XVIII." *Anuario de Historia del Derecho Español* 23 (1953): 329–69.

———. "La avería en el comercio de Indias." *AEA* 2 (1945): 515–698.

Chonuigote, Nicolás. "La derrama del Cuzco." *Revista Histórica* 14 (1941): 297–304.

Chuecos, H. García. *Hacienda colonial venezolana. Contadores mayores e intendentes de ejército y real hacienda.* Caracas, 1946.

Cordoncillo, J. M. "La real lotería en Nueva España." *AEA* 18 (1961): 193–331.

Costeloe, Michael P. "The Administration, Collection, and Distribution of Tithes in the Archbishopric of Mexico, 1800–1860." *The Americas 23* (1966): 3–27.

———. *Church Wealth in Mexico: A Study of the 'Juzgado de Capellanías' in the Archbishopric of Mexico, 1800–1856.* Cambridge: Cambridge University Press, 1967.

Cuello Martinell, M. A. "La renta de los naipes en Nueva España." *AEA* 12 (1965): 231–335.

Cruchaga, M. *Estudio sobre la organización económica y la hacienda pública de Chile.* Madrid: Editorial Reus, 1929.

Domínguez Ortiz, A. "Los caudales de Indias y la política exterior de Felipe IV." *AEA* 13 (1956): 311–83.

"El papel sellado." *BAGN* 2 (1931): 327–28.

Emeth, Omar. "El libro de cuentas de un negrero en 1621." *RCHG*, no. 10 (1913), pp. 274–86.

Fonseca, Fabian de, and Urrutia, Carlos de. *Historia general de la real hacienda.* 6 vols. Mexico: Imprenta por V. G. Torres, 1845–53.

Gallardo y Fernández, F. *Origen, progreso y estado de las rentas de la corona de España, su gobierno y administración.* 7 vols. Madrid: Imprenta Real, 1805–08.

Góngora, Mario. "Los 'Hombres Ricos' de Santiago y La Serena a través de las cuentas del quinto real." *RCHG*, no. 131 (1963), pp. 23–46.

Guzmán Lozano, E. "Breve historia de las alcabalas en México." *Jus* 10 (1943): 17–62; 11 (1943): 21–41.

Haring, C. "Ledgers of the Royal Treasurers in Spanish America in the Sixteenth Century." *HAHR* 2 (1919): 173–87.

Kroeber, C. B. "The Mobilization of Philip II's Revenue in Peru, 1590–1596." *Economic History Review,* 2d ser. 10 (1958): 439–49.

Hoffman, P. "The Computer and the Colonial Treasury Accounts: A Proposal for a Methodology." *HAHR* 50 (1970): 731–40.

———, and Lyons, E. "Accounts of the Real Hacienda, Florida, 1565 to 1602." *Florida Historical Quarterly* 48 (1969): 57–69.

Lira González, Andrés. "Aspecto fiscal de la Nueva España en la segunda mitad del siglo XVIII." *HM* 17 (1968): 361–94.

Maniau, J. *Compendio de la historia de la real hacienda de la Nueva España.* Mexico: Imprenta de la Secretaría de Industria y Comercio, 1914.

Mariscal Romero, P. "Los bancos de rescate de Platas." *AEA* 20 (1963): 313–97.

Molina, E. "La hacienda pública durante la época colonial." *RCHG* 1 (1911): 648–56; 2 (1916): 68–81.

Moreyra Paz-Soldán, M. "Cartas y un informe sobre el Tribunal Mayor de Cuentas del virrey Marqués de Montesclaros." *Revista Histórica* 18 (1949): 311–30.

———. "Valor histórico de los libros de contabilidad haciendaría colonial." *Revista Histórica* 22 (1955–56): 311–55.

Moxo, Salvador de. *La alcabala. Sobre sus origines, concepto, y naturaleza.* Madrid: Consejo Superior de Investigaciones Científicas, 1963.

Palacio Atard, V. "La incorporación a la corona del Banco de Rescates de Potosí." *AEA* 2 (1945): 723–38.

Parry, J. H. *The Sale of Public Offices in the Spanish Indies under the Hapsburgs.*

Ibero-Americana, 37. Berkeley and Los Angeles: University of California Press, 1953.

Ramírez Cabañas, J. *Mercedes y pensiones, limosnas, y salarios en la Real Hacienda de la Nueva España.* Mexico, 1945.

Ramírez Díaz, L. "El Tribunal y Real Audiencia de Cuentas. Los origines en Castilla y el Tribunal de Cuentas del Perú." *Revista Histórica* 27 (1964): 352–92.

Rodríguez, María Encarnación. "Los caudales remitidos desde el Perú a España por cuenta de la real hacienda. Series estadísticas, 1651–1739. *AEA* 21 (1964): 1–24.

―――. "La contabilidad virreinal como fuente histórica." *AEA* 23 (1966): 1523–42.

―――. "Una quiebra bancaria en el Perú del siglo XVIII." *Anuario de Historia del Derecho Español* 26 (1956): 707–39.

Romero, Emilio. *Historia económica y financiera del Perú. Antiguo Perú y Virreynato.* Lima: Imprenta Torres Aguirre, 1937.

Rumeu de Armas, A. *Historia de la previsión social en España. Cofradías, gremios, hermandades, montepios.* Madrid: Editorial Revista de Derecho Privado, 1944.

Sánchez Bella, I. "La jurisdicción de hacienda en Indias (*s.xvi y xvii*)." *Anuario de Historia del Derecho Español* 29 (1959): 176–227.

―――. *La organización financiera de las Indias. Siglo XVI.* Sevilla: La Escuela de Estudios Hispano-Americanos, 1968.

Santos Martínez, P. "Reforma a la contabilidad colonial en el siglo XVIII (El método de partido doble)." *AEA* 17 (1960): 525–36.

Smith, Robert S. "Sales Taxes in New Spain, 1575–1770." *HAHR* 28 (1948): 2–37.

Stapff, Agnes. "La renta del tobaco en el Chile de la época virreinal." *AEA* 18 (1961): 1–63.

Ulloa, Modesto. *La hacienda real de Castilla en el reinado de Felipe II.* Rome: Libreria Sforzini, 1963.

Werner, Theodor Gustav. "Europäisches Kapital in iberoamerikanischen Montanunternehmen des 16. Jahrhunderts." *Vierteljahrschrift für Sozial-und Wirtschaftsgeschichte,* no. 48 (1961), 18–55.

Wright, Irene A. "Rescates: With Special Reference to Cuba, 1599–1610." *HAHR* 3 (1920): 333–61.

PRICES AND WAGES

Borah, Woodrow. *New Spain's Century of Depression.* Ibero-Americana, 35. Berkeley and Los Angeles: University of California Press, 1951.

―――, and Cook, Sherburne F. *Price Trends of Some Basic Commodities in Central Mexico, 1531–1570.* Ibero-Americana, 40. Berkeley and Los Angeles: University of California Press, 1958.

Carmagnani, Marcello. *El salario minero en Chile colonial: su desarollo en una sociedad provincial: El Norte Chico, 1690–1800.* Santiago: Centro de Historia Colonial, 1963.

Florescano, E. "La historia de los precios en la época colonial de Hispanoamérica: Tendencias, métodos de trabajo, y objectivos." *Latinoamerica. Anuario Estudios Latinoamericanos* 1 (1968): 111–29.

―――. *Precios del maiz y crisis agricolas en México, 1708–1810.* Mexico: El Colegio de México, 1969.

Gould, J. D. "The Price Revolution Reconsidered." *Economic History Review,* n.s. 17 (1964): 249–66.

Hamilton, Earl J. *American Treasure and the Price Revolution in Spain, 1501–1650.* Cambridge, Mass.: Harvard University Press, 1934.

——. "Monetary Problems in Spain and Spanish America, 1751–1800." *Journal of Economic History* 4 (1944): 21–48.

——. "Use and Misuse of Price History." *Journal of Economic History* 5 (1944): 47–60.

——. *War and Prices in Spain, 1651–1800.* Cambridge, Mass.: Harvard University Press, 1947.

Lohmann Villena, G. "Apuntaciones sobre los precios en la Lima del siglo XVI." *Revista Histórica* 29 (1966): 79–104.

Nadal, Jorge. "La revolución de los precios españoles en el siglo XVI. Estado actual de la cuestión." *Hispania* 75 (1959): 504–29.

Romano, Ruggiero. "Historia de los precios en historia colonial hispanoamericana." In *Temas de historia económica hispanomericana.* Paris, 1966.

——. "Movimiento de los precios y desarrollo económico: El caso de Sudamérica en el siglo XVIII." *Desarrollo Económico* 3 (1963): 31–55.

COINAGE AND MINTS

"Acunación de monedas en los últimos años de la colonia, 1805–1814." *BAGN* 6 (1935): 276–304.

Aiton, A. S., and Wheeler, B. "The First American Mint." *HAHR* 11 (1931): 198–215.

Álvarez, Juan. *Valores aproximadas de algunas monedas hispanoamericanas, 1497–1777.* Buenos Aires: Talleres Gráficos del Ministerio de Agricultura de la Nación, 1917.

Burzio, Humberto. *La ceca de la Villa Imperial de Potosí y la moneda colonial.* Buenos Aires: Peuser, S.A., 1945.

——. *Diccionario de la moneda hispanoamericana.* 3 vols. Santiago: Fondo Histórico y Bibliográfico José Toribio Medina, 1956–58.

——. "La moneda de la tierra y de cuenta en el régimen monetario colonial hispano-americano." *Boletín de la Real Academia de la Historia* 124 (1949): 201–08.

——. "El oficio de ensayador en América en el período hispánico." *Numisma* 2 (1952): 65–77.

——. "El peso de oro hispanoamericano." *Historia* 4 (1956): 9–24.

——. "El 'peso de plata' hispanomericano," *Historia* 3 (1958): 21–52.

Carbo, L. A. *La historia monetaria y cambiaria del Ecuador desde la época colonial.* Quito, 1953.

Carrera Stampa, M. "The Evolution of Weights and Measures in New Spain." Translated by R. S. Smith. *HAHR* 29 (1949): 2–24.

Domingo Figuerola, L. "Contribución al estudio de la ceca de Potosí." *Numisma* 7 (1957): 47–65.

Domínguez Ortiz, A. "La falsificación de moneda peruana a mediados del siglo XVII." In *Homenaje a D. Ramón Carande.* Madrid: Sociedad de Estudios y Publicaciones, 1963.

García Martínez, B. "El sistema monetario de los últimos años del período novohispano." *HM* 17 (1968): 349–60.

García Ruiz, Alfonso. "La moneda y otros medios de cambio en la Zacatecas colonial." *HM* 4 (1954): 20–46.

Heiss, Aloiss. *Descripción general de las monedas hispano-cristianas.* 3 vols. Madrid: R. N. Milagro, 1865–69.

Jara, Álvaro, "Dans le Pérou du XVIᵉ siècle: la courbe de production des métaux monnayables." *AESC*, 22 année (1967): 590–603.

Lluis y Navis-Brusi, J. "La falsificación de moneda ante las Leyes de Indias." *Numisma* 7 (1957): 41–70.

Luengo Muñoz, Manuel. "Sumaria noción de las monedas de Castilla e Indias en el siglo XVI." *AEA* 7 (1950): 325–66.

Mateu y Llopis, Felipe. "La creación de la moneda americana por Carlos V." *Boletín de la I Exposición Iberoamericana de Numismática y Medallística*, no. 3 (1958), pp. 51–55.

————. *La moneda española.* Barcelona: Editorial Alberto Martín, 1946.

Meek, Wilbur T. *The Exchange Media of Colonial Mexico.* New York: King's Crown Press, 1948.

Moll, Bruno. *La moneda.* Lima: Librería Internacional del Perú, 1949.

Moreyra Paz-Soldán, M. *Apuntes sobre la historia de la moneda colonial en el Perú. El reglamento de la casa de moneda de 1755.* Lima, 1938.

————. *Los quintos reales y las pragmáticas secretas sobre la moneda.* Lima, 1953.

————. "La técnica de la moneda colonial. Unidades, pesos, medidas y relaciones." *RHA*, no. 20 (1945), p. 347–67.

————. "La tesorería de la Casa de Moneda de Lima bajo juro de heredad y comprada por los Condes de San Juan de Lurigancho." *Revista Histórica* 15 (1942): 106–42.

————. "La tesorería y estadística de acuñación colonial en la casa de moneda de Lima." *Universidad Católica del Perú. Instituto de Investigaciones Históricas. Cuadernos de Estudios*, vol. 2, no. 4, pp. 3–56.

Nesmith, R. S. *The Coinage of the First Mint of the Americas at Mexico City, 1536–1572.* New York: American Numismatic Society, 1955.

Ortiz Mena, Raúl. *La moneda mexicana.* Mexico: Editorial América, 1942.

Pradeau, A. F. "Esquema del número aproximado de monedas mexicanas." *Numisma* 7 (1957): 61–64.

————. *Historia numismática de México desde la época precortesiana hasta 1823.* México: Banco de México, 1950.

————, ed. *Don Antonio de Mendoza y la Casa de la Moneda de México en 1543.* México: Antigua Librería Robredo, 1953.

Quintana, Miguel A. *Los ensayos monetarios como consequencia de la baja de la plata.* México: Imprenta Galas, 1931.

Rubio Mañé, J. I. "Acuñación de oro y plata, 1733–1791." *BAGN* 17 (1946): 491–501.

Sánchez Pérez, P. "Leyes de la moneda de oro y plata desde la fundación de la casa de moneda en la Nueva España, 1536 hasta 1947." *Memorias de la Academia de la Historia* 18 (1959): 383–401.

Sayous, André E. "La circulation de métaux et de monnaies au Pérou pendant le XVIᵉ siècle." *Revue d'Économie Politique*, 42ᵉ année (1928): 1300–17.

————. "Les procédés de paiement de la monnaie dans l'Amérique espagnole pendant la première moitié du XVIe siècle." *Revue Économique Internationale* 4 (19e année): 271–304.

Stuardo Ortiz, Carlos, and Eyzaguirre Escobar, Juan. "Las primeras monedas de cobre que circulan legalmente en Chile." *Numisma* 3 (1953): 43–52.

Zavala, Silvio. "Apuntes históricos sobre la moneda del Paraguay." *TE* 13 (1946): 126–43.

MINING

Bakewell, P. *Silver Mining and Society in Colonial Mexico: Zacatecas, 1546–1700.* Cambridge: Cambridge University Press, 1971.

Bargallo, M. *La minería y la metalurgia en la América Española durante la época colonial.* México: Fondo de Cultura Económica, 1955.

Brading, D. A. "La minería de la plata en el siglo XVIII: El caso Bolaños." *HM* 18 (1969): 317–33.

————. "Mexican Silver Mining in the Eighteenth Century: The Revival of Zacatecas." *HAHR* 50 (1970): 665–81.

————. *Mines and Merchants in Bourbon Mexico, 1763–1810.* Cambridge: Cambridge University Press, 1971.

Cobb, G. "Supply and Transportation for the Potosí Mines, 1545–1640." *HAHR* 29 (1949): 25–45.

Crespo Rodas, A. "La fundación de la villa y asientos de minas de Oruro." *Revista Histórica* 29 (1966): 304–26.

Diffie, B. W. "Estimates of Potosí Mineral Production, 1545–1555." *HAHR* 19 (1940): 275–82.

Floyd, Troy S. "Bourbon Palliatives and the Central American Mining Industry, 1765–1800." *The Americas* 18 (1961): 103–27.

Friede, Juan. "La introducción de mineros alemanes en América por la Compañia Welser de Augsburgo." *BANH* 44 (1961): 286–91.

Garces G., J. A. *Las minas de Zamora. Cuentas de la Real Hacienda.* Quito, 1957.

Hamilton, Earl J. "Imports of American Gold and Silver into Spain, 1503–1660." *The Quarterly Journal of Economics* 43 (1929): 436–72.

Hanke, Lewis. *The Imperial City of Potosí. An Unwritten Chapter in the History of Spanish America.* The Hague: Nijhoff, 1956.

Haring, C. H. "American Gold and Silver Production in the First Half of the Sixteenth Century." *The Quarterly Journal of Economics* 29 (1915): 433–79.

Helmer, M. "Edelmetalle Perus in der Kolonialzeit." *Saeculum* 13 (1962): 293–300.

Howe, Walter. *The Mining Guild of New Spain and its Tribunal General, 1770–1821.* Cambridge, Mass.: Harvard University Press, 1949.

Iglesia y Auset, Francisco de la. *Los caudales de Indias en la primera mitad del siglo XVI.* Madrid, 1904.

Jara, Álvaro. "La producción de metales preciosos en el Perú en el siglo XVI." *Boletín de la Universidad de Chile,* no. 44 (1963), pp. 58–64.

————. *Tres ensayos sobre economía minera hispanoamericana.* Economía Minera Hispanoamericana, 1. Santiago: Universidad de Chile, 1966.

Lang, M. F. "Martín López and the Chilapa Quicksilver Mines, 1658–1670." *RHA* 69 (1970): 41–62.

————. "New Spain's Mining Depression and the Supply of Quicksilver from Peru, 1600–1700." *HAHR* 40 (1968): 632–41.

Lohmann Villena, G. *Las minas de Huancavelica en los siglos XVI y XVII*. Seville: La Escuela de Estudios Hispano-Americanos, 1949.

Matilla Tascón, A. *Historia de las minas de Almadén*. Vol. 1, *Desde la época romana hasta el año 1645*. Madrid: Gráficas Osca, 1958.

Miró, Luis. "Bartolomé de Medina, Introductor del beneficio de patio en Nueva España." *HM* 13 (1964): 517–31.

Moreno, A. M. "La explotación minera del valle del Supia en el siglo XVIII." *RI* 3 (1942): 117–26.

Moreyra Paz-Soldán, M. "En torno a dos valiosos documentos sobre Potosí." *Revista Histórica* 20 (1953): 161–236.

Motten, C. G. *Mexican Silver and the Enlightenment*. Philadelphia: University of Pennsylvania Press, 1950.

Nordenskiöld, E. *Sydamerika. Kampen om guld och silver, 1498–1600*. Uppsala: J. A. Lindblad, 1919.

Palacio Atard, V. "El asiento de la mina de Huancavelica en 1779." *RI* 5 (1944): 611–30.

Probert, A. "Bartolomé de Medina: The Patio Process and the Sixteenth-Century Silver Crisis." *Journal of the West* 8 (1969): 90–124.

Restrepo, V. *Estudio sobre las minas de oro y plata de Colombia*. Bogotá: Imprenta de Silvestre y Compañía, 1888.

Rodríguez Casado, V. "Huancavelica en el siglo XVIII." *RI* 2 (1941): 83–92.

Soetbeer, A. *Edelmetall-produktion und Werthverhältniss zwischen Gold und Silver seit der Entdeckung Amerika's bis zur Gegenwart*. Gotha: J. Perthes, 1879.

Tomayo, J. L. "La minería de Nueva España en 1794." *TE* 10 (1943): 287–319.

Velarde, Carlos E. *Historia del derecho de minería hispano americano*. Buenos Aires: Talleres Gráficos Argentinos de L. J. Rosso y Cia., 1919.

Wagner, H. R. "Early Silver Mining in New Spain." *RHA*, no. 14 (1942), pp. 49–71.

West, R. C. *Colonial Placer Mining in Colombia*. Baton Rouge: Louisiana State University Press, 1942.

————. *The Mining Community of Northern New Spain: The Parral Mining District*. Ibero-Americana, 30. Berkeley and Los Angeles: University of California Press, 1949.

Whitaker, A. P. "The Elhuyar Mining Missions and the Enlightenment." *HAHR* 31 (1951): 557–85.

————. *The Huancavelica Mercury Mine*. Cambridge: Harvard University Press, 1941.

AGRICULTURE, GRAZING, INDUSTRY

Anderson, L. *El arte de la platería en México*. Mexico: Editorial Porrua, 1956.

Barros Arana, D. *Riquezas de los antiguos jesuitas de Chile*. Santiago: Imprenta de O. L. Tornero, 1872.

Barrett, W. *The Sugar Hacienda of the Marqueses del Valle*. Minneapolis: University of Minnesota Press, 1970.

Bazant, J. "Evolución de la industria textil poblana, 1554–1845." *HM* 13 (1964): 473–516.

Beltrán, Román. "Primeras casas de fundición." *HM* 1 (1952): 372–94.

Bermúdez Miral, O. "La polvora durante la colonia." *RCHG* 130 (1962): 116–56.

Berthe, Jean Pierre. "Sur l'histoire sucrière américaine." *AESC*, 1ᵉ année (1959), 135–41.

Borah, Woodrow. *Silk Raising in Colonial Mexico.* Ibero-Americana, 20. Berkeley and Los Angeles: University of California Press, 1943.

Bruman, H. J. "Early Coconut Culture in Western Mexico." *HAHR* 25 (1945): 212–23.

Cappa, Ricardo. *Estudios críticos de la dominación española en América.* Vols. 7–10. Madrid: G. del Amo, 1889–97.

Carrera Stampa, M. "Las ferias novohispanos." *HM* 2 (1953): 319–42.

Chávez Orozco, Luis. *Breve historia agrícola de México en la época colonial.* Mexico, 1958.

Coni, Emilio A. *Agricultura, comercio, e industria coloniales (siglo XVI–XVIII).* Buenos Aires: El Ateneo, 1941.

Cosío Villegas, D. "El comercio de azúcar en el siglo XVI." *TE* 5 (1938): 571–85.

Dusenberry, W. H. "Ordinance of the Mesta in New Spain, 1537." *The Americas* 4 (1948): 345–50.

———. "Woolen Manufacture in Sixteenth-Century New Spain." *The Americas* 4 (1947): 223–34.

Febres Villaroel, O. "La crisis agricola en el Perú en el último tercio del siglo XVIII." *Revista Histórica* 27 (1964): 102–99.

Fernández y Fernández, Ramón. "Historia del trigo en México." *TE* 1 (1934): 429–44.

Florescano, E. "El abasto y la legislación de granos en el siglo XVI." *HM* 14 (1965): 567–630.

———. "El problema agrario en los últimos años del virreinato, 1800–1821." *HM* 20 (1971): 477–510.

———. "Meteorología y ciclos agricolas en las antiguas economías: El caso de México." *HM* 17 (1968): 516–34.

Gagliano, J. A. "The Coca Debate in Colonial Peru." *The Americas* 20 (1963): 43–63.

Giberti, H. C. E. *Historia económica de la ganadería argentina.* Buenos Aires: Editorial Raigal, 1954.

Guerra y Sánchez, R. *Azúcar y población en los Antilles.* Havana: Cultural S.A., 1944.

Guthrie, C. L. "Colonial Economy, Trade, Industry, and Labor in Seventeenth-Century Mexico City." *RHA*, no. 7 (1939), pp. 103–34.

Hammett, B. R. "Dye Production, Food Supply, and the Laboring Population of Oaxaca." *HAHR* 51 (1971): 51–78.

Helmer, Marie. "Commerce et industrie au Pérou à la fin du XVIIIᵐᵉ siècle." *RI* 10 (1950): 519–26.

Lamas, A. "El pósito colonial." *TE* 23 (1956): 90–112.

Lee, R. "American Cochineal in European Commerce, 1526–1625." *JMH* 23 (1951): 205–24.

———. "Cochineal Production and Trade in New Spain to 1600." *The Americas* 4 (1948): 449–73.

Lida, Clara E. "Sobre la producción de sal en el siglo XVIII: salinas de Peñón Blanco." *HM* 14 (1965): 680–90.

Marquez Miranda, F. *Ensayo sobre los artífices de la platería en el Buenos Aires colonial.* Buenos Aires: Imprenta de la Universidad, 1933.

Matesanz, José. "Introducción de la ganadería en Nueva España, 1521–1535." *HM* 14 (1965): 533–66.

Mellafe, R. "Agricultura e historia colonial hispanoamericana." In *Varios temas de historia económica hispanoamericana,* pp. 23–32. Paris: École Pratique des Hautes Etudes, VIe section, 1965.

Miranda, J. "Notas sobre la introducción de la mesta en la Nueva España." *RHA,* no. 17 (1944), pp. 1–26.

Moreno Toscano, Alejandra. "Tres problemas de la geografía del maíz, 1600–1624." *HM* 14 (1965): 631–55.

Mosk, Sanford A. "Spanish Pearl Fishing Operations on the Pearl Coast in the Sixteenth Century." *HAHR* 17 (1938): 392–400.

Muro Arias, Luis F. "Herreros y cerrajores en la Nueva España." *HM* 5 (1956): 337–72.

Ratekin, M. "The Early Sugar Industry in Española." *HAHR* 34 (1954): 1–19.

Real Díaz, J. J. "Las ferias de Jalapa." *AEA* 16 (1959): 167–314.

Ringrose, D. "Carting in the Hispanic World: An Example of Divergent Development." *HAHR* 50 (1970): 30–51.

Sandoval, F. *La industria del azúcar en la Nueva España.* Mexico: Universidad Nacional Autónoma de México, 1951.

Santos Martínez, P. *Historia económica de Mendoza durante el virreinato, 1776–1810.* Madrid: Gráficas Orbe, 1961.

Smith, R. S. "Indigo Production and Trade in Colonial Guatemala." *HAHR* 39 (1959): 181–211.

———. "Retail Stock of a Guatemalan Store, 1780." *HAHR* 26 (1946): 60–65.

Toledo, E. B. "El comercio de mulas en Salta, 1657–1698." *AIIH* 6 (1962–63): 165–90.

Torre Revello, J. *El gremio de plateros en las Indias occidentales.* Buenos Aires: Imprenta de la Universidad, 1932.

Toscano, S. "Una empresa renasientista de España: la introducción en cultivos y animales domésticos euro-asiáticos en México." *Cuadernos* 5 (1946): 143–98.

Vásquez de Warman, Irene. "El pósito y la alhóndiga en la Nueva España." *HM* 17 (1968): 395–426.

Vidart, D. *La vida rural uruguaya.* Montevideo: Uruguay, Depto. de Sociología Rural, 1955.

Weber, D. J. "Spanish Fur Trade from New Mexico, 1540–1821." *The Americas* 24 (1967): 122–36.

LAND, LABOR, AND TRIBUTE

Arcila Farías, E. *El régimen de la encomienda en Venezuela.* Seville: Escuela de Estudios Hispano-Americanos, 1957.

Borah, W. "Los tributos y su recaudación en la audiencia de Nueva Galicia durante el siglo XVI." In *Historia y sociedad en el mundo de habla española: Homenaje a José Miranda,* ed. B. García Martínez et al., pp. 27–48. Mexico: El Colegio de México, 1970.

Borde, Jean, and Góngora, M. *Evolución de la propriedad rural en el valle del Puargue.* Santiago: Editorial Universitaría, 1956.

Calderón Quijano, J. "El Banco de San Carlos y las comunidades de indios de Nueva España." *AEA* 19 (1962): 1–144.

Carmagnani, M. "La opposición a los tributos en la segunda mitad del siglo XVIII." *RCHG* 39 (1961): 158–95.

Chevalier, F. *Land and Society in Colonial Mexico: The Great Hacienda.* Berkeley and Los Angeles: University of California Press, 1963.

———. "Signification sociale de la fondation de Puebla de los Angeles." *RHA,* no. 23 (1947), pp. 105–30.

Corbitt, D. C. "Mercedes and Realengos: A Survey of the Public Land System in Cuba." *HAHR* 19 (1939): 262–85.

Crespo Rodas, A. "La 'Mita' de Potosí." *Revista Histórica* 22 (1955–56): 169–82.

Curtin, P. *The Atlantic Slave Trade: A Census.* Madison: University of Wisconsin Press, 1969–.

Fals-Borda, O. *Campesinos de los Andes: Estudio sociológico de Saucio.* Bogotá: Universidad Nacional, 1961.

———. "Indian Congregations in the New Kingdom of Granada. Land Tenure Aspects, 1595–1850." *The Americas* 13 (1957): 331–52.

Fajardo, M. D. *El régimen de la encomienda en la provincia de Vélez. Población indigena y enconomia.* Bogotá: Universidad de los Andes, 1969.

Fernández de Recas, G. *Mayorazgos de la Nueva España.* Mexico: Biblioteca Nacional de México, 1965.

García Martínez, G. *El marquesado del valle. Tres siglos de régimen señorial en Nueva España.* Mexico: El Colegio de México, 1969.

Gibson, Charles. "Llamamiento General, Repartimiento, and the Empire of Acolhuacan." *HAHR* 36 (1956): 1–27.

Goldwert, M. "La lucha por la perpetuidad de las encomiendas en el Perú virreinal, 1550–1600." *Revista Histórica* 12 (1955–56): 336–60; 13 (1957): 207–45.

Góngora, Mario. *Origen de los "inquilinos" de Chile central.* Santiago: Universidad de Chile, Seminario de Historia Colonial, 1960.

Greenleaf, Richard E. "The Obraje in the Late Mexican Colony." *The Americas* 23 (1967): 227–50.

———. "Viceregal Power and the Obrajes of the Cortés Estate, 1659–1708." *HAHR* 48 (1968): 365–79.

Herrera, G. "Las encomiendas de indios y el departamento de Loreto." *Revista Histórica* 3 (1908): 254–60.

Jara, A. "Los asientos de trabajo y la provisión de mano de obra para los no encomenderos en la ciudad de Santiago, 1586–1600." *RCHG* 225 (1957): 21–95.

———. "Importación de trabajadores indígenas en el siglo XVII." *RCHG* 224 (1956): 177–212.

———. *El salario de los indios y los sesmos del oro en la tasa de Santillán.* Santiago: Universidad de Chile, 1961.

———. "Salario en una economía caracterizada por les relaciones de dependencia personal." *RCHG* 233 (1965): 40–60.

——, ed. *Tierras nuevas, expansión territorial y ocupación del suelo en América* (*siglos XVI–XIX*). Mexico: El Colegio de México, 1969.

Jiménez Rueda, J. "Tasaciones de tributos, 1531–1569." *BAGN* 20 (1949): 63–104.

Keith, R. G. "Encomienda, Hacienda, and Corregimiento in Spanish America: A Structural Analysis." *HAHR* 51 (1971): 431–46.

Kirkpatrick, F. A. "The Landless Encomienda." *HAHR* 22 (1942): 765–74.

Lamas, A. "Las cajas de comunidades indígenas." *TE* 24 (1957): 298–337.

Lockhart, James. "Encomienda and Hacienda: The Evolution of the Great Estate in the Spanish Indies." *HAHR* 49 (1969): 411–29.

López Sarrelangue, D. "Los tributos de la parcialidad de Santiago de Tlaltelolco." *MAMH* 15 (1956): 129–224.

McBride, George. *The Land Systems of Mexico.* New York: American Geographical Society, 1923.

Mellafe, R. *La introducción de la esclavitud negra en Chile.* Santiago: Universidad de Chile, 1959.

Miranda, J. *La función económica del encomendero en los origines del régimen colonial. Nueva España, 1521–1531.* Mexico: Universidad Nacional Autónoma de México, 1965.

——. "La tasación de las cargas indígenas de la Nueva España durante el siglo XVI excluyendo el tributo." *RHA*, no. 31 (1951), p. 77–96.

——. *El tributo indígena en la Nueva España durante el siglo XVI.* Mexico: El Colegio de México, 1952.

Ots Capdequi, J. M. *España en América: El régimen de la tierra en la época colonial.* Mexico: Fondo de Cultura Económica, 1959.

——. "El tributo y la mita en la época colonial." *RI* 1 (1940): 76–117.

Peña y Camara, J. de la. *El tributo: sus origenes, su implantación en Nueva España.* Seville, 1934.

Ramón, Jose Armando de. "La institución de los censos de los naturales en Chile, 1570–1750." *Historia* (Universidad Católica de Chile) 1 (1961): 47–94.

Salvat Monguillot, M. "El régimen de encomiendas en los tiempos de la conquista." *RCHG* 132 (1964): 5–58.

Scholes, F. V. "Tributos de los indios de la Nueva España." *BAGN* 7 (1936): 185–226.

Simpson, L. B. *The Encomienda in New Spain: The Beginning of Spanish Mexico.* Berkeley and Los Angeles: University of California Press, 1966.

——. *Exploitation of Land in Central Mexico in the Sixteenth Century.* Ibero-Americana, 36. Berkeley and Los Angeles: University of California Press, 1952.

——. *Studies in the Administration of the Indians in New Spain.* Vol. 1, *Laws of Burgos;* vol. 2, *The Civil Congregation.* Ibero-Americana, 7. Berkeley: University of California Press, 1934.

——. *Studies in the Administration of the Indians in New Spain.* Vol. 3, *The Repartimiento System of Native Labor in New Spain and Guatemala.* Ibero-Americana, 13. Berkeley: University of California Press, 1938.

——. *Studies in the Administration of the Indians in New Spain.* Vol. 4, *The Emancipation of the Indian Slaves and the Resettlement of the Freedmen, 1548–1553.* Ibero-Americana, 16. Berkeley and Los Angeles: University of California Press, 1940.

Vásquez, M. C. *Hacienda, peonaje, y servidumbre en los andes peruanos.* Lima: Editorial Estudios Andinos, 1961.

Verlinden, C. "El régimen de trabajo en México: Aumento y alcance de la gañancía. Siglo XVII." In *Historia y sociedad en el mundo de habla española: Homenaje a José Miranda,* pp. 225–46. Mexico: El Colegio de México, 1970.

Wiedner, David L. "Forced Labor in Colonial Peru." *The Americas* 16 (1960): 357–83.

Zavala, S. *De encomiendas y propriedad territorial en algunas regiones de la América española.* Mexico: Antigua Librería Robredo de J. Porrua e Hijos, 1940.

———. *La encomienda* indiana. Madrid: Imprenta Helénica, 1935.

———. *Los esclavos indios en Nueva España.* Mexico: Colegio Nacional, 1967.

———. "Origines coloniales del peonaje en México." *TE* 10 (1944): 711–48.

———. "Los trabajadores antillanos en el siglo XVI." *RHA,* nos. 2–3 (1938), pp. 31–67, 60–94.

Zurkalowski, E. "El establecimiento de las encomiendas en el Perú y sus antecedentes." *Revista Histórica* 6 (1923): 254–69.

POPULATION

Aguirre Beltrán, Gonzalo. *La población negra de México, 1519–1810. Estudio etnohistórico.* Mexico: Ediciones Fuente Cultural, 1946.

Aschman, H. *The Central Desert of Baja California: Demography and Ecology.* Ibero-Americana, 42. Berkeley and Los Angeles: University of California Press, 1959.

Audera, V. *La población y la inmigración en Hispanoamérica.* Madrid: Ediciones Cultura Hispánica, 1954.

Barón Castro, R. *La población de El Salvador. Estudio acerca de su desenvolvimiento desde la época prehispánica hasta nuestros dias.* Madrid: Consejo Superior de Investigaciones Científicas, 1942.

Bendicente, F. C. *Contribución al estudió de la población argentina.* Santa Fe: Imprenta de la Universidad, 1943.

Berthe, J. P. "La peste de 1643 en Michoacán: Examen crítico de una tradición." In *Historia y sociedad en el mundo de habla española: Homenaje a José Miranda,* ed. B. García Martínez et al., pp. 247–62. Mexico: El Colegio de México, 1970.

Besio Moreno, N. *Buenos Aires, puerto del Rio de la Plata, capital de la Argentina: estudio crítico de su población, 1536–1936.* Buenos Aires: Talleres Gráficos Tuduri, 1939.

Borah, W. "América como modelo? El impacto demográfico de la expansión europea sobre el mundo no europeo." *Cuadernos Americanos* 6 (1962): 176–85.

———. "Francisco de Urdiñola's Census of the Spanish Settlements in Nueva Vizcaya." *HAHR* 35 (1955): 398–402.

———. "The Historical Demography of Latin America: Sources, Techniques, Controversies, Yields." In *Population and Economics. Proceedings of Section V of the International Economic History Association, 1968,* ed. Paul Deprez, pp. 173–205. Winnipeg: University of Manitoba Press, 1970.

———, and Cook, S. F. *The Aboriginal Population of Central Mexico on the Eve of the Spanish Conquest.* Ibero-Americana, 45. Berkeley and Los Angeles: University of California Press, 1963.

————. "Conquest and Population: A Demographic Approach to Mexican History." *Proceedings, American Philosophical Society* 113 (1969): 177–83.

————. *The Population of Central Mexico in 1548: An Analysis of the Suma de visitas de pueblos.* Ibero-Americana, 43. Berkeley and Los Angeles: University of California Press, 1960.

Boyd-Bowman, P. "La emigración peninsular a America, 1520–1539." *HM* 13 (1963): 165–92.

————. *Indice geobiográfico de 40,000 pobladores de América en el siglo XVI.* Vol. 1, *La época antillana, 1493–1519.* Bogotá: Instituto Caro y Cuevo, 1964. Vol. 2, *1520–1539.* Mexico: Editorial Jus, 1968.

————. "La procendencia de los españoles de América, 1540–1559." *HM* 17 (1967): 37–71.

————. "Regional Origin of the Earliest Spanish Colonists of America." *PMLA,* 1956, pp. 1157–72.

Colmenares, G. *Encomienda y población en la provincia de Pamplona, 1549–1650.* Bogotá: Universidad de los Andes, 1969.

Cook, N. D. *Padrón de los indios de Lima en 1613.* Lima: Universidad Mayor de San Marcos, 1968.

Cook, S. F. *The Conflict between the California Indian and White Civilization.* 2 vols. Ibero-Americana, 21, 22. Berkeley and Los Angeles: University of California Press, 1943.

————. *The Extent and Significance of Disease among the Indians of Baja California, 1697–1773.* Ibero-Americana, 12. Berkeley: University of California Press, 1937.

————. *The Historical Demography and Ecology of the Teotlalpan.* Ibero-Americana, 33. Berkeley and Los Angeles: University of California Press, 1949.

————. "The Incidence and Significance of Disease among Aztecs and Related Tribes." *HAHR* 26 (1946): 320–35.

————. "The Population of Mexico in 1793." *Human Biology* 14 (1942): 499–515.

————. *Population Trends among the California Mission Indians.* Ibero-Americana, 17. Berkeley and Los Angeles: University of California Press, 1940.

————. "The Smallpox Epidemic of 1797 in Mexico." *Bulletin of the History of Medicine* 7 (1939): 937–69.

————. "Smallpox in Spanish and Mexican California, 1770–1845." *Bulletin of the History of Medicine* 7 (1939): 153–91.

————. *Soil Erosion and the Population in Central Mexico.* Ibero-Americana, 34. Berkeley and Los Angeles: University of California Press, 1949.

————, and Borah, W. "La despoblación del México Central en el siglo XVI." *HM* 12 (1962): 1–12.

————. *Essays in Population History: Mexico and the Caribbean.* Vol. 1. Berkeley and Los Angeles: University of California Press, 1971.

————. *The Indian Population of Central Mexico, 1531–1610.* Ibero-Americana, 44. Berkeley and Los Angeles: University of California Press, 1960.

————. "On the Credibility of Contemporary Testimony on the Population of Mexico in the Sixteenth Century." In *Suma antropológica en homenaje a Roberto J. Weitlaner,* pp. 229–39. Mexico: Instituto Nacional de Antropología y Historia, 1966.

————. *The Population of the Mixteca Alta, 1520–1960.* Ibero-Americana, 50. Berkeley and Los Angeles: University of California Press, 1968.

————. "The Rate of Population Change in Central Mexico, 1550–1570." *HAHR* 37 (1957): 463–71.

Cook, S. F., and Simpson, L. B. *The Population of Central Mexico in the Sixteenth Century.* Ibero-Americana, 31. Berkeley and Los Angeles: University of California Press, 1948.

Cooper, Donald. *Epidemic Disease in Mexico City, 1761–1813. An Administrative, Social, and Medical Study.* Austin: Unversity of Texas Press, 1965.

Crosby, Alfred W. "Conquistador y Pestilencia: The First New World Pandemic and the Fall of the Great Indian Empires." *HAHR* 47 (1967): 321–37.

Cuesta, L. "La emigración gallega a América." *Arquivos do Seminario de Estudios Gallegos* 4 (1932): 141–217.

Deprez, P., ed. *Population and Economics.* Winnipeg: University of Manitoba Press, 1970.

Díaz Vial, R. "Situación de los libros parroquiales." *Revista de Estudios Históricos* (Santiago), no. 10 (1962), pp. 109–22.

Dobyns, Henry F. "Estimating American Population. I. An Appraisal of Techniques with a New Hemispheric Estimate." *Current Anthropology* 7 (1966): 395–460.

————. "An Outline of Andean Epidemic History of 1720." *Bulletin of the History of Medicine* 37 (1963): 493–515.

Friede, J. "Algunas observaciones sobre la realidad de la emigración española a América en la primera mitad del siglo XVI." *RI* 12 (1952).

————. "The 'Catálogo de Pasajeros' and Spanish Emigration to America to 1550." *HAHR* 31 (1951): 331–48.

————. "Demographic Changes in the Mining Community of Muzo after the Plague of 1629." *HAHR* 47 (1967): 338–43.

————. *Los quimbayas bajo la dominación española.* Bogotá: Talleres Gráficos del Banco de la República, 1963.

Gerhard, P. "Descripciones geográficas (Pistas para investigadores)." *HM* 17 (1968): 618–27.

————. *México en 1742.* México: J. Porrua, 1962.

González, E. R., and Mellafe, R. "La función de la familia en la historia social hispano-americana colonial." *AIIH* 8 (1965): 57–71.

Guitierrez del Arroyo, I. "Alcaldías y corregimientos en México de 1777." *HM* 7 (1957): 532–35.

Hernández y Sánchez Barba, M. "La población hispanoamericana y su distribución social en el siglo XVIII." *Revista de Estudios Políticos* 52 (1954): 111–42.

Keller K., Carlos. "El Norte Chico en la época de la formación de la república." *RCHG* 123 (1956): 15–49.

Klein, H. S., and Carmagnani, M. "Demografía histórica: la población del obispado de Santiago, 1777–1778." *BACH* 32 (1965): 57–74.

Konetzke, Richard. "Documentos para la historia y crítica de los registros parroquiales en las Indias." *RI* 7 (1946): 581–86.

————. "La emigración de las mujeres españolas a América durante la época colonial." *Revista Internacional de Sociología* 3 (1945): 123–50.

————. "La emigración española al Río de la Plata durante el siglo XVI." *Miscelanea Americanista* 3 (1952): 297–353.

————. "Las fuentes para la historia demográfica de Hispano-América durante la época colonial." *AEA* 5 (1948): 267–323.

————. "Legislación sobre inmigración de estranjeros en América durante la época colonial." *Revista Internacional de Sociología* 3 (1945): 263–99.

Kubler, George. *The Indian Caste of Peru, 1795–1940: A Population Study Based upon Tax Records and Census Reports.* Washington, D.C.: United States Government Printing Office, 1952.

————. "Population Movements in Mexico, 1520–1600." *HAHR* 22 (1942): 606–43.

Lerner, V. "Consideraciones sobre la población de la Nueva España (1793–1810) según Humboldt y Navarro y Noriega." *HM* 17 (1968): 327–48.

Lobo, E. M. L. "Imigracão e colonizacão no Chile colonial, 1540–1565." *Revista de História* (São Paulo) 35 (1967): 39–60.

Lópéz Sarrelangue, D. E. "Población indígena de la Nueva España en el siglo XVIII." *HM* 12 (1963): 516–30.

Manrique Castañeda, L. "Notas sobre la población de Santa María Chignecatitlan en México." *Anales of the Instituto Nacional de Antropología e Historia* 16 (1963): 199–225.

Mendizabal, M. O. "Demografía del siglo XVI, 1519–1594. Consequencias demográficas del choque de la cultura occidental con las culturas indígenas de México." *Boletín de la Sociedad Mexicana de Geografía y Estadística,* vol. 48, pt. 2, pp. 301–41.

Miranda, J. "Evolución cuantitativo y desplazamiento de la población de Oaxaca en la época colonial." *Estudios de historia novo-hispano* 2 (1968): 129–47.

Morales Padrón, F. "Colonos canarios en Indias." *AEA* 7 (1951): 399–441.

Moreno, J. L. "La estructura social y demográfica de la ciudad de Buenos Aires en el año 1778." *AIIH* 8 (1965): 151–70.

Neasham, V. A. "Spain's Emigrants to the New World, 1492–1592." *HAHR* 19 (1939): 147–60.

Ortiz y San Pelayo, F. *Los vascos en América.* Buenos Aires: J. Roldán, 1913.

Pérez Guerrero, E. *Colonización e inmigración en el Ecuador.* Quito: Editorial Casa de la Cultura Ecuatoriana, 1954.

Pilar Charco, María del. "La población de Potosí en 1779." *AIIH* 8 (1965): 171–80.

Rodríguez Arzua, J. "Las regiones españolas y la población de América, 1509–1538." *RI* 7 (1947): 695–748.

Rosenblat, Angel. *La población de América en 1492—Viejos y nuevos cálculos.* Mexico: El Colegio de México, 1967.

————. *La población indígena y el mestizaje en América.* 2 vols. Buenos Aires: Editorial Nova, 1954.

Rosini, B. "El censo de 1771." *AIIH* 6 (1962–63): 43–57.

————. "Estructura demográfica de Jujuy: s. XVIII." *AIIH* 8 (1965): 119–50.

Rubio, Angel. "La emigración extremeña a Indias en el siglo XVI." *RCHG* 109 (1947): 140–88; 110 (1947): 56–124.

Saco, J. A. *Historia de la esclavitud de la raza africana en el nuevo mundo.* 4 vols. Havana: Habana Cultural, 1938.

Sánchez-Albórnoz, C. *Despoblacion y repoblación del valle del Duero.* Buenos Aires: Instituto de Historia de España, 1966.

Sánchez-Albórnoz, N. "Estudio sobre la demografía histórica del Valle de Santa María." *Universidad* (Santa Fe, Argentina), no. 62 (1964), 93–104.

————. "Les registres paroissiaux en Amérique Latine." *Revue Suisse d'Histoire* 17 (1967): 60–71.

————. "Perfil y proyecciones de la demografía histórica en la Argentina." *AIIH* 8 (1965): 31–56.

Sastrón, M. *Colonización de Filipinas. Immigración peninsular.* Manila: Malabon, 1897.

Sauer, Carl. *Aboriginal Population of Northwestern Mexico.* Ibero-Americana, 10. Berkeley: University of California Press, 1935.

Simpson, L. B. "The Population of Twenty-Two Towns of Michoacán in 1554. A Supplement to Cook and Simpson, *The Population of Central Mexico in the Sixteenth Century.*" *HAHR* 30 (1950): 248–50.

Warren, Finton. "The Caravajal Visitation: First Spanish Survey of Michoacán." *The Americas* 19 (1963): 404–12.

Zelinksky, Wilbur. "The Historical Geography of the Negro Population of Latin America." *Journal of Negro History* 34 (1949): 153–221.

BRAZIL

General Works

Azevedo, J. L. de. *Épocas de Portugal económico.* Lisbon: Livraria Clássica, 1929.

Braudel, F. "Au Portugal: avant et après les grandes découvertes." *AESC,* 4ᵉ année (1949): 192–97.

Boxer, C. R. *The Dutch in Brazil, 1624–1654.* Oxford: Clarendon Press, 1957.

————. *The Golden Age of Brazil, 1695–1750.* Berkeley: University of California Press, 1962.

————. *Salvador de Sá and the Struggle for Brazil and Angola, 1602–1686.* London: University of London, 1952.

Dornas Filho, J. *Aspectos da economia colonial.* Rio de Janeiro, 1958.

Ferreira Lima, H. *Formacão economica do Brasil (período colonial).* Rio de Janeiro: Editôra Fundo de Cultura, 1961.

Furtado, C. *The Economic Growth of Brazil. A Survey from Colonial to Modern Times.* Berkeley and Los Angeles: University of California Press, 1963.

Godinho, V. de Magalhaes. *História econômica e social de expansão portugesa.* Lisbon: Terra-Editora, 1947.

Lemos Britto, J. G. de. *Pontos de partida para a história econômica do Brasil.* São Paulo: Companhia Editôra Nacional, 1939.

Martins, I. P. de. *Introducão à economia brasileria.* Rio de Janeiro: J. Olimpio, 1961.

Prado, Caio. *The Colonial Background of Modern Brazil.* Berkeley and Los Angeles: University of California Press, 1967.

Silva Rego, A. de. *O ultramar Português no sèculo XVIII, 1700–1833.* Lisbon: Agência-Geral do Ultramar, 1967.

Simonsen, R. *História econômica do Brasil.* 2 vols. São Paulo: Companhia Editôra Nacional, 1937.

Trade and Navigation

Alves, M. "O comércio marítimo e alguns armadores do século XVIII na Bahia." *Revista de História* (São Paulo) 17 (1965): 133–42.

Baiao, A. *O comèrcio do Pau Brasil.* Lisbon, 1923.

Boxer, C. R. "Brazilian Gold and the British Traders in the First Half of the Eighteenth Century. *HAHR* 49 (1969): 454–73.

Canabrava, A. Piffer. *O comércio portugês no Rio da Prata, 1580–1640.* São Paulo, 1944.

Ellis, M. "Estudo sobre alguns tipos de transporte no Brasil colonial." *Revista de História* 1 (1950): 495–516.

Godinho, V. de Magalhães. *L'économie de l'empire portugais aux XVe et XVIe siècles.* 2 vols. Paris, 1958.

———. "Le Portugal, les flottes du sucre et les flottes de l'or, 1670–1770." *AESC*, 5e année (1950): 184–97.

Lobo, E. M. L. "As frotas do Brasil." *Jahrbuch für geschichte von Staat, Wirtschaft und Gesellschaft Lateinamerikas* 4 (1967): 465–88.

Mauro, F. *Le Portugal et l'Atlantique au XVIIe siècle, 1570–1670.* Ports-Routes-Trafics, 10. Paris: SEVPEN, 1960.

Mello, A. R. de. "Contrabando e bandeirismo no segundo quartel do século XVII." *Revista de História* 9 (1958): 341–52.

Nunes Dias, M. "A organizacão da rota atlantico do ouro da mina e os mecanismos dos resgates." *Revista de História* 11 (1960): 369–98.

———. "As frotas do cacau da Amazonia, 1756–1777. Subsidios para o estudo do fomento ultramarion portuges no século XVIII." *Revista de História* 13 (1962): 363–77.

———. "Fomento e mercantilismo: política portugesa na Baixada Maranhense, 1775–1778." *Jahrbuch für Geschichte von Staat, Wirtschaft und Gesellschaft Lateinamerikas* 2 (1965): 257–334.

Verge, P. *Flux et réflux de la traite des nègres entre le Golfe de Bénin et Bahia de Todos os Santos du XVIIIe aux XIXe siècle.* The Hague: Mouton and Company, 1968.

Vivieros, J. de. *História do comércio do Maranhão, 1612–1894.* 2 vols. São Luis, 1954.

Trading Companies

Diégues, M., Jr. "As companhias privilegiados no comércio colonial." *Revista de História* 1 (1950): 309–38.

Freitas, G. de. "A Companhia Geral do Comércio do Brasil, 1649–1720." *Revista de História* 2 (1951): 307–29, 85–110, 313, 344.

Nunes Dias, M. "A tonelagen da frota da Companhia Geral do Grão-Pará e Maranhão, 1755–1788." *Revista de História* 15 (1964): 113–40.

———. "Fomento ultramarino e mercantilismo: a Companhia Geral do Grão-Pará e Maranhão, 1755–1788." *Revista de História* 17 (1966): 359–429, 47–120, 367–416; 18 (1967): 99–148, 10–166.

Finance, Taxation, Accounting, Crown Revenue

Caetano, M. Do *Conselho Ultramarino ao Conselho do Imperio Colonial.* Lisbon: Divisão de Publicações e Biblioteca, 1943.

Cardozo, M. "The Collection of Fifths in Brazil, 1695–1709." *HAHR* 20 (1940): 359–79.

Mendes da Luz, F. P. *O Conselho da India.* Lisbon, 1952.

Rosa, R. "Os antecedentes do Tribunal de Contas no Brasil." *RIHGB,* no. 180 (1943), pp. 35–62.

Prices

Godinho, V. de Magalhaes. *Prix et monnaies au Portugal.* Paris: Colin, 1955.

Rodrigues Leite, F. "Preços em São Paulo seiscentista." *Anais do Museu Paulista* 17 (1963): 41–121.

Mining, Coinage, Mints

Braudel, F. "Moedas e civilizacões. Do ouro do Sudão a prata da Amerika." *Revista de História* 4 (1953): 67–83.

Cardozo, Manuel. "The Brazilian Gold Rush." *The Americas* 3 (1946): 137–60.

Ellis, M. "Contribuicão ao estudo do abastecimento dos zonas mineradoras do Brasil no século XVIII." *Revista de História* 9 (1958): 429–64.

———. "Pesquisa sobre a existencia do ouro e da prata no Planalto Paulista nos séculos XVI e XVII." *Revista de História* 1 (1950): 51–72.

Lima, A. de. *História dos diamantes nas Minas Gerais. Século XVIII.* Rio de Janeiro: Edições Dois Mundos, 1945.

Sombra, S. *Historia monetária do Brasil colonial.* Rio de Janeiro: Ofkinas Gráfkas da Emp. Almanak Laemmert, 1938.

Agriculture, Grazing, Industry

Abrantes, Visconde de. "Qual a origem da cultura e comércio de anil entre nos e quaes as causas do seu progresso e da sua decadencia." *RIHGB,* no. 15 (1888), pp. 42–60.

Alden, Dauril. "The Growth and Decline of Indigo Production in Colonial Brazil: A Study in Comparative Economic History." *The Journal of Economic History,* 25 (1965): 35–59.

———. "Manoel Luís Viera: An Entrepreneur in Rio de Janeiro during Brazil's Eighteentr-Century Agricultural Renaissance." *HAHR* 39 (1959): 521–37.

———. "Yankee Sperm Whalers in Brazilian Waters and the Decline of the Portugese Whale Fisheries, 1773–1801." *The Americas* 20 (1964): 267–88.

Alves, J. *História das secas. Séculos XVII a XIX.* Fortaleza, 1953.

Amaral, L. *História geral da agricultura brasileira.* 3 vols. Saõ Paulo: Companhia Editora Nacional, 1939–40.

Cruz, E. "A exportacão da madeira do Pará para Portugal, no século XVIII." *RIHGB,* no. 234 (1957), pp. 38–43.

Ellis, M. "Aspectos da pesca de Bahia no Brasil colonial." *Revista de História* 8 (1957): 415–62.

———. *O monopólio do sal no estado do Brasil, 1631–1801.* São Paulo, 1956.

Escragnolle Tauny, A. de. *História do café no Brasil.* Rio de Janeiro: Departamento Nacional do Café, 1939.

Lippmann, E. O. von. *História do açucar.* 2 vols. Rio de Janeiro: Leuzinger, S.A., 1942.

Novais, F. A. "A proibicão das manufacturas no Brasil e a política econômica portugesa do fundo século XVIII." *Revista de História* 17 (1966): 145–66.

Nunes Dias, M. "Colonizacão da Amazonia, 1775–1778." *Revista de História* 18 (1967): 471–90.

Raffard, H. The Sugar Industry in Brazil. London, 1882.

Wanderly Pinho, J. *História de um engenho do Reconcavo, Matoim–Novo Caboto–Freguezia, 1552–1944.* Rio de Janeiro: Z. Valverde, 1946.

Population

Alden, Dauril. "The Population of Brazil in the Late Eighteenth Century: A Preliminary Survey." *HAHR* 43 (1963): 173–205.

Ramos, Arthur. *Las poblaciones del Brasil.* Mexico: Fondo de Cultura Económica, 1944.

Saraiva, A. J. "Le Père Antonio Vieira S.J. et l'esclavage des noirs au XVII⁰ siècle." *AESC,* 22⁰ année (1967): 1289–1309.

Soares de Souza, J. A. "A populacão de São Paulo, em 1766 e 1772." *RIHGB,* no. 223 (1954), pp. 3–15.

11

QUANTITATIVE RESEARCH IN LATIN AMERICAN HISTORY OF THE NINETEENTH AND TWENTIETH CENTURIES

by William Paul McGreevey

The success of the "new economic history" in answering narrow but important questions about the course and causes of economic change in the United States has served as a stimulus to quantitative historical research in other areas and subfields of history. Research in Latin American history since independence is no exception. Historical studies of economic change, demography, politics, and social welfare which make abundant use of quantitative data have been published or are in the works. Nonetheless, the achievements are small when compared to developments in North American history. Much remains to be done—and much can be done. A principal concern of this chapter is to indicate useful paths which can be followed to increase the efficiency of scholars in quantitative research and to promote satisfactory results from the investment of scholarly effort and research funds.

Despite the gains made in recent years, quantitative research on Latin America since independence is less developed than similar work for other areas. Only the economic history of the years 1810–1945 has received much attention; quantitative research on political and social subjects is in its infancy. Yet, as my bibliography of source materials (pp. 490–501 below) will indicate, the possibilities for quantitative research in a wide range of historical fields are quite good. A major barrier has been the dispersion of

Partial financial support for the preparation of this chapter was supplied by a grant to the University of California, Berkeley, from the Ford Foundation. The Center for Latin American Studies at Berkeley provided typing and clerical assistance; Mrs. Eloyde Tovey, librarian at the University Library, Berkeley, took major responsibility for preparation and annotation of the bibliography. I extend my thanks to them, but retain responsibility for any errors.

materials. There are 24 Latin American countries, if one includes the recently established free states. Since the early nineteenth century, their governments have kept separate statistical records which have never been drawn together into a central place. This dispersion contrasts with the relative concentration of materials on the same areas during their colonial epochs. The student of the earlier period can undertake quantitative research at the Archivo de Indias in Seville, at Simancas, at the British Museum or Public Record Office in London, and in one or two major libraries in the United States. (No central archival reserve exists for the former Portuguese empire.) With materials for the nineteenth and early twentieth centuries scattered in myriad local archives, however, research has been less effective for the nineteenth century than for the eighteenth. Only for the years since 1945 has the United Nations Economic Commission for Latin America (ECLA) gathered systematic economic (and more rarely sociological) data which can provide the basis for study of the area as a whole. For earlier years only individual countries can be treated, with the hope that at some date successful international comparisons will become feasible as the collection of quantitative material grows.[1]

Just as the Latin American situation creates a special problem of data scatter, it increases the number of cases of successful or arrested change. A sovereign national government is in most cases the ideal body to assemble many types of statistical information: its ability to gather information is clearly superior to that of local or supranational units. In contrast to states of continental size—the United States, Russia, China, and India—Latin America shows a long history of many governments with a wide variety of territorial extent, size and density of population, economic and social problems and policies, and even one state of continental size.

For very few countries (and those unrepresentative of the rest of the world) is there a quantitative record against which to test models of social, political, and economic change. Only a dozen countries, nearly all Western European or "born free," to use the phrase of Louis Hartz, make up the sample for quantitative comparative studies of historical change before World War II. Successful quantitative research in Latin America can greatly increase that list of countries.

The penchant for comparative historical studies has led to a number of interesting and fruitful generalizations about the processes of economic and social change. But whatever the merits of those generalizations in explaining events in the North Atlantic area or Japan, there can be no assurance of their successful transplanting to tropical soil. The analysis of social classes, for example, and particularly the "historical function" of the bourgeoisie would seem to be very different in the Latin American context from any generalizations based on European experience.[2] More specific hypotheses about economic change have also proved to be difficult to apply to less developed countries. For example, Gerschenkron's suggestion that the strain of backwardness can influence the speed and character of industrialization does not explain much of the pattern of industrialization in Latin America.[3]

There is a natural tendency to analyze Latin America using the same categories that have been applied to the North Atlantic Community, since Latin American society is an offspring of the Iberian peninsula. Yet the substance of socially significant history is in many cases quite different. The temporal power of the Church had receded in most of Europe before the eighteenth century ended, but in Latin America the economic power of the Catholic church remained a major political and social issue throughout the nineteenth century. Yet only recently have competent quantitative studies of the social, economic, and political roles of the Church begun to emerge.[4] These reveal the crucial role of clerical decision making in the possibilities for economic progress and social change. For example, church-related organizations were the largest source of liquid capital throughout Latin America from the seventeenth to the middle of the nineteenth century. The Church also managed innumerable liens (*censos*) on real property for the support of Church activities and individuals. Moreover, Church organizations as a body were probably the largest holders of cultivable lands leased for private use. Through these mechanisms the Church had control of the major asset of Latin America—land. But this control was exercised with no view to stimulating the economic progress of the area. Loans were given almost exclusively against agricultural mortgages, so that manufacturing and mining were impeded by the lack of loanable funds. Loans were given indiscriminately for the purchase of titles of nobility, for foreign travel, or for real improvements to property, nearly always at the low rate of 5 percent per annum. Capital was not allocated to its most efficient use; rather, it was rationed in terms of other goals established by the hierarchy, such as favoritism, repression of change, and the accumulation of social and political power among the clergy.

In several Latin American countries Church holdings were "intervened" or returned to the national patrimony for resale and distribution during the nineteenth century. Given the political, social, and economic power of the Church, these acts of seizure of Church wealth were of paramount importance. Yet only surface aspects of these changes have been examined. Careful quantitative research sensitive to the peculiarities of the Church's role in Latin America will produce results of interest to the comparative social historian.

The Church remained in nineteenth-century Latin America the last strong representative of supranational power. The suppression of such power is a problem of general concern in the formation of new states. The Church in Latin America is at once an example of the peculiarities of Latin American history and of the possibilities for comparative history in the Latin American area. And there *are* materials available which will permit effective quantitative research. In the past, Latin American historians have tended to assume that the statistical data are meager and fixed in quantity, poor in quality, and scanty in rewards for investigation. Yet my bibliography of statistical documents (pp. 490–501 below)—which is but a sample of possible sources of data—indicates the richness of available materials.

Argentina may be an atypical case because of the affluence of that country as early as the 1890s, but a glance at its range of statistical materials in published compendia of data indicates the potential for historical research. The first Argentine census was taken in 1869. The materials available in that collection are believed to be sufficient to form the basis for national income benchmark estimates. If the team of Argentine social and economic historians who have worked sporadically on the problem of estimating national income for that epoch are successful, then Argentine data will have been pushed back as far into the past as those of Japan and most other major countries. The potential for economic statistics seems quite high.[5]

Analysis of social change and political participation can also be pushed back into the last quarter of the nineteenth century. For example, data on immigration are available in great detail from 1869 and hence encompass the main period of immigration after 1880.[6] The Argentine Ministry of Justice and Public Instruction published statistical data on education, crime, and related social problems as early as 1863, well before the population was swollen by immigration. Hence these sources could be used to prepare a comprehensive quantitative investigation of the impact of massive immigration on society. Many other social questions may also be investigated through this collection of data.

Of all quantitative materials, the most abundant and greatest in temporal dimension are periodic censuses. A fairly complete listing of these is provided in a publication of the Population Research Center, University of Texas.[7] Census compilations before the 1940s are plagued with large errors of underenumeration in many countries, but these materials are rich in their potential utility for social and economic history. They have been used for studies of secular trends in vital rates, internal migration, and racial mixture. Germani, di Tella, and others have used Argentine census data on labor force distribution and urbanization to analyze trends in the rise of the middle classes, in the ecological background of voting behavior, and in social disorganization.

Other countries have not provided census materials as rich as those of Argentina. Uruguay, an equally developed nation, conducted no national census between 1908 and 1963. Haiti did not conduct a census until 1950. There was no census in Bolivia between 1900 and 1950, or in Ecuador between 1906 and 1950. In contrast to the smaller countries, Mexico has had a long tradition of census taking (the earliest dates from 1560). One generalization may be possible: the larger countries have a more complete record of census taking. Brazil's first census was conducted in 1872, and seventeen volumes of results were published between 1873 and 1876. Subsequent censuses occurred in 1890, 1900, 1920, 1940, 1950, and 1960. Collver has pointed out that the lack of vital statistics for Brazil makes it impossible to estimate historical birthrates from existing census data; however, there are many other uses for the existing data.[8]

Aside from population census data, statistics of economic output appear to be the most available type of quantitative data for Latin America. Despite the difficulties of estimating aggregate economic output, a number of nineteenth- and twentieth-century estimates are worth noting here (see table 11.1). To maximize comparability between estimates originally in a wide variety of currencies for varied points in time, all figures in table 11.1 were changed to U.S. dollars of 1950 purchasing power.

Table 11.1

Per Capita National Product of Selected Latin American Countries
and the United States, Various Years, 1800–1966
(U.S. dollars of 1950 purchasing power)

	Argentina	Brazil	Chile	Colombia	Cuba	Jamaica	Mexico	U.S.
1800		50						
1805							90	
1825					170			
1830						173		
1845								246
1850	159	43				141		
1855			110					322
1870				100		137		339
1890	345					141		
1895							84	
1900	356	106			279			754
1905			190					
1910	434				352	155	107	
1920	430				407		122	
1925				121				1187
1930	434				246	185	123	
1935							108	
1940	498				188			
1945					347		172	
1950	575	230						1874
1955	571							
1960	461	232	301	248	357	309	257	
1966	558	190	355	229			376	3300

SOURCE: For details on sources, see William P. McGreevey, "Recent Research on the Economic History of Latin America," *Latin American Research Review* 3 (1968): 89–117.

A common set of causal elements may in the past have influenced changing levels of living throughout the area. Despite great differences in the timing and character of export expansion, in domestic industrialization, and in the development of autonomous national political decision making, the rank order of the countries included in table 11.1 did not change significantly between 1850 and 1960. The countries and their relative positions in levels of living are indicated in table 11.2. There is no case in which any country changed its relative position dramatically enough to rise or fall more than a single place. Some possible explanations for this are (1) that Latin American countries continued throughout this period to be too dependent on exogenous forces affecting their economies for their own policies to have any effect on their relative backwardness; or, alternatively, (2) that local conditions determining the course and rate of economic change were much more similar than we have believed. These explanations obviously hide a wealth of more specialized hypotheses.

Table 11.2

Relative Positions in Levels of Living of Selected Latin American Countries

	1850	1960
Argentina	2	1
Cuba	1	2
Jamaica	3	3
Chile	4	4
Mexico	6	5
Colombia	5	6
Brazil	7	7

NOTE: This table is based on interpolation and extrapolation to 1850 from available estimates as shown (table 11.1), and on the 1960 and 1965 data on per capita product. The Spearman rank correlation coefficient for the two series was significant at the .05 level. For sources, see note to table 11.1.

Unfortunately, data on total and per capita national product do not extend much beyond those which are the bases for table 11.1. The improvement and broadening of the basic data needed to provide credible estimates of total and per capita product for periods from 1850 to the present could engage economic historians for some years. A useful project which could begin immediately is a restudy of national output estimates made by ECLA for Argentina (1900–50), Brazil (1925–50), Chile 1925–50), and Colombia (1925–53). The methodology used in those pathbreaking studies requires a full description and review. This work might then provide the basis for extension of output estimates into the past. Ideally, the work would be coordinated with that of members of the research staff of the Banco de México, who have been revising Mexican national output estimates for the years from 1895 to 1960.[9]

Foreign trade and trade-related statistics provide another substantial body of quantitative data. In addition to the Latin American statistics, those of major European trading partners and the United States can be used in cross-checks and consistency checks to achieve greater accuracy than is attainable with data gathered only domestically. Such checks will eventually produce improved estimates of visible trade, shipping and insurance payments, and the net positions of foreign investors. This quantitative work is important because there are such divergent views among historians (without access to reliable quantitative data) on the role of foreign trade, investment, and the varieties of imperialism practiced within Latin America. Especially for Latin American countries, which have only incomplete and inaccurate trade records, the records of the industrialized countries offer supplementary and alternative sources of data.

Foreign trade helps us to study some changes in the domestic economy and society. For example, the dissolution of the textile-handicrafts group in the nineteenth century in Mexico, Ecuador, Colombia, and northeast Argentina was caused by growing imports of cotton textiles. Monographic studies of this question have been conducted for Mexico and Argentina, but there has been no general integration of this work to examine the suggestive hypothesis of "ruralization" in Latin America resulting from the Industrial Revolution, i.e., the transformation of diversified economies into extreme specialization and dependence on foreign trade.[10] Since the timing of the decline of local crafts was related partly to the volume of imports of foreign manufactures and partly to the rise of factory manufacture within Latin America, this subject must be approached with great care. Its importance may be gauged, however, by the large percentage of the labor force employed in cottage handicrafts before the incursion of foreign goods—more than 20 percent in Colombia in 1870, and perhaps as much in some other countries.[11]

On those aspects of the domestic economy which have never been recorded independently by statistical agencies outside of Latin America, there is less chance for consistency checking. Agricultural statistics, for example, have rarely been gathered with care and attention. A report of the British consul in Bogotá on Colombian agriculture in 1888 begins:

> As no statistics are procurable upon any point connected with agriculture in Colombia, a report on the subject can only consist of a general account of the various crops grown in different parts of the country, of the nature and capacity of the soils and climate, together with such few notices of the methods pursued and their results as can be gathered from personal observation, and the very contradictory information to be obtained from private individuals.[12]

The paucity of data on domestic (as opposed to export) agriculture has been reflected in the scholarly literature. Fewer than 5 percent of all publications on Latin American economic history in the last 20 years have been devoted to the rural subsistence sector of the economy.[13]

Since industrialization did not begin in Latin America until the twentieth century, there is a much greater opportunity for developing a full body of information on the industrial sector of the economy than on most other sectors. Local censuses of industry, as well as limited reports prepared for local and national governments, can be used to provide a better picture of industrial development. For example, industrial censuses were taken as early as 1922 in the city of Medellín and continued at intervals until the first Colombian national census of industry in 1945. These local data have never been used in a study of the industrial history of Colombia. In many other areas of Latin America, such sources will in time provide a more complete picture of nascent industrialization. My bibliography of Argentine statistical materials contains many items of this type. Concentrated urban growth makes study of large-scale manufacturing relatively easy, since most factories are located in a few large cities.

Data on the economy have been the most used of historical statistics; almost untouched is the vast array of educational, social, and judicial data. As a consequence of widespread concern with education, there has been a long history of the provision of educational data on numbers of children in school, numbers of teachers and schools, and expenditures for education. Since a society's investment in education is among the best available indicators of social inequality and possible trends toward equality, changes in that investment (and in the schooling rate, particularly at the secondary school level) can provide insights into the pace and character of social change. The potential for quantitative analysis in this area is, thus far, largely undetermined because of a lack of scholarly enterprise.[14]

Social history is, however, the second best developed field, after economic history, in the availability and use of statistical data. For example, James Wilkie has made a careful study of the role of the Mexican government in changing social conditions in Mexico since the Revolution of 1910.[15] His work utilizes extensively the data on illiteracy, the use of Indian languages, the level of urbanization, consumption of corn (as opposed to wheat), style of dress (shoes or *huaraches*), and sanitation. He then aggregates these indicators into a general index of poverty which enables him to compare the several states and the nation in 1910 and 1960. One may question whether these items constitute a true index of poverty; nevertheless, Wilkie's work makes our understanding of the revolutionary and post revolutionary changes much more specific than the many nonquantitative appraisals which preceded it.

Studies of earlier epochs in Mexican social history have moved toward the utilization of descriptive statistical techniques. The monumental *Historia moderna de México* edited by Daniel Cosío Villegas is concerned with the years 1867–1911.[16] In it many scholars have collaborated to give a picture of social, political, and economic life in rich quantitative detail not previously available.

It is in Mexico that social history appears to be most advanced in the use of quantitative data and statistical techniques. Unfortunately, quantitative investigations of political behavior in the past will probably not yield much in the case of Mexico. Mexican legislatures have usually acted as rubber stamps for *caudillo* presidents, so that roll-call analysis for most periods will not be fruitful. Elections have on occasion been so rigged that voting data cannot be assumed to convey useful information about the opinions of the electorate.

One important investigation in the field of politics has been undertaken by David Bushnell of the University of Florida.[17] He has assembled the vast array of electoral statistics for the Republic of Colombia and used them, along with Argentine data, for an essay on comparative political history. Bushnell contrasts the movement toward universal suffrage in the two countries until it was achieved in 1853 (though it was subsequently abrogated in Colombia); in so doing he relates the extension of the franchise to the rise of liberalism and the attitudes of elites toward the poor. This study uses quantitative techniques as an adjunct to intellectual and political history.

Scholars trained as economists make up a substantial share of all those who have published quantitative historical investigations, although even more of the scholars in economic history have been trained in law or history. A useful distinction can be made between the approaches to quantitative history in Latin America which have been followed by the Europeans and those of the "new" economic historians of the United States. French historians (e.g., Pierre Chaunu) have concerned themselves with the gathering of quantitative data—particularly of prices—and rather less with techniques of analyzing those data. In contrast, research of the last decade on American economic history has made use of quantitative techniques, but always with a close tie to the formulation and testing of hypotheses drawn from economic theory. Each style has its advantages and drawbacks. Quantitative work in what I shall call the "European style" builds the corpus of available data, but neither the utility nor the direction in which such data are augmented is determinate, since there are few hypotheses to direct the work. The method of the new economic history builds data along established lines in terms of relevant hypotheses, but data are built along such narrow lines that they may very well be of no use in the analysis of broader or different questions.

Estimates of the number of scholars in different categories who have worked on some aspect of the quantitative economic history of Latin America between 1750 and 1960 are provided in table 11.3. The estimates are based on an examination of over 700 books and articles published in the field since 1945. The total of 175 probably overstates the numbers available for quantitative work since it includes anyone who has published at least one article useful to a quantitative history of Latin America. Some of these scholars have died, and others would probably not want to undertake quantitative investigations.

How might more of these scholars be persuaded to undertake quantitative research in Latin American history? There are problems peculiar to each of the groups in table 11.3. Many of the historians will shrink from statistical endeavors on the ground that the techniques are unfamiliar and difficult to learn. In contrast, most economists tend to be concerned only with contemporary policy issues. Europeans, whether historians or economists, may in the past have been deterred from doing quantitative research simply because of the difficulties of reaching Latin American archives or securing funds to support research. Increased research funds may help greatly with European scholars, but collaborative programming is an even more central need for scholars in the Americas. Latin Americans already have research materials easily available and most urgently need support of their universities for released time from teaching duties.

Table 11.3

Estimated Number of Scholars Who Have Published Results of
Quantitative Research in Latin American History, 1955–69

Continental Origin, Type of Training	Number of Scholars
North American Historians	50
Latin Americans Trained in Law	50
North American Economists	35
Latin American Economists	20
European Historians	10
European Economists	10
TOTAL	175

SOURCE: William P. McGreevey, *A Bibliography of Latin American Economic History,* 1760–1960 (Berkeley: University of California, Center for Latin American Studies, 1969).

There currently exists no formal structure of training for quantitative research in Latin American history. An ideal approach would be to offer a regular summer workshop on quantitative research in Latin American history, providing instruction in statistical techniques—particularly the handling of time series data and testing procedures—and in substantive problems of investigation using quantitative data. Such a workshop could operate effectively with two or three instructors and perhaps as many as 20 students. In only a few years this kind of program could add numbers and quality to the scholarly work force in this field and achieve the economies of scale associated with a larger number of workers in the area.

The most substantial sources of support for research have always been universities and other centers of higher education, through salaried support of affiliated scholars. In private correspondence a European social historian has argued that the failure of Latin American universities to support quantitative historical research through appropriate appointments of scholars to their faculties has retarded development of this field. The situation is changing slowly in Latin America, but the historical profession will for some time be dominated by a generation with a traditional view of what kinds of research a historian should do.

If North American and European universities show their approval through growing support for quantitative historical research, however, Latin American universities will increase their support for scholars with such interests. The gathering and analysis of numbers require the perspective and special skills of those who have lived in the society under study. Continuing growth of the small group of Latin Americans in the field of quantitative history will make the work of foreign scholars more effective. It is a fact of academic life that a North American or European must spend the greater part of his life at his home university and away from the primary statistical data which are his raw materials. A collaborator in Latin America can complement the foreign scholar. The collaborator cannot be replaced by a research assistant—foreign and domestic scholars must work together as colleagues for full effectiveness.

Compared with the salaries provided by American universities to their teaching staffs, assistance from philanthropic foundations or government agencies is small. Nonetheless, it provides the crucial margin necessary for field research and the acquisition of materials. One hesitates to recommend that more meetings be sponsored, yet progress in this field requires regular communication between scholars. In several fields of historical research the investigator wishes to encounter only the doorkeeper at the archives and the documents there. Quantitative research in Latin American history, however, cannot style itself on that model. At the least it now requires face-to-face interchange of progress reports. Meetings for that purpose would be an ideal use for part of an increment of funds made available through foundations and government.

Thus far, scholars at work on quantitative questions in Latin American history have presented their data and analyses in scattered form. There has been no effort similar to the joint enterprise of United States government officials and scholars (under the auspices of the Social Science Research Council) to bring together United States official data and private calculations. In Latin America, private sources of data remain completely separated from official statistics. Latin American government officials have but a marginal interest in the compilation of data about the past. Once a program of scholarly research is under way, however, there is a high probability that official organizations (in one country perhaps the central bank; in another, an industrial development branch of the government; in still another, an autonomous research institute or foundation) will aid the project by facilitating access to government statistics and providing personnel and funds for the publication of results. But given the initial indifference of government officials, private scholars will have to move well along toward the stage of publication of statistical data before seeking government assistance.

What return can be expected from the efforts and funds directed toward quantitative approaches to Latin American history? The goals should be, first and most easily defined, the preparation, analysis, and assembly of data in the form of statistical histories for the major Latin American countries; and second, the expansion of research opportunities for nonquantitative historians who can use these statistical histories to elaborate a more broadly informed and quantitatively based literature of Latin American history.

Once scholars begin to assemble and publish quantitative data, other organizations will come forward with similar publications. In those cases in which public officials or private individuals have custody of records which they have not previously made public, statistical histories may stimulate the publication of currently unavailable materials. If this development occurs, the indirect results of the sponsorship of quantitative research may be greater than the direct results. For example, most private records of ecclesiastical landholdings and their purchase after disamortization in the nineteenth century have never been made public.

Work on quantitative history in several countries will give rise to external economies for the several collaborating groups working independently. Quantitative materials are potentially adaptable to comparative historical analysis, and thus statistical projects in several countries will complement each other. The pay off of adding each additional scholar to the corps at work on quantitative history will exceed substantially the individual research projects. In scholarly work of this kind, the whole is greater than the sum of its parts.

The division of labor within single-nation collaborative efforts can spread across national boundaries. Although it takes a long time to become familiar with data sources in a single country (as the size of the section on Argentina in my bibliography will attest), once a particular kind of statistical information—e.g., age-sex distributions in early censuses—is mastered, it can readily be used in several countries. An excellent example of such cross-country historical demography is Collver's study, *Birth Rates in Latin America*. As the range of readily available historical data grows, we can expect more such comparative studies.

Historical statistics can make a richer picture of the past available to many scholars. The product of research is denser, more compact, and hence cheaper to use than the results of narrative history. Quantitative historical research will lower the cost to other scholars of obtaining useful information about the past, an acutely important factor in the area of historical statistics. This kind of economy itself recommends support for quantitative research in Latin American history. If within the next decade we are able to provide in statistical compendia some of the body of data appropriate to analyses of social and economic change for five to eight countries, then we will have produced a significant addition to both man's knowledge about economic and social change and the possibilities of cumulative increase in that knowledge.

NOTES

1 Two series of ECLA publications are of importance for historical data. The early issues of *Economic Survey of Latin America,* especially those for 1948 and 1949, contain statistical data not elsewhere available; and the nine-volume series, *Analyses and Projections of Economic Development* (1955–66), provides detailed statistical data used by ECLA for global programming of economic development. Unpublished statistical appendixes to several volumes in the latter series are more useful than the aggregate published data.
2 In this regard one might consider the analysis of social change in Frederick B. Pike's *Chile and the United States, 1880–1962* (Notre Dame, Ind.: University of Notre Dame Press, 1963). Marxist historians have long been trying to apply the notion of class struggle to the Latin American context, but without notable success.
3 Albert O. Hirschman, ed., *Latin American Issues: Essays and Comments* (New York, The Twentieth Century Fund, 1961), p. 5.
4 On Mexico, see Michael P. Costeloe, *Church Wealth in Mexico. A Study of the "Juzgado de Capellanías" in the Archbishopric of Mexico, 1800–1856* (London: Cambridge University Press, 1967); Jan Bazant, "Desamortización en 1856," *Historia Mexicana,* no. 62 (1964), pp. 193–212; Frederick B. Pike, ed., *The Conflict between Church and State in Latin America* (New York: Knopf, 1964). On Colombia, see Germán Colmenares, *Las haciendas de los jesuitas en el nuevo reino de Granada* (Bogotá: Universidad de los Andes, 1969). On Chile, see Arnold J. Bauer, "Chilean Rural Society, 1830–1890" (Ph.D. diss., University of California, Berkeley, 1969). These are but a sample of the literature on the subject; they differ from earlier works, however, in an effort to present quantitative data in a systematic manner.
5 Roberto Cortés Conde, "Problemas del crecimiento industrial de la Argentina, 1870–1914," *Desarrollo económico* 3 (1963): 143–71; Aldo Ferrer, *La economía argentina* (Mexico City: Fondo de Cultura Económica, 1963); Tulio Halperín Donghi, "La expansion ganadera en la campaña de Buenos Aires, 1810–1852," *Desarrollo económico* 3 (1963): 57–100.
6 See República de Argentina, Dirección de inmigración, *Memoria* (Buenos Aires, 1869–1920 annually).
7 Population Research Center, *International Population Census Bibliography. Latin America and the Caribbean* (Austin: University of Texas, Bureau of Business Research, 1965).
8 O. Andrew Collver, in *Birth Rates in Latin America: New Estimates of Historical Trends and Fluctuations* (Berkeley: Institute of International Studies, University of California, 1965), p. 75, also provides a useful evaluation of census data from the point of view of their utility in substituting for reliable vital statistics.
9 Enrique Pérez López et al., *Mexico's Recent Economic Growth: The Mexican View* (Austin: University of Texas Press, 1967).
10 Handicrafts and early efforts at manufacturing in Mexico are the subject of the excellent study by Robert A. Potash, *El Banco de Avío de México. El fomento de la industria, 1821–1846* (Mexico City: Fondo de Cultura Económica, 1959).

11   República de Colombia, Oficina General de Estadística, *Anuario estadístico, 1875* (Bogotá, 1875), pp. 23 ff.
12   W. J. Dickson to the Marquis of Salisbury, 18 October 1888, no. 446 in the Reports of the Annual Series of Diplomatic and Consular Reports.
13   William Paul McGreevey, "Recent Research on the Economic History of Latin America," *Latin American Research Review* 3 (1968): 108.
14   Elizabeth Connealy, "The Evolution of Brazilian Education in the Nineteenth Century" (unpublished paper, Berkeley, 1967).
15   James W. Wilkie, *The Mexican Revolution: Federal Expenditure and Social Change since 1910* (Berkeley and Los Angeles: University of California Press, 1967).
16   Daniel Cosío Villegas, ed., *Historia moderna de México*, 8 vols. (Mexico City: Editorial Hermes, 1955–65).
17   David Bushnell, "El sufragio en la Argentina y en Colombia hasta 1853." *Revista del Instituto de Historia del Derecho XIX* (Buenos Aires, 1968), pp. 11–29.

BIBLIOGRAPHY

GENERAL GUIDES TO THE STATISTICS AND LITERATURE OF ECONOMIC AND SOCIAL HISTORY

Baughman, James P. "Recent Trends in the Business History of Latin America." *Business History Review* (BHR), vol. 39, no. 4 (1965), pp. 425–38.
Bushong, Allen D. "Doctoral Dissertations on Pan-American Topics. Accepted by United States and Canadian Colleges and Universities, 1961–65." *Latin American Research Review*, vol. 2, no. 2 (1967), supplement.
————, and Kidder, Frederick E. "Theses on Pan American Topics." Washington, D.C.: Pan American Union, 1962.
Hispanic American Historical Review (*HAHR*), Historiographical Series:
    Arnade, Charles W. "The Historiography of Colonial and Modern Bolivia." *HAHR*, vol. 42, no. 3 (1962), pp. 333–84.
    Barager, Joseph R. "The Historiography of the Rio de la Plata Area since 1830." *HAHR*, vol. 39, no. 4 (1959), pp. 588–642.
    Griffith, William J. "The Historiography of Central America since 1830." *HAHR*, vol. 40, no. 4 (1960), pp. 548–69.
    Potash, Robert A. "The Historiography of Mexico since 1821." *HAHR*, vol. 40, no. 3 (1960), pp. 383–484.
    Smith, Robert Freeman. "Twentieth Century Cuban Historiography." *HAHR*, vol. 44, no. 1 (1964), pp. 44–73.
    Stein, Stanley J. "The Historiography of Brazil, 1808–1889." *HAHR*, vol. 40, no. 2 (1960), pp. 234–78.
    Szaszdi, Adam. "The Historiography of the Republic of Ecuador." *HAHR*, vol. 44, no. 4 (1964), pp. 503–50.
Humphreys, R. A. *Latin American History: A Guide to the Literature in English.* London: Oxford University Press, 1958.
Inter-American Statistical Institute. *Statistical Activities of the American Nations, 1940.* Washington, D.C.: Pan American Union, 1941.
————. *Bibliography of Selected Statistical Sources of the American Nations.* Washington, D.C.: Pan American Union, 1947.

Jones, Tom Bard. *A Bibliography on South American Economic Affairs: Articles in Nineteenth Century Periodicals.* Minneapolis: University of Minnesota Press, 1955.

Normano, João F., ed. *The Economic Literature of Latin America: A Tentative Bibliography.* 2 vols. Cambridge, Mass., Harvard Univ. Press, 1935.

Ragatz, Lowell J. *Statistics for the Study of British Caribbean Economic History, 1763–1833.* London, 1928.

Stein, Stanley J. "Latin American Historiography: Status and Research Opportunities." In *Social Science Research on Latin America,* edited by Charles Wagley. New York: Columbia University Press, 1964.

Zimmerman, Irene. *Guide to Current Latin American Periodicals: Humanities and Social Sciences.* Gainesville: University of Florida Press, 1961.

DOCUMENTARY SOURCES

International Sources

References in this section relate to League of Nations and United Nations publications. Latin American data are included only as a lesser part of the whole of worldwide coverage. The period of League of Nations publications (1920–1930s) makes them particularly useful for research on the period of incipient industrialization in Latin America.

International Institute of Agriculture. *Les grands produits agricoles: compendium de statistique, 1924–1938.* Rome, 1944. Data were taken from the regularly published *International Yearbook of Agricultural Statistics* for the purpose of reshaping and recombining yearly figures to form one vast at-a-glance reference tool covering the production, commerce, and consumption of the world's agricultural products.

League of Nations. *Industrialization and Foreign Trade.* Geneva, 1945. This study traces the growth of industry and trade in the world since the 1870s and examines in detail the effects of industrial growth in the past on the trade of other countries. An annex gives indexes of manufacturing from 1870 to 1938 and statistics of world trade from 1871 to 1938, presented in tabular form by country and product and with yearly world totals.

United Nations. *Yearbook of National Accounts Statistics.* New York, 1947–. This publication gives information provided by banks or offical agencies of the natonal governments. It superseded *Statistical Papers, Series H* (Statistics of national income and expenditure), of which ten issues were published.

———. *Yearbook of Food and Agricultural Statistics.* Pt. 1, *Production;* pt. 2, *Trade/Commerce.* Washington, D.C.: United Nations, F.A.O., 1947–57. This superseded *International Yearbook of Agricultural Statistics.* The statistics it gives are official ones supplied by the governments.

———. *Economic Survey of Latin America.* Lake Success, N.Y.: United Nations, Economic Commission for Latin America, 1948. Early issues contain historical statistics on Latin American economic development; later issues have become contemporary reportage.

———. *Economic Bulletin for Latin America.* Vol. 1– and supplement. Santiago, Chile: United Nations, Economic Commission for Latin America, 1956. This appears biannually and contains statistics on current economic conditions and trends in Latin America.

————. *Statistical Bulletin for Latin America*. New York: United Nations, Economic Commission for Latin America, 1964.

United States and Inter-American Sources

American Geographical Society. *A Catalogue of Maps of Hispanic America; Including Maps in Scientific Periodicals and Books and Sheet and Atlas Maps with Articles on the Cartography of the Several Countries and Maps Showing the Extent and Character of Existing Surveys*. 4 vols. Map of Hispanic America, publication 3. New York, 1930–32.

Childs, James Bennett. *The Memorias of the Republics of Central America and the Antilles*. Washington, D.C., 1932.

Gregory, Winifred, ed. *List of the Serial Publications of Foreign Governments, 1815–1931*. New York, 1932. The Latin American entries are by country, sub-arranged by issuing agency. Holdings of libraries in the United States—including government, public, and university—are indicated wherever they are known.

Grubbs, Henry A. *A Tentative Guide to Manuscript Material in Latin American Libraries*. Cambridge, Mass., 1936.

Harvard University Library. *Widener Library Shelflist*. Widener Collection, vols. 5–6 (Latin America). Cambridge: Harvard University Press, 1967.

Hill, Rosco R. *The National Archives of Latin America*. Cambridge, Mass., 1945.

International Bureau of the American Republics. *Commercial Directory of the American Republics; Comprising the Manufacturers, Merchants, Shippers and Banks and Bankers Engaged in Foreign Trade, together with Names of Officials, Maps, Commercial Statistics, Industrial Data, and Other Information Concerning the Countries of the International Union of American Republics*. 2 vols. Washington, D.C., 1897–98.

Jones, Cecil Knight. *A Bibliography of Latin American Bibliographies*. 2d ed. Washington, D.C., 1942. This listing includes bibliographies, collective biographies, histories of literature, and some general and miscellaneous works for references purposes.

McGregor, John. *Commercial Statistics of America; a Digest of Her Productive Resources . . . with the Addition of the Spanish American Republics*. London, 1847.

Pan American Union. *Foreign Trade Series*. Nos. 1–[214]. Washington, D.C., 1918–50.

————. *Index to Latin American Periodical Literature, 1929–1960*. 8 vols. Boston, Mass.: Columbus Memorial Library, 1962.

Phelps, Elizabeth, ed. *Statistical Activities of the American Nations, 1940: A Compendium of the Statistical Services and Activities of 22 Nations of the Western Hemisphere, together with Information Concerning Statistical Personnel in these Nations*. Washington, D.C., 1941.

Savage, Thomas, ed. *Manual of Industrial and Commercial Intercourse between the United States and Spanish America*. San Francisco, 1889.

Taueber, Irene B. *General Census and Vital Statistics in the Americas; an Annotated Bibliography of the Historical Censuses and Current Vital Statistics of the Twenty-One American Republics, the American Sections of the British*

Commonwealth of Nations, the American Colonies of Denmark, France, and the Netherlands, and the American Territories and Possessions of the United States. Census Library Project. Washington, D.C.: Government Printing Office, 1943.

U.S. Bureau of the Census. *Argentina: Summary of Biostatistics. Maps and Charts, Population, Natality, and mortality statistics.* Washington, D.C.: Government Printing Office, 1945.

Argentina: Sample Materials from a Major Country

This section is intended as a sample of official sources for the quantitative history of a single country. Argentina probably has the most complete documentation available for any country in the region. Census materials for Argentina as a whole begin with the year 1869; these are not listed here because they are relatively easy to locate.

General Statistical Sources

Argentine Republic, Dirección General de Estadística. *Registro estadístico de la República Argentina.* Vols. 1–21. Buenos Aires, 1864–[86].

———. *Anuario.* Buenos Aires, 1892–1914. This gives comprehensive social and economic statistics for provinces, cities, zones, with comparative statistics included throughout. It was continued by the Ministerio de Hacienda as *Estadística del Comercio y de la Navegación.* The commercial information was continued to be issued by the Dirección General de Estadística as *Anuario del Comercio Exterior.*

Argentine Republic. *Anuario Oficial de la República Argentina.* Vol. 1. Buenos Aires, 1912. This is a compendium of statistical material emanating from the Ministerios del Interior, Relationes Exteriores y Agricultura. It is no longer published.

Argentine Republic, Dirección General de Estadística. *Resúmenes estadísticos retrospectivos.* Buenos Aires, 1914. This includes data on commerce (imports, exports), finance (national and municipal budgets, 1894–1913), governmental revenue and expenditures for the 50 years preceding 1914, immigration and emigration (a 44-year résumé), agriculture (1909–13), railroads and earnings (1857–1913), shipping (retrospective statistical survey) mails and telegraph (1895–1913), and school population (public and private instruction in 1912).

———. *Extracto estadístico de la República Argentina.* No. 1. Buenos Aires, 1916.

Argentine Republic, Dirección de Economía Rural y Estadística. *Informes y estudios de la Dirección . . . Emilio Lahitte.* 3 vols. Buenos Aires, 1916–20.

Argentine Republic, Dirección General de Estadística. *Intercambio económico de la República, 1910–1917,* directed by Alejandro E. Bunge. Buenos Aires, 1918. This is a detailed analysis of trade, prices, and balance of payments for the 1910–17 period by an Argentine economist.

———. . . . *Informe . . . Dirección General de Estadística.* Nos. 1–100. Buenos Aires, 1923–45. This quarterly publication contains statistics on economic activities. Foreign trade is treated in greatest detail.

———, Consejo National de Estadística y Censos. *Boletín censal y estadístico* (Buenos Aires), vol. 1 nos. 1–15 (20 June–1 Dec. 1945).

Argentine Republic, Dirección General de Estadística. *Síntesis estadística mensual.* Vols. 1–9, with supplements. Buenos Aires, 1947–55. This superseded Argentine

Republic, Ministerio de Agricultura, *Boletín Estadístico*. The monthly statistical bulletin keeps up to date the information presented in the *Anuarios* of various agencies as well as the periodic *Censos*.

Argentine Republic, Secretaria de Asuntos Económicos. *Producto e ingreso de la República Argentina en el período 1935/54*. Buenos Aires, 1955.

Argentine Republic, Consejo National de Desarrollo. *Mapas y estadísticas de la República Argentina*. Buenos Aires, 1962. Collation of economic statistics from various sources published since 1940.

Boeri, Lelia I. Catálogo de estadísticas publicadas en la república Argentina. 2 vols. Buenos Aires: Instituto Torcuato di Tella, Centro de Investigaciones Económicas, 1963.

Boston, Massachusetts, First National Bank. *The Situation in Argentina; Monthly Bulletin of the Buenos Aires Branch of the First National Bank of Boston*. Buenos Aires, 1925–.

Mendoza (province), Argentine Republic. *Censo general de población y riqueza de Mendoza. Ley 1398. Cultivos permanentes, 1942*. Mendoza, Argentina: Instituto Técnico de Investigationes y Orientación Económica de la Producción, 1943.

The Review of the River Plate (Buenos Aires). Published since Dec. 1891, first weekly, now every ten days. A British-owned financial, shipping, and trade journal devoted to weekly reports on the Argentine economy. The statistics are derived from government agencies.

Revista de Economía Argentina (Buenos Aires). Published monthly since July 1918.

General Statistics on the Province and City of Buenos Aires

Buenos Aires, Dirección General de Estadística. *Anuario estadístico de la provincia de Buenos Aires*. Vol. 1. La Plata, 1881–[1926]. This was continued by the Oficina de Estadística General as *Registro estadístico de la provincia de Buenos Aires*, 1898–1923.

Buenos Aires, Comisión Directive del Censo. *Censo general de la provincia de Buenos Aires demográfico, agrícola, industrial, comercial y, verificado el 9 de octubre de 1881*. Buenos Aires, 1883. This commercial and demographic census includes historical data on population growth since 1822.

―――. *Censo general de la población, edificación, comercio e industrias de la ciudad de Buenos Aires, levantado en los días 17 de agosto, 15 y 30 de septiembre, 1887*. 2 vols. Buenos Aires, 1889. This was the second census of the city of Buenos Aires, the first having been included in the national census of 1869. Questions asked in the census of 1887 were age, parentage, civil status, color, occupation, religion, national origin, place of residence, whether or not literate. The census also included contemporary analyses of commercial activities and social services in addition to historical data on vital statistics and racial composition of the population.

Buenos Aires, Dirección General de Estadística. *Demografía*. La Plata, 1895–1907 (annually). This title varies; in 1895 it was published as *Memoria demográfica*. The volumes for 1896–97 were published in the *Anuario de la Provincia de Buenos Aires*. The data are cross-classified by age, sex, and nationality; a report on causes of mortality is included.

Buenos Aires, Bolsa de Cereales. *Memoria y informe de la Comisión Directiva de la Bolsa de Cereales*. Buenos Aires, 1899–1900, 1913–14. This is an annual report of production; movement into Buenos Aires; and prices of food crops for livestock, grains, seed crops, vegetable commodities, flax, etc. It includes statistics on price fluctuations in the cereals market, volume of trade, etc.

Buenos Aires. *Censo general de población, edificación, comercio, e industrias de la Ciudad de Buenos Aires; levantado en los días 11 y 18 de septiembre, de 1904, bajo la administración del Señor Don Alberto Casares.* Buenos Aires, 1906.

————. *Censo general de población, edificación, comercio, e industrias de la ciudad de Buenos Aires; levantado en los días 16 al 24 de octubre de 1909 bajo la administración de Don Manuel J. Guiraldes, por Alberto B. Martinez.* 3 vols. Buenos Aires, 1910. Contains statistical information on economic, social, and political activities in the city of Buenos Aires. Information ranges from voting habits to public services and financial activities.

Buenos Aires, Comisión Técnica Encargada de Realizar el Cuarto Censo General de la Ciudad de Buenos Aires. *Cuarto censo general, 1936; 22 X-1936.* 4 vols. Buenos Aires, 1938–40.

Buenos Aires, Departamento de Policía. *Boletín de estadística y jurisprudencia; delitos en general, suicidios, accidentes, y contravenciones diversas.* Buenos Aires, 18??–[1942].

Statistics on Foreign Commerce

Argentine Republic, Ministerio de Hacienda. *Estadística general del comercio exterior, 1870–1880.* Buenos Aires, 1870–80.

————. *Estadística del comercio y de la navegación.* Vols. 1–13. Buenos Aires, 1880–92.

Argentine Republic, Dirección General de Estadística. *El comercio exterior argentino.* Nos. 1–236. Buenos Aires, 1882–1945.

Argentine Republic, Dirección de Comercio e Industria. *El comercio internacional argentino.* Nos. 1–11. Buenos Aires, 1908–20.

Argentine Republic, Dirección General de Estadística. *Anuario estadístico . . . comercio exterior.* Buenos Aires, 1915–47. This yearbook of foreign trade is probably the most complete compilation for the period covered. Much retrospective data is included.

————. *. . . Noticia sumaria del comercio exterior argentino en el decenio, 1910–1919.* Buenos Aires, 1920.

Agriculture and Livestock Production

Argentine Republic, Ministerio de Agricultura. *Memoria presentada al honorable Congreso por el Ministro.* Buenos Aires, 1899–1949. This includes data on agricultural production and exports as well as information on the extractive and service industries. The 1899 edition provides figures on the number and localization of immigrant workers.

————, Ministerio de Agricultura. *Boletín estadístico.* Buenos Aires, 1900–46. A monthly summary of agricultural and pastoral production.

Argentine Republic, Dirección de Economía Rural y Estadística Agrícola. *Estadística agrícola.* Buenos Aires, 1902–04, 1917–18.

Argentine Republic, Dirección de Economía Rural y Estadística. *Informes y estudios de la Dirección de Economía Rural y Estadística.* Buenos Aires, 1908–[20].

Argentine Republic, Comisión del Censo Agropecuario. *Censo agropecuario nacional. La ganadería y la agricultura en 1908 . . . Censo levantado durante la presidencia del Dr. José Figueroa Alcorta por una comisión.* 3 vols. Buenos Aires, 1909.

Argentine Republic, Dirección de Economía Rural y Estadística. *Anuario agrope-cuario.* Buenos Aires, 1932– annually. The 1935 edition contains comparative figures for the period 1930–35 on matters relating to agricultural production—costs, wages, land tenure, financing.

Argentine Republic. *Censo algodonero de la República Argentina, año 1935–36.* Junta Nacional del Algodón, no. 16. Buenos Aires, 1936.

Argentine Republic, Dirección de Economía Rural y Estadística. *Informaciones estadísticas agropecuarias.* Vols. 1–7. Buenos Aires, 1937–43.

Argentine Republic, Dirección de Algodón. *La industrialización de fibra de algo-dón en la República Argentina, 1938–1955.* Buenos Aires, 1938–55. This lists annual production statistics for processing of cotton fibre, manufacture of thread, etc. Retrospective figures to 1914 are given in some cases.

Argentine Republic, Comisión Nacional del Censo Agropecuario. *Censo nacional agropecuario. Año 1937.* 2 vols. Buenos Aires, 1940.

Argentine Republic, Dirección Nacional de Estadísticas y Censos. *Censo nacional agropecuario de 1952: existencia de ganado vacuno, porcino, y lanar: Resulta-dos Provisionales.* Buenos Aires, 1953.

————. *Censo nacional agropecuario, 1960.* 3 vols. Buenos Aires, [1960]

Commerce and Industry

Argentine Republic, Dirección General de Estadística. *Estadísticas comerciales y monetarias.* Buenos Aires, 1905–07.

Argentine Republic, Dirección de Comercio e Industria. *Estadística industrial y comercial; boletín nos. 1–27, 1908–1919.* Buenos Aires, 1908–19. Each number is devoted to a different subject: banks and securities, telephones, newspaper pub-lication. Also included are reports on specific provincial and territorial com-merce and industry.

————. *Información comercial e industrial.* Nos. 1–38. Buenos Aires, 1919–22.

Argentine Republic, Dirección General de Estadística y Censos de la Nación. *Esta-dística industrial.* Buenos Aires, 1938–44 (for 1934/35–1941). An industrial census for 1935.

Argentine Republic, Dirección Nacional del Servicio Estadístico. *IV censo general de la nación: censo industrial de 1946.* Buenos Aires, 1952.

Argentine Republic, Dirección Nacional de Estadística y Censos. *Censo industrial, 1954.* Buenos Aires, 1960.

Finance

Argentine Republic, Caja Nacional de Ahorro Postal. *Memoria y balance general.* Buenos Aires, 1915–.

Argentine Republic, Comisión del Censo Hipotecario Nacional. *Censo hipotecario nacional al 31 de diciembre de 1936.* Buenos Aires, 1938.

Banco Central de la República Argentina. *Memoria anual.* Buenos Aires, 1935–. Gives descriptions of foreign and domestic finance and monetary conditions supported by statistical tables; also lists prices of commodities, exports, food-stuffs, etc.

————. *Boletín estadístico.* 1935–48; new series, 1958–. A monthly survey of in-vestment conditions and financial activities of the public and private sectors.

Banco de la Nación Argentina. *Memoria y balance general* [Annual report and balance sheet]. Buenos Aires, 1891–.

Banco Hipotecario Nacional. *Memoria anual.* Buenos Aires, 1887–[1947].

Banco Industrial de la República Argentina. *Memoria y balance. Ejercicio.* Vols. 1–13. Buenos Aires, 1944–56.

Government Revenues and Expenditures
Argentine Republic, Ministerio de Hacienda Pública. *Memoria sobre el estado de la hacienda pública.* Part 1. Buenos Aires, 1834.
———. *Memoria del departamento de hacienda.* Buenos Aires, 1863–. This annual summary of private and public financial sectors includes government income and expenditures, investments, public debt. Later *Memorias* include reports of national commercial and savings banks, the Port of Buenos Aires, customs, coinage.
———. *Estadística de la aduana de Buenos Aires, 1861–69.* Vols. 1–9. Buenos Aires, 1863–.
Argentine Republic, Junta de Administración del Crédito Público Nacional. *Memoria de la Junta de Administración del crédito público.* Buenos Aires, 1864–1928.
———. *Informe del presidente del crédito público nacional.* 5 vols. and atlas. Buenos Aires, 1881–88.
Argentine Republic, Contaduría General de la Nación. *Memoria . . . correspondiente al año 1912 [?]–1953 [?].* Buenos Aires, [1912–53]. Tabulated accounts of budgets, income, and expenditures of the national government and all its agencies, including the national university of Buenos Aires.

Transport, Public Works, and Utilities
Argentine Republic, Dirección General de Ferrocarriles Nacionales. *Estadística gráfica de los ferrocarriles en explotación, 1857–1935.* 11 pages, 96 diagrams. Buenos Aires, 1937.
———. *Estadística de los ferrocarriles de la república.* Buenos Aires, [1892–1935].
Argentine Republic, Ministerio de Obras Públicas. *Memoria.* Buenos Aires, 1884–1948.
———. *Boletín de obras públicas.* Buenos Aires, 1900–(annually). Contains statistical data on water supply, purification, sewage and disposal, etc. Also includes budgets and costs of national and provincial projects for amplification and improvement of public facilities.

Labor
Argentine Republic, Departamento Nacional del Trabajo. *Boletín.* Nos. 1–48. Buenos Aires, 1907–21. Monthly information on working conditions, wages, strikes, and occupational structure of the labor force.
———. *Anuario estadístico del trabajo.* Buenos Aires, 1913–24.
———. *Boletín informativo.* Nos. 1–246. Buenos Aires, 1918–42.

Immigration
Argentine Republic, Dirección de Inmigración. *Memoria.* Buenos Aires, [1869–1920]. Contents include annual immigration and emigration totals by nationality, occupation, sex, civil status, and age; destination of the immigrants by Argentine localities; and figures on internal migration. The 1913–15 volumes give a decennial résumé of immigration figures, including the number of skilled workers entering each year (i.e., 1903–14).
———. *Informe de estadística.* Buenos Aires, [1923]. This report covers national and provincial migratory movement, including interior and exterior travel by Argentinians. It gives retrospective and comparative figures on immigration back to 1857.

————. . . . *Resumen estadístico del movimiento migratorio en la República Argentina, años 1857–1924.* Buenos Aires, 1925.

Police

Argentine Republic, Departamento de Policía. . . . *Policía de la provincia de Buenos Aires. Boletín mensual de estadística.* Vols. 1–9. [La Plata], 1891–1903.

Education

Argentine Republic, Ministerio de Justicia e Instrucción Pública. *Memoria . . . Anexos* . . . Buenos Aires, [1863–1936] (annually). Volume 1 presents statistics on the work of the courts and information on crime and criminals (vital and social statistics). Volumes 2–3 contain statistical material on all aspects of public instruction, including budget for public education, universities, colleges, technical, and professional schools.

Argentine Republic, Oficina Central del Censo. *Censo escolar nacional correspondiente a fines de 1883 y principios de 1884.* 3 vols. Buenos Aires, 1885.

Argentine Republic, Dirección del Censo Escolar de la Nación. *Censo escolar de la nación.* 4 vols. Buenos Aires, 1943. This census provides demographic information on persons of school age in all provinces and detailed information on the illiterate portion of Argentina's population.

————. *El analfabetismo en la Argentina; estudio comparativo desde 1869 a 1943; informe de la Dirección del Censo Escolar de la Nación.* Buenos Aires, 1944.

————. *Censo escolar de la nación; la distribución por zonas de la población argentina y su relación con los hechos culturales, económicas, y sociales.* 2d ed. Buenos Aires, 1946. A comparative study for the period 1869 through 1943, and a statistical analysis of the 1943 school census showing the role of urbanization in the growth of literacy. Includes detailed statistics on illiteracy by age, sex, place of birth (foreign or national), and region.

Argentine Republic, Departamento de Documentación y Información Educativa. *Serie estadística educativa.* Buenos Aires, 1960–. A statistical analysis of school population, including charts on educational facilities, students, and teachers for preprimary through university facilities. Figures are broken down for each province by age, sex, grade levels achieved, etc.

Martinez, Alberto B. . . . *Recensement général d'éducation levé le 23 mai 1909 pendant la présidence de M. le Dr. Jose Figueroa Alcorta et le ministère de la justice et de l'instruction publique de M. le Dr. Rómulo S. Naon.* 3 vols.: vol. 1, School population; vol. 2, Educational statistics; vol. 3, Monograph studies. Buenos Aires, 1910.

SECONDARY MATERIALS

Aubrey, Henry G. "The National Income of Mexico." *Estadística, Inter-American Statistical Institute* (Washington, D.C.), June 1950, pp. 185–98.

Baer, Werner. "Regional Inequality and Economic Growth in Brazil." *Economic Development and Cultural Change* 12 (1964): 368–85.

Bauer, Arnold J. "Chilean Rural Society, 1830–1890." Ph.D. dissertation, University of California, Berkeley, 1969.

Bazant, Jan. "Desamortización en 1856." *Historia Mexicana,* no. 62, pp. 193–212.

————. *Historia de la deuda exterior de México, 1823–1846.* Mexico City, 1968.

Borah, Woodrow, and Cook, Sherburne F. "Marriage and Legitimacy in Mexican Culture: Mexico and California." *California Law Review* 54 (1966): 946–1008.

Brandenburg, Frank. *Desarrollo de la empresa privada latinoamericana.* Bogotá: Ediciones Tercer Mundo, 1965.

Brito Figueroa, Federico. *Historia económica y social de Venezuela.* 2 vols. Caracas: Universidad Central de Venezuela, 1966.

Bushnell, David. "El sufragio en la Argentina y en Colombia hasta 1853." *Revista del Instituto de Historia del Derecho XIX* (Buenos Aires), 1968, pp. 11–29.

Chaplin, David. *The Peruvian Industrial Labor Force.* Princeton, N.J.: Princeton University Press, 1967.

El Colegio de México. *Estadísticas económicas del Porfiriato. Fuerza de trabajo y actividad económica por sectores.* Mexico City: El Colegio de México, n.d.

Collver, O. Andrew. *Birth Rates in Latin America: New Estimates of Historical Trends and Fluctuations.* Berkeley: Institute of International Studies, University of California, Berkeley, 1965.

Colmenares, Germán. *Las haciendas de los jesuitas en el nuevo reino de granada.* Bogotá: Universidad de los Andes, 1969.

Connealy, Elizabeth. "The Evolution of Brazilian Education in the Nineteenth Century." Unpublished paper, Berkeley, 1967.

Corporacion de Fomento de la Producción. *Veinte años de labor, 1939–1959.* Santiago, 1962.

Cortés Conde, Roberto. "Problemas del crecimiento industial de la argentina, 1870–1914." *Desarrollo ecónomico,* vol. 3, nos. 1–2 (1963), pp. 143–71.

———, and Gallo, Ezequiel. "El crecimiento ecónomico de la argentina. Notas para su análisis histórico." *Anuario del Instituto de Investigaciones Históricas, Universidad Nacional del Litoral, Argentina,* no. 6 (1962–63), pp. 265–335.

Corwin, Arthur F. *Spain and the Abolition of Slavery in Cuba, 1817–1886.* Austin: University of Texas Press, 1967.

Cosio Villegas, Daniel, ed. *Historia moderna de México.* 8 vols. Mexico City: Editorial Hermes, 1955–65.

Costeloe, Michael P. *Church Wealth in Mexico. A Study of the "Juzgado de Capellanías" in the Archbishopric of Mexico, 1800–1856.* London: Cambridge University Press, 1967.

The Cuban Economic Research Project. *A Study on Cuba. The Colonial and Republican Periods.* Coral Gables, Fla., 1965.

Davis, Kingsley. "The Place of Latin America in World Demographic History." *The Milbank Memorial Fund Quarterly,* vol. 42, no. 2, pt. 2 (1964), pp. 19–47.

Diaz Alejandro, Carlos F. "An Interpretation of Argentine Economic Growth since 1930." *The Journal of Development Studies* 3 (1967): 14–41, 155–77.

———. The Argentine Tariff, 1906–1940. Oxford Economic Papers, New Series, XIX, pp. 75–90.

Di Tella, Guido, and Zylmelman, Manuel. *Las etapas del desarrollo económico argentino.* Buenos Aires: Editorial Universitaria de Buenos Aires, 1967.

Di Tella, Torcuato S. *La teoría del primer impacto del crecimiento ecónomico.* Santa Fe, Argentina: Instituto de Sociología, Facultad de Filosofía y Letras, Universidad Nacional del Litoral, 1965.

———. "La controversia sobre la educación en Argentina: Sus raíces." *Revista Mexicana de Sociología,* 28th year, vol. 27, no. 4 (1966), pp. 855–88.

Ely, Roland T. *Cuando reinaba su majestad el azúcar.* Buenos Aires: Editorial Sudamericana, 1963.

Encina, Francisco A. *Nuestra inferioridad económica, sus causas, sus consecuencias.* Santiago: Editorial Universitaria, 1955.

Fals Borda, Orlando. *Subversion and Social Change in Colombia.* New York: Columbia University Press, 1969.

Ferrer, Aldo. *La economía argentina.* Mexico City: Fondo de Cultura Económica, 1963.

Furtado, Censo. *The Economic Growth of Brazil. A Survey from Colonial to Modern Times.* Berkeley and Los Angeles: University of California Press, 1963.

Germani, Gino. *Política y sociedad en una época de transición de la sociedad tradicional a la sociedad de masas.* Buenos Aires: Editorial Paidós, 1962.

––––––, and Di Tella, Torcuato, eds. *Argentina, sociedad de masas.* Buenos Aires: Instituto Torcuato Di Tella, 1965.

Glade, William P. *The Latin American Economies: A Study of Their Institutional Evolution.* New York: Van Nostrand, 1969.

Goodrich, Carter. "Argentina as a New Country." *Comparative Studies in Society and History* 7 (1964): 70–88.

Gordon, William E. "Imperial Policy Decisions in the Economic History of Jamaica, 1664–1934." *Social and Economic Studies,* 1957, pp. 1–28.

Graham, Richard. "A British Industry in Brazil: Rio Flour Mills, 1886–1920." *Business History Review,* vol. 7, no. 1 (1966), pp. 13–38.

Halperín Donghi, Tulio. "La expansion ganadera en la campaña de Buenos Aires, 1810–1852." *Desarrollo económico* 3 (1963): 57–110.

Hirschman, Albert O., ed. *Latin American Issues: Essays and Comments.* New York: Twentieth Century Fund, 1961.

Joslin, David. *A Century of Banking in Latin America. Bank of London and South America Limited, 1862–1962.* London: Oxford University Press, 1963.

Kroeber, Clifton B. *The Growth of the Shipping Industry in the Río de la Plata Region, 1794–1860.* Madison: University of Wisconsin Press, 1957.

Leff, Nathaniel H. *The Brazilian Capital Goods Industry, 1929–1964.* Cambridge: Harvard University Press, 1968.

––––––. "Long-term Brazilian Economic Development." *Journal of Economic History* 29 (1969): 473–93.

Levin, Jonathan V. *The Export Economies. Their Pattern of Development in Historical Perspective.* Cambridge: Harvard University Press, 1960.

López Cámara, Francisco. *La estructura económica y social de México en la época de la reforma.* Mexico City: Siglo XXI Editores, 1967.

McGreevey, William Paul. "Recent Research on the Economic History of Latin America." *Latin American Research Review* 3 (1968): 89–117.

––––––. *An Economic History of Colombia, 1845–1930.* Cambridge: Cambridge University Press, 1971.

––––––. *A Bibliography of Latin American Economic History, 1760–1960.* Berkeley: University of California, Center for Latin American Studies, 1969.

Mamalakis, Markos, and Reynolds, Clark W. *Essays on the Chilean Economy.* Homewood, Ill.: Richard D. Irwin, Inc., 1965.

Merkx, Gilbert W. "Legalidad, cambio político, e impacto social en los cambios de presidentes latinoamericanos, 1930–1965." *Revista latinoamericana de sociología* 4 (1968): 421–40.

Mexico, Secretaria de Economía, Dirección General de Estadística. *Estadísticas sociales del Porfiriato, 1877–1910*. Mexico City, 1956.

Morgan, D. J. "Imperial Preference in the West Indies and in the British Caribbean, 1929–55: A Quantitative Analysis." *Economic Journal*, vol. 72, no. 285 (1962), pp. 104–33.

Morse, Richard M. "Recent Research on Latin American Urbanization: A Selective Survey with Commentary." *Latin American Research Review* 1 (1965): 35–74.

Ortiz, Ricardo M. *Historia económica de la Argentina*. 2 vols. Buenos Aires: Ediciones Pampa y Cielo, 1964.

Pérez López, Enrique, et al. *Mexico's Recent Economic Growth, The Mexican View*. Austin: University of Texas Press, 1967.

Pike, Frederick B. *Chile and the United States, 1880–1962*. Notre Dame, Ind.: University of Notre Dame Press, 1963.

————, ed. *The Conflict Between Church and State in Latin America*. New York: Knopf, 1964.

Potash, Robert A. *El Banco de Avío de México. El fomento de la industria, 1821–1846*. Mexico City: Fondo de Cultura Económica, 1959.

Sánchez-Albornoz, Nicolas. "Les régistres paroissiaux en Amérique Latine, Quelques considérations sur leur exploitation pour la démographie historique." *Revue Suisse d'Histoire* 18 (1967).

Scott, Robert E. *Mexican Government in Transition*. Urbana: University of Illinois Press, 1964.

Smith, Peter H. "Social Mobilization, Political Participation, and the Rise of Juan Perón." *Political Science Quarterly*, vol. 84, no. 1 (1969).

————. *Politics and Beef in Argentina*. New York: Columbia University Press, 1969.

Spiegel, Henry W. "A Century of Prices in Brazil." *Review of Economics and Statistics*, vol. 30, no. 1 (1948).

Stein, Stanley J. *Vassouras. A Brazilian Coffee County, 1850–1900*. Cambridge: Harvard University Press, 1957.

————. *The Brazilian Cotton Manufacture: Textile Enterprise in an Underdeveloped Area, 1850–1950*. Cambridge: Harvard University Press, 1957.

Véliz, Claudio. *Historia de la Marina Mercante de Chile*. Santiago: Ediciones de la Universidad de Chile, 1961.

Vera Valenzuela, Mario. *La política económica del cobre en Chile*. Santiago: Ediciones de la Universidad de Chile, 1961.

Vernon, Raymond. *The Dilemma of Mexico's Development*. Cambridge: Harvard University Press, 1965.

Wilkie, James W. *The Mexican Revolution: Federal Expenditure and Social Change since 1910*. Berkeley and Los Angeles: University of California Press, 1967.

Williams, Eric. *Capitalism and Slavery*. Chapel Hill: University of North Carolina Press, 1944.

Wionczek, Miguel S. *El nacionalismo mexicano y la inversión extranjera*. Mexico City: Siglo XXI Editores, 1967.

Wood, Donald. *Trinidad in Transition. The Years After Slavery*. London: Oxford University Press, 1968.

12

QUANTITATIVE DATA FOR JAPANESE
ECONOMIC HISTORY

by Kozo Yamamura and Susan B. Hanley

After overcoming his initial dismay at the first sight of rows of dusty volumes bearing nondescript titles in Japanese, the historian will be delighted to discover that the output of statistical data on Japan has grown at a rate even faster than that of the economy of modern Japan. The Japanese data compare favorably, in quantity as well as in quality, with those of any other nation at comparable stages of development.

Japan abounds in statistical materials for both the Tokugawa (1600–1867) and post-Restoration periods, materials valuable for economic, political, social, and other historical studies. But discussions of types of available data, their accessibility, their reliability, and problems of their use are meaningful only in the light of specific meanings of the term *quantitative data*. We may distinguish three meanings.

The first meaning of the term is simply that of numerical records of any type, aggregate or nonaggregate, to be used as supporting evidence without reference to an analytical framework. In that sense, a historian will find the amount of quantitative material available in Japan overwhelming. He will also find that, though a fair number of studies has been made by Japanese historians who have investigated numerical records of all types, much remains to be done. A historian with a thorough knowledge of written Japanese studying the Tokugawa period and the early years of Meiji could use the numerical records contained in *han* (domain) documents, village records of all kinds, merchants' account books, and various types of private records.

In its second usage, quantitative data mean one or more sets of data, preferably time series for an extended period, which can be used as the major materials of research. In this sense, the availability and reliability of data and the problems of their use depend on the individual researcher's purpose, his scale of research, and his command of the language. The field is wide open, especially for those who are willing to dig into Tokugawa sources, which are well guarded from all but the most dedicated scholars by discouragingly obscure grammar and nearly illegible calligraphy. Even Tokugawa records can be made to serve as ingredients for time-series or cross-sectional analyses of statistically meaningful dimensions. The prime examples of what can be done are the current studies being undertaken on Tokugawa population and on prices.[1] The field becomes even wider with the beginning of the Meiji period. However, even data which are often used and apparently reliable demand careful scrutiny if they are to show something more than a general trend. For example, a set of Meiji government data for iron output may be reliable enough to show the growth rate of the iron industry, but not to compare the annual growth rates of the iron industry and another industry. We shall illustrate this problem later by a discussion of the use of rice-productivity data in estimates of the general rate of economic growth for the Meiji-Taisho periods (see pp. 511–13 below).

Finally, quantitative data can refer to sets of data which are consistent with one another for the purpose of theoretical analysis. In this case, the available materials must be evaluated by entirely different criteria. In such an analysis, a researcher seeks to determine the specific theoretical significance of such data within a given analytical framework, and, in most cases, this means that the data must be synthesized or "reconstructed" from what is available. For example, data on investment in the Keynesian sense which can be used in a theoretically acceptable national income accounting system could not have been gathered before such concepts existed. Scholars in Japan are now trying to reconstruct and improve earlier reconstructions of "synthetic" data.

This chapter will discuss what kinds of sources exist for the three genres of data defined above, how accessible these sources are, what problems may be encountered in the use of specific kinds of materials, and what directions may be taken by those interested in such research.

KINDS OF STATISTICAL DATA

Statistical sources can be divided into two basic categories. The first are premodern sources, dating from the Tokugawa period (in some cases, even earlier) and the early Meiji years. These data must be used with caution, but, if carefully selected in relation to the type of study being undertaken, they lend themselves to rather sophisticated research. The second category contains modern statistics with which more analytically oriented statistical studies can be conducted, mostly within the framework of economic history. These modern statistical materials date from the late 1880s and visibly increase in quantity and reliability at the beginning of the twentieth century. By the time of World War I, good modern statistics become available.

The Tokugawa or premodern data can be subdivided into several basic categories. The first is that of the official records, mostly of the individual *han* or domain; some, however, are from the Bakufu or national administration, and others are from large cities such as Edo (Tokyo) and Osaka. At the Bakufu level, these records consist of aggregate population statistics, *daimyo* genealogies, lists of government offices and positions, and numerous fiscal and other accounts.

The records at the higher levels of government were compiled in most cases from records of surveys conducted at lower levels; hence they tend to be more formal and less reliable than lower-level sources. For example, the Bakufu production figures for the various han became formalized in the seventeenth century and are meaningless, as far as actual production is concerned, for the last two centuries of the Tokugawa period. They do reflect the political position of a han, but such concerns are usually outside the scope of a quantitative study. The Bakufu figures in this case show some sort of pattern for the earlier years, though they cannot be used to ascertain basic and detailed trends.

The han records follow much the same line. The basic problem is that such records no longer exist for a great many han, but some of the records that do exist are extremely complete. Han records include lists of samurai and other retainers; stipend figures; income and expenditures for the han; data concerning schools, temples, shrines, extraordinary expenses, and projects; and numerous other kinds of data of interest to social, political, and economic historians.

A second category of Tokugawa data is that of the local material, based on a village or group of villages.[2] Surviving data include copies of records handed up to the han administration such as the *shūmon-aratame-chō* (religious investigation records) and the *kenchi-chō* (cadastral registers), copies of which were left with the village headmen. Much of the material at this level deals with village finance—village expenditures on irrigation, salaries for officials, and entertainment of domain officials—and with landholdings. Such data exist for many villages in Japan, and countless villages and towns have taken the trouble and expense to have local histories written. Administrative and financial affairs tended to be similar at the village level throughout the country during the Tokugawa period, but one cannot always use the detailed records of one village or even a select group of villages to make up a representative picture of Tokugawa Japan.

A third category of sources for the Tokugawa period is private records. These include data ranging from diaries containing information on crops, weather, and farm prices to the account books of private merchants. Again, such records may be hard to use, as it is often difficult to determine how representative they were, but they supply information impossible to obtain in any other way. For the mid- to late-Tokugawa period, the importance of these private quantitative data cannot be overemphasized. For example, the quantitative data in *Fudasashi Jiryoku* [Records of rice dealers], *Ryōgae nendaiki* [Chronicles of money changers] and its companion data volumes, and *Bōchōfūdo chūshin an* [Proposals for the development of the Bōchō region] are extremely important yet little used (see bibliographical appendix below, items 10, 1, 8, respectively). Though the examples cited in this chapter are limited, most serious students of the Tokugawa period should have little difficulty locating an appropriate body of quantitative data for meaningful research.

Moving on to post-Restoration materials, one immediately notes that the data in the first genre, numerical records, continue to increase; but a more visible development is the sudden appearance, almost a flooding, of the genre of data which can be used for cross-sectional or time-series analyses. Many of these data were collected by the Meiji government and newly established local governments. A cursory examination shows that many of these are of value to historians interested in the political, social, and economic changes which swept Japan in the early years of Meiji.

The data made available by nongovernmental bodies are also valuable. In the beginning of the 1880s, various types of newly incorporated firms and banks began to produce large quantities of data which have not been fully analyzed. Recently, Furushima, Shibagaki, and others have begun to make use of them.[3] But western scholars have hardly touched these sets of data or the often extremely useful data imbedded in company histories.[4] All in all, in planning possible uses for the second genre of data, a researcher must be prepared to face an acute *embarras de richesses* after the Russo-Japanese War. This apparent superabundance has its problems, but our advice is to plan a research program with the assurance that the necessary data do exist and that the only limitation is the researcher's patience.

Japan is extremely well endowed with the third genre of data for the years following the Restoration, especially with statistics used by theoretical economists. For the last ten years particularly, the Ministry of International Trade and Industry, the Economic Planning Agency, and other government agencies on one hand, and academic institutions and scholars on the other, have begun to reconstruct series of data based on theoretical economic concepts. These series are as good as, if not better than, those of any other nation in coverage and reliability. They are "synthesized" from the second genre of data originally issued by the government and found in earlier works of Japanese economists. The series include most of the standard economic data such as GNP, agricultural output, industrial production, the sectoral composition of industries, and general price and wage series, as well as more detailed price series for specific commodities and wage statistics for specific occupations. Though attempts have been made to carry back these data to dates as close to 1868 as possible, the earliest reliable series for any econometric analysis start from the 1890s.[5]

The examples here stress economic history, but sets of data which can be used by historians interested in political, social, and other aspects of modern Japanese history exist in abundance. If the politically or socially oriented historian is interested in using data at a level comparable to those used in the "new economic history," he will find excellent statistics on education, justice, demography, politics, and numerous other subjects which have barely begun to be analyzed by the Japanese.

It is clear that the available data vary from scattered records of village population and merchants' price records in the Tokugawa period (or even earlier) to the highly synthetic data being published by Hitotsubashi University. The amount of data increases over time, and reliability and coverage improve even more rapidly, but even during the Tokugawa period the stream of data is a wide river of usable material. A historian who chooses Tokugawa or Meiji Japan as the area for his research finds that the availability of quantitative data is not the serious problem it is for medieval Europe or earlier Japanese periods. The traditional (but now diminishing) reluctance of Japanese historians to conduct more quantitative research, and Westerners' reluctance to enter the world of the mysterious East and cross the formidable language barrier, have kept a large quantity of data untapped.

AVAILABILITY OF SOURCES

The variety of sources is so great and the number of materials so large for both the premodern and modern periods that any researcher's major problem is how most efficiently to locate the best sources. As the problems are different for each period, we shall deal with them separately. Because of our own fields of interest, the examples and suggestions here are largely from economic history, but a historian doing any kind of quantitative research on Japan can expect to encounter much the same situation. Although an exhaustive compilation of bibliographical suggestions is beyond the scope of this study, our suggestions here and in the bibliographical appendix may help guide the researcher to useful sources.

If one does not have a definite procedure for finding data on the Tokugawa period, the process of searching can be most discouraging. As John W. Hall notes, in *Japanese History: A Guide to Japanese Reference and Research Materials*, "The vast majority . . . of source materials lies unknown or unused in storage places long forgotten or largely inaccessible." [6] The best way to start is by consulting the comprehensive bibliographies, of which Hall's book is one of the most useful. An annotated bibliography in English with titles both in transliteration and in Japanese characters, it lists not only the most important bibliographical sources and secondary works for every branch of history but also the major archival collections with their locations and brief descriptions of their most important material. This work was published in 1954 and has not yet been updated.

There are other comprehensive bibliographies, both in English and in Japanese, too numerous to be listed here. However, any economic historian, after taking a look at the English bibliographies, will find that the most indispensable source for secondary materials is the Honjō bibliography, written in Japanese.[7] This contains a listing by field of all books and journal articles on economic history in Japanese; in addition, it contains a supplementary listing of English works. The bibliography was originally issued in 1933 and has been updated in additional volumes. It is to be found in every major university library in the United States and on the shelf of every economic historian in Japan.[8]

An important source for private records beginning with the Tokugawa period is the *Kinsei shomin shiryō mokuroku* [A guide to the availability and location of private records], published in 1952.[9] Its three volumes list documents preserved in numerous libraries, universities, and private collections throughout Japan. The more than 10,000 entries give the names of the various documents, their nature, the time periods covered, the quantity of materials, and the names and addresses of the holders. They are extremely helpful to anyone attempting to determine what sources exist for a particular region or village or what sources of a certain type exist in various areas of Japan.

After scanning the major bibliographies, the researcher's step is to seek out historians in Japan working in his field and to find the archives and major libraries likely to contain relevant materials. This is essential because of the language difficulties in dealing with Tokugawa sources and, even more important, the scattered nature of Japanese sources and the often obscure locations of even important documents. Anyone contemplating a study involving a region or local area must do some basic digging for materials in Japan; due to the nature and location of the materials, no comprehensive research can result from the use of printed materials alone or from depending just on works found in American libraries.

One heartening change, particularly since World War II, is the increasing compilation and publication in printed form of important documentary sources. These include (1) local and regional histories containing a large variety of quantitative evidence which can be used in various types of historical research, and (2) the reproduction in printed form of numerous private records which up until now were accessible only to the small number of Japanese who read Tokugawa calligraphy (for examples, see bibliographical appendix, items 9, 10).

Given the abundance of data, a researcher needs to begin his search for post-1868 data by consulting bibliographical works. Henry Rosovsky's *Quantitative Japanese Economic History, An Annotated Bibliography* is the best source for a bird's-eye view.[10] It includes 467 annotated entries for the categories of national income, population and labor force, production (agriculture and industry), foreign trade, prices and wages, labor relations, money and banking, and public finance, education, law, and other areas. For most purposes, the annotations are sufficient to guide the would-be user; for those 393 entries which were available in the United States as of the late 1950s, it lists library locations.

After a careful examination of Rosovsky's work, the next logical step is to examine a few larger sources in Japanese. One of the most complete of such sources, and one which can be recommended highly, is the *Tōkei shiryō kaidai* [a guide to statistical materials], published in 1936 by Zenkoku tōkei chōsa-kikan rengō-kai (Federation of Statistical Research) under the auspices of the Prime Minister's Office.[11] This extensive guide contains annotated statistical data from the early 1890s to the year of its publication. Its 9,917 entries refer to almost all data published by all levels of government, educational institutions, and private agencies and firms; they include data useful in political, social, military, economic, and demographic research, as well as studies in local history. The 23 categories include land and climate, population, agriculture, forestry, mining, manufacturing, commerce and finance, transportation and communications, trade and industrial organizations, exports and imports, prices, public finance, labor and social welfare, education and religion, law enforcement, and the Diet and elections.

A more up-to-date bibliographical compilation of even greater importance is the two-volume *Hitotsubashi Daigaku shozō tōkei shiryō mokuroku* [catalog of statistical data in the possession of Hitotsubashi University], which lists all the statistical data held by the university.[12] The coverage of this lengthy work is excellent, reflecting the university's long-standing interest in acquiring statistical material, especially from the 1880s on. It is difficult to use because no entry is annotated, and it takes time to be able to identify worthwhile series by title and publisher. For this reason, scholars should approach this catalog after the Rosovsky volume and the *Tōkei shiryō kaidai*.

There are other compilations which some historians may profitably consult. One is *Tōkei kankei ko-shiryō mokuroku* [A bibliography of old statistical materials], published by the Library of the Statistics Bureau of the Prime Minister's Office.[13] This undated 130-page booklet is valuable for its lists of all statistical publications issued between 1868 and 1893 by the government, encompassing data in the fields of politics, population, economics, and law enforcement. It includes such items as *Karokushikyū torishirabe-chō* [A report on the stipends paid to the former samurai], published in 1873, and *Jiso-zei hōkoku-sho* [A report on the land tax], published in 1868. Several other more commonly known sources which researchers can profitably examine are those by Minobe and Matsukawa, Nishioka, Masaki and Matsukawa, and Okazaki.[14]

One recent series has special importance for the future of quantitative research in Japanese economic history. It is the *Estimate of Long-Term Economic Statistics of Japan Since 1868,* edited by Professors Kazushi Ohkawa, Miyohei Shinohara, and Mataji Umemura of Hitotsubashi University.[15] The result of a decade of work by a group of economists at the university's Economics Research Institute, it will, when completed, consist of 13 volumes. Each volume is divided into three parts: findings, estimating procedures, and statistical tables. Summary statements of the estimating procedures and the headings and technical remarks of the statistical tables are given both in Japanese and in English. As the editors have emphasized, the data were estimated in the framework of what economists call "the national income accounting system." For example, in volume 9, *Agriculture-Forestry,* the emphasis is on estimating continuous long-term series of outputs, inputs (including investments), and prices, not on data concerning structural changes and other institutional aspects which can be found elsewhere. The bibliography of the sources used for the estimates in each volume is useful in scouting out related data sources and in identifying articles and books which discuss the theoretical issues involved in the estimating procedures for specific areas. Though the editors are the first to disclaim definitiveness or completeness, their work will be valuable for a long time to come.

Unlike the Tokugawa period, study of the post-Restoration period requires only the ability to read printed Japanese. In many books, such as *The Estimate of Long-Term Economic Statistics,* the table headings appear both in Japanese and in English. Thus the modern statistics are much more accessible than the earlier ones.

Let us add a special note of warning about many of the impressive-looking multivolume series which purport to include numerous statistical data but which do not include references to the sources. The best rule of thumb is that a serious historian should refrain from any use of data cited unless the original source can be verified. More often than not, commissioned authors are extremely casual in ascertaining the reliability and/or specific nature of data they adopt from second- and even thirdhand sources. Though there are exceptions, most of the multivolume series published by private firms are far from helpful, especially for those who have not yet learned the subtleties of Japanese academia and publishing enterprises.

PROBLEMS AND CHARACTERISTICS

A researcher's experience depends on the subjects and therefore on the sets of data he chooses. One may encounter only a few minor problems while another is beset by varying definitions of entries, changes in coverage (geographical, enumerative, etc.), inconsistencies in methodology, and serious inaccuracies. It is useful to discuss what can be done with various types of data and what problems one may encounter in using specific sets of data, especially analytically constructed models making use of modern economic concepts.

Three examples of problems follow. The first concerns the reliability of official statistics in the Meiji-Taisho periods and ways in which the data can be improved. The second and the third examples, from the Tokugawa and modern periods respectively, show problems in using partial or disaggregated data to try to obtain as complete an aggregate view as possible.

The first example we shall call the case of the "Rumbles in the Rice-fields," to borrow Henry Rosovsky's apt phrase. The "rumbles" originated with James Nakamura's 1966 book on *Agricultural Production and the Economic Development of Japan, 1873–1922*, which claims that the official statistics for the period are totally unreliable because they understate the level of agricultural output considerably for the early part of the series.[16] Nakamura bases his argument on evidence that the official figures for the early 1870s were subject to underreporting by peasants (and collaborating local officials) who wished to minimize their tax burdens. Peasants, he argues, resorted to rather extensive concealment, underreporting of the actual size of cultivated land, and underestimation of the yield of registered land.

Nakamura's claim was accompanied by agricultural production figures which he "reconstructed." According to his new estimates, the annual growth rate of agricultural output from 1878 to 1882 and from 1913 to 1917—during the crucial 35 years—ranged between 0.8 and 1.2 percent. This estimate was considerably lower than earlier ones, such as Ohkawa's 2.4 percent, often used in his and Rosovsky's joint work. As one article puts it:

> How different the growth rates are between Ohkawa's *The Growth Rate of the Japanese Economy* which is primarily based on the official statistics and Nakamura's who completely defies the reliability of the official statistics! For the initial phase of industrial spurt, in terms of gross output, the rates of growth of production and labor productivity in *GRJE* are double as great [sic] as in Nakamura and that of land productivity nine times as great as in Nakamura.[17]

The magnitude of the difference between these estimates is enough to affect one's interpretation of the whole pattern of economic development in Japan. If Nakamura is correct, the Japanese economy did not benefit by an agricultural spurt which enabled reallocation of resources for the purpose of industrialization, but its development was, as Nakamura puts it, much more like "the development of the economically advanced countries in the West than indicated previously; that is, Japan's development was much less unique than previously believed." [18]

Nakamura's "revisionism" was so fundamental as to evoke challenges to his estimates on several grounds. Here we need examine only the gist of the rumbles to indicate the major points of the debate. Hayami and Yamada question Nakamura's estimate because

> Nakamura's agricultural production statistics would give daily per capita calorie consumption for 1878–87 equal to or even larger than 2290, the average of fifteen years from 1913 to 1927. In other words, the conjecture of Nakamura on agricultural production and productivity in the early Meiji period is presuming the income elasticity of calorie consumption was zero in Japan at the level of income less than 200 U.S. dollars at 1958 prices. All of the international evidence are [*sic*] defying such presumption.[19]

They also find Nakamura's estimate inconsistent with available data on the rate of increase in the use of fertilizers, the known improvements in rice-seeds, and irrigation and drainage facilities. Their own estimate of fertilizer use of 2.53 tons per hectare is close to the official data of 2.36 ton/ha., as compared to Nakamura's estimate of 3.22 ton/ha., for the base period between 1878 and 1882.[20] As a result, they defend the accepted "spurt" thesis of Japanese economic development.

Rosovsky's critical review of Nakamura's volume is a thorough challenge to his views and estimates. He criticizes Nakamura for arbitrary selection of rice yields for his base year, failure to take full cognizance of regional variations in yields, and failure to account for known technological advances which influenced productivity.[21] Rosovsky's methodological objection is the crux of the debate:

> The official series purport to tell us what actually happened in Japan from one year to the next. Villages reported, information was collected at prefectural levels, and eventually totals were recorded by the bureaucrats in Tokyo. Theoretically these quantities take into account bumper crops in Kyūshū, crop failures in Tōhoku, and the possibility of a farmer quarrelling with his wife and consequently raising less rice than usual in 1899. In other words, it is a measure of actual performance—although it may be a false and unsuccessful measure. What Professor Nakamura substitutes is a measure of expected performance, or a kind of normal value —if his assumptions are correct.[22]

Nakamura, however, had made a fundamental point in criticizing the uncritical use of government data by Ohkawa and Rosovsky. Their retort was that any revision of official statistics must be made with extreme caution, for revisions can be even more distorting than the unquestioning acceptance of official data. The net result of this debate to date has been a reevaluation of the official statistics compiled by the Japanese economists Yamada and Hayami, which appears to be the accepted standard at present. Despite the fact that Nakamura's estimates have not been widely accepted as he presented them, it is evident, as Rosovsky himself concedes, that "none of us will ever again use these series uncritically, and this is Professor Nakamura's great contribution." [23]

The lessons of this debate are clear. First, historians wishing to examine fundamental issues of economic history must endeavor to obtain as accurate a set of data as possible. There is a constant need for economic historians to reevaluate quantitative data in the light of appropriate new theoretical concepts, statistical techniques, and newer and better analytical tools. Second, there are as yet many fundamental issues of Japanese economic history which need to be examined with the use of quantitative data. The fact that such a basic issue as the estimates of rice production and productivity is still being discussed is encouraging to those willing to labor in the field of Japanese economic history. It is still a young field, relatively rich in raw data and rewarding for those wishing to investigate important questions with the aid of quantitative evidence. Third, new findings and hypotheses, even those subsequently proved wrong, should challenge existing ones to generate the heat which provides energy to move knowledge forward. Quantitative economic history should be able to convert this energy into light.

Our second example involves the problems found in attempting to use partial or disaggregated data as the core of a research project, specifically the difficulties encountered in studying the population of the Tokugawa period, an area of research largely ignored by most Japanese scholars until the last several years. Studies by the past generation of Japanese scholars have been chiefly descriptive, with no visible attempt at statistical analysis. But under the direct influence of new methods of analyzing premodern demographic data developed in Western Europe, and generally under the influence of the increasing use of statistical analysis in historical research, a small number of scholars in Japan have begun detailed quantitative analyses of the Tokugawa population.[24] The wide variety of available sources in this field offers promising opportunities for any scholar willing to undergo time-consuming training to acquire the necessary language and statistical skills and also to do extensive fieldwork.

The basic problem involved in studying the Tokugawa population is that the reliability of the available aggregated figures has not yet been established, and the more reliable data exist only for small units such as villages of a few hundred or for time periods too short to allow for a meaningful time-series analysis. The basic levels of sources exist. The first are aggregated data such as the national survey carried out approximately every six years from 1721 on. These statistics are by han, and similar statistics exist for regions within various han. Examples of such statistics exist for Okayama and Yonezawa. These statistics show fairly accurately the trends within many of the han, but to what extent they can be considered reliable has yet to be established. Sekiyama Naotarō analyzes these national statistics in a number of his works and illustrates differences in regional population trends, but further analysis awaits the establishment of the reliability of these figures.[25] And a closer look at the Okayama totals compared with the han statistics shows that Sekiyama's totals for this han at least do not include the population figures for the castle town.

The national and han statistics originated at the village level. The most basic population records are the *ninbetsu aratame-chō* and the *shūmon aratame-chō*, village census and religious investigation records. Where these records still exist, they often offer a complete picture of the population trends for a village, usually purporting to contain the name, age, and relationship to the head of household of every person in a village over a certain age (most commonly one year). The problem in using these sources is, first and foremost, the accessibility of the materials; the second difficulty, for the foreign scholar, is in reading and interpreting these records, often full of wormholes and written in cursive script, sometimes by ill-educated village headmen or priests.

A good deal of searching on one's own will uncover new village records, but still there are few *shumon aratame-chō* which will permit extensive time-series analyses. A promising hint and a long trip to some mountain village may result in the discovery of only a single register for one year in the possession of an old man whose ancestors were the headmen of the village in which he lives. One good means of uncovering data is through the Mombushō Shiryōkan in Tokyo and the universities in which population research is being carried on. But often the best source of information for anyone wishing to use local sources is a visit to the appropriate department of the prefectural university in the area in which possible materials may exist. The *Kinsei Shomin Shiryō Shozai Mokuroku*, referred to earlier in this chapter, should of course be consulted.

Even when the *shūmon aratame-chō* or other basic sources have been found, there is the problem of deciphering them, and for statistical analysis an accurate reading of all pertinent data is essential. Some *shūmon aratame-chō* are available in print, but the major sources published to date are disappointing. These include a five-volume series containing *shūmon ninbetsu on-aratame-chō* for Echizen-no-kuni or Fukui han and a similar volume for the Hōi area of Mikawa-no-kuni in the present Aichi prefecture.[26] A number of scholars spent hundreds of hours of painstaking work copying these documents for publication, but unfortunately either their methods of ferreting out the original resources were inadequate or numerous registers were missing. While the materials can be used for comparisons of family composition in some cases or totals of village population changes, they are inadequate for either complete time-series analyses of one or more villages or accurate cross-sectional studies of a number of villages.

Thus the fundamental task in arriving at general observations is to maintain a balance between aggregate figures of questionable reliability and reliable partial figures on the village level. Statistics for the Tokugawa period share the common weakness of being scattered in region and time, making it extremely difficult for historians to use them as ingredients for more general observations. This is not to say that Tokugawa data cannot be successfully used as a basis for quantitative historical research. For the historian willing and able to strike the delicate balance between use of advanced statistical techniques on given amounts of aggregate data and skillful use of scattered and often incomplete data in a more traditional manner, the Tokugawa period is now open for quantitatively oriented studies in nearly every field of history.

Our third example comes from regional economic studies, one of the more important neglected areas in Japanese economic history. It was selected to show the difficulties involved in gathering regional data and in attempting to aggregate or compare these data. These difficulties must be faced in the intensive examinations of regional economies which are useful in unmasking the considerable variations hidden in national or aggregate studies. Aggregation presents constant problems if the available regional data are not directly comparable because of differences in coverage, reliability, or methods of collection.

Each researcher finally decides which series of data can be aggregated and which sets of regional data are comparable for his purposes. Thus this example is intended only to show possible sources and basic problems and difficulties in gathering regional data. Even though political units may not be the most economically meaningful building blocks, a prefecture (*ken*) is used as the basic regional unit, as it is frequently the only subdivision for which data are available, especially for a long-run analysis.

Prefectural data are generally found in two places: (1) national publications, usually of the central government or one of the newspapers or economic research institutes, which frequently include data broken down by prefectures; (2) the prefectures' own statistical volumes, which are generally the best sources of detailed information. Researchers must also examine several available bibliographies and catalogs, some of which are for a particular topic, showing which Japanese libraries hold the specific data needed. Let us examine each type of data in turn.

Nationwide Data

The first place to look for prefectural data is where the work of collection and standardization has already been done, namely, among the statistical publications of the several offices of the central government. Detail, of course, increases as one moves from general to specific areas. The most general publication is the *Tōkei Nenkan* [Annual statistics], which, under various names and issuing agencies, contains data from 1882 to the present except for a gap during World War II.

Though the contents of the *Tōkei Nenkan* vary over the years, each volume includes data on population, agricultural output, fishing, mining, construction, banking, internal trade and commerce, communications, wages, labor disputes, etc. Caution must be exercised in using the prefectural data in those volumes. For example, data on population, one of the major subdivisions in the *Tōkei Nenkan,* are acceptable for most purposes only after 1920, and even then the data were collected by family registration rather than by more modern census techniques. To use the population data, therefore (and this applies as well to other sets of data in these volumes), one must begin by examining the sources used.[27]

The *Ōkurashō Nempō* [Annual reports of the Ministry of Finance], are a major source of economic statistics below the level of the *Tōkei Nenkan.* These contain data on prefectural government revenue and expenses and local bond issues. Information on bank branches, capital, and deposits by prefecture can be found in several of the annual publications of the Banking Bureau (*Ginkōkyoku*) of the Ministry of Finance. Production, first presented in a single volume published by *Nōshōmushō* (Ministry of Commerce and Agriculture), is later treated separately in the *Nōrinshō* (Ministry of Agriculture and Forestry) series for agriculture and the *Kōjō Tōkeihyō* [Statistics of factories] series for industry.[28] Rather complete descriptions of these and other relevant volumes along with details on changes in the names of publications and issuing agencies can be found in the Rosovsky bibliography. Its annotation usually indicates whether or not the material is classified by prefecture, but coverage varies so widely that the only sound approach is to examine the publications themselves. The first issue of the *Nōshōmu Tōkeihyō* [Statistics of agriculture and commerce] in 1886 includes, for example, information by prefecture on area planted; crops raised; output of various crops; head of cattle on hand and slaughtered; numbers of factories having steam engines, water wheels, or neither; output of a number of industrial commodities; prices for 25 commodities by location; and average monthly prices, usually in the Tokyo or Osaka markets.

A look at commodity prices reveals some of the problems involved. When computing a value series using physical output figures, it can be highly misleading to combine a prefectural series with one of the price series presented in the "national" publications, depending on the purpose at hand. National publications usually show prices in some central city market, and prices in the prefecture may have been quite different. Another large problem area is the extent of coverage. The *Nōshōmu* volume discussed above presents data by prefecture but includes anywhere from 9 to 46 prefectures, depending on the series. Annotation is not extensive, and it is difficult to tell, for example, whether a certain prefecture actually had no factories equipped with water wheels or simply did not report them. To deal with such problems one must go to the publications of the prefectures with missing figures or perform some sort of interpolation using other government statistics. Still another problem lies in the fact that not all prefectures were created at the same time. Nara, for example, was part of Ōsaka, and Kagawa part of Ehime, until the late 1880s. Fortunately, however, some of the data are classified not only by *fuken* (prefectures) but by *kuni* (provinces), so that a reasonable approximation to a series for Nara prefecture can be carried backward in time by using the figures for Yamato-no-kuni, which are included with the Ōsaka figures.

In general, we have continuous and reasonably reliable production series from the 1880s. Some others, such as *Kaisha Tōkeihyō* [Statistics of firms], did not start until 1921; still others are not available until 1946. A researcher should begin by examining, along with the Rosovsky monograph, the Yūshōdō microfilm catalog, since this firm has begun to market some of the above-mentioned data. The most relevant are the company's 378 reels of the complete collection of official data submitted to the central government by the prefectures during the 1880s.[29] Researchers should also examine the forthcoming volume on regional economic statistics of the Hitotsubashi series of long-term economic statistics, which was mentioned earlier. This should help to fill in the larger part of a frustrating void: the lack of prefectural time-series.

Prefectural Statistics

The very profusion of prefectural statistics is in itself a mixed blessing. On the one hand, a great variety of information has been compiled; on the other, considerable effort must be expended to get at it all. In 1884 an order went out to the prefectures under the signature of Yamagata Aritomo, then home minister, prescribing the format in which prefectural statistics would henceforth be published. This order set forth 284 required entries, ranging from health and education to production and prices. Since that time all the prefectures have published statistics, called first *Fuken Tōkeisho* [Prefectural statistics] and, in recent times, *Nempō* or *Nenkan* [Annual reports]. Some prefectures had already started publishing statistical annuals, eight of them as early as 1873, and the order of 1884 was a major effort to standardize and increase coverage.

Perhaps the next major step in this field was the issue of microfilm collections of the statistical publications. Yūshōdō has assembled them in two groups—one for the Meiji period and another for the Taishō and Shōwa periods, up to 1945. The material in the first group is described in an index to the microfilm, and both are discussed in English in the current company catalog.[30] The Meiji collection, although of great value, is by no means complete. A full cross-section is not available until 1911, although at least some material for each prefecture is reproduced from 1889 on. Several long, unbroken series are available, notably for Tokyo since 1876 and for Yamaguchi and Fukuoka since 1879. Conspicuous gaps in important prefectures include Hyogo from 1893 to 1899 and Aichi for 1900–01 and 1903. By 1885 coverage is about half complete, and up to 1910 it varies from between 32 and 45 prefectures out of a total of 47.

The *Fuken Tōkeisho* could be described as a *Tōkei Nenkan* scaled down one level, since the coverage for each prefecture is roughly as wide as for the national volumes. An example of these volumes is the *Tōkyō-fu Tōkeisho,* which includes data for Tokyo prefecture for 1878–82. It is a large source (379 tables) containing many kinds of information, much of it presented by *gun* (county) or *ku* (ward). Items covered include land use, agriculture, population and vital statistics, finance, shrines, industry, transport, education, taxes, government expenditures, and disasters. The agriculture section includes the results of some experimental efforts such as the use of foreign seeds and the performance of cotton transplanted from Aichi.[31]

By 1925 this publication had settled into a more standard mold and had expanded considerably. Most tables give prefecture-wide totals for 1918–25 and an area breakdown for the final year. For example, population figures are given for the city of Tokyo (Tokyo-shi, comprising 15 wards), Hachiōji city, 8 counties, Oshima, Hachiōji-jima, and Ogasawara Guntō (Bonin Islands). Special items include tables of railway shipments of major commodities into Tokyo broken down by originating prefecture, individual taxpayers in 18 tax brackets, and banking statistics on major quasi-public banks in Tokyo and those headquartered elsewhere but having branches in Tokyo, along with aggregate figures for private banks and savings banks in Tokyo.[32]

Several cities have also published statistical information, in some cases almost as elaborate as that for prefectures.[33] In the *kenshi* (prefectural history), some of which run to as many as 30 volumes, tidbits can be gleaned; and although this can be an extremely arduous task, one may be rewarded with long time series otherwise available only in many issues of a statistical publication. For example, the history of Iwate prefecture contains data on public finance in the prefecture from 1897 to 1941.[34] Some data are presented in short tables with yearly annotation, such as that (on p. 1244) for textile production for 1888–97. Most of the *kenshi* are arranged chronologically, so that data from the Meiji period on (the most useful statistics) can be found in the later volumes. The individual volumes are arranged by topic within a period. Village and town histories can be equally complete and elaborate.

Bibliographies and Catalogs

For regional history, there are several bibliographies and catalogs that help in locating specific items. Their use may save time in searching and possibly in computation.

While the microfilm publications solve many problems, readers who wish to work with specific prefectural statistics will find the Diet Library Catalog extremely helpful.[35] This gives Japanese library locations of prefectural volumes from about 1876 to June 1956, but it indexes only the *Fuken Tōkeisho.* A wider range of publications within narrower geographic areas can be found in the bibliographies *(mokuroku)* published by political units, frequently city or prefectural libraries. Examples are *Ōsaka shiryō mokuroku* and *Kyōdo shiryō kaisetsu mokuroku,* both of which deal mainly with Osaka City but also contains sections on the entire Ōsaka-*fu* area.[36]

Occasionally one may come upon a long series for a particular prefecture, usually in some specialized field. Nishioka's work is useful in locating a wide range of prefecture-centered materials published up to the early 1950s. Some materials of this sort may also be found in the *Keizaigaku bunken kihō,* which is published quarterly. Another bibliography, dealing with many statistical publications, is that by Minobe and Matsukawa. It is arranged by topic and describes the publications in some detail. Included is an appendix arranged by issuing office and giving details such as frequency of issue, compilers, publishers, dates started, number of pages, and price. One section covers prefectural statistics, including standard items and also special items such as income estimates. This volume covers only publications from 1950 and 1956 but is reputed to be a sequel to Masaki and Matsukawa, which presumably treats earlier material.[37]

These descriptions cover only the major sources of the quantitative data available for quantitative regional studies. There are many possible sources that fill the gaps left by official data. Histories of banks founded under the Banking Act of 1876 are often excellent sources of quantitative data on such items as deposits, loans, industrial output, and flows of commodities for the region in which the bank is located. Some of the bank histories, rich in data, are in fact competent economic histories of the region.[38] So are some company histories. For those wishing to recapture the economic life of early Meiji, the histories of those companies which came into being in the late 1870s or soon after are excellent guides; they also provide useful data on their regions.

In the case of both bank or company histories and local histories, the search for a specific series of data for a particular prefecture is difficult because there as yet exists no comprehensive catalog for such a search. But since, as the Japanese would put it, these histories are "the wide base of a triangle"—the peak being the official data—they should be carefully examined, using available bibliographical works such as *Shakai Kagaku Kenkyū, Hompō shashi mokuroku,* and *Shashi jitsugyōka denki mokuroku.*[39]

No one can hope to overcome the difficulties of gathering regional quantitative data with less than a many-faceted effort. But, as is shown by the many quantitative studies requiring data which are not readily available from official sources or special series, the necessary quantitative data are available for those who seek them. As Professor Furushima and others have amply shown, this task is worth all its attendant tedium, muscle pains, frustration, and the disappointment of not finding an index for books published before the 1950s.[40]

New interests, issues, and even fads exercise considerable power in determining what is attractive or important in research, and the choice of approach and topic is a highly personal matter. With these provisos, a number of areas are inviting. Both the authors' interests and the state of research on Japanese history cause us to center our suggestions around economic history, but there are analogous needs for research in other fields as well.

The first suggestion is to continue to make every effort to improve available quantitative data for economic theoretical concepts for use in quantitative historical research. Though the efforts of many, including those involved in the new Hitotsubashi series, continue to make substantial advances in this respect, the work is far from complete. Also, new analytical concepts and tools constantly demand new sets of data. This is an endless task which requires the participation of an increasingly large number of historians. Another aspect of this data "reconstruction" is also in need of historians' attention: in spite of constant use of the governmental data, we do not yet know exactly how those data were compiled. For example, in the case of rice output, the Hitotsubashi series adopted "the official data without any revision" for the period after 1890 because the editors found no "significant discontinuities or inconsistencies in the statistics or other appropriate reason for revision." [41] The rice output data apparently met the requirements of these editors, but their only test was theoretical consistency with other sets of available data in the framework of the national income accounting system. Even if that were the most important test for quantitative analysis, the fact remains that there have been no systematic studies or evaluations of the actual methods used by the Meiji government in compiling the large number of data it collected.

The importance of examining all available official records concerned with the description of actual methods of data collection cannot be overemphasized. The task is a difficult and tedious one, but a historian who is prepared to examine these records, compile his findings, and present an analysis of the original method used can contribute significantly toward filling a large gap in our knowledge. Just as no self-respecting Japanese parents ever fail to examine thoroughly the genealogy of their son's prospective bride, historians willing to shoulder the burden of investigating the "genealogy" of the Japanese quantitative data could perform a significant service which economists have so far neglected.

A second area of research is no less important. That is to make a fuller use of existing data to investigate (1) the patterns of development of individual, or a selected group of, industries; (2) the development of the capital market and intersectoral flow of resources; and (3) the interactions and variations of regional economic growth patterns. This last point has been touched upon earlier, but brief comments are in order for the first two areas. This suggestion to make fuller use of data applies equally to all aspects of Japanese history.

The industry studies available, with a few possible exceptions, are not quantitative; that is, quantitative evidence tends to be relegated to a few tables and not used as the chief, or even an important, ingredient of research. Carefully structured quantitative studies of industries, individually or for a selected group, are still wanting in Japanese economic history. Available quantitative evidence for factor and product markets can, if used imaginatively, go far in explaining the various patterns of development and the role of the market in the growth of the national economy; this will yield the insights into economic growth which depend on close examination of units smaller than the national economy.

Capital markets and intersectoral flows of resources are necessary and promising areas for research. Such difficulties as the need to combine numerical records embedded in various sources and the relative lack of "clean" data have deterred many economic historians. But research in these areas is long overdue. E. S. Crawcour laments our ignorance:

Firstly, we do not yet know to what extent these resources [mobilized for industrialization] depended on increases in agricultural productivity and to what extent the transfer was effected by re-allocating existing resources. Clearly the two go together and rising productivity makes reallocation much easier. Secondly, we do not know how far industrial growth depended on resources from agriculture and how far it was financed by traditional industry. Either way the growth of traditional industrial output was just as important as that of agriculture. Thirdly, it is hard to distinguish "traditional" from "modern" in the industrial expansion of the Meiji period. If it were possible to produce output and employment series by "traditional" and "modern" sectors they would certainly give a far less dramatic . . . picture of structural transformation than that reflected by the standard sectoral classification.[42]

These questions have direct bearing on the "Rumbles in the Ricefields." Along with them are other problems awaiting answers: What was the role of the Zaibatsu banks in accumulating and supplying capital to industry during the early phase of industrialization? When and how, if ever, did a unified capital market emerge? What role did the capital market play in transferring resources intersectorally and interregionally?[43] These are a few of the many questions which require our immediate attention. Historians, familiar with similar questions for other nations and aware of their complexities, but free from the overzealous demand of some economists that all necessary data be neatly labeled and easily manipulated, may be best equipped to investigate these questions using quantitative methods.

Another need, which may have been evident in our discussion of quantitative data for regional studies, is to compile as complete a census as possible of the histories and records of all levels of political units, companies, and banks, with special emphasis on the quantitative data they contain. A few of these attempts are available in Japanese, but none, to our knowledge, are satisfactory in coverage and annotation. It would be extremely desirable to have a catalog in English of all these histories and records, showing which are available in the U.S. and which are held by whom in Japan. The data contained in the *History of the Mitsui Bank* or the five-volume history of the Oji Paper Company may be no less useful than national statistical publications for certain researches. The process of compiling will require time, patience, teamwork, and funds. But especially since some listings are already available, a bibliography and inventory to complement that of Henry Rosovsky can be written.

In spite of the postwar interest in Japan as a field of academic research, quantitatively-oriented historical research still awaits the concerted efforts of historians. In the final analysis, it is the historians of various persuasions and training who must put together and discover what is substantive in the quantitatively oriented history of Japan. Historians have a unique training for finding the most significant threads in an abundance of evidence such as exists in quantitative language for Japan. As the "Rumbles in the Ricefields" show, new sets of quantitative evidence are capable of suggesting new interpretations of the most fundamental developments. For those willing to make the necessary investments, the time is ripe, the field uncrowded, and the intellectual problems challenging.

NOTES

1 See articles by Hayami Akira on the Tokugawa population in the journals of Keio University; Susan B. Hanley, "Population Trends and Economic Development in Tokugawa Japan: The Case of Bizen Province in Okayama," *Daedalus*, Spring 1968, pp. 622–35; Susan B. Hanley and Kozo Yamamura, "Population Trends and Economic Growth in Preindustrial Japan," in *Historical Population Studies.* ed. D. V. Glass and Roger Revelle (London: Edward Arnold, 1972). For studies on various Tokugawa price series, see bibliographical appendix below, items 3 and 4; also Sydney E. Crawcour and Kozo Yamamura, "The Tokugawa Monetary System, 1787–1867," *Economic Development and Cultural Change,* vol. 18, no. 4 (July 1970).

2 For an indispensable discussion of pre-Meiji village records, see John W. Hall, "Materials for the Study of Local History in Japan: Pre-Meiji Village Records," *Occasional Papers,* no. 3 (Ann Arbor: University of Michigan Press, Center for Japanese Studies, 1952), pp. 1–14.

3 T. Furushima, *Sangyōshi* [A history of industries] (Tokyo, 1966); K. Shibagaki, *Nihon kinyū shihon bunseki* [An analysis of Japanese financial capital] (Tokyo, 1965).

4 See sources cited in n. 39 below.

5 Yasuba Yasukichi expresses the same view after making a careful analysis of industrial statistics in his "Senzen no Nihon ni okeru kōgyō tōkei no shinpyō-sei ni tsuite" [On the reliability of the prewar Japanese industrial statistics], *Osaka Daigaku Keizai-gaku,* vol. 17, nos. 2–3 (Dec. 1967), pp. 76–95.

6 John W. Hall, *Japanese History, A Guide to Japanese Reference and Research Materials* (Ann Arbor: University of Michigan Press, 1954), p. 4.

7 Honjō Eijirō, *Kaihan Nihon keizaishi bunken* [Revised bibliography of Japanese economic history] (Tokyo, 1933). Despite the title, this source is much more than just a bibliography of economic history. Honjō covers works in all the social sciences in a comprehensive fashion.

8 Ibid.; idem., *Nihon keizaishi shin-bunken* [New bibliography of Japanese economic history] (Tokyo, 1942); Honjō Eijirō, Yoshikawa Hidezō, and Matsuyoshi Sadao, *Nihon keizaishi daisan bunken* [Bibliography of Japanese economic history, Number Three] (Tokyo, 1953).

9 Nihon Gakujutsu Shinkō-kai, *Kinsei shomin shiryō shozai mokuroku* [A guide to the availability and location of private records), 3 vols. (Tokyo, 1952).

10 Henry Rosovsky, *Quantitative Japanese Economic History, An Annotated Bibliography and a Survey of U.S. Holdings* (Berkeley: University of California Press, 1961).

11 See also Statistics Bureau, Office of Prime Minister, *Hompō genkō tōkei shiryō kaidai* [A guide to current statistical materials in Japan] (Tokyo, 1951). This is an updated version of the 1936 edition mentioned in the text. But its coverage is smaller, as it drops more of the earlier data of the original version than it adds of the post-1936 data.

12 These volumes were compiled by the Economic Research Institute of the Hitotsubashi University for its own use, but academic historians can obtain permission to see them.

13 This is available at the Economic Research Library, Hitotsubashi University.

14 R. Minobe and S. Matsukawa, *Tōkei chōsa sōran* [A compendium of statistical surveys] (Tokyo, 1956); Hideo Nishioka, *Nihon kenbetsu chishi mokuroku* [The catalog of prefectural histories of Japan] (Tokyo, 1955); C. Masaki and S. Matsukawa, *Tōkei chōsa gaido bukku* [A guidebook for statistical research] (Tokyo, 1951); F. Okazaki, *Tōkei kenkyū bunken* [Sources for statistical research] (Tokyo, 1925).

15 *Estimate of Long-Term Economic Statistics of Japan since 1868* [*Tōyō keizai shimpōsha*], ed. K. Ohkawa, S. Shinohara, and M. Umemura. The titles of all 13 volumes are: 1. National Product; 2. Population and Labor Force; 3. Capital Stock; 4. Capital Formation; 5. Savings and Currency; 6. Personal Consumption Expenditures; 7. Government Expenditures; 8. Prices; 9. Agriculture-Forestry; 10. Mining-Manufacturing; 11. Textiles; 12. Railroads and Electric Utilities; 13. Regional Economic Statistics. Volumes 3, 6, 7, 8, 9, and 12 have been published; the rest were scheduled to appear in the following order: 4, 5, 2, 1, 10, 11, 13.

16 Henry Rosovsky, "Rumbles in the Ricefields," *Journal of Asian Studies*, vol. 27, no. 2 (February 1968), pp. 347–60; James I. Nakamura, *Agricultural Production and the Economic Development of Japan, 1873–1922* (Princeton, 1966).

17 Yujirō Hayami and Saburo Yamada, "Agricultural Productivity at the Beginning of Industrialization," in *Agriculture and Economic Development: A Symposium on Japan's Experience*, ed. B. F. Johnston and Kazushi Ohkawa (Princeton and Tokyo, 1970), p. 107.

18 Nakamura, *Agricultural Production*, p. 131.

19 Hayami and Yamada, "Agricultural Productivity," p. 10.

20 Ibid., appended table 1.

21 Rosovsky's article criticizes Nakamura's work on a few other factual and methodological grounds, which we do not intend to cover.

22 Rosovsky, "Rumbles in the Ricefields," p. 34 (draft version, quoted by permission of the author).

23 Ibid., p. 359.

24 Japanese historical demography centers around Professor Hayami Akira's group at Keio University.

25 For example, Sekiyama Naotarō, *Kinsei nihon no jinkō kōzō* [The population structure of Tokugawa Japan] (Tokyo, 1958).

26 Saku Takashi, *Echizen-no-kuni shūmon ninbetsu on-aratame-chō*, 5 vols. Tokyo: Yoshikawa Kōbunkan, 1967–70; Aichi-ken Hōi chihō-shi hensan iinkai, *Mikawa-no-kuni Hōi chihō shūmon jimbetsu aratame-chō* (Tokyo, 1961).

27 For example, good starting points are Irene Taeuber, *The Population of Japan* (Princeton, 1958); Ministry of Health and Welfare, Institute of Population Problems, *Meiji shonen ikō Taisho 9-nen ni itaru danjo nen sei betsu jinkō suikei ni tsuite* [On population estimates by sex and age from the early years of Meiji to 1920] (Tokyo, 1962).

28 Ministry of Finance, *Ōkurasho Nempō* [Annual report of the Ministry of Finance], 1875–1943, 1950– (annually); idem., *Ginkō Sōran* [Survey of banks], 1875– (annually); *Zenkoku ginkō shisan fusai hyō* [Data on assets and liabilities of banks in the nation], 1875– (annually); Ministry of Agriculture and Commerce (*Nōshōmushō*), *Nōshomu tōkeihyō* [Statistics of agriculture and commerce], 1879–1923 (annually); idem., *Kōjō tōkeihyō* [Statistics of factories], 1919– (annually); Ministry of Agriculture and Forestry, *Nōrinshō tōkeihyō* [Statistics of agriculture and forestry], 1924–40 (annually).

29 Ministry of Commerce and Industry (*Shōkōshō*), *Kaisha Iōkeihyō* [Statistics of firms], 1921–46 (annually); Yūshōdō Film Publishing Company Ltd., *Meiji nenkan fuken tōkeisho shūsei* [Index to prefectural statistics of Meiji years] (Tokyo, 1964); idem., *Fuken shiryō maikurofuirumu han, kaisetsu, saimoku* [Microfilms on prefectural material, annotations, and details] (Tokyo, 1964); idem., *Yūshōdō Microfilm Publications, General Catalogue, 1967–68* (Tokyo, 1966); idem., *Fuken shiryō* [Materials on prefectures] (Tokyo, 1964), microfilms.

30 See n. 29 above.

31 Tōkyō-fu, Shōmuka Tōkei Kai, *Tōkyō-fu tōkeisho* [Statistics of Tokyo], 2 vols. (Tokyo, 1884). One delightful item is a 50-page list of all the bridges in Tokyo, classified by source of construction funds and giving the name, location, material, length, width, date and cost of construction, and body of water spanned. It includes 173 bridges called *Ishibashi* (stone bridge), one of which is said to be made of wood. The Japanese bureaucrats rank among the most zealous groups of data-gatherers anywhere.

32 Ibid. (Tokyo, 1927). For Osaka, see Ōsaka-fu, *Ōsaka-fu tōkeisho* [Statistics of Osaka] (Osaka, 1925).

33 One of the better volumes is *Ōsaka-shi tōkeisho* [Statistical yearbook of Osaka City]. For major cities, it is possible to get fairly good time series after 1910. These data usually include figures on land, population, education, public health, religion, agriculture and forestry, commerce, companies, money and banking, manufacturing, transportation, military affairs, police, courts and prisons, construction, social welfare, civil officials and finance.

34 Iwate Prefecture, *Iwate Kenshi* [The history of Iwate Prefecture], vol. 9 (Iwate, 1964).

35 Kokuritsu Kokkai Toshokan (The Diet Library), *Todōfuken tōkei sōgō mokuroku* [A comprehensive catalog of prefectural statistics] (Tokyo, 1958).

36 Osaka Shiritsu Toshokan (The City Library of Osaka), *Osaka shiryō mokuroku* [A catalog of materials on Osaka] (Osaka, 1963); Kanagawa Kenritsu Toshokan (The Prefectural Library of Kanagawa), *Kyōdō shiryō kaisetsu mokuroku* [An annotated catalog of materials] (Yokohama, 1960).

37 Nishioka, *Nihon kenbetsu chishi mokuroku;* Council of Japanese Academic Societies, Section 3, *Keizaigaku bunken kihō* [Quarterly bibliography of economics]; Minobe and Matsukawa, *Tōkei chōsa sōran;* Masaki and Matsukawa, *Tōkei chōsa gaido bukku.*

38 For a description of some of the better bank histories, see Kozo Yamamura, "The Role of Samurai in the Development of Modern Banking In Japan," *Journal of Economic History,* vol. 27, no. 2 (June 1967). For those interested in regionally oriented industry studies, company histories are essential, as they often cover regional wage differentials, sources of inputs, and market and other relevant data.

39 T. Katō, "Ginkōshi shōkai" [Introduction to bank histories], in *Shakai Kagaku Kenkyū* [Research in the Social Sciences], vol. 6, no. 4 (1955); Shiga University, *Hompō shashi mokuroku* [A catalog of company histories in Japan], in *Hikone Ronsō* [Annals of Hikone], vol. 33 (1956); Tokyo University, *Shashi, jitsugyōka denki mokuroku* [A catalog of company histories and businessmen's biographies], November 1964 (monograph).

40 Furushima, *Sangyōshi.*

41 Ohkawa et al., *Estimate of Long-Term Economic Statistics of Japan since 1868,* p. 131.

42   E. S. Crawcour, "Japan, 1868–1920," *Agricultural Development in Asia*, ed. R. T. Schand (Berkeley, 1969), p. 21.

43   *Cf.* W. W. Lockwood, *Economic Development of Japan* (Princeton, 1954), preface.

BIBLIOGRAPHICAL APPENDIX

This brief appendix lists only 23 samples which should be included in a more comprehensive bibliographical work. The items were selected on the basis of their relative importance in terms of quality, coverage, and general interest. All the items examined, and especially those described below, show that: (1) the supply of useful quantitative data of all types continues to increase for the period between 1868 and 1940, and (2) increasingly large efforts are being made by Japanese economic historians to make more quantitative evidence available for the period before 1868.

The large quantity of data available for the pre-World War II periods and the increasingly large quantity available for the post-1945 years make a full-scale bibliographical work on the quantitative data for historical research on Japan, economic or otherwise, highly desirable. For example, numerous company, bank, and local histories have never been catalogued in any comprehensive manner in English. The Rosovsky monograph (n. 10 above) and other sources cited in n. 39 could serve as valuable cores should the work be undertaken.

1   Mitsui Takasumi. *Ryōgae nendaiki* [Chronicles of money-exchanging]. 3 vols. Tokyo: Iwanami Shoten, 1932 (vol. 1), 1933 (vols. 2, 3). The original version was written by Takahara Kyūbei in 1845, and Mitsui Takasumi edited and annotated it for publication. The first two volumes provide detailed descriptions of money exchange markets, rates of exchange, and various kinds of coins circulated from the late seventeenth century to the first half of the eighteenth century. The first volume emphasizes activities of *hon ryōgae nakama* (exchangers specializing in gold and silver coins), while the second volume deals with *waki ryōgaeya* (dealers in other types of coins). The last volume contains research by Mitsui using the materials in the first two volumes and other sources. It discusses meanings and conditions of changes in rates of exchange and demands for numerous kinds of coins and contains 16 color charts of rates and demands for various kinds of coins from as early as 1692.

2   House of Mitsui, *Ōsaka kingin beisen narabi ni hibi sōbahyō* [Daily market prices of gold, silver, rice, coins, and bills of exchange of Osaka]. 2 vols. Tokyo: House of Mitsui, 1916. These two large volumes were compiled from 119 volumes of daily notes (*nikki-roku*) of the House of Mitsui and include some of the more valuable and reliable data for the Tokugawa economy between 1805 and 1871. The data included are exchange rates of gold in silver, exchange commission rates (*kawase keiki*) for gold and silver bills, exchange rates of coins (*zeni*) in silver, and the price of rice traded in Osaka. All quotations are daily and include the high and low for each day. The first 35 pages of Vol. 1 are an excellent guide for those who wish to use these data.

3   Miyamoto Mataji, ed. *Kinsei Ōsaka no bukka to rishi* [Prices and interest rates of premodern Osaka]. Tokyo: Toppan Insatsu, 1963. This book contains prices

and interest rates for the period between the 1830s and 1870s. Prices gathered from a wide variety of sources yield time series on wages, costs of transportation, and numerous goods ranging from household items to commercial goods such as rice and wine. Interest rates were taken from records of the House of Kōnoike and include amounts of loans, interest rates, periods of loans, names of borrowers, purposes of loans, and other information. The first two chapters are excellent general discussions of histories of prices and detailed descriptions of prices and interest rates of Japan. This is undoubtedly one of the best of the recent books published on the Tokugawa economy.

4   Kyoto Daigaku Kinsei Bukkashi Kenkyūkai (A Research Association to Study Price Fluctuations from the Fifteenth to Seventeenth Centuries). *Jūgo-jūnana seiki ni okeru bukka hendō no kenkyū* [A study on price fluctuations from the fifteenth to seventeenth centuries]. Kyoto: Nakamura Insatsu, 1962. These prices were compiled from records of temples and shrines in and around Kyoto for the period between 1451 and 1650. The more than 100 items cover such topics as rice, coins of various kinds, gold, silver, vegetables, cloth, and numerous household goods. All time series, with a few exceptions, include the source, time, price, and unit of measurement. The introduction to this volume is useful for its detailed descriptions of measurement units, relative values of monies, and various types of markets of the period.

5   Irimajiri Yoshinaga. *Tokugawa bakuhansei no kōzō to kaitai* [The structure and dissolution of the Tokugawa system]. Tokyo: Yūshōdō, 1963. Though this book is on the structure and dissolution of the Tokugawa Bakufu's politico-economic system, it uses quantitative evidence liberally throughout. The data, often applying to a village or kuni, are skillfully used to illustrate and analyze the *bakuhan* system. Most frequently used are data for agricultural outputs, yields, shares of landlords and peasants, occupations, and population. This is an excellent guidebook to the numerical records of the period. The author, a leading economic historian on the Tokugawa period, shows how case studies and regional investigations can be used in writing vivid and valid history.

6   Waseda Daigaku Keizai Gakkai (The Economic Research Association of Waseda University). *Ashikaga Orimonoshi* [A history of weaving in Ashikaga]. 3 vols. Tokyo: Choyōkai, 1960. These three volumes contain approximately 450 statistical tables relating to structure, output, financing, cooperative unions, prices, etc. of the cotton-weaving industry in and around Ashikaga, formerly a village and now a city north of Tokyo. It is one of the most exhaustive studies of a local economy from the late Tokugawa period to around 1940. Given the importance of the industry in the economic development of Japan, the data and analyses in these volumes merit special attention.

7   Taiwan Ginkōshi Hensankai. *Taiwan ginkōshi* [The history of the Bank of Taiwan]. Tokyo: Dainihon Insatsu, 1964. This volume of over 1,400 pages is one of the best bank histories and in effect an economic history of Taiwan with special emphasis on finance and banking. It covers the period from 1900 to the end of World War II, a time when Taiwan was under Japanese rule, and it contains much discussion useful for political and diplomatic as well as for economic history. The volume is rich in data throughout, and the appended statistical tables contain most of what economic historians usually wish to find.

8 Suzuki Naoji. *Edo ni okeru kome torihiki no kenkyū* [A study on Rice-trading in Edo]. Tokyo: Kashiwa Shobō, 1965. This is a good work on the rice market of Edo during the Tokugawa period. It contains data on the rice output of han actively marketing in Edo, prices, shipment, and payment patterns. It is also one of the better books for reference to sources which may need to be investigated further.

9 Rinji Kokusai Tōkei Kyoku (The Special Bureau of National Bond Statistics). *Kokusai tōkei* [Statistics of national bonds]. Tokyo: Insatsu-kyoku, 1908. The volume includes data on amounts, rates of interest, holders, purposes (military, fiscal, industrial promotion, colonial administration, etc.) of all national bonds from the beginning of Meiji to 1910. The data are available, in 305 tables, for each of the bond issues during the period. The volume is worthy of close attention by historians interested in government financing and the role of the government in general in the economic development of Japan during the Meiji era.

10 Osaka Zeikan (Osaka Tariff Bureau). *Osaka zeikan enkakushi* [A history of the Osaka Tariff Bureau]. Imaoka Kōbunsha, 1908. This is a republication of the 1902 volume entitled *Zeikan enkaku chōsa hōkokusho* [A research report of the Tariff Bureau]. Though it is a descriptive history of the functions and roles of the Osaka Tariff Bureau, it contains data on tariff rates, duties collected on exports and imports, the volume and type of commodities passing through the bureau and costs of warehousing, and in some cases costs of shipping. It will be useful to those interested in Osaka and its position in international trade during the period between 1868 and 1898.

11 Kagaku Gijitsu Chō, Shigen Chōsakai (Resources Research Section, the Bureau of Scientific Technology). *Nihon no shigen mondai* [Japan's natural resource problems]. 2 vols. Tokyo: Kagaku gijitsu chō, 1961. The resources covered are water, forests, and food in volume 1; energy, iron and steel, textiles, pulp, artificial resin and rubber, ocean and regional resources in volume 2. Although not conceived as data sources, these volumes contain a good amount of data on technological changes, output, and efficiency of resource use. The descriptive text is also useful for basic knowledge of the resources concerned. These volumes could also be used to trace sources of further data.

12 The Bank of Japan. *Meiji ikō hompō shuyō keizai tōkei* [Major economic statistics of Japan since Meiji]. Tokyo: Bank of Japan, 1966. The volume contains 140 series of data in about 600 pages, both quantitative data in an economic theoretical sense and data which reflect institutional changes. The content is similar to that found in the annual volumes of the Bank of Japan statistics. Though its comprehensiveness, explanations of sources and methods used, and titles in English make this volume handy, most of the series start only during the Shōwa period (after 1926).

13 Nippon Rōdō Undō Shiryō Iinkai (A Committee on Materials of the Japanese Labor Movement). *Nippon rōdō undō shiryō* [Materials on Japanese labor movement]. Vol. 10. Tokyo: Chūō Kōron, 1959. The tenth volume of this series includes data on prices, output, population, employment, hours of work, labor conditions, labor unions, family budgets, and welfare for the period between the early Meiji years and 1940. The data are not limited to those relating

directly to the Japanese labor movement. As this 600-page volume is accompanied by sources of each series of data, the researcher can use it to scout further.

14   Nakayama Ichirō, et al. *Chushō kigyō kenkyū* [Studies on small and medium firms]. 6 vols. Tokyo: Tōyōkeizai, 1960–61. Of the several serial publications on the subject, these six volumes are by far the best. The period covered is from the early Meiji (in some cases even before) to 1960. The title of each volume describes the contents accurately: 1. The development of small and medium industries; 2. Statistical analyses of small-medium firms; 3. A survey of statistics on small-medium firms (in 175 tables); 4. The economic structure of small-medium firms in export industries; 5. The reality of technological progress in small-medium industries; 6. Regional economies and the structure of small-medium firm conglomeration. Volumes 2 and 3 contain both quantitative data in the economic theoretical sense and quantitative data to reflect institutional or structural changes. Numerous types of data are included for comparison with data for large firms. For the development of Japanese industries, these six volumes are indispensable in their descriptions, analyses, and data.

15   The Prefectural Library of Yamaguchi Prefecture. *Bōchōfūdo chūshin an* [Proposals for the development of the Bōchō region]. 21 vols. and index vol. Yamaguchi-kenritsu Toshokan, 1961. This is one of the most comprehensive documents on a han economy and can be used by various types of historians, especially economic historians. The documents have been scarcely touched to date because the original 395 barely legible handwritten folios were available only at the Yamaguchi Prefectural Library. The period covered in these volumes is the first decade of the Tempō period, 1830–41, when the documents were compiled. For a study of Chōshū han in the late Tokugawa period, these volumes are essential.

The index or research guide (*kenkyū yōran*) conveniently indexes the contents of all 21 volumes and includes explanations of historical words used, maps, administrative organizations of various levels of local governments down to the village level, names and locations of temples, *shukuba* (post-towns), and villages. The economic data include: output of agricultural products (rice, maize, cotton, tobacco, tea, etc.); amount of cultivated land; taxes paid in kind or in cash, all on a regional and village base; household consumption expenditures; costs of seeds; detailed data on planting, weeding, harvesting, and types and quantity of labor used; types and quantities of fish harvested; holdings of domestic and draft animals by household and by village; and holdings of gold and silver by village and by household. These volumes also include demographic data by village, class, and household. The noneconomic data include: detailed information on officials such as *daikan* (district magistrates) and *ōmetsuke* (police), changes in the han and village administrative structures; names and numbers of *gōshi* (country samurai, often former peasants who had become *gōshi* by buying the so-called *gōshi*-shares) and samurai; and other data showing changes in the political structure of the late Tokugawa period.

The most profitable use of these volumes might be to analyze both noneconomic and economic data to investigate the changes in the social and economic positions of samurai and peasants in the Tempō period.

16 The Prefectural Library of Kōchi Prefecture. *Chōsokabe chiken-chō* [Records of land registration for Chōsokabe domain]. 19 vols. Kōchi Kenritsu Toshokan, 1963. This is one of the rare documents on land use and landholding patterns in the late sixteenth century. The records are for the Chōsokabe han, a part of the present Kōchi prefecture. The data are for the period between 1587 and 1598, and the original documents, now in the possession of the Kōchi prefectural library, were compiled at the end of the seventeenth century.

The statistics include: size of landholding, area cultivated, and area left fallow, by village and by household; agricultural labor; land owned or leased by temples and shrines; village population by social class; taxes paid by household and by village; and detailed occupational breakdown by village. These records are a rare source of quantitative data on the pre-Tokugawa economic and social structure.

17 Meguro Ward. *Meguro-ku shi* [A history of Meguro ward]. Compiled by the Tokyo Municipal University Research Association. Tokyo: Meguro-ku, 1960. This is one of a very large number of excellent local histories offering varied and numerous statistical data. Both volumes are long, each about 1200 pages. Volume 1 contains a good general history; volume 2, the source volume, includes a surprising quantity of social, political, and economic data from about the 1620s, when Meguro ward was a part of Musashino-no-kuni. Patient researchers can find relatively long time series on landholding, occupation, class structure, population, family composition, and law enforcement to use for intertemporal comparisons. This work is typical of numerous local histories which are potentially extremely useful. As with all other local histories, a major problem, in addition to the limited geographical area covered, is the necessity to read Japanese relatively rapidly in order to find specific materials in the large bulk of the study.

18 Kitamura Village History Editorial Association. *Kitamura sonshi* [A village history of Kitamura Sonshi] Hensan-kai, 1960. This is an example of a good, well-written village history. The village is located in Sorachi *gun* (county) in Hokkaidō. The history is useful for quantitative evidence of the process of the gradual settlement of Hokkaidō; government efforts and subsidies for the development of the island; and social, political, and economic changes of a village in Hokkaidō. Some quantitative data go back to the early eighteenth century.

19 Local History Research Institute, The Faculty of Law, Meiji University. *Izu Shimoda*. Tokyo: Meiji University, 1962. This is a useful and interesting 753-page history of an important port city familiar to all students of Japanese history. Though no time-series analysis can be attempted, some of the data on taxation, stipends paid to samurai, landholdings, and the construction of houses and temples start as early as 1588. Anyone interested in the rapidly changing social and economic aspects of a region affected by the waves of *kaikoku* (opening of the nation) and *kurofune* (the black ships) will find the history worthwhile.

20 Hitotsubashi University Fudasashi Jiryaku Publication Committee. *Fudasashi*

Jiryaku [Records of rice dealers]. 3 vols. Tokyo: Sōbun-sha, 1966. This is an important source of historical data of which only a fraction has yet been used by Japanese scholars. It includes data for 1724–1817 on the quantities and market prices of rice originally given to samurai as stipends. The rates of interest charged to, and the amounts borrowed by, samurai from *fudasashi* using the stipend rice as collateral are also included, along with the costs of transporting rice. To examine the Tokugawa economy in general and to evaluate the economic status of the samurai class in particular, this is some of the most important quantitative evidence yet unused. It is an example of the immense amount of unused data which can only be fully utilized through use of a computer.

21 Takaoka Commercial High School. *Toyama baiyakugyō-shi* [The historical material of the Toyama medicine peddlars]. 2 vols. Kaimeidō, 1935. These two volumes include descriptions and statistics, including prices and sales volume, of all aspects of the development and growth of this well-known Japanese industry, which dates from the 1740s. The medicine peddlars occupy a position analogous to that of the Yankee peddlars in United States economic history. The importance of the industry in the Toyama region makes these two volumes valuable sources for the quantitative history of a local economy in a changing politico-social environment.

22 Nomura, Kanetarō. *Mura meisai-chō no kenkyū* [A study of village records]. Tokyo: Yūhikaku, 1949. The village records, *mura meisai-chō* (literally "detailed reports on villages"), were compiled by village headmen or, in some instances, by han officials themselves for various administrative and economic purposes. They include data on landholdings, agricultural production, peasant income, tax assessments and the proportions to be paid in cash and in kind, village resources (population and stocks of assets, i.e., houses, irrigation systems, animals, various types of nonarable land) and various types of data on village administration, law enforcement, and social organizations. The records in this volume are for 109 villages between 1736 and 1744. The volume contains the original data as well as Nomura's brief observations. Some quantitatively oriented historians should ask a new set of questions of the data and analyze these records much more extensively than Nomura did.

23 The Kanazawa Municipal Library. *Kaga han nōsei seiji keizaishi shiryō* [Historical materials on the agricultural policies, politics, and economic history of Kaga-han]. Kanazawa Kenritsu Toshokan, 1964. The library reproduced the original handwritten version of the original 98 booklets (in 15 large folios) in the possession of the Kanazawa Prefectural Library. The contents therefore are useful only for those able to read Tokugawa calligraphy or those working with specially trained Japanese personnel.

The reward for examining this difficult source is great. These volumes include data, for the period between Bunsei (1818–30) and late Tokugawa, on numerous aspects of han agriculture at various levels; on political and administrative aspects of the han; and on numerous other political and social, as well as economic, changes of a han in the late Tokugawa period. This is a rich mine of quantitative data.

13

QUANTITATIVE RESOURCES FOR THE STUDY OF INDIAN HISTORY

by Morris David Morris

The materials discussed in this chapter are those which an economic historian would normally encounter. I am not concerned here with the possibilities of applying quantitative methods to nonquantitative materials, but only with reporting on those types of data which quite obviously lend themselves to the development of time series. Whatever the limitations of my study, even within these restrictions there are large amounts of data of interest to social as well as economic historians.

When I refer to "Indian" history, I concern myself with South Asia or at least with what are now India, Pakistan, and Bangladesh. I know nothing about the materials in the Himalayan states, Nepal, Sikkim, and Bhutan. Nor am I able to say anything very precise about Ceylon. However, a casual inspection of the work done on that country and discussions with G. Obeyesekere suggest that in general my comments about the subcontinent will be applicable to Ceylon.[1]

I will consider only materials generated after 1500, since I am not sufficiently familiar with the early periods to be able to say anything useful about the potential for quantitative study of pre-1500 data.[2] Nor will I say anything about the obvious possibilities which exist for the period after 1947. However, these chronological limitations (1500–1947) are hardly confining; rather than a paucity of materials there is an embarrassment of riches. In fact, the possibilities for work with quantitative data in the history of India are so enormous that I have been forced to restrict myself to an unsatisfactory general description of what is available.

The reader should not assume that all available materials are European.

I would like to express my thanks for the generous advice I received from a number of people. Among those who gave me the benefit of their specific knowledge are Ian Catenach, K. N. Chaudhuri, D. R. Gadgil, K. Mukerji, T. Raychaudhuri, Sourin Roy, and J. N. Sharma.

It is one of the widespread fictions of scholarship that South Asian society had no sense of history.[3] It is also generally assumed that indigenous materials for the study of Indian history, particularly quantitative materials, were extremely limited. These are notions which seem to have derived from particular developments in Indological scholarship on the one hand and the special preoccupation with the British connection on the other.[4] Whatever their origins, such preconceptions are certainly not valid. Studies of Indian history can draw on a range and amount of vernacular materials that possibly rival those available for European regions during the same period.

Today South Asia is an economically underdeveloped region, but historically it supported a highly sophisticated civilization, the operation of which generated substantial amounts of quantitative data. In the post-1500 period, there were at least two powerful indigenous imperial administrative systems (the Mughal and Maratha empires); a large number of smaller (but still European-sized) states; and a congeries of native religious, political, and commercial enterprises which either required quantitative data for their functioning or produced it in the course of their activities. Some of these institutions, like the Mughal and Maratha empires, came to an end in the early nineteenth century. But many princely states survived, and new ones were established under British rule; materials flowed from these sources right up to the end of the period under consideration. The great pilgrimage centers continued to function. In fact, greater political security and transportation improvements probably increased their numbers and extended their scales of operations. Indigenous commercial activities continued to generate data within traditional economic sectors. And the expansion of commerce probably increased the supply of materials, not only here but from the more modern forms of indigenous activity.

Added to these native sources are, of course, the more obvious materials produced by Europeans who came into the region in one capacity or another—as commercial entrepreneurs, in some social role, or as officials of an imperial authority. We have quantitative materials generated on a scale and of a significance undreamed of by scholars outside the field. For example, the records of the English East India Company are a rich mine of data: "There are at least 48,000 volumes of manuscripts at the India Office covering the two and a half centuries of the East India Company's official existence, an average of approximately 200 per decade."[5] The records of the Company and its successor, the India Office, show the possibilities on an even grander scale; they "consist of some 150,000 volumes" plus "a large number of unsorted papers and collections of files, and about 10,000 volumes of official publications of the central and provincial governments of India and the Indian states."[6] This description does not include the large amounts of official materials which never left India.[7] In fact, even historians who have worked on South Asian materials are largely unaware of the scale on which quantitative data exist and the research opportunities which they offer.

The substantive unfamiliarity with these materials and their possibilities is a result of at least three specific characteristics of much of the writing of South Asian history. For one thing, to a large extent the questions which have preoccupied most historians have not lent themselves to answers embodying quantitative elements.[8] But even where quantification would have been useful, the essentially polemic orientation of much scholarship has meant that quantitative data have rarely been used seriously or creatively. Rather, they have been used as decoration, illustrating propositions and conclusions which have been arrived at in other ways.[9] A third characteristic, now beginning to change slightly, has been the rather surprising reluctance of scholars of the modern period to use vernacular materials, nonquantitative or quantitative.[10]

In the past decade or so there has been a slight increase in the willingness to use quantitative data for historical purposes. A major bar to their extensive use has been the obvious one: very few historians are prepared to handle such materials with any degree of confidence (or competence). But even where the scholars have been technically competent, the quality of the results has usually left much to be desired. This last phenomenon raises problems that I will consider briefly in my discussion of the use of available data.

I ought to warn against any misinterpretation of my enthusiasm in the following section about the availability of quantitative material. Elsewhere I have advanced the view that for a number of reasons South Asia was never able to develop a stable political apparatus with a sturdy administrative underpinning.[11] Moreover, the administrative systems were never as impressive in operation as the historical description of formal structures would suggest.[12] These conditions indicate some of the limits to the quantitative data the historian can expect to find. But the exact nature and quality of the quantitative materials available can be determined only when scholars get seriously interested in them. At this point, let me turn to a brief description of those materials.

AVAILABLE QUANTITATIVE MATERIALS

Mughal Empire Materials

Data from the Mughal Empire were generated in the course of imperial administration. The efforts of the Emperor Akbar (1556–1605) and his finance minister, Todar Mal (d. ca. 1590), produced a host of administrative surveys and apparently a continuous flow of certain kinds of data. The amount of information is apt to be exaggerated because of a tendency to overestimate the efficiency and centralized character of Mughal rule. But even if the system had been as efficient as some have claimed, it would have furnished material relating mostly to tax matters. Other substantial types of information would not have been provided.

A number of scholars are working on this period; the major concentration of research on Mughal India is to be found at Aligarh University. The leading student of the quantitative materials, Irfan Habib, has written a major study of the economic and social history of the period and has provided an introduction to the relevant bibliography.[13] Habib has built on the pathbreaking work of W. H. Moreland, a scholar of profound quantitative concerns. Referring in his classic volume, *India at the Death of Akbar,* to the interpretative difficulties imposed by "the exuberant language of the sixteenth century," Moreland wrote: "The only possible corrective is to fix the attention on quantities and I have attempted throughout to arrive at numerical estimates, actual or relative as the available data permit, of the various factors which composes the stream of economic life." [14] Moreland's work provides useful leads to the sources and to the interpretation of quantitative data of the period. A bibliography of his writings has been prepared by Margaret Case.[15]

Maratha Empire Materials

Apart from other collections, the so-called Peshwa *Daftar,* the records and correspondence of the Maratha Empire, are located in Poona, 120 miles southeast of Bombay. This collection, consisting of 27,000 bundles of records in Marathi and some 8,000 files in English, covers the period 1714–1818.[16] Some of these have been translated and published, but although the published materials are of interest to diplomatic and political historians, they contain none of the quantitative data.

Tapan Raychaudhuri, professor of history at the University of Delhi, has suggested that the Peshwa *Daftar* might well yield information on tax revenues, prices, agricultural output, and possibly even area under cultivation in the regions represented.[17] D. R. Gadgil, for many years director of the Gokhale Institute of Politics and Economics, informed me that the material is "specially full for the period 1750 to 1820." His assistant, investigating records relating to internal customs and excises, came up with promising material. One of Gadgil's students is completing a thesis on "financial accounts during the regime of the Peshwa Madhavrao I 1761–72." Apparently the quantitative material is extensive.

> But as there is little detailed knowledge of the working of the then revenue, administrative and other systems, and as the detailed material of the village and *pargana* [district] level is not continuous or full, the research student has found it difficult to piece together a detailed meaningful account. However, this is the first time that the Maratha records have been treated from this point of view.[18]

Gadgil's reference to the lack of detailed knowledge of the working of the then revenue, administrative, and other systems suggests one major difficulty in working with traditional materials: our lack of knowledge of how the institutions which produced the data functioned. Moreover, traditional materials were frequently written in scripts that modern scholars have difficulty reading, in this case a cursive Marathi. Clearly the use of these materials will require scholars with special training in the relevant scripts and in the technical details of Maratha administration.

Princely State Materials

In addition to these records of imperial administrations, the records of many separate pre-British political entities (to which one might apply the possibly inappropriate British term *princely states*) have survived. For example, a great trove of documents relevant to the economic history of a number of Rajasthan states—Bikaner, Jodhpur, Mewar, Jaipur—have been identified in the Rajasthan State Archives by Satish Chandra and S. P. Gupta.[19] The material has not been catalogued, not to mention indexed.

Added to the official materials, apparently, there are still extant large and important complementary private collections in the custody of former ruling families and *jagirdars* (great estate holders). "Records in the possession of *mahajans* [in this region apparently hereditary village officers], temples, *muafidars* [traditional grant holders of a special type], etc., are also extremely important for a study of economic life, but no systematic collection of these have [*sic*] been made as yet." [20]

Only the State Archive material has been sampled in any detail. The survey suggests that some Bikaner records go back to the sixteenth century, but they have yet to be deciphered and analyzed. The Jodhpur records apparently start in the early eighteenth century. In the Jaipur collection, the largest, some records date back to 1648. The main body of materials begins around 1664, but even after this date there are gaps. From 1709 continuous files are available, and the various series continue until at least 1830. Depending on the date at which specific British administrative forms were introduced, some files continue to the end of the nineteenth century. They include materials that reflect changing crop patterns, agricultural productivity, land utilization, prices, etc. For example:

> There is sufficient material in the Jaipur *pargana* records to enable a detailed study being made of local prices of food grains, cash crops, etc., from the middle of the seventeenth century onwards and also to compute the relative prices of cash-crops to food grains and of copper, silver and gold to one another. This would be an extremely useful supplement to information in the European sources regarding the movement of prices in the coastal areas.[21]

Another source of princely state materials is the Hyderabad (now Andhra) State Archives. I have seen some of this material but have not had a chance to examine it in detail. From Raychaudhuri's description these records very likely constitute a Central India counterpart to the Rajasthan materials already described.[22] In addition, there is also the Inayet Jang collection, which has been transferred from Hyderabad to the National Archives in Delhi. According to Raychaudhuri,

> The Inayet Jang collection, going back to the early 17th century and covering a period of about a century and a half, contains information on prices. Processing this mass of data will require collaboration between statisticians, historians, economists and, of course, experts on revenue matters who have a thorough knowledge of Perian revenue documents. The last mentioned animal belongs to a declining species to be found mainly in Hyderabad and probably some of the princely states. To the best of my understanding, for the type of work required they are not to be found among the professional historians, even the technically best equipped among them.[23]

Kerala Materials

In this area, too, I am indebted to Raychaudhuri for information. His letter is worth quoting not only for the materials to which he refers but also for his comment on some of the difficulties of using them.

> During my wanderings as an official of the National Archives I have come across huge collections of documents containing quantitative information which are by no means negligible but are little known outside the world of archivists in this country. One collection which I found most impressive was the archives at Ernakulum, Kerala, consisting of the revenue records of the local princes. Maintained in palm leaf scrolls in neat bundles these records which are still in use for the settlement of disputes go back in many cases to the 16th century and one broken series relating to the royal household contains information such as the detailed breakdown of the cost of shipbuilding in the 14th century. In 1958, when I saw these records, I could trace only one person—a petty clerk at the Archives— who could decipher the grandham script in which these records were written. (The ordinary scholars of old Malayali would probably be unable to handle the relevant technicalities.) If he is dead by now probably one will require fresh research to decipher these documents. The only idea regarding the quantity of records at Ernakulum I can give you is that there are two large rooms full of them stacked ceiling high.[24]

The materials of traditional Rajasthan, Hyderabad, and Kerala were generated in the course of the administrative activities of typical princely states. It is likely, therefore, that such archives exist (or did exist) in large volumes in many other parts of the subcontinent. These materials, with their great research potential, have not been properly identified as yet. Those that outside archivists have noted have neither been catalogued nor worked over.

Miscellaneous Indigenous Materials

In addition to materials generated by sovereignties, quantitative data can be found arising out of the activities of temples, genealogists, village officials, and merchants. For example, B. N. Goswamy has pointed to the great potential in the records kept by priests at centers of pilgrimage. He tells us that the records of five northwest Indian centers with which he is familiar have been "maintained with remarkable continuity over the past 350 years or so."

> It may be possible, for instance, with the help of these records to ascertain, among other things, at a given point of time, in an area, the population of a village or town or region, the distribution of castes in that area, the hierarchy of the social order, the relative position of the professions, the pattern of migration from one place to another, and so on. Considerable work of demographic interest may thus be possible from the records of a place like Haridwar for large parts of India, or at a place of relatively restricted interest like Rameshwaram (Madras) or Gaya (Bihar) or Jagannathpuri (Orissa) for the regions which they serve. . . . It may be possible again for us not only to study the situation at a fixed point of time, but also the developments in it over a period of time.[25]

Large quantities of village records were generated in the pre-British period. For example, in western India land revenue was collected not by government officers but through a hierarchy of intermediaries. Each intermediary from the village headman up had to provide the security of a banker. Each had his own accountants and record keepers (*mehtas*) who produced quantitative information. These records were not official, and, as a result, they were not taken over by the British. It is unclear how and where such materials have survived.[26] One study (in Marathi) which apparently has drawn on such data as well as on family records is a history of Nagaon, a small west coast village in the Kolaba district, during the period 1760–1840. The book was based on the papers of the Adhikari family, the mehtas of the Angres, who were then the ruling group.[27]

One additional source has been uncovered and is being used by a group of anthropologists. These are genealogical and other records kept by a caste of professional bards in the Gujarat. The oldest volume uncovered dates from 1740, although some of the genealogies go back much farther. This particular material comes from western India, but there is no reason to doubt that similar data are available elsewhere in the country.[28]

Merchants maintained elaborate correspondence and account books, and one encounters occasional references to them. I am certain that much of this kind of material still exists in family records that antedate the period of British rule, but I know of no place where they are available nor of any English-language studies which have used such materials.[29]

Thus far I have considered pre-British indigenous sources having their origins in activities largely independent of contact with the West. Whatever the promise for quantitative work implicit in these materials, it is dwarfed by the data that Europeans generated and the vernacular materials that were a direct response to European influence.[30]

East India Companies Records

The first great body of quantitative data was generated by the Portuguese and other European companies trading to the East. In general they contain information on foreign trade, but there is a fair amount of material on local prices, interest rates, freight charges, etc. The records of the Portuguese, which are not well known to many students of South Asian history, contain not only foreign trade data but fiscal materials relating to the small regions that the Portuguese ruled in India. They are to be found in archives in Lisbon and Goa.

The records of the English East India Company, covering a period of more than 250 years, reflect its activities as trader and then as the governing representative of Parliament. Initially the main preoccupation of the company was commercial, and the quantitative data in the records are, of course, very extensive. When, after 1760, the company became increasingly preoccupied with administrative obligations, its records reflect the growing concern with the revenues and expenses of government. There are no really good guides to the quantitative data in the Company's records, but the best general one is by William Foster. Furber's *John Company at Work* has an impressive bibliography which, while limited in some respects, suggests some of the quantitative possibilities of the eighteenth century materials.[31]

Although some foreign trade data have been published for the seventeenth and eighteenth centuries, much more is available for that period and later.[32] For example, K. N. Chaudhuri of the London School of Oriental and African Studies has surveyed the material carefully and reports that it is possible to develop very detailed foreign trade figures for the period 1793–1947 entirely from materials in London.[33] Sourin Roy, deputy director of the National Archives of India, confirms Chaudhuri's further judgment that there are Calcutta port books, now the property of the Calcutta Port Trust, from which one could construct elaborate series of import and export prices.[34] These records could be supported by the *Prices Current* produced from 1853 fortnightly and later weekly by the Calcutta Chamber of Commerce.[35] I have not been able to check on the situation elsewhere, but it seems likely that Bombay, Madras, and Karachi would yield similar materials.[36]

The records of the Dutch East India Company also contain enormous amounts of quantitative data. Raychaudhuri, who has given a great deal of attention to these materials, writes that detailed time series can be constructed for the volume and value of foreign trade, for prices of commodities, for numbers of ships visiting various ports, and occasionally even for the output of particular commodities in specific localities. Furber, too, has pointed out that the Dutch records are very detailed. For example, referring to trade coming through Cochin between 1723 and 1742, he tells us that "every ship, every cargo was meticulously recorded in Cochin. The careful reproduction of these hundreds of entries, and the use of a computer upon them would be a great service to India's economic history." [37] In addition to the English and Dutch company records, which are the most productive sources of quantitative data, one should not neglect the archives of the French and Danish companies nor those of the Ostend Company at Antwerp.[38]

The European company records provide quantitative data on other subjects, but until about 1760 these were only by-products of foreign trade activities. However, the British East India Company records after that date and Government of India sources from 1858 reflect the expanding territorial control and the increasing need for quantitative information of all sorts. Settlement reports and other surveys concerned with the generation of land revenue provided vast amounts of data about the rural sector. But it was only gradually that the formal statistical apparatus was constructed. By the late 1860s and early 1870s, as Stokes tells us, "a great administrative machine had been created entirely novel to English experience. . . . The careful overhaul of the land revenue system in the revised settlements being effected in most of the provinces, the registration of deeds, the census of population, and the compilation of statistics, all these were giving by the [eighteen] seventies a new precision and certainty to the working of the machine." [39]

I do not propose to describe the development of the Indian statistical apparatus. Suffice it to say that in 1867 the first annual *Statistical Abstract Relating to British India* was published. It contained annual data for the 25-year period 1840–65 on public finance, foreign trade, education, railways, postal services, public works, etc. From that date onward, the tide of official data has risen. In 1871 "a central secretariat was established to collect and disseminate statistical information. The first census of British India was taken in 1872. From this work, headed by W. W. Hunter, there eventually emerged the massive *Imperial Gazetteer of India*. Kipling satirized the Indian passion for statistics in his delightful parody of Swinburne's 'Atlanta in Calydon', entitled 'Chorus of the Crystallised Facts' with which he ends his poem 'The Masque of Plenty.' " [40] From 1881 the decennial census has provided quantitative data of a scope and quality that most developed countries would be proud to claim.[41]

In 1884 the first annual issue of *Prices and Wages in India* was published, with price data carried back to 1873. About the same time, annual estimates of agricultural output and acreage began to appear, although detailed data for all the principal crops on an all-India basis were not published until the last decade of the nineteenth century.[42]

The variety of officially published series continued to proliferate, but to my knowledge there is no detailed description of the quantitative data that have become available over time. Even in the absence of any complete bibliographic apparatus, it is safe to suggest that from at least 1840 (and possibly even earlier) the official published statistical materials are extensive enough to compare with those available for the United States or Britain.[43] In fact, if one compares them with the materials in *Historical Statistics of the United States* (HSUS), it becomes obvious that with some exceptions all the tables in HSUS would find their statistical counterparts in some Government of India publication.[44] My comparison, of course, says nothing about the quality of the Indian data.

In the absence of a single definite source, I shall cite a few works that can be used to penetrate the maze of Indian official statistical sources. Two very general descriptions of the development of modern Indian official statistics have been provided by Lord Meston and H. A. F. Lindsay.[45] There is a rather more detailed note on statistical data presented by Finlay Shirras to the Indian Industrial Commission.[46] Much of the statistical material published in the nineteenth century can be found listed in Frank Campbell's *Index Catalogue,* which refers to annual provincial administration reports, gazetteers, parliamentary commissions, and most publications of the various government agencies.[47] Inasmuch as a great many of the statistical presentations originally began appearing as parliamentary papers, a useful guide is the special index published in 1909.[48] Unfortunately, there are no similar lists for the twentieth century. However, it is possible to work backwards from certain recent bibliographies. The most obvious source is the three-volume *Guide to Current Official Statistics,* which claims to refer to "all recurrent publications of statistical interest issued by the Department of the Central Government . . . and other relevant publications." [49] These volumes contain some description of the contents of each publication listed, definitions of the categories used, comments on methods of data collection and compilation, and occasionally some remarks on data weaknesses. Infrequently the length of time during which a specific series has been published is noted. Inasmuch as these volumes are guides to "current" publications, references are almost never made to sources or series no longer being issued. This defect can be remedied partly by the bibliography in Anstey's *The Economic Development of India.*[50] The citations in this book are not always very precise, but they help to identify publications with quantitative data and time series for the early twentieth century that are not reported in the sources already mentioned.

There are two additional specific weaknesses on the bibliographic side. Possibly the most important is the absence of guides to the provincial and local statistical publications. Frank Campbell's *Index Catalogue* does give some leads for the nineteenth century, but I know of no source that even begins to be helpful for the period from 1900 on. The other weakness is the lack of easily available guides to the quantitative data on any specific problem. This situation is more easily overcome. One can always get started by making use of the bibliographic apparatus (not always adequate) which is to be found in almost any serious study on a subject.

The guides which I have discussed so far help us only with the published Government of India statistical series and with the most general record sources. But official activity generated records at local levels as well. Frequently the quantitative data are much more detailed here because they have not been consolidated and summarized for higher-level bureaucratic convenience. For example, in what is now the state of Uttar Pradesh in North India, the unpublished proceedings of the provincial Board of Revenue—filling 582 fat files for the years 1832–55 apparently contain a large amount of statistical materials provided by district officers. And any extant files of district officers and divisional commissioners probably contain additional quantitative information never even forwarded to the provincial offices.[51]

These, however, are only the records generated by local British officers. Below them, typically at the village level, vernacular records were also produced for official purposes. Metcalf reports that in the several district collectorates in Uttar Pradesh there exist great collections of never-used Urdu-language village records which provide detailed tenurial data for all the villages of this enormous province from the time of the first British revenue settlements in the mid-nineteenth century to the present.

> [The historian] can obtain . . . detailed information . . . on such important aspects of agricultural economics and social organization as land tenure and land use, size and distribution of holdings between castes, patterns of cropping and crop yields, the nature and extent of sales, mortgages, and inheritance of land, village subdivisions, kinship groupings, the rights of tenants, and the customary relations between agriculturists and other castes with regard to access to village lands, wells, and groves. Furthermore, and of crucial importance to the historian, this information is available not just for the recent past, but often over a continuous span of one hundred years.[52]

Officially generated local records of this sort exist in many Indian regions. A. M. Shah has described these and other kinds of vernacular records available in the Gujarat.[53]

In addition to the official vernacular records are certain kinds of private materials relating to the countryside. For example, detailed rent statistics can readily be obtained from the estate papers of *zamindari* and *taluqdari* families. Various scholars have encountered such rent rolls. In recent years the abolition of *zamindari* rights eliminated the legal significance of these records, and unfortunately they are now being destroyed at a very rapid rate.[54]

The subject of vernacular materials brings to mind the possibility of tapping the account books of merchants, particularly for price data. In 1902 Theodore Morison wrote, "These old account books still exist in many districts." In fact, Morison made use of some of them in his article on nineteenth century price behavior.[55] My colleague, Edward B. Harper, has been working on a set of account books maintained by a Havik Brahman farmer from the Malnad region of South India; he tells me that such account books are common among this group and often go as far back as a century. Local price data are also available for the nineteenth and twentieth centuries in the vernacular press.

Additional sources of important quantitative materials may be family and caste histories, although it is difficult to know how significant these are. Maureen Patterson reported in 1965 that between 1914 and 1963 64 Maratha family histories (in Marathi) had been published and at least 30 more were being prepared. In some cases the materials date back to the early eighteenth century. Miss Patterson has suggested the possibilities of quantitative data in these family histories, from the "age-old and well known Brahman tendency towards classification and quantification." In fact, her description indicates that, in addition to other obvious social data, the biographies may yield considerable demographic data, including changing life expectancies.[56]

So much for the indigenous materials, virtually unknown and certainly untouched by scholars.[57] For other nonofficial materials containing large amounts of quantitative data, the most obvious sources are the industry association materials. The best known of these are the annual reports of the Bombay Millowners Association, going back to 1875 (with the same data going back to 1865); the Indian Jute Mills Association, beginning in 1884; and the Ahmedabad Millowners Association, starting in 1891. There are, of course, a number of others. In addition, some individual firms have masses of quantitative data still available. Industrial enterprises like the Tata Iron and Steel Company and managing agencies like Andrew Yule and Company are merely two cases in point.

I could, of course, go on at increasingly tedious length but to no great purpose. The evidence is convincing enough that the quantitative data and the possibilities of quantitative research are very great. I will now turn briefly to the question of how these masses of materials can be most efficiently exploited.

USE OF AVAILABLE DATA

My first proposition is that the development of a catalog of sources should *not* have a first order of priority. True, there are no easy ways of finding materials. Yet anyone who has worked for any length of time on Indian subjects will have relatively little trouble identifying the prime sources of quantitative data appropriate to his needs. The main problem is, instead, retrieving the material and (even more important) making it useful once it has been abstracted from the sources. The scholar who is not a South Asian specialist but who wants to use quantitative evidence for comparative purposes will not be interested in spending time working through unprocessed sources. He needs easy access to properly developed, carefully explained data whose quality and limitations are clear.

Having spent a great deal of time working with fairly obvious types of Indian data, I believe that in the present state of scholarship on Indian history the need is for a *Historical Statistics of India* (HSI), more or less the equivalent of the *Historical Statistics of the United States*. As a main priority of scholarly activity, such a project would certainly economize on research time. It would also contribute directly to improving the quality of scholarship in the field. In the absence of such a publication, each scholar must construct the series he needs from the raw material. Inasmuch as it is the series and not the manner of its construction that is crucial, the historian tends to publish the final result in whatever form is most convenient for him. Typically the series cannot be used properly by anyone else, because the method of its construction and summation was not made explicit. This means that scholar after scholar must in turn go back to the original sources and painfully put the same data together again. Obviously, any published compilation that reduced the burden of this task would be helpful.[58]

There is a more important qualitative benefit implied by this proposal, however. A great many historians are not trained to handle quantitative materials; when they do, their statistical constructions suffer from egregious weaknesses. Even when the scholar has some awareness of statistical method, he is strongly tempted to construct his historical series from the most easily available sources without applying any critical tests to the data.[59] I know from my own experience how great the temptation is to build up statistical material without seriously exploring the limitations of the data or attempting to make explicit the assumptions under which they were generated. Take, for example, the difficulties inherent in the widely used Bombay Mill-owners Association (BMOA) data, one of the major sources on industrial growth since 1865. On one occasion when I made use of the association's employment data, I did point out some of their defects. But my needs were limited, and I made no serious effort to work out a corrected employment series.[60]

It is clear that a careful reconstruction of the BMOA employment, investment, and output data (based only on the raw data in the BMOA annual reports) would yield much better (and probably quite different) statistical evidence about the history of the Indian cotton textile industry.[61] The same point can be made, I think, about virtually every time series that scholars have used to interpret India's economic and social behavior. Each series has its individual defects of classification, collection, or definition which need identifying, and virtually none of this work has been done as yet.[62]

Time would be saved by the simple process of extracting basic series from the cumbersome and frequently inaccessible official reports and publishing them along with the available definitions and classificatory information that typically accompany such data. This in itself would aid future research.[63] But, obviously, complete and carefully constructed statistical series, each with a complete critical apparatus appended, would be even more useful. With such information in easily accessible form, scholars would be less prone to draw inappropriate historical conclusions. Moreover, after a large number of important series had been published, it would be possible to grapple with some absolutely basic questions. For example, if we could get a relatively small number of solid statistical series laid out, we might be able to deal with the vexing issue for which, even today, we cannot find a convincing answer: in per-capita terms did the Indian economy in the nineteenth century grow, remain stagnant, or decline? This problem alone shows how desperately a *Historical Statistics of India* is needed. Within the space of little more than a year, three economists arrived at three completely different conclusions about economic growth in nineteenth century India. As might be expected, one argued that per-capita income fell, the second argued that it rose, and the third claimed that it remained constant.[64]

This is not the place to work out the details of a project that would ultimately yield a *Historical Statistics of India*. The idea is not entirely utopian, nor should it be terribly costly. Inasmuch as many scholars are forced to collect data from the records, only a modest financial incentive would be necessary to induce them to organize this material for publication as raw series. There are also scholars who are forced by the exigencies of their work to build up time series and process the results. Incentive would not have to be very great to obtain such results for publication. It might also be possible to encourage students in India to produce, and universities to accept, the construction of critically evaluated time series as Ph.D. dissertations. If, as they are produced, such series and critical notes could be published in an appropriate journal—such as *The Indian Economic and Social History Review*—gradually the groundwork would be laid for a volume of *Historical Statistics of India*.

The costs of financing such an enterprise should not be particularly great if the statistical material is produced mainly as the by-product of normal scholarly activities of faculty and their students. But the implementation of this kind of project would require the establishment of some sort of permanent overseeing committee. This committee would have to decide on the priority of materials to be developed, a decision partially determined by the work that scholars are otherwise doing. The committee would have to set standards for the arrangement, classification, and presentation of the data and would ultimately determine the acceptability of work done.

There is one substantive matter about which I feel strongly. The great temptation is to present data on an all-India basis. But the most important feature of Indian economic and social life is the fact of regional diversity. For economic historians, regional data are absolutely essential in order to identify differential rates of growth and economic change over time. Clearly, regional disaggregation would reveal patterns of behavior quite different from those which emerge when only all-India aggregated data are employed.[65] A major task of any committee involved in the kind of enterprise I have described would be to concentrate much scholarly effort upon regional and local statistical series.

NOTES

1 For example, a reading of G. Obeyesekere, *Land Tenure in Village Ceylon* (Cambridge: Cambridge University Press, 1967), suggests some data sources similar to those available in India.
2 The distinguished economic historian, W. H. Moreland, commented in his *India at the Death of Akbar: An Economic Study* (Delhi: Atma Ram and Sons, 1962), "There is, I fear, little prospect that adequate materials for a similar study of earlier periods [before the end of the 16th century] will ever become available" (p. v).
3 For a trenchant comment on this point, see M. N. Srinivas's introduction to the article by A. M. Shah and R. G. Shroff, "The Vahivanca Barots of Gujarat: A Caste of Genealogists and Mythographers," in *Traditional India: Structure and Change*, ed. Milton Singer (Philadelphia: The American Folklore Society, 1959), pp. 41–42. In fact, the entire article (pp. 40–70) is an interesting refutation of the traditional view.
4 For some of the historiographical characteristics reflected in the writing of Indian history, see Morris David Morris and Burton Stein, "The Economic History of India: A Bibliographic Essay," *The Journal of Economic History*, vol. 21, no. 2 (June 1961), pp. 179–207.
5 Holden Furber, *John Company at Work* (Cambridge: Harvard University Press, 1951), pp. viii–ix.
6 Rajeshwari Datta, "The India Office Library: Its History, Resources, and Functions," *The Library Quarterly*, vol. 36, no. 2 (April 1966), p. 122. The entire essay (pp. 99–148) is a useful description of the collections at the India Office Library. Another useful guide to the Library and the collections is S. C. Sutton, *A Guide to the India Office Library* (London: Her Majesty's Stationery Office, 1952).
7 For a rather general description of local official records in one region of North India, see Thomas R. Metcalf, "Notes on the Sources for Local History in North India," *The Journal of Asian Studies*, vol. 26, no. 4 (August 1967), pp. 665–75. While there are no guides to the local materials, V. C. Joshi is now in the final stages of preparing a *Guide to Sources of Modern Indian History* under the auspices of the Indian Institute of Public Administration in New Delhi. This guide should serve as a major first step toward making known what local materials are available.
8 Of course, this has been a characteristic of historical work on other parts of the world as well. However, in the last generation there has been a shift toward quantitative work elsewhere that has not yet found a parallel development in work on South Asia.
9 See, for example, T. Raychaudhuri's pointed review of Pradip Sinha's *Nineteenth Century Bengal: Aspects of Social History*, in *The Indian Economic and Social History Review*, vol. 3, no. 3 (Sept. 1966), pp. 318–20. An example of the intellectually revolutionary results that can be obtained by the imaginative application of simple quantitative tests to a rather traditional question is Dharma Kumar's *Land and Caste in South India: Agricultural Labour in the Madras Presidency during the Nineteenth*

Century (Cambridge: Cambridge University Press, 1965). A review article which points out the importance of the study is Morris David Morris, "Economic Change and Agriculture in Nineteenth Century India," *The Indian Economic and Social History Review*, vol. 3, no. 2 (June 1966), pp. 185–209. The forthcoming work of Professor Bernard S. Cohn on early 19th century social mobility promises to provide equally significant evidence of the important results that can be obtained from the use of quantitative data.

10   One need only refer to any study of the British period published since 1947 to discover the truth of this proposition. See the rather tart comments made by A. M. Shah in "Social Anthropology and the Study of Historical Societies," *The Economic Weekly*, special number (July 1959), pp. 953–62. While Shah's comments are addressed to anthropologists, they are equally applicable to historians.

11   Morris David Morris, "Towards a Reinterpretation of Nineteenth Century Indian Economic History," *Journal of Economic History*, vol. 23, no. 4 (Dec. 1963), pp. 608–18.

12   Sir Josiah Stamp once quoted a statement of Harold Cox's which should illustrate the point:

> When I was a very young official in India I remember going to my superior officer with a very elaborate problem based upon statistics, and when I had explained it to him he said to me, "Young man, when you are as old as I am you will not rest so heavily on statistics. The Government can collect statistics, add and subtract, advance them to the *n*th power, derive formulae and pass Acts of Parliament upon those statistics, and all the while the figures upon which they have been based have been made up by the *chowtydar* (village watchman), who just puts down what he damn well pleases."

Cited in the discussion of Lord Meston, "Statistics in India," *Journal of the Royal Statistical Society*, vol. 96, pt. 1 (1933), p. 16.

13   Irfan Habib, *The Agrarian System of Mughal India, 1556–1707* (New York: Asia Publishing House, 1963). Habib's discussion of "The Jama and Hasil Statistics," pp. 395–409, gives some idea of the kinds of data available.

14   Moreland, *India at the Death of Akbar*, p. vi.

15   Margaret, H. Case, "The Historical Craftsmanship of W. H. Moreland, 1868–1938," *The Indian Economic and Social History Review*, vol. 2, no. 3 (July 1965), pp. 245–58.

16   Maureen L. P. Patterson, "Chitpavan Brahman Family Histories: Sources for a Study of Social Structure and Social Change in Maharashtra," in *Structure and Social Change in Indian Society*, ed. Milton S. Singer and Bernard S. Cohn (Chicago: Aldine, 1968), pp. 397–411.

17   Letter from T. Raychaudhuri, 6 October 1967.

18   Letter from D. R. Gadgil, 23 August 1967.

19   My discussion is based on Satish Chandra and Satya Prakash Gupta, "The Jaipur Pargana Records," *The Indian Economic and Social History Review*, vol. 3, no. 3 (Sept. 1966), pp. 303–15.

20   Ibid., p. 303.

21   Ibid., p. 313.

22   There is a brief and very general description by V. K. Bawa in "The State Archives of Andhra Pradesh," *The Quarterly Review of Historical Studies*, vol. 6, no. 1 (1966–67), pp. 20–24.

23   Letter from T. Raychaudhuri, 6 October 1967.

24   Ibid.

25   B. N. Goswamy, "The Records Kept by Priests at Centres of Pilgrimage as a Source of Social and Economic History," *The Indian Economic and Social History Review*, vol. 3, no. 2 (June 1966), pp. 175, 179–80. For the entire description, see pp. 174–84.

26   For a discussion of these records, cf. A. M. Shah, R. G. Shroff, and A. R. Shah, "Early Nineteenth Century Village Records in Gujarat," in *Contributions to Indian Economic History*, vol. 2, ed. T. Raychaudhuri (Calcutta: Firma K. L. Mukhopadhyay, 1963), pp. 89–100.

27   For a reference to this study, see S. V. Avalaskar, "Some Notes on the Social Life in Nagaon in the Early 19th Century," *The Indian Economic and Social History Review*, vol. 3, no. 2 (June 1966), pp. 169–73.

28 Shah and Shroff, "The Vahivanca Barots of Gujarat," pp. 40–70; Shah, "Social Anthropology and the Study of Historical Societies," pp. 953–62; Shah, Shroff, and Shah, "Early Nineteenth Century Village Records in Gujarat," pp. 89–100.

29 The failure to use such sources can be noted by reference to D. R. Gadgil, *Origins of the Modern Indian Business Class: An Interim Report* (Vancouver: University of British Columbia, Publications Centre, 1967). This sophisticated albeit brief description of the Indian business community in mid-18th century depends almost exclusively on English-language sources. See also the plea for the development of indigenous sources in Holden Furber, *Bombay Presidency in the Mid-Eighteenth Century* (New York: Asia Publishing House, 1965), pp. 45–46, 69.

30 For readers unfamiliar with the materials of South Asian history, three general bibliographic sources are particularly useful: Maureen L. P. Patterson and Ronald B. Inden, *South Asia: An Introductory Bibliography* (Chicago: University of Chicago Press, Syllabus Division, 1962); J. Michael Mahar, *India: A Critical Bibliography* (Tucson: University of Arizona Press, 1964); Bernard S. Cohn, *The Development and Impact of British Administration in India: A Bibliographic Essay* (New Delhi: The Indian Institute of Public Administration, 1961). For a survey of work in economic history, see Morris and Stein, "The Economic History of India."

31 Great Britain, India Office, *A Guide to the India Office Records, 1600–1858*, ed. William Foster (London: Eyre and Spottiswoode, 1919); Furber, *John Company at Work*, bibliography.

32 For the earlier period, see Bal Krishna, *Commercial Relations between India and England, 1601–1757* (London: Routledge, 1924); Kristoff Glamann, *Dutch-Asiatic Trade, 1620–1740* (Copenhagen: Danish Science Press, 1958); W. H. Moreland, *From Akbar to Aurangzeb* (London: Macmillan, 1923).

33 Letter from K. N. Chaudhuri, 12 July 1967. Chadhuri is currently well along on a massive statistical analysis of the East India Company's trade with India.

34 Letter from S. Roy, 1 July 1967.

35 Geoffrey W. Tyson, *The Bengal Chamber of Commerce and Industry* (Calcutta: Bengal Chamber of Commerce and Industry, 1952), pp. 27–28.

36 As evidence of what else is possible, my colleague, D. C. North, in the course of a general study of international freight rates, has established the feasibility of constructing a series of freight rates between London and India that begins with the opening of the East India traffic and continues without a break to 1914.

37 Furber, *Bombay Presidency in Mid-Eighteenth Century*, p. 44.

38 Furber, in *John Company at Work*, has a bibliographic introduction to these materials. Reference should also be made to the bibliographic leads furnished in Glamann, *Dutch-Asiatic Trade*; T. Raychaudhuri, *Jan Company in Coromandel, 1605–1690* (The Hague: Nijhoff, 1962); and Indira Narang, "The Ostend Company's Records and the 'Instructions' of Alexander Hume," *The Indian Economic and Social History Review*, vol. 4, no. 2 (March 1967), pp. 17–37.

39 Eric Stokes, *The English Utilitarians and India* (Oxford: Oxford University Press, Clarendon Press, 1959), pp. 280–81.

40 Ibid.

41 Kingsley Davis, *The Population of India and Pakistan* (Princeton: Princeton University Press, 1951). As part of the 1961 Census of India publication schedule, the registrar general approved a research project to be carried out under the direction of B. and D. Bhattacharya of the Socio-Economic Research Institute of Calcutta; this will ultimately result in the publication of eight volumes of "pre-Census estimates of population in India." One volume is intended to reproduce all identifiable estimates of population up to 1800. Each of the seven subsequent volumes will compile estimates available for one of the seven decades preceding the appearance of the first full-scale Census of India. The first published volume, for 1820–30, contains 37 estimates of population either for India as a whole or for regions, districts, or individual towns. See Census of India 1961, *Report on the Population Estimates of India, 1820–1830*, ed. Durgaprasad and Bibhavati Bhattacharya (Delhi: Manager of Publications, 1965). Another volume, for 1811–20, was reported ready to go to press in 1971; and two more, covering 1801–10 and 1831–40, were in progress.

42 George Blyn, *Agricultural Trends in India, 1891–1947: Output, Availability, and Productivity* (Philadelphia: University of Pennsylvania Press, 1966), pp. 39 ff.

43 Reserve Bank of India, *Banking and Monetary Statistics of India* (Bombay: Reserve Bank of India, 1954), contains rupee and sterling debt series from 1820–21 and import and export data on gold and silver from 1834–35. The *Statistical Abstract* contains series which begin in 1840.

44 U.S. Bureau of the Census, *Historical Statistics of the United States, Colonial Times to 1957* (Washington, D.C.: U.S. Government Printing Office, 1960).

45 Lord Meston, "Statistics in India," *Journal of the Royal Statistical Society*, vol. 96, pt. 1 (1933), pp. 1–20; H. A. F. Lindsay, "India's Trade and Industrial Statistics, Past, Present and Future," ibid., vol. 97, pt. 3 (1934), pp. 399–422.

46 Indian Industrial Commission, *Minutes of Evidence 1916–17*, vol. 2 (Calcutta: Superintendent of Government Printing, 1917), pp. 778–869. This is a particularly useful introduction to the discussion of the quality of the statistical data.

47 Frank Campbell, *Index Catalogue of Indian Official Publications in the Library of the British Museum* (London: British Museum, 1900).

48 Great Britain, India Office, *Annual Lists and General Index of the Parliamentary Papers Relating to the East Indies Published during the Years 1801 to 1907 Inclusive*, House of Commons, vol. 64, no. 89 (London: His Majesty's Stationery Office, 1909).

49 Office of the Economic Advisor, Ministry of Commerce and Industry, Government of India, *Guide to Current Official Statistics:* vol. 1, *Production and Prices*, 4th ed. (Delhi: Manager of Publications, 1949); vol. 2, *Trade, Transport and Communications, and Finance*, (Lucknow: Government Branch Press, 1945); vol. 3, *Public Finance, Education, Public Health, Census, Labour, Consumption of Commodities, and Miscellaneous* (Delhi: Manager of Publications, 1948).

50 Vera Anstey, *The Economic Development of India*, 3d ed. (London: Longmans, Green, 1949).

51 See Thomas R. Metcalf, "Notes on the Sources for Local History in North India," *Journal of Asian Studies*, vol. 26, no. 4 (August 1967), pp. 665–75. There is also a useful description of some of the available rural survey materials in Karunamoy Mukerji, *Agriculture, Famine, and Rehabilitation in South Asia* (Santiniketan: Visva-Bharati, 1965), pp. 202 ff. What is particularly interesting is Mukerji's description of the rediscovery of the J. C. Jack survey papers (pp. 205 ff.).

52 Metcalf, "Sources for Local History in North India," p. 671.

53 Shah, "Social Anthropology and the Study of Historical Societies," pp. 959–62; Shah, Shroff, and Shah, "Early Nineteenth Century Village Records in Gujarat," pp. 89–100. For a detailed description of these village records, see Oscar Lewis, *Village Life in Northern India: Studies in a Delhi Village* (Urbana: University of Illinois Press, 1958), pp. 329–47. A recent report that describes available village materials in careful, explicit detail is Tom G. Kessinger's "Historical Materials on Rural India," *The Indian Economic and Social History Review*, vol. 7, no. 4 (Dec. 1970), pp. 489–510.

54 Metcalf, "Sources for Local History in North India," pp. 672–73.

55 T. Morison, "The Instability of Prices in India before 1861," *Journal of the Royal Statistical Society*, vol. 65, pt. 3 (Sept. 1902), pp. 513–25.

56 Patterson, "Chitpavan Brahman Family Histories." In addition to the material Miss Patterson describes, there are also, for example, the censuses made by Saraswat Brahmans of their own economic and social conditions in 1896, 1911, 1922, 1932, 1945, and 1956. See Census Working Committee, Kanara Saraswat Association, *The Chitrapur Saraswat 1956 Census Report and Directory* (Bombay: The Kanara Saraswat Association, 1956).

57 It is startling to realize that even Indian scholars have neglected the enormous potential of these sources. When writing about the period of European contact, they exhibit an almost exclusive preference for official and English-language sources.

58 A large amount of scholarship depends on a relatively limited number of types of statistical information. At least initially it would be fairly easy to establish obvious orders of importance.

59 In fact, most of the very interesting national income estimates exhibit this failing. For a survey of the literature, see M. Mukherjee, "A Preliminary Study of Growth

of National Income in India, 1857–1957," in International Association for Research in Income and Wealth, *Asian Studies in Income and Wealth* (Bombay: Asia Publishing House, 1965), pp. 71–103; and M. Mukerji, "National Income," in *Economic History of India, 1857–1956,* ed. V. B. Singh (Bombay: Allied Publisher's Printing, Limited, 1965), pp. 661–703.

60 Morris David Morris, *The Emergence of an Industrial Labor Force in India* (Berkeley: University of California Press, 1965), pp. 213–16. I also discuss the defects of official wage data, place of origin statistics, and caste data (pp. 219–37).

61 For example, a simple adjustment of the Bombay employment data to allow for second- and third-shift working after 1930 yields a much more rapid rate of growth than is suggested by the uncorrected data; this might contribute to a revision of our notions of interwar economic performance in India.

62 Blyn's *Agricultural Trends in India* and Davis's *Population of India and Pakistan* represent two important exceptions to these structures. For some ideas on the weakness of data being collected even currently, cf. A. Rudra, "National Income Estimates: Why Not Discontinue Them?" *The Economic Weekly,* 4 February 1961, pp. 209–13.

63 The Reserve Bank of India's *Banking and Monetary Statistics of India* is an obvious example of the advantages of having even simple compilations available.

64 See George Rosen, "A Case of Aborted Growth: India, 1860–1900," *The Economic Weekly,* 11 August 1962; V. V. Bhatt, *Economic Weekly,* special number (July 1963), pp. 1229–36; Morris, "Reinterpretation of Nineteenth Century Indian Economic History." I am not implying that answers to important questions will be found merely by compiling statistics; solid theoretical work and further empirical work will still be essential. However, if we had better statistical evidence we might narrow the range of possibilities. We might at least indicate the direction of movements of national and per-capita income, if not their rates.

65 For some additional comments on the need for regional data, see Morris and Stein, "Economic History of India," pp. 194–96; and Morris David Morris, "Values as an Obstacle to Economic Growth in South Asia: A Historical Survey," *Journal of Economic History,* vol. 27, no. 4 (Dec. 1967).

CONTRIBUTORS

WILLIAM O. AYDELOTTE is professor of history at the University of Iowa, a specialist in modern British political history, and one of the pioneers of quantitative history in this country. Recently a collection of his essays on the application of quantitative methods to history was published under the title *Quantification in History* (1971).

SUSAN B. HANLEY received her Ph.D. in history from Yale in 1971. She is now a research associate of the Population Institute, East-West Center, Honolulu. She is a specialist in the demographic and economic history of Tokugawa Japan.

DAVID HERLIHY, formerly of the University of Wisconsin, is professor of history at Harvard University and a specialist in medieval economic history and northern Italy in the fourteenth and fifteenth centuries. His best-known works are *Pisa in the Early Renaissance* (1957) and *Medieval and Renaissance Pistoria* (1967). He is now collaborating on a project for the computer processing of a fifteenth-century Florentine tax census.

ARCADIUS KAHAN is professor of economics at the University of Chicago and a specialist in modern Russian economic history, particularly agrarian history. He is now investigating capital formation during early industrialization in Russia and structural changes in the economies of continental Europe.

DAVID S. LANDES is professor of history at Harvard University and a specialist in modern European economic history. His best-known works are *Bankers and Pashas* (1958) and *The Unbound Prometheus* (1969).

JUAN J. LINZ is professor of sociology and political science at Yale University. The author of books on Spanish business and Andalusian local elites, he has published papers on "The Party System of Spain: Past and Future" in Lipset and Rokkan, eds., *Party Systems and Voter Alignments;* and on the Spanish authoritarian regime in Allardt and Rokkan, eds., *Mass Politics,* and in Huntington and Moore, eds., *Authoritarian Politics in*

Modern Society. He has also published methodological papers on comparative sociology. He is presently writing a monograph on the political elite of Spain, 1869–1972, and on Spanish intellectuals, of which a first chapter appeared in *Daedalus* in 1972.

VAL R. LORWIN is professor of history at the University of Oregon and a specialist in the economic and social history of modern Western Europe. Among his best-known works are *The French Labor Movement* (1954) and his contribution to *Political Oppositions in Western Democracies* (1966).

WILLIAM PAUL MCGREEVEY, formerly of the University of California, Berkeley, is now a senior economic advisor with the Department of Economic Affairs, Organization of American States. He is a specialist in the economic history of modern Latin America. His best-known work is *An Economic History of Colombia, 1845–1930* (1971).

MORRIS DAVID MORRIS is professor of economics at the University of Washington and a specialist in Indian economic history. His best-known work is *The Emergence of an Industrial Labor Force in India* (1965).

BIRGITTA ODÉN is professor of history at the University of Lund and a specialist in modern Swedish political and social history, public finance, and migration. Among her published works are *Rikets uppbörd och utgift* (1955), *Kopparhandel och statsmonopol* (1960), and *Kronohandel och finanspolitik* (1966).

JACOB M. PRICE is professor of history at the University of Michigan, Ann Arbor, and a specialist in eighteenth-century British history and European economic history. His works include *The Tobacco Adventure to Russia* (1961) and *France and the Chesapeake* (1972).

JAMES J. SHEEHAN is associate professor of history at Northwestern University and a specialist in modern German political and social history. His best-known work is *The Career of Lujo Brentano* (1966). He is now working on a social history of the liberal movement in nineteenth-century Germany.

JOHN J. TEPASKE is professor of history at Duke University and a specialist in the colonial period of Latin American history. His best-known work is *The Governorship of Spanish Florida, 1700–1763* (1964). He is now working on a quantitative study of the activities of the treasuries of Mexico and Peru, 1519–1810, and a more general administrative-social study of the viceroyalty of Peru, 1700–60.

CHARLES TILLY is professor of sociology and history at the University of Michigan, Ann Arbor, and a specialist in urbanization and its political implications. His best-known work is *The Vendée* (1964). He is now working on a large-scale quantitative study of mass violence in modern France.

Louise Tilly is instructor in history at Michigan State University and a specialist in modern European economic and social history. She is now working on a study of the working class of Milan in the late nineteenth century.

Kozo Yamamura is professor of Asian studies and economics at the University of Washington and a specialist in Japanese economic history. His best-known work is *Economic Policy in Postwar Japan* (1967). He and Susan Hanley are now working on a study of the economic and demographic history of Tokugawa Japan.

INDEX